Music of Latin America and the Caribbean

Mark Brill

University of Texas, San Antonio

Prentice Hall

Boston   Columbus   Indianapolis   New York   San Francisco   Upper Saddle River
Amsterdam   Cape Town   Dubai   London   Madrid   Milan   Munich   Paris   Montréal   Toronto
Delhi   Mexico City   São Paulo   Sydney   Hong Kong   Seoul   Singapore   Taipei   Tokyo

Editorial Director: Craig Campanella
Editor in Chief: Sarah Touborg
Executive Editor: Richard Carlin
Vice President of Marketing: Brandy Dawson
Executive Marketing Manager: Kate Mitchell
Associate Managing Editor: Melissa Feimer
Senior Operations Specialist: Brian Mackey
Cover Designer: Suzanne Behnke
Manager, Visual Research: Beth Brenzel

Cover Image: © chantal cecchetti/Fotolia.com
Senior Media Director: David Alick
Full-Service Project Management:
MPS Limited, a Macmillan Company
Composition: MPS Limited, a Macmillan Company
Printer/Binder: RR Donnelley
Cover Printer: RR Donnelley

Photo credits: **p. 34** Linda Whitwam © Dorling Kindersley, Courtesy of Catedral de Arequipa; **p. 36** Reprinted with permission from Bernardino de Sahagun "Codice Florentino" 3 vols, Mexico City, Biblioteca Medicea and Archivo General de la Nacion, 1979; **p. 49** Alex Robinson © Dorling Kindersley; **p. 53** Lebrecht Music & Arts Photo Library; **p. 64** Picture Desk, Inc./Kobal Collection; **p. 64** Picture Desk, Inc./Kobal Collection; **p. 74** DAVID SACKS Getty Images, Inc.—Taxi; **p. 89** Eugene Gordon; **p. 99** Rivera, Diego. Emiliano Zapata, 1928. Mural, 2.05 x 1.46 m. Court of Fiestas, Level 3, South Wall. Secretaria de Educacion Publica, Mexico City, Mexico. © Banco de Mexico Diego Rivera Museum Trust/Art Resource, N.Y; **p. 116** Robert Fried/robertfriedphotography.com; **p. 124** © Jan Butchofsky-Houser/CORBIS; **p. 136** Getty Images, Inc./Frank Miceiotta/Stringe; **p. 188** © GREG JOHNSTON/DanitaDelimont.com; **p. 204** North Wind Picture Archives; **p. 207** Private Collection/The Bridgeman Art Library; **p. 226** Andy Crawford © Dorling Kindersley; **p. 228** Alex Robinson © Dorling Kindersley; **p. 246** Getty Images Inc.—Stone Allstock; **p. 246** Getty Images Inc.—Michael Ochs Archives; **p. 263** David Ashby © Dorling Kindersley; **p. 280** Getty Images Inc.—Hulton Archive Photos; **p. 293** Stock Connection; **p. 305** Paul Loven/Image Bank/Getty Images; **p. 308** Picture Desk, Inc./Kobal Collection; **p. 310** © Dorling Kindersley; **p. 310** © Dorling Kindersley; **p. 317** Viesti Associates, Inc.; **p. 319** Nature Picture Library; **p. 348** Private Collection/The Bridgeman Art Library; **p. 360** AGE Fotostock America, Inc.; **p. 383** Fundacion Victor Jara

Library of Congress Cataloging-in-Publication Data
Brill, Mark.
Music of Latin America & the Caribbean / Mark Brill. — 1st ed.
p. cm.
Includes bibliographical references and index.
ISBN-13: 978-0-13-183944-1 (alk. paper)
ISBN-10: 0-13-183944-6 (alk. paper)

1. Music—Latin America—History and criticism. I. Title.
II. Title: Music of Latin America and the Caribbean.
ML199.B75 2010
780.98—dc22

2010032779

10 9 8 7 6 5 4 3 2 1

Prentice Hall
is an imprint of

ISBN 10: 0-13-183944-6
ISBN 13: 978-0-13-183944-1

www.pearsonhighered.com

CONTENTS

INTRODUCTION

The great diversity and the sheer amount of music in Latin America and the Caribbean makes capturing all of it in a single text impossible, yet the scope and breadth of Mark Brill's adventurous text is vast and impressive. Addressing a general lack of understanding and awareness of Latin American and Caribbean cultures that applies as much to music majors as to non-majors, the author focuses little on musical transcriptions; instead, a more literary and historical approach informs the listening experience but does not define it. The text's greatest strengths are its candid reporting of historical and political processes and the author's excellent selection from such a vast field as Latin American and Caribbean music. Because of its strong historical approach to a dynamically changing musical soundscape, this text surpasses other introductory texts to Latin American and Caribbean music. No doubt other books address the needs and preferences of some professors, yet this text is of timely and singular importance in attempting to provide an unbiased historical perspective informing each chapter. Mark Brill's approach satisfies a need for a comprehensive historical picture—missing in more specialized music narratives—of the complicated developments that have produced the immense variety of what one might call Music of Latin America and the Caribbean. There is no way to teach it all, but by emphasizing the processes of musical development in the Americas, Dr. Brill helps students to grasp the big picture and gain a larger understanding that they can apply to their specific research projects.

Although not explicitly stated as such, the main arguments and conclusions of this text are that individual histories throughout Latin America and the Caribbean have similar roots but have developed uniquely subsequent to the radical changes brought about by colonization and globalization over the past half century. As such, the text is ethnomusicological in nature, firmly rooted in examining cultural histories and ideas in order to understand the deeper significances of music in its local manifestations.

Dr. Brill does a great job of establishing the social and musical contexts, naming and describing the instruments and how they're played, and always providing the names of more genres he can't address. Students and the general reader will want to take a break from the text to listen to the CD examples that accompany the text or search the Internet for additional examples. The more readers listen to the examples and engage with the reading, the better they will understand how the music summarizes the points made in the text. The text leads us to many doors, but it is up to the reader to open them to see what is on the other side. Sidebars are provided to call attention to important details.

Dr. Brill's text provides what other texts have not. Top on the list of praises are those leisurely walks through the critical historical past, in which the author does not equivocate the facts, allowing the stunning realizations that come with knowing the simple truths about things. Dr. Brill provides those dimensions of human understanding missing in other texts. For example, Dr. Brill distinguishes the Caribbean from Latin America in that English, Dutch, African, and Asian languages and cultures intersect these island cultures as much and sometimes more than the romance languages and cultures of French or Spanish; hence this text discusses music of "Latin America and the Caribbean." And, although in the United States we have come to appropriate the terms "America" and "American" for ourselves, in this text you will see the terms applying to America the continent and Americans, its diverse inhabitants. Mestizos everywhere, those who claim ancestry to multiple racial streams (remember that "race" is merely a social construction) have fused elements of all cultures and icons of musical cultures permeate the people's musics. With the musics come characters that tell stories of the past, the present, and those things yet to come; with the musics comes the desire to dance; and with the musics comes the will to live against screaming poverty and political anxiety. Dr. Brill captures the complicated histories and inner characters of the peoples whose musics he introduces us to in his discussions, and thus his text is essential for anyone interested in Latin America and the Caribbean, and primarily in their musics.

Dr. Brill brings a solid foundation to a complex, multicultural subject by teaching us the historical trajectories that have brought us to this moment. Instructors now have a strong fundamental text on which to build their lectures, and students learn details of particular traditions that allow them to connect them from one region to another. The classroom teacher can rest assured that the students are reading contemporary historical accounts, many of which never made it into history books in the past. Instructors are given the flexibility and freedom to build on those histories as they select listening examples for classroom analyses, to plug in their own expertise in the continuum of things, indeed, offering new continua in the classroom.

Although most useful for undergraduate courses, this text has much to offer the general interested reader. Dr. Brill assists the novice reader at any age in his understanding of the music and cultures that are his focus. Indeed, limiting the scope of this project was and continues to be a challenge, but in a day when students have easy access to sites such as YouTube, names of musicians and genres and bits of information of any kind can lead to further personal research instantly on the Internet. This text provides a great deal of information to aid the student in online research. As Dr. Brill writes: "There is work for anthropological and ethnomusicological research for generations. Hopefully, the richness and historical importance of Latin American music that this textbook is attempting to convey will inspire students to undertake such work in years to come" (p. 27). To further enable such research, the text spills over to a Web site that includes what could not be included in a single text.

In Chapter 1, Dr. Brill seeks to establish a fundamental history of precolonial music cultures. He submits that "Modern students of pre-colonial cultures are hampered by a scarcity of primary documents and artifacts. Any conclusions drawn from these studies, particularly in relation to music, must be taken with caution at the outset, since the record is often incomplete and misleading" (p. 7). Dr. Brill grapples with the contradictions whenever possible, anticipating student questions. Ultimately it is the life of the instruments and the music they make today that takes the foreground. Chapter 2 focuses on processes surrounding the establishment and development of classical music brought from Europe. This is especially important because these traditions today reflect 500 years of ongoing evolution in the Americas. Dr. Brill highlights genres that proved to be seminal for secular music as well, such as the *villancico*. We learn also how nationalism has expressed itself through art music. Chapter 3 provides a comprehensive history and overview of music in Mexico, offering ample historical contextualization. Chapters 4 and 5 address developments specific to the Spanish Caribbean (Cuba, Puerto Rico, and the Dominican Republic) and similarly on the English- and French-speaking Caribbean (Jamaica, Trinidad, Haiti, Guadeloupe and Martinique, and the transnational Garífuna of Belize and Honduras). Chapters 6 through 9 focus on South America, beginning with Brazil, Colombia and Venezuela, the Andean Region (Peru in particular), and the Southern Cone (especially Argentina and Chile). All of these chapters are comprehensive and direct the reader to a variety of recordings, about 60 of which are included in the accompanying CDs

Among the innovative aspects of Dr. Brill's text, he includes *nueva canción* as a widespread American (including the U.S.) phenomenon. He is able to discuss the impact that globalization has had on genres like *reggae, cumbia, tango, mariachi, salsa*, and others as they have become transcultural. He puts to rest many previously anecdotal misunderstandings about the origins of instruments and genres, revealing the ethnic origins of particular traditions and supplying connections that clearly mark musical developments in their evolutions, as in the Cocolo bands of the Dominican Republic. He provides a comprehensive view of the cultural diversity of Latin America and the Caribbean with strong connections to the pulse on the people and current trends.

This is an exciting new contribution to music scholarship. The text offers a strong foundation in music history as well as additional resources that enable students to undertake their own special projects in areas not covered in the text itself; for example, Dr. Brill has provided additional information on about indigenous musics, which arguably could be the focus of an entire text in themselves. With this new resource, we have made a monumental leap into twenty-first-century awareness and understanding of the universe that exists south of the United States and that will continue to shape U.S. musical culture over time.

Brenda Romero

Associate Professor,
Coordinator of Ethnomusicology,
University of Colorado

1

Music of Latin America and the Caribbean

An Overview

INTRODUCTION

If you have cracked open the pages of this book, you have undoubtedly, at some point in your life, been intrigued, moved or even excited by the sounds and rhythms of Latin America and the Caribbean. You may also be aware, by the same measure, of the vast diversity of musical styles and genres that pervade the western hemisphere. The study of Latin American music can be tremendously fulfilling, though a one-semester study can only begin to do the subject any justice. The vastness of Latin American music can be appreciated by considering the aesthetic, cultural, and geographic range of the following genres, all of which fall under its designation: Argentine tango, Jamaican reggae, eighteenth-century Latin Masses, Tex-Mex ballads, Peruvian panpipe melodies, Afro-Brazilian drumming, and any number of hip-hop–derived urban dances that have emerged throughout the continent. These varied styles have in common their creators, Latin Americans all, recipients and transmitters of a particular mix of cultures that defines them and provides them a sense of identity.

Music is the expression of people's lives. It is many other things, too. But at its core, music serves as the conduit for humans to express themselves, to identify to themselves and to others who they are, and to establish a sense of belonging. Through music, humans are able to say: "Amidst this huge, imposing world, among this complex set of relationships that make up human civilization, *this* is who *I* am." This reality is no more apparent than in the thousands of musical cultures that have emerged and evolved in Latin America. The slave recalling her ancestral spirits on a far away continent; the Aztec warrior who saw his ancient civilization crumble to dust; the *guajiro* farmer, forsaken in a distant island, longing nostalgically for the Spanish homeland he would never again see; the modern youth eking out a living in modern urban ghettos; all these individuals were able to say through their music: *This* is who *I* am.

The study of Latin American and Caribbean music, like that of all music, requires stylistic and aesthetic considerations. But it also requires reflection on issues of history, geography, religion, and ethnicity. A theme that seems to emerge in virtually every Latin American culture is the tension between the "refined" music of the elite and the "coarse" music of the underclass. Latin American society in general has well-defined social classes that are rarely upset, except by violent political upheavals. The Spanish conquistadors, in their characterization of Aztec and Inca music as "barbaric" and "uncivilized," were taking their own worldview as an absolute standard for musical artistry. In so doing, they were also establishing a long tradition of musical intolerance—quickly adopted by the Portuguese, French, Dutch, English, and others—that has pervaded the continent (including the northern part) until modern times. Prejudices have been around for half a millennium and are still present in many Latin American societies. Even today, many consider certain styles, such as Mexican *norteños* or Puerto Rican *reggaetón* as "low-class" music. Add to that racial prejudices: "This music is too Black (or too Indian)" is an implied—and occasionally verbalized—judgment often rendered by a country's elite who are usually of European descent. Yet attitudes change, and another constant seems to be that what one generation considers objectionable, future generations will embrace.

To complicate matters, the accepted distinctions between art, folk, and popular music are often problematic in Latin America, where cross-pollination between styles and genres have sometimes rendered their categorization meaningless. Folk music is generally defined as the music of the people, often anonymous and steeped in tradition and community ritual, and associated with the uneducated working classes, usually in rural areas. Popular music typically emerges in urban settings, composed by known individuals and circulated throughout the community at all levels, often with commercial considerations. Art—or classical—music has traditionally been defined as the music of the elite and educated members of a society, a music that is studied, written down and performed in more formal settings. But what is one to make, for example, of the Martinican *kwadril*, a dance derived from the classical balls of the eighteenth-century French salons, integrated into the Afro-Caribbean folk drumming traditions, and one of the source components of the decidedly popular *zouk* of recent years? Attempting to classify the *kwadril* in terms of art, folk, or popular music seems a rather artificial endeavor, though it does illustrate the process of transformation the style, like so many others, has undergone.

This process of transformation is the result of intricate social and economic factors that affect composers, performers, and audiences. Much of the music of Latin America began as folk music, typically learned at a young age by a member of the community, and perhaps specifically tied to a ritual that emerged in the context of the church, the village, the farm, the plantation or the slum. But in the first half of the twentieth century, these traditions were greatly affected by the economic development that engulfed the continent and the pronounced urban migration that ensued. Time and again, we find examples of rural people migrating to urban areas, bringing their music with them. Invariably, the result is a new style of music, distinct from that of the city dwellers who were already there, but also different from the country dances and ballads the migrants left behind. For whenever rural folk traditions transform into urban styles, its performers often abandon the ritual and religious context of the music. The urban *samba* of Brazil, the Andean *huayno* and *sanjuán*, the Argentine *cuarteto*, and countless others are examples of urban styles associated with those recently arrived who now constitute a poor, urban underclass.

At about the same time that the great urban migrations were occurring—and not coincidentally—many countries began adopting a distinctly nationalist outlook. Nationalism, a movement that took hold in political, artistic, and literary circles in Europe in the nineteenth century, became an important factor in the Americas in the twentieth century, as countries across the hemisphere began embracing rural folk music and art as the truest expression of culture, nation, or ethnic background. One result was that the art music establishment often adopted these folk styles, and one began finding in the concert hall the *tangos*, sambas, *sones*, and *rumbas* that had previously been the domain of the village, the *barrio*, the nightclub, or the carnival parade.

Perhaps more importantly, the folk traditions often also became the preferred form of popular music. Over and over, one can trace the transformation of a given folk music tradition, first into the sophisticated art music of the upper classes, and subsequently into the popular music of the middle classes. By the second half of the twentieth century, dozens of folk music traditions were being transformed radically by the forces of modernization and globalization, undergoing a process of popularization that usually included the infusion of foreign elements, the use of modern electric instruments (usually borrowed from rock-and-roll), and the adoption of a modern pop beat. In the process, many of the traditional elements were abandoned, particularly those that pertained to African or Native elements, as commercial entrepreneurs, in order to appeal to wider middle-class audiences, attempted to modernize and "sanitize" the music. Almost simultaneously, in different parts of the continent, the Cuban *son* tradition led to *salsa*, Jamaican Rastafarian drumming yielded *reggae*, Andean rhythms infused the Peruvian *chicha*, the Mexican *corrido* engendered *tejano*, and the Trinidadian *calypso* brought about *soca*. (These styles and transformations are all examined in subsequent chapters.)

Yet the process of transformation is often mysterious, its causes frequently left unexplained. Thus for reasons still unclear, the 1980s and 1990s saw a hemispheric confluence of accordion-based popular styles. The simultaneous rise of the Colombian *vallenato*, Mexican *tejano*, Brazilian *forro*, Argentine *chamamé*, Louisiana *zydeco*, and other folk styles into national popularity and even international prominence occurred for reasons that cannot be entirely explained by social, economic, political, or aesthetic factors. The accordion, formerly a quintessential folk instrument, all at once seemed to conquer the realm of popular music in Latin America.

Another mystery is the often-irrelevant effect of political borders on the evolution of the continent's music. Through processes that are hard to distinguish, styles as disparate as the Cuban *bolero*, the Colombian *cumbia*, the Argentine tango, and Mexican *música ranchera* have spread virtually unencumbered across the continent. Many of these styles are nationalistic in nature, with features that Cubans, Colombians, Argentines, or Mexicans proudly identify as uniquely theirs. Yet there is also perhaps something Latin American about these styles that transcends their places of origin and that appeals to inhabitants of the entire continent, and in some cases, of the entire world. It is tempting to attribute this phenomenon to the fact that adjacent countries have similar cultures and languages. Yet the same process applies to countries that do not share a historical or cultural past. Thus, Jamaican reggae beats, the product of African and English culture, quickly spread through the Spanish, French, and Dutch Caribbean, and thereafter to the rest of the world. Moreover, dozens of Latin American and Caribbean styles have been adopted at some point by the Anglo-dominated United States, most famously during the "Latin Craze" of the 1930s and 1940s.

Much of Latin America's folk music has been transformed and re-created outside of its original context, often in some commercial venue or as an attempt to recover a lost tradition. This transformation does not in any way invalidate the music or even render it somehow "inauthentic." In recent years, Latin America has been a major contributor to the emergence of so-called "world music," a phenomenon to which some critics and academics have reacted negatively, objecting to its pop orientation, its homogenous uniformity, its mass-media dissemination, and its Western influences. By contrast, they regard forms that originate in community rituals as sacred and "authentic" representations of a pure and unadulterated culture. This supplanting of the traditional by the popular is often blamed on the forces of globalization and modernization. In truth, this is undoubtedly so. The meaning of the music in terms of its function and social representation is unquestionably altered by this transformation, and in the process, much of the individuality that brought it about is unquestionably lost. (In reviewing this manuscript, I myself was amazed—and somewhat saddened—to notice how many times I have related that a traditional folk style is now played by electric guitars, bass, synthesizers, and drum sets. The incredible diversity of Latin American music is diminished when all the styles adopt essentially the same instrumentation.)

Yet attempting to stop the forces of globalization by rejecting the music they engender seems a fruitless—even counterproductive—endeavor. For Latin America, globalization began in 1492, and the current trends are only the latest in an evolutionary process that is now more than half a millennium old. For better or for worse, "world music" is here to stay, and should be recognized and evaluated on its own merits, not excluded from serious study because of its mass-media orientation. Moreover, the issue of authenticity is one that must be treated carefully. To say that a Santería drumming ritual in a remote area of Cuba is "authentic," whereas a glossy, pop-oriented salsa performance at the Latin Grammy Awards is "inauthentic" is to miss the point of the meaning of music. Both extremes—and everything in between—are *real* music, performed by *real* musicians in front of *real* audiences. There is nothing fake—or inauthentic—about either. They are simply different musical expressions of people's lives, derived from vastly different social contexts. One may, of course, aesthetically prefer one to the other, but they must both be recognized and respected as equally valid musical expressions. They are both important parts of the vast panoply that we call "Latin American Music," and to ignore one in favor of another is to paint only half of the picture.

But does this mean one cannot make educated judgments as to the inherent quality of certain types of music? Most critics and musicologists have reached the conclusion, based not on subjective predilection but on the analysis of objective musical evidence, that Wolfgang Mozart was a "better" composer than, say, Antonio Salieri. Can one apply the same informed judgment to the vast array of folk, classical, and popular styles in Latin America? Only, I submit, if these judgments are rendered within a genre, not between genres. Clearly, some reggae songs are "better" than others, and some salsa tunes are also "better" than others, based on objective criteria as to what constitutes a good reggae or salsa song. But there is no valid rationale—certainly not the issue of authenticity—to conclude that reggae is a better (or worse) genre of music than salsa. Similarly, there is no basis, other than personal aesthetic preference, to declare that any of the three major categories of music—art, folk, and popular—is better or worse than the others.

As you study the various styles and genres found in Latin America, you would do well to temporarily withhold judgment of the musics you encounter, particularly those you are unfamiliar with. Learn as much as you can within each genre. Study the music, listen to the recordings, learn about the customs and rituals that led to the style's emergence and the social or religious contexts that influenced it. Understand why the music emerged and what function it serves. Most importantly, understand what the music means to the performers and their audiences. Then—and only then—can you start making qualitative judgments about the music you hear; only then will you be able to say "this samba is better than that samba."

INDIGENOUS CULTURES BEFORE 1492

Prior to the first major encounter between Europeans and Americans in 1492, the continent was home to thousands of different cultures whose diversity was as widespread as its geographical landscape. From the tundra of the arctic to Tierra del Fuego in southern Argentina, in arid deserts, steamy jungles, and some of the highest mountain ranges in the world, Americans made their homes, raised their families, and constructed civilizations. They also made music, in spiritual ceremonies, in rites of passage, and for their pleasure and entertainment.

Most current theories hold that the continent was populated during the last ice age, between twelve and twenty thousand years ago. As much of the water froze into glaciers, the ocean level fell, revealing a land bridge between Siberia and Alaska called Beringia. Nomadic hunter-gatherers crossed this land bridge from Asia onto the American continent—or perhaps sailed along the coast—finding an uninhabited new land whose rich bounty ensured not only survival but also prosperity. Within a millennium, the entire continent had been populated. Countless hunter-gatherer societies emerged, each developing in time its customs, rituals, and musical traditions. As in most—perhaps all—aboriginal societies, the first music making undoubtedly revolved around either makeshift percussion instruments—perhaps as basic as striking a rock with a stick—or of the human voice: a mother singing a lullaby to her child, a young hunter imitating the song of a bird, a family mourning the death of a parent, or an entire village chanting to unseen forces. The earliest known instruments in the Americas consist of percussion instruments made from gourds, seeds, and animal claws or hooves, as well as flutes made from wood, cane, and animal and even human bones.

Many of these hunter-gatherer societies died out as the result of war, famine, or migration. Others persisted for millennia, adapting to changing conditions, sometimes surviving the European invasion even into the twentieth century (such as the famous Yanomamo who still live in the Venezuelan rainforest, much as their ancestors did for untold generations). Around 3000 BCE, still others evolved into agrarian societies, domesticating important New World crops—notably potatoes and maize (corn)—which would in time revolutionize the eating habits and the economic development of the entire world. It is from some of these agrarian societies that emerged a few prominent and powerful civilizations whose achievements rivaled and often surpassed those in other parts of the world.

The three leading civilizations on the American continent prior to the arrival of the Europeans were the Mayas from Mesoamerica (a term that literally means "middle America" and that refers to southeastern Mexico, Guatemala, Belize, and Honduras); the Aztecs from central Mexico; and the Incas who lived in the Andean region of what is today Peru, Ecuador, Bolivia, and surrounding areas. These societies created massive architectural monuments, dominant political organizations, and lucrative economic systems. They achieved a high level of military prowess and governed complex social structures and religious beliefs—usually enforced by powerful clergy—that dictated the everyday life of their inhabitants. They also contained the majority of the population of the Americas, though the exact number remains unknown—and controversial. The number of inhabitants of the American continent in 1492 has been estimated as low as 20 million and as high as more than 100 million.

Pre-Columbian Music

Modern students of pre-colonial cultures are hampered by a scarcity of primary documents and artifacts. Any conclusions drawn from these studies, particularly in relation to music, must be taken with caution at the outset, since the record is often incomplete and misleading. Historical events have made the study of Native societies in pre-Columbian times a challenging task. The first wave of destruction came with the conquistadors, who readily seized as much gold and silver and as many precious objects as they could, in the process destroying many artifacts and monuments. Subsequent European settlers, fearing indigenous uprisings and preoccupied with forcefully establishing their political and religious dominance, often systematically destroyed as many elements of Native culture as they could and attempted to change the mindset and philosophies of the Natives, including their musical tendencies. Much of the knowledge that pertained to Native music disappeared, including written manuscripts that described musical ceremonies, carvings of instruments on temple walls, and even a large number of musical instruments. Almost completely lost was the music itself, for pre-Columbian America probably had no system of musical notation, relying instead on oral transmission. Those elements that did survive tended to be filtered through the eyes of Spanish writers, creating an outlook that was rarely complimentary. Since the Conquest, centuries of neglect have further contributed to the demise of cultural elements to the point where only a small fraction of the Native patrimony survives. Thus while historians, archaeologists, and anthropologists have sometimes been able to reconstruct ceremonies and musical instruments, what the music actually sounded like remains mostly a mystery.

Pre-Columbian Cultures as Seen by Europeans

In early colonial accounts, music and musical rituals are typically described only when they contravene Christian theocratic ideology, and adjectives such as "primitive," "barbaric," "demonic," and "uncivilized" are common. Some descriptions, for example, disparage Native music for its lack of harmony and polyphony, concepts that in sixteenth- and seventeenth-century Spain had reached their highest points of musical artistry. Overly complex syncopated rhythms were considered barbaric, and dissonances, rather than being judged as part of an overall tonal system, were dismissed as out of tune.

The perception of aboriginal cultures did not much improve after the end of the colonial period. Generations of historians and travelers, particularly during the nineteenth century, often commented on how "primitive" and "backwards" the original inhabitants of the Americas had been, with arguments that frequently took on racist overtones and that were used as justification for the European colonization of the continent. Europeans argued, for example, that American Native societies had failed to invent the wheel, which had been part of the Western and Middle Eastern world for millennia. Rarely was it pointed out that there were no significant American draft animals to pull carriages, negating the need to invent carriages, thus rendering the wheel by-and-large superfluous. (As it turns out, the abstract concept of a wheel—a circular gyrating mechanical system that repeats a specific task—did in fact exist in the Americas, and could be seen for example in the water and windmills of various indigenous groups.) By the same token, the dearth of domesticated animals meant that Americans were not exposed to diseases that evolved from cows, pigs, or fowl, and lacking such immunities, became vulnerable to European epidemics in the sixteenth century. Other factors that contributed to their general state of civilization were the natural and geographic features that isolated the American continent, and the relatively late arrival of its inhabitants.

RECOMMENDED READING   For an in-depth exploration of the causes that have led to the emergence of different levels of historical development, read *Guns, Germs and Steel: The Fates of Human Societies*, by Jared Diamond (W. W. Norton, 1997).

Modern understanding of Native musical cultures is thus derived from the following sources:

- a few surviving pre-Columbian codices, as well as several post-Conquest volumes written by Native Americans;
- writings by conquistadors and missionaries who encountered Native cultures;
- modern studies of pre-Columbian and colonial Native languages, literature, art, and history;
- archaeological studies of pottery, sculptures, murals, tombs, structures, and original musical instruments; and
- anthropological studies of musical practices of modern Native groups, many of whom still speak aboriginal languages and maintain traditions only partially modified by five centuries of contact with Europeans.

Because of problematic nature of these sources, and of the huge human diversity on the American continent, few generalizations can be made about its music. Nevertheless some common characteristics emerge from the historical record:

- There were no string instruments in America prior to European contact. Indigenous music was played entirely by wind instruments (aerophones), percussion (idiophones and membranophones), and the human voice.

- Similar instruments could be found in various parts of the continent, including:
  - drums with heads made from the skins of wild animal such as deer or jaguars (since there were no cows, sheep, or goats);
  - shakers made from gourds containing shells, pebbles, or seeds, the antecedents of the modern *maracas*;
  - rasps made from serrated gourds or hollow sticks, the antecedents of the modern *güiro*;
  - conch shells, used extensively from northern Mexico to Argentina;
  - clay whistles and ocarinas; and
  - flutes, the most prominent melodic instrument, found everywhere including North America, in a large variety of scales and ranges, and made from different materials, including cane, wood, and bone. Both notched flutes (with a carved notch in the upper-rim to facilitate blowing) and duct-flutes (with a mouthpiece that directs the player's breath) were common. The flute was often considered the closest representation of the human voice.
- Native music was often—in some cases almost entirely—related to religious rituals and ceremonies.

Colonial writings focus on the large-scale ceremonial and religious aspect of music, and indicate that the main outlets for Native musical expression were religious ceremonies. Yet music was also a function of everyday life in the village and in the home and was also associated with war and conquest.

Pre-Hispanic civilizations also had highly developed literature, rhetoric, poetry, and drama traditions that reflect an emphasis on metaphor and symbolism, colored by an overpowering faith in the spirit world. The Native view of the universe revealed a fatalistic belief in destiny, underlined by a deep sense of humility and melancholy. Aztec, Maya, and Inca mythology purvey a sense of pessimism, both in the relationship between the various deities and between gods and humans. These tendencies towards melancholy and pessimism were remarkably similar to those of the Spaniards, who reinforced them in subsequent centuries. They can still be found among the music of their modern descendants, particularly in the Andean region. Epic stories display a natural acceptance of suffering and are reflected in the penitent traditions introduced by the Spanish.

1492 AND THE ADVENT OF SYNCRETISM

Perhaps the most useful term in the study of Latin American history, culture, and music is **syncretism**, defined as a process of mutual influence and adaptations among different religious or cultural traditions. In a syncretic process, two (or more) cultures merge and combine to form a new culture, drawing from—but wholly distinct from—its sources. A syncretic study of Latin America examines how dozens of groups emerged as the result of a mixture of primarily European, African, and Native cultures, and how these cultures evolved under vastly different historic, economic, and social circumstances. In time, a profound cultural and musical fusion came to dominate, and the styles of all three continents came to constitute the musical heritage of most modern Latin Americans.

Yet one must tread carefully when discussing syncretism in the context of a colonial society or run the danger of unconsciously absorbing the prevailing colonial paradigm. When a dominant culture melds with a dominated culture, more often than not it is the latter that must adopt the characteristics of the former. Africans and Natives were forced to adopt the customs, languages, and religions of the Europeans, and not the other way around. But the syncretic process is long and complex and does not merely involve the adoption of the elements of one culture by another. Rather, it concerns the creation of a third, distinct culture, one in which issues of cultural control are eventually no longer applicable—or at least far less pronounced. Thus, modern Mexico is a syncretic society, dominated by a Mestizo culture that is mostly (though not completely) devoid of issues of Spanish and Native cultural domination.

The White Legend and the Black Legend

Christopher Columbus's arrival in the New World in October 1492 began a process of cultural transformation that continues to this day. The presence of Spain, Portugal, and other European nations in the Americas has been controversial almost from their first arrival on the continent. Their exact roles continue to elude consensus. As early as the eighteenth century, two opposing views of the European—and specifically Spanish—role in the development of the American continent emerged, and they continue to inflame passions to this day. The so-called **White Legend**, formed by conservative, pro-colonial thinkers, emphasizes the achievements of Spanish culture and portrays the Spaniards as saviors, bringing economic prosperity and spiritual salvation to the inhabitants of the New World. By contrast, the **Black Legend**, product of the liberal, nationalistic movement, sought to dismiss such contributions, depicting the Spaniards as bloodthirsty, opportunistic conquerors bent on the destruction of the Native Americans for the purpose of advancing their own enrichment. Both of these views must be approached cautiously, as neither correctly tells the full story. The truth, as always, can be found somewhere in the middle.

To be sure, Spain's military powers, maritime abilities, strong nationalism, and Catholic faith were major factors in the shaping of the hemisphere. Having triumphantly expelled the Moors in 1492 after more than 700 years of occupation, the Spanish ambition knew no bounds, and the discovery of the American continent that same year was seen as God's will that Spain should reach its glorious destiny. At the same time, its European rivals were being overtaken: France and England were occupied with internal political and military struggles, and Portugal was focused on exploring the Asian route it had recently established. As a result, the Americas in the sixteenth century were wide open for Spanish exploration, conquest, colonization, and conversion.

There is a crucial distinction between colonialism in Latin America and that which occurred in the New England colonies. The British and Dutch, seeking religious and economic asylum, came to the northern continent to find new places to live and prosper, for the most part independently from the homeland. They brought with them their possessions, their farming tools, their Bibles, and their families. A fairly homogeneous transplant of the culture ensued, fueled by the vision of recreating the civilization left behind in the new, bountiful land. The presence of Native populations was contrary to that vision, and as a result indigenous peoples were at first segregated and ultimately mostly eradicated. By contrast, the Spanish conquistadors were not disaffected, religiously persecuted citizens bent on recreating Spain in America. Rather, at least in the first century, they were agents of the Spanish Crown whose mission was to provide new wealth to the national treasury and to serve as emissaries of the Church charged with the salvation of souls. After the initial search for gold had proved illusory, the Spaniards set out to create wealth by intense silver mining operations and agricultural production that required the presence of a large work force. Latin America was "one vast commercial enterprise," as one historian put it, not a haven for freedom-seekers. Thus, unlike the British and Dutch colonists, the goals of the Spanish emissaries could be attained only by preserving the Native populations, and not by eradicating them.

The Black Legend incorrectly perpetrated the myth that the Spaniards were intent on causing widespread death and destruction in the new lands. To be sure, the early conquistadors were brutal, violent individuals, usually more interested in gaining personal wealth and power than in any consideration for the Crown treasury. The Black Legend had it right when it told of massive enslavement and exploitation, and the Spaniards certainly did not hesitate to eliminate individuals who got in their way. But they did not set out to wipe out Native societies, as massive genocide was contrary to their vested interests. The Church saw the Native inhabitants of the colonies as potential converts and by the Crown as a source of forced labor. In theory, Native Americans were "free" Spanish subjects, though this status, without means of enforcement, seldom had any relation to the way Natives were treated, and when labor was not given voluntarily, it was extracted by force. Moreover, the brutality of the Spanish Conquest was often somewhat mitigated, even at times restrained, by the presence of missionaries who brought a moral imperative to the Conquest, an imperative unknown to the New England pilgrims and their descendants. In the eyes of the Spanish clergy, the Natives of the American continent were lost children of God who had to be protected both from the violence of the landowners and from the evils of idolatry. Conversion of the Natives was a primary reason for the Conquest itself, one that gave an aura of legitimacy to the Spanish expeditions in the New World.

The Black Legend further accuses the conquistadors of cultural genocide, and in this respect it is often accurate. Any element of the culture that could lead to national identity or the challenge of authority, or that might perpetuate the Native religions, was usually systematically destroyed. The amount of art, music, poetry, literature, and scientific knowledge that was lost to posterity is incalculable. Yet the Spaniards' aim was not to obliterate the Native civilizations, but rather to subjugate them under Spanish command. Conquerors like Hernán Cortes and Francisco Pizarro quickly recognized that the Aztec and Inca civilizations had been in place for centuries and were well organized and efficient. Rather than destroying the structures, the Spaniards merely replaced traditional forms of government with their own, preserving many elements of Native society that were the same or similar. Native populations were integrated into colonial society, albeit at its lowest level.

Yet from their first contact with Spaniards, the Native population very quickly began to decrease. The vast majority of deaths that occurred in the first hundred years of the colony were caused not by brutal exploitation but by European diseases inadvertently brought by the invaders and against which Americans had no immunity. Smallpox was introduced by accident on April 23, 1520, when the conquistador Pánfilo de Narváez landed in Veracruz, on the east coast of Mexico. Even casual contact brought contagion, which then traveled rapidly through the countryside, carried by Native traders and envoys. The devastation, once begun, was unstoppable. Fatalities were catastrophic in especially dense areas, often decimating entire ethnic groups, and in the process facilitating the conquest of the territories by the Europeans.

Other diseases quickly followed, including tuberculosis, typhoid, influenza, measles, and dysentery. They did not abate after the initial catastrophic contact, but rather continued their deadly march across the continent. Within a few years, millions of Native Americans had died. By the seventeenth century, population losses of 90 percent were not uncommon. In Mexico, the Native population declined from an estimated 25 million in 1519 to slightly over one million in 1605. In the Andes, close to 90 percent of the Inca population expired within a decade of first contact with Europeans. To this day, heretofore isolated communities in the Amazonian jungle still quickly succumb to European germs they have never before encountered. Whether or not the indigenous populations survived the military and biological conquest affected the subsequent racial and social composition of the lands they had previously inhabited. Thus in places like Mexico and Peru, a significant number of Native inhabitants survived the Conquest, while most Caribbean islands quickly lost their entire Native populations.

Racial Syncretism and the Problem of Racial Categories

Perhaps the most important factor in the development of Latin American society was that, unlike the New England colonists, the male Spanish conquerors did not bring their families with them, which very quickly led to a mixing of European, African, and American races. The forced mixing of these populations inevitably led to widespread racial syncretism, which almost instantly brought about many levels of discrimination. The ethnic and racial distinctions have been the source of much semantic confusion across the continent, because many countries referred to dissimilar segments of their population by similar names. The most contentious classification—"Indian"—derived from Christopher Columbus's mistaken belief that he had reached the Asian continent, became pervasive worldwide and remains so to this day. (In this textbook I have avoided using the terms "Indian" and "Amerindian" in favor of the more accurate "Native," indigenous," or "aboriginal." Moreover, I use the term "Native American" to refer to the original inhabitants—and their descendants—of the entire continent, not merely those of the United States.)

In places that received large numbers of African slaves, such as Brazil and the Caribbean, there emerged a fusion of European and African religion, culture, and music called generally *Mulatto*. By contrast, in places where the African presence was less pronounced, such as Mexico, Guatemala, and Peru, a melding of European and Native characteristics became the dominant culture: the *Mestizo*. Together these fusions pervaded every aspect of colonial society and eventually led to the emergence of modern Latin America.

The term *Mestizo* varies from country to country. In general it refers to a person of mixed European and indigenous ancestry. Yet historically there was also a language and cultural component to the term, and it was understood that Mestizos spoke Spanish and had adopted European dress and customs, even if they were of pure indigenous ancestry. Conversely, persons of mixed blood but who spoke no Spanish were referred to as *indios*. In the Andean region, lower-class Mestizos were also referred to as *cholos*, while upper-class persons of mixed ancestry were called *cruzados*. In Central America, Mestizos are also called *ladinos*, a term originally used in Spain to denote Spanish Jews. In Brazil, a Mestizo who lived in the interior, spoke Portuguese, and interceded with the indigenous populations was called a *caboclo*, whereas a Mestizo who lived on the coast was called a *carioca* and was considered socially superior to the *caboclo*. In Louisiana, *Mulattos* were legally equivalent to Blacks, while in Haiti and Brazil they traditionally constituted a social and economic elite, enjoying respectable status far above that of the Black population. In Brazil, Venezuela, and other countries, Mulattos were also called *pardos*, or "spotted ones."

The term *Creole* is also problematic. (Its very origins are unknown: it may be derived from the Portuguese *crioulo*—literally someone raised by the master of the house—or it may come from a West African language called *Kreyol*.) In some Spanish-speaking countries such as Mexico and Peru, *criollo* refers to White descendants of the early European settlers—as opposed to the *peninsulares*, those born in the mother country who emigrated to the Americas. But in the West Indies, *Creole* came to mean a person of mixed European and African descent, usually speaking a dialect of French, English, or Spanish that was also called *Creole*. Meanwhile, in the Guyana territories on the South American coast, a *Creole* was an American-born descendant of African slaves, as opposed to one born in Africa.

To further complicate matters, the Europeans often set up complex systems of racial classification, which were used for preferential treatment, and that established definitions such as *morisco* or *quadroon* (a person whose ancestry is one-quarter Black), *albino* or *octoroon* (one-eighth Black), and so forth, as well as *castizo* (a person whose father is a Native and whose mother is European). A person of mixed Native and African ancestry was called *lobo* in Mexico, *zambo* in the Andes, and *griffe* in English-speaking countries. The confusion even extends to White European designations: in Cuba, rural descendants of Spaniards named *guajiros* are unrelated to the *guajiros* of Venezuela and Colombia, the most populous indigenous groups from those countries.

Many of these terms can be offensive to modern sensibilities, having derogatory implications that often allude to cultural or even biological inferiority. (*Mulatto* means "small mule" in Spanish.) Enlightened modern societies, while acknowledging socio-historical constructions of race, no longer embrace these distinctions, but rather consider ethnicity in terms of historical, social, economic, political, and cultural characteristics. The music of a Trinidadian calypso singer is interesting not because of the blood in her veins, but because of the historical, cultural, religious, and aesthetic factors that combined to produce it.

The Emergence of Mestizo Culture

The Spanish conquest had been devastating to the Aztec and Inca empires, but many of the Native societies that had been previously subjugated—if they survived the European diseases—welcomed their newfound freedom. Some of them went their own way, retreating to remote areas that had traditionally been their homes and remaining relatively isolated, often in jungles and rain forests such as the Amazon and in the interior of southern Mexico and Central America. Other groups were mountain-dwellers or desert tribes, for example in the Peruvian *Altiplano* or the deserts of northern Mexico. These isolated groups continued to preserve their evolving religion, language, and customs and had a greater independence in their historical development.

Most Natives in the Americas, however, did not belong to isolated cultures in remote areas but rather lived in pre-Columbian urban centers that were now readily accessible to the Europeans. The colonial period was by-and-large not good to them. Millions lost life, resources, and ethnic identity through enslavement, missionary evangelization, and forced conscription in colonial armies. Often ethnic groups were wholly removed from ancestral lands, forced to adapt to new rural environments or urban centers. Missionaries were constantly on alert to spot and eradicate vestiges of Native religions, while landowners kept Native cultures on a tight leash, lest a strong national-ist movement emerged that might lead to revolt, something that did occur more than a few times. In time, the gradual emergence of a dominant Mestizo culture absorbed thousands of Native cultures, and their religions, languages, custom, and identities were lost or altered in the process.

Yet some Native societies were able to survive under the yoke of the European occupiers, due to their ability to change and adapt to evolving circumstances, even to thrive in the face of adversity and destruction. Pragmatism was often a central tenet of the Native way of life, of its outlook towards the future. Long-held customs and beliefs could be altered, even abandoned, to ensure survival. This process was naturally smoother when both old and new cultures held common facets. While the infusion of Spanish and Portuguese elements drastically influenced Native culture, for example in the alteration of their dress, work, and music habits, many aspects of their culture nonethe-less managed to survive, such as the Native diet or the structure of familial interrelationships. Though age-old farming systems were disrupted, agriculture as a practice was generally unaffected by the European presence, and efforts to introduce wheat and other European staples failed to replace the Native dependence on corn. In many cases, lower levels of Native political hierarchy were preserved, as were many traditional features of domestic life.

Conversely, Native populations had an extraordinary influence on colonial society, art, and culture. The Native aesthetic, which had been developed and nurtured over centuries, was not eradicated at the time of the Conquest, but was instead channeled in new directions. Their artistic penchants were preserved and are evident in colonial painting, architecture, sculpture, and music. The Natives embraced Spanish crafts and quickly learned to express themselves in European styles and media—so successfully that they often rivaled their Spanish counterparts. Colonial artistic traditions emerged that syncretically fused elements from both Spanish and Native (as well as African) cultures, complementing the technical and aesthetic elements of each into novel and wholly original syncretic styles.

Mestizo Music

The fall of the Aztec and Inca empires forever changed the nature of musical life on the American continent. Native music of subsequent centuries, even that of completely isolated groups, was henceforth devoid of pre-Colombian large-scale ceremonial elements or sophisticated musical systems. But because of their ability to adapt, the Natives reinterpreted their musical traditions and reapplied them to a new reality, recouping whatever musical remnants they could from the debris of their fallen civilizations. Whether in colonial churches, in heavily populated urban centers, or in remote rural villages, thousands of musical traditions continued to evolve in the Americas, all of them syncretic to various degrees.

An important transformative factor was the introduction of string instruments, which, as noted earlier, had been completely unknown on the American continent. The sudden appearance of lutes, rebecs, guitars, violins, and harps forced a new approach to timbre, performance technique, and instrument construction on the inhabitants of the Andes, whose music was dominated by wind instruments, and those of Mesoamerica, whose music had been percussion-based. Other instruments followed suit, from mandolins and shawms to trumpets, organs, and accordions. Similarly, African drums and marimbas had an enormous influence on some Native traditions. Particularly notable is the fact that one European string instrument—the guitar—in time became dominant throughout the continent.

These instruments brought not only new sonorities to the region but also new ways of combining different sonorities. True to form, Native Americans quickly began making these new instruments their own, and many instruments soon became hybridized, yielding new variations that had been unknown in Europe, with corresponding tuning systems, performance techniques, and composition ideals. Perhaps the most prominent example is the *charango*: a small Andean guitar, made from the shell of an armadillo, that had been unknown to both the Europeans and the ancient Incas.

By the same token, the Natives began using new instruments in ways no European ever did, in religious observances, harvest ceremonies, or courtship rituals that were specific to the Americas. Instruments such as the harp and the guitar, rather than just playing a melody or a complex polyphonic accompaniment, were often exclusively strummed to provide harmony, or played as rhythm and percussion instruments, to the point where they were sometimes classified as drums. European musical forms were also adapted to Latin American needs and practices, as were new concepts of harmony, particularly the sophisticated system of counterpoint that defined the continent's classical tradition and influenced its folk and popular styles. Throughout the colonial period, and into the nineteenth and twentieth centuries, much of the Native music patrimony would be influenced by—and in turn greatly modify—European and African music. Five hundred years into the process, the results are as diverse and wide-ranging as any other element of Latin American culture, yielding the amazing array that today constitutes Latin American and Caribbean music.

European Cultures in America

For centuries, European conquerors, soldiers, priests, settlers, bureaucrats, farmers, and travelers brought with them their worldviews—their cultures, customs, values, social mores, religions, and laws. They also brought with them their music, dances, instruments, and poetic forms, with all their social and religious implications, for music was for the Europeans, as it is for any human civilization, an integral part of who they were. Much of their cultural identity was represented by the sounds emanating from the colonial churches and the aristocratic salons, in much the same way that the drums of the African slaves or the *huéhuetls* of the Native Mexicans were a direct statement of their own existence.

Numerous musical traditions, many of them descended from Spanish medieval folk music and poetry, accompanied the settlers across the ocean and quickly became ensconced in colonial society. These included song forms such as *villancicos, romances, guarachas, jácaras, chanzonetas, tonadas,* and *tonadillas.* European dances were also prevalent in the Americas, including the *pavana, pasacalle, minuete, jota, malagueña, tarantela,* and *seguidilla,* as well as some Black-influenced dances such as the *cumbée.* The origin of other dances remains in question; dances such as the *fandango, petenera, sarabanda,* and *paracumbe* seem to have emerged concurrently on both the American and European continents. Whether homegrown or imported, these popular songs and dances nonetheless readily acquired a distinct American flavor, influenced by Native and Black elements. Usually introduced in the salons of the elite, they were quickly adopted by rural people and transformed into folk dances. As we shall see in later chapters, they developed in different ways, with hundreds of local variations, yielding a rich variety of forms and styles.

Yet many of these diverse forms also retain common elements, even 500 years after their introduction. Thus one can find throughout the continent the traditional dance called *zapateado* (from the Spanish word *zapato*—shoe), derived from the flamenco dancing of Andalusia. With lively rhythms and rapid toe-and-heel work, it is a courtship dance, with the men holding their hands behind their backs and striking the ground forcefully with their heels while the women make subtle advances by lifting the hems of their long skirts. The *zapateado* can be found in many parts of Latin America, from the Andes to Cuba and Mexico, where the most prominent example is the *jarabe tapatío*. Another shared characteristics is the competitive nature of many Latin American song traditions, found for example in the Colombian *vallenato*, the Venezuelan *gaita*, the Argentine *payada de contrapunto*, and the Trinidadian *calypso*. Still another element many of these forms have in common is a particular rhythmic device called the ***sesquiáltera***.

The Latin American *Sesquiáltera*

The *sesquiáltera* (also known as *hemiola* in Western art music) is a polyrhythmic technique found throughout Latin America. It is a device that juxtaposes duple and triple meters, and is most often seen when $\frac{3}{4}$ and $\frac{6}{8}$ rhythms are combined: three groups of two eighth notes alternate with two groups of three eighth notes. To fully understand the concept of the *sesquiáltera*, try clapping or singing the following rhythmic patterns:

1 2 **3** 1 2 **3** 1 2 **1** 2 **1** 2   **1** 2 3 **1** 2 3 **1** 2 1 **2** 1 **2**
>   >   > > >   >   >   > > >

Another way of playing the *sesquiáltera* is:

1 and **2** and **3** and **1** and 2 **and** 3 and **1** and **2** and **3** and **1** and 2 **and** 3 and
>   >   >   >   >   >   >   >   >   >

One of the most famous examples of *sesquiáltera* occurs in the song "America" from the musical *West Side Story* by Leonard Bernstein and Stephen Sondheim. Bernstein deliberately infused the music with the rhythmic complexity of the *sesquiáltera* to evoke the Puerto Rican culture that is an important element of the plot.

I like to **be** in A- **me** - **ri** - **ca**   **O**kay by **me** in A- **me** - **ri** - **ca**
1 2 3 **1** 2 3 **1** 2 **1** 2 **1** 2   **1** 2 3 **1** 2 3 **1** 2 **1** 2 **1** 2
>   >   > > >   >   >   > > >

When the uneven patterns are played simultaneously by different instruments (rather than sequentially, as in the examples), the resulting syncopations can be thrilling and exhilarating. The *sesquiáltera* is derived from medieval rhythmic practices, and before that from Arabic music that influenced the Spanish Peninsula. Brought over by the Spaniards in their *villancicos* and *tonadas*, today it is widespread throughout the continent and can be found, for example, in the Mexican *son jarocho*, the Venezuelan *joropo*, the Paraguayan *polca*, the Chilean *cueca*, the Argentine *zamba* and *chacarera*, and in various Andean styles, all of which are examined in later chapters.

The most widespread European poetic forms are the *décima* and the *copla*. *Coplas* ("couplets" or "verses") typically consist of four lines with either an **a b a b** or **a b c b** rhyming scheme. The *décima* is a classical poetic form that emerged in Spain in the sixteenth century, mostly in the works of the poet and guitarist Vicente Martinez de Espinel, who himself was strongly influenced by medieval Moorish poetry. *Décima* literally means "tenth," an allusion to the form of the poem: ten lines, divided in five pairs or couplets, with the following rhyme scheme: **a b b a a c c d d c**. Both *coplas* and *décimas* are octosyllabic—with eight syllables per line. The influence of Spanish songs and the *décima* form are commonplace throughout Latin America, for example in the Cuban *punto*, the Peruvian *socabón*, the Mexican *canción*, the Panamanian *pindín*, and the Colombian *vallenato*.

The Emergence of African Culture

The epidemics of the New World posed a problem for the Europeans, who needed a large workforce to build their cities, mine their silver and copper mines, till their fields, and work their plantations. They quickly turned to another source of labor found in yet a third continent: Africa. The slave trade had begun with the Portuguese in the middle of the fifteenth century, and as early as 1505, the first Africans were being imported to Cuba. Within a few decades, Spanish, Dutch, and British slave traders joined the Portuguese in shipping their human cargo across the Atlantic. This was the so-called "Middle Passage," the second in a three-legged journey that brought European manufactured goods to the coast of Africa, where they were exchanged for humans. These were then taken to the Americas and traded for crops such as cotton, sugar, coffee, and tobacco, which were then brought back to Europe, completing the cycle. Between 1505 and 1888, the year slavery was finally outlawed on the continent, as many of twenty million slaves were forcibly brought from Africa under the most inhumane conditions. Physical torture and psychological humiliation took their toll on the Africans in the cramped and suffocating cargo bays of the slave ships. An estimated two million did not survive the voyage; those who did were condemned to a life of brutal toil with no hope of returning to their homeland and little prospects of freedom.

Half of the imported slaves went to the Caribbean, another third to Brazil. As a result of this forced migration, most of the American lands today form part of the African Diaspora—the diffusion of African people from their original homeland to other parts of the world. The slaves were captured or bought mostly in West Africa, in what is now Senegal, Guinea, Ivory Coast, Ghana, Togo, Benin, and Nigeria, and in Central Africa, in modern Gabon, Congo, Angola, Zambia, Zimbabwe, and Mozambique. They seldom spoke the same language, and they belonged to various—often enemy—ethnic and cultural groups, including prominently the Ewe, Ashanti, Yoruba, and Mandinga. Significantly, they brought with them much of their cultures, religions, and musics, all of which in turn influenced to various degrees the cultural development of the new European dominion. Though one can make few broad generalizations about the myriad African-influenced musical styles found on the continent, some musical traits were often shared by many cultures. Thus, and taking into account any number of exceptions, one can survey the music of the African inhabitants of the New World and note the following characteristics:

- The music tends to have complex rhythms and syncopations, often based on patterns such as the *clave, tresillo,* and *cinquillo* (examined in later chapters).
- The form of the music tends to be open-ended and in two parts (AB), as opposed to the symmetrical, closure-oriented three-part form (ABA) typical of European music.
- Songs tend to consist of short repeated phrases in call-and-response form, as opposed to long elaborate melodies. Think of the famous lyrics from the Jamaican folk song, "Banana Boat Song":

    Call: *Hey mister tally-man, tally me bananas.*
    Response: *Daylight come an' I want go home.*

- The drum tends to be the instrument of choice, with some important distinctions:
    - Upright-drum practices, in which the drummer sits in front of a standing drum, are of West-African origin.
    - Horizontal-drum techniques, in which the drummer sits astride a horizontally laying drum, playing it between his legs, are derived from Central African practices.
    - The marimba and thumb-piano, both of African origin, are also widespread.
- Most importantly: African inhabitants of the Americas almost invariably adopted European and Native traits, instruments, forms, and styles, and combined them with their own. In a word, their music became syncretic.

But Africans faced different challenges in different places. The nature of colonial culture varied throughout the Americas, and was affected by myriad factors such as climate, language, religion, geographical terrain, and so on, as well as the complex differences of the various European source cultures. These differences combined with the varied cultural characteristics of the Africans themselves, resulting in musical traditions that were extremely diverse. Mixing African and European cultures did not automatically yield a generic result, as can be attested by the marked differences between Brazilian samba, Cuban rumba, Jamaican reggae, and Dixieland jazz. Moreover, the African presence was not felt uniformly across the continent. In countries such as Mexico and Peru, disease decimated but did not result in the complete annihilation of Native populations, negating the necessity to bring large numbers of African slaves to these areas. The syncretic dynamic thus worked very differently in these countries, though it was equally pronounced.

Religious Syncretism

Syncretism is also evident in the religious devotion that was a key aspect of colonial life, from Mexico to the Caribbean and from Brazil to the Peruvian *Altiplano*. The missionaries realized from the beginning that attempting to destroy Native culture completely would be counterproductive to their efforts at conversion. Instead, a conscious attempt was made to incorporate some elements of the Native worldview into the transplanted European culture, creating a completely new entity. Aware of their susceptibility to ceremony and their propensity for splendor, the missionaries did their best to lure and charm the new converts by making religious celebrations, processions, and festivals a source of joy. Every aspect of evangelization was geared towards facilitating the Native's embracing of Christianity, including lavish ceremonies, expressive rituals, colorful temples, appealing icons, statues, paintings, and other objects of devotion. Familiarizing the Natives with the physical characteristics of the new faith would inevitably draw them into its moral and spiritual concepts. Churches and cathedrals were deliberately constructed over the foundations of the destroyed Native temples, in order to make clear in the minds of the Natives that the new religion was to supplant the old. Buildings and altars were impressively ornamented with breathtaking murals, sculptures, flowers, and tapestries, and brightly illuminated for masses and services. Continuous use of music in the services was of course one of the main manifestations of this affinity for ceremony. By emphasizing the grandeur of the Christian celebrations, the missionaries attempted to increase the faith of the new converts and improve the morale of the recently subjugated peoples.

Throughout Latin America, celebrations were held for local patron saints and Catholic feasts, each displaying a distinct emotion. Thus, Christmas would be a time of joy, with loud and colorful celebrations that included intricate crèches and gift offerings, while Easter rituals were more subdued and solemn, reflecting anguish and penitence, but also hope for salvation. Processions were loud, expensive, lengthy, and elaborate, and followed a path that was sumptuously decorated and lined with thousands of men, women, and children. Natives carried images of the local patron saint, as well as candles, crucifixes, or offerings, while penitents walked for miles on bloody knees, as some continue to do today. Music, singing and dancing, eating and drinking, fireworks, costumes, decorations, flowers, and even intricate floats all helped to celebrate the Virgin or a particular saint. Ecstatic self-flagellations took place inside the church during Easter, in the midst of large amounts of candles and flowers. These celebrations and processions have continued uninterrupted for centuries and are still held in many places in Latin America. Religious celebrations also served as community social affairs, to commemorate an important visiting dignitary, or to honor the death of a local leader.

They often included supplications to ward off disease or crop failure, or rituals of thanksgiving.

The Spaniards also introduced dance, drama, and pantomime as means of conversion. Traditional Spanish dance-dramas such as *Morismas, Matachines,* and *Moros y Cristianos* illustrated the medieval battles between Moors and Christians, with the Christians invariably triumphing over the infidel, providing a moral undertone meant to influence the Natives whose religious convictions might be suspect. Assorted *Pastorellas, Pasiones, Comedias a lo Divino*—stylized representations of the Passion of Christ—were imported from Spain, where they had been popular throughout the Middle Ages, and quickly assumed an American flavor. Other theatrical works such as *entremeses, jácaras,* and *mojigangas* incorporated elements of Spanish, Native, and Black culture. Designed for religious instruction and moral edification, these plays were mostly doctrinal in nature: reenactments of scripture, the life of Christ, the story of John the Baptist, or historical events such as the capture of Jerusalem. Titles included *The Fall of the First Parents, The Annunciation of the Nativity of Saint John, The Annunciation of our Lady,* and *The Nativity of St. John the Baptist.* The newly converted Natives, who saw in them a lighter side of the otherwise heavy and solemn Catholic rite, readily accepted them. Actors, singers, and dancers were all Native, and they often spoke and sang in Native tongues. Performances in Spanish invariably included Native words and expressions that delighted the audiences. Musical accompaniment included strumming guitars, flutes and whistles, castanets, drums, and maracas. Representations usually involved scenes of mock fighting with wooden swords, masks, and costumes, and there was often much clandestine drinking involved, both by participants and spectators. The tradition of the edifying play continues virtually uninterrupted to this day, and religious ceremonies throughout Latin America are still immersed in splendor that rivals that of their colonial, and indeed of their pre-Columbian, ancestors.

Yet the missionaries' strategy of supplanting the old religion with the new backfired somewhat, for although the Natives did worship at the new sites and in new ways, the substitution of old temples and ceremonies with new ones provided a measure of spiritual continuity that permitted the banned faith to thrive (albeit covertly) alongside Christian doctrine. The Aztec, Maya, and Inca pantheons were similar to those of the Greeks and Romans in that they were open to new beliefs and new deities. They had detailed and complex mythologies that traditionally incorporated the gods of conquered peoples, which were then freely worshiped. It was thus not particularly difficult for them to accept Christ into their religious tradition. Christianity was compatible with their own rites, which were tolerant at their core. More difficult was the missionary's demand that the Natives worship *exclusively* at the Christian altar, that they surrender their previous beliefs and customs. For the most part, the Natives were not beholden to the idea of religious exclusivity, of the adoption of one faith at the expense of all others. Though Christianity was often accepted with ease, many Natives were unable or unwilling to abandon the traditions that had guided their families and villages for centuries.

As a result, Native religions endured, at first alongside (but separate from) Christianity, and increasingly in a mixture of interconnected Christian and Native beliefs that adapted to the specific needs of the populace. Native celebrations, feasts, and processions were combined with the Christian faith and held away from the watchful eyes of priests and church officials. Idols would find their way onto altars, hidden under crosses or stashed away in church walls. Often, Native and Christian deities were deliberately merged to facilitate worship. Thus, the Virgin Mary became associated with Tonatzin, the mother of the Aztec gods, and as a result became more readily accepted as the Virgin of Guadalupe. Another example was the *Guelaguetza*, an ancient Zapotec ceremony of thanksgiving that took place in Oaxaca in July, which was seamlessly transformed into the feast of the Virgin of Mount Carmel, celebrated on July 16, a tradition that still continues.

Meanwhile, African slaves were developing their own religions, based on communications with the ancestral spirits who dwelled in the African continent. To shield these activities from the disapproving eyes of the plantation owners and church authorities, the ancestral spirits were given Christian identities. For example, the Afro-Cuban Santería spirit called Babalú Aye, the father of the world, was closely identified with St. Lazarus. Over time the two deities—and the two faiths—came to be intermingled and fused together. The adoption of Christianity, ironically, also injected into slave culture a yearning for spiritual liberation that often developed into a form of resistance and, frequently, revolt.

Thus, Christianity melded with Native or African religions (and often both) throughout the Americas, creating new syncretic forms of worship that survive to this day. These belief systems are not a rejection of Christianity. For the most part, their followers are sincere Christians who complement their beliefs with those followed by their forefathers for centuries. Modern church officials have often taken a pragmatic approach to syncretic religions. Priests and missionaries in remote areas—often Natives themselves—casually accept Native elements in church and consider them not dangerous idolatry but rather an opportunity to reinforce the faith of the flock. Nor is there contradiction between the faiths: while Christianity emphasizes salvation and eternal life, Native rites—at least in practice—are often more concerned with fertility, disease, and crop failure, as well as social concepts such as love, revenge, and community status. A key element of many African rites is communication with an African homeland most practitioners have never seen. In most cases, the rituals provide an important sense of identity.

Perhaps the most widespread example of syncretic celebration on the continent is that of carnival. Spelled car**ni**val in English, car*na*val in Portuguese and Spanish, and termed *Mardi Gras* in French-speaking countries, it is celebrated in different ways—even on different dates—depending on the country. Most countries on the continent have some kind of carnival celebration, with the most famous ones taking place in Rio de Janeiro, Trinidad, and New Orleans. It usually takes place prior to Lent, a final release before the rigors of fasting. The common elements of carnival are exuberant local color, costumes, parades, and music and dancing derived from European, African, and Native traditions. In the southern hemisphere's warm summer, the carnival season can last throughout the extended period between New Year's and Lent. The revelry reaches a fever pitch during the five days between the Friday and Tuesday before Ash Wednesday.

The syncretic process was not limited to culture, race, and religion, but extended to all aspects of life including agricultural practices and food preparation. Africans introduced culinary customs that revolved around bananas and cassava. Europeans introduced grains such as oats, wheat, and rice, and livestock such as horses, donkeys, cattle, sheep, and pigs. They also brought alien flowers, weeds, vegetables, fruit trees—and rats. Some of the imported crops came to dominate the Americas, particularly sugar and coffee. Europeans also provided technology, for example wagons pulled by beasts of burden, plowshares, and textile techniques. The influence also went in the other direction. Two American crops, corn and potatoes, virtually ended famine in Europe, producing much higher yields than wheat and rice, and growing where those crops would not. Corn could be fed to domesticated animals, and thus revolutionized Europe's meat and dairy products. Cotton was an invaluable commodity rarely found in Europe, but plentiful in the Americas, as were chilies, tobacco, squash, pineapples, tomatoes, sunflowers, peanuts, turkeys, chocolate, rubber, rare hardwoods, and coveted dyes, notably that of the Mexican cochineal. And of course there's the music, whose syncretic evolution will take up most of the chapters in this textbook.

MODERN NATIVE SOCIETIES

More than half a millennium after Columbus first landed in America, Native societies maintain an important cultural—and occasionally political—presence in many Latin American countries. The proportion of indigenous population is naturally greatest in the former Maya, Aztec, and Inca lands: Bolivia (55 percent), Peru (45 percent), Ecuador (25 percent), Guatemala (40 percent), and Mexico (30 percent). Conversely, other areas saw the virtual eradication of the Native population, so that in many countries, the Native percentage remains in the single digits, and is sometimes less that one percent. Pre-Columbian languages have splintered into various dialects, so that there are dozens of modern versions of Maya, and over 40 versions of Quechua. Some studies have identified more than two thousand separate languages in Latin America.

Cultural—and musical—consideration of modern Native groups must be undertaken with caution. An important point to remember is that the populations that inhabited the Americas in 1492 usually bear little resemblance to any current inhabitants of the continent, even those, like Mexico's Lacandones or Venezuela's Yanomamo, that have remained in relative isolation. As a rule, human societies evolve, and, while the music, customs, and religions of these tribes may be unrelated to European or African ones, they also are distinct from those of their ancestors of half a millennium earlier.

The dangers faced by Native groups during the colonial period have not always let up in modern times. In every country on the continent, Native groups have been marginalized to various degrees. Forced labor, conscription, exploitation, political pressure to assimilate, and loss of resources and ancestral lands have continued to erode the integrity of traditional societies. Having finally become somewhat resistant to age-old European diseases, many Native groups are increasingly threatened by new ones such as AIDS and dengue fever. Additionally, the intensified destruction of the rain forest in recent years has seen a precipitous decline in the viability of many indigenous groups.

In the twenty-first century, modern forces of globalization and modernization continue to conspire against traditional societies, notably by encouraging urban migration of their youth. In many areas, Protestant missionaries have replaced Catholic ones, claiming, like their colonial counterparts, to have the best interest of the Natives in mind, providing them not only with the word of God but also literacy, education, and health practices. Most Native communities have to balance their economic development with the threat of acculturation, and the continuous dilemma is often how to achieve a better way of life without sacrificing traditional character. Too often, the arrived-at solutions result in entire Native groups—along with their languages, religions, and musical customs—being absorbed into the dominant Mestizo or European culture or altogether disappearing from the American continent.

Indigenous Music Today

It is in this context that music has become an important signifier of ethnic identity. In the face of hardship and sometimes even annihilation, a Native group survives through its music and other cultural elements which often serve important familial, social, and religious functions. Similar traditions can be found across the continent including healing ceremonies, relationships with nature and animals, worship of totems and deities, and contact with—or protection from—the supernatural. Rituals dedicated to the agricultural cycle are also prominent, including the cultivation of corn or cassava, the harvest, and the rainy season, as are rites of passage such as births, courtship rituals, funeral ceremonies, naming ceremonies, and war practices. Non-members of Native cultures should be careful in how they judge these rituals and the music that accompany them. In many Native worldviews, the present is but one moment in the evolving continuum. From this point of view, there is no such thing as a pure, indigenous style, there never has been and never will be. An Aztec warrior would not identify the music in 1450 as the true "authentic" music, but as an instantaneous snapshot of a continuing process. The music of his modern descendants is just as valid a snapshot, even if it includes European and African instruments and practices. And while some modern Native musicians have deliberately espoused the "pure and unadulterated" music of their ancestors for political or self-identity purposes, this too is a modern attitude.

In the twenty-first century, indigenous music is increasingly being recognized as an integral part of Latin American cultures. Important studies by prominent ethnomusicologists are continuously being published, and Native traditions are becoming commercially successful in a global market. Additionally, local and regional festivals and conferences dedicated to Native music have emerged, including prominently the First Indigenous Music Festival of the Americas, held in Mexico City in 2003, the first event to bring together Native musical traditions from all points of the continent.

The countries that have the most prominent Native musical styles are, not surprisingly, the former Maya and Aztec lands (explored in Chapter 3) and those of the Inca civilizations (discussed in Chapter 8.) Additionally, however, there are literally thousands of aboriginal groups of different sizes, with millions of individuals inhabiting the continent from Alaska to Tierra del Fuego. All these groups have musical traditions that have undergone a wide range of syncretic evolution, to the point where it is often difficult to draw a clear line between purely indigenous music and the (usually) Mestizo folk music that gradually evolved from it. Attempting to explore and describe all of these musical cultures is beyond the scope of this textbook. Instead, a few of the most prominent are explored at logical places.

LATIN AMERICA TODAY

The American Continent consists of four major areas: North America, Central America, South America, and the Caribbean. North America consists of Canada, the United States, and Mexico. The seven countries of Central America are Guatemala, El Salvador, Honduras, Nicaragua, Costa Rica, Panama, and Belize, all of whose inhabitants speak Spanish except for Belize, where English is the predominant language. South America contains 12 independent countries: Venezuela, Colombia, Ecuador, Peru, Bolivia, Chile, Argentina, Uruguay, Paraguay (where the predominant European language is Spanish), Brazil (where Portuguese is spoken), Guyana (formerly British Guyana), and Suriname (formerly Dutch Guyana). Additionally, South America contains French Guiana, still a possession of France. Finally, the Caribbean contains 13 independent countries and about a dozen territories still dependent on France, Britain, the Netherlands and the United States. Of the 35 countries and dozen territories in the hemisphere, only Bolivia and Paraguay are landlocked.

A question that often surfaces is "What exactly is Latin America?" One traditional definition encompasses those areas in the western hemisphere whose inhabitants predominantly speak Romance languages—those derived from ancient Latin—especially Spanish and Portuguese. Another definition puts it as the entire landmass south of the Rio Grande—the borderlands between the United States and Mexico—plus certain islands of the Caribbean. Yet these definitions, based on commonalities of language and culture, have always been difficult to sustain, and are becoming increasingly so. Problematic are the Guyanas, very much part of the South American continent but separated from their neighbors by history, language, and culture. Another problematic issue is that of the Caribbean, with its array of multicultural and multilingual islands. But the real obstacle to achieving an accurate definition is the increasing migration of peoples within the continent, as well as from outside the hemisphere. This textbook takes the firm position that Latin America includes the entire western hemisphere, for the days when Latin American culture and society began on the southern shores of the Rio Grande are quickly falling behind us. Indeed, in the twenty-first century, the entire continent—including the United States and Canada—is now infused with elements of Latin American music and culture. If the previous definitions are still used for historical and political convenience, the distinctions have little meaning to those interested in studying the region's music.

The text continues with a discussion of the European-based art music tradition, examining styles from different countries and different eras. We then consider in turn six major geographical areas on the continent, concentrating on the folk and popular music of each: Mexico and Central America, the Caribbean, Brazil, Northern South America, the Andes, and finally the Southern Cone. Though the United States has historically been an integral part of the evolution of Latin American music, it does not get its own chapter. Instead, its contributions are examined in conjunction with the evolution of various styles in other countries. Thus, discussion of the emergence of salsa in New York and of Tex-Mex in the borderlands appears in the Caribbean and Mexico chapters, respectively.

My intent is not to relate the entire musical life of each country, for that would prohibitively extend the size of this textbook. Rather, I explore the principal local styles and genres, and discuss foreign ones only if they have had a particular impact on the musical development of the country. Moreover, neighboring countries often share similar cultural and musical evolutionary processes, for example the syncretic melding of European, African, and Native elements, the development of carnival traditions, or the influence of rock music on traditional folk styles. I describe these processes in detail at logical places but then try to limit their full recounting for every culture, region, and country, trusting the reader to make the appropriate connections.

Much of the music of Latin America is still unknown and undiscovered, and much of it is in danger of being lost through globalization, modernization, or simply because the people themselves are disappearing or being absorbed into the dominant culture. In isolated towns and villages, from the mountains of Mexico, Peru, and Chile to the jungles of Guatemala, Panama, and Brazil, and to sparsely inhabited Caribbean islands, people are making music that no outsider has ever heard, let alone documented, published, or recorded. For every success story such as that of the Garífuna (an Afro-indigenous tribe from Central America whose music has become famous virtually overnight), there are hundreds or perhaps even thousands of other styles and traditions that are practiced by a few villages, or even a few families. There is work for anthropological and ethnomusicological research for generations. Hopefully, the richness and historical importance of Latin American music that this textbook is attempting to convey will inspire students to undertake such work in years to come.

A NOTE ON THE ACCOMPANYING CDs
AND THE RECOMMENDED LISTENING

The more than 40 musical examples on the CDs that accompany this text are representative of just some of the styles discussed in subsequent chapters. For hundreds of other styles, I have listed **Recommended Listening** examples, taken for the most part from commercially available compact discs. In many cases, more than one example is recommended. In this increasingly digital world, it is more and more possible to acquire single tracks rather than entire CDs. There are also several useful compilations that are also commercially available. Of note are the original field recordings of the ethnomusicologist Alan Lomax that have recently been released and that provide an invaluable insight into many Latin American cultures. Two compilations that nicely complement this textbook are *Africa in America: Music from 19 Countries* (Corason Records) and *Raíces Latinas* (Smithsonian Folkways), which together offer examples of more than 50 different styles from all over Latin America. Yet another important source of ancillary materials is the JVC/Smithsonian Folkways Video Anthology of Music and Dance of the Americas, which provides extensive video footage of more than 150 music tradition on the American continent, most of which are covered in this textbook. Finally, the recent explosion of Internet-based video examples—notably those found on YouTube.com—has provided an invaluable resource for both students and teachers of Latin American and Caribbean music. Virtually every stylistic example discussed in the text can be illustrated by a video readily available on the Internet. However, as of this writing, there is no reliably fixed source for these video examples, and many of them are prone to disappear overnight. I have thus not provided readers with specific Internet sources, trusting them to do the appropriate Internet searches on their own.

2

The Classical Tradition

INTRODUCTION

For many—perhaps most—people, the first thing that comes to mind when confronted with the idea of Latin American music is one of the popular styles that has recently become prominent, styles such as salsa, reggae, *tejano*, or samba. Much of the world is unaware that Latin America has a classical tradition that is as long and rich as some of the practices in Europe. American polyphonic masterpieces were written well before the birth of William Shakespeare. Fabulous organs were played in American churches and cathedrals decades before the pilgrims landed at Plymouth Rock, and sumptuous operas were performed on the continent long before the United States came into existence.

Classical—or the preferred term, "art"—music has often been defined as a learned tradition, studied and analyzed in an academic setting, transmitted in written form, performed in formal concerts for attentive audiences, and composed by known composers, as opposed to anonymous works. Yet these definitions are problematic in Latin America, since many of its folk and popular traditions also have those characteristics. Everywhere in Latin America, the integration of low and high culture has always been a matter of course—a trait inherited from Spain, where Christian, Muslim, and Jewish traditions had always been incorporated into society and reflected in the music. Modern proponents of Latin American art music still do not hesitate to include elements from the folk or popular realms, and vice-versa.

The terms "art" and "classical" can apply to the learned music of any country. (India and Japan, for example, have important classical music traditions.) For our present purposes, however, the terms will refer only to the Western art music tradition that began in Europe during the Middle Ages and expanded to the Americas in the sixteenth century and later to other parts of the world. The broad styles of Western art music—Renaissance, Baroque, Classical, Romantic, and Modern—each had their equivalents in the New World. These will be examined in turn, though to study the classical traditions of each of the almost 50 countries and territories that constitute Latin America and the Caribbean is beyond the scope of this textbook. Instead, general stylistic trends will be presented, highlighted by representative works of prominent composers from throughout the continent.

THE COLONIAL PERIOD

From a purely utilitarian point of view, music fulfilled very specific functions during the colonial period, addressing the needs of society at large. For missionaries and priests, it served to evangelize and later to sustain Christian ideology. For the civil authorities, music was used to commemorate specific events, such as the arrival of a viceroy or archbishop, or the death of a monarch. For the Spanish immigrants and their descendants, it served to establish a spiritual and emotional connection with the far-off homeland. For the Natives, and later for a growing number of Mestizos and Blacks, music was a spiritual conduit, but also a form of entertainment and public diversion, an escape from an often-brutal existence. Landowners called *encomenderos* ("land trustees") profited from both the religious elements and the entertainment aspect of music, which helped preserve political control and authority by appeasing the Native work force.

Within a century after the arrival of the Spaniards in the Americas, much of the continent had been organized under viceroyalties, which were ruled by a viceroy (a "vice-king," one who stands in for the king). These viceroyalties eventually included New Spain (including Mexico and the Caribbean and stretching as far north as California), New Granada (present-day Colombia, Ecuador, and Venezuela), La Plata (Bolivia, Paraguay, Uruguay, and Argentina), and Peru (which also included present-day Chile). Additionally, Brazil was ruled by the Portuguese and had its own system of colonial organization.

Spanish and Portuguese immigrants brought with them their songs, ballads, and dances, which became the root of much of Latin America's folk music. But in the beginning, much of the art music revolved around the church, as it did in Europe. Within a few years, the Church established itself on the continent with an extensive bureaucracy, the founding of missions and dioceses, and the building of churches and cathedrals. The Church hierarchy also included the founding of several chapters of the notorious Spanish Inquisition, charged with cleansing the land of heresy.

It was in these missions, churches, and cathedrals that colonial musical life flourished, for the Catholic priests and missionaries had brought with them the rich music traditions that had been part of the European church for over a thousand years. Friars belonging to monastic orders, such as the Franciscans, the Dominicans, the Augustinians, and the Jesuits, established missions wherever feasible. From California to Tierra del Fuego, in urban centers, and in remote islands, mountains, deserts, and jungles, thousands of missionaries set out to convert Native Americans to the Christian faith. In the process, they also set up important educational systems, at the basis of which was musical instruction, resulting in the widespread diffusion of Western European musical practices across the continent. Many of the missionaries themselves became first-rate composers, and their choirs and orchestras often consisted exclusively of Native musicians.

Recommended Viewing: For a depiction of missionary work in colonial South America, see the 1986 film *The Mission*, which also contains a remarkable music score.

In the ensuing centuries, churches were built in virtually every city, town, and village, and the church music tradition became widespread. Important musical centers included Mexico City, Puebla, Oaxaca, and Valladolid (Mexico), Bogotá (Colombia), La Paz and Sucre (Bolivia), Guatemala City (Guatemala), Cuzco and Lima (Peru), Montevideo (Uruguay), Buenos Aires (Argentina), and Santiago (Chile). The first American cathedral was established in Santiago in Cuba (1522), soon followed by those in Mexico City (1528), Puebla (1531), Lima (1543), Sucre (1553), and many others.

Colonial Church Music

European church music at the time of the conquest consisted primarily of two types, both of which were readily transplanted to the New World. The first was plainchant (often referred to as Gregorian chant), which had emerged in the Middle Ages and was the foundation of all church music throughout Europe. It is an unaccompanied, religious vocal style that is monophonic, meaning it has a single melodic line (though that line can be sung by many singers in unison). There are literally thousands of chants, one for just about every aspect of the Catholic liturgy. Almost from the very beginning, the rich medieval chant repertoire was brought to the New World, and it quickly became the backbone of ceremonial music in churches and missions throughout the continent. In various places in Latin America, such as certain towns in the state of Michoacán, Mexico, the chant tradition has survived continuously down to our time.

The second transplanted style was Renaissance polyphony, which had begun in Europe in the first half of the fifteenth century. Polyphony simply means "many voices," and the style is one in which two, three, four, or more voices are superimposed upon one another. The most skillful composers of Renaissance polyphony were those who successfully combined the rhythmic and melodic elements of the various voices and produced an interesting and harmonious sound. Polyphonic works were most often written for and performed in church, but several types of secular polyphony also emerged.

During the Renaissance, Spain was one of the most important musical centers in Europe. The Golden Age of Spanish music occurred during the 75-year period between 1525 and 1600, corresponding almost exactly with the age of Spanish empire building. This confluence was no coincidence: The common link was the great wealth that the colonies were generating, since societies that acquire great resources often stimulate, produce, and support great art. Spanish polyphony was greatly influenced by the choral innovations developed in Venice, Italy, and in particular by the use of multiple choirs. Extremely intricate polyphony became the vogue in Spain during this period. Thousands of exalted works were written by dozens of Spanish composers, most prominently among them Cristóbal de Morales, Francisco Guerrero, and Tomás Luis de Victoria. Their works were the height of a polyphonic style that emphasized smooth lines, complex imitative voices, and above all a reliance on aural beauty that sought to honor the divine.

Because of Spain's musical affinity, the New World received numerous Renaissance musicians and composers whose early years had been spent in extraordinary musical surroundings. They took the journey across the Atlantic, bringing with them the works of the Spanish masters, which were then performed in churches and cathedrals throughout the land. Important music libraries and archives began emerging all over Latin America and the Caribbean. More importantly, the compositional style itself was transported wholesale, and it was not long before Renaissance works were being composed on American shores. Polyphony and polychorality reached new heights throughout the colonies, and composers delighted in displaying and honing their contrapuntal virtuosity.

New World churches and cathedrals had elaborate musical organizations, the larger ones having multiple choirs and a panoply of instrumentalists. At the center of this music world was the chapelmaster, typically the most important and talented musician in the region. The chapelmaster (*maestro de capilla* in Spanish and *mestre de capela* in Portuguese) was at once composer; choral and orchestral conductor; teacher of voice, organ, and composition; business manager of the choir and orchestra, and administrator of the entire musical establishment. Rarely an ordained priest, he was often also charged with musical education, not only of his own musicians, but of members of the general public as well. Most important of all, the chapelmaster was the artistic director of the musical establishment, making decisions regarding the composition of the choir and orchestra, selection of the musical program, and performance of the music for the masses, offices, special feasts, and other church ceremonies. Many of the cathedral chapelmasters are recognized primarily as important composers, and much of the colonial musical heritage is owed to them.

In the early years of the colony, musical activity emulated Spanish tradition, and the repertoire was mostly Spanish, complemented by occasional Italian and Flemish works. Some of the Spanish musicians who emigrated to the Americas during the sixteenth century were Pedro de Gante, Juan Navarro, Hernando Franco, and Juan Xuárez, who became Mexico City's first chapelmaster in 1539. Of the sixteenth-century composers in New Spain, it was Franco who achieved the greatest quality and sophistication. Franco became chapelmaster of the Mexico City Cathedral in 1575, and his works are on par, and often superior to, many of his Renaissance counterparts across the ocean. In particular, his series of *Magnificats* and his "Salve Regina" represent some of the finest music of the early colonial period. In South America, the most important sixteenth-century composer was Gutierre Fernández Hidalgo, who was successively chapelmaster in Bogotá, Quito, and Sucre (then known as La Plata). Like Franco, Hidalgo is remembered for his *Magnificats* and several *Salve Reginas*.

> **Recommended Listening:** "Salve Regina" and "Magnificat Quarti Toni" by Hernando Franco, from the CD *Masterpieces of Mexican Polyphony*.

> **Recommended Listening:** "Salve Regina" and "Magnificat Secundus Tonus" by Gutierre Fernández Hidalgo, from the CD *Musique à la Cathédrale Santa Fé de Bogotá*.

Soon thereafter, Criollo (American-born of European descent) musicians began writing important church compositions, and by the seventeenth century, the continent could boast numerous composers who had achieved great skill, including Juan de Herrera, chapelmaster of the cathedral in Bogotá from 1703 to 1738, and Francisco López Capillas, Mexico City chapelmaster from 1654 to 1674.

> **Recommended Listening:** "Misa de Difuntos a 5 voces: Kyrie eleison" by Juan de Herrera, from the CD *Musique à la Cathédrale Santa Fé de Bogotá*.

> **Recommended Listening:** "Alleluia: Dic nobis, Maria" by Francisco Lopez Capillas, from the CD *Masterpieces of Mexican Polyphony*.

The size and design of colonial cathedrals often allowed the presence of two separate and distinct choirs on either side of the altar, a facet that was readily exploited by composers seeking to expand their musical language. Polychoral compositions by Juan de Araujo (Lima and Sucre), Antonio de Salazar (Mexico City), and Juan Gutiérrez de Padilla (Puebla) represent an advanced achievement in this style, to a degree that was not reached in Europe during the Renaissance. Though polychorality did exist in Europe, particularly in the music associated with Venice, most European musicians in the seventeenth century had moved on to a different—Baroque—style, which the Americans were not particularly concerned with. In a very real sense, Latin American composers were able to extend the ideals of the Renaissance to a degree that was no longer possible in Europe. They had an additional century and a half to further explore the possibilities of modality, counterpoint, polyphony, and polychorality.

> **Recommended Listening:** "Ut Queant Laxis" by Juan de Araujo, from the CD *New World Symphonies: Baroque Music from Latin America*.
>
> **Recommended Listening:** "Salve Regina for 8 voices" by Juan Gutiérrez de Padilla, from the CD *Masterpieces of Mexican Polyphony*.

CDI, Track 1: Renaissance Polyphony: *Missa Ego flos campi: Agnus Dei*

Music: Juan Gutiérrez de Padilla
Instrumentation: two four-voice choirs
Notes: Padilla's Mass makes use of two choirs that respond antiphonally to each other. The Agnus Dei, the final movement of the Catholic Mass, is a prayer that is normally repeated three times in its entirety. Here Padilla assigns each phrase antiphonally to both choirs, who toss it back and forth between them, before coming to a cadence (pause or ending). The material often appears in imitation within one choir, then reappears in the other choir, providing a texture of double imitation.

0:00	Agnus Dei	*Lamb of God*
0:55	Qui tollis peccata mundi,	*Who takes away the sins of the world,*
1:05	Miserere nobis,	*Have mercy upon us,*
1:37	Dona nobis pacem.	*Grant us peace.*

Instrumental Music

Not all colonial art music was vocal, and instrumental music quickly gained a foothold in the New World. Numerous instruments, including oboes, trumpets, horns, cornets, sackbuts (early trombones), violins, *bajónes* (bass viols), and flutes had been present in American cathedral orchestras as early as 1575. In addition, *orlos* (a kind of oboe), fifes, harps, guitars, mandolins, *jabelas* (Moroccan flutes), dulcians (early bassoons), *rabeles* (rebecs), *chirimía* (an oboe-like instrument), and *vihuelas* (a kind of guitar) were common, as well as a large selection of Native instruments. By the seventeenth century, all of the major musical centers had a strong contingent of instruments at their disposal. Instruments were used in religious feasts to complement the voices in *villancicos, jácaras,* and *chanzoneta,* which are discussed below. By the eighteenth century, full instrumental accompaniments were expected in church performances.

Exceptional organs also pervaded the colonies. As in Europe, the organ was a key device in Christian worship, and the powerful sounds emitting from the bellows and pipes complemented the monumental colonial architecture and emphasized the solemnity of Christianity to the assembled congregation. The artistry of Spanish organ building was at its peak during this period, and it often surpassed even that of Dutch and German artists. As a result, many magnificent organs were imported from Spain, and soon organs began to be built in the New World as well, such as the organ of the Mexico City Cathedral, built in 1735, which still exists. The most spectacular instruments were of course those in the great cathedrals, but organs were present everywhere in the country, and small towns in rural Guatemala, Peru, or Paraguay could boast of intricate instruments that would make

Organ at the Arequipa Cathedral, Arequipa, Peru. Linda Whitwam©Dorling Kindersley, Courtesy of Catedral de Arequipa.

many European cities envious. The mission churches in the Pueblos of present-day New Mexico, the northernmost part of New Spain, received shipments of dulcians and *chirimías* as early as 1626, and by 1664 they each had their own organ.

Musical Syncretism

The missionaries who undertook the conversion of the Natives in the early years of the colony were often trained musicians. They immediately immersed themselves in Native cultures and learned the Native languages and quickly realized that the Natives had used music almost exclusively as a religious element. They thus developed the concept of missionary work through music, based on the idea that musical training of the Natives would parallel and thus facilitate their religious conversion and their moral uplifting. Singing schools were quickly founded in Mexico, Guatemala, Peru, and as far north as New Mexico. Biblical passages were readily translated into Native languages, turned into song and taught to the Natives. Christian words were interjected into existing Native melodies, reinforcing the new faith with familiar elements of Native culture.

Personal reports from the clergy to the Spanish King praising Native musical ability.

"Experience teaches us how much the Indians are edified by its sacred music for they are great lovers of music, and the religious who hear their confessions tell us that they are converted more by music than by preaching, and we see them come from distant regions to hear it, and desire to learn it."

—Juan de Zumárraga, Bishop of Mexico City, in a letter to King Charles V, 1540.

"I have composed verses in which [the Natives] can see how God made Himself man to save the world; how he was born of the Virgin Mary without sin; and in them they learn the commandments of this God who saved them."

—Pedro de Gante, Franciscan Missionary, in a letter to King Felipe II, 1558.

The missionary work, as well as the presence of so many talented European and Criollo musicians, led to the widespread musical training of the Native population throughout the continent, but particularly in Mesoamerica and the Andes. Because musical expression was inherent to Native religious worship, the Natives smoothly adapted to European singing, and many soon excelled at it. Colonial accounts from both Mexico and the Andes describe (often with great surprise) the Natives' ability to learn how to read and sing chant and polyphony, and to play instruments such as organs, and a variety of wind and string instruments. The Natives were able to share among themselves the

Aztec natives learning to sing in the European style. Courtesy Archivo General de la Nación, Mexico.

European tradition and teachings acquired from the Spaniards, so that soon the culture was sufficiently diffused to allow highly regarded Native choirs to develop throughout the countryside. They also acquired the technical skills necessary to support the spread of European music, creating splendid music libraries by painstakingly copying books brought over by Spanish clerics and musicians. Skilled artisans who had always been able to make their own instruments, the Natives also learned to make credible imitations of European instruments. Soon, even the smallest villages had their own singers and instrumentalists.

It was not long before Natives became accomplished composers in their own right, including Don Hernando Franco, a *Cacique* (Native upperclass) composer and musician at the Mexico City Cathedral, and a pupil and namesake of the chapelmaster Hernando Franco. The Cacique Franco is credited as the composer of two hymns dedicated to the Virgin, written in the Náhuatl language, "Sancta Maria in Ilhuicac cihuapille" ("Saint Mary Heavenly Lady") and "Dios Itlazonantzine" ("Beloved Mother of God"). In Lima, Peru, an anonymous Quechua Native wrote a hymn in his Native language called "Hanacpachap Cussicuinin" ("Joy of the Heavens"). The celebrated composer Juan Pérez Bocanegra included it in one of his hymn compilations, and, in 1631, it became the first example of printed polyphony in the New World. In Oaxaca, Mexico, a Zapotec Native named Andrés Martínez wrote an entire Latin Mass in 1636. But perhaps the most important and celebrated Native composer was Juan Mathías, also a Zapotec, who became chapelmaster of the Oaxaca cathedral in 1655, the first Native musician to reach such a high post. His eight-voice *villancico* "Quien sal aqueste dia disfraçado" remains a fine example of colonial church music. These and other works exhibit unusual traits in terms of structure, harmony, and melody, which point to a Native aesthetic that colors the European religious music.

> **Recommended Listening:** "Quien sal aqueste dia disfraçado" by Juan Mathías, from the CD *Baroque Music of Latin America*.

> **Recommended Listening:** "Sancta Maria in Ilhuicac cihuapille" and "Dios Itlazonantzine" by Don Hernando Franco, from the CD *El Siglo de Oro en el Nuevo Mundo–Villancicos e oraciones del '600 Latinoamericano*.

> **Recommended Listening:** "Hanacpachap cussicuinin" from the CD *Boston Camerata: Nueva España*.

The *Villancico*

The most important secular genre in both Spain and colonial Latin America was the *villancico*, a vocal song form that originated in medieval Spain and allowed for loose structures and diverse compositional styles. A *villancico* could be a free-style folkish composition or a solemn work strictly in accordance with Renaissance rules of counterpoint. *Villancicos* were semireligious songs of faith and praise, but were nonliturgical and always in vernacular languages such as Spanish, Portuguese, or Native dialects, never in Latin. The genre, exempt from the formal and stylistic rigidity that applied to other forms, evolved freely, and upon its arrival in the Americas, its flexibility allowed it to absorb the vast, though often subtle, influences of the different ethnic groups. Many composers, such as Juan Gutiérrez de Padilla, continued to compose *villancicos* in the old European style, including *gitanillas* ("gypsy *villancicos*") and *gallegos* ("from Galicia"), parodying Spanish accents and dialects. But for the most part, the genre quickly developed past its Iberian counterpart, becoming the mainstay of secular composition in the Americas. In retrospect, it reached a measure of richness and originality that placed it at the pinnacle of New World composition, though at the time it was viewed as a secondary genre.

Sor Juana Inés de la Cruz

An important writer of *villancicos* was the famous seventeenth-century nun Sor Juana Inés de la Cruz, one of Mexico's greatest literary figures. She was a poet, historian, theologian, musician, and composer, and wrote learned theological and historical essays. Known in Europe as "the Tenth Muse," she rose above the prejudices that surrounded her and established a following that has only grown exponentially in the last three centuries. Sor Juana, who lived in Puebla, displayed a degree of passion and intellectual achievement that would have stood out anywhere, and that placed her at the zenith of colonial culture. Extremely adept in music, she wrote many compositions and an important musical treatise.

She also wrote the texts to many *villancico* cycles that were subsequently set to music by various composers, notably Miguel Matheo Dallo y Lana, chapelmaster at the Puebla cathedral, and Juan de Araujo, a Spaniard who worked most of his life in the cathedrals in Lima and Sucre.

RECOMMENDED LISTENING   "Por celebrar del Infante" by Juan de Araujo, text by Sor Juana Inés de la Cruz, from the CD *Sor Juana Inès de la Cruz: Le Phénix du Mexique*.

Composers of *villancicos* were often the same church and cathedral musicians who wrote sacred masses and other liturgical works. In Latin American churches and cathedrals, the *villancico* came to occupy an important position, particularly for Christmas celebrations, but also for the various feasts held throughout the year, such as Corpus Christi, Pentecost, Epiphany, and the feasts for the Virgin Mary and St. Peter. By the seventeenth century, the *villancico* had evolved into a form that was well established, usually consisting of an initial *estribillo* (refrain) sung by the choir, followed by a *copla* (stanza) sung by a soloist or group of soloists, sometimes immediately repeated, before returning to the *estribillo*.

Villancico cycles consisted of seven to ten poems set to different meters that were sometimes sung in church services to entertain the public after each responsorial. The last *villancico* was usually light and cheerful, with comical situations and stories, and often included the imitation of African or Native accents and dialects, and even the mocking of the Spaniards themselves. Aspects of African culture had appeared in Spanish *villancicos* as early as the fifteenth century, owing to important slave population in Spain and Portugal, most from Guinea and Angola. As a result, these *villancicos* came to be called *negros, negrillos,* or *guineos.* When the genre was transported to the American continent, the *villancico guineo* went with it, and because of the increased racial and cultural diversity in the New World, it took on a new life and intensity. *Guineos* were usually in $\frac{6}{8}$ meter, and often sought to parody the language, accent, and pronunciation of ethnic groups, and their texts were a mixture of Spanish, Portuguese, Native dialects, and African (especially Yoruba) languages, usually deliberately distorted in a humorous and disparaging way, often making them incomprehensible.

By the seventeenth century, the *guineo* had become a convention, no longer necessarily attempting to duplicate the language of African slaves, but often composed simply out of custom, in places where no Africans had ever lived. Some *villancicos* were so infused with dance rhythms that they in turn were called by the names of the dances, such as the *tocotín*, of Aztec origin, and the *paya*, which combined elements from Mulatto, African, and Mestizo culture. These genres were permeated with popular characteristics, sung in African or Native languages and accompanied by Native instruments, but still answering to the harmonic and even formal demands of the Spanish homeland. European dances such as the *sarabande* and the *chaconne* also began to change, infused with *guineo* and Native elements. Throughout Latin America, from Mexico to Cuba and Puerto Rico, from Colombia and Venezuela to Chile and Argentina, African- and Native-influenced compositions had an important impact on the development of popular and folk styles, affecting the development of *romances, décimas, aguinaldos,* and countless other genres. The Portuguese composer Gaspar Fernández, chapelmaster at the Guatemala and Puebla Cathedrals, wrote over 250 *villancicos,* including many *guineos,* as well as a dance and song type called *Mestizo e indio* in the Náhuatl and Talxcala languages; these forms reflect Native cultures, combining polyphonic imitation with the rhythmic configuration characteristic of many indigenous melodic and rhythmic elements.

> **Recommended Listening:** "Gallego: Si al nacer o minimo" by Juan Gutiérrez de Padilla, from the CD *Boston Camerata: Nueva España.*
>
> **Recommended Listening:** "Duerme Niño Descanza" by Gaspar Fernández, from the CD *Villancicos de la Catedral.*
>
> **Recommended Listening:** "Mestizo e indio: Tleycantimo choquiliua" by Gaspar Fernández, from the CD *Villancicos y danzas criollas.*
>
> **Recommended Listening:** "Mestizo e indio: Xicochi xicochi conetzintle" by Gaspar Fernández, from the CD *Boston Camerata: Nueva España.*
>
> **Recommended Listening:** "Negrillo: Dame albricia mano Antón" by Gaspar Fernández, from the CD *Boston Camerata: Nueva España.*

CDI, Track 2: *Villancico*: "Tururu farara con son"

Music and Lyrics: Gaspar Fernández
Instrumentation: Baroque guitar
Notes: Fernandez wrote this *villancico guineo* in honor of the Virgin Mary. The title words are vocables meant to imitate African singing, as are some elements of the music. The accompaniment of the baroque guitar is in $\frac{6}{8}$, while the text appears in syncopation against it. Try to clap the guitar pattern: (**one**-two-three-**four**-five-six) and notice how the words enter on all the "wrong" beats.

Tururu farara con son para san pura vira mia Si parida san María san ispañol su coraçon.	*Tururu farara with music for my pure, holy life Saint Mary, the Spanish saint of your heart.*

Art Music in Colonial Brazil

As in most of Latin America, the music of the Catholic Church played an important part in Brazilian culture, though in the sixteenth and seventeenth centuries, it was far less pronounced than the vigorous musical activity found in the Spanish colonies, partly due to a strongly secular Portuguese government. It was not until the eighteenth century that Brazil developed an active art music tradition. Thus whereas music manuscripts from the mid-1500s survive in Spanish America, the earliest known Brazilian example is from the relatively late date of 1759.

In Brazilian churches and cathedrals, polyphonic hymns and other works predominated, along with traditional Latin plainchant. The Brazilian church establishment was organized in a similar fashion to that of the Spanish colonies, with the central religious authority being the bishop or archbishop, headquartered in a cathedral. Cathedral music was prominent in large cities such as Bahia and Pernambuco, and to a lesser extent in São Paulo, Rio de Janeiro, and Minas Gerais, where an economic boom in the second half of the eighteenth century spawned an impressive musical culture. In theory, colonial musical life revolved around the cathedral's traditional music hierarchy, from the chapelmaster and the organist down to the choirboys. But in practical terms, Brazilian church music was centered not in the cathedrals of the large urban centers, but rather in the missions of the Jesuits, who were the most important Christian presence in Brazil, as well as in brotherhoods called *irmandades*. These guild-like organizations had their precedents in medieval Portugal, and the practice took on a new life in Brazil. Most musicians of any stripe, from cathedral organists and chapelmasters to plantation slaves, belonged to one of the many *irmandades* that grew in colonial Brazil and survive to this day.

Just as colonial authorities in Spanish America quickly incorporated Native populations into their singing and music-making traditions, so too did Brazil educate a large number of African slaves in music, partly to counter the African drumming traditions that were omnipresent on Brazilian plantations. Slaves and Natives were taught to sing, play, and compose in the European style, performing in churches and on plantations and ranches, where they would form makeshift orchestras. Eventually Native, Black, and Mulatto composers made important contributions to the Brazilian church music tradition, for example Luis Álvarez Pinto, chapelmaster in the city of Recife, who wrote many pieces in a late-Baroque style, including, most prominently a 1760 *Te Deum*. European songs and dance forms were also popular in the salons of the Brazilian gentry, where polkas, waltzes, and minuets were the order of the day. These were eventually infused with Brazilian rhythms, and they engendered popular dances such as the *maxixe*. Similarly, European song styles such as the *modinha* were quickly adopted by African and Native Brazilians and were transformed into popular styles. These are discussed extensively in Chapter 6 .

Recommended Listening: "Te Deum laudamus" by Luís Álvares Pinto, from the CD *Negro Spirituals au Brésil Baroque*.

The American Baroque

In Europe, the musical style changed drastically around 1600, when Renaissance vocal polyphony was replaced by a more secular, instrument-based style. This was the beginning of the Baroque period, and it was most prominently displayed in a recently invented genre that became extremely popular throughout Europe: opera. For the next two hundred years, European music reveled in dramatic secular genres, purely instrumental chamber music, and church music that relied heavily on the sounds of violins and harpsichords, a style developed first in Italy and known as *concertato*—with various elements functioning together, or "in concert."

Yet Renaissance polyphony continued to rule American churches and cathedrals for more than a century after it had been abandoned across the ocean, and the first American operas did not appear until a century after their European counterparts. This was partly due to the inherent conservatism of Spanish colonial administration, which closely controlled all aspects of colonial life and which usually perceived any change as a threat to its rule. As the seventeenth century progressed, the colonies began experiencing a dual musical personality, still clinging to the polyphonic traditions of the Renaissance but also slowly acknowledging the newer harmonic and melodic language and the innovative use of orchestral instruments.

Some musicologists, critics, and historians have commented, usually negatively, on this lag between European and American musical evolutions, citing this fact as evidence that Latin American art music was somehow inferior to European music, and often referring to it as antiquated, superficial, derivative, and unimaginative. In truth, though, the Spanish colonies evolved at their own pace, and the music they produced responded to a completely different set of social, racial, religious, and political circumstances. Colonial music was the recipient of distinctly American aesthetic elements that made up for the waning European influences. The infusion of Native, Mestizo, and African characteristics took music in new directions that were impossible in the homeland, touching on themes and making use of language and rhythmic patterns that were beyond European sensibilities and capabilities. To judge American music by European standards is to ignore the particular characteristics of American music, negating music's nature as a signifier of cultural identity. American music was different from European music simply because America was different from Europe.

In any event, by the eighteenth century, the *concertato* style finally began emerging in the works of American composers. This was due in part to a number of Italian composers that came to the Americas, notably the Jesuit Domenico Zipoli, who lived and worked in Argentina in the 1710s and 1720s; Roque Ceruti, who came to Peru in the first half of the eighteenth century; and Ignacio Jerusalém, who became chapelmaster in Mexico City at mid-century. Additionally, the works of some of the great Italian composers such as Vivaldi, Pergolesi, Corelli, and Lully began finding their way across the Atlantic. American church musicians increasingly composed secular and dramatic works, indulging in the new harmonic language of the Baroque, with increased instrumentation, a simpler, more homophonic approach, and liberal use of a bass accompaniment called *basso continuo*. Solo church singing, which had been forbidden even in Spain, now began appearing, with a strong operatic emphasis. Inevitably, this secular style came to dominate musical life in the colonies, even in the midst of the most solemn Catholic rituals.

Colonial Architecture

Ornate Baroque churches and cathedrals complemented the highly ornamented musical and artistic style. This was principally the result of the works of the Churrigueras, a long-standing family of sculptors and architects from Madrid. The Churrigueras, which included brothers José Benito, Joaquín, and Alberto, developed a style that quickly pervaded much of Spain and dominated the construction of churches in the Americas. This architecture has come to be known as *churrigueresco*. Its characteristics are extremely elaborate and symmetrical ornamentation on the façade and in the interior of buildings, in particular with the use of spiral columns, depictions of angels in flight, and magnificent gold-plated altars.

Colonial Opera

Spain had its own tradition of light opera and musical theater called zarzuela, developed in the 1650s for the court of King Philip IV. Like most musical theater, it often included spoken dialogue interspersed with musical numbers and could range from serious drama and tragedy to low comedy and slapstick. Popular song was always a facet of the music. The most important dramatist associated with *zarzuela* was Pedro Calderón de la Barca, and the first great composer of the genre was Juan de Hidalgo. In the second half of the seventeenth century, *zarzuela* was transferred to the Americas, where it competed with Italian opera, at first at the courts of the viceroys and other dignitaries, and eventually in theaters open to the public, such as Mexico City's Teatro Coliséo, founded in 1670.

The first opera composed on the American continent was *La Púrpura de la Rosa* ("The Blood of the Rose"), written in Lima in 1701 by Tomas de Torrejón y Velasco to celebrate the coronation of Philip V. One of the most prominent composers in South America, Torrejón was chapelmaster in Lima for more than half a century, and his works were known throughout the continent and in Europe. The text of *La Púrpura de la Rosa*, by Calderón de la Barca, tells the story of the mythological love triangle between Venus, Mars, and Adonis. The various characters reflect both drama and comic relief; inevitably, love triumphs over destiny. The opera highlights many of the allegories present in the Greek myth. Its literary text is well reflected in the music, where solo arias alternate with choral sections. Torrejón combines the *zarzuela* style with local *jácara* dances with which he had become familiar in Peru.

> **Recommended Listening:** "Huid pastores" and "Jácaras" by Tomas de Torrejón y Velasco, from the CD *The Harp Consort: La Púrpura de la Rosa*.

The second American opera was *La Parténope,* which premiered in Mexico City at the palace of the viceroy on May 1, 1711. *La Parténope,* of which only the libretto survives, was composed by Manuel de Zumaya, one of the finest composers to have emerged on the American continent. Zumaya (sometimes spelled Sumaya) was born in Mexico City in 1684, and probably traveled to Italy early in his career, where he learned the Baroque operatic style. At age 31, he became chapelmaster at the Mexico City cathedral and for the next quarter century remained the head of one of the most important musical institutions, influencing musical developments throughout New Spain and in other parts of the colonies.

Zumaya revolutionized the musical establishment in Mexico City, forcing it into the fold of the Baroque style. Though still required to compose a certain number of a *cappella* (purely vocal) works, he championed the modern *concertato* style, which then swept throughout the colonies. He composed works with orchestral accompaniment and solo parts which often resemble operatic arias, and his *villancicos* reflect a more European (and in particular Italian) style than those of his contemporaries. He expanded the melodic and harmonic language he inherited, and his use of counterpoint was innovative and daring. He was the first important colonial composer to use orchestral instruments as a matter of course, and he expanded the composition of the cathedral orchestra, not only to satisfy the demands of European compositions, but also to accommodate his own progressive works. By mid-century, due in part to Zumaya's efforts, the instrumental style pervaded secular and religious music, and colonial orchestras began to assert independence from the choirs and started performing on their own.

> **Recommended Listening:** "Celebren, publiquen" by Manuel de Zumaya, from the CD Chanticleer: Mexican Baroque.

Baroque: "Celebren, publiquen"

Music and Lyrics: Manuel de Sumaya
Instrumentation: violins, violoncellos, double bass, organ
Notes: Though still polychoral, Sumaya's celebration of the Virgin reflects many characteristics of the Baroque era, chief among them the *concertato* orchestral accompaniment. It also reveals a more secular approach to composition: Although the theme is still religious, the lively tempo, continuous bass line and joyful outlook point to a more humanistic view of the world.

Estribillo	Refrain
Celebren, publiquen,	*Praise, proclaim,*
entonen y canten,	*intone and sing,*
celestes Amphiones,	*heavenly Amphions*
con métricos ayres,	*with metric tunes,*
las dichas, las glorias,	*the good fortune, the glory,*
los gozos, las paces,	*the joy, the peace*
con que hoy a su Reyna	*with which today*
la corte flamante	*its Blessed Queen*
recibe gloriosa	*the Heavenly Host*
admite gozosa	*receives amidst*
y aplaude triunfante.	*triumphant applause.*
Y al elevarle la Angélica	*And as the Angelic Host raises Her up*
milicia a dichas, a glorias,	*to good fortune, to glory,*
a gozos, a paces,	*to joy, to peace,*
cada cual reverente la espera	*each one in his heavenly station*
deseoso en su clase	*reverently awaits her*
por Pura, por Reyna,	*as the Pure One, as Queen,*
por Virgen, por Madre.	*as Virgin, as Mother.*

Meanwhile, Brazilian colonial music also struggled to adapt to the modern musical developments. Though there had been scattered examples of secular works in the eighteenth century, it was not until 1808 that a Brazilian secular style truly emerged. The Portuguese royal court, fleeing Napoleonic upheavals, established its capital in Rio de Janeiro, and the European-style court of King João VI became an important musical center. Many Portuguese composers followed the court to Brazil, and opera soon became popular, affecting the development of much subsequent music. The greatest of the composers at court was undoubtedly the José Maurício Nunes García, of Mulatto heritage, who had gained prominence as the chapelmaster at the Rio de Janeiro Cathedral starting in 1798. He eventually became King João's *mestre de capela* and became closely associated with the court, receiving numerous awards, commissions, and appointments. He was a brilliant keyboard player and wrote many secular and sacred works for the royal chapel. Like Zumaya, he was a transitional figure, composing in a classical style with a marked operatic influence.

> **Recommended Listening:** "Missa de Nossa Senhora do Carmo: Agnus Dei" by José Maurício Nunes García, from the CD *Brazilian Baroque: Terra de Santa Cruz.*

The Fall of the Colonial System

Two important factors altered the evolution of colonial music and culture during the eighteent century: the increasingly secular climate brought on by the European Enlightenment, and the decline of the Spanish empire in terms of power, wealth, and influence. Spain, with its stringently Catholic faith, had fervently resisted the secular ideals that had engulfed much of Europe since the seventeenth century, and it shielded its precious colonies from these new philosophical developments. But by the middle of the eighteenth century, Enlightenment ideals cautiously infiltrated colonial thought, fueled by scientific and philosophical treatises that were smuggled in by knowledgeable Criollos and French and British travelers. This gradual importation of libertarian notions soon brought about a marked reform in intellectual and political life. Objective criteria, empirical data, and scientific method were adopted as the principal source of knowledge. An attitude of skepticism increasingly questioned the established social and religious order, as well as the political power of governing bodies at all levels, from the Viceroy and the Archbishop to the local mayor and the country deacon. Enlightenment concepts of equality and individual liberty challenged issues such as slavery and absolute monarchy. Secularization caught fire and was manifested throughout society, in the streets, fields, town halls, and most notably, in the churches.

The seeds of discontent and nationalism had taken root, nourished by the intellectual restlessness of the educated elite and the social and economic dissatisfaction of the Native and Mestizo classes. Inevitably, the Criollos actively called for independence from Spain, a land they had never seen and with which they had few connections. Militarily, economically, and aesthetically, Spain had ceased to be a world power, and by 1800, it had lost all of its international influence, mostly to the British Empire. Within a few decades, it would lose most of its territories in the Americas. This period also saw a drastic redefinition of the role of the colonial Church, with an acknowledged decline of its wealth and power. The necessity for rigorous evangelization had all but vanished, except in California and parts of the South American interior. From its position as an almost equal partner in the civil administration of the colonies, the Church became increasingly fractured and unstable. Its financial conditions and philosophical crisis led to its divestment in the cultural health of colonial society, yielding to the civil authorities the mantle of protectors and promoters of culture.

The collapse of colonial institutions and ideals precipitated the fall of an aesthetic tradition that had evolved for almost three centuries, best exemplified by the decline of the once-great musical chapels across the land. Cathedral music was assaulted by the preponderance of European dramatic works, which were adopted enthusiastically by the Criollo elite, as well as by the spread of popular and folk styles favored by the ever-growing Mestizo class. Plainchant and polyphonic sacred works were increasingly in competition with secular operas, *zarzuelas*, *romances*, and *chanzonetas*. Irreverent processions, temporal plays, and musical pageants that reflected a worldly, humanistic approach began replacing the pious dramatic representations and the musical events of a purely spiritual nature that had hitherto been the norm. Composition of the semireligious *villancico* declined and was ultimately abandoned. There was also a renewed interest in and appreciation of Native cultures, a facet that would come to influence much of the music that would follow.

The liberation of social, political, and religious institutions resulted in a marked aesthetic evolution. By the end of the eighteenth century, the colonial mind—and with it its literature, art, architecture, and music—emerged from its excessively ornamented Baroque tendencies in favor of a more Classical approach, one which emphasized logic and clarity, with well-defined concepts and structures, balanced and symmetrical phrases, and a refined elegant aesthetic. The Classical style, best exemplified in Europe in the works of Wolfgang Mozart and Joseph Haydn, was adopted by several transitional figures on the American continent, including Esteban Salas y Castro, who worked at the cathedral in Santiago de Cuba, and José de Oregón y Aparicio, chapelmaster at Lima. After three centuries of colonial rule, Latin America and its music were about to enter a new era, one colored by an often-violent struggle for independence and by a proud nationalism that would inspire its own particular brand of Romanticism.

THE NINETEENTH CENTURY: ROMANTICISM IN AMERICA

Inspired by the American and French revolutions, and more recently by the successful struggle for Haitian independence in 1804, Latin Americans soon launched independence movements of their own. The first crack in Spain's American empire came in Mexico in 1810, soon followed by uprisings throughout the continent, many of them led by the Venezuelan general Simón Bolívar. By mid-century, Spain's possessions in America were seriously curtailed, and with the Cuban Revolution of 1898 and the ensuing Spanish-American War, Spain lost control of the Americas altogether.

The independence movements, not surprisingly, yielded much patriotic fervor and engendered a sense of nationalism that was reflected in the arts, including in music. In Europe, where political revolutions were also occurring, Romanticism was in full swing, infused with deep emotion, proud nationalism, and a reverence for individual achievement. These ideals were most prominently evident in the works of Ludwig van Beethoven and the generation of composers that followed him, and were in turn adopted by Latin American artists and thinkers who were fired up by the successful struggles for independence. Local and regional cultures, having endured three centuries of often-brutal control and repression, were ready to explore their own individuality. Art and music flourished in the nineteenth century, often sponsored by the newly formed governments, which established important opera houses, theaters, and conservatories. The Americas quickly shed their reliance on sacred music and turned to the secular genres that dominated the European music scene: art songs, piano character pieces and opera. (Unlike Europe, however, an important symphonic tradition did not develop in the Americas in the nineteenth century).

Música de salón ("chamber music") became an important facet of nineteenth-century American society. It had its beginnings at the tail end of the colonial period, with composers such as the Mexicans Antonio Sarrier and José Mariano Elízaga redefining the cultural identity of the Criollo ruling class, whose salons became awash in refined and graceful dances such as the waltz, and in romantic songs that were often influenced by Italian opera or

German *lieder* (art songs). Before long, homegrown singing and dancing styles emerged, colored by local and regional dance rhythms, and by Black and Native characteristics. Mexican composers such as Tomas León, Melesio Morales, and Julio Ituarte inserted folk dances like the *jarabe* and the *huapango* into their music, introducing a sense of nationalism that would continue to grow throughout the nineteenth and twentieth centuries. In Cuba, the salons of Havana and Santiago became infused with popular and folk rhythms and melodies. The leading Cuban composer was Ignacio Cervantes, a virtuoso pianist who had trained at the Paris conservatory. His compositions, notably his set of 36 Cuban dances, incorporate both Afro-Cuban and White *guajiro* elements, and display disparate influences such as tangos and *habaneras*, usually characterized by markedly syncopated rhythms.

> **Recommended Listening:** "Ecos de México" by Julio Ituarte, from the CD *Ecos de México*.
>
> **Recommended Listening:** "Netzahualcóyotl" by Melesio Morales, from the CD *Almíbar*.
>
> **Recommended Listening:** "Danzas cubanas" by Ignacio Cervantes, from the CD *A Treasury of Cuban Piano Classics*.

Military bands that developed during the wars of Independence were another important facet of nineteenth-century music throughout the Americas. Eventually, their role evolved from a militaristic one to one of popular entertainment. To this day, makeshift brass ensembles and formal marching bands retain an important presence throughout the continent. This style is reflected most prominently in many of the continent's national anthems, for example Venezuela's, written by Juan José Landaeta in 1810, or Mexico's, written by the Spaniard Jaime Nunó in 1854.

> **Recommended Listening:** "Venezuela" and "Mexico" from the CD *The Regimental Band of the Coldstream Guards: Collections of National Anthems, Vol. 2*.

The Mexican dictator Porfirio Díaz, who ruled almost continuously from 1876 to 1911, sought to emulate European culture in all respects. Under his often-despotic rule, Mexican aristocracy developed a social order that was sophisticated, elegant, and refined. As a result, fin-de-siècle Mexico became an important center for opera, song, and piano music. One of the most important Mexican composers in this era was Manuel M. Ponce, who wrote music in many genres, but whose more than 150 songs were particularly popular in the well-mannered salons of the Mexican elite. His most famous song, "Estrellita" ("Little Star") continues to be popular throughout the world. Ponce wrote a lot of his guitar music for the legendary guitarist Andrés Segovia, who was responsible for popularizing it throughout the world. Ponce's compositions had an important impact on twentieth-century Mexican nationalism.

Romantic piano music was also very popular with the Mexican upper classes, and many piano virtuosos emerged. Most prominent among them were Ricardo Castro and Juventino Rosas, an Otomí Native, who composed many important works, including the 1891 hit "Sobre las olas" ("Over the Waves"), which became one of the most famous waltzes in the world.

Recommended Listening: "Estrellita" (Vocal version) by Manuel M. Ponce, from the CD Jose Carreras in Concert.

Recommended Listening: "Sobre las olas" (Orchestral version) by Juventino Rosas, from the CD *Valses Mexicanos 1900*.

Recommended Listening: "Sobre las olas" (Piano version) by Juventino Rosas, from the CD *Rosas: Works for Piano*.

CDI, Track 3: Romantic Song: "Estrellita"

Music and Lyrics: Manuel M. Ponce
Instrumentation: string orchestra, harp, woodwinds
Notes: Ponce wrote Estrellita for voice and either piano or orchestra. It has become a staple of the orchestral repertoire, and has also become popular as an arrangement for numerous jazz ensembles, for solo violin, and for solo guitar (as heard in this recording). Written during the reign of Porfirio Díaz (though published in 1914 after Díaz's fall), the song epitomizes the elegance, romanticism and nostalgia of the Porfiriato. The famous opening figure soars an octave-and-a-half to reach the little star in the distant sky, the contour of the melody reflecting the imagery of the song. Yet despite the anguish and heartache, the song retains a feeling of sentimental tenderness.

Estrellita del lejano cielo,	*Little star of the distant sky,*
Que miras mi dolor, que sabes mi sufrir.	*You see my pain, you know my suffering.*
Baja y dime si me quiere un poco,	*Come down and tell me if she loves me a little,*
Porque yo no puedo sin su amor vivir.	*Because I cannot live without her love.*
¡Tu eres estrella, mi faro de amor!	*You are my star, my beacon of love!*
Tu sabes que pronto he de morir.	*You know that soon I shall die.*
Baja y dime si me quiere un poco,	*Come down and tell me if she loves me a little,*
Porque yo no puedo sin su amor vivir	*Because I cannot live without her love.*

Romantic Opera

Opera became the primary facet of Latin American and Caribbean art music during the nineteenth century, as sumptuous theaters throughout the continent produced the great European works, as well as quality dramas by American composers. By this point, *zarzuela* light opera had had a long tradition on the continent, a tradition that continued unfettered in many countries such as Cuba and Mexico, though now with a more nationalistic bent. It was Italian Romantic opera, however, that saw the Latin American craze for the genre reach new heights, particularly with the works of the Italians Gioacchino Rossini, Gaetano Donizetti, Giovanni Bellini, and Giuseppe Verdi. The Italian penchant for drama and beautiful soaring melodies called *bel canto* ("beautiful singing") appealed to audiences everywhere, and the style of aria writing was adopted by many composers. Later in the century, operas by composers from France (such as Georges Bizet and Giacomo Meyerbeer) and Germany (including most prominently Richard Wagner) also became popular.

Important opera houses and theaters were constructed in almost every major city starting in the late eighteenth century, including the Teatro del Coliséo and Teatro de Bellas Artes in Mexico City, the Teatro Municipal in Santiago de Chile, and the Theatro Municipal and Theatro Régio in Rio de Janeiro. Perhaps the most important center of opera on the continent in the nineteenth century was the Argentine capital, Buenos Aires, which had over a

Theatro Municipal, Rio de Janeiro, Brazil. Courtesy Dorling Kindersley Media Library.

dozen opera houses, most prominent among them the Teatro de la Ranchería, Teatro Coliséo, and the legendary Teatro Colón, which opened in 1857 in its original incarnation. Before long, Latin America had become a mandatory part of the "grand opera tour," as important companies and famous performers traveled across the continent, received at every stop by adulating audiences. The stops included Mexico City, Havana, Bahia, Rio de Janeiro, and Buenos Aires, as well as New York, Atlanta, Charleston, and New Orleans.

So great was the passion for Italian opera that Latin American composers began writing it themselves, in the Italian language and style, but with a marked penchant for Native themes and elements. One such opera was *Guatimotzín* (1871), written by the Mexican composer Aniceto Ortega, which displays many aspects of Aztec culture. Other Mexican composers of Romantic opera included Luis Baca, Cenobio Paniagua, and Melesio Morales. In Cuba, Eduardo Sanchez de Fuentes wrote important dramatic works and ballets, while in Argentina, Francisco Hargreaves and Juan Gutiérrez composed operas that incorporated elements from Argentine folk music.

Brazil also became an important center for Italian opera. In the 1700s, Spanish operas and *zarzuelas*, performed in Spanish, had become a big part of Brazilian culture. By the nineteenth century, Brazilian composers and audiences had also embraced the Italian style. The first Brazilian opera was José Maurício's *Le due jemelle*, written in 1809 to celebrate Queen Maria's birthday, though the score no longer exists. The chapelmaster Marcos Portugal wrote 35 Italian operas and over 20 comic operas in the Portuguese language. Another important landmark in Brazilian opera was *A noite de São João* (1858), written by Elias Álvares Lobo. But the most important nineteenth-century composer of operas—not only in Brazil but in all of the American continent—was undoubtedly Antônio Carlos Gomez. Born in São Paulo, Gomez displayed great musical talent at a young age. At 23 he moved to Rio de Janeiro to study at the Imperial conservatory and there became acquainted with the latest Italian operas. His interest piqued, he traveled to Italy to learn the *bel canto* craft firsthand. It was not long before he achieved great success with several operas, both in Brazil and in Italy, where he was accepted and admired by many of the luminaries of Italian music, including Giuseppe Verdi himself. His most successful opera was *Il Guarany*, which premiered at La Scala opera house in Milan in 1870, and which brought him great fame and wealth. Set in 1660, *Il Guarany* (the title refers to a Native tribe of Brazil and Paraguay) is a love story between a Native chief and the daughter of a Portuguese explorer. Though it is thoroughly Italian in its approach, style, and language, it does contain exotic themes and romanticized Native songs and dances that greatly appealed to European audiences who hungered for exotic foreign cultures. It was equally successful in Brazil, and many of its themes, including the overture, have become part of the Brazilian cultural consciousness.

Recommended Listening: "Overture" and "Act I: Sento una forza indomita" by Antonio Carlos Gómez, from the CD *Il Guaran–Domingo, Villaroel, Alvarez, Neschling*.

THE TWENTIETH CENTURY: NATIONALISM IN AMERICA

The pride engendered by the continent's wars of independence thus fueled a nationalist aesthetic, reflected in the music of various nineteenth-century composers, who drew from folk and popular styles and from Native and African rhythms and melodies. But it was only in the twentieth century that nationalism really emerged as a coherent political, social, and artistic movement. Native, African, folk, and popular music became not only acceptable but desirable by art musicians and intellectuals and soon became a staple at all levels of society. This latest phase of syncretism, wherein Native or African melodies, rhythms and instruments were once again incorporated into European forms and styles, was but the next step in a process that had been ongoing for more than four centuries.

This nationalism was combined with a particular modern aesthetic that mirrored European developments. Almost simultaneously with the Latin American nationalists, composers such as the Russian Igor Stravinsky, the Hungarian Béla Bartók, the Czech Leos Janácek, and the North American Aaron Copland were collecting folk tunes from their own countries and incorporating them into their music. However, Latin American composers who emulated the atonal and avant-garde developments of their European counterparts were generally overshadowed by those who pursued a nationalist idiom. Though every country in Latin America and the Caribbean developed some form of nationalist music, the three most prominent proponents were the Mexican Carlos Chávez, the Brazilian Heitor Villa-Lobos, and the Argentine Alberto Ginastera.

The Aztec Renaissance

In Mexico, a popular rebellion arose in 1910 against the dictatorship of Porfirio Díaz. This was the Mexican Revolution (not to be confused with the war of independence of a century earlier), which lasted more than a decade. It spawned yet another wave of nationalistic pride, as well as a generation of artists, composers, and literary figures that emulated Mestizo and Native culture. This movement is called informally *el Renacimiento azteca*, or the Aztec Renaissance (see Chapter 3). In music, it manifested itself as a reaction to the dominance of European styles, particularly Italian opera. Seeking an alternative, composers turned for inspiration to the musical elements of pre-Conquest Natives. They sought to evoke the world of American aborigines before the arrival of the Europeans, for they saw in Native music and art the true identity of Mexico and Mexican culture. "Indianism" and "primitivism" became important and desirable aesthetic characteristics. The music resulting from this movement was often tinged with melancholy at the loss of a past it attempted to recapture, or at least evoke.

The movement was rooted in the works of composers such as Manuel M. Ponce, José Rolón, and Candelario Huízar but really took hold when Carlos Chávez adopted a pronounced Native aesthetic and incorporated it into his music. Chávez attempted to recreate the spirit of Native music and

Native rituals where—he claimed—one could find the true soul of the indigenous Mexican. He developed precise theoretical ideals derived from his studies of the music of the Ancient Aztecs and of contemporary Native groups such as the Yaquis and the Seris. He often quoted Native melodies in his compositions, but rather than simply arranging and orchestrating them, he set out to recreate a Native aesthetic based on musical, historical, and cultural elements. Whereas Ponce had used a piano or string quartet to suggest folk aesthetics, Chávez made extensive use of Aztec instruments like the *huéhuetl* drum and *teponaztli* slit-drum, *ayacachtli* rattles, various flutes and sea conchs, as well as folk instruments such as marimbas and *guitarrones*. He used these in combination with the standard instruments of the orchestra, which he skillfully manipulated to recreate the sounds and sonorities of Native music. He relied on asymmetrical rhythms, with structures that emphasized repetition of short melodic fragments. Most important was his use of pentatonic scales and his reliance on minor thirds and perfect fifths, which gave the music a distinct, if stereotypical, quality.

Chávez's most celebrated work is *Sinfonía india* ("Indian Symphony," 1936), which uses Native instruments and melodies from the Yaqui and Seri tribes as well as strong, pounding rhythms that evoke the primal rituals inherent in aboriginal Mexican culture. His ballets *El fuego nuevo* ("The New Fire," 1921) and *Los cuatro soles* ("The Four Suns," 1925) are based on Aztec mythology. The chamber piece *Xochipilli-Macuilxóchitl* (1940), named after the Aztec god of music, celebrates the joy and pageantry of ancient Aztec festivals. Its instrumentation consists mostly of Aztec winds and percussion instruments, but also includes a trombone that plays offstage and imitates the sound of a sea conch.

Chávez was also an educator, conductor, and promoter of Mexican culture. Like Ponce, he did not write exclusively in a nationalistic language, and much of his output consists of abstract music with no evident cultural reference. But it was his nationalistic works that put him squarely on the international stage. Other Aztec Renaissance composers included Blas Galindo, José Pablo Moncayo, and Silvestre Revueltas, whose tone poem *Sensemayá* (1938), inspired by a Cuban snake-killing ritual, used unusual rhythms based on Native and Afro-Cuban vocal patterns. The Aztec Renaissance was very influential throughout the Americas, as well as in Europe and especially in North America, where it was espoused and championed by the composers Aaron Copland and Leonard Bernstein.

> **Recommended Listening:** "Xochipilli-Macuilxóchitl" by Carlos Chávez, from the CD *Carlos Chávez: Chamber Works*.
>
> **Recommended Listening:** "Symphony No. 2 ('Sinfonía India')" by Carlos Chávez, from the CD *Leonard Bernstein: Latin American Fiesta*.
>
> **Recommended Listening:** "Sensemayá" by Silvestre Revueltas, from the CD *Leonard Bernstein: Latin American Fiesta*.
>
> **Recommended Listening:** "Huapango" by José Pablo Moncayo, from the CD *Huapango*.

Brazil

Brazilian nationalist composers also began quarrying the fertile sources of their folk and popular styles. As early as the 1890s, Alexandre Levy and Alberto Nepomuceno, and later Camargo Guarnieri, were incorporating *modinhas, maxixes, choros,* and sambas into their piano, chamber, and vocal works. But the most important nationalist composer was Heitor Villa-Lobos. Born in Rio de Janeiro in 1887, Villa-Lobos's musical training consisted of the formal "high art" education he received from his father and the "street" genres and styles he acquired from Brazilian popular culture, many of which were then considered unworthy of "real" musicians. Much to his father's chagrin, Villa-Lobos developed no such prejudices and readily embraced the folk music of Native and Black Brazilians, as well as the popular urban styles such as *modinhas, choros,* patriotic songs, and sambas. A prolific composer with more than a thousand compositions, Villa-Lobos's best works can be found among his various art songs, as well as his works for solo guitar, piano, and string quartet.

Villa-Lobos's music reflects a syncretic duality. On the one hand, he loved and respected the art music of the great European masters and engaged in the modern styles that were the rage in Europe in the 1920s and 1930s, such

Brazilian composer Heitor Villa-Lobos. Courtesy Lebrecht Music & Arts.

as impressionism, expressionism, and neoclassicism. On the other hand, he saw in the popular music of his day the manifestation of the human spirit, and, like Chávez, he envisioned a music that reflected the true nature and identity of his countrymen. Villa-Lobos traveled extensively throughout Brazil, assimilating and recording a vast array of local and regional folk styles, many of which were later reflected in his compositions. In so doing, he promoted their acceptance among high-society Brazilians who had hitherto looked down on them. Villa-Lobos was also an important educator, infusing musical nationalism into the Brazilian pedagogical system. As a result, the popular styles he was promoting gained nationwide acceptance, fostering a sense of nationalistic pride in an entire generation of Brazilians.

His most famous works are undoubtedly the cycle of nine *Bachianas Brasileiras*, a set of orchestral works for various combinations of instruments that reflect his syncretic outlook. The works are loosely based on the compositional process of Johann Sebastian Bach, and the forms, texture, and contrapuntal methods of the Baroque composer can be discerned in the *Bachianas*. But harmonically, melodically, and especially rhythmically, the *Bachianas* reflect a Brazilian sensitivity, and as such are a true representation of the syncretic process that Villa-Lobos was trying to achieve. *Bachiana No. 5* was written for voice and eight cellos, and contains a soaring soprano aria, underscored by rhythmic figures that originate in the lively Afro-Brazilian rhythms of the northern city of Bahia.

> **Recommended Listening:** "Galhofeira" by Alberto Nepomuceno, from the CD *Nepomuceno: Piano Works*.

> **Recommended Listening:** "Dansas Brasileiras" by Camargo Guarnieri, from the CD *Leonard Bernstein: Latin American Fiesta*.

> **Recommended Listening:** "Bachiana brasileira No. 5: I. Aria (Aria–Cantilena)" by Heitor Villa-Lobos, from the CD *Bidu Sayao: Opera Arias and Brazilian Folksongs*.

CDI, Track 4: Twentieth-Century Nationalism: *Bachianas brasileiras No. 2*, "O trenzinho do Caipira"

Music: Heitor Villa-Lobos (1933)
Instrumentation: strings, woodwinds, brass, piano, celesta, bass drum, snare drum, cymbals, triangle, tambourine, Brazilian percussion
Notes: The four movements of *Bachiana No. 2* describe various facets of life in Brazil. The fourth section, subtitled "The Little Train of Caipira," recalls a 1931 journey Villa-Lobos took on a train which transported *caipira*—agricultural workers—in the northeastern province of São Paolo. It depicts the small steam-engine locomotive huffing and puffing through the countryside, finally reaching its destination and slowly coming to a halt.

The piece is divided into two sections, separated by a pause in which the train stops to pick up more workers. Each section is highlighted by an occurrence of the train theme, first heard in the violins, then (after the train resumes its journey), in the oboes and flutes. To depict the mechanical sound effects of the train, Villa-Lobos used several Brazilian percussion instruments, including *reco-reco* scrapers, *ganza* metal shakers, and *chocalho* gourd shakers. (These are described in detail in Chapter 6.) The chugging train itself is portrayed by a repeating ostinato pattern in the piano, cellos, timpani, and *reco-reco* scrapers, with increasing and decreasing tempos.

0:00	Train gets underway and begins speeding up; hissing steam depicted by *chocalhos*.
0:28	Brass flourishes, as train begins moving rapidly through the countryside.
0:37	Train theme (first phrase) in violins, with woodwind and brass accents.
0:56	Train theme (second phrase) at higher pitch.
1:15	Closing phrase repeated several times.
1:32	Change in texture and orchestration, announcing a stop.
1:46	Train comes to a stop; strident horns and clarinets mimic train whistle; high violin harmonics portray squeaking brakes.
1:56	Train resumes.
2:01	Train theme (first phrase) now in woodwinds, with percussion and brass accents.
2:19	Train theme (second phrase) at higher pitch.
2:37	Closing phrase repeated several times.
2:59	Brass mimic train whistle, announcing the final destination.
3:11	Train begins to slow down; slow cellos, woodwind trills.
3:40	Train comes to a stop; high violin harmonics portray squeaking brakes.
4:02	Final locomotive chug: loud, accented chord.

Argentina

Argentina also saw an important nationalist movement arise in the twentieth century. With the inauguration of the new Teatro Colón in 1908, Buenos Aires continued to be one of the important opera centers in Latin America. Nationalist composers wrote operas whose stories were drawn from various myths and legends from Argentina and the rest of the continent. Others sought to portray facets and characteristics of Argentine life, using or evoking its rich folk music. Alberto Williams composed *gauchescas*, piano pieces infused with indigenous elements and with the folk music of the rural lifestyle of the pampas and the *gaucho* cowboys (discussed in Chapter 9). Felipe Boero's opera *El Matrero* (1929) used folk tunes and a *gaucho* dance called *pericón*. Luis Gianneo wrote important works that made use of the tango, rural folklore traditions, and even Native characteristics. Juan José Castro's piano and orchestral music, including his *Sinfonía argentina* (1934), also evoked various aspects of Argentine life, including the tango and the *gaucho*.

But the most important Argentine composer of art music was Alberto Ginastera. Born in Buenos Aires in 1916 of Spanish and Italian parents, he received musical training at a young age. He became somewhat of a child prodigy, writing two of his most famous works, *Danzas argentinas* and the ballet *Panambí*, before age 21. In 1945, after a visit to the United States, he founded an association called the League of Composers, and like Chávez and Villa-Lobos, also established important schools and institutions dedicated to the study of music.

Ginastera was a very versatile musician, composing in just about every genre, including ballets, orchestral works, operas, concertos for various instruments, piano pieces, guitar works, and a great deal of chamber music. He also composed important film scores. His early style incorporates the rhythms of the *pampas* and of rural folk music. His manipulations of orchestral color evoke the life of the *gaucho* in an almost surreal way, with folk tunes presented with a great deal of lyrical simplicity. The ballets *Panambí*, which premiered in 1937 at the Teatro Colón in Buenos Aires, and *Estancia* (1941), best illustrate Ginastera's approach to nationalism. *Estancias* recreates life on an *estancia*—a *gaucho* cattle ranch. The composer quotes various folk tunes, and incorporates narrations from the nineteenth-century *gaucho* literary epic *Martín Fierro*. The final section of the ballet incorporates a fast *gaucho* dance called the *malambo*. By the mid-1950s, however, Ginastera had moved away from the nationalism of his youth and towards some of the avant-garde developments of his European contemporaries, in an increasingly abstract idiom he called "new-expressionism."

> **Recommended Listening:** "El rancho abandonado" and "Milonga popular: Arroro Indígena" by Alberto Williams, from the CD *Coming from Latin America*.

> **Recommended Listening:** "El tarco en flor" by Luis Gianneo, from the CD *Escenas Argentinas*.

> **Recommended Listening:** "Milonguero, tango" by Juan José Castro," from the CD *Magali Goimard: Argentine Piano Music*.

> **Recommended Listening:** "Estancia: Danza final (Malambo)" by Alberto Ginastera, from the CD *London Symphony Orchestra-Alberto Ginastera: Panambí/Estancia*.

> **Recommended Listening:** "Danzas argentinas Op. 2: No. 3: Danza del gaucho matrero" by Alberto Ginastera, from the CD *Alberto Ginastera: The Complete Piano Music, Vol. 1*.

Other Nationalist Styles

Every country in Latin America and the Caribbean looked to its folk traditions to develop a nationalistic language. In Colombia, Guillermo Uribe Holguín used the *bambuco* folk dance as a source of inspiration. In Peru, Rosa Mercedes Ayarza de Morales composed music with elements of Peruvian folk songs and dances such as *festejos* and *marineras*. In Paraguay, twentieth-century nationalism was most evident in the symphonic compositions of José Asunción Flores, who took the popular genre he had created—the *guarania*—and turned into an important art music form that reflected the character of the Native Guaraní of Paraguay. His most prominent works include symphonic poems such as *María de la Paz, Mburicaó,* and *Víctima del mal de Chagas,* and art songs such as *India, Paragua-pe,* and *Panambi Vera.* Paraguay also developed an important nationalist *zarzuela* tradition in the twentieth century, with folkloric themes tied to the Guaraní character of the nation. The first of these was the 1913 *Tierra Guaraní* by Nicolino Pellegrini. After the middle of the century, the team of composer Juan Carlos Moreno González and librettist Manuel Frutos Pane created a number of important *zarzuela* hits, which included *La tejedora de Ñandutí, Korochire,* and *María Pakuri.*

In Cuba, there was a movement called *Afrocubanismo* that aimed to deliberately incorporate elements of Afro-Cuban folklore into art music, including percussion instruments and syncopated rhythms. Its principal proponents were Amadeo Roldán and Alejandro Caturla. Roldán's ballet *La Rebambaramba,* which aims to describe life in Havana during the Feast of the Epiphany in the 1830s, contrasts elements of European, *guajiro,* and African traditions. Caturla studied in Paris, where he acquired a European idiom, but eventually returned to the sounds of his Native island for inspiration. He sought to recreate the sonorities of both *guajiro* and Afro-Cuban folk music with orchestral instruments, and to evoke Cuban rhythms and harmonies. Caturla also set to music many of the texts of the celebrated Cuban writer and musicologist Alejo Carpentier.

Another important proponent of Cuban art music was the pianist Ernesto Lecuona, who excelled in both classical and popular music. He wrote classics such as *Siboney,* which was later turned into a popular *son,* as well as important orchestral suites, such as the 1919 *Andalucía,* which includes the famous dance *Malagueña.* Lecuona is also known for writing important film scores, even receiving an Academy Award nomination in 1942 for the film *Always in My Heart.* Cuban *zarzuela* also had an important presence during this period, with a distinctive Cuban sound, particularly in the works of Lecuona and Gonzalo Roig, who wrote the famous *Cecilia Valdés.* A movement similar to Cuban *Afrocubanismo* and Mexican *Indianism* emerged in Haiti called *Negritude* (discussed in Chapter 5), which sought to emulate Black culture. In art music, the movement was led by three prominent Haitian composers: Robert Geffard, Ludovic Lamothe, and Justin Elie, all of whom made extensive use of Afro-Caribbean folk melodies and rhythms.

> **Recommended Listening:** "Suite española: Andalucía (Malagueña)" by Ernesto Lecuona, from the CD *Nohema Fernández: Serenata cubana.*

> **Recommended Listening:** "Berceuse campesina" by Alejandro Caturla, from the CD *Nohema Fernández: Serenata cubana.*

> **Recommended Listening:** "Preludio cubano" by Amadeo Roldán, from the CD *Nohema Fernández: Serenata cubana.*

> **Recommended Listening:** "Danse capoise" by Ludovic Lamothe, from the CD *Vision of Ludovic Lamothe.*

Latin American Modernism

Art-music developments in Europe and the United States during the second half of the twentieth century cannot be easily categorized. Following the harmonic, rhythmic, timbral, and aesthetic liberation that had occurred in the first decades, composers continued to stretch the musical envelope in hundreds of directions. Consequently, the post-war era saw an explosion of styles and techniques, and composers reached such a level of individuality that there were almost as many distinct styles as there were composers.

Latin American and Caribbean composers followed suit, expanding their styles beyond nationalism, and readily embracing modernism and such avant-garde techniques as alleatory, microtonal, and electronic music, as well as dozens of other stylistic avenues. In Mexico, Julian Carrillo and Mario Lavista explored the possibilities of orchestral timbre. Lavista, in particular, composed a number of remarkable film scores, including *Flores de papel* and *Cabeza de Vaca*. In Cuba, José Ardevol, who had at one time been an ardent supporter of nationalism, adopted a more modern approach. In 1942, he led a group of composers, the *Grupo de Renovación Musical*, who purported to liberate Cuban music and infuse it with various avant-garde elements. The Venezuelan Antonio Estevez wrote important choral works in a modernist style. Significant Argentine composers included Carlos Guastavino, who wrote important art songs, and more recently Pablo Ortiz, who has explored electronic and computer techniques in his theater and film music.

But nationalism was not abandoned altogether. Many composers continued to mine the rich history of folk and popular music. The Mexican composer Arturo Márquez infused his compositions with the traditional Mexican *danzón* styles. In Argentina, Ástor Piazzolla reinvented the tango, literally calling it the *nuevo tango* (discussed in Chapter 9), and permeating it with elements from the popular, classical, and jazz idioms. The *nuevo tango* was influential on a whole generation of Argentine composers, notably Osvaldo Golijov, who was also influenced by Jewish and klezmer music. Yet, unlike the work of earlier composers such as Ginastera and Villa-Lobos, the music of post-war nationalist composers, though based on popular and folk styles, mostly reverted back to the concert hall, rarely embraced by popular audiences.

Recent years have seen the reemergence of much of the colonial musical legacy, as various scholars set out to explore and revive this virtually forgotten tradition. Led by UCLA's multi-faceted and tireless Robert Stevenson, a generation of musicologists have uncovered, transcribed, published, and performed many of the works found in the dusty archives of Latin American churches, cathedrals, and missions. Similar studies are being undertaken in all aspects of Latin American art music, from colonial church music to nineteenth-century Romanticism and twentieth-century nationalism and modernism. These studies time and again confirm that Latin America's contributions to Western Art music rivaled—and in some cases surpassed—those of Europe and North America.

3

Mexico

CHAPTER SUMMARY

Introduction

Historical Overview
- The Mayas and Other Early Mexican Cultures
- The Aztecs
  - Aztec Instruments
  - Aztec Music
- The Conquest and the Colonial Period
- Mexican Independence

Mexican Celebrations
- Patriotic and Religious Celebrations
- Day of the Dead

Mexican Native Traditions
- Modern Maya Music
- Modern Aztec Music
  - *Los concheros*
- Other Native Traditions

Mexican Folk Music
- *Canción*
- *Orquesta típica*
- Mexican Dances
- The *son*

Regional Traditions
- Southeastern Mexico
  - *Danzón* and *bolero*
  - *Son jarocho*
  - *Son huapango*
  - The Marimba

- Central and Western Mexico
  - The *charro*
  - *Canción ranchera* and *mariachi*
  - *Son, jarabe,* and *bolero*
- The Borderland Region
  - *Corrido*
  - *Dueto* Singing
  - *Música norteña* and *conjunto*
  - *Tejano* and Tex-Mex
  - *Banda*

Popular Music in Mexico
- *Música Tropical*
- Pop
- *Nueva trova*

INTRODUCTION

Mexico is a land of mountains and valleys, of sunshine and rain, of ancient mystery, myth, and ritual. Tall sierra ranges, thick tropical jungles, arid deserts, heavenly beaches, and high plateaus contribute to a varied landscape that is mirrored in Mexico's people and culture, and of course, in its music. Because much of the terrain is hard to traverse, many areas in Mexico remained—and continue to remain—relatively isolated, resulting in a variety of cultural and musical styles that evolved independently. One can still find areas where pre-colonial traditions have continued almost unfettered, and towns and villages where only Native languages are heard. There are considerable racial and ethnic differences, distinct levels of economic development, and well-defined social classes. This vast geographic, cultural, social, and economic diversity is administered from a centralized government in Mexico City, one of the largest cities in the world. Because of its proximity, Mexico has become the most familiar Latin American country to residents of the United States. Indeed, much of the current territory of the United States was at one time part of Mexico. But throughout much of its history, Mexico has also had important European connections, particularly with Spain and France.

HISTORICAL OVERVIEW

Present-day Mexico was home to two of the three dominant civilizations on the American continent prior to the arrival of the Europeans: the Mayas and the Aztecs. But hundreds of other indigenous groups lived throughout the territory, sometimes independently of unfolding historical events. Their descendants still populate much of the country, perpetuating newer versions of their age-old customs and traditions.

The Mayas and Other Early Mexican Cultures

The Mayas represented the pinnacle of several thousand years of continuous social, political, economic, and artistic evolution. They were only the most prominent—and eventually the most influential—of dozens of civilizations that emerged in central and southern Mexico starting around 3000 BCE. These included the Olmecs on the Gulf coast; the civilizations of Cholula and Teotihuacán in central Mexico; the Otomís, Purépecha, and Toltecs in the north; and the Zapotecs and Mixtecs in the south. Though these groups spoke different languages and were often at war with each other, they shared many cultural characteristics, partly the result of Aztec imperialism, which stretched throughout Mexico and as far south as Nicaragua and the Caribbean region. The conquest of an ethnic group, whether military or cultural, rarely resulted in its destruction. Knowledge acquired over millennia—of an agricultural technique or the construction of a particular instrument, for example—was never lost but instead passed on to succeeding cultures. These societies were all agrarian, with a dependence on corn and other crops. Their ingenious *chinampa* system of agriculture resulted in an enormous biodiversity that allowed for the development of large city-states. Many of them built imposing cities and monuments that still survive, and produced similar art and architecture. They had an advanced knowledge of mathematics and astronomy, with a numbering system that included a zero, and a calendar that had 365 days and even accounted for leap years. They also shared musical features, and one can find similar performance traditions and musical instruments among the Maya, Toltec, Otomí, Purepecha, Zapotec, and Aztec cultures. Perhaps most importantly, the various civilizations in Mesoamerica shared religious rituals and beliefs, often venerating the same deities, which represented fundamental elements of nature—sun, rain, earth, sky, and animals such as deer and jaguars—as well as basic human activities—fertility, war, and death.

In the midst of this dynamic cultural cross-fertilization emerged the Mayas, a civilization that would ultimately achieve a lasting and prominent place in the history of Mesoamerica. Around the year 200, they began to establish a stronghold in present-day Guatemala, and from there their influence extended both north and south. Part of their success was due to their agricultural system, as well as to their domination of the lucrative canoe trade along the east coast of Mexico and Central America. Eventually, the Mayas came to occupy much of southeast Mexico and the Yucatán peninsula, as well as Guatemala, Belize, and Honduras. Theirs was not always a centralized empire, but more often a set of rival city-states that competed economically—and often militarily—with each other. Impressive cities developed, such as Chichen Itza and Uxmal in the Yucatán Peninsula, Copán in Honduras, Palenque and Bonampák in Chiapas, and Tikal in Guatemala. Most of these cities were interconnected by a complex network of roads called *sacbés*.

Much of the music of the Maya was played on wind instruments: clay ocarinas and whistles, highly ornamented with animal, human, or divine images, as well as flutes and panpipes made from wood or cane reeds, some of them with two or even three chambers, attesting to the Maya's ability to perform music with harmonic accompaniment. Surviving Maya codices portray a *kayum*—an upright cylindrical drum played with the hands. Rattles and jingles were usually made from pods, seeds, and occasionally rattlesnake tails. Other percussion included water drums, conch shells, and turtle shells. They also had a slit-drum called *tunkul* or simply *tun*, though there is disagreement as to whether they developed it on their own or adopted it from the Aztec *teponaztli* (discussed below). It was still in use when the Spaniards arrived and continued to be an important instrument in Maya festivals throughout the colonial period and is still present today. Another important instrument was a long, thin trumpet made out of cactus stalks, used for both ceremonial as well as warfare purposes. A famous set of murals in Bonampák displays these impressive—and somewhat otherworldly—trumpets.

> **Note on recommended listening:** Various modern artists have attempted to recreate some of the music of the Mayas, Aztecs, and Incas, many of them engaging in valuable research involving instruments and ceremonial practices. Nevertheless, since we have no actual music from these cultures—no melodies or rhythms—these recreations, however well researched and informed, must ultimately come down to guesswork. This of course does not render them invalid as musical artifacts. They are important contemporary compositions that reflect the aesthetics and values of twentieth- and twenty-first-century artists. Some of them are thus recommended later in this and other chapters as examples of modern indigenous music. But no actual examples of pre-Columbian music are recommended since, regrettably, none exist.

The Aztecs

Sometime around the ninth century, the Maya civilization mysteriously began to collapse for reasons not entirely understood by modern historians. Within a few decades, their descendants had reverted to a subsistence-level economy, scratching a living among the ruins of their once-glorious cities. Other civilizations arose to prominence such as the Toltecs, Tlaxcaltecas, Purépecha, Otomís, Zapotecs, and Mixtecs. Eventually, however, one tribe emerged which would control virtually all of Mesoamerica until the arrival of the Europeans.

They called themselves *Mexica* (meh-SHEE-ka), from which the Spanish conquistadors and missionaries later coined the term *Mexico*. The Mexica were one of seven nomadic groups that spoke *Náhuatl* (NAH-wah-til). The term *Aztec* is from the Náhuatl *aztecatl*, "coming from Aztlán," their mythical, ancestral homeland known to have been somewhere in the north, perhaps as far as what is now the southwestern United States. Sometime in the twelfth century, the Mexica left Aztlán and arrived in the Valley of Mexico. A key Mexica myth held that Huitzilopochtli, god of war and of the sun, had commanded them to seek an eagle perched on a cactus clutching a snake and to build their home at this site. According to the legend, the Aztecs wandered the land until they came upon just such a sight in 1325, on an island in the center of Lake Texcoco (though in reality they were confined there by the local ruler). There they founded the city that would be at the center of their empire: Tenochtitlán, the site of modern Mexico City. Today, Huitzilopochtli's vision is reproduced in countless Mexican symbols, including most prominently on the Mexican flag.

The Aztecs extended their small island with artificial "floating gardens" called *chinampas* (a Mayan invention), which in time anchored on the shallow lakebed and became islands themselves, with canals intertwining between them.

Tenochtitlán was admired by the first Spaniards who saw it as one of the most beautiful cities in the world, with a population estimated at 250,000 in 1519. At its center were the religious temples and buildings of the nobility, dominated by two great pyramids, 60 meters high, and dedicated to the sun god Huitzilopochtli and the rain god Tlaloc. The vast market in Tlatelolco sold goods from throughout the empire, visited by more than 50,000 people daily. Eventually, the Aztecs built a political, military, and economic empire that extended from the Pacific to the Gulf of Mexico, and from the central plateaus to Central America. It was not so much a centralized bureaucracy as an extended zone of influence that collected tribute from other city-states who pledged theoretical allegiance to them. Aztec society was hierarchical, with the nobility and clergy at the top, a middle class of warriors, artisans, and traders, and a lower class of agrarian workers. At the bottom were the slaves, who could buy their freedom but otherwise had few rights. One of the most controversial aspects of Aztec society was their religious practice of human sacrifice, by which captured war prisoners and other important figures were put to death to appease the gods. Though human sacrifice was widely practiced, it was not on the massive scale reported by some conquistadors. To the regret of many Mesoamericans, the practice of executing humans for religious purposes did not end with the arrival of the Europeans but was continued by the Inquisition during the colonial period, a fact that somewhat tempered the European claim of moral superiority.

AZTEC INSTRUMENTS Surviving accounts of Aztec culture specify the importance of music in their society, which was geared toward religious rituals and ceremonies. More recently, historians and archaeologists have confirmed the Aztecs' extraordinary fondness of music, conditioned by centuries of religious composition and performance. These studies reveal a highly evolved music culture and reflect an organized society that relied on strict hierarchical authority. Every aspect of music—performance, music education, instrument making, composition, and dance—was ritualized according to long-established rigid rules. Several instruments symbolized—and even personified—the deities themselves and were thus idolized and offered human sacrificial blood. Other instruments were infused with magical powers, played at specific times during the ritual. Often instrument makers intricately decorated them with paintings or carvings depicting deities, warriors, or animals. Instruments and voices were prized if they had a clear, loud, high-pitched sound, which would best communicate with the gods. Yet when the conquistadors first heard these high-pitched voices, they considered them out of tune.

The two most prominent Aztec instruments were a set of drums called the *teponaztli* and the *huéhuetl*, originally powerful deities who illegally brought music to the human world and who as a result were banished to earth by the gods. Both instruments served important ceremonial functions, but were also used in battle to rally warriors and frighten enemy troops. The *teponaztli* is a horizontal slit-drum (an idiophone) made from a hollow tree trunk sealed at both ends, with an incision cut along the body of the instrument in the shape of an elongated "H." The two vibrating keys that result are of different lengths, and when struck with rubber mallets called *olmaitl*, they produce different

Musical instruments at the court of the Aztec emperor.

Aztec dancers accompanied by *huéhuetl* and *teponaztli* drums.

pitches (typically two or three half steps apart) whose timbre is not unlike that of a marimba. Ceremonial *teponaztlis* could measure five feet in length, though smaller ones were carried around the neck into battle. *Teponaztli* players could verbally transmit rhythms to each other by using a system of rhythmic syllables, not unlike the *bols* used in the music of India. *Teponaztlis* were common throughout the region, with various names such as *quiringua* and *teponagua*, *tunkul* in the Maya lands, and *mayohuacán* (or *mayohavau*) of the Taíno and Siboney Natives on various Caribbean islands, the periphery of Aztec imperialism. They are still commonly seen on religious altars on important Catholic feast days.

The lower-pitched *huéhuetl*, a footed drum (a membranophone), was made from—and named after—the *ahuehuete* tree, a cypress that is used for ceremonial purposes throughout central Mexico. The drumhead, made from deer or jaguar skin, could be tuned, and a skillful player could play an interval of a fifth. The drum stood upright on three "feet," with the player striking the single head with bare hands. (Contemporary Danza Azteca groups continue to use it today, although players usually now use two mallets.) Surviving codices often depict the *huéhuetl* and the *teponaztli* together, and they probably exchanged complex rhythms. Both also served melodic functions and were subject to very careful tuning, for only the correct harmony would please the gods.

The Aztecs had a variety of wind instruments, including a vertical clay flute called *chililihtli*. Other flutes were made of reed, bone, or wood, including a double flute called *tlapitzalli*, with one mouthpiece and two chambers, each with its own set of finger holes. Double flutes allowed a musician to play two pitches simultaneously, thus providing rudimentary harmony, either by providing a drone to accompany a melody or by doubling the melody itself. (There is some evidence that the Aztecs might have had triple and quadruple flutes as well.) Another prominent wind instrument was the *atecocoli*, a conch shell that was used extensively as a trumpet in ceremonies invoking Tlaloc, the rain god. The Aztecs also had a variety of high-pitched whistles, panpipes, and clay ocarinas called *huilacapitztlis*. Percussion instruments included the *omichicahuaztli*, a serrated *güiro*-like rasp made of wood or bone scraped by a stick, and the *áyotl*, a turtle shell that was struck with wood or antler mallets. Several rattles were used, including the small *cacalachtli*, made out of clay and used to invoke protection for the crops; the long, thin *chicahuaztli*, somewhat like a rain stick; and the *ayacachtli*, made from gourds containing seeds or pebbles, not unlike *maracas*. Metal jingles of various types called *coyolli* were common, worn especially by dancers around the neck and wrists. Ankle shakers named *ayoyotes* were made from shells, dried nuts and seeds, or animal hooves, claws, and bones.

AZTEC MUSIC   According to Aztec mythology, music was given to the people by Quetzalcoatl and Tezcatlipoca, the gods of sky and wind. Music was wholly associated with religious ceremonies that integrated it with poetry, movement and dance, prayer, theater, and costumes, all performed within dramatic architectural settings. More than being a decorative complement, music was part of the process itself, an integral part of the culture. It appears to have been performed exclusively in a community setting rather than for individual or familial purposes: there are no records of music being performed for its own sake, or of dancing, singing, and instrumental music performed apart from religious ceremonies. (This highly stylized tradition does not, of course, preclude the existence of music's function as part of everyday life, present in virtually every human culture: lullabies, children's games, works songs, etc.)

Ritual music was composed and performed by *cuicapiztles*, a privileged class of professional musicians who constituted an integral part of Aztec bureaucracy. They were trained at specific schools for music and dancing called *cuicacallis* ("houses of song") in which only the most talented boys and girls, beginning at age 12, were allowed to enroll. It was considered an honor to become a full member of the singing class, and they enjoyed great reward, honor, and privilege, often exempt from taxes or tribute. In exchange, they had to perform at an incredibly high level. Music did not merely accompany the ceremony—music *was* the ceremony. An error in the music meant an error in the ritual observance, and therefore was an insult to the gods. As a result, nothing short of perfection was acceptable from the dancers and musicians. The Aztec performance requirements are legendary: training was relentless, all music was performed by memory, and a wrong pitch, missed drumbeat, or misstep was punishable by having the performers' hands cut off and sometimes even by death. The incentive for perfect performance was understandably great, a fact that was confirmed by Hernán Cortés himself who brought some dancers and musicians back to Spain to perform for the king and the Pope, who were duly impressed.

Musicians in the *cuicacallis* were expected to compose new songs and ritual ceremonies for virtually every day of the Aztec calendar, but also for theatrical festivals and poetry readings and contests. Epic songs narrated historical or mythical stories, usually in praise of a great warrior or member of the nobility. (Modern scholars have seen in these epic songs one of the origins of the Mexican *corrido*, discussed later in this chapter.) The Aztecs had a pronounced penchant for aesthetic beauty, which was manifested particularly in their admiration for both flowers and music. Poetry and song—called *cuicatl*, or "flowery speech"—were particularly popular and seen as the greatest art forms. Renowned poet/philosophers called *tlamatinime* ("knowers of things") included the Aztec emperor Axayácatl and the revered Texcoco ruler Nezahualcóyotl, whose poetry is filled with imagery of nature and divine symbolism. Much Aztec poetry has survived in its original Náhuatl language and often reflects the thoughts and feelings of everyday citizens of the Aztec empire, rather than the official pronouncements of emperors and priests. Poems often have multiple levels of sophisticated symbolism and can allude simultaneously to relationships between individuals, between members of the social hierarchy, and between humans and gods, nature, and the ancestral world.

Aztec festivals were invariably magnificent and dazzling to Spanish eyes. Buildings and pyramids were lavishly decorated with flowers. Sumptuous religious ceremonies, both solemn and festive, involved outdoor processions, human sacrifices, and the consumption of food and fermented beverages. The music conveyed strong emotions: sorrowful laments, joyful celebrations, or fervent praise. Musicians and dancers with extravagant costumes performed various categories of dance and song, each with distinct steps and accompaniment, including, for example, the *macehua*, a solemn penitent dance used to implore the gods for protection, and the *mitote*, a large-scale dance/celebration that lasted for several hours, in which the entire community participated. *Mitotes* were held in the grand plaza of Tenochtitlán or any town square or large courtyard, often to welcome an important dignitary. They included hundreds and even thousands of people forming concentric circles, at the center of which musicians would play the *teponaztlis, huéhuetls*, and other instruments. The first circle included the priesthood and nobility as well as the elderly, and the outer circles contained the rest of the assembly by order of age and social class, all dancing carefully choreographed steps to the vibrant music, moving in perfect synchronization and singing in unison in a soft voice. The inner circles, having less area to cover, danced more slowly, while the outer ones moved at a brisk pace, but all in perfect lockstep. As the celebration evolved, the tempo, pitch, and dynamic level of the dance would rise, finally reaching an exciting climax.

Missionary Fray Diego Durán describes an Aztec celebration in honor of the goddess Xochiquetzalli.

"My favorite dance was performed with rose garlands with which they crowned and surrounded themselves. On the main *momoztli* [altar] of the temple of their great god Huitzilopochtli, they constructed a house of roses and some hand-made trees filled with scented flowers, under which they seated the goddess Xochiquetzalli. As they danced, young boys descended dressed as birds and butterflies, beautifully attired with lavish feathers, green and blue, red and yellow. They climbed the trees and passed from limb to limb, drinking the dew from the roses. The gods now emerged, represented by Indians dressed like the ones on the altar, and with blowguns they started shooting at the mock birds in the trees. The flower goddess [Xochiquetzalli] arose and received them, taking them by the hand, and sitting them next to her, bestowing on them the great honor and recognition they deserved . . . this was the most beautiful, lavish and solemn dance these people had, and few times have I seen such a marvelous dance . . . I have seen dancing accompanied by lovely songs that were sometimes so mournful that it filled me with sadness and I listened with a heavy heart . . . "

—Fray Diego Durán, *Historia de los indios de la Nueva España*, 1581

The Conquest and the Colonial Period

On April 21, 1519, a small band of Spanish warriors, equipped with a few horses and guns, arrived on the east coast of Mexico, in what is now Veracruz, and began making its way to the interior. They were led by Hernán Cortés, a rebellious young Spanish captain who had boldly set out to discover new lands. In November, they entered Tenochtitlán, where Cortés met the Aztec emperor Motecuhzoma II (known by Mexicans today as Moctezuma and by North Americans as Montezuma). For the next several months, Aztecs and Spaniards eyed each other suspiciously, and eventually hostilities broke out. The vastly outnumbered Spaniards made a hasty retreat on June 30, 1520, the so-called *Noche Triste*—the Night of Sorrows. But Cortés quickly regrouped his army, made important allies among the enemies of the Aztecs, and on August 13, 1521, he re-conquered the city, executed the Aztec nobility, and destroyed most of the temples, monuments, libraries, and books. Thus came the end of the Aztec empire.

In its place, Cortés established one of the most important Spanish colonies, which he called New Spain. From the ruins of the Aztec city in the middle of Lake Texcoco arose Mexico City, literally built with the rubble of the demolished temples and palaces. Today, one can visit some of the ancient structures of the Templo Mayor that have been uncovered by recent excavations in the Zócalo, still Mexico City's central plaza. (Most of Lake Texcoco was drained during the colonial period.) Other important cities quickly emerged, notably Puebla, Guadalajara, Oaxaca, as well as Veracruz on the east coast, which served as the gateway to Cuba and Spain, and Acapulco on the southwest coast, where an important trade route was established to the Philippines and the Far East.

The Spaniards had a dual mission in the Americas. The colonists, many of them descendants from the original *conquistadors*, were bent on achieving great wealth through vast farming and ranching operations called *encomiendas*. To govern them, a vast complex civil bureaucracy quickly emerged, at the head of which was the viceroy. But the second goal of the Spanish Conquest was the evangelization of the Natives, a mission that was sanctioned by the Spanish monarchy, with special authority derived from the Pope in Rome. To achieve their aim, the Church dispatched priests and bishops who lived in churches and cathedrals, and Franciscan, Dominican, and Augustinian missionaries who lived in rural areas and whose task was the conversion of the Native populations. Impressive churches and cathedrals quickly emerged, notably the Mexico City Cathedral, begun in 1530. Soon churches could be found in virtually every major town and village in the country.

Both church and civil authorities realized early on that the most efficient way of achieving their goals was not to tear down entire Native civilizations and rebuild them from scratch, but rather to incorporate existing Native elements into the Spanish, Catholic fold. One strategy was to simply redirect aspects of Native religion, art and culture, for example by building cathedrals on the same sites as the old temples, to provide a sense of religious continuity.

Native artists were employed to decorate the new churches, providing a familiar place of worship. Since music had been an important part of Aztec religious ceremonies, the Spanish priests emphasized it in Catholic services, to make the new converts feel at home in the new religion. The Spaniards were engaging in a process of deliberate and coerced syncretism: very quickly much of the Native population accepted the new faith, though the priests were less successful in eradicating the old system of beliefs. For centuries, even to this day, many Mexican Natives and Mestizos have continued to worship the ancient deities even as they simultaneously—and sincerely—practice their Catholic faith.

The Virgin of Guadalupe

Perhaps the most important facet of syncretism in Mexico was the appearance, on December 12, 1531, of the Virgin of Guadalupe on the site of the shrine of Tonantzin, the mother of the Mexica gods. Neo-Hispanic mythology has it that the dark-skinned Virgin appeared to an Aztec peasant named Juan Diego. The sighting of a European deity *as* a Native, *by* a Native shows the extent to which the two religions and cultures had melded, even within 10 years of the conquest. Some modern historians claim that Juan Diego never existed, and that the Virgin was a clever invention by the Spaniards to more easily convert the Native population. In any event, whether myth or reality, the Virgin became a signal to the converted peoples that they were an integral component of the nature of the world, part of the "master plan" that was dictated by European theology, a concept strongly advocated by the missionaries themselves. For almost five centuries, the Virgin of Guadalupe has remained a symbol of Mexican nationalism and today is a sign of divine intervention in Catholic communities around the world.

European diseases were devastating to Mexico's Native people, but because of the huge numbers of inhabitants, the population was not completely eradicated as it had been, for example, on some of the Caribbean islands. The fraction of the indigenous population that proved resistant to smallpox and other afflictions was large enough to permit their survival. This readily available work force was quickly enslaved by the *encomendero* landowners, and as a result, the Spaniards were not as pressed to import African slaves to Mexico. Still, as many as 200,000 slaves and free Africans populated some of the coastal areas in Mexico, notably in the eastern state of Veracruz, in the Yucatán Peninsula, and in the southwestern states of Guerrero and Oaxaca, where their descendants survive today. Mexico's Black population and its contributions to Mexican culture have been largely ignored by historians and anthropologists bent on tracing the origins of Mexican society exclusively to their Spanish and Native roots.

As everywhere else in the Americas, neo-Hispanic culture was syncretic in nature. Led by Criollos—Mexican-born descendants of Europeans—the culture was increasingly infused with the growing Mestizo population. Painting, architecture, literature, and music all acquired distinct Native and Mestizo traits, which eventually distinguished them from the arts in Spain. Churches and cathedrals, based on an ornate Spanish architectural style called *churrigueresco*, soon acquired their own lively characteristics. In time, colonial Mexico became less of a Spanish cultural outpost and acquired its own character and identity.

Mexican Independence

By the nineteenth century, Criollo society had developed a deep resentment of Spanish intrusion. Led by the priest Miguel Hidalgo, Mexico called for revolt on September 16, 1810, and after an extended and bloody conflict, the insurgent forces were victorious in 1821. Soon thereafter, they declared a constitutional government, one that for the first time attempted social and cultural integration. The war of independence, however, was only the first in a series of conflicts that would mark Mexican history throughout the century. The 1836 secession of Texas was followed by a series of conflicts between Mexico and the United States, the end result of which was that the United States seized half of Mexico's territory: the present states of Texas, Arizona, New Mexico, California, and parts of Colorado and Louisiana. Soon thereafter, the French Emperor Napoleon III, wishing to emulate his famous uncle, sought to expand the French empire in the Americas, and proceeded to invade Mexico. The so-called "French Intervention" lasted for five years beginning in 1862, during which time a Mexican empire was established, led by the Austrian Prince Maximilian of Hapsburg. The French adventure proved to be short-lived, and in 1867, they were expelled and Emperor Maximilian was executed.

From 1876 to 1911, Porfirio Díaz held the presidency almost continuously, effectively becoming Mexico's dictator. This era, known as the *Porfiriato*, was one of important economic development and modernization, as Mexico transitioned from an agrarian, rural society to a more sophisticated modern nation. But it was also a period of political repression and growing inequality, with peasants working the land as virtual indentured servants, as their ancestors had in colonial days, and with a growing disconnect between the common people and the mostly White elite. In 1910, the Mexican Revolution was launched, a bloody conflict that deposed Díaz and saw a complicated succession of leaders rise and fall, as well as the emergence of colorful revolutionaries such as Pancho Villa and Emiliano Zapata, who have since become mythical figures in Mexican history. The constitution of 1917, which still governs Mexico, overturned traditional social structures, instituted important land distribution reforms, and instilled progressive ideals of social equality. A new sense of nationalism emerged, which contributed to the emergence of the so-called Aztec Renaissance.

The Aztec Renaissance

The early decades of the twentieth century saw the advent of various nationalist move-ments across the continent. One of the most prominent and influential was loosely known as *el Renacimiento azteca*—the Aztec Renaissance—an intellectual, cultural, and artistic movement that took its cue from the progressive ideals of the Revolution and the new constitution. Its proponents celebrated Native and Mestizo contributions to Mexican soci-ety while nominally rejecting foreign influences. Increasingly, this resentment was directed more towards the growing political, economic, and cultural encroachment by the United States than towards the waning European influences. For the next several decades, many artists and intellectuals contributed to this cultural reemergence in literature, poetry, painting, dance, and music. Important figures included writers such as Octavio Paz and José Vasconcellos, and composers such as Carlos Chávez and Silvestre Revueltas. There also arose a generation of prominent painters and muralists, led by Diego Rivera and Frida Kahlo (Rivera's wife), which also included José Clemente Orozco, Rufino Tamayo, and David Alfaro Siqueiros. These artists, writers and composers were fiercely nationalistic and incorporated many features of Native and Mestizo culture into their works.

After internal peace was restored in 1921, the political process became rela-tively democratic, though it was dominated by one political party, the Institutional Revolutionary Party (PRI), which won every presidential elec-tion from 1929 to 2000. For much of the twentieth century, Mexico, keenly aware of the enormous influence of its northern neighbor, followed an inde-pendent streak that often put it at odds with the United States. Today, Mexico is a dynamic, modern country that is attempting to emerge into the industrial world while struggling with poverty, social inequality, drug cartels, environmental degradation, and the urban problems of one of the largest cities in the world. Like so many countries in the hemisphere, Mexico strives to balance modernization and the preservation of its cultural heritage. Thus, for example, traditional Day of the Dead rituals are increasingly infused with incongruous, commercially produced U.S. Halloween paraphernalia. The recent opening of a Wal-Mart shopping center within sight of some of Mexico's most ancient pyramids—an event that caused great controversy— is symptomatic of the identity conflicts that Mexico (along with the rest of the world) is experiencing.

Yet, some places in Mexico still retain the charm of bygone ages, such as the colonial towns of Guanajuato, San Miguel de Allende, and Oaxaca. Travelers, commentators, and historians often refer to the notion of "Old Mexico," an elusive concept typically imbued with a deep sense of nostalgia. Mexicans of a certain age will wistfully recall the elegance of the late-nineteenth century *Porfiriato* or the romance of the revolutionary upheavals. More often than not, however, the longing for "Old Mexico" does not refer to a particular period, but to a generic sense of the past. This, too, is part of Mexico, a crucial element of the country's nationalism, found most profoundly in its music.

MEXICAN CELEBRATIONS

Mexico is a land of celebration, as attested by the myriad feasts and fairs that mark the calendar, each with its own individual tradition, but all linked by culinary and melodious delights. These religious *fiestas* can be traced to Mexico's multifaceted past, with roots in pre-encounter days, bolstered by colonial Catholic feasts. Since every day is a saint's day, there are always fiestas somewhere in Mexico. Sometimes, the fiestas become week- or even month-long regional affairs and are called *ferias*, such as the summer Guelaguetza festival in Oaxaca. Fiestas and *ferias* are a time to commune with neighbors and with the saints, who are always guests of honor. The saints are human, thus the celebrations are always lively, rarely solemn, and never restrained. Festivals have become elaborate colorful affairs where fun and courtship abound, with many different styles of music, dances, costumes, decorations, theater, and fireworks. Weddings and baptisms are always a source of joy and an occasion to celebrate life. Elaborate parties such as *posadas* and *fandangos* take place at home, in taverns, or at a communal meeting place and often become semi-public gatherings drawing in neighbors and passers-by.

At the center of everything lies music and food, inexorably intertwined and always present at virtually any get-together—whether a formal fiesta, an extended Sunday afternoon meal, or a light evening supper. Evening strolls in town squares invariably lead to encounters with guitar trios or marimba ensembles entertaining diners and amorous couples. Vendors sell amulets, candles, food and drink, pottery, and toys, often belting out dissonant but enthusiastic songs, advertising their wares. One still finds wooing serenaders with guitars, crooning romantic renditions of "Las mañanitas" (traditionally sung in early morning), though much of the town youth will flock to the local disco to hear the latest *techno* offerings from Europe or the United States. In the villages, where Spanish is rarely spoken, mothers and grandmothers still prepare mouth-watering dishes as they sing ancient Native tunes to their daughters.

Patriotic and Religious Celebrations

The most important patriotic celebration begins on the night of September 15 and culminates on September 16—Independence Day—commemorating the day in 1810 when Mexico began its liberation from Spanish rule. By contrast, November 20 celebrates the Revolution of 1910, a century later. May 5—*Cinco de mayo*, celebrating the 1862 Mexican victory against French occupying forces, is a somewhat minor holiday in Mexico but has gained much more importance in the United States, an occasion for Mexican Americans to celebrate their heritage. Whereas carnival is prominent in some coastal regions, notably Veracruz, it is overshadowed by the celebrations of *Semana santa*—Holy Week.

Vivid (and often bloody) reenactments of the Crucifixion are common sights on Good Friday. A more gentle tradition is that of *cascarones*—Easter eggs filled with confetti and cracked over the heads of family members. Another important religious celebration is the Feast of the Virgin of Guadalupe (December 12), which features penitents walking on bloodied knees, making their way for miles to the Basilica of Guadalupe in Mexico City. Christmas celebrations span about a month: starting in mid-December, *posadas* take place in which revelers assemble in candlelight processions, knocking on neighborhood doors and seeking "shelter," re-enacting Joseph and Mary's wanderings through Bethlehem. Shelter is always refused, until the revelers arrive at the host's house, where they are finally admitted, and a great fiesta ensues, with singing, dancing, food, piñatas, and elaborate Nativity scenes. Christmas Day is of course central to the celebrations, but the traditional exchange of gifts does not occur until January 6, to commemorate the arrival of the gift-bearing kings, and when the Christmas season finally comes to an end.

Day of the Dead

Día de los Muertos—Day of the Dead—celebrations have occurred in Mexico in some form or another for at least three millennia. The Aztecs believed the deceased returned to the world and had to be honored by the living. Their death rituals, which could last more than a month, were shocking to the Spaniards who did their best to eliminate them, though ultimately, they merged syncretically with Catholic customs to produce the tradition that is popular today. One aspect of this syncretism was their association with the closest "death holidays" Christianity had to offer: All Saints' Day and All Souls' Day, which occur on November 1 and 2. Today, *día de los Muertos* is observed throughout the country, and even in some parts of the United States. Like their Aztec ancestors, modern Mexicans have a very personal relationship with death, not fearing it or shunning it, but embracing it as a necessary part of life: Celebrating death is as common as celebrating life, perhaps even more so. The festivities involve visiting the cemetery where offerings are made to the deceased, who are guests of honor. Dead children are honored on November 1, adults the following day. But the preparations start weeks and even months earlier, as village markets (and, increasingly, modern supermarkets) start offering colorful *día de los Muertos* trappings.

During the celebration itself, cemeteries are surrounded by vendors hawking food, drink, and decorations. Graves are cleaned and intricately decorated, while in the family home rudimentary or elaborate altars are constructed with offerings that can include flowers and garlands, votive candles, toys, paper streamers, pictures of the deceased, and colorful crosses, as well as food, drink, and cigarettes. The flower of preference is an orange marigold called *cempasuchi*—"flower of the dead." The offerings help the dead travel on their journey to and from the netherworld. Images of death abound, often derived from Aztec culture, for example the veneration of skulls as trophies and ritual objects. Skeleton masks and costumes called *calacas* are widespread, representing death itself, and often bear colorful names such as *La Flaca* ("the skinny one") or *La Huesada* ("the bony one"). Perhaps the most iconic image is that of the sugar skull that bears the name of the deceased. Picnics are held on family plots, with elaborate meals that are shared with the deceased guests. *Copal* incense is burned to guide the dead back home. The deceased's favorite food and drink are prepared, as well as *pan de muerto* pastries, decorated with skulls or skeletons. Tequila, beer, or the Aztec cornmeal drink called *atole* are prominent. The favorite music of the deceased is played and dancing ensues. As in all Mexican celebrations, fireworks are ever-present. The more elaborate celebrations include setting up banquet tables and hiring *mariachis*. In some places, all-night candlelight vigils occur.

MEXICAN NATIVE TRADITIONS

About 30 percent of modern Mexicans are indigenous. Some of the most prominent groups include the Náhuatls, Mayas, Zapotecs, Mixtecs, Otomís, Totonacas, Mazahuas, Huastecos, Tarahumaras, Purépechas, Yaquis, Seris, and Huichols. Though Spanish is the most common language, more than 60 Native languages are spoken by more than 10 million people, including most prominently several versions of Maya in the Yucatán Peninsula, Zapotec and Mixtec in the southern regions, and Náhuatl in and around Mexico City.

Modern Maya Music

Though the Spaniards nominally conquered all of southeastern Mexico and Guatemala, the Maya have maintained a semblance of political and cultural independence that has lasted until modern times. Today, most Mayas continue to remain isolated from mainstream cultures in Mexico, Guatemala, Belize, and Honduras. There are more than 4 million speakers of one of the many Maya dialects, all of which differ substantially from the language spoken at the height of their civilization 1,500 years ago. These dialects are so widespread that Merida, the capital of the state of Yucatán, has radio stations that regularly broadcast in them. Because of the Mayas' isolation, the Catholic Church was also not always successful in its mission of converting them. In the second half of the twentieth century, that task was taken up by a number of evangelical Protestant organizations, mostly from the United States. In some towns in Chiapas, Yucatán, and Guatemala, there is still a palpable tension between the Mestizo Catholics—who usually hold political and economic power—and the Protestant Indios who remain politically, economically, and linguistically marginalized.

Several Maya groups were able to maintain their musical traditions, preserving the instruments of their ancestors, including wooden trumpets, conch shells, and the *xul* cane flute, which can be played either vertically or transversally. Percussion instruments include rattles and jingles called *chin-chines*, tortoise shells struck with a stick, two-headed drums made from deer leather called *kjom*, clay pots called *cántaros*, and water-drums called *bulalek*. The *tunkul* slit-drum can still be found in the Maya lands, still part of traditional dances, sometimes played singly, but often with two or more playing simultaneously. Modern Mayas will often combine these ancestral instruments with European ones such as the harp, the violin or the oboe-like *chirimía*, or African instruments such as the marimba—the most popular instrument in Chiapas and Guatemala. A common instrumentation consists of a marimba, a *xul* flute and *chin-chines*. And of course guitars of different shapes and sizes are common, including large 12-string guitars and the small *jarana* (ha-RA-na), with 6 to 12 strings arranged in pairs.

Because virtually no Maya music survived the Conquest, it is difficult to determine whether the complex, asymmetrical rhythms found in modern Maya music reflect those of their pre-Columbian ancestors or those of marimba-playing techniques fundamentally of African origin. To modern Mayas, of course, the question is academic: Lively rhythms reflect their present identities, regardless of how the traditions came to be. What is incontrovertibly a legacy of the ancient past is the ritualistic nature of modern Maya music, though now syncretically combined with Christian feasts and celebrations. Dramatic representations and Catholic processions dedicated to a specific patron saint are common in cities, towns, and villages, as are carnival dances and Christmas *posadas*, popular in both Mexico and Guatemala. Modern-day shamans and other members of the community engage in healing ceremonies, blowing *xul* flutes and ocarinas, and chanting prayers and songs that invoke the spiritual powers of nature or of a specific deity. Songs in Maya dialects are also used for other ritual purposes: births, funeral songs, courtship rituals, exorcisms, entertainment for children, prayers for rain and for the harvest. Yet others are narrative epics of historical or mythological import.

Two important Maya dances found throughout the Yucatán Peninsula are the *mayapax*, which celebrates the Maya struggle for independence during the nineteenth century, and the *jarana*, the traditional (and official) dance of the state of Yucatán. (*Jarana* also refers to the small guitar mentioned earlier.) The *mayapax* tends to be more somber and ceremonial, the *jarana* more festive. Both dances include the *sesquiáltera* (combining $\frac{3}{4}$ and $\frac{6}{8}$ rhythms), and can be accompanied by Mestizo instruments such as violins, trumpets, *jaranas*, snare drums, and bass drums made from hollowed out trees, or by traditional Maya instruments such as conch shells, *tunkuls*, and water-drums. Recent instrumental additions have come from Afro-Caribbean *música tropical* styles, for example cowbells, *timbales, güiro*, and *claves*. Female dancers wear the traditional *huipil*—a white dress with colorful embroidery—and flowers and colorful ribbons in their hair. Both are danced at local *fiestas* or events such as baptisms, weddings, and bullfights. They are also often performed at many of the region's archeological sites, in honor of ancient Maya deities, and increasingly, as fancy dramatic representations geared to tourists.

The *ix tolil*—"ribbon dance"—was an ancient dance performed by warriors in honor of the Maya sun god Kinich Ahau and mentioned in 1593 in the *Books of Chilam Balam*. A modern derivation called *Los xtoles* (shee-TO-less) is still performed and praises the sun with a pentatonic melody that is allegedly descended directly from the ancient version and is often cited as one of the oldest melodies in the world. Other contemporary Maya dances include *las cofradías* ("the brotherhoods"), *la conquista* ("the conquest"), *el venado* ("the deer"), and *el agua* ("the water"). In urban areas, many of these rituals and celebrations have become forms of ethnic and regional identity, a process that often takes on political overtones. In more remote isolated areas, they continue to be the fabric of everyday life, not necessarily signifying a greater symbolism, instead quietly reflecting the communal relationship that humans have with each other, with nature and with the spiritual world.

> **Note:** As mentioned earlier, virtually no music survives from pre-colonial Mexico. As a result, recommendations of Maya and Aztec music are either attempts to historically recreate those styles, or musical examples of contemporary Maya and Aztec Natives.

> **Recommended Listening:** "Sun chilan" and "Katzkatz sun" by Florencio Mess, from the CD *Maya K'ekchi Strings*.

> **Recommended Listening:** "El Mishito," "Fragmento del Rabinal Achí," and "Entrada del baile de los güegüechos," from the CD *Music from Guatemala, Vol. 1*.

> **Recommended Listening:** "Son Sventa N'ahaul San Lorenzo" and "Bat'i son martomail," from the CD *Explorer Series: Mexico – Fiestas of Chiapas and Oaxaca*.

> **Recommended Listening:** "Mayan Ancestral Music" and "Songs for Our Ancestors" by Xavier Quijas Yxayotl, from the CD *Mayan Ancestral Music*.

Modern Aztec Music

Post-Conquest descendants of the Aztecs are usually referred to as "Náhuatls" or "Náhuas," named after the language they speak. There are currently more than 2.5 million Náhuatls, the largest of the country's indigenous groups. They live mostly in rural areas of central Mexico, around Mexico City. Like many other groups, they were able to preserve some of their ancestral music customs and features. Many communities still use the *teponaztli* and *huéhuetl*, as well as reed and clay flutes, conch shells, tambourines, rain sticks, donkey jaws used as scrapers, gourd rattles filled with seeds or pebbles, metal jingles, as well as the *ayoyote* ankle shakers made from shells, hooves, claws, or bones. Their traditional instruments are often syncretically complemented by guitars, harps, violins, and *chirimías*, and their rituals contain elements from both Native and Christian beliefs. Because of its geographically and historically central position, Aztec culture was channeled into Mexican folklore to a greater degree than that of other Native groups. Many of the *sones* and *danzas* discussed later in this chapter were influenced to some extent by the music of the Aztecs, and other indigenous communities such as the Otomí and the Mazahuas also have adopted Aztec musical features.

One result of the Aztec Renaissance discussed earlier was the revival—or re-energizing—of various folk music traditions, including prominently the emergence of *ballets* (or *bailes*) *folklóricos*, professional dance companies dedicated to the performance and preservation of the country's Native and Mestizo folk dances (as well as dances of Spanish origin such as *Matachines* and *Moros y Cristianos*, discussed in Chapter 1). The most prominent of these are the Mexico City-based Ballet Folklórico de México de Amalia Hernández (founded in 1952) and the Ballet Folklórico Nacional de México Aztlán de Silvia Lozano (founded in 1960), but hundreds of groups have emerged throughout Mexico. They are usually highly organized troupes whose members are named after various characters from the conquest, including *generales, sargentos,* and *soldados.* The leader of the dance is the *Capitán de Conquista,* charged with maintaining order and setting the tone and pace of the performance. Aztec dancing—called *mi'totiliztli*—has always been part of the cultural landscape in Náhuatl villages and communities throughout central Mexico. But with the advent of the *ballets folklóricos,* the dances have transcended their ritualistic nature and become popular on a national level, not only with tourists and visitors, but also with the Mexican people, who see them as important symbols of ethnic and national identity. Their popularity has also extended to the United States, where the Mexican-American community has embraced Native and folk dancing as a way to reconnect with its roots.

LOS CONCHEROS   Many pre-colonial dances, notably the large-scale *mitote* and the *macehua* prayer dance, survived into modern times, performed at Náhuatl ritual ceremonies and in public performance by the *ballets folklóricos.* The solemn *macehua,* in particular, was influential on one of the most prominent Náhuatl dances, the *danza de los concheros*—"the shell dancers"—so-called because it is traditionally accompanied by a small guitar made from the shell— or *concha*—of an armadillo, as is the Andean *charango.* Still popular in traditional settings in towns and villages around Mexico City, *los concheros* is also one of the staple dances in the repertoire of a typical *ballet folklórico. Los concheros*—along with the *concha*—emerged within a decade of the fall of the Aztec empire. The term refers both to the dancers and to a collection of dances that symbolically recreate many of the events of the Conquest, with names such as *la conquista* ("the Conquest"), *la batalla* ("the battle"), *la alabanza* ("the praise"), and *el sacrificio* ("the sacrifice"). It also recreates the pilgrimage of Natives to the shrine of the dark-skinned Virgin of Guadalupe and is thus celebrated prominently on December 12, though it can occur at any time and place. Like its Aztec predecessor, *los concheros* is a solemn dance, now imbued with both Native and Catholic beliefs, reflecting a need to find one's place both within the Aztec cosmology and the Christian faith. It is also a tribute to Aztec ancestors, particularly those who fought valiantly against the European invader.

While many Aztec dances are traditionally limited to men, *los concheros* includes both men and women, though it is not a couples' dance or courtship ritual and the dancers seldom touch. The ceremony begins with the burning of *copal* resin as an offering to the deities. Successive dances are then performed, each entailing carefully choreographed steps and complex theatrical representations of historical and cosmological events. Dancing involves vigorous footwork, with much twirling, crouching, and jumping, alternately facing up towards the sky and leaning down to the ground. Dancers represent animals such as jaguars and eagles, or elements such as fire, sun, sky, and water. They form complex geometric shapes, most prominently the sign of the cross, but also circles that represent the earth. The steps all have symbolic meanings that venerate nature and the gods. Dances reflect both the agrarian and warring aspects of pre-colonial Aztecs, addressing concepts of war and conquest, but also of fertility and the harvest. The duality of the Aztecs' worldview is prominent, such as the opposition between day and night, dark and light, good and evil, life and death, feminine and masculine, and so on. A full ceremony can last several hours and requires much agility and physical stamina.

Traditional male attire consists of scant but heavily decorated loincloths, complemented by capes, jewels, body and face paint, wrist and ankle rattles, and magnificent feather headdresses and shields. Women formerly wore similar costumes, but in time came to wear *huipiles* and other Mestizo folk costumes. (In secular *ballets folklóricos*, women often reclaim their traditional attire.) Flowers, always important in ancient Aztec rites, are prominent here too. In its traditional form, *los concheros* is accompanied by the *huéhuetl* and *teponaztli*, as well as by conch shells and the *concha* guitar. The dancers accentuate the beats with rattles and *ayoyote* ankle shakers. In more modern versions, other instruments can also be found, including flutes, guitars, snare drums, and *chirimías*. The blowing of conch shells, usually as a summons to the gods or to rally warring troupes, is an obligatory part of the dance, providing dramatic theatricality. All participants sing Native songs (usually composed in the twentieth century) which set pre-colonial Aztec poetry. These songs, like the dance itself, are considered a form of prayer.

> **Recommended Listening:** "Nawi Ollin Teotl Kwikatl" and "Ni Witzilipochli Kwikatl" by Tzotzollin, from the CD *Mexihkateokwikameh – Sacred Songs of the Aztecs*.

> **Recommended Listening:** "Copal Offering to the Four Directions" and "Xipe Totec" by Xavier Quijas Yxayotl, from the CD *Aztec Dances*.

> **Recommended Listening:** *Concheros* Suite: "Toque de flauta triple," "La pasión," "¡Que florezca la luz!," "La cruz," and "Xipe" by Sones de México Ensemble, from the CD *¡Que Florezca! (Let It Bloom)*.

Other Native Traditions

In addition to Maya and Aztec music, there are hundreds of traditions still performed by Natives from other groups, too numerous to explore in depth in this textbook. Some of the most prominent in the states of Puebla and Veracruz are *los negritos* ("the Black men") and *los quetzales*, in which dancers wear colorful circular headdresses made from quetzal feathers. Also in Veracruz is *la Malinche*, a dance that represents Hernán Cortés's Native interpreter and concubine, a figure much reviled by male Mexican intellectuals. In Michoacán, *los viejitos* ("the elderly men") involves colorful masks and vigorous dancing. In the coastal Mixteca mountain range, *los tejorones* depicts the hunting and killing of a jaguar, in full regalia that includes jaguar skins and masks. *Los huehues* is performed during the celebration for the dead in November. In Oaxaca, dozens of Native dances can be found, including prominently *la pluma* ("the feather"), a prominent component of the Guelaguetza summer festival, in which dancers in large feather headdresses honor the sun, accompanied by flutes, percussion, and rattles. Jalisco has *la conquista* and Michoacán has *los cuauileros*, both of which recreate battles between Spaniards and Natives. These dances have a wide range of accompaniment, from a simple drum-and-whistle, to *jaranas*, harps, violins, and various rattles and percussion instruments.

Perhaps the most famous Native dance in Mexico is *los voladores* ("the flyers"), traditionally performed by Huastec and Totonaca Natives of Puebla and Veracruz. *Los voladores* involves four or six dancers who climb to the top of a 100-foot pole from which they then hurl themselves upside down, attached by a rope that rotates 13 times around the pole before the dancers reach the ground. Atop the pole stands another dancer playing a flute and a small drum and performing complex dance steps. The ceremony is fraught with religious imagery and symbolism: the phallic pole—the tree of life or cornstalk—connects the earth and sky, while the flyers themselves can represent the deities, the deceased who are liberated from earthly constraints, or the corn silk revolving down the stalk. The four flyers making 13 revolutions represent the 52 years of the Aztec calendar. Because of its dramatic nature, *los voladores* has become a favorite dance throughout the country, adopted by Native and Mestizo dance groups, and it is often performed for tourists who stand in awe of the dangers inherent to the ceremony.

> **Recommended Listening:** "Danza de los negritos," "Danza de los voladores," and "Danza de los viejitos" from the CD *Misas y fiestas mexicanas*.

MEXICAN FOLK MUSIC

Though Mexico's folk music is rooted in Native traditions, it was also influenced by its immigrants and foreign connections, not only with Spain, but also its Caribbean neighbors—notably Cuba—as well as the United States. In addition to the formal church music and festive pageantry discussed in Chapter 2, Mexico benefited from the adoption of the rich and abundant Spanish folklore. Spanish dances and folk songs, mostly from Andalusia, Galicia, and Estremadura, found their way to Mexico, as well as literary forms such as the *copla*, the *décima*, and the *romance*. These forms were quickly adopted by the indigenous, Mestizo, and African populations, who then infused them with their own cultural expressions, leading to the development of a folk tradition that was quintessentially Mexican.

Canción

The eighteenth century saw the emergence of the Mexican *canción* (lit. "song"), a Spanish-language lyric song form that became popular throughout the country. In the nineteenth century, the *canción* was influenced by Italian opera and Spanish light opera called *zarzuela*. Some romantic *canciones* developed in the salons of the elite and eventually spread to rural areas, while others originated in the Mexican countryside. The Mexican Revolution had a major impact on songwriting, and some of the popular songs that have become famous throughout the world emerged during this period. These include "La adelita," "Allá en el Rancho Grande," "Valentina," and "La cucaracha," though in some of these cases new texts were added to pre-existing melodies. One of the most famous and beloved songs is "Cielito lindo," which all styles from every part of Mexico have appropriated. The text was taken from a previously existing eighteenth-century song, but the version that is popular today probably emerged at the beginning of the twentieth century. Another important song is "La mañanitas," which celebrates a person's saint day, and which has become as prevalent as "Happy Birthday" has in the United States.

> **Recommended Listening:** "Cielito lindo" by Los Camperos de Valles, from the CD *El Triunfo (Sones de la huasteca).*
>
> **Recommended Listening:** "Cielito lindo" and "Las mañanitas" by *Mariachi* Vargas de Tecalitlán, from the CD *Serie Platino: 20 Éxitos.*

Orquesta típica

Mexico also adopted many imported European instruments, including horns, oboes, harps, violins, and the ubiquitous guitar in many forms and sizes. In some isolated areas, these instruments evolved independently, sometimes resulting in unusual local variations, with atypical tunings and singular playing techniques. In urban areas, a strong tradition of orchestral music developed, particularly during the eighteenth and nineteenth centuries, mostly associated with Spanish theater, Italian opera, and *zarzuela*. This led to the development of rudimentary orchestras called *orquestas típicas*, ensembles that quickly began performing traditional Mexican folk music alongside their more formal repertoire. They flourished during the late nineteenth-century dictatorship of Porfirio Díaz, who sought all manner of refinement and sophistication. The first *orquestas típicas* consisted of 10 to 20 musicians playing psalteries, marimbas, and flutes, although guitars, harps, and violins soon became the instruments of choice. They played at weddings, patron-saint festivals, patriotic celebrations, and community dances and also gave formal concerts. Their repertoire consisted of *sones, boleros,* and *danzones,* but eventually also included foreign dances such as *rumbas* and foxtrots. Some prominent *orquestas típicas* included the Orquesta Típica Lerdo, founded by Miguel Lerdo de Tejada in 1901, which became prominent throughout Mexico and toured the United States, introducing much of the Mexican repertoire north of the border.

Lerdo's orchestra was distinct for two important reasons. It was the first Mexican music to be recorded: A few wax cylinders, recorded by Thomas Edison in 1904, have survived, including the song "Consentida". Additionally, Lerdo's rendition of "Marcha de la alegría" was the first broadcast of the legendary Mexico City radio station XEW.

During the 1930s, jazz and U.S. popular tunes entered into the *orquesta típica* repertoire, and, after World War II, they began adopting the polkas and waltzes that were popular among the accordion-based *conjunto* players in the borderlands, adding a level of sophistication to what many considered a rural style. They also began playing the *ranchera* songs of the *mariachis* in an effort to appeal to the mainstream Mexican audience. As a result, by the middle of the twentieth century, *orquestas típicas* became particularly popular in the west and borderland regions. Important *orquestas* also arose in various part of the southwestern United States, notably those of Beto Villa in Texas, Pedro Bugarín in Arizona, and Lalo Guerrero in Los Angeles.

> **Recommended Listening:** "La cucaracha" by Orquesta Pájaro Azul and "Jesusita en Chihuahua" by Orquesta del Norte, from the CD *Mexican-American Border Music, Vol. 1: An Introduction: The Pioneer Recording Artists*.

Mexican Dances

Spanish dances such as the *malagueña*, the *fandango*, and the slow, dramatic *jota* were present in the eighteenth century. The nineteenth century saw the importation of the polka in the borderland region, as well as the waltz and its local variation, the heavily syncopated *vals criollo*, (which was condemned by the colonial Inquisition as being too salacious). In the south, the Cuban *habanera* arrived along with the *danzón*. By the 1920s, the Argentine tango and the U.S. foxtrot were popular in dancehalls throughout the country, soon followed by Caribbean dances such as the *mambo* and the *rumba*. Today, each of Mexico's 32 states has its own official dance and many more that are unofficial. Thus Jalisco has the *jarabe*, Veracruz has the *huapango*, Nuevo León has the *lanceros*, and Yucatán has the *jarana*. A dance style with distinctly African influences is the *Yanga*, from the town of the same name on the coast of Veracruz, the center of Afro-Mexican culture. Many of these folk dances have similar steps that vary slightly from region to region. They are often danced on large wooden stages called *tarimas*. Dancing couples often participate in the musical texture with the *zapateado*, virtuosic and vigorous foot stomping that essentially functions as a percussion instrument, providing a rhythmic—often syncopated—counterpoint to the complex melodies played by the instruments. For the woman, too, the traditional dance figure is the *zarandeo*, in which she twirls her flowing skirt like a fan, signaling her availability to her partner. The visual effect of the colorful skirt nicely complements the aural effect of the footwork.

The *son*

The most prominent dance in Mexico is the *son*, which is not to be confused with the Cuban *son montuno*, although the Mexican version was influenced by the Cuban one, as well as by colonial dances such as the *malagueña*, the *fandango*, and the *habanera*. It was originally most popular in the southern tropical regions, though it can now be found throughout the country. Like many dance styles, the *son* has also developed an important parallel song tradition, which usually uses the *copla* poetic form: verses consist of four lines, with eight syllables per line, and with rhymes in the second and fourth line. Vivacious instrumental introductions and interludes accentuate the verses, which are often improvised.

Traditional *sones* often deal with elements of nature such as plants and animals, with hidden veiled meanings that refer obliquely to women and the pursuit of love. Many *sones* have regional differences and are named for their place of origin, for example the *son veracruzano* (from Veracruz), *son julisciense* (Jalisco), *son calentano* (Guerrero), *son michoacano* (Michoacán), *son arribeño* (a competitive dance from the Sierra Gorda), or *son chileno* (derived from Chile's *cueca* and imported to Guerrero by prospectors and soldiers in the nineteenth century). Various Native groups have also adopted the *son* into their own Native traditions, such as the *abajeño* from the Purépecha people of Michoacán and the *istmeño* ("from the isthmus") of the Zapotec people of Oaxaca, recently popularized by the Oaxacan singer Lila Downs. Often, different traditions will share many of the standard songs in the *son* repertoire, the differences coming in performance style, instrumentation, rhythm, inflection, tempo, and so on. Two *sones* in particular have been very influential in the development of the genre: "La sandunga" and "La llorona." Though they both originated in the southern state of Oaxaca, their mournful qualities have made them popular in most of the *son* traditions throughout the country.

> **Recommended Listening:** "La sandunga" and "La llorona" by Lila Downs, from the CD *La sandunga*.

REGIONAL TRADITIONS

Because of the extreme musical diversity found throughout Mexico, it is hard to make broad stylistic generalizations. Indeed, every region and state has its own local traditions, as do many cities and towns, which are often isolated from those of neighboring areas. Nevertheless, three very broad geographical distinctions can be made, useful in attempting to categorize Mexico's music. The southeastern region—tropical, warm, and humid—developed certain musical tendencies that were closely connected to Cuba and Central America. This area includes the states of Veracruz on the east coast, Oaxaca in the South, Chiapas on the Guatemalan border, and the Yucatán Peninsula. By contrast, central Mexico, with its arid deserts and high mountains, is dominated by a distinct rural, cowboy culture. It includes states such as Michoacán, Durango, and Jalisco. Finally, the northern borderland region has developed various characteristic styles, and includes states such as Chihuahua, Coahuila, Nuevo León, Tamaulipas, as well as the U.S. border states that were formerly part of Mexico. At the crossroads of these three broadly conceived aesthetic tendencies sits Mexico City, the cosmopolitan capital that absorbed every style in the country and developed some of its own.

Historically, many Hispanics living in the southwestern part of the United States became avid consumers of music from Mexico's central and northwest regions—*norteña, corrido, mariachi*, and so on. By contrast, Hispanic populations in other parts of the United States—including Florida, New York, and Chicago—have tended to be more interested in the music of southeastern Mexico, as well as Caribbean styles such as salsa, *cumbia*, and *reggaetón*. By the beginning of the new millennium, however, *mariachi*, salsa, *cumbia*, and other styles had become popular throughout the country.

Southeastern Mexico

DANZÓN* AND *BOLERO   The east coast of Mexico received many genres from its Caribbean neighbors that it then made its own, developing traditions that came to rival and even surpass the original versions. Two of the most important are the *danzón* and *bolero*, the former a dance, the latter a song style. Both were originally inherited from Cuba, and their emergence is discussed at length in Chapter 4. In the late nineteenth century, the *danzón* gained an important foothold in the Yucatán Peninsula and the coast of Veracruz. By 1916, the Cuban Orchestra of Tomás Ponce was active among the dancehalls on the Mexican coast and in the capital, popularizing the *danzón* for decades thereafter. The romantic rhythms still stir up feelings of nostalgia among Mexicans of a certain age, recalling the elegance of the dancehalls of the 1930s and 1940s. The U.S. composer Aaron Copland, on a visit to Mexico, became familiar with *danzón* music and evoked its elegant rhythms in his 1936 orchestral piece *El Salón México*.

> **Recommended Listening:** "Nereidas" and "Juárez" by Danzonera Mandinga de Luis González Pérez, from the CD *Lo mejor del danzón: Colección RCA 100 años de música*.

The *bolero* is a vocal style infused with Afro-Cuban influences that eventually came to surpass its Caribbean cousin, becoming one of the most successful imports in Mexico. As recounted in Chapter 4, by the 1940s the *bolero* had abandoned the *son* orchestras in favor of the guitar trio. This ensemble usually consists of two guitars playing *bolero* rhythms with a third player performing virtuosic improvisations on a high-pitched instrument (typically a *tres* in Cuba, a *cuatro* in Puerto Rico, and a *requinto* in Mexico). But the major attribute of a successful trio is the ability to blend all three voices in close harmony.

With the guitar trio, the *bolero* came to dominate much of the popular music of Mexico and the other Spanish-speaking countries for the next few decades. This so-called golden age of the *bolero* saw the emergence of hundreds of successful trios, including Los Tres Ases, Los Tres Diamantes, and Los Tres Caballeros. But the undisputed leaders were the Trio Los Panchos, comprised of lead singer Johnny Albino, guitarist Chucho Navarro, and virtuoso *requinto* player Alfredo Gil. Gil's improvisation abilities and vocal arrangements placed Los Panchos at the top of the genre, and made them one of the most successful Latin groups ever. Their distinctive three-part harmony came in part from having spent several years in New York, where they became intricately familiar with the jazz scene. They brought a harmonic sophistication not previously heard in the *bolero* tradition. Their many hits included a 1964 collaboration with the New York–born singer Eydie Gormé, a collaboration that produced some of their best recordings.

CDI, Track 5: *Bolero*: "Sabor a mí"

Music and Lyrics: Álvaro Carrillo
Instrumentation: two guitars, *requinto*, bass, conga drums, maracas, cowbell
Notes: This 1964 recording by Eydie Gormé and Los Panchos highlights Alfredo Gil's virtuosity on the *requinto* and Gormé's lilting vocals. The introduction and the accompaniment of the verses have a marked chromatic descent: Listen as every few measures the harmony descends a half step, eventually reaching a cadence. By contrast, the chorus is more harmonically and rhythmically static, with strong syncopated beats emphasized by the percussion.

Tanto tiempo disfrutamos de este amor,	*We've enjoyed this love for so long,*
Nuestras almas se acercaron tanto así,	*Our souls have grown so close together*
Que yo guardo tu sabor,	*That I've still got a taste of you*
Pero tú llevas también sabor a mí.	*But you also carry a taste of me.*
Si negaras mi presencia en tu vivir,	*If you'd denied my presence in your life,*
Bastaría con abrazarte y conversar.	*It would be enough to embrace and speak with you.*
Tanta vida yo te di,	*I gave you so much life,*
Que por fuerza tienes ya sabor a mí.	*That you necessarily have a taste of me.*
Chorus	
No pretendo ser tu dueña.	*I don't pretend to be your owner.*
No soy nada, yo no tengo vanidad.	*I am nothing, I have no vanity.*
De mi vida doy lo bueno.	*Of my life I give what is good.*
Soy tan pobre que otra cosa puedo dar.	*I am so poor there is nothing else to give.*
Pasarán más de mil años, muchos más.	*Many more than a thousand years will pass,*
Yo no sé si tenga amor la eternidad.	*I don't know if eternity holds any love.*
Pero allá tal como aquí,	*but there as here,*
en la boca llevarás sabor a mí.	*your lips will always carry a taste of me.*

0:00	**Instrumental Introduction:** Short figure in *requinto* sets the mood and harmony, followed by short pause.
0:02	Pronounced figure in *requinto*, accompanied by gently swaying guitars and percussion; chromatic descent.
0:20	**Verse 1:** Gormé accompanied by instruments and male voices humming in the background, descending chromatically.
0:38	Short *requinto* figure marks transition between verses.
0:40	**Verse 2:** Johnny Albino sings second verse; humming replaced by descending guitar figure.
1:00	**Chorus:** Gormé returns for chorus; strong rhythmic syncopations emphasized by cowbell and conga drums.
1:19	**Verse 3:** Gormé sings third verse.
1:38	*Requinto* solo recalls introductory theme, with more intricate improvisations.
1:59	**Chorus:** Close harmony by male voices.
2:17	**Verse 3:** Gormé repeats third verse; male voices humming in the background.
2:38	Last line repeated one last time, with all four singers rising an octave above.
2:43	Song ends with opening guitar chord.

The first important Mexican *bolero* was "Nunca," by the talented but short-lived Yucatec songwriter Guty Cárdenas. Other Mexican singer/songwriters quickly followed, notably the great singer and composer Agustín Lara, who became immensely popular throughout Latin America. With either guitar or piano accompaniment, Lara developed a sensitive and idiosyncratic style that remains popular today. Many female singers also achieved great success with the *bolero*, including Amparo Montes from Chiapas and Toña la Negra from Veracruz, as well as the Argentine actress and tango singer Libertad Lamarque. Female composers also left their mark on the Mexican *bolero*, including Ema Elena Valdelamar, who wrote songs such as "Mil besos" and "Mucho corazón"; Maria Grever who composed "Júrame" and "Cuando vuelva a tu lado"; and Consuelo Velázquez, whose 1941 "Bésame mucho" became an international sensation.

With the explosion of youth pop culture in the 1960s, the *danzón* and *bolero* fell into relative disfavor, relegated to increasingly distant and romantic memories of "Old Mexico." Yet they regained some of their earlier popularity towards the end of the century, on the coattails of the salsa explosion. From the popular idioms of Luis Miguel and Julio Iglesias to the operatic style of Plácido Domingo and the films of the Spanish director Pedro Almodóvar, traditional *boleros*, *trovas*, *danzones*, and *canciones* of the golden age have revived a sense of romanticism and nostalgia of earlier generations.

Recommended Listening: "Nunca" by Guty Cárdenas, from the CD *Inmortales de la Trova Yucateca.*

Recommended Listening: "Rayito de luna" by Trio los Panchos, from the CD *Recuerdos.*

Recommended Listening: "La última noche" and "Piel Canela" by Eydie Gormé and Los Panchos, from the CD *Eydie Gormé canta en español con los Panchos.*

Recommended Listening: "Solamente una vez" and "Aventurera," from the CD *Agustín Lara: 40 temas originales.*

Recommended Listening: "Alma mía" by Libertad Lamarque, "Arráncame la vida" by Toña la Negra and "Inolvidable" by Amparo Montes, from the CD *Voces inolvidables del bolero: Colección RCA 100 años de música.*

SON JAROCHO   The most famous style of *son* is undoubtedly the *son jarocho* (ha-RO-cho) from southern Veracruz. It has been around for at least two centuries, and was strongly infused with Afro-Caribbean elements during the colonial period. Typical *jarocho* ensembles consist of one or two *arpas* (harps with 32 to 36 strings), the four-string *requinto* guitar, and various versions of the *jarana* guitar, discussed earlier. The *jarana* player vigorously strums the chords, providing the harmonic and rhythmic accompaniment to the melodic *arpas* and *requinto*, which in turn engage in fast virtuosic dialogue, often of a competitive nature. The competition is also verbal, as the instrumentalists take turns improvising verses. *Jarochos* are also couples' dances, with stylized courtship gestures that get more suggestive as the dance progresses, mimicking the mating rituals of animals. Opposing lines of dancers face each other, with their head and torso held erect and immobile, while their feet perform complex steps, including the *zapateado* and the female *zarandeo*.

The *son jarocho* is fast and energetic, with African-derived rhythmic patterns and pronounced syncopations and percussive effects, including prominently the ubiquitous *sesquiáltera*. Much of the music—from the lyrics to the percussive accompaniment and complex melodies—is improvisatory and in a constant state of flux, with performers never giving the same performance twice. Attempts to establish the "original" version of a piece are usually pointless, though recordings by prominent musicians have diminished the improvisatory nature of *jarocho*, providing a permanent and thus, in the eyes of some, "correct" version. Legendary performers include Lino Chavez and Andrés Huesca, who appeared in many Mexican films in the 1930s and 1940s, and who introduced the style to the United States. More recent was the singer and harp player Graciana Silva—"La Negra Graciana"—who performed in her Native Veracruz for decades before making her first recordings in the 1990s. The most famous of all Mexican *sones* is "La bamba," a *jarocho* popularized in the United States as a rock-and-roll anthem by Richie Valens

Jarana and harp players from Veracruz, Mexico. Photo: David Sacks/Getty Images.

in the 1950s and again by Los Lobos in the 1980s. But "La bamba" had been popular in Veracruz since at least the first part of the century and, because of the *son*'s improvisatory nature, hundreds of its verses have been identified.

> **Recommended Listening:** "El cascabel" by Lino Chavez, from the CD *Lino Chávez, Vol. 1.*

> **Recommended Listening:** "La bamba" and "El siquisiri" by La Negra Graciana, from the CD *La negra graciana: Sones Jarochos.*

CDI, Track 6: *Son jarocho*: "La bamba"

Music and lyrics: traditional
Instrumentation: two harps, guitar, *jarana*
Notes: In this recording, by José Gutiérrez and Los Hermanos Ochoa, the instrumentalists trade-off singing the verses, each ending with a chorus. Notice that the familiar words "bamba-bamba," made famous in several popular versions, are not part of the traditional chorus.

Para cantar la bamba me hallo contento	*To sing the bamba I am content*
Porque me la acompaño con mi instrumento.	*Because I accompany myself on my instrument.*
Que tilín, que tilín	*Tilín, tilín*
Que repiquen campanas de Medellín.	*May the bells ring from Medellín.*
A las morenas quiero desde que supe	*I like dark women since I learned that*
Que morena es la Virgen de Guadalupe.	*The Virgin of Guadalupe is a dark woman.*
Chorus	**Chorus**
Ay arriba y arriba, arriba iré.	*Oh, up and up, up I go.*
Yo no soy marinero, por ti seré.	*I'm not a sailor, but for you I will be.*
¿Cómo quieres que tenga la cara blanca,	*How can you want my face to be White,*
Si soy carbonero fe Tierra Blanca?	*Since I'm a coal miner from the White Country?*
¿Para que me dijiste que estabas sola	*Why did you tell me that you were alone*
Si estabas con tu amante, falsa traidora?	*When you were with your lover, you lying traitor?*
Una vez que te dije que eras bonita,	*Once when I said you were beautiful,*
Se te puso la cara coloradita.	*Your face turned a little red.*
Allá viene la bamba del otro lado,	*Here comes the bamba, from the other side,*
De esa tierra morena que es Alvarado.	*From that brown land called Alvarado.*
Ay le pido de corazón:	*Oh, I beg you from my heart:*
Que se acabe la bamba y venga otro son.	*Let's end this bamba, so another son may start.*

SON HUAPANGO   The rich and lush territory east of the Sierra Madre Oriental is known as *La Huasteca,* a region that in the nineteenth century saw the emergence of the *son huapango* (sometimes called *son huasteco*). *Huapango* is a Native word that refers to the act of dancing on a wooden stage. In modern usage, the term also refers to the large-scale celebrations at which these dances are performed. *Huapango* is different from the *jarocho* in the southern part of Veracruz in that the melody is played by the violin rather than the harp, with the accompaniment provided by a *jarana* and a five-course guitar called *guitarra quinta.* Like the *jarocho,* the *huapango* is rhythmically complex, with frequent polyrhythms that often mix different meters. *Huapango* vocalists often sing in pairs, in call-and-response form with a distinct high falsetto voice. *Zapateado* dance steps are also part of the festivities.

> **Recommended Listening:** "El guajolote" by Los Camperos de Valles, from the CD *El triunfo (Sones de la Huasteca).*

> **Recommended Listening:** "El mil amores" and "La Malagueña," from the CD *El huapango: Sones huastecos.*

CDI, Track 7: *Son huapango*: "El caballito"

Music and lyrics: traditional
Instrumentation: violin, *guitarra quinta*
Notes: "El caballito" ("The Pony") displays the features of a traditional *huapango*: high-pitched and falsetto singing, singers trading off verses, and the syncopated $\frac{6}{8}$ rhythm. In the first verse, the guitar player uses a vigorous strumming technique called *rasgueo*, while in the second verse he switches to *pespunteo*, in which he rapidly plucks the melody on a single string.

Voy a salir a campear hasta San Luis Potosí.	*I am going out into the countryside all the way to San Luis Potosí.*
A ver si puedo lazar un caballito que vi,	*To see if I can rope a little horse that I saw,*
Para llevarme a pasear a una muchacha de aquí.	*So that I can go riding with a young girl from here.*
Es bonito ser vaquero, vestido de caporal.	*It's nice to be a cowboy, dressed up like a foreman.*
Con su chamarra de cuero y su reata de lazar,	*With his leather vest and his lariat for roping*
Lazar a medio potrero para poder manganear.	*Roping out in the pasture to able to do rope tricks.*
Si gasto mil pesos diarios, no siento ni el padecer.	*If I spend a thousand pesos a day, I won't even feel the strain*
Olvida ya tus agravios, procura ser mi mujer,	*Just forget your concerns, get to be my woman,*
Que besando yo tus labios, aunque dure sin comer.	*And me kissing your lips, even if I go without eating.*

THE MARIMBA Though *marimbas* can be found throughout Mexico, it is in the southern state of Chiapas, as well as in neighboring Guatemala, that the instrument developed to its highest level in terms of construction, performance, and repertoire. Chiapas, with its tropical climate and thick rain forest, has historically remained fairly isolated from the rest of Mexico. There have been marimbas in the region since the 1540s, just a few years after the Spaniards arrived, bringing with them African slaves who then recreated the instrument from their ancestral homeland. (Its name is of Bantu origin, meaning "many sounds.") Natives of Chiapas, or *Chiapanecos*, pride themselves on being some of the best marimba players—*marimberos*—in the world. The instrument is an integral part of the culture, from the largest cities to the smallest villages. Entire families are often dedicated to the instrument, and it is not uncommon to find three generations of a single family in front of an instrument. Marimbas can be heard virtually everywhere in Chiapas, from social events such as weddings and birthdays to masses and religious ceremonies, as well as formal concerts. They can always be found on neighborhood streets, at town markets, or entertaining diners and evening strollers on the *zócalo* (central square) in the capital Tuxtla Gutierrez, in neighboring Oaxaca, or across the border in Guatemala.

In Chiapas, marimbas are often referred to as "singing trees." They are xylophone instruments with wooden keys. Suspended underneath each key is a resonating chamber, originally made from bamboo, cane, or a calabash gourd but now usually consisting of a wood cylinder. The most distinctive feature of the marimba *chiapaneca* is a natural membrane normally made of pig tripe that rests inside the resonator, making it hum and reverberate, much like a snare drum. This effect, called *charleo*, is undoubtedly of African origin, where this is still a regular practice. The keys are struck with rubber mallets called *bolillos*, which come in various sizes and levels of hardness.

On early marimbas, the keys were arranged diatonically—with only the white keys of the piano—reflecting the African roots of the instrument. By the turn of the twentieth century, the keyboard could be arranged chromatically—with both white and black keys of the piano. These modern marimbas are called *marimba doble*—"double"—while the diatonic instrument is called *marimba sencilla*—"single." Marimbas come in various sizes: the most common are the tenor marimba, which spans four-and-a-half octaves, and *the marimba*

Marimba band from Antigua, Guatemala. Photo by Eugene Gordon.

grande, which spans six-and-a-half. A smaller, less common instrument is the *marimba tiple*. The traditional marimba ensemble consists of four players standing in front of a single marimba *grande* (another African feature) playing the melody, the countermelody, the harmonic accompaniment, and the bass, though occasionally only two or three will play, resulting in a thinner texture. Alternatively, a single musician can play the melody on a small *tiple*, with the accompaniment played by the other three on a *grande*. Marimbas can also be accompanied by guitars, double bass, *jaranas*, and percussion. Each player will have one, two, or even three mallets in each hand. An important performance element is the sustained mallet roll—rapidly and repeatedly striking a single key, much like a drum roll—that emphasizes a specific pitch or chord.

Much of the marimba repertoire consists of traditional *sones*, love songs, and folk and popular Mexican tunes. In remote villages, rudimentary marimbas sing out ancient melodies native to Chiapas and Guatemala. In the nineteenth century, *marimberos* also incorporated many of the popular European dances such as waltzes and polkas. But these days the best *marimberos* are versed in wide-ranging styles, from European classical music to the latest offerings of U.S. jazz and pop music. Some of the most important events in Chiapas are the state-sponsored marimba competitions, which attract thousands of players from the entire state. The honor and pride of a community, as well as significant monetary prizes, ride on the competition. The golden age of the marimba occurred during the 1930s and 1940s, when a number of marimba groups emerged from Chiapas and popularized the style in Mexico City and throughout the country. These groups usually consisted of four brothers, as evidenced by the ensemble names: Hermanos Gómez, Hermanos Paniagua, Hermanos Marín, and the most famous of all, Hermanos Domínguez, from the town of San Cristóbal de las Casas, where today the main theater is named after them. The four Domínguez brothers were Abel, Ernesto, Armando, and the leader Alberto, an exceptional musician and composer who wrote popular songs such as "Frenesí" and "Perfidia."

Recommended Listening: "El tilingo lingo" by Marimba Lira de Oro, from the CD *Al son de la marimba: Colección RCA 100 años de música.*

CDI, Track 8: Marimba: "La zandunga"

Music and lyrics: traditional
Instrumentation: marimba, bass, drum set
Notes: "La zandunga" is a famous Zapotec dance from the state of Oaxaca, with the typical $\frac{3}{4}$ meter of a waltz. The form is strophic, with the chorus (at 0:00, 1:02, and 2:00) alternating with the verses. At the onset of the second verse (1:32), the texture changes dramatically, reflecting a more improvisatory approach. Notice the *charleo*—the snare effect of the marimba—as well as the sustained mallet rolls to emphasize a particular note.

Central and Western Mexico

The central and western states of Mexico are not unlike the western United States, with a romantic mythology that revolved around ranching, horses, and the cowboy. The arid deserts, high mountains, and wide-open expanses were the perfect setting for the lonely, roaming adventurer, where fortunes could be made, and where bandits and revolutionaries could escape and live freely.

THE *CHARRO* Indelibly linked to western Mexico is the *charro*—the Mexican cowboy. The *charro* tradition is not only derived from ranching and cattle herding (as in the United States), but also from a warrior culture that contributed to Mexico's seemingly endless military conflicts in the nineteenth century, and even back to the conquistador's self-identification as romantic errant knights. The *charro* has a strict code of conduct; he is a *caballero* ("gentleman/horseman"), as gallant and chivalrous as any medieval knight, and honor, virtue, and pride are as important to him as ranching skills. Regalia are an integral part of the *charro* and include colorfully embroidered vests and tight woolen pants embellished with silver studs, the obligatory wide-brimmed sombrero, and cowboy boots with spurs. All *charros* wear guns and occasionally ammunition belts called *bandoleras*. They participate in *charreadas*, more sophisticated and picturesque versions of U.S. rodeos. Basic skills such as steer-catching, bull- and bronco-riding, and roping proficiency have always been part of the competition, though with a more refined and elegant character. Being a *charro* is also being an artist, and the art form is called *charrería*. At the center of the *charro* culture is the horse, and proficient horsemanship is prized above all other skills. The extensive training applies as much to the steed as it does to the rider. One aspect of the competition, for example, involves making the horse dance as a *mariachi* plays on, and to perform elegant rope tricks while mounted. Mexican horsemen are some of the best in the world, and it is no accident that Mexico has traditionally performed well at international equestrian competitions.

Charrería is a form of cultural identity that encompasses not only the actual *charros*, but much of the rest of the country as well, as many Mexicans who have never ridden a horse can nevertheless identify with its proud nationalist attitudes. *Charros* have become national symbols, always performing in patriotic parades, for example. They are mentioned in the Mexican national anthem, and even have their own holiday (September 14). Often, the passion for *charrería* is hereditary, and some of the most distinguished horse ranches in Mexico have been in the same family for generations, each member contributing once again to the *charro* mystique. *Charro* culture is heavily male, infused with a degree of machismo cloaked as gallantry. Nevertheless, women have an important role to play, either as the *china*, the virtuous young maiden, always wearing woolen shawls and sequined skirts, to whom the *charro* dedicates his valor; or as the *charra*, the hardy cowgirl who is allowed to enter the male circle only if she is as tough as the *charros* themselves. *Charras* can shoot guns, smoke cigars, and drink tequila with the men; their outfits are as ornate as their male counterparts, and include sombreros, guns, and long, flowing skirts that force them to ride sidesaddle.

A special ritual of the *charro* culture is the serenade, one of the most prominent aspects of courtship in the region. Ideals of honor dictated that the gallant *charro* could only court the virtuous *señorita* by means of the *serenata*, wherein he would stand in the street under the maiden's window, backed by his full *mariachi*, freely expressing his love and adoration in song. The young lady would peek from behind the curtain, or, more daringly, come out on the balcony to accept the professions of love. Often the *charro*'s adoration was idealized in the manner of the medieval songs of courtly love, a love that was frequently unattainable or unrequited. The typical—now almost stereotypical—song for serenade was "Las mañanitas," also used as Mexico's birthday song of choice.

CANCIÓN RANCHERA AND MARIACHI   The center of *charrería* is the western state of Jalisco (ha-LEES-co), which has as its capital the beautiful colonial city of Guadalajara and which also contains—perhaps not coincidentally—the town of Tequila, origin of the famous spirit distilled from the giant agave cactus. In Jalisco emerged the musical style most closely associated with *charro* culture: *canción ranchera*, played by the ubiquitous *mariachi*. *Canción ranchera*—"ranch song"—has its origins in the country songs from the area's ranches and haciendas, where few instruments or often a single guitar served as accompaniment. Many of these songs became popular in nationalist theater productions in the nineteenth century, usually accompanied by an *orquesta típica*. But it was not until it adopted the *mariachi* instrumentation towards the end of the century that the *canción ranchera* became firmly enshrined as the most prominent genre in Mexico.

The *mariachi* ensemble is as closely connected to the *charro* as his horse and his spurs, and it is the element of *charrería* that has transcended its own culture and become internationally popular. *Mariachi* players are in theory *charros* themselves, and since the 1930s have adopted the elaborate *charro* outfits. The term *mariachi* may have originated from the Native Coca language of Jalisco (now extinct) and referred to a wooden *tarima* dance platform. (It is not, as legend long had it, a derivation of the French word *marriage*.) The ensembles themselves have been around for more than two hundred years in some form, principally in Jalisco, but also in the adjacent states of Nayarit and Colima. Today, the term refers not only to the musical style but also to the musicians and to the ensemble itself. Traditional *mariachis* consisted of five instruments: two violins, a harp, a *guitarra de golpe* (a small low-pitched five-string guitar), and a *vihuela* (a high-pitched Spanish ancestor of the guitar). This instrumentation originated in the nineteenth-century Spanish theater orchestras that performed in Guadalajara and throughout the western states. By the end of the century, the instruments were adopted by groups in isolated and rural areas, who adapted them to their folk aesthetic. In the early twentieth century, trumpets were added, as well as the *guitarrón*, a larger and thicker guitar with six strings and a relatively short neck that provides a deep bass.

Today, *mariachis* typically consist of eight to ten violins (often playing in three-part harmony), two or three trumpets, guitar, *vihuela*, and *guitarrón*. The timbral differences between the instruments provide a distinct aural contrast that can be striking and is an integral part of *mariachi* music. The harp occasionally makes an appearance but is most often omitted, mostly because *mariachis* frequently wander freely in a specific venue, and the harp would limit their mobility. In recording sessions, entire symphony orchestras can complement a *mariachi*, as can marimbas, saxophones, and even synthesizers. An important part of the music is its intricate rhythmic complexity, with thrilling syncopations and *sesquiálteras*. *Mariachi* lyrics are sung by a soloist or by the entire ensemble, sometimes in call-and-response form. The typical *mariachi* voice is loud and passionate, emulating the bel-canto style of Italian opera, but also rustic and untrained, reflecting the genre's origins as country/folk music. Yells and whistles—either from the audience or by the players themselves—are an integral part of the music. Reflecting their *charro* origins, *mariachi* songs are often infused with masculine themes that tell tales in which the men are virtuous but forsaken, while the women are unfaithful and disloyal. Others display the *charro's* love of nature and of the horse culture, or his regional pride and national patriotism.

The first *mariachi* to enter the national stage was *Mariachi* Vargas de Tecalitlán, to this day the most prominent in Mexico. Its founder and patriarch was Gaspar Vargas, who in 1898 took his ensemble from Guadalajara to Mexico City, where it became extremely popular with the working classes, although for most of the elite who frequented the elegant salons of the *Porfiriato*, the music remained backward country music. In the 1930s, the Aztec Renaissance sparked a new interest in the art and folklore of the Mexican people. The populist President Lázaro Cárdenas, who wanted to foment a sense of nationalism, hired *Mariachi* Vargas to play at his inauguration, and thereafter *mariachi* music was widely featured in political campaigns and gained widespread interest and support from all levels of society. During this period, *Mariachi* Vargas was led by Gaspar's son Silvestre, and soon thereafter by the legendary Rubén Fuentes, who for more than half a century would be the most important presence in *mariachi* music. Fuentes professionalized the genre and arranged most of the repertoire in the form we know today, with a strong emphasis on the trumpets. Because of Fuentes, the so-called Mexico City style came to dominate *mariachi* music, largely overshadowing the traditional styles in Jalisco, which still used the original, strings-only instrumentation. Fuentes was also was a pioneer in the recording industry, and worked in radio, film, and television, collaborating with some of the greatest performers of the genre. It is through film in the 1930s, 1940s, and 1950s that *mariachi* music finally reached every corner of the republic, its dominant status finally assured. Not coincidentally, *Mariachi* Vargas played on the soundtrack of many of these films, cementing its standing as the premiere *mariachi* in the country.

Recommended Listening: "Guadalajara" and "Los arrieros" by *Mariachi* Vargas de Tecalitlán, from the CD *Serie platino: 20 éxitos*.

Recommended Viewing: For an integral look at *charro* and *mariachi* culture, see the 1936 film *Allá en el Rancho Grande*, the first (and arguably best) in a long list of films in the *charro* genre.

SON, JARABE, AND BOLERO The principal form of *mariachi* music is the *son jali-sciense* ("from Jalisco"). It shares much of the same repertoire with its *jarocho* and *huapango* cousins, and as in those traditions, the music is often meant to be danced, once again with the ubiquitous *zapateado* foot work. While most *mariachi* music is rural in character, a parallel urban dance style also emerged, though the same ensembles typically play it. This is the *jarabe* (ha-RA-bey), technically a col-lection of dances fused together. The term *jarabe* (like the Venezuelan *joropo*) is derived from the Arabic word *jarop*, which literally describes a sweet liquid mix-ture used for medicinal purposes. (The English word "syrup" is also a relative.) A traditional *jarabe* dance suite can include *sones* and *huapangos*, as well as European dances such as the waltz, the polka, and the Spanish *jota* and *fandango*, all stylized with regional folk elements. In the nineteenth century, *jarabes* often consisted of five dances, though today up to seven can be included, appearing in a specific order according to function. Not surprisingly, traditional *jarabes* often include courtship dances. The female dancer—the *china*—entices then avoids her partner, who seeks to win her favors by displaying his dancing abilities, all in *zapateado* and *zarandeo*. The lyrics of the songs and the movements of the bodies can be quite spicy: the Inquisition banned a suggestive *jarabe* from the late eigh-teenth century for being too scandalous.

Although the *jarabe* is the primary dance form of Jalisco, with examples such as the *jarabe de la botella*, or the *jarabe largo*, it is not exclusively from that state, and other regions have examples of it as well, for example Oaxaca's *jarabe mixteco*. The most well known is the *jarabe tapatío* ("from Guadalajara"). One of its dances, the *fandango*, has become famous throughout the world as the Mexican Hat Dance. Emerging in the early nineteenth century, the *jarabe tapatío* was declared the national dance of Mexico by President Benito Juárez during his struggle against the French in the 1860s. Since then, its constituent dances have become standardized. In 1918, the Russian dancer and choreographer Anna Pavlova, on a Mexican tour, became familiar with it and incorporated it into her repertoire, which resulted in its worldwide dissemination. It is from Pavlova's production that the tradition arose of men and women dancing around a sombrero, the most familiar element of the dance to non-Mexicans.

Recommended Listening: "Jarabe tapatío" by *Mariachi* Vargas de Tecalitlán, from the CD *Serie platino: 20 Éxitos*.

CDI, Track 9: *Son mariachi*: "La negra"

Music: Alberto Lomelí (1926)
Lyrics: Fidencio Lomelí
Instrumentation: violins, trumpets, *vihuela*, guitar, *guitarrón*
Notes: Rhythmic complexities lend an exhilarating feel to this piece which, like many sones, makes extensive use of the *sesquiáltera*, juxtaposing duple and triple meters.

But there are also complex syncopations as the instruments and voices play against each other. Count out the rapid **one**-two-**three**-four-**five**-six pattern as you listen, then notice how the instruments and the voice play against this pattern. For example, in the first verse, the voices enter on an offbeat and with a different meter, so that the vocal accents do not coincide with the instrumental ones. The word "Negrita" in Spanish is normally accented on the middle syllable. Here, however, the outer syllables are emphasized, adding yet another dimension of ambiguity to the already complex rhythm.

Negrita de mis pesares,	*Dark woman of my sorrows*
Por tu amor ando llorando.	*For your love I am weeping.*
Negrita de mis pesares,	*Dark woman of my sorrows*
Por tu amor ando llorando.	*For your love I am weeping.*
A todos díles que sí,	*To all of them say yes,*
Pero no les digas cuando	*But do not tell them when*
Así me diras a mí,	*That is what you will tell me,*
Por éso vivo penando!	*That is why I live in pain!*
¿Cuando me traes a mi negra?	*When will you bring me my woman?*
Que la quiero ver aquí.	*Because I want to see her here,*
Con su rebozo de seda,	*With the silk shawl*
Que le traje de Tepíc.	*That I brought her from Tepíc.*
¿Cuando me traes a mi negra?	*When will you bring me my woman?*
Que la quiero ver aquí.	*Because I want to see her here,*
Con su rebozo de seda,	*With the silk shawl*
Que le traje de Tepíc.	*That I brought her from Tepíc.*

0:00	**Instrumental Introduction**. Slow, pronounced trumpet introduction leads to gradually increasing tempo in $\frac{6}{8}$ rhythm, marked by repeating notes in trumpets and violins, supported by percussive chords in vihuela and guitar, and a rising arpeggio in guitarrón.
0:15	Trumpets and violins drop out, only to accentuate strong syncopations.
0:23	Trumpets and violins reenter, not with repeating notes heard earlier but with an undulating melody, complemented by a lively grito ("yell").
0:35	After slight pause, undulating melody becomes syncopated.
0:45	**Verse 1:** Chorus of singers enters off the beat. Violins double the singers; vihuela, guitar and guitarrón continue percussive rhythm.
1:03	Syncopated repeated notes of introduction return in trumpets and violins.
1:06	Undulating melody in trumpets and strings (×3).

1:18	Descending figure in trumpets (×3).
1:31	Simpler version of descending figure in trumpets (×6, each with slight variations).
1:57	**Verse 2:** Singers enter, once again off the beat, with violins doubling the melody.
2:13	Descending figure in trumpets (×3).
2:27	Simpler version of descending figure (×2).
2:35	Descending figure with trumpet arpeggios in straight triple rhythm (×2).
2:43	Descending figure with trumpet arpeggios back in $\frac{6}{8}$ rhythm (×2 1/2).
2:54	Sudden pause leads to typical *mariachi* ending: three ascending notes, another tension-creating pause, and the final closing chords.

In the 1930s, *mariachi* singers began adopting the southeastern *boleros* into their own styles. Thus was born the *bolero ranchero*, which melded the two traditions and was popularized by a number of singers who became superstars. These included Chavela Vargas, Lola Beltrán, Lucha Reyes, Lucha Villa, Jorge Negrete, and the legendary Pedro Infante, who also had an important film career tragically cut short by a plane crash in 1957. Perhaps the greatest composer in the genre was José Alfredo Jiménez, who wrote more than four hundred *ranchera* songs, including some of the most essential pieces of the repertoire. Today, the most prominent interpreter of *ranchera* music is undoubtedly the Jalisco-born Vicente Fernández. Known as *El Rey*—"The King"—Fernández has also had an important film career, continuing the legacy of the *charro* films that began in the 1930s. *Mariachis* and their music remain more popular than ever across the country, present whenever there is a celebration such as a birthday, a baptism, a wedding, or a funeral. Mexico City's famed Plaza Garibaldi and Guadalajara's Plaza de los *Mariachis* are *mariachi* epicenters, where dozens of bands congregate nightly to perform or seek engagements. Several *mariachi* festivals have emerged, including the weeklong *Mariachi* Vargas Extravaganza, organized by Rubén Fuentes in the 1990s, as well as the Encuentro Internacional del *Mariachi* held in Guadalajara. *Mariachi* music has also become something of an international sensation, thanks in part to Linda Ronstadt's 1987 album *Canciones de mi padre*, produced with the help of Fuentes, which is widely regarded as the album that fomented interest in *mariachi* music outside of Mexico, and especially in the United States.

Recommended Listening: "Amorcito corazón" by Pedro Infante, from the CD *Pedro Infante: Boleros de oro*.

Recommended Listening: "Ay Jalisco no te rajes" by Jorge Negrete, "La negra" by Silvestre Vargas and "Guadalajara" by Lola Beltrán, from the CD *Jalisco, La Tierra del Mariachi*.

Recommended Listening: "El rey" and "Si nos dejan" by José Alfredo Jiménez, from the CD *Lo mejor de José Alfredo Jiménez*.

Recommended Listening: "El rey" and "Volver, volver" by Vicente Fernández, from the CD *Vicente Fernández Historia de un ídolo. Vol. 2*.

Recommended Listening: "Los laureles" by Linda Ronstadt from the CD *Canciones de mi padre*.

The Borderland Region

In the first half of the twentieth century, Mexican popular music—including the recording and film industry—was dominated by *mariachi* and *ranchera* music, whose influence extended as far away as Mexico City and Los Angeles. But in the northern borderlands, another style was emerging, one that was wholly different from the mainstream *mariachi* style and that would ultimately challenge *mariachi's* dominance. This new style was best exemplified in three distinct but related genres: *corrido*, *dueto* singing, and música *norteña*.

CORRIDO   The *corrido* is a narrative ballad, a literary genre whose storytelling aspects define the genre. (The name comes from the verb *correr*—to run, and literally means a song that "runs on.") *Corridos* developed from the Spanish (and specifically Andalusian) *romances*, which recounted heroic narratives. These *romances* in turn had their roots in the *canciones* of medieval troubadours and epic songs of the Moorish occupation, the most famous of which is that of El Cid, the Spanish knight who successfully fought the Moors. Some ethnomusicologists have also linked the *corrido* with Aztec and Maya traditions of epic poetry and storytelling. It is thus a continuation of an ancient art that existed on both continents before 1492. In a time and place where radio and newspapers were scarce, the *corrido* served as a source of information, preserving and transmitting oral history from town to town and from one generation to the next.

Part of the success of the *corrido* comes from its musical simplicity, with standard, undeviating rhythms and simple chord structures. A typical *corrido* will be in $\frac{3}{4}$ waltz rhythm (*boom-chic-chic boom-chic-chic*) or $\frac{2}{4}$ polka rhythm (*oom-pah oom-pah*). Most of the time, the singer accompanies him- or herself with a guitar or *vihuela*, with a standard three-chord progression that rarely changes throughout the song. Melodic accompaniment historically came from the accordion, though in modern times, and particularly during recording sessions, *corridos* can be played by *norteña* ensembles with amplified guitars and accordion, electric bass, and a drum set. The complexity comes in the language, and *corridos* can easily have 30 or 40 verses. Since the point is to provide as much information as possible, *corridos* generally do not have a refrain, which would waste time by repeating previously heard text. Each verse has four to six octosyllabic lines. The simple melody remains the same for all verses. Beyond that, each *corrido* has its own poetic structure and its own rhyme scheme, with variations in stress and intonation. Like the troubadours of old, *corridistas* have traditionally been good improvisers, and itinerant singers still travel markets and town squares, accompanying themselves with their *vihuela*, inventing humorous and ribald verses to delighted tourists in exchange for a tip.

The typical *corrido* narrative has a three-part structure. In the preface, the singer/narrator establishes the context of the story, often providing exact dates, places and names of the protagonists, and the reason for telling the story. The second part presents the action. In the closing section, the narrator outlines the moral of the story and then takes his or her leave, usually with a short *despedida* (farewell) to both the characters and the audience. The narrator strives for realism, particularly in violent or tragic stories. Though there might be some moral or philosophical commentary at the beginning and end, it is the central, action-filled section that defines a *corrido*, for these are epic poems that recount deeds of bravery, injustice, or infamy.

Corridos were widespread in the late 1700s, though the earliest known example was written in Texas in 1808. An important early *corrido* was "La pulga" ("The Flea"), written by Pepe Quevedo in 1821. *Corridos* described many of the historical developments of the nineteenth century, for example the French presence in the 1860s and the dictatorship of Porfirio Díaz. A key theme of nineteenth-century *corridos* was the violence and injustice resulting from the Mexican-American War and the annexation of almost one-half of the Mexican territory by the United States. Thus began in popular folklore a marked animosity towards the Anglo-American "gringo," an attitude that would remain an important part of the culture for the next century and a half. While *corridos* could be found all over Mexico, they would thereafter be inexorably linked with the borderlands.

But it was during the violent revolution in the first decades of the twentieth century that *corridos* emerged as a major national genre. They became a source of nationalist pride and an important oral history of the Mexican Revolution, written and retold by often-illiterate eyewitnesses who wanted the world to know what they had seen. They were also character studies of important men and women, military figures, bloodthirsty bandits, or ordinary common folk who achieved fame through courage or injustice. Through these *corridos* we see the human aspects of historical figures such as Pancho Villa and Emiliano Zapata and get an inside look at their military operations. We also witness aspects of everyday life during those momentous times, for example the crucial contributions of the *soldaderas*—women who followed the regiments, cooking and providing favors for their soldiers, and occasionally taking up arms themselves. *Corridos* tell stories of heroes and tyrants, of oppression and injustice. Villains are often Anglo-American, while Mexican

Revolutionary General Emiliano Zapata, as painted in 1928 by Diego Rivera.

bandits are romanticized as they fight or evade U.S. lawmen; soldiers and generals show courage or cowardice; common folk are oppressed by the forces of the tyrant, or by fate. Other historical figures make appearances: Teddy Roosevelt, César Chávez, and former Mexican President Vicente Fox (referred to as "El Zorro"). But *corridos* can address other subjects as well, for example bullfighting and the *charro* lifestyle, natural or human disasters, farm workers, the poor and destitute, and of course themes of love, deception, betrayal, and crimes of passion. *Corridos* can be tragic, humorous, ironic, and satirical, sometimes all at once. Many were—and are—subversive to the established order.

> **Recommended Listening:** "El güero estrada" by Los Alegres de Terán, from the CD *Mexican-American Border Music, Vol. 1: An Introduction: The Pioneer Recording Artists.*

CDI, Track 10: *Corrido:* "Gregorio Cortez"

Music and Lyrics: traditional
Instrumentation: accordion, *bajo sexto* guitar, bass
Notes: There are dozens, if not hundreds of recordings of this popular ballad, which recounts the (mostly) true events of Gregorio Cortez, a legendary figure who, in 1901, evaded capture after being unjustly accused by Texas lawmen. His "David versus Goliath" story came to symbolize relations between Anglo-Americans and Mexican Americans in the borderland region. Though corridos are most often performed with a single guitar, this 1958 recording by Los Hermanos Banda makes use of a full *conjunto*, interjecting elaborate accordion passages between verses.

En el condado del Carmen miren lo que ha sucedido:	*In the county of El Carmen look what has happened:*
Murió el sherife mayor, quedando Román herido.	*The sheriff is dead, and Roman is wounded.*
Otro día por la mañana, cuando la gente llegó,	*The following morning, when the people arrived,*
Unos a los otros dicen, no saben quien lo mató.	*Some to the others said, they don't know who killed him.*
Anduvieron informando, como tres horas después,	*They were investigating, and about three hours later,*
Supieron que el malhechor era Gregorio Cortés.	*They found the wrongdoer had been Gregorio Cortés.*
Insortaron a Cortés por toditito el estado.	*Cortés was wanted throughout the state;*
Vivo o muerto que se aprehenda, porque a varios ha matado.	*Alive or dead may he be caught, for several he has killed.*
Decía Gregorio Cortés, con su pistola en la mano,	*Said Gregorio Cortés, with his pistol in hand,*
"No siento haberlo matado; al que siento es a mi hermano."	*"I'm not sorry for having killed him; it's my brother I feel sorry for."*
Decía Gregorio Cortés con su alma muy encendida,	*Said Gregorio Cortés with his soul aflame,*
"No siento haberlo matado; la defensa es permitida."	*"I'm not sorry for having killed him; self-defense is permitted."*
Gregorio le dice a Juan: "Muy pronto lo vas a ver.	*Gregorio said to Juan, "Soon you will see.*
Anda, háblale a los sherifes que me vengan a aprehender."	*Go on, tell the sheriffs to come and take me."*
Decían los americanos "¿Si lo vemos qué le hacemos?	*The Americans would say: "If we see him, what shall we do?*
Si le entramos por derecho, muy poquitos volveremos."	*If we face him head on, very few will return."*
Agarraron a Cortés; ya terminó la cuestión,	*Now they caught Cortés; now the case is closed.*
La pobre de su familia la lleva en el corazón.	*His poor family, he carries in his heart.*

As the twentieth century progressed, the themes of the *corrido* changed. Important *corridistas* included Víctor Cordero, who wrote "Juan Charrasqueado" in 1940, a murder ballad that became popular nationwide and that was retold in several films. Though the advent of the electronic age and mass-media no longer necessitated the *corrido* as a preserver or transmitter of information, the genre nevertheless survived and even flourished. After World War II, themes of the Mexican Revolution were replaced by more pressing concerns in the northern borderlands: the plight of migrant farm workers and the injustices of a landowning society. Protagonists of *corridos* were no longer heroic military leaders but victims of U.S. social injustice. *Corridos* relating to the migrant-rights movement led by César Chávez became common and were used extensively to foment unionization and promote social action in both Mexico and the United States. As such, the *corrido* became an important signifier of cultural identity for several generations of Mexican Americans.

By the 1980s, as Mexico continued on its path of modernization and urbanization, the most common subject of *corridos* was the drug trafficking that flourished on the northern borderlands, and particularly in the state of Sinaloa. There are so many *corridos* on the subject of *narcotrafficantes*—drug dealers—that they can now claim their own subcategory: the *narcocorrido*. Many were commissioned by the druglords themselves in an effort to create a romantic mythology, portraying them as latter-day versions of the quixotic, authority-defying bandits of the revolutionary era. The stereotypical image of the *narco* drug-dealer, with dark glasses, cowboy boots, machine guns, and pickup trucks is as iconic today as the Mexican bandit, with his *sombrero* and *bandoleras*, was one hundred years ago. *Narcocorridos* continue the tradition of naming specific names and places, and of subversive defiance of authority, resulting in censorship attempts by political leaders. Other *corridos*, however, take the opposite view, pointing to the bloody violence and murder caused by the drug trade.

The most prominent exponent of modern *corridos* is the legendary Sinaloa band Los Tigres del Norte, which, starting in the 1970s, made important contributions to *tejano*, *norteña*, and *corridos*, infusing their music with distinct rock and *cumbia* influences, a strong electric guitar presence, and sophisticated sound effects which made their concerts impressive. Their music portrayed real people and vivid situations that ordinary folks could relate to. Los Tigres del Norte are credited with creating the *narcocorrido* with their 1972 hit "Contrabando y traición" ("Contraband and Betrayal"), which tells a story of love, betrayal and murder in the midst of the drug trafficking world. Other important singers of modern *corridos* include Los Broncos de Reynosa, and the short-lived but now-legendary Chalino Sánchez, who met a violent end that mirrored the subjects he was singing about.

Recommended Listening: "Contrabando y traición" by Los Tigres del Norte and "El crimen de Culiacán" by Chalino Sánchez, from the CD *Corridos y narcocorridos*.

DUETO SINGING   While *corrido* and *conjunto* were essentially rural genres, a more urban singing style emerged in towns and cities like Monterrey, Brownsville, San Antonio, and Los Angeles. These were *duetos*, female duos that sang *rancheras*, *boleros*, and *corridos* in close harmony, often accompanied by a lone guitar. Female duo singing had been popular in the late nineteenth century, and the earliest recordings of the style were made on wax cylinders in the early 1900s. Some of those early pioneers included Rosa and Luisa Villa as well as the Padilla Sisters, a Los Angeles duo whose recordings quickly became famous and were widely imitated. Because the accordion was still associated with the working class, record companies who were targeting middle-class audiences opted instead for simple guitars, *orquestas típicas*, or even *mariachis* for *dueto* accompaniment.

Dueto singing, consisting primarily of female singers, was an unusual phenomenon in a predominantly masculine culture, one that allowed these women to achieve a measure of respect and achievement they might otherwise not have attained. Yet in spite of their prominence, they often had to adapt to a male-oriented industry: Songwriters and recordings studios were dominated by men, as were the working-class bars and *cantinas* the women often sang in. Their songs still spoke of the virtue of men and the treachery of women. Though a few managed to break through the barriers of patriarchal society, by and large the singers were still expected to follow traditional roles. More than a few were forced to abandon their singing careers upon marriage, for it was felt their roles as wives and child-bearers would be adversely affected.

The most important proponents of this style of singing were members of the talented Mendoza family, which for years performed at dances and variety shows on both sides of the border. One member of the family in particular stood out and became the first star among borderland musicians: Lydia Mendoza. Born in Houston in 1916, she was a child prodigy, learning to sing and to play guitar and violin at a young age from her mother and grandmother. The family made its first recording in 1928, when Lydia was only 12, and soon thereafter she began doing live radio performances in San Antonio, which increased her visibility. Solo recordings quickly followed, including the song that in 1934 would become the first *norteña* hit and that would propel Mendoza to stardom: "Mal hombre". Her career launched, she would spend the next seven decades intermittently touring and recording, releasing more than 60 albums and becoming a legend in the process. Mendoza's appeal rested on her clear and energetic voice and her ability to sing in various styles and genres, including *rancheras*, *boleros*, *corridos*, *jarochos*, and *mariachi* songs, and even opera arias and art songs. Her guitar-playing ability was well known, and often her 12-string guitar would be her only accompaniment. At other times, though, she would eagerly meld her voice with that of accordion-based *conjuntos*, *orquestas típicas*, or *mariachis*. Mendoza had many nicknames, including *Reina del Tejano* ("Queen of Tejano"), *Cancionera de los Pobres* ("Singer of the Poor"), *Alondra de la Frontera* ("Lark of the Border"), and *Gloria de Texas* ("Glory of Texas"). Mendoza blazed the trail for the music careers of many other women, including her two sisters María and Juanita, as well as Chelo Silva, the Cantú Sisters (Nori and Ninfa), the Hernández Sisters (Carmen and Laura), and Rosita Fernández.

Recommended Listening: "Sueño en Río Grande" by Las Hermanas Padilla, from the CD *Mexican-American Border Music, Vol. 1: An Introduction: The Pioneer Recording Artists*.

Recommended Listening: "Aunque en miles calles vivas" by La Familia Mendoza, "Piensa en mi" by Lydia Mendoza, and "Postas de retrocarga" by Las Hermanas Degollado, from the CD *Mexican-American Border Music, Vol. 1: An Introduction: The Pioneer Recording Artists*.

Recommended Listening: "Mal hombre" and "Pero hay qué triste" by Lydia Mendoza, from the CD *Mal hombre and Other Original Hits from the 1930s*.

Recommended Listening: "Se me fue mi amor" by Carmen y Laura Hernandez, from the CD *Tejano Roots: The Women (1946–1970)*.

MÚSICA NORTEÑA **AND** *CONJUNTO*   The labels *música norteña* and *conjunto* are closely related but not completely interchangeable. They refer to a style that emerged from—and parallel to—the *corrido* in the twentieth century. *Conjunto* means "ensemble," referring to the fact that this music was played by more than one person, unlike the *corrido*, which was often a solo genre. *Música norteña* simply means "music from the north." An important contributing factor to the emergence of *norteña* was the presence of German and Czech Mennonites who settled in central and south Texas and northern Mexico in the late nineteenth and early twentieth centuries. These immigrants brought with them much of their own culture, including folk dances and the diatonic button accordion, both of which would come to have a huge influence on the music of the region. *Norteña* is, admittedly, an unusual syncretic form, melding elements from wildly dissimilar and contrasting cultures, yet whose results turned out to be one of the most successful styles in Latin America. (Flaco Jiménez, one of the great modern performers of *norteña*, has famously compared it to "a mixture between a German Shepherd and a Chihuahua.")

By the turn of the century, amateur Mexican musicians in the borderlands took up the accordion and began learning German and Bohemian folk dances such as *polkas, waltzes, mazurkas*, and *redowas*, and infusing them with elements from the *corrido*, the *huapango*, and other Mexican genres, making them faster, wilder, and more powerful than their European versions. Soon, other instruments were added to create a *conjunto*, including a rural drum made from goatskin called *tambora de rancho* and a *bajo sexto*, a, 12-string bass guitar. Despite the complexity of some of the dances of origin, *norteña*, like *corrido*, eventually settled into two typical rhythmic configurations: the triple-meter waltz and the duple-meter polka. These borderland musicians began playing in *cantinas*, dancehalls and at community dances called *fandangos. Norteña* thus emerged as dance music rather than as a vocal genre. Before long, it was the preferred music of the working classes in the borderlands, popular with German, Czech, and Mexican patrons, who were attracted to its rowdy energy and its sexual suggestiveness. Significantly, it was not popular among local Anglo-Americans, who considered the accordion a low-class instrument and the dances insidious, an attitude that has somewhat survived to this day.

Recommended Listening: "Es un capricho (Polka)" by Bruno Villareal, from the CD *Mexican-American Border Music, Vol. 1: An Introduction: The Pioneer Recording Artists*.

By the 1930s, *norteña* was establishing itself as an important regional genre, gaining popularity throughout the borderlands and beyond. This was partly due to two factors. The first was the advent of important musicians who took *norteña* in bold new directions and whose tremendous influence on the style can be felt to this day. First among these was Narciso Martínez, known as *El Huracán del Valle* ("The Hurricane of the Valley"), the son of migrant farm workers who lived in the Rio Grande Valley. Born in 1911, he became a virtuoso of the accordion and radically transformed its technique, de-emphasizing the bass and chord capabilities of the instrument in favor of right-hand virtuosity. As a result, the *bajo sexto* began to assume a more prominent role, particularly with the contributions of Martínez's accompanist Santiago Almeida. The result was a bold, exciting, and energetic style, which became widely imitated by *norteña* musicians for decades. Other important musicians included Beto Villa and Don Santiago Jiménez, who in the 1930s added a double bass, thus forming what would become the standard *conjunto* instrumentation of accordion, *bajo sexto*, and bass.

The other important factor was the sudden interest by U.S. record companies that had previously been successful recording Appalachian country singers and African-American blues. Seeking new material, they discovered the music of the borderlands and began recording Martínez, Jiménez, Lolo Cavazos, and others, as well as Lydia Mendoza and the *dueto* singers. *Norteña* soon began airing on borderland radio stations, record sales quickly flourished, and its commercial success became as pronounced as that of American country and blues. With the advent of World War II, the national record companies stopped promoting much of the folk music that had been their staple for over a decade. Not to be outdone, local companies emerged that continued the music's dissemination, notably the Texas label Ideal, founded by Armando Marroquín in 1946, which for decades thereafter recorded many *norteña* artists, including Narciso Martínez himself, who appeared on Ideal's first release. After World War II, *norteña* continued to mature, with musicians such as Valerio Longoria, who replaced the *tambora de rancho* with a modern drum set and transformed the *conjunto* into a vocal genre, singing boleros and *rancheras* to what had previously been a purely instrumental genre. Soon thereafter, Tony de la Rosa added the modern drum set and electric bass. Other important bands from this period included Los Alegres de Terán, Los Relámpagos, and the Conjunto Bernal, led by Paulino Bernal, who took *norteña* to a new level of polished virtuosity.

Recommended Listening: "La pollita (vals)" by Narciso Martínez and Santiago Almeida, "Ella es mi delirio" by Andres Berlanga and Francisco Montalvo, and "El rancho grande" by Santiago Jimenez, from the CD *Mexican-American Border Music, Vol. 1: An Introduction: The Pioneer Recording Artists.*

Recommended Listening: "Que me gano con llorar" by Conjunto Trio San Antonio and "Sin tu cariño" by Valerio Longoria, from the CD *Mexican-American Border Music, Vol. 1: An Introduction: The Pioneer Recording Artists.*

Recommended Listening: "La Margarina" and "Pensamiento" by Conjunto Bernal, from the CD *Conjunto Bernal: 16 Early Hits.*

TEJANO AND TEX-MEX   Mexican Americans in Texas, or Tejanos, were heavily influenced by 1950s and 1960s rock-and-roll, as well as by American country-western, blues, and rhythm and blues. They transformed *música norteña* from a rural, ethnic folk music to a glossy urban pop style, and deemphasized the *corrido*. In the process it adopted a new name: *tejano* ("Texan"). Though the accordion was still a fixture, musicians now added electric guitars, electric bass, drums, and eventually synthesizers, trumpets, and saxophones, in an ensemble that came to be known as *orquesta*. New artists emerged, including prominently the virtuoso accordionist Ramón Ayala, who began making more complex arrangements. A new dance form eventually became prominent: *cumbia*, derived from the Colombian dance of the same name, discussed later in this chapter. Conversely, U.S. rock-and-roll and pop music were also influenced by *norteña*, yielding a new syncretic style called Tex-Mex, whose most prominent proponents included Freddy Fender, the Sir Douglas Quintet, Sam the Sham and The Pharaohs, and The Champs, whose song "Tequila" became an international hit.

Many traditionalists resisted these new changes, complaining that *tejano* had become more Americanized, and that it was selling out, pandering to middle-class assimilated Mexican Americans at the expense of the traditional *conjunto*, which still mirrored the values of the working class. Two of the musicians instrumental in the development of *tejano* and its popularization beyond the borderlands were the sons of Santiago Jiménez: Santiago Jiménez Jr. and especially Leonardo "Flaco" Jiménez, who combined his virtuosic accordion playing with rock rhythms. One of the most popular and recognizable *tejano* stars, Flaco Jiménez collaborated with a number of U.S. and European rock and pop artists, notably Ry Cooder, Bob Dylan, Emmylou Harris, and The Rolling Stones. Other important *norteña* and *tejano* groups have emerged, many who pride themselves on their northern geographic origin, as evidenced by their names: Los Relámpagos del Norte, Los Cadetes del Norte, Los Rieleros del Norte, Los Dinámicos del Norte, Los Bravos del Norte, and, most prominently, Los Tigres del Norte, discussed earlier in this chapter.

Yet in spite of the modernization of the style, *tejano* continued to remain fairly provincial, limited in popularity to the borderlands, and unable to break into either the U.S. or Mexican mainstream or to take advantage of the salsa phenomenon that was occurring in New York and Miami. In the 1980s, several bands had some success, including La Mafia, a Houston-based group that turned *tejano* songs into romantic pop ballads. They became the first *tejano* band to break into American mainstream pop music, though their presence there was relatively short-lived. Since the heyday of the *dueto* singers in the 1950s, a number of female singers have broken into the male-dominated *norteña* and *tejano* world. These include the San Antonio-born Tish Hinojosa, who has created a brand of folk music permeated with the sounds of Texas and northern Mexico. But the most famous of the female *tejano* singers was Selena Quintanilla (known mostly by her first name), who made important contributions and became extremely popular in Texas and northern Mexico before her murder in 1995 at age 23. Born in Lake Jackson, Texas, Selena skyrocketed to international success, releasing several albums that won numerous awards, notably 1994's *Amor prohibido*. With Selena, *tejano* finally broke into the U.S. pop scene, appealing not only to the vast Spanish-speaking market, but to mainstream U.S. audiences as well. Other important *tejano* artists who have enjoyed popular success include Emilio Navaira, Rick Trevino, and Jay Perez, and the groups Los Kumbia Kings, Intocable, Los Tigrillos, Pesado, and Duelo. The Texas Tornados was an assembly of many *tejano* luminaries, including Flaco Jiménez, who added elements of U.S. country-western music to the traditional *tejano* sound.

Yet modern *norteña* is by no means monolithic, and many bands adhere to various styles: some have saxophones, others have marimbas; some are more strongly influenced by American rock, others by salsa and *cumbia*; the traditional *conjunto* continues to be popular in the borderlands and among immigrants both in the United States and throughout Mexico, with many regional variations, and continues to thrive in other parts of the world. Record sales of *música norteña* have continued to climb, surpassing all other styles of Mexican music. All-*norteña* radio stations have proliferated everywhere in the United States, and *norteña* is now a major presence in nightclubs and on the concert circuit in both countries. Its survival and success in the face of the onslaught of U.S. popular music points to its importance as a signifier of national, class, and ethnic identity. It remains the music of the Latino working class.

> **Recommended Listening:** "Ay te dejo en San Antonio" and "Juárez" by Flaco Jiménez, from the CD *The Best of Flaco Jiménez*.

> **Recommended Listening:** "Nuestra canción" and "Estás tocando fuego" by La Mafia, from the CD *Estás tocando Fuego*.

> **Recommended Listening:** "Amor prohibido" and "Bidi bidi bom bom" by Selena, from the CD *Amor prohibido*.

> **Recommended Viewing:** For a glimpse of the modern world of *tejano*, see the 1997 film *Selena*, a biography of Selena Quintanilla.

BANDA   Yet another style related to *norteña* is *banda*, derived from wind bands—and particularly military bands—that were popular throughout

Mexico in the nineteenth century. In the twentieth century, in the states of Sinaloa, Durango, and Zacatecas, these wind bands began adopting *mariachi* and *norteña* characteristics. *Banda* became primarily a vocal genre, with two- and three-part singing of traditional *corridos, rancheras,* and *boleros,* as well as more recent styles such as *cumbias.* A typical *banda* consists of 15 to 20 musicians who play brass instruments such as trumpets, trombones, and tubas, and woodwinds such as clarinets and saxophones. An instrument particular to *banda* is a low-pitched tuba-like instrument called the *tambora,* which provides the bass for these ensembles. Bass drums, snare drums, cymbals, and other percussion instruments usually accentuate the music but do not provide a steady background rhythm, as that is the role of the *tambora.* Like much of *norteña, banda* remained a local or regional style until the 1980s and 1990s, when it jumped on the *norteña* bandwagon and developed more widespread popularity, including in the southwestern United States. Some of the most prominent performers of *banda* include Banda el Recodo, Banda Jerez, Julio Preciado, El Coyote, and Yolanda Pérez. A subcategory of *banda* music is the *pasito duranguense* ("little step from durango"), a style that emphasizes elaborate ornamental passages in the clarinet and faster tempos designed for dancing, including highly syncopated polka and *cumbia* rhythms. In the United States, the style has been particularly popular in Chicago, home to many immigrants from Durango. Important *duranguense* bands include Grupo Montéz de Durango, Conjunto Atardecer, and Los Horoscopos de Durango.

> **Recommended Listening:** "La india bonita" by Banda Típica Mazatlán, from the CD *Mexican-American Border Music, Vol. 1: An Introduction: The Pioneer Recording Artists.*

> **Recommended Listening:** "El sinaloense" by Banda Sinaloense el Recodo, from the CD *Lo mejor de lo mejor.*

> **Recommended Listening:** "Camino a Tepehuanes" by Montez de Durango, from the CD *En vivo desde Chicago.*

POPULAR MUSIC IN MEXICO

Música Tropical

The worldwide popularity of Afro-Cuban music which started in the 1930s also extended to Mexico and had an important effect on the development of Mexican music. As noted above, the *bolero* and *danzón* were adopted and developed in Mexico, becoming important styles in their own right. Other Afro-Cuban styles, including the rumba, mambo, conga, and later, salsa, also made important strides in Mexico, which developed its own Caribbean music tradition, called generally *música tropical.* Cuban and other Caribbean musicians immigrated to Mexico, including notably Pérez Prado—"the King of the Mambo"—who, beginning in 1949, became the anchor of the *música tropical* scene for the next three decades, performing at popular cabarets and appearing in various films.

Recommended Viewing: For a look at the 1940s and 1950s cabaret scene in Mexico, including footage of Pérez Prado, Agustín Lara, Los Panchos, and many others, see the 1950 *"cabaretera"* melodramas *Aventurera* and *Perdida*.

Mexico also partook of the *salsa* and *merengue* explosion of the 1970s and 1980s, producing several bands of note, but another Latin style would dominate *música tropical* in the last decades of the century and into the new millennium. This was *cumbia* (discussed in depth in Chapter 7), which became as prominent in Mexico as it was in its native Colombia. Starting in the 1960s, important Colombian *cumbia* artists such as Carmen Rivero, Luis Carlos Meyer, and La Sonora Dinamita began touring in Mexico. Before long, Mexican *cumbia* bands emerged, performing in dancehalls and fiestas, and the style could soon be heard on radio stations across the country. It was—and continues to be—particularly popular with the working classes. Mexican *cumbia* and *música tropical* in general differ from their Caribbean cousins in that they do not emphasize Afro-Caribbean percussion instruments to the same extent. Instead, they rely on electric guitars, bass, and synthesizers. Percussion is provided by a drum set, though sometimes conga drums can be present. *Cumbia* songs can be slow romantic pop ballads or fast dance tunes. One of the first Mexican *cumbia* stars was Mike Laure, who had a number of hits in the 1960s, including "Banda borracha" and "Tiburón a la vista." The Afro-Mexican singer Rigo Tovar was instrumental in modernizing *cumbia* in the 1970s, injecting it with rock elements such as electric guitars and synthesizers. Tovar became an idol of the working classes, and was one of the most successful musicians in the 1970s and 1980s. Other important proponents of Mexican *cumbia* include Los Bukis, Los Yonics, Los Temerarios, Fito Olivares, and Los Ángeles Azules. Various regional *cumbia* styles also emerged, including the DJ record-spinning *cumbia sonidera* in central Mexico; *cumbia grupera* on the Gulf Coast; *cumbia villera*, a slower form which became popular in urban slums; and *cumbia norteña*, a style widespread in the borderlands and the U.S. southwest that adopted *conjunto*'s characteristic accordion and *bajo sexto* instrumentation. *Cumbia rap* has also recently emerged, combining the traditional style with urban rap and hip hop sensibilities, for example with the contributions of the Mexican band Los Chicos del Barrio, or the Texas group Los Kumbia Kings, fronted by A. B. Quintanilla, brother of Selena. After disbanding in 2006, Los Kumbia Kings later reformed into two groups: Los Super Reyes and the Kumbia All-Starz. Mexican *cumbia* remains popular with the working classes, while in the United States it remains one of the staples of the Hispanic community, competing with *tejano* and *banda* on U.S. radio stations and dancehalls.

Recommended Listening: "El pescador" by Carmen Rivero y Su Conjunto, from the CD *Econo Series: A Bailar la Cumbia*.

Recommended Listening: "Banda borracha" and "Tiburón a la vista" by Mike Laure, from the CD *Lo mejor de Mike Laure*.

Recommended Listening: "Matamoros querido" and "Sirenita" by Rigo Tovar, from the CD *La Historia de un ídolo*.

Pop

As virtually everywhere in the world, Mexico had a resurgence of pop music after the 1960s that was heavily influenced by U.S. styles. Mexican pop fused various traditions such as *ranchera* and *bolero* with glossy production values, achieving its shiny sound with sophisticated string orchestras or standard rock instrumentations. A long list of Mexican pop icons can be drawn, artists who sometimes had lasting appeal but who more often than not reached incredible heights of popularity for a short time only to be forgotten within a few years. Unlike some of the folk-based styles such as *tejano* and *cumbia*, which have gained widespread popularity in the United States, the glossy, youth-oriented pop music that has emerged in Mexico has only sporadically broken into the U.S. market. Some of the standout pop artists who emerged in the 1960s and 1970s include Johnny Laboriel, Angélica María, Juan Gabriel, and José José. An important figure is the U.S.-born singer Vikki Carr, who has sung in both Spanish and English. While her early career focused on American jazz and pop music, she later achieved much crossover success with *boleros* and Latin pop. By the 1980s, many youth-oriented pop groups were mirroring the success of the "boy bands" from other parts of Latin America. These included the groups Flans and Timbiriche, both of which achieved some level of success throughout the continent. From Timbiriche arose several singers who later became successful solo pop artists, notably Paulina Rubio and Thalía. Many pop stars, including Lucía Méndez and Veronica Castro, started their careers on popular *telenovela* soap operas. Other prominent stars in the last few decades include Luis Miguel and Gloria Trevi.

> **Recommended Listening:** "No tengo dinero" and "Sera mañana" by Juan Gabriel, from the CD *15 Años: Baladas éxitos.*

> **Recommended Listening:** "Cuando calienta el sol" and "Que seas feliz" by Luis Miguel, from the CD *Luis Miguel: Grandes éxitos.*

> **Recommended Listening:** "Gavilan o Paloma," "Lo que no fue, no será" and "Nave del olvido" by José José, from the CD *The Best of José José.*

Nueva trova

The 1960s also saw a continent-wide explosion of folk-based singing traditions called generally *nueva canción*, which emerged principally in Chile but which also included the Cuban *nueva trova*. Mexico had several important representatives in this style, notably the singer/songwriters Amparo Ochoa, Gabino Palomares, and Oscar Chávez. These and other artists wrote and performed songs—often simply accompanying themselves with a guitar—about social injustice inherent in Mexican society, the conditions of the poor and the working class, and the oppression of Native peoples. Ochoa also recorded songs about feminist issues—one of the first Mexican artists to do so—and as such gained an important following. Her songs reflected the social fight against injustice being waged throughout the continent, and in solidarity with the Chilean people, she recorded an album denouncing the violence of the

Chilean dictator Augusto Pinochet. Perhaps the most prominent Mexican *nueva trova* song is "La maldición de Malinche," composed by Palomares and popularized in a recording by Ochoa. The song spoke of the anger and sorrow that resulted from Mexicans' welcoming foreign invaders with open arms, from the Spanish Conquest to the U.S. cultural and economic invasion of the twentieth century. Another important artist was the short-lived Rodrigo González, nicknamed Rockdrigo, who in the 1980s developed a personal style called *música rupestre* ("cave music"). His songs, which are often both melancholy and humorous, addressed urban problems such as the poverty, traffic, pollution, and overpopulation that affected Mexico City, and the impossibility of living there. Perhaps ironically, Rockdrigo was killed in the 1985 Mexico City earthquake, though his songs greatly influenced the emerging *rock en español* movement in Mexico and as far away as Argentina.

> **Recommended Listening:** "La maldición de Malinche" by Amparo Ochoa, from the CD *Por siempre*.

> **Recommended Listening:** "Por tí" and "Macondo" by Oscar Chávez, from the CD *Oscar Chávez: 20 éxitos*.

> **Recommended Listening:** "Estación del metro Balderas" and "Balada del asalariado" by Rockdrigo, from the CD *Hurbanistorias*.

4

The Spanish-Speaking Caribbean

CHAPTER SUMMARY

Introduction to the Caribbean
- Caribbean History
- Caribbean Culture
- Native Musical Traditions
- African Religions and Rituals
- Modern Caribbean Music

Cuba
- Introduction
- Historical Overview
- Instruments and Elements of Cuban Music
- The African Roots of Cuban Music
  - Santería
  - Other Afro-Cuban Rhythms
- The Spanish Roots of Cuban Music
- Cuban Dance Music
  - *Son montuno*
- The Cuban Song Tradition: *Trova* and *Bolero*
- Cuban Music Leaves the Island
- Cuban Music Since the Revolution
  - *Nueva trova*
  - *Salsa*
  - The 1990s

Puerto Rico
- Historical Overview

- Spanish Roots: *Jíbaro* Music
  - *Décima* and *Seis*
  - *Aguinaldo*
  - *Danza*
- African Roots
  - *Vejigantes*
  - *Bomba*
  - *Plena*
  - *Bomba* and *Plena* in the Twentieth Century
- Puerto Rican Popular Music
  - *Reggaetón*

The Dominican Republic
- Afro-Dominican Styles
  - *Palos*
  - *Cocolos*
- Syncretic Styles
  - Merengue
  - *Bachata*

INTRODUCTION TO THE CARIBBEAN

The Caribbean consists of more than one hundred inhabited islands and thousands more that are uninhabited, stretching across more than 2,000 miles from the southern tip of Florida to the coast of Venezuela. There are about 40 million inhabitants in the Caribbean, almost a third of whom live in Cuba alone. The region is extremely diverse: in addition to Native, Spanish, and African influences, important contributions have been made by French, English, Swedish, Danish, Dutch, and East Indian cultures, all of which would seemingly set them apart from the Spanish- and Portuguese-speaking countries that make up the bulk of Latin America. Yet even a brief overview reveals a shared cultural, historical, and musical bond, and that the islands are an integral part of the development and emergence of the Americas as a whole. While languages and specific historical circumstances may differ, cultural experiences and broad historical trends—the most obvious being slavery and European colonialism—are shared among most of the countries in the hemisphere. As in much of the rest of the Americas, ethnic groups throughout the Caribbean have succeeded in combining elements of their source cultures. The intense racial, social, cultural, religious, and musical syncretism found in places like Jamaica, Trinidad, and Haiti is very closely related to that found in Brazil, Cuba, and Mexico. The French *zouk* and *kongo* and the English reggae and calypso are intricately bound to the Spanish *bomba* and *rumba,* and even to the Brazilian *samba* and *bossa nova.*

Caribbean History

Together, the islands of the Caribbean Sea were home to several million inhabitants before the arrival of the Europeans. The Siboney and Taínos had lived in the region for thousands of years, mainly in Cuba and Jamaica. Around 200 BCE, Arawaks from South America began populating the southern islands. More than a millennium later, yet another group began a war-like migration from South America, displacing many island inhabitants. These were the Caribs, after whom the sea was eventually named. All of these groups were able seafaring people, and the canoe-based trade system they developed resulted in mutual cultural exchanges that lasted until the arrival of the Europeans.

The region's history and culture have typically been measured from colonial and postcolonial perspectives, though other views have recently emerged. The Caribbean is of course where Christopher Columbus first landed in the Americas, making the cluster of islands the site for the first modern encounter between Europeans and Americans. The landing on the island of Guanahani (renamed San Salvador) on October 12, 1492, placed the Caribbean squarely at the center of European ambition. (Because Columbus thought he had landed in Asia, the islands were called the Indies, and eventually, upon recognition of the mistake, the West Indies.) Thereafter, the Caribbean became the intersection of much of the continent, the place where European powers went first before expanding their sights.

The sudden European awareness of the territories that existed across the Atlantic engendered a centuries-long land-grab as their economic potential became readily apparent. The Spanish, intent on preserving the region for themselves, quickly built fortresses in Cuba, Puerto Rico, and Hispaniola, though these proved mostly futile as other European powers began their own colonial efforts. There ensued a trans-Atlantic geopolitical cat-and-mouse game that would last for almost half a millennium, as the Spanish, English, Danes, Swedes, French, and Dutch jockeyed for economic and military leverage, turning the sea into their personal playground. Often hiring pirates to do their dirty work, they captured, colonized, raided, bartered, surrendered, and recaptured their various possessions, waging centuries-long military conflicts, trade wars, and economic embargos. As a result, some islands changed hands more than 20 times during the colonial period.

In the process of colonization, the original inhabitants were mostly annihilated. In the northern islands, the Siboney, Taínos, and Arawaks were eradicated within a few generations of the arrival of the Europeans, mostly by disease. In many of the southern islands, the Caribs held out for several centuries before finally succumbing. Native culture had little influence on subsequent events in most of the Caribbean, though subtle traces of it remained in the historical record and can be discerned in popular culture even now. Today, a few descendants of the Caribs still inhabit regions of Dominica, Belize, Brazil, and the Guyanas.

The islands were rich in forest lumber, minerals, and gold and precious metals, all of which were duly exploited. Eventually, important crops were developed: bananas, tobacco, coconuts, coffee, citrus products, cocoa, and spices. But it was sugar—"brown gold"—in particular that brought great wealth to the colonizers of the Caribbean. Sugar satisfied the European sweet tooth, as well as the demand for cheap rum distilled from it. Huge plantations emerged throughout the region, producing not only the crops destined for European markets but also spawning a way of life that would last for more than 400 years and that can still be found on some of the islands.

The plantations system meant an increased need for labor, and, the original inhabitants having been mostly eradicated, millions of slaves were brought to the Caribbean, making it an important part of the African Diaspora. The nineteenth century saw the abolition first of the slave trade and then of slavery itself. Slaves in the British islands were the first to be emancipated in 1833, while those on Spanish islands were the last in 1880. But the demand for labor did not decrease, and to meet it, indentured servants—in a system that in practice was not very different from slavery—were brought in from Africa, India, China, and the Middle East. As a result, many of the inhabitants of the Caribbean are of Indian and Middle Eastern descent.

Towards the end of the nineteenth century, a new factor influenced the political and economic development of the Caribbean: involvement by the United States, most prominently in Cuba and Puerto Rico during the Spanish-American War in 1898, but also in the Virgin Islands, Haiti, and the Dominican Republic. With few exceptions, the Caribbean was not part of the nineteenth-century revolutionary movement that brought independence to most of Latin America. Haiti did achieve independence in 1804, as did Cuba nearly a century later, but most of the islands remained under European dominion until the rash of independence movements in the 1950s and 1960s. Many islands became autonomous nations; others remained loosely attached to their colonizing power, notably the British Commonwealth; others still, including French Martinique and Guadeloupe, did not achieve independence at all but remain constituent parts of the original colonial powers. Today, there are 13 independent nations in the Caribbean: Antigua and Barbuda, the Bahamas, Barbados, Cuba, Dominica, Grenada, the Dominican Republic, Haiti, Jamaica, Saint Kitts and Nevis, Saint Lucia, Saint Vincent and the Grenadines, and Trinidad and Tobago. The rest of the islands remain territories dependent on Venezuela, France, Britain, the Netherlands, or the United States.

The Caribbean is intricately linked with the sea and with warm tropical climates, a geographical reality that has resulted in many of the islands becoming important ports of call that fomented trade and tourism and that has contributed to the emergence of art, literature, and music. Throughout the region, the prevalence of sugarcane has contributed to a centuries-old tradition of rum production, including a spiced variety found on many of the islands. One of the legacies of colonialism is that many Caribbean economies still rely on single crops and concentrated land ownership, while a majority of inhabitants barely survive on a subsistence level. As a result, the Caribbean contains some of the poorest countries in the world. The twentieth century saw the development of new industries, including petroleum production and tourism, which have become important parts of some Caribbean economies. Cruise ships have made the Caribbean easily accessible, and many islands have become a favorite playground for millions, mostly from Europe and the United States, attracted by the colorful music and cultures and by the warmth and beauty of sandy beaches and picturesque scenery. Carnival season in particular is immensely popular among both islanders and tourists.

Caribbean Culture

In spite of the common history and culture it shares with its Latin American neighbors, the Caribbean does nonetheless stand apart in terms of culture and especially music. Virtually every one of the inhabited islands had to contend with its own particular set of racial, religious, historical, and geographical factors, and thus developed its own culture and music, its own secular celebrations and religious rituals. The more varied the background, the more syncretic the culture. Islands that were ruled by more than one colonial power, such as Trinidad or Dominica, have divergent styles that draw from many influences. By contrast, islands such as Cuba that had only one colonial power saw a more straightforward evolution of their European and African mix.

This diversity is particularly apparent in the region's linguistic differences. The French, English, Spanish, and Dutch imposed their languages on the islands, though some islands were controlled in succession by two or more countries. Slaves and immigrants also spoke languages that originated in various parts of Africa, India, the Middle East, and even the Caribbean itself. From this veritable Babel-like sea, complex dialects have emerged that combine many of the source elements, often distorting words from one or more European languages. Thus, Francophone islands have dialects called *kwéyol* (Creole) or *patois* (pronounced pah-TWA); Anglophone islands have various versions of *pidgin*, while the Dutch Antilles speak *papiamentu*. For more than four hundred years, these languages have been transmitted orally, resulting in widely diverse spellings and pronunciations as well as dialects that differ from island to island, sometimes even within regions of a particular island. Another example of the region's cultural diversity can be seen in the national sports: Baseball is the sport of choice in most of the Spanish Caribbean, while soccer rules in French-speaking islands and cricket is king in most English-speaking islands.

Native Musical Traditions

Native Caribbean cultures, particularly that of the Taínos, had several instruments that could be also found in Central and South America. Most prominent were the *maracas*, gourds filled with seeds that were rhythmically shaken and that were reportedly larger than their popular descendants. Some claim that the name comes from a Native group that inhabited the shores of the Maraca River in Brazil and that eventually migrated to the Caribbean. The *güiro* was a serrated gourd that was scraped. The Taínos also used conch shells, as did dozens of other cultures throughout the continent, as well as reed or bone flutes, some of which have survived into modern times. The Native inhabitants of the Caribbean also used the *mayohuacán* (or *mayohavau*), a drum with an incision that created two vibrating tongues, similar to the Aztec *teponaztli*. Music was important in the religious rituals of Caribbean civilizations, though little of it survives today. Early writers described in particular the *areito*, a community song and dance form that was used to convey the history of the people and other important knowledge. By one account, the *areito* would involve several hundred dancers assembled in a circle and could

Carib native drummers from the island of Dominica.

take several hours or even an entire day as the elders passed on their knowledge to the assembled youth. Today, various artists from the Caribbean use the term *areito* to refer generally to a song or dance, though these modern incarnations have no relation to the pre-Columbian dance.

African Religions and Rituals

As virtually everywhere in Latin America, slavery was central to the development of island traditions. The slaves were ethnically diverse, originating from different African tribes and speaking a multitude of languages. Very often, they were from enemy tribes, and the violence carried into the New World. But regardless of their point of origin or their final destination, slave culture was at the root of a religious, musical, and artistic syncretism that melded African, European, and, eventually, East Indian customs to create a unique Caribbean folklore. A common trait of Caribbean slave culture was the struggle for liberation, both on a personal level and—eventually—as a nation. On many islands, escaped slaves called *Maroons* (*marrons* in French, *cimarrones* or *marrones* in Spanish) established clandestine communities where they lived in relative peace and prosperity, a few of which survive to this day. Some of these communities developed a culture of resistance and served as bases for rebellion. Active resistance throughout the region greatly influenced the development of Afro-Caribbean history, religion and music. Conversely, state and religious authorities struggled to control Afro-Caribbean culture and religion, very often through its music. Their success or failure often determined the evolutionary course of the various islands, with enormously diverse results.

Wherever African slaves were present in the Americas, African religions were sure to emerge and survive, providing them with a spiritual continuity and sense of identity. Many Afro-Caribbean religions are still prominent in the Caribbean, notably the various *Santería* rites in Cuba, *vodou* in Haiti, *kumina* and the more recent Rastafarian movement in Jamaica, as well as dozens of other spiritual traditions on some of the smaller islands. Often, the rituals have shed their spiritual content, and are sustained by secular musical components—the drumming and dancing traditions. In spite of this, most inhabitants of the Caribbean are Christians—Roman Catholic in the French and Spanish colonies, Protestant in the English and Dutch colonies. There are also important Hindu, Jewish, and Muslim populations found throughout the islands.

Modern Caribbean Music

Despite their extreme diversity, the islands share certain commonalities that are at the root of most of the music. Perhaps most importantly, the collective experience of slavery, imbued with memories of the African continent and the struggle for freedom, infuses every Caribbean island. African instruments were essential to the music of the slaves, and they eventually shaped most Caribbean societies, regardless of race or ethnicity. The primary African instrument, of course, was the drum, which, with its complex rhythmic practices, supported a culture that yearned to reconnect with the comfort of the African homeland. One of the drum's uses was as a means of communication, and for this reason, some Europeans fearing rebellion often repressed or banned its use, though even in these cases, the drumming traditions often continued to thrive underground. Conversely, on other islands, drumming was believed to make the slaves work harder, and were thus allowed and even encouraged. As a result, Caribbean drums developed in different ways on various islands, and appear in a tremendous diversity of shapes and sizes, with myriad performance techniques and functions. Afro-Caribbean music also included various singing styles, particularly those that involve a soloist and chorus in call-and-response form. African dancing also contributed to the vivid rhythms, still on display for example in Santería rites and Trinidadian carnival. Many of the secularized dances have made their way into popular styles all around the world. Slave celebrations and festivities using drum ensembles were often allowed and even encouraged by the Europeans, as long as they maintained at least a secular outward appearance.

But the Europeans also had a rich history of music in the Caribbean, particularly in the form of songs and dances that were brought over from the continent, often performed by Black musicians at the social balls of the White elite. Inevitably, a syncretic fusion emerged: some music was purely European, some was purely African; most was a mixture of the two. Some was purely vocal, some was purely instrumental. A good deal of it was meant for dancing. While African music relied heavily on percussion/vocal ensembles, its European counterpart was often performed on string and wind ensembles. New religious styles developed, used to connect with God, nature, or the ancestral spirits; some music was meant for entertainment or for ritual healing; many forms developed during slavery days as children's ring songs, work songs, and songs for special occasions such as weddings and funerals. Sometimes music was used for communication and eventually for rebellion. Later, songs became conduits for history or political commentary. Still later, music was used to entertain the millions of tourists that flocked to the islands.

In the second half of the twentieth century, the music of the Caribbean became the world's second-most popular and influential, after that of the United States. From the fertile Caribbean emerged *merengue* and *salsa, rumba* and *mambo, trova* and *nueva canción,* calypso and mento, reggae and ska, *compas, soca* and *zouk.* Many of these styles have become extremely popular on every continent. Important salsa and reggae festivals are regularly held in Europe, Asia and the United States. Many Caribbean artists have shot to stardom, including most prominently Harry Belafonte, Bob Marley, Peter Tosh, Celia Cruz, Gloria Estefan, Ricky Martin, Lauryn Hill, Wyclef Jean, and the Fugees. Yet in spite of all the glamour and the attention these artists and genres have received, traditional folk music still thrives in the villages and towns, often far removed from the glitzy hotels and sandy beaches. Caribbean music is perhaps best expressed in the various festivals in the region, the most prominent of which is carnival, though there are hundreds of other celebrations throughout the region, including Muslim holidays such as Eid-ul-Fitr and Hosay, and Hindu holidays such as Phagwah and Diwali.

Though there are many ways to categorize the various Caribbean styles, perhaps the most logical is to divide them by language, since African traditions blended in similar ways within a specific European culture. The largest and most prominent Spanish-speaking islands are Cuba (capital: Havana), the Dominican Republic (Santo Domingo), and Puerto Rico (San Juan). The principal French-speaking islands are Haiti (Port-au-Prince), Martinique (Fort-de-France), and Guadeloupe (Pointe-à-Pitre). The main English-speaking islands are Jamaica (Kingston), the Bahamas (Nassau), Barbados (Bridgetown), and Trinidad and Tobago (Port-of-Spain). Some islands, such as Dominica and tiny Carriacou, have had a musical tradition and influence that is disproportionate to their size.

Alan Lomax

Much of the folk music of the Caribbean is extremely well documented, thanks to the efforts of the famed ethnomusicologist Alan Lomax, who in 1962 traveled to several islands and recorded much of the music he found there. Many of these traditions have subsequently faded and disappeared from their places of origin, often replaced by more commercial styles from neighboring islands or from the United States. In the course of his investigations, Lomax recognized important connections—which he called "creolization"—between the musics found on the various islands, as well as with the music of African Americans in the southern United States. Lomax's remastered recordings (with extensive liner notes) have recently been released by Rounder Records in a collection of over 100 CDs that offer a remarkable view of this music.

CUBA

Introduction

Cuban music is perhaps the most popular and influential in Latin America. Dancehalls and record stores across the world are wholly dedicated to the sounds and rhythms of this medium-sized island of 12 million inhabitants. Yet one cannot categorize Cuban music into a single style, for the island has been affected by diverse racial, social, historical, and geographical identities. Nothing in Cuba—and certainly not its music—fits neatly into homogeneous categories. Complex racial and class divisions, social prejudices, and political leanings have shaped virtually every aspect of Cuban society, most notably its music: Some styles have been (and continue to be) seen as "White," associated with the traditional ruling class; others are seen as "African," often linked with poverty, illiteracy, and, historically, with traditional religions. Most are a complex mixture. Because Cuba was zealously protected from encroachment from the other European powers, the Spanish elements of Cuban culture remained fairly isolated throughout its colonial history, mostly unaffected by English or French developments in the region. While some styles and genres, for example the music associated with some Afro-Cuban religions, have rarely been heard outside the island until recent years, others, such as the *son* and the rumba, have had a wide impact on Cuba's Caribbean and North American neighbors, as well as Europe and Asia. They have even made a full-circle return to Africa, their continent of origin.

Historical Overview

Cuba is the largest Caribbean island, and it has played central roles in the affairs of two historical world powers. It was the crown jewel of the Spanish Empire, even after larger and sometimes wealthier colonies such as Mexico and Peru came into—and then departed—the Spanish sphere. It was also the last major colony to achieve independence, in 1898. The twentieth century saw its proximity to the United States—it is famously only 90 miles from the Florida coast—become a major factor in its development.

Columbus claimed Cuba for Spain on his first voyage, on October 29, 1492, just two weeks after he arrived on the continent. By 1514, the entire island was conquered by Diego Velázquez de Cuéllar, who founded several towns, including Havana, which officially became Cuba's capital in 1607. Within a few generations, the 300,000 Taíno and Siboney Natives were eradicated, so that by 1557, only about 2,000 remained. Today, little remains of Cuban indigenous music and culture. The island became the first European outpost in the Americas—the first Spanish colony and the first American diocese. It also quickly became one of most lucrative, as the Spaniards established wealthy cattle ranches called *encomiendas*, and later plantations that would produce sugarcane, tobacco, and rum. The colonial period often juxtaposed the gentility of European culture with the brutality of the slave-based agricultural system, both of which are reflected in Cuba's music and culture. The first record of African slaves brought to Cuba dates from 1513, establishing a precedent that would quickly be adopted throughout the Americas, not only by the Spanish, but also by English, French, Dutch, and Portuguese slave traffickers. Between 1521 and 1870, more than 1.5 million slaves were brought to Cuba, almost 10 percent of all slaves brought to the Americas. Traditionally, Cuban slaves had been allowed to purchase their freedom, which led to an increased ethnic and racial melding and the creation of an important Mulatto class.

Because Cuba had been the wealthiest colony—in 1820 it became the world's largest producer of sugar—the Spanish grip remained tighter than elsewhere on the continent. Eventually, however, an independence movement emerged in the 1860s, largely propelled by the Afro-Cuban inhabitants of the island. Slavery was abolished in 1886, and a few years later, the war of independence, led by Antonio Maceo and the poet José Martí, finally led to Cuba's freedom in 1898. Yet Cuba's period of self-determination was short-lived. Sensing Spain's weakness, the neighboring United States saw an opportunity and started the Spanish-American War, which essentially transferred control of Cuba (as well as Puerto Rico and the Philippines) from Spain to the United States. Though Cuba technically gained its independence, in practice it had simply replaced one colonial power with another. For the next six decades, the United States would take an active role in the political, economic, and social life of the island, often supporting corrupt and violent dictatorships in the process. Soon, most of Cuba's farmland, sugar production, manufacturing industries, railways, mining output, and public utilities were owned by U.S. companies. United States tourism became an important part of the economy, and major cities like Havana and Santiago became tourist spots and gambling meccas, replete with high-priced hotels, night-clubs, casinos, and houses of prostitution, many of them connected to U.S. organized crime.

Yet the average Cuban worker profited little from the economic boom, and by the 1950s wide resentment at American excesses began to grow. When Fidel Castro waged an insurgency in the mid-1950s, the second revolution had begun. On January 1, 1959, after a three-year guerilla campaign, Castro's army overthrew the government of Fulgencio Batista and quickly implemented social and economic reforms, which, among other things, nationalized U.S. companies in Cuba. The United States countered by implementing a trade embargo and other measures which effectively pushed the Castro regime into the Soviet sphere. By the early 1960s, Cuba was declared a communist nation. The tensions that followed were marked by events such as the Bay of Pigs invasion (1961) and the Cuban missile crisis (1962). Eventually, a standstill was achieved, and since then, Cuba and the United States have stared at each other uneasily across the 90 miles of water that separates them.

The Castro revolution had a profound effect on the racial composition of the island. Afro-Cubans traditionally have been strong supporters of Castro. In 1959, two-thirds of Cubans were White, the remaining third Mulatto or Black. In the half century since the revolution, the ratio has reversed itself, and the White majority has become an ever-shrinking minority. An important factor in the development of the Cuban nation was the half million Cubans who emigrated, mostly to Miami, in the decades after the revolution. Exercising great political influence in the United States, they saw themselves as the fighting soul of a subjugated people, but in practical terms, the mostly wealthy exiled community was instrumental in exacerbating the continuing entrenchment and enmity between the two countries, and—counter-productively—the continued oppression of the Cuban people. Most of the Cuban émigrés—particularly in the Miami community—are White, and the antipathy between Cuba and Miami has often been charged with racial overtones.

Instruments and Elements of Cuban Music

The instruments used in Cuban music are derived from a variety of sources, though some emerged on their own as new, original instruments. The most important European instrument in the Caribbean was the guitar. It was introduced into the region early on, and quickly engendered many variations in size, tuning, and number of strings. In Cuba, the most popular guitar is the *tres* or *tres cubano*, a small six-string folk guitar, arranged in three courses of two strings, tuned either in unison or in octaves. Other variations of guitar-like instruments are the cittern and the small *bandurria*, each with 12 strings.

Not surprisingly, given Cuba's important West African roots, a prevalence of percussion instruments has dominated the Cuban sound and engendered an important rhythmic proclivity. *Maracas*, remnants of Cuba's aboriginal Taíno population, are pairs of round gourds filled with dry seeds to which a handle has been attached. Tuned to slightly different pitches, they are shaken rhythmically, one in each hand, to provide a driving percussive presence in the upper registers of Cuban ensembles. The *güiro* is a hollow and serrated calabash gourd that is scraped with a stick or a metal wire scraper. Its origins are Taíno, but Africans quickly adapted it to their own music-making. The *cencerro* (or *ekón*) is a cowbell typically made of copper, and often used to mark the *clave* rhythm. Cowbells can be found in many African and Latin American cultures. *Chéqueres* are gourds draped with beads similar to African shakers. A *quijada de burro* is, literally, a "donkey jawbone," though these days it is often made of wood. It is struck like a cowbell or scraped like a *güiro*.

Most prominent among the numerous Cuban drums are the *congas*, tunable drums played with the palm of the hand. They are made of wood, with a single leather head, and are also known as *tumbadoras* or simply *tumbas*. They come in various sizes, from the large bass *tumba* to the medium *tres por dos* and the small high-pitched *niño* or *quinto*. Perhaps the oldest of the African instruments, it began as a hollow tree trunk covered with goat or antelope hide. Later, the development of European cooperage (or barrel making) allowed for the production of more sophisticated conga drums. Derived from the European timpani, the *timbales* are a pair of short tunable drums, made out of metal, played with drumsticks, and mounted on a stand that may also hold

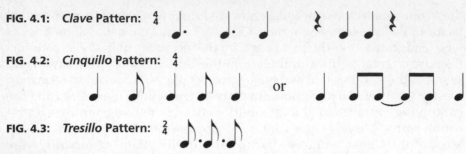

FIG. 4.1: *Clave* **Pattern:**

FIG. 4.2: *Cinquillo* **Pattern:**

or

FIG. 4.3: *Tresillo* **Pattern:**

cowbells and a wood block. **Bongos** are pairs of small drums, one slightly higher pitched than the other, held between the knees and struck with the tips of the fingers. Of African origin, they are used in particular by soloists to show virtuosity. They are also known as *gemelos*, or twins.

Claves, also known as *palitos* ("little sticks"), are cylindrical hardwood blocks that are struck together. Again, one is slightly higher pitched than the other. Perhaps no other facet of Cuban music explains the concept of syncretism better than the clave: they are neither African nor Spanish, but a distinctly Cuban creation derived from elements of both cultures. But the word *clave* also refers to a rhythmic pattern that can be played by these and other percussion instruments, including most prominently the *cencerro* cowbell. Many Caribbean genres rely on the rhythmic *clave* as a device that underlies and shapes the music. The most popular, popularly known as the 3-2 *clave*, is shown in Fig. 4.1, a two-measure phrase with a strong syncopation. There are many variations of this clave, most repeating the two-bar figures, either in duple or $\frac{6}{8}$ time. The clave rhythmic pattern is of West African descent, and musicians in Ghana and Togo use similar devices in their drumming patterns. Other prominent patterns are the *cinquillo* and *tresillo*, shown in Fig. 4.2 and 4.3.

Montuno: The term *montuno* has many definitions that are not always grasped by outsiders, even in context. Literally, the term means "from the hills" and refers to the inhabitants of the mountainous regions of the Sierra Maestra, in the Oriente district of Cuba. It is from this region that the *son* developed, and thus the tradition of the *son montuno*. But the term quickly came to describe two specific musical elements of the *son* and later, of salsa: a repeated rhythmic figure that the piano or guitar will vamp on; and the final section of a *son* in which a soloist and chorus alternate lines in a call-and-response style, while the instrumentalists improvise over it.

The African Roots of Cuban Music

As in many countries in Latin America, Cuban music inherited important characteristics from both its African and European ancestries. But in Cuba, the racial, ethnic, cultural, and religious elements blended and cross-pollinated to an extent not seen anywhere on the continent except perhaps Brazil, so that, even by the beginning of the twentieth century, few of the traditions remained in their pure, original form. The African influences themselves were not homogeneous, but were derived from four major ethnic groups: the Bantu from Central Africa, in what is now Angola, Congo, and Mozambique; the Yoruba, from West Africa in what is now Nigeria and Benin; the Ibo and Carabali, from Nigeria; and the Ewe/Fon, from the West African Kingdom of Dahomey, in present-day Ghana, Togo, and Benin.

The most prominent elements of African culture are music and religion, both inexorably linked, and both drawing from Catholic and African traditions. Today, Catholics represent almost half the population; about 2 percent of Cubans follow African-derived religions exclusively and most others practice a hybrid of African and Christian rites. Afro-Cuban religions include the Bantu *palo monte* and *abakua*, as well as the Ewe/Fon *regla arará*, which developed in the Matanzas district. But the most dominant expression of Afro-Cuban religion is Santería ("saint-worship"), which mixes Catholicism with Yoruba rites. While these syncretic religions have rarely been known outside of Cuba until recent years, their music and dance, especially that of Santería, have served as the source of much of Caribbean music for centuries.

SANTERÍA   Rites and ceremonies related to Santería can go by various names including *lukumi*, *regla de ocha*, *yoruba*, and *espiritismo*. Modern Santería performances range from closed ceremonies in rural villages, to spontaneous drumming and dancing in the streets of Havana, to shiny traveling productions designed mainly for tourists. Santería relies heavily on dancing and music, and particularly on drumming traditions that are specific to various rituals. Both men and women participate in Santería ceremonies. A number of songs and rhythms are performed called *orus*, directed towards the *orishas*, ancestral deities whose origins can be traced to West Africa, where they are still very much present today. The *orishas* represent a link both to the spiritual realm and to the ancestral lands that lay across the Atlantic. To conceal the nature of their beliefs from the Spaniards, African slaves would give them a Christian identity, and over time, the two belief systems came to meld into one syncretic religion. Practitioners pray to their *orisha* while simultaneously singing to the equivalent Christian saint. Conversely, contemporary feast day celebrations will honor the specific saint whose feast it is, but also his or her equivalent *orisha*. The several dozen *orishas* have specific names and characteristics: Ochún is the *orisha* of love, femininity, and rivers, and identified with Our Lady of Charity; Changó is the *orisha* of fire, thunder, lightning, war, and masculinity, and equivalent in Christianity to Saint Barbara; and Babalú Aye, the father of the world, is identified with Saint Lazarus.

The principal means of Santería expression are *bembé* and *batá* drumming and singing, two distinct but closely related traditions. The sacred *batá* drums are three double-headed hourglass-shaped drums whose spiritual force—known as *aña*—is used to communicate with the spirits. The smallest *batá* drum is called *Okónkolo* or *Omelé*, the medium drum is *Itótele* and the largest is *Iyá*, the "mother" of the drums. They are placed horizontally on the player's lap and played on both heads, usually accompanied by the *ekón* cowbell and *chéquere* gourds. The three drums thus produce six distinct sounds that are used to recreate African tonal languages, including prominently that of the Yoruba. A chorus of singers chants liturgical texts in a call-and-response structure, over complex interlocking rhythmic patterns or cycles. In sacred

Cuban *batá* drums and other percussion instruments.

bembé ceremonies, which have their own set of drums, *orishas* can take possession of the dancers to communicate with the world.

> **Music Example:** "Babalú Ayé" by Los Muñequitos de Matanzas, from the CD *Ito Iban Echu: Sacred Yoruba Music of Cuba*.

CDI, Track 11: Afro-Cuban Ritual: "Yemayá olordo"

Music and Lyrics: Traditional
Instrumentation: *batá* drums
Notes: Yemayá is the Orisha of rivers and the sea. She is also the mother of all living things, and is thus the goddess of fertility and the protector of children. Always appearing in white and blue, she is associated with the Virgin of Regla. In this recording by Los Muñequitos de Matanzas, the singer chants incantations to Yemayá in the Yoruba language, to which the choir responds in turn. Meanwhile, the *batá* drums engage in a similar dialogue, exchanging complex cyclic patterns .

OTHER AFRO-CUBAN RHYTHMS During the colonial period, slaves and free Blacks were often prohibited from participating in regular celebrations such as carnival or *Día de Reyes* (Epiphany), so they created their own associations called *cabildos*, religious brotherhoods that served important social and economic functions. (Similar organizations existed throughout Latin America, sometimes called *hermandades* or *cofradías* in Spanish and *irmandades* or *cofrarias* in Portuguese.) The *cabildos* performed their own celebrations and street parades named *comparsas*, elaborate affairs with colorful costumes that usually represented the *orishas*. Exotic food and drink were always part of the celebrations, including generous doses of rum and beer, and of course continuous music and dancing. From these *comparsas* emerged a variety of Afro-Cuban music genres, including prominently the *conga* and the *rumba*, which, though they are derived from Santería rhythms, are secular in nature. After independence, these genres continued to flourish, and by the mid-twentieth century, the *comparsas* were often used for political purposes, to endorse or defeat a given candidate. Like the *samba* schools of Brazil, contemporary *comparsas* are organized by city and even by neighborhood, each steeped in traditions that dictate the music, the dancing and the costumes, particularly during the carnival season.

The *conga* (literally, a dance from the Congo) is the principal dance and musical form associated with carnival, and after which the conga drum is named. Starting in the 1940s, Desi Arnaz and others popularized the dance in the United States, where it was called the *conga line*. Thereafter it gained worldwide appeal, probably due to the simplicity of the steps (1-and-2-and-3, kick! 1-and-2-and-3, kick!) and the ease with which large numbers of people can spontaneously break into dance. Other important carnival dances include the *cocoyé* and the *mozambique*.

Recommended Listening: "Medley of Carnival Congas" from the CD *Afro-Cuba: A Musical Anthology*.

The *rumba* has its roots in Bantu fertility rites. Traditionally performed with drums and *claves*, it emerged among the sugar plantations on the western side of Cuba and among the dock workers of Matanzas. In the 1930s, various *rumba* bands began popularizing the dance across the island, often in nightclubs and cabarets. Soon thereafter, the *rumba* was introduced to the United States and became popular worldwide. In its new international incarnation, it became infused with jazz and popular elements and eventually became an important ballroom dance. Variations of the *rumba* include the *yambú*, a slow dance for couples; the *columbia*, a dynamic dance for men designed to show off manly attributes; and the *guaguancó*, an intensely suggestive dance which involves male pelvic thrusts called *vacunao* ("vaccination," symbolizing sexual penetration), while the female dancer performs the *botao* ("rejection"), defending her honor by using her skirt to prevent him from getting too close. During the seventeeth and eighteenth centuries, other important Afro-Cuban dances emerged including the *gatatumba*, the *cumbé* (or *paracumbé*), the *cariaco*, the *masucamba*, the *mulata*, the *sopimpa*, and the *zarambeque*, though many of these dances have since vanished. Since the 1950s, the most famous proponents of Afro-Cuban rituals have been Los Muñequitos de Matanzas.

Recommended Listening: "Parece mentira" by Los Muñequitos de Matanzas, from the CD *Rumba caliente*.

African characteristics have remained important in modern popular songs, which still make references to the *orishas* and make use of complex rhythms. Santería itself has become an important religion that transcends the shores of the island. Like vodou in Haiti and *candomblé* in Brazil, it remains both a serious religious experience and a way for clever entrepreneurs to infuse the music and culture with exoticism. Afro-Cuban music, already powerful on its own merits, is often "complemented" by a certain dangerous exoticism in glossy production designed to appeal to tourists, excited by what they perceive as primal drums and the sight of chicken blood. Yet in the villages of the Cuban interior, musicians continue to perform the rhythms that their ancestors played in Cuba and before that in Africa itself.

The Spanish Roots of Cuban Music

Throughout much of the colonial period, music was divided according to social, economic, and racial lines. While the Black and Mulatto slaves (and, later, working classes) developed their African-based rhythms, the White elite favored the songs and dances of their European heritage. The style that comes closest to a pure Hispanic expression is that of the *guajiros*, rural farmers from the eastern part of the island whose Spanish ancestry dates back to the early days of the colony. *Guajiras* are wistful and melancholy ballads that evoke the Spanish homeland. They make extensive use of Spanish poetic forms such as the *punto* and the *décima*, as well as the competitive *controversia*, in which two singers improvise lyrics in a contest of verbal skill. The instrumental accompaniment usually consists of guitars and other Spanish colonial string instruments, with occasional percussion instruments.

In colonial cities, poor Whites and Mulattos also developed their own popular songs called *guarachas*, associated with bars, brothels, and places of ill repute. *Guarachas* were loosely based on the refined Spanish *tonadilla*, but their style was coarse and unsophisticated. *Guarachas* are in two parts, a fast section in triple meter and a slower section in duple meter. Played with guitar and *tres* accompaniment, their suggestive lyrics are humorous observations of everyday life or satirical critiques of local officials. *Guarachas* also engendered a dance that was equally suggestive, to the point of being scandalous. In the nineteenth century the *guaracha* was exported to Puerto Rico where it continued to evolve. In the twentieth century, the Cuban *guaracha* was absorbed by many of the rhythmically intense popular styles that emerged on the island and in New York. Many of the subsequent *son* and *salsa* singers—most prominently Celia Cruz—came to be known as *guaracheras*.

> **Recommended Listening:** "Lagrimas Negras" by Los Guaracheros de Oriente, from the CD *Cuba Romantica: Nostalgia Guajira*.

Cuban Dance Music

In rural areas, the Spanish-derived *zapateado* was widespread, while in the cities, the urban gentility engaged in *bailes de salon* (ballroom dances) such as

FIG. 4.4:   Habanera Rhythm Pattern: $\frac{2}{4}$

minuets, waltzes, quadrilles, and *rigodones* that were popular in Europe in the eighteenth and nineteenth centuries. Particularly popular in the salons of the Cuban upper classes was the *contradanza*, related to the French *contredanse* and any number of English figure dances. Unlike these, which were danced by the group as a whole, the *contradanza* was danced by couples, and led by a caller called the *bastonero*. It consisted of four set figures: the slow *paseo* and *cadena*, followed by the fast *sostenido* and *cedazo*.

It was not long before Cubans were developing their own dances, including the famous *habanera* (literally, a dance from Havana), with its African syncopations and swaying rhythms (see Fig. 4.4). One *habanera* known as "El areglito," written by the Spanish composer Sebastian Yradier in the 1840s, was picked up by Georges Bizet who inserted it into his opera *Carmen*. It quickly became the most famous *habanera* in the world. Since then, various other European composers have written their own versions of the suggestive dance.

Recommended Listening: "La habanera" by Ernesto Lecuona, from the CD *Lecuona Plays Lecuona: Ultimate Collection*.

Despite its African rhythmic influence, the *habanera*, along with other dances such as the *garande* and the *guiriguay*, mostly reflected the European proclivities of the Spanish gentility, in great contrast to the lively rhythms emanating from the drums in the slave quarters. Yet this division was not destined to last much longer. By the middle of the nineteenth century, European dances were slowly becoming "Africanized," infused with the syncopation that characterizes rhythms such as the *clave* and the *cinquillo*, and as such came to be adopted by the urban working classes, performed in the dancehalls that dotted the slums of Havana, Matanzas, and Santiago. The White gentility vehemently resisted these developments, objecting to the large numbers of Afro-Cuban musicians and dancers, and especially to what they perceived as inflammatory and subversive rhythms, which lent the new dances a pronounced sensuality. But like most attempts to control the direction of popular trends, their efforts proved futile in the end. For the next century, Afro-Cuban cultural elements continued to displace the power structures of the White elite, though not without struggles and protestations.

Examples of these new dances included the *cariaco*, the *caringa*, the *chanchamele*, and the *apobanga*. Some were short-lived, while others, such as the *upa* and *merengue*, made their way to neighboring islands and strongly influenced the Dominican Republic. In Cuba, the most lasting result of this stylistic evolution was a new hybrid genre called the *danzón*. Created by bandleader Miguel Failde in Matanzas in the 1870s, it combined African rhythms with European-style dancing. *Danzón* was played by a European-style string-and-wind orchestra, with flute and violin improvisations, that also included a piano, bass, and percussion instruments such as the timbales and the *güiro*. While the tried-and-true European *contradanza* remained ensconced in high society, the more exotic *danzón* quickly became popular throughout the island, especially among the Black and Mulatto populations. It also became associated with the wars of independence at the end of the century, and thus became the first important nationalistic style in Cuba. It continued to gain popularity after 1900, as did dance offshoots such as the *danzonete*, the *charanga*, and the *chachachá*. Important twentieth-century performers of these styles include the Orquesta Original de Manzanillo and the Orquesta Aragon.

> **Recommended Listening:** "La Patti Negra" by Orquesta de Pablo Valenzuela, from the CD *Cuban Danzón: Before There Was* Jazz.

> **Recommended Listening:** "Negra Bombón" by Arcaño y sus Maravillas, from the CD *Melao*.

> **Recommended Listening:** "El Bodeguero" by Orquesta Aragon, from the CD *Cuban Originals: Orquesta Aragon*.

SON MONTUNO The *son montuno*, another syncopated dance style popularized by nightclub bands, is the most important genre in Cuban music. The *son* existed in Spain before the Conquest, and it was transmitted to many parts of Latin America, but especially to Cuba and Mexico. (The Mexican *son* is explored in Chapter 3). The Cuban *son montuno* first emerged during the period of independence in the mountainous regions of the Sierra Maestra in the Oriente (eastern) province. It had a smaller orchestration than the *danzón* and other popular music of the time: Guitars replaced the wind and string sections, and a strong emphasis was put on percussion: *clave*, maracas, *güiro*, and bongos. Occasionally, a trumpet and double bass were added to the ensemble. A typical *son* has a melodic opening section called *largo*, followed by a rhythmic *montuno*, in which the soloist will improvise short lines and the chorus repeats a given phrase, in call-and-response fashion.

Amidst the chaos of the first decade of Cuban independence, the *son* outgrew its rural origins and in the 1910s made its way to Havana, where it quickly adopted some of the characteristics of the *guaracha*, and was quickly banned by the authorities as subversive. In an ironic twist, the Black and working class *son* was seen as a threat to the established and elegant *danzón*, though a generation earlier it was the latter that had been attacked for precisely the same reason.[1] Once again, though, the new style quickly became popular in Havana—even in the salons of the elite—and soon engulfed the rest of the island. The first generation of important *son* bands in the 1910s and 1920s included the Sexteto Habanero, the Sexteto Occidente, and Ignacio Piñeiro's Septeto Nacional.

> **Recommended Listening:** "Tres Lindas Cubanas" by the Sexteto Habanero, from the CD *Sextetos y septetos cubanos*.

---

[1]A similar ironic parallel occurred in the United States with the advent of both jazz in the 1920s and rock and roll in the 1950s. Both faced accusations of being "too Black" and therefore subversive. But many members of the generation that had earlier embraced jazz later came to repudiate rock and roll for the same reason. In turn, the rock and roll generation often reacted negatively to the advent of rap and hip hop in the 1980s and 1990s.

Recommended Listening: "Echale salsita" by the Septeto Nacional de Ignacio *Piñeiro*, from the CD *50 Aniversario: Septeto Nacional de Ignacio Piñeiro*.

Recommended Listening: "El Son de la Loma" by the Septeto Nacional de Ignacio *Piñeiro*, from the CD *Son de la loma*.

CDI, Track 12: *Son Montuno:* "Mayeya, No juegues con los santos"

Music and Lyrics: Ignacio Piñeiro (1928)
Instrumentation: guitar, *tres*, bass, trumpet, clave, bongos
Notes: This *son* by the legendary Septeto Nacional invokes the spirits of Santería to ensure a lover's faithfulness. The warning not to toy with the spirits is reinforced by references to the necklaces of the Orishas, the colors yellow (an allusion to the *orisha* Ochún) and blue (Yemayá), and the summoning of Ori Baba in the *montuno* section (which begins at 1:30).

Mayeya, no quiero que me engañes,	*Mayeya, do not deceive me,*
Respeta los collares,	*Respect the necklaces,*
No juegues con los santos.	*Do not toy with the spirits.*
No pretende engañarme con ese cuento,	*Don't pretend to deceive me with that tale,*
Porque todo' en Cubita no conocemos.	*Because we all know each other in Cuba.*
El que no lleva amarillo, se tapa con azul	*He who does not wear yellow, covers himself with blue.*
Montuno	
Entra Ori Baba . . .	*Come, Ori Baba . . .*

By the 1930s and 1940s, the number of *son* bands had grown exponentially. Up until this period, conga drums had been prohibited because of their potential for social and racial unrest. The prohibition ended in the 1930s, and many *soneros* quickly began using congas to deepen the rhythm section of their orchestras, giving the style a percussive boost that would further enhance its popularity. This period also saw the rise of many of the luminaries of Cuban music including La Sonora Matancera, Trio Matamoros, Compay Segundo, Chano Pozo, Beny Moré, the bass player Israel "Cachao" López, and the blind and colorful bandleader Arsenio Rodríguez.

Sones can be classified into many categories. The most prominent is the *son montuno* ("from the hills"). Other types include the *conjunto, changüi* (from Guantánamo), and the *sucu-sucu* (from the island of La Juventud). Hybrid versions of the *son* have also emerged, with hyphenated names that display the fusion of the genres: *son-bolero, son-Afro-Cubano, son-guajira, son-pregón,* and *son-guaracha.* The most famous *son* is undoubtedly "Guantanamera," written in 1928 by Joseito Fernández, with lyrics based on a poem by the Cuban independence fighter José Martí. It tells the story of a young *guajira* from the town of Guantánamo, and to this day has remained a worldwide symbol for Cuban music and culture.

> **Recommended Listening:** "Guantanamera" by Compay Segundo, from the CD *Calle Salud [New Version]*.

After 1950, the *son* began branching out in different directions. One branch continued to expand and evolve into a louder and flashier style. Piano and trumpets were added, and eventually electric keyboards and bass joined the ensemble. Percussion sections were expanded, notably with the addition of timbales, setting the stage for the *salsa* phenomenon that would emerge in the 1970s. Meanwhile, a more traditional branch of *son* quietly continued to emphasize the subtlety of its early *guajiro* and Afro-Cuban roots, and for decades continued to entertain audiences in the neighborhoods of Havana. In the 1990s, some of these early *soneros* made an international splash when they were reintroduced as The Buena Vista Social Club, a makeshift group which included Compay Segundo, Ibrahim Ferrer, Eliades Ochoa, and the *bolero* singer Omara Portuondo. The success of the group revived not only the traditional *son*, but also the *bolero* and *trova* that had been popular at mid-century. Though the recording project—and the accompanying Oscar-winning film—suggest that these musicians were relics of a pre-revolutionary nostalgic era, awaiting "rediscovery," they had in fact been active musicians during most of their lives, and had continued to promote a style that had never been abandoned, let alone forgotten.

> **Recommended Listening:** "Chan-Chan" by The Buena Vista Social Club, from the CD *Buena Vista Social Club*.
>
> **Recommended Viewing:** The documentary film *The Buena Vista Social Club* (1999).

The Cuban Song Tradition: *Trova* and *Bolero*

In addition to the Afro-Cuban drumming genres like the *rumba* and to the syncretic dances such as the *danzón* and the *son*, there is another equally important tradition in Cuba: the popular song. Two distinct styles of popular song have emerged from Cuba in the past century and a half: the *trova* and the *bolero*. Both were shaped by Spanish *zarzuela* and *flamenco* singing, as well as by nineteenth-century popular songs in Spain, Mexico, and other Spanish-speaking countries. The word *trova* has its roots in the medieval itinerant singer/songwriters known as *troubadours* and *trouvères*. The *bolero* was a dance first popularized—perhaps even invented—in the 1780s by the Spanish dancer Sebastian Cerezo, who introduced it at the Spanish court. Yet the Spanish dance, which is in triple meter, is only distantly related to the Cuban song form, which is typically in duple meter (see Fig. 4.5).

FIG. 4.5: *Bolero* **Rhythm Patterns:**

Like so much Cuban music, both the *trova* and *bolero* first emerged in the eastern part of the island, in and around Santiago. *Trovas* and *boleros* were unapologetic in their romanticism, speaking of love (usually unrequited), the sorrow of longing, the anger of jealousy, and the pain of betrayal. But they also spoke of freedom and revolution, particularly at the turn of the nineteenth century, when independence was a common cause. Whether the singer was a lovelorn romantic or an idealistic revolutionary, the guitar was always a faithful companion with whom one shared one's troubles. A syncopated guitar strumming called *ravado* added a particular poignancy to the songs. An important characteristic of both *trova* and *bolero* is the combination—and often juxtaposition—of major and minor keys, a facet found throughout Latin American song styles, for example in the Ecuadorian *pasillo*. The use of both modes nicely corresponds to the emotional ambivalence of the themes of these songs, which speak simultaneously of love and pain, of optimism and pessimism, of hope and despair. Often, the verse will begin in the minor key, turning to a more hopeful major key in the refrain, only to return to the gloom of the minor in the next verse.

One of the first important *trovas* was "La bayamesa"—"the girl from Bayamo," an eastern town steeped in Cuban history. Founded in 1513, it is Cuba's second oldest town and is also the place where the Cuban independence movement first made its stand in 1868. The rebel leader Carlos Manuel de Céspedes, remembering a song he had composed for a girlfriend decades earlier, now wrote new patriotic words for it, and "La bayamesa" quickly became popular among the revolutionary fighters. After independence, it became the national anthem and remains so to this day.

José Pepe Sánchez, born in 1856, became the father of the Cuban *bolero* when he wrote "Tristezas". He was also an important singer and teacher, and was influential on an entire generation of songwriters who popularized the *trova* and *bolero*. The most important of these was certainly the long-lived singer Sindo Garay, who wrote yet another song entitled "La bayamesa", and who introduced innovations in guitar playing and harmony singing. The *trova* and *bolero* traditions thrived in nineteenth-century Havana, popular with the theater-and-café crowd, and eventually in the elite social circles of the capital. The *trovadores* themselves lived vicarious, bohemian lifestyles that fueled their creativity. By the twentieth century, new artists began to emerge, including Maria Teresa Vera, the first of many female Cuban stars, and whose trova "Veinte años" became a classic. Perhaps the most important *trovador* in the twentieth century was Ignacio Villa, nicknamed Bola de Nieve ("Snowball"), whose particular refined vocal ability made him an international star.

Recommended Listening: Trova: "La bayamesa" by the Buena Vista Social Club, from the CD *Buena Vista Social Club*.

Recommended Listening: Trova: "Veinte años" by Maria Teresa Vera, from the CD *Veinte años*.

Recommended Listening: Trova: "Ay, amor!" by Bola de Nieve, from the CD *Ay, amor!*

Recommended Listening: *Bolero*: "Tristezas" by Trio Los Soles, from the CD *Historia del Bolero en el Siglo XX, Vol. 1.*

In the 1920s, the *bolero* was adopted by the *son* orchestras, and a hybrid was born, the *bolero-son*, songs with traditional structure and rhythm, but now with the orchestration of the *son*, and with the added *montuno* chorus. *Soneros* such as Beny Moré quickly adopted the *bolero* and made it their own. The *bolero* continued to adapt to the changing styles, and new hybrids kept appearing, including the *bolero-mambo*, the most popular of which was "Quizás, quizás," by Osvaldo Farrés.

Recommended Listening: *Bolero-son*: "Siboney" by the Sexteto Nacional, from the CD *Music of Cuba: 1909–1951.*

Recommended Listening: *Bolero-mambo*: "Quizás, quizás" by Desi Arnaz and His Orchestra, from the CD *Babalu.*

In the 1940s, the *bolero* was transformed yet again, adopted by a new ensemble that came to typify the style for the next several decades: the guitar trio. This was considered the golden age of the *bolero*, as trios from Cuba, Mexico, and Puerto Rico became extremely popular throughout Latin America. (The *bolero*'s golden age is further explored in Chapter 3). Throughout the 1940s and 1950s, the *trova* and the *bolero*—and a new offshoot, the *filín*—continued to evolve and yield fine compositions, maintaining an important following in Spanish-speaking countries. With the advent of rock and roll, however, Latin music in general lost some of its international luster, and the *trova* and *bolero* fell to the wayside, popular mostly with an older generation that associated the song styles with a deep sense of nostalgia. In Santiago, the establishment of the state-sponsored salon *La Casa de la Trova* in 1968, dedicated to preserving and performing songs in the old style, was soon followed by the emergence of similar establishments all over Cuba. Today, fans flock to these houses of music to take in a style that once appeared to be moribund. By the same token, recent artists have undertaken to revitalizing the old *bolero* tradition, resurrecting the songs that the trios played decades earlier.

Recommended Listening: "Adoro" by Los Tri-O, from the CD *Parece que fue ayer.*

Recommended Listening: "Contigo aprendí" by Lucrecia, from the CD *Mis boleros.*

Cuban Music Leaves the Island

The U.S. presence in Cuba in the first half of the twentieth century greatly stimulated its music, and some of the most famous Cuban musicians got their start at the countless nightclubs on the island, notably the famous Tropicana nightclub that opened in 1939. As had been the case for centuries, foreign styles continued to influence the development of Cuban music, this time from the U.S. popular culture scene, with pop entertainers such as Frank

Sinatra and Nat King Cole, and jazzmen such as Dizzy Gillespie and Stan Kenton. In turn, North Americans took in the mysterious exoticism of the Latin rhythms, which conveyed a hot, sultry, even dangerous atmosphere. It wasn't long before elegant and sophisticated Cubans with ruffled shirts and long evening gowns became the rage in the streets of New York, both on Broadway and in predominantly Hispanic East Harlem. This was the beginning of the so-called "Latin Craze," a movement in the United States and Europe that revered the music of Latin America, particularly Cuba, but also other Latin American styles and artists, notably the Brazilian Carmen Miranda and the Peruvian Yma Súmac. This rage for all things Latin would continue for two decades, finally abetting with the advent of rock and roll in the late 1950s.

The first Cuban musician to make it big in the United States was Don Azpiazú and His Orchestra, who in 1930 arrived in New York with the singer Antonio Machín and the song "El manisero" ("The Peanut Vendor"). The song became one of the biggest hits of the era, and brought about a craze for Cuban culture and music. Many artists quickly followed suit, including Xavier Cugat, Miguelito "Mr. Babalú" Valdés, and Machito and his Afro-Cubans. The most famous of these early émigrés was Desi Arnaz, who popularized the conga in the United States, and who would later have a second career as the husband and co-star of television's Lucille Ball. In later years, this generation of Cuban musicians working in the United States came to be known, mostly inaccurately, as "the Mambo Kings." By the 1940s, many dancehalls and nightclubs in New York had sprung up that were dedicated exclusively to Latin— and especially Cuban—music. These included the Copacabana and the Palladium, both of which would rival the Tropicana in Havana for years to come. The bands that played at these nightclubs popularized hundreds of Cuban songs and dances that were often categorized under the rubric *rumba* (or even the misspelled *rhumba*) though in fact these pieces had little to do with the Afro-Cuban dance of that name, and were more akin to the *son* or *danzón*.

Recommended Listening: "El manisero" by Don Azpiazú, from the CD *Don Azpiazú & His Havana Casino Orchestra*.

Recommended Viewing: For a glimpse of the New York Latin Music scene in the 1950s, see the film *The Mambo Kings* (1992).

By the late 1940s, another genre began supplanting the pseudo-*rumba* craze. This was the famous *mambo*, which combined *rumba* rhythms with a jazzy Big Band sound. Never one of the traditional dances of Cuba, the *mambo*'s exact origins remain unclear. It seems to have emerged in Havana in the 1930s, and several musicians lay claim to its invention. In any event, the undisputed king of the *mambo* was Pérez Prado, who infused Cuban rhythms with a wildly original style. His sparse but dramatic orchestral arrangements which emphasized brass instruments, his complicated steps, designed to maximize the drama, and his famous "huh!" shout at important structural points made the *mambo* style unmistakably his own. Prado left Cuba for Mexico City in 1949, where he became instantly successful as a band-leader, and from where his songs became known throughout the world. Together the new *rumba* and the *mambo* fueled the worldwide frenzy for Latin music in the 1940s and 1950s. In Britain, the ballroom dance studio of Pierre and Doris Lavelle were the first to set formal choreography to these dances, and as a result they would become staples of ballroom dancing for decades to come.

Recommended Listening: "¡Qué rico el mambo!" by Pérez Prado, from the CD *The Original Mambo King*.

Inevitably, the new exotic sounds were bound to fuse with the other popular music that had dominated the North American music scene during that same period: jazz. Because of the syncopated rhythms that found their origins in Africa, Cuban music was a natural fit with jazz. Afro-Cuban jazz quickly became popular in both countries, and increasingly Cuban bands made appearances at such hallowed jazz spots as the Apollo and the Cotton Club. It was not long before U.S. jazz leaders such as Dizzy Gillespie, Stan Kenton, and Charlie Parker sought out Cuban percussionist to play in their bands, including Chano Pozo, Patato Valdés, and Ramon "Mongo" Santamaría.

Recommended Listening: "Mango Mangue" by Charlie Parker and Machito and His Orchestra, from the CD *South of the Border: The Verve Latin-Jazz Sides*.

A key figure in the evolution of Cuban music was Tito Puente, a New Yorker of Puerto Rican origin. Born in Spanish Harlem in 1923, he was a continuous presence in the New York Latin music scene for more than 60 years, bridging the two waves of Latin music popularity. A child prodigy who later studied at Juilliard, he played with—and absorbed the styles of—many of the Cuban musicians that were all the rage in the 1940s, including Machito and Arsenio Rodríguez. Despite his youth and origins, he came to be identified with that generation of Cuban "Mambo Kings." He was a virtuoso percussionist, particularly on the timbales and the vibraphone, and he composed and expertly arranged much of his own music. His concerts always exuded great energy and showmanship. In the 1950s, Puente continued to collaborate with musicians such as Mongo Santamaría, Johnny Pacheco, and Ray Barretto, contributing to every Latin style during that period, including the *danzón*, the *mambo*, the *chachachá*, Latin jazz, Big Band music, and even the *bossa nova*. In 1952, at age 29, he was invited to a Cuban event that celebrated a half century of Cuban music—the only non-Cuban musician so invited. In the 1970s, Puente became a major force in the development of *salsa*. His song "Oye cómo va," released in 1962, did not emerge onto the national consciousness until another Latin musician, the young Carlos Santana, covered it in 1970, whereupon it became a huge rock hit. Puente often joked that he had been disgruntled that Santana's meteoric rise had been based in part on Puente's song, but his annoyance quickly dissipated when Santana's royalty checks began to arrive. His many nicknames included "El Rey de los Timbales" and "El Rey del

Mambo," but he was often known simply as "El Rey"—The King. Puente died in 2000, having released more than 100 albums.

> **Recommended Listening:** "Ran Kan Kan" and "Oye Como Va" from the CD *Oye Como Va: The Dance Collection*, by Tito Puente.

The United States was not the only country where Cuban music became popular. Because of its proximity, Mexico became an important destination for Cuban composers, singers, and bandleaders, notably Tomás Ponce, Beny Moré, and Pérez Prado. In particular, the Yucatan Peninsula and the Gulf Coast shared with Cuba an ethnic and historical background, reflected in their common Caribbean sensibilities. It was often easier for residents of Veracruz and Merida to reach Havana than Mexico City. The *danzón* and the *bolero* became very popular in Mexico, which in turn developed its own style of Romantic song and social dances. (See Chapter 3.) Many Cuban musicians also migrated to Europe in the twentieth century, including Antonio Machín, who went to Spain in the 1930s. Paris became an important center for Cuban—and thereafter all of Latin American—music, particularly at the famed La Coupole nightclub, which to this day offers nightly salsa dancing and music.

Cuban Music Since the Revolution

The 1960s were not kind to Cuban music in general, whether in Havana and Santiago or in New York and Miami. The reasons have less to do with politics than with the youth-oriented explosion of popular culture that emerged during that decade. As virtually everywhere else in the world, the predominance of U.S. and British pop and rock and roll had a very depressing effect on Cuban music. In this context, Latin rhythms came to be seen as old-fashioned icons associated with an older generation not to be trusted. The 1959 revolution also unquestionably altered Cuba's musical evolution, though in the long run, Castro's socialist regime became an important supporter of the music landscape. The most visible consequence was the emigration of several prominent musicians who left Cuba for greener pastures, typically to the United States. The earlier musical exodus of the so-called "Mambo Kings" continued after 1959, but now with far less fanfare. Musicians such as Olga Guillot and La Lupe appealed to new audiences in New York and Miami, while the legendary *son* band La Sonora Matancera, which featured a young singer named Celia Cruz, now found itself permanently performing in the United States. Cruz's success came from her ability to inject the Santería rhythms she had learned in her youth into the *son* and *guaracha* styles performed by the Sonora Matancera.

At home, the immediate effects of the revolution were severe, as tourism ground to a halt and the nightlife momentarily dried up. Within a few years, however, the government adopted a traditional socialist plan, with generous state support of musicians, but also with government censorship and restrictions on content. The regime unfailingly provided economic support for arts and culture, including relatively high salaries and free health care and education. While the bigger stars often went into exile for lucrative contracts,

Tito Puente and Celia Cruz.

ordinary musicians usually found their situation improved by the regime change. Moreover, the government's hostility towards American pop and rock, which it viewed as capitalistic and decadent, resulted in the preservation, more-or-less intact, of some of the styles that had propelled Cuban music prior to the revolution. The old *soneros* who had come to prominence decades earlier still maintained an important presence. Cuba relied on its rich tradition, and the *sones* of yesteryear were glorified as the "authentic" legacy of the island.

But new developments began popping up as well. The *pachanga* and the *pilón* became popular—if short-lived—dance styles in the early 1960s. Perhaps the most popular group during this period was Los Zafiros, who offered a Latin version of the doo-wop groups that had been popular in the United States for over a decade. New bands included Irakere, with Chucho Valdes, Paquito D'Rivera, and Arturo Sandoval, who continued to experiment with jazz and *son* rhythms. The pop-oriented Los Van Van offered an accessible sound and style that, not incidentally, was ideologically in tune with the Castro regime. As in most socialist states, the artistic course has been shaped to a great extent by ideology and politics. Even as some forms of expression were supported and touted as great achievements of Cuban culture, censorship prevented others from emerging and evolving. The bottom line is that for half a century, Cuban music more or less continuously maintained its place among the most vibrant and original musical styles in the world.

NUEVA TROVA　In the late 1950s and early 1960s, a continent-wide folk song phenomenon emerged that became one of the most important musical and ideological movements of the twentieth century. It occurred spontaneously throughout North and South America, embodied particularly in the Chilean *nueva canción* (explored in Chapter 9). In the United States, the movement was epitomized by singers such as Bob Dylan and Joan Baez, who attempted to bring a degree of seriousness to a culture that was too often dominated by light-weight glossy rock and roll. Much of the music consisted of socially committed protest songs that were solidly grounded in left-wing politics and concepts of social justice. This youth-oriented music was often initially rejected as evidence of an insidious counterculture by the governments they criticized.

Revolutionary Cuba was ideologically in tune with this movement. The old *trova* song tradition, though never abandoned, had seen a dramatic decline in popularity since its heyday in the first half of the century. Like their counterparts across the globe, Cuban youth looked down on the romantic song and dance styles of their elders, and instead embraced a new singing style that merged political consciousness with the guitar songs from earlier in the century. This new revitalized version of the *trova* was called, originally enough, *nueva trova*, while the old style came to be known as *vieja trova* or *trova tradicional*. In the years leading up to and following the Revolution, Fidel Castro looked to contemporary revolutionary songs as a serious counter to the fluff that dominated U.S. airwaves. The most famous of these was Carlos Puebla's "Hasta siempre Comandante," which told the melancholy story of Ernesto "Che" Guevara, one of the heroes of the Cuban Revolution. Ironically, many other protest songs were originally viewed with suspicion by the Castro regime, though by the late 1960s, *nueva trova* musicians were widely accepted across the island, and throughout the Spanish-speaking world. The movement was officially recognized in 1967 with the Encuentro de la Canción Protesta, a music festival in Havana that brought together dozens of musicians from 18 countries across the hemisphere and that spawned hundreds of similar festivals in subsequent years. The most important of the Cuban *nueva trova* singer-songwriters were Silvio Rodríguez, Noel Nicola, Vicente Feliú, Pablo Milanés, and Sara González.

> **Recommended Listening:** "Yolanda" by Pablo Milanés, from the CD *Cancionero*.

> **Recommended Listening:** "Unicornio" by Silvio Rodríguez, from the CD *Cuba Classics 1: Canciones Urgentes*.

CDI, Track 13: *Nueva Trova*: "Hasta siempre Comandante"

Music and Lyrics: Carlos Puebla (1965)
Instrumentation: guitar, bass, conga drums, maracas, bongos
Notes: After the assassination of Ernesto "Che" Guevara in Bolivia in 1965, his iconic image became a counterculture symbol around the world. This melancholy salute to the revolutionary hero, here performed by the composer Carlos Puebla, remains a powerful

hymn in Cuba and throughout Latin America. The opening guitar figure serves as a transition between verses and chorus. The percussion lends this performance a sultry feeling that reflects the mystery of the man who had become a legend even before his death.

Spoken: La primera canción esta escrita cuando nuestro comandante en jefe leyo la carta de despedida del Che.

Aprendimos a quererte
Desde la histórica altura,
Donde el sol de tu bravura
Le puso un cerco a la muerte.

Chorus
Aquí se queda la clara,
La entrañable transparencia,
De tu querida presencia
Comandante Che Guevara.

Tu mano gloriosa y fuerte
Sobre la historia dispara,
Cuando todo Santa Clara
Se despierta para verte.

Vienes quemando la brisa
Con soles de primavera,
Para plantar la bandera
Con la luz de tu sonrisa.

Tu amor revolucionario
Te conduce a nueva empresa,
Donde esperan la firmeza
De tu brazo libertario.

Seguiremos adelante
Como junto a ti seguimos.
Y con Fidel te decimos:
Hasta siempre Comandante.

Spoken: *The first song was written when our commander-in-chief [Fidel Castro] read Che Guevara's farewell letter.*

We learned to love you,
From the historical heights,
Where the sun of your courage
Put a barrier around death.

Chorus
Here remains the clear,
Heart-warming transparency
Of your beloved presence
Comandante Che Guevara.

Your strong and glorious hand
Takes a shot at history,
When the whole of Santa Clara
Awakens to see you

You come burning the breeze
With suns of spring,
To plant the flag
With the light of your smile

Your revolutionary love
Leads you to new missions,
Where they await the firmness
Of your liberating arm.

We shall go on,
Together we'll follow you.
And with Fidel we say:
Till forever Comandante

Meanwhile, in the United States, Latin music's decline in popularity led to the closing of many prominent nightclubs, most notably the Palladium in 1964. A brief craze, the soul-influenced *boogaloo*, had a surge in the late 1960s, spurred by Ray Barretto's "El Watusi" and Joe Cuba's "Sock It to Me Baby", but it too proved to be short-lived. Cuban music—indeed, Latin music in general—began to fade in the United States, relegated to the hotel ballrooms of the Borscht Belt in the Catskill Mountains, where it still catered to an older, mainly Jewish audience. Record labels were making far more money selling Elvis and the

Beatles to U.S. youth than the remnants of a Latin tradition that appealed mainly to their parents. By 1965, a casual fan surveying the Latin music scene in the United States would undoubtedly have surmised that the glory days of Cuban music were over and that, like the Big Band sound or Dixieland jazz, it was becoming increasingly irrelevant to popular culture, a relic to be remembered with fond nostalgia and little else. Such an observer could not have foreseen the explosion that in the following decades was to thrust Cuban music once again to the forefront of pop culture, eclipsing its previous popularity, not just in Havana and New York but across the entire globe. That explosion, of course, was *salsa*.

SALSA The resurgence of Latin music was not meant to occur on the sunny islands of the Caribbean but rather in the urban streets of New York City. In contrast to the urbane, sophisticated bandleaders who propelled the New York Latin music scene in the 1930s and 1940s, Cuban musicians in the United States after the 1960s identified much more with the *barrios*, the ethnic neighborhoods they shared with Puerto Ricans and Dominicans in East Harlem and Queens. It is from these *barrios* that the salsa movement emerged, the most important Cuban style to develop outside of Cuba. The term itself (which simply means "sauce") conveys the mixture of exotic hot spices that is often identified with Caribbean cultures, and more importantly, with the colorful neighborhoods of New York.

The exciting new sound was developed by U.S.-born or U.S.-based musicians such as Jimmy Sabater and the trombonist Willie Colón, a Puerto Rican from the Bronx who collaborated with vocalist Héctor Lavoe and Panamanian songwriter Rubén Blades to celebrate the experiences of *barrio* life. The epicenter of the *salsa* movement was New York's Fania Records, founded in 1964 by the Dominican flutist Johnny Pacheco. Fania Records was the "Latin Motown" and early on signed and promoted most of the luminaries that went on to define *salsa* for decades, including pianist Eddie Palmieri, *conguero* Mongo Santamaría, drummer Ray Barretto, and later, Tito Puente and Celia Cruz. With the Castro regime tightly controlling musical exports, these musicians could no longer look to the island as a direct source of inspiration, so they began to develop their own version of the Cuban sound.

Salsa shed the romantic expressivity of the *son* in favor of a faster, livelier rhythm. Like the *son*, it has two parts: the main body of the song, followed by the faster *montuno*, where the singer and chorus alternate quickly in call-and-response style. Bass, piano, and brass (usually trumpets and trombones) play important roles, with improvisatory sections that draw directly from Latin jazz. Percussion instruments are invariably at the forefront, particularly the timbales, congas, and bongos. Unlike the traditional *son* groups, salsa bands have often become spectacular outfits with smooth production values, flashy lighting, and dazzling choreography—often by scantily clad backup singers performing fabulous dance moves on stage.

Salsa's roots are decidedly in the Cuban *son* and in the Afro-Cuban drumming tradition, but also in the Puerto-Rican *bomba* and *plena*. Many of the first generation of *salseros* were in fact from Puerto Rico or of Puerto Rican descent, causing some to claim that *salsa* is more a Puerto Rican phenomenon than a Cuban one. But *salsa* is also a pan-Caribbean (and even pan-American) development, influenced by styles and cultures from numerous countries including Panama, the Dominican Republic, Venezuela, Colombia, and even Brazilian *samba*. Combined with the ever-present jazz influence, the result was a rich musical gumbo that in the 1970s infected the Spanish-speaking areas of New York and Miami, as well as Mexico, Central and South America, and the Caribbean (but, significantly, not Cuba). Soon, other countries began infusing features of the hot new style into their own traditions, notably the Colombian *cumbia* and the racing Dominican *merengue*.

> **Recommended Listening:** "Pedro Navaja" and "Siembra" by Ruben Blades, from the CD *Siembra*.

> **Recommended Listening:** "La Murga" by Willie Colón, from the CD *Best of Willie Colón*.

CDI, Track 14: *Salsa*: "Las calaveras"

Music and Lyrics: Elvis Botero (1988)
Instrumentation: trombones, piano, bass, *güiro*, conga drums
Notes: This 1988 hit by the Colombian group The Latin Brothers shows the extent of salsa's expansion throughout Latin America. The accompaniment consists of the continuous *montuno* piano pattern, complemented by the bass and percussion. Over that pattern, the singer (Brigido "Macondo" Chaverra) and the trombone choir (a trademark of Colombian and Venezuelan salsa) trade off melodic statements. The lyrics reflect concerns with race and class that were historically present in Colombia: The poor Black man was beloved by the (presumably) Black townspeople; the White landowner was not. The moral of the story is that in death all are equal, and that any advantage obtained in life is only temporary. This message is reinforced in the call-and-response section (also called *montuno*), which begins at 2:33. The chorus of musicians, in a comical nasal voice meant to depict singing skeletons, repeat the moral of the story, while the soloist expands on the theme.

Se murió el negro Simón,	*Simón the Black man has died,*
El fruterito del pueblo.	*The town fruit seller.*
Como querían a ese negro	*How that Black man was beloved*
En toda la población.	*Throughout the town.*
Y murió el viejo pipón. "Cuál pipón?"	*And the old fat man died. "What fat man?"*
El hacendado del pueblo.	*The town's wealthy landowner.*
Y a los dos los enterraron	*And both were buried*
En el mismo cementerio.	*In the same cemetery.*
Y a los dos los enterraron	*And both were buried*
En el mismo cementerio.	*In the same cemetery.*
Miren que casualidad	*And what a coincidence,*
Si a la fosa van a dar.	*They'll be placed in the same grave.*

Miren que casualidad	*And what a coincidence*
Si a la tumba van a dar.	*They'll be placed in the same tomb.*
Al rico le hicerion carrosa,	*The rich man got a fancy hearse,*
Al negro sencillo ataúd.	*The Black man a simple coffin,*
Que lo adornaban con flores	*Adorned with flowers*
De la Negra Sepherina.	*By the Black woman Sepherina.*
Y una marcha funeral	*And I saw a funeral march*
Veo pasando que camina,	*Passing by,*
Y una marcha funeral	*And I saw a funeral march*
Veo pasando que camina,	*Passing by,*
Y yo me le pegué atras	*And I fell in behind*
Pa' presenciarla en seguida.	*To witness it directly.*
Y el elenco concluyó	*And the gathering came to an end*
Porque la noche llegó.	*At nightfall.*
Y dormían los dos difuntos	*And the two dead men slept,*
El negrito y el pipón.	*The Black man and the fat man.*
Y dormían los dos difuntos	*And the two dead men*
En un eterno sopor.	*Slept together in eternal rest.*
Después de un tiempo pasado,	*After some time passed,*
Pa' terminar mi relato,	*To finish my story,*
Me fuí para el campo santo	*I went to that cemetery*
Y encontré dos calaveras.	*And found two skeletons.*
Ellas no tenían nariz	*They didn't have any noses*
Pero sé que blancas eran.	*But they were both White.*
Ellas no tenían nariz	*They didn't have any noses*
Pero sé que blancas eran.	*But they were both White.*
Y que paso, si al final, camará . . .	*And wouldn't you know it, in the end, comrade. . . .*

Montuno: Las calaveras todas blancas son.	**Montuno:** *All skeletons are White on the inside.*

Soloist:	**Soloist:**
Multicolores por fuera,	*Multicolored on the outside,*
Por dentro un solo color.	*On the inside only one color.*
No importa como te mueras,	*It doesn't matter how you die,*
Si solo es un vasilón.	*It is all just a joke.*
Como el gordo y el negrito,	*Just like the fat man and the Black man,*
El frutero y el pipón.	*The fruit vendor and the landowner.*
No hay diferencia de raza,	*There's no difference*
Ni tampoco religión.	*In race or in religion.*
Es el color de la tuya y la mía,	*It is the color of yours and mine*
Como la del mundo entero.	*And everyone else's in the world.*
Aquello del campo santo,	*That business from the cemetery,*
Un mensaje verdadero.	*A real message.*
Asi que componte garallón!	*So pull yourself together man!*
Aprovecha lo que queda, Mancual	*Take advantage of what's left,*
Y no pierdas la ocasión.	*and don't miss the opportunity.*

Si al final lo que queda de tí,	*For in the end what's left of you,*
De Roberto,	*Of Roberto,*
de Luis o de mí es la calavera.	*Of Luis or myself is the skeleton.*
Fijate porque razón	*Think of why*
Hay tanta calavera	*There are so many skeletons.*
Si te llevan al panteón	*If they take you to the cemetery,*
Y tu sabes lo que queda.	*You know what will remain.*

U.S. mainstream culture had to wait for the meteoric rise—and equally meteoric decline—of disco in the late 1970s before it too was infected by the Latin phenomenon. In the 1980s, much of the U.S.'s first contact with Latin music took place with the sounds emerging from South Florida. Miami's Little Havana neighborhood was home to an older generation of Cuban exiles who for more than two decades had combined a politically charged and sometimes violent anti-Castro rhetoric with a deep nostalgia for pre-revolutionary Cuba. But a newer, more forward-looking generation was beginning to assimilate the rhythms of their Cuban past with U.S. pop culture. In particular, the Miami Sound Machine, founded by Emilio and Gloria Estefan, successfully blended shiny contemporary U.S. pop with the rhythms of *son* and *salsa*, most notably in their 1985 hit "Conga", a reworking of the 1940s carnival dance. Other important artists emerging from South Florida include Willie Chirino, and the recent emigrée Albita.

> **Recommended Listening:** "Conga" by Gloria Estefan and the Miami Sound Machine, from the CD *Gloria Estefan–Greatest Hits*.

Meanwhile, back in Cuba, musicians kept developing their own styles, often based on their rich history, but they were increasingly influenced by events outside the island. Cuban musicians in the 1970s and 1980s, did not use the term *salsa*, but other names such as *songa*, the style espoused by Los Van Van. *Salsa* itself, long banished from its homeland, finally came full circle in the late 1980s when some of the *salseros*, including the Venezuelan Oscar D'León, began performing in Cuba, returning to the island its missing musical legacy. The Cubans readily embraced the new style and without missing a beat developed their own version called *timba*, which quickly rose to popularity first within Cuba, and eventually abroad, with such bands as NG La Banda. The timing for *salsa*'s homecoming was propitious, as the revitalization of Cuba's music scene became an important source of revenue for the hard times that Castro's cash-strapped regime would soon endure.

THE 1990s   The fall of the Soviet Union in 1991 greatly affected Cuba's economy and had a major impact on musical developments. The Castro regime began emphasizing tourism, directed mostly towards Europe and Latin America. Controls and regulations on musicians were significantly relaxed, allowing them to perform outside of Cuba—even in the United States—while still maintaining a base on the island. Many of the up-and-coming *timba* bands began touring and even recording abroad, notably in Spain, providing a lucrative source of foreign capital. The proliferating demand for Cuban music also meant that many musicians who had been around for decades on the island suddenly gained an international following, most notably the now-famous integrants of the Buena Vista Social Club, discussed earlier. Afro-Cuban sounds also began morphing with other styles, including rock, pop, Brazilian sounds, jazz, and rap, and fusion bands were popping up everywhere. Carlos Varela took the *nueva trova* tradition and infused it with a 1990s alternative-rock style. Rap music, first heard by Cuban youth over the airwaves that came across from Miami, began making inroads. Many Cuban Latin rap artists took their African roots seriously and incorporated them into their music. The appropriately named group Orishas combines traditional Afro-Cuban drumming, *son* orchestration, and rap cadences to promote an innovative contemporary style that is distinct and original. Cuban hip-hop and house music began appearing in Havana clubs, just as their Cuban American counterparts were appearing in clubs in New York and Miami.

Recommended Listening: "Represent" by Orishas, from the CD *A lo Cubano*.

By the turn of the millennium, things looked much brighter on the island than they had a decade earlier. The result of the Castro reforms was the continuing survival—indeed, the flourishing—of Cuba and its music into the twenty-first century. Latin music continues to shine brightly both in Cuba and in the United States. The Tropicana still delights tourists in Havana with the sounds of its past and present, while New York and Miami remain important centers for a new generation of Cuban musicians. The forefathers of these *salseros*, those who left the island in the glory days of the 1930s, could probably not have predicted the heights to which their music would rise.

PUERTO RICO

Historical Overview

Puerto Rico, though much smaller than Cuba, has had a history similar to that of its western neighbor. Until the twentieth century, it had been occupied by only one European power—Spain—despite numerous English and Dutch attempts to capture it. In 1508, the Spaniards, led by Juan Ponce de León (later discoverer of Florida) established an important settlement near the present capital of San Juan, including military forts to repel foreign invaders. Significant tobacco, coffee, and sugar plantations were established in coastal areas, though the island never reached the level of wealth that Cuba, Haiti, or Jamaica did, and its importance was more strategic than economic. By the same token, the lack of large agricultural operations meant that slavery was not as pronounced. Having managed, like Cuba, to avoid the nineteenth-century revolutionary movements of the continent, Puerto Rico was absorbed by the United States in 1898 during the Spanish-American War. The island became an official U.S. territory in 1917, and in 1952 became the Commonwealth of Puerto Rico, an autonomous part of the United States. Since 1917, all Puerto Ricans have been

U.S. citizens, and in the 1950s, a large Puerto Rican exodus to the U.S. occurred. Today, most inhabitants of the island are Roman Catholic and speak Spanish. Many Puerto Ricans demand complete independence from the United States, while others support statehood for the island.

Cuba and Puerto Rico share a common identity based on Spanish and African elements. Puerto Rico was never overshadowed by Cuba's musical prominence and managed to develop its own styles, many of which have become influential abroad. These include African-influenced styles like *bomba* and *plena*, and Spanish styles like the *danza, décima, seis*, and *aguinaldo*. Moreover, Puerto Rican musicians have taken Cuban styles such as the *son, bolero*, and *salsa* and made them their own, often matching and even surpassing them in terms of quality and popularity. Some of the best *salsa* musicians, *bolero* trios, and *son* orchestras have emerged from Puerto Rico. The island has also developed some unique instruments, notably the *cuatro*, a small high-pitched guitar, with a body in the shape of a violin or sometimes rounded like a lute. Though earlier versions of the instrument had four or eight strings (*cuatro antiguo*), the modern *cuatro* typically has 10 strings, arranged in five courses of double strings. The *cuatro* is the national instrument of Puerto Rico and has become a symbol of cultural identity.

Spanish Roots: *Jíbaro* Music

Because the African presence was not as pronounced as it was in Cuba and other parts of the Caribbean, Puerto Rican music is strongly influenced by Spanish elements, particularly from the southern region of Andalusia. A rural culture emerged among the *jíbaros*, poor ranchers and farmers from Puerto Rico's coffee plantations, akin to the Cuban *guajiros*. *Jíbaro* music was based on Spanish folk songs, ballads, dances, and literary traditions, but it became increasingly infused with local instruments, rhythms, and attitudes. By the twentieth century, many artists had recorded much of the *jíbaro* heritage, including Ramito, Baltazar Carrero, Marcial Reyes, El Gallito de Manatí, El Jibarito de Lares, Chuito el de Bayamón, Andrés "El Jíbaro" Jiménez, and the group Mapeyé.

DÉCIMA* AND *SEIS An important *jíbaro* literary style is the *décima*, a type of poetry embraced by Puerto Ricans of all classes and ethnic groups. *Décimas* are improvisatory, with spontaneous verses that must follow a particular metric structure, rhyme scheme, and specific rules relating to the number of syllables, vowels, and accented words. Verbal dexterity is a sought-after and much-admired quality. Often, rival *décima* singer/poets compete against each other: they are given the first line and must improvise extemporaneously the rest of the poem. They perform for large crowds at public festivals, private get-togethers and political rallies.

This popular poetry manifested itself musically in a song-and-dance style called *seis* ("six"), supposedly because the original dance consisted of six couples performing a complex contra dance. The social dancing aspect of the *seis*, however, was quickly abandoned, and it remained an important folk-song tradition, performed at parties and celebrations that often lasted late into the night. Singers invent *décima* verses as they go along, accompanied by a small ensemble that plays lively rhythms, typically in $\frac{2}{4}$. The simple melodies are played on the *cuatro*, accompanied rhythmically by guitars and a *güiro*, though in times past other instruments were used including the *bordonúa* bass guitar, as well as higher-pitched guitars such as the *tiple*. The subject matter can be about social or political issues, or it can be humorous observation about members of the audience. *Seises* are particularly popular during the Christmas season, and as a result, many people in modern times have come to associate them with Christmas carols, unfairly discounting their role in year-round celebrations. Over sixty types of *seis* exist, each dictating certain rules as to rhythms, tempo, melody, rhyme scheme, number of lines, number of syllables, and so on. They are named after specific places in Puerto Rico (*seis bayamonés, seis cayeyano, seis de oriente, cante jondo de Vieques*), certain types of instrumental techniques, (*seis bombeao, seis zapateao*) or after a certain composer or performer (*seis de andino, seis de la enramada*). Others merely have fanciful or descriptive names (*seis del juey, seis de culebra*). Some of the most prominent *seises* include the fast and lively *seis chorreao* and the slower, minor mode *seis mapeyé*.

> **Recommended Listening:** "Jíbaro del cuento" by Ramito, from the CD *Ramito: Puerto Rico's Favorite*.

> **Recommended Listening:** "Seis mapeyé" and "Seis chorreao" by Marcial Reyes, from the CD *Puerto Rico in Washington*.

> **Recommended Listening:** "Cante jondo de Vieques" by Edwin Colón Zayas, from the CD *Bien Jíbaro!: Country Music of Puerto Rico*.

AGUINALDO *Aguinaldos* are Puerto Rican Christmas carols, sung throughout the Christmas season, but particularly popular on the Feast of the Epiphany (January 6). They use improvised *décima* texts, usually in six-syllable lines. Accompanied by the usual *cuatro* and guitar ensembles, they are usually religious songs, though secular *seises* have also come to be part of the repertoire. Like the Dominican *arguinaldo*, the Trinidadian *parang*, and the Mexican *posada*, *aguinaldos* are performed by *parrandas*: groups of revelers, musicians, friends, and neighbors who parade from house to house, "begging" for food and drink in exchange for songs. Dancing, drinking, and eating follow, after which the *parranda* moves on to the next house.

> **Recommended Listening:** "Aguinaldo" by Edwin Colón Zayas, from the CD *Bien Jíbaro!: Country Music of Puerto Rico*.

DANZA The songs and dances of the rural *jíbaros* were not always popular in the salons of the urban gentility, which looked to their Spanish counterparts for social entertainment. As elsewhere in the Caribbean, European ballroom dances were popular in Puerto Rican salons. In the 1840s, the *habanera* was introduced. Its sensual rhythm and vitality—as well as its African influences— appealed to Puerto Rican youth disenchanted with the stiff European dances of their forefathers. Soon, Puerto Ricans developed their own style called simply *danza*, which in time became both a dance and song form. The father of *danza* was the pianist Manuel Gregorio Tavárez, who wrote important early examples of the style. His pupil Juan Morel Campos wrote more than three hundred *danzas*. By 1900, the sophisticated form was adopted by Puerto Ricans of all classes throughout the island. *Danza* composers wrote about love, sensuality, and romance, reflected in the fact that many *danzas* have women's names as titles. The most famous *danza* is also Puerto Rico's national anthem: "La borinqueña", a sentimental and romantic dance composed by Felix Astol. (*Borinquén* is the Taíno word for the island of Puerto Rico.)

Danza is played by traditional string or wind orchestras, including prominently the *bombardino*, a low brass instrument similar to a tuba, though it is smaller and higher-pitched. Like most dances, the *danza* is usually in triple meter and consists of clearly defined sections with a complex series of internal repeats. It begins with the *paseo*, an eight-bar promenade in which the men, clad in White ties and tails, lead the women around the dance floor, showing off the charm and beauty of their partners. The women, elegantly dressed in ballroom gowns, hold their fans suggestively, subtly communicating their intentions. After the obligatory bows and curtseys, the dancing begins in three distinct sections, each usually of 16 bars. The steps have evolved over the years, but at their core there remains a sensuality that is underscored by the syncopated rhythms and that has caused the dance on occasion to be banned. Some *danzas* are fast, lively, and festive, others slow, romantic, and elegant. Today, many Puerto Ricans associate the *danza* with elegant days of yore, a romantic reminder of simplicity and love, and the style provokes a deep sense of nostalgia and melancholy.

> **Recommended Listening:** "Laura y Georgina" by Orquesta Euterpe, from the CD *Lamento Borincano–Early Puerto Rican Music: 1916–1939.*

> **Recommended Listening:** "Sara" by Quinteto Borinquén, from the CD *Lamento Borincano–Early Puerto Rican Music: 1916–1939.*

> **Recommended Listening:** "La Borinqueña" by Rafael Alers, from the CD *Danzas, Vol. 5 – La Borinqueña* (ANSONIA).

African Roots

African religions and drumming traditions were less pronounced in Puerto Rico than in Cuba, Jamaica, or Haiti. They were nonetheless crucial to the island's musical development and form an important part of Puerto Rican heritage. Whereas the mountainous interior was mostly populated by White *jíbaros*, most Puerto Rican slaves lived in large plantations in coastal communities such as Loíza, Arroyo, Guayama, Cangrejos, Mayagüez, Cataño, and Ponce.

VEJIGANTES A curious tradition that emerged during the Puerto Rican carnival is that of the *vejigante*, a mythological character that has its origins in medieval Spain and was later influenced by African elements. The tradition revolves around masks that were formerly made from inflated cow bladders (*vejiga* means bladder), though these days they are made from cardboard or papier-mâché. Intended to scare away evil spirits, the masks are colorfully painted and worn with wild costumes adorned with capes and bat wings. *Vejigantes* can be found throughout the island but are particularly popular in Loíza and Ponce, strongholds of Afro-Caribbean culture. Every town has its own *vejigante* characters, including *Caballero* ("Spanish knight"), *El Viejo* ("old man"), *La Loca* ("crazy woman"), and colorful dragons and horned spirits whose task is to ward off evil. Lively *vejigante* revelers parade on the streets, mainly during the carnival season, but also during other celebrations such as the feast of St. James.

BOMBA The most important Afro-Puerto Rican style is *bomba*, derived from Yoruba rhythms of West Africa, which emerged during the colonial period, possibly as early as the seventeenth century. Not allowed to practice their African religions, slaves appended their spiritual beliefs to Christian celebrations, particularly the feast of Santiago Apostol (St. James the Apostle, celebrated on July 25). The result were the *bailes de bombas*, slave get-togethers that celebrated events such as weddings and baptisms but that were only permitted on Sundays. The dances at these celebrations quickly became a means of identity, a source of spiritual strength and occasionally a form of resistance. Though the feast of Santiago is still one of the most important festivals, particularly in the northern town of Loíza, *bailes de bombas* today occur at any important religious celebration or social event. They often evolve into large-scale jam sessions called *bombazos* or *descargas*.

Bomba is primarily a dance tradition, with call-and-response singing, accompanied by drums made from discarded rum barrels called *barriles*. The principal instruments are the low-pitched *buleador* (or *segundo*) and the high-pitched improvising *subidor* (or *primo*). Complex counter-rhythms are provided by one maraca and the *cuas*, two hardwood sticks that are played on the side of the drums, in the fashion of the Martinican *ti-bwa*. Rituals begin after a circle is formed, with a loud call by a female singer called *laina*. The drumming then begins, and the chorus responds to the *laina*'s call. At the heart of *bomba* is the double dialogue between the singer and chorus on one hand, and the dancers and drummers on the other. As in some traditions in French-speaking islands, the dancers dictate the rhythms to the drummers. One of the dancers will challenge the *subidor*, dancing a sequence of steps called *piquetes*. The drummer must answer the challenge by improvising his response—the *repiqueo*—which aims to convey and mimic the dancer's movements. Other challenges, each faster and livelier than the last, keep the level of energy at a fever pitch. Songs typically contain few lyrics, with the soloist improvising short variations on a principal idea—usually commenting on community events—and the chorus responding after each variation.

Bomba encompasses many rhythmic styles, some recalling specific African traditions such as *sicá, yubá, babú, güembé, corvé, belén*, and *cunyá*. Others are named after European styles, such as *holandé* ("from Holland") and *leró* ("the roses"), a French Creole word adopted from nearby Haiti, in which the dancers imitate the figures formed in the French quadrille. *Bombas* also have regional variations, since the island is divided by its mountainous interior: northern *bombas* are traditionally sung by men, southern ones by women.

Recommended Listening: Bomba: "Yuba la Marilé" by Hermanos Ayála, from the CD *Bomba de Loíza*.

CDI, Track 15: *Bomba*: "Camino a Mayagüez"

Music and Lyrics: Traditional
Instrumentation: *buleador* and *subidor* drums, maracas
Notes: Guateque Ballet Folklórico is a dance troupe from Corozal dedicated to the performance and preservation of Puerto Rico's folk music. This traditional *bomba* tells of the musical encounters that occur while traveling to two towns on opposite sides of the island. Similar phrases are repeated and recombined in call-and-response form. The rhythm of the chorus is different than that of the verses, and each plays differently against the background rhythms in the drums. But the real interest lies in the competition between the drummers and the dancers (here of course unseen), who try to outdo each other.

Chorus	Chorus
Anda y ve, anda y ve. Camino de Guayama, camino a Mayagüez.	Go and see, go and see. On the road to Guayama, on the road to Mayagüez.
Ay cuando yo estaba enfermo, nadie me vino a ver. Camino de Guayama, camino a Mayagüez.	Oh, when I was sick, no one came to see me. On the road to Guayama, on the road to Mayagüez.
Ay sonaron los barriles, camino a Mayagüez. Estan sonando bomba, camino a Mayagüez.	The drums were playing, on the road to Mayagüez. They are playing the bomba, on the road to Mayagüez.
Camino de Guayama, que yo no declare.	On the road to Guayama, that I did not reveal.
Camino de Guayama, y con vos a Mayagüez.	On the road to Guayama, and with you to Mayagüez.
Que suena me la bomba, que suena me la bien. Camino de Guayama, camino a Mayagüez.	Play me a bomba, and play it well for me. On the road to Guayama, on the road to Mayagüez.
Camino de Guayama, que yo no declare	On the road to Guayama, that I did not reveal.
Están sonando bomba, y que suena me la bien	They are playing the bomba, and play it well for me.

Camino de Guayama, camino a Mayagüez.	*On the road to Guayama, on the road to Mayagüez.*
Me dame esa maraca, y que suena me la bien	*Give me that maraca, and play it well for me.*
Camino a Mayagüez, camino a Mayagüez.	*On the road to Guayama, on the road to Mayagüez.*
Y suena me esa bomba, y que suena me la bien.	*An play me that bomba, and play it well for me.*

PLENA In the second half of the nineteenth century, many *jíbaros* from the mountains and former slaves from the plantations migrated to urban coastal areas in search of a better life. It was in cities such as San Juan and Ponce that White country music met the rhythms of the Black *bomba*, and a new syncretic form emerged called *plena*. From the Spanish *jíbaro* folk tradition, *plena* took its narrative song aspects and the use of melody instruments such as the *cuatro* and the *bombardino*. From the African *bomba* it borrowed the drums and percussion and the call-and-response structure, here called *soneo*. *Plena* was also influenced by immigrants form other Caribbean islands, particularly Jamaica and Barbados. Just as the *seis* and *décima* had been a source of cultural identity for the White *jíbaros*, and *bomba* had been for the Black slaves, *plena* now became identified with the urban working class, which encompassed both races and—increasingly—a mixture of the two. By the turn of the twentieth century, as Puerto Rico became a U.S. possession, the musical elements of *plena* were in place, and a dance tradition soon developed along the sugar-growing southern coast, particularly in the southern city of Ponce.

As in *bomba*, *plena* drums include the lower-pitched *buleador* (here sometimes called *seguidor*), which establishes the main rhythms, and the higher-pitched, improvisatory *subidor* (or *requinto*). *Güiros*, cowbells, *maracas*, and *claves* provide accented rhythms. But *plena* also includes melodic and harmonic instruments, notably the *cuatro* and other guitars, and occasionally horns, *bombardinos*, and even accordions. An important percussion instrument is the *pandero*, a tambourine-like drum without cymbals. The *soneo* call-and-response structure, borrowed from the *bomba*, is also similar to the *montuno* in the Cuban *son*. Some *plena* ensembles reflect the *seis* instrumentation, with only a *cuatro*, guitar, *güiro* and a single *maraca*. *Plenas* are usually in $\frac{2}{4}$ time.

Plena was mostly a social dance for couples that occurred at informal get-togethers or urban nightclubs. Unlike *bomba*, however, dance occupies a lesser role, with no dialogue between drummers and dancers, and with more emphasis on the lyrics and singing. It was also an expression of community, functioning as a device for oral communications, to the point where it was known as *El periódico cantado* ("the singing newspaper"). Singers would travel from town to town, narrating current events and telling tales of the happenings in the next community, in the capital, or abroad, of historical accounts, news of the harvest, weather reports, social and political commentary and satire, and light-hearted, humorous, and even racy gossip. Through the lyrics of the *plena*, one can take stock not only of the events that affected the members of a community, but also their state-of-mind, their dreams and aspirations, their sorrows and regrets.

CDI, Track 16: *Plena*: "Tanta vanidad"

Music and Lyrics: Rafael Hernández
Instrumentation: drums, three *pandero* tambourines, accordion, guitar, *cuatro*
Notes: On its face a love song, "Tanta vanidad" is a commentary on the social and political corruption of Puerto Rico in the 1920s. The call-and-response singing is accompanied by a continuous figure in the accordion and percussion.

Chorus	Chorus
Tanta vanidad, tanta hipocresía. Si tu cuerpo, despues de muerto, Pertenece a la tumba fría.	*Such vanity, such hypocrisy. Since after death, your body Belongs to the cold grave.*
Cuando bajes a la tumba, sin orgullo y sin rencores, Te pondré un ramo de flores donde tu cuerpo reposa. Que descances en la fosa, recuerdo de mis amores.	*When you descend into the grave, without pride or bitterness, I'll put some flowers where your body lies. May you rest in your tomb, reminiscence of my love.*
Si vieran que sufro tanto, al matar tu hipocresía, Tu manida, tu pasilla, tu modo de proceder. Cuenta te, cuenta mujer, que mucho vale la vida.	*If you could see how much I suffer, as your hypocrisy kills Your home, your walk, your way of life. Tell yourself, woman, how much life is worth.*
Y si yo muero primero, vente a mi tumba a rezar, Alli para demostrar que tu amor era sincero. Y si tú mueres primero, iría a tu tumba a rezar.	*And if I should die first, come pray at my grave, To demonstrate that your love was true. And if you should die first, I will pray at your grave.*
Y con esto me depido. Adiós mi línda mujer. Nos volveremos a ver donde no haya hipocrecía. Aunque sea en la tumba fría, yo siempre te he de querer.	*And now I take my leave. Goodbye beautiful woman. We will see each other where there is no hypocrisy. Even if in the cold grave, I will always love you.*

BOMBA AND PLENA IN THE TWENTIETH CENTURY   Most ensembles in Puerto Rico play both *bomba* and *plena* almost interchangeably. The first generation of great *pleneros* included Manuel Jiménez—known simply as "El Canário"— who starting in 1914 composed and recorded more than a thousand songs. In 1925, while living in New York, El Canário was the lead singer for the legendary Trio Borinquén, but he soon left the group and had even greater success composing and performing *plenas* and *bombas*, firmly establishing the styles' popularity in the United States, where they greatly contributed to the U.S. "Latin Craze" of the 1930s and 1940s. Taking their cue from the Cuban *soneros*, artists such as trumpeter César Concepción and trombonist Mon Rivera offered a more stylish and sophisticated Big Band version of *plena*. Another important *plenero* was the percussionist Rafael Cortijo, whose band included the singer Ismael "Maelo" Rivera. Perhaps the most prominent was the legendary Don Rafael Cepeda—"the Patriarch of the Bomba and the Plena"—who composed hundreds of *bombas* and *plenas*, many of which remain at the center of the repertoire.

> **Recommended Listening:** "Cortaron a Elena" by Canário y su Grupo, from the CD *Voces del milenio, Un recuerdo histórico Vol. 2.*
>
> **Recommended Listening:** "Pídele a Eleggua [Bomba Sicá]" and "Bombón de Elena" by the Cepeda Family, from the CD *Dancing the Drum.*
>
> **Recommended Listening:** "Bombón de Elena" by Cortijo y su Combo con Ismael Rivera, from the CD *Juntos otra vez.*

When Latin music's popularity declined in the United States in the 1960s, the Puerto Rican styles were no exception. Soon thereafter, however, *bomba* and *plena* began contributing to the complex Cuban, Dominican, and Jamaican sounds emerging from the New York *barrios* that ultimately resulted in the *salsa* phenomenon. *Salsa* owes a lot to its Puerto Rican roots, and many of the early luminaries were Puerto Rican or of Puerto Rican descent, including Héctor Lavoe, Bobby Valentin, Tito Puente, Willie Colón, and Eddie Palmieri. Later, artists such as Eddie Santiago, Gilberto Santa Rosa, and the group El Gran Combo solidified Puerto Rico's *salsa* credentials. But *salsa*'s meteoric rise, ironically, had the effect of obscuring the styles that helped create it. In the 1960s and 1970s, *bomba* and *plena* began to change, becoming more "salsified," adopting a shiny modern personality and glossy production values, in the process shedding their roots as the music of common folk of Puerto Rico. Still based on traditional drum rhythms, *bomba* now added more (usually Cuban) percussion as well as bass, guitar, and brass. Ensembles performed in theaters or nightclubs, concentrating more on the music than on the crucial dialogue between dancers and drummers that were at the root of the style.

The styles received a strong boost when the New York-born *salsa* trombonist Willie Colón made a series of important recordings in the 1970s. Colón's music reintroduced *bomba y plena* to a younger generation of Puerto Ricans who had been enamored with *salsa* and who regarded their own folk music as an antiquated relic of the past. By the 1990s, their increasing popularity once again provided a sense of national pride and identity to modern

Puerto Ricans. Today, they are enjoying a resurgence, in both their modern *salsa*-shaped version and their classic folk-based iterations. Groups such as Plena Libre, Plenealo, and the New York-based Los Pleneros de la 21 are at the forefront of the movement. Other important artists include the Ayála Brothers, who have popularized the northern *bomba* from Loíza, and the group Paracumbé, which specializes on the *bomba* from southern Puerto Rico.

> **Recommended Listening:** *Plena:* "Pena de amor" by Willie Colón and Mon Rivera, from the CD *There Goes the Neighborhood*.

> **Recommended Listening:** *Plena:* "Plena de San Anton" by Los Pleneros de la 21 from the CD *Somos Boricuas: Bomba y plena en Nueva York*.

Puerto Rican Popular Music

Puerto Rico has also developed a pop music tradition that has produced a number of music stars at home and in the United States. Most prominent were the boy bands that were wildly successful in the 1980s, including Los Chicos and especially Menudo, which became a worldwide sensation and paved the way for the U.S. boy-band phenomenon in the 1990s. Some members of these bands went on to have successful solo careers, notably Chayanne, formerly of Los Chicos, and Menudo's Ricky Martin, who had worldwide hits with "María, Livin' La Vida Loca", and "The Cup of Life", which was the official song for the 1998 soccer World Cup.

The protest songs that emerged throughout Latin America in the 1960s, such as the Cuban *nueva trova* and the Chilean *nueva canción*, also appeared in Puerto Rico, with groups like Haciendo Punto en Otro Son, Teatro de Guerrilla, Conjunto Trapiche, and La Rueda Roja, and artists such as Roy Brown, Andrés "El Jíbaro" Jiménez, and Antonio Cabán Vale, popularly known as "El Topo." They wrote socio-political protest songs that, short of being revolutionary, had a strong leftist bent that addressed problems in Puerto Rican culture such as social injustice, minority rights, poverty, unemployment, and political repression. Some were linked to the movement for Puerto Rican independence and, more recently, to the U.S. Navy's use of the island of Vieques as a firing range, inflicting environmental damage, cancer-causing agents, and occasional civilian casualties. As everywhere, these artists were concentrated in the universities and relied on literary traditions and the works of distinguished poets and writers such as Juan Antonio Corretejer and José Luis González. Often, these folk songs were performed by a solitary singer with his or her guitar, or adopted the traditional Puerto Rican instrumentation—*cuatro*, guitar, *güiro*, and *maraca*. Others shed their folksy *trova* feel and adopted *salsa*, rock, or rap to deliver their message.

> **Recommended Listening:** "Son de Vieques" by Andrés Jiménez, from the CD *Son de Vieques*.

REGGAETÓN With hip-hop and rap styles gaining popularity across the world in the 1990s, it was almost inevitable that Latin styles would emerge that combined urban beats with Afro-Caribbean rhythms. One such style was *reggaetón* (or *reguetón*), which began in the 1970s when Jamaican immigrants, hired to work on the Panama Canal, brought reggae and soca with them to Panama. Local deejays such as Nando Boom and El General quickly developed a Spanish-language form of reggae, which soon made its way to other Spanish-speaking countries of the region, mostly through underground channels, for it was still too obscure to break through the surface of the reggae, *salsa*, and pop music that dominated Latin American record charts. By the 1990s, Puerto Rican hip-hop artists (including the New York-born Vico C) combined this Panamanian reggae with rap and techno house music, slowed down its frantic soca pace, and added traditional *bomba y plena* rhythms. The result was *reggaetón*, which became one of the most important Afro-Caribbean styles since the emergence of *salsa* and *reggae* a generation earlier. *Reggaetón* instantly became a phenomenon in Puerto Rico and soon became widely popular throughout Latin America and the Spanish Caribbean. By the turn of the millennium, it had found its way to the United States, first in Latin communities of Miami and New York, and soon thereafter in the commercial mainstream, as well as many European markets. The first *reggaetón* song to become a hit in the United States was "Oye mi canto" by the rapper N.O.R.E. Others quickly followed, including "Gasolina" by Daddy Yankee. Important *reggaetón* artists include Tego Calderón, Don Omar, Héctor y Tito, Zion Lennox, Trébol Clan, Tempo, Mickey Perfecto and Ivy Queen, who has been called the "Celia Cruz of Reggaetón." Latin pop artists such as Enrique Iglesias and Shakira have released *reggaetón* remixes of many of their hits, and other artists such as Wyclef Jean, Cypress Hill, and 50 Cent have also jumped on the *reggaetón* bandwagon.

 Reggaetón's catchy rhythms and rapid Spanish lyrics are underscored by a driving, energetic beat, reminiscent of *bomba*'s *subidor*, but produced by an electronic drum machine. Like hip-hop, it is primarily a youth-oriented style that reflects the angst of the Black urban underclass. It speaks of the difficulties of street life, of urban crime and gangs, of racism and the police, and of unsentimental tales of love, cheating, and sex. Like some rap music, it can be brutally misogynistic and violently anti-authoritarian, and as such has met with some of the same parental, societal, and political resistance that rap has experienced in the United States. In the new millennium, *reggaetón* is the music of choice at Latin American parties and night clubs, where it is danced to a grinding, sexually suggestive dance style called *perreo*—"doggie-style."

 Recommended Listening: "Gasolina" by Daddy Yankee, from the CD *Barrio Fino*.

 Recommended Listening: "Salte del medio" by Tego Calderón, from the CD *El Abayarde*.

 Recommended Listening: "Como mujer" by Ivy Queen, from the CD *En mi imperio*.

THE DOMINICAN REPUBLIC

The Dominican Republic shares the island of *La Española* (or Hispaniola) with Haiti. Columbus landed on the island on his second voyage and there established the settlement of Santo Domingo. Like Puerto Rico, it began as an important colony, and then languished for much of the colonial period as the Spaniards concentrated on wealthier lands. As a result, they were not as zealous in protecting it from the French settlers that began arriving in the 1600s. After a few minor conflicts, the Spanish ceded the western third of the island to France in 1697. In the eighteenth century, the French Saint Domingue became one of the wealthiest colonies, while the Spanish Santo Domingo lay mostly fallow and underdeveloped, and—significantly—received just a fraction of the slave population that lived on the western side. Santo Domingo achieved independence in 1821, but soon thereafter Haiti invaded and unified the entire island under one government. The arrangement proved uncomfortable to many Dominicans, particularly the White elite who objected to being ruled by a predominantly Black country. In 1844, the Dominicans revolted, and the Dominican Republic was founded. The United States twice occupied the country during the twentieth century. Most Dominicans today are Catholic and Spanish-speaking, and have inherited racial and cultural traits from Spain, Africa, and, to a lesser extent, the Taíno Natives. Notwithstanding the fact that the Dominican population is 80 percent Mulatto, 15 percent Black, and 5 percent White, many Dominicans have traditionally viewed the country as a "White society," in contrast to the Haitian "Black society" on the other side of the island. In spite of this predisposition, African heritage remains very pronounced in Dominican culture and is evidenced in its folklore, myths, popular arts, cuisine, and, of course, its music, particularly in its most famous style: *merengue*.

The Dominican Republic has developed a few instruments of its own, including the *guayo* (or *guayano*), a scraper originally used to grate the cassava plant, and the *güira*, a serrated metal cylinder that is scraped by a metal fork, related to the Cuban *güiro*, though the latter is usually made from a gourd. The *tambora* is the most prominent drum, used to produce *merengue*'s famous galloping rhythm. It is a short and squat wooden drum, traditionally made from hollowed-out tree trunks, with two goat-skin heads, one side played with a hardwood stick, the other with a bare palm. The *maraca ocoeña* (from the Ocoa region in the south) is a wooden cylinder shaker, with seeds that hit against nails that have been tacked into the wood. The *gayumba* has a string attached to two sticks affixed to a hole in the ground, not unlike the Brazilian *berimbau*. The *marimbula* (or rumba box) features large plucked metal pitched tongues, similar in concept to the African *mbira* thumb piano. Another important instrument is the accordion, introduced in the nineteenth century by German tobacco traders.

Afro-Dominican Styles

African-derived traditions and religions survive in secluded areas in the south and the western border region. As in many other parts of the Caribbean, the *calenda* was very popular, one of the first dances to become popular on slave plantations, and the source of much of the music that followed. An important subsequent tradition was the *salve regina* (or simply *salve*), a nonliturgical singing style with a call-and-response structure and accompanied by complex polyrhythms played on *atable* drums and other percussion. Other celebrations called *velas* or *velaciones* celebrate the feasts of specific saints throughout the country. Call-and-response work songs, known as *cantos de hacha* ("axe songs") or *cantos de siembra* ("sowing songs"), emerged on the plantations and remain popular.

> **Recommended Listening:** "Salve a San Antonio y Oh Libué" by Música Raíz, from the CD *Palos, Salve, Gaga y Congos*.

> **Recommended Listening:** "Pindó mamá pindó" and "Ay Lola Eh" from the CD *Caribbean Island Music: Songs and Dances of Haiti, the Dominican Republic and Jamaica*.

PALOS   Perhaps the most prominent Afro-Dominican style is a drumming tradition called interchangeably *palos* ("trees") or *atables* ("drums"). There are dozens of regional variations, most of which include a large bass drum called *palo mayor* and one or two higher-pitched drums called *alcahuetes*. The drums have a single, cowhide head and are played by hand, accompanied by a *güira* and either regular *maracas* or *maracas ococñas*. Call-and-response singing, as well as dances called *bailes de palos*, are part of the rituals. *Palos* are often performed by *cofradías*, Afro-Dominican religious organizations similar to Cuban *cabildos* and Brazilian *irmandades*. Because Blacks were usually excluded from most levels of society, these colonial brotherhoods offered social services to its members, and served as important centers of Afro-Dominican culture. Modern *cofradías* are usually dedicated to the rites of a specific saint, for example *Nuestra Señora de los Dolores* (Our Lady of Sorrows) or *El Espíritu Santo* (The Holy Spirit), and over the centuries, they have developed distinct drumming traditions dedicated to their saint. Ritual and musical elements differ, though most *cofradías* preserve the standard instrumentation and call-and-response singing structure. Many include elaborate processions, and *salves* are often sung as part of their ceremonies, which also include rituals for the elders, the dead, and the ancestral spirits. Thus the *cofradía* of *El Espíritu Santo* in Villa Mella developed a tradition called *congos*, with burial ceremonies and rituals that commemorate the dead. Conversely, the *cofradía* of *San Juan Bautista* in Baní holds a festival called *sarandunga*, which includes a somber processional singing style called *morano*, and distinct *bailes de palos* called *bomba* and *capitana*, as well as the *jacana*, a courtship dance in which the men pursue the reluctant women.

> **Recommended Listening:** "Calunga" and "Ya lo ve" from the CD *Caribbean Island Music: Songs and Dances of Haiti, The Dominican Republic and Jamaica*.

> **Recommended Listening:** "Leyenda congo" and "Kikondé" by Música Raíz, from the CD *Palos, salve, gaga y congos*.

COCOLOS   Because of its proximity, Haiti has been an important influence, and certain Dominican communities have developed their own vodou and *rará* traditions (discussed in Chapter 5). Additionally, a small but significant number of immigrants came from English-speaking islands in the second half of the nineteenth century, mostly from the Bahamas, British Virgin Islands, and the Turks and Caicos islands. Called *cocolos* by the locals, they came to work in the Dominican sugar industry and on the construction of the railroad. They were concentrated in the port cities, particularly around Santo Domingo, La Romana, and San Pedro de Macorís. The *cocolos* provided another layer of syncretic melding, adding their Anglophone traditions to the Spanish, French, and African elements already present. Specifically, they brought a lively and colorful style similar to that of the *tuk* bands of Barbados, themselves reminiscent of the fife-and-drum corps of the British army. *Cocolo* bands, consisting of tin-whistles, kettle drums, bass drum, and triangles, perform in fancy street parades called *guloyas*, which take place during feast days, carnival, and other celebrations. *Guloyas* recreate British dances, with dancers on stilts wearing masks and colorful costumes, though much of the music and dancing is derived from African traditions. One of the most prominent of these *guloyas* is called *el momise*, based on the British Mummer's Plays that take place during the Christmas season, and which recreate biblical and mythological stories such as St. George and the Dragon.

Syncretic Styles

European ballroom dances like the *quadrille* and the *contradansa* were also popular with the White upper classes of the Dominican Republic, inevitably leading to the emergence of regional folk dances, including most prominently the elegant *tumba*, danced in groups like a *quadrille*, with partners rarely touching except by the hand. Others included the *chenche*, the *carabiné*, and the fast *mangulina*, all prevalent in the south; the *balsié* in the east; the *zapateo*, similar to the Cuban dance of the same name; the *chivo florete* in the Samaná peninsula; and the *yuca*, which imitates the harvest of the yuca plant. But the most important Dominican dance is, by far, the *merengue*.

MERENGUE   *Merengue*, the Dominican national dance, has become a phenomenon throughout the world, its popularity on par with that of *salsa* and reggae. It is a dancing and singing style that is closely linked to Dominican identity, reflecting the nation's Spanish and African origins, and reinforced by the fact that it appeared just as the republic was emerging from Spanish and Haitian control. The name *merengue* seems to have no connection with the egg white and sugar confection of the same name (meringue, in English) and is probably a derivation of an African word. Popular myth has it that *merengue* originated at the battle of Talanquera, during the 1844 war against Haiti. According to the story, a Dominican soldier named Tomás Torres, thinking the battle was lost, deserted his post. The battle, however, was won, and afterwards Torres's fellow soldiers ridiculed him in what became the first *merengue*. A more likely origin lies in an Afro-Cuban dance called the *upa*, which was brought to Puerto Rico and the Dominican Republic in the 1840s. The *upa*, evidently similar to the famous *habanera*, had a variation called *merengue*. Whatever its origin, the dance entered Dominican society in the 1840s, and within a decade was appearing as a closing dance at the end of a ball. It was fast and lively,

with separate couples holding each other close, and with simple but suggestive choreography that involved a pronounced movement of the hips. The
dance would become increasingly fast as it neared its conclusion.

Merengue did not become an instant sensation. Newspapers reported
that the dance was confused, disorganized, and inelegant, in contrast to the
more refined set dances like the time-honored *tumba*. The White gentility soon
dismissed it as crass, lewd, and sinful—even criminal and demonic. Their crit-
icisms often reflected a subtle—and sometimes not so subtle—racial bias,
implying that the wild *merengue* was "too Black." Ironically, many later
Dominican critics reversed course and denied any African traits in the
merengue, attributing the style only to a mixture of Spanish and country
rhythms, in contrast to the overtly Black styles such as *palos* and *rará*. This
prejudice still exists today in parts of Dominican society, despite the fact that
merengue has clear African influences: ethnomusicologists have found connections with Yoruba rhythms of West Africa, and even with the Bara tribes of
Madagascar who had a small but important presence in the Caribbean in the
eighteenth century.

In contrast to the negative reaction of the White gentility, *merengue* became increasingly popular with rural farmers and the urban working classes,
attracted by its close physical contact between couples. By the 1860s, *merengue*
had become popular throughout the island, even as the gentility held on to
the dying *tumba*. On the other side of the island, Haiti developed a similar,
guitar-based style called *méringue*, which is slower, softer, and smoother, and
with French Creole lyrics. Dominican commentators, always weary of the influence of Haitian culture, also minimized the relationship between the
Haitian and Dominican styles.

In its early stages, *merengue* was played with the traditional wind and
string ensembles of aristocratic salons. As it moved into working-class neighborhoods and out to the countryside, traditional folk instruments were increasingly visible: a variety of *bandurrías* and guitars including the *tres*, the *tiple*, and
the Dominican *cuatro*, a small guitar similar to the Puerto Rican instrument of
the same name, but with fewer strings. But it is the *tambora* drum and the *güira*,
which have become the typical instruments of the genre. The most prominent
characteristic of *merengue* is the triplet figure that accents every beat in a $\frac{2}{4}$ or
$\frac{4}{4}$ meter, providing a fast driving pulse known as *el caballito*—"the little horse,"
because of its lively galloping rhythm. (See Fig. 4.6).

It is this rhythm that lends the *merengue* its unsettling sense of constant
motion, which in turn suggests apprehension and anxiety. The galloping
rhythm is produced on the double-headed *tambora*, held horizontally on the
knees, in three rapid motions: the stick in the right hand strikes one head, the
bare palm of the left hand strikes the other head, and the stick in the right
hand strikes the frame of the drum, producing a sharp sound.

FIG. 4.6: *Merengue* **Rhythm Pattern:** 4/4

CDI, Track 17: *Merengue*: "Juanita Morey"

Music and Lyrics: Pedro Reynoso
Instrumentation: *güira, tambora, marimbula* thumb-piano.
Notes: In this classic *merengue*, the "caballito" galloping rhythm is more prominent on the *güira*, while the *tambora* provides African-based syncopated rhythms and the *marimbula* plays the bass notes. Each phrase of the song is repeated, a feature typical of many merengues.

Juanita Morel, oye tu merengue.	*Juanita Morel, listen to your merengue.*
Entre las mujeres, que tu eres mi derriengue.	*Among women, you are my downfall.*
Orarorara, yorirorara	*Orarorara, yorirorara*
Entre las mujeres, que tu eres mi derriengue.	*Among women, you are my downfall.*
En mi cacería, alli mate unas palomas.	*When I went hunting, I shot some pigeons.*
Y no te sale nada, pos tay de embromona.	*Nothing works out for you, since you're such a prankster.*
Orarorara, yorirorara	*Orarorara, yorirorara*
Y no te sale nada, pos tay de embromona.	*Nothing works out for you, since you're such a prankster.*

Almost from the start, *merengue* developed as a singing style as well as a dance, with songs that dealt with political, historical, and popular events, and the more sordid aspects of life such as crime and prostitution, reflected in coarse and sometimes vulgar lyrics. The first important composer of *merengues* was the Dominican general Juan Bautista Alfonseca, who in the 1860s popularized the style with several now classic compositions. In the 1870s, a new development altered the merengue: the arrival from Germany and Austria of the accordion. Legend has it that in the town of Santiago de los Caballeros, in the wealthy agricultural region of Cibao, there was a nightclub of dubious repute called *El Perico Ripiao* ("The Ripped Parrot"). It was there that, for the first time, the local *merengue* band replaced the soft-sounding guitars with the accordion, which could be better heard over the percussion. The singers also added the nasal vocal timbre that subsequently became typical of the style. This accordion-based version quickly spread throughout the rural communities of Cibao and thereafter throughout the country. The style came to be known as *merengue Cibaeño* or *merengue típico*, and its instrumentation, consisting of accordion, *güira*, and *tambora*, was called *perico ripiao* and became the standard Dominican ensemble. Around the turn of the century, many classic *merengues típicos* were written by composers such as Juan F. García, Juan Espínola, Julio Alberto Hernández, and the accordionist Francisco "Ñico" Lora.

Recommended Listening: "Sectional Merengue Cibaeño" by Ñico Lora y su Conjunto and "Santiago" from the CD *Merengue: Dominican Music and Dominican Identity*.

Recommended Listening: "Loreta" by Angel Viloria from the CD *Angel Viloria: Merengues Vol. 3*.

CDI, Track 18: *Merengue típico*: "Apágame la vela"

Music and Lyrics: Bienvenido Brens
Instrumentation: accordion, *güira*, *tambora*
Notes: The suggestive lyrics and double entendres of this song are common facets of merengue. The accordion and the nasal quality of the singing identify this style as *perico ripiao*, as opposed to the more traditional merengue heard on the previous track. The energetic drumming and call-and-response singing still reflect Afro-Dominican influences.

Ayer me dijo una bruja que tengo vela prendia,	*Yesterday a witch told me that my candle was lit.*
Una la prendo de noche y otra la prendo de dia.	*I light one at night, and the other during the day.*
Chorus	
Y apágame la vela, Maria (x8)	*Blow out my candle, Maria*
Pa terminarla porfia me voy a enganchar a la guardia.	*To finish it off at last, I'm going to recruit the guards.*
Una coje la pistola y la otra la polaina.	*One will take the gun, the other the trousers.*

By the first decades of the twentieth century, *merengue* still struggled to break into the graces of the elite upper classes. An offshoot style emerged during the first U.S. occupation (1916–1924) called the *pambiche* (derived from the English "Palm Beach"), a slower version that mocked U.S. soldiers who tried to perform it. But it was not until the 1930s that *merengue* finally acquired a degree of national respect when the dictator Rafael Trujillo embraced it as an important part of Dominican heritage. Trujillo, of working-class roots, portrayed himself as a man of the people and rejected the lofty pretenses of the society elite in favor of a more populist outlook. He cleverly recognized *merengue*'s identification with the Dominican people, and specifically embraced the accordion-based *típico* style, which he soon incorporated into his political campaigns. It quickly became associated with Trujillo's policies and even with Trujillo himself, and it was not long before it turned into the national symbol of the republic.

Though it dominated the urban dancehalls, the style retained its improvisatory character, its acoustic rustic sound, and the traditional orchestration of accordion, *güira*, and *tambora*, but now also added a marimba or a double bass. Later, saxophones and trumpets complemented the accordion-based melodies, and foot-pedal bass drum supplemented the rhythms of the *tambora*. *Merengue* had finally become mainstream—though much of it by force: Trujillo required every dance band and radio station in the country to perform it. Prominent *típico* artists included Tatico Henríquez, Dionisio Mejía, El Trio Reynoso, and Luis Kalaff and the Alegres Dominicanos. In recent years, a number of contemporary virtuoso accordionists have kept the *típico* style healthy and popular in its home country, including Francisco Ulloa, El Ciego de Nagua, Rafaelito Román, and El Prodigio.

> **Recommended Listening:** "Pambiche: En la batea" from the CD *Merengue: Dominican Music and Dominican Identity*.

> **Recommended Listening:** "La Salve de Las Antillas" by Luis Kalaff y Alegres Dominicanos, from the CD *Luis Kalaff: Merengue Vol. 3*.

> **Recommended Listening:** "Se acabo la esclavitud" by Dionisio Mejia, from the CD *Guandulito*.

> **Recommended Listening:** "India de los ojos verdes" by Francisco Ulloa, from the CD *Francisco Ulloa: 20 Grandes Éxitos*.

In the 1940s, some *merengue* dance bands shed the accordion and other elements of the *típico*, and—taking their cues from the Cuban *son* orchestras—emphasized the brass section and added percussion such as *conga* drums. This *merengue de orquesta* soon became popular in other Caribbean islands and in the New York Latin music scene, where it took its place alongside Cuban and Puerto Rican styles. Some of the most famous bands included Luis Alberti's Orquesta Presidente Trujillo, Papa Molina y la Super Orquesta San José, and Antonio Morel y su Orquesta. The first merengue hit was Alberti's "Compadre Pedro Juan", written for the daughter of an aristocratic family from Santiago, and as such devoid of suggestive lyrics. A ballroom version also became popular in the 1950s, smoother and with an introductory *paseo* promenade, followed by a relatively slow waltz-like dance, with men and women dancing close together.

> **Recommended Listening:** "Compadre Pedro Juan" by Ñiñi Vásquez, from the CD *Merengue: Dominican Music and Dominican Identity*.

> **Recommended Listening:** "Negrito del Batey" by Papa Molina, from the CD *Merengues de Siempre*.

By the 1960s, as many Dominicans emigrated to the United States, *merengue* became more visible in New York *barrios* where it competed with Cuban *salsa* and Puerto Rican *plena* and *bomba*. The *merengue*, which decades earlier had left its country roots in favor of a more sophisticated ballroom style, now returned to the streets with a new generation of musicians. In the process, it too was transformed, adopting many of the elements of *salsa*, jazz, and rock and roll. Synthesizers, electric guitars and bass were added, and the saxophone had a much more prominent role. The tempo increased, and the strong, galloping rhythms were more pronounced than ever, still played on *tamboras* but complemented by congas and maracas. Merengue also adopted *salsa's montuno*, the rapid call-and-response between soloist and chorus. The 1960s generation of *merengue* artists included Johnny Ventura, Wilfrido Vargas, and Luis Pérez.

> **Recommended Listening:** "Mosaico 1: La Agarradera/Bovine/Cabo E'vela/Mami/Me Llaman Chu" by Johnny Ventura y Su Combo, from the CD *Johnny Ventura: El hombre y su música*.

> **Recommended Listening:** "Abusadora" by Wilfrido Vargas y sus Beduinos, from the CD *Serie platino*.

By the 1980s and 1990s, *merengue* still dominated the Dominican urban landscape, and maintained an important presence in other parts of Latin America and North American cities like New York and Miami. In modern discos and nightclubs, *salsa* bands play *merengue* and *plena* interchangeably, and *merengues* are often danced with *salsa* steps that have little relation to the original choreography. Much of the music has suffered the trappings of commercialization, with empty glossy production values and pop artists with superstar mentalities often ignorant of the music's rich history. Yet some artists still produce fine representatives of the style, including Millie Quezada and Juan Luis Guerra, who has developed a slower, more lyrical and socially-conscious version of *merengue* that incorporates jazz and *bachata*. Like many Latin American styles, *merengue* adopted some of the Black-based urban music emanating from North American inner cities, leading to inevitable hybrids such as *merenhouse*, which adopted electronic techno and house, and *merenrap*, which added rap and hip-hop. Important proponents of these new styles include Raúl "El Presidente" Acosta, who has had a strong impact in the New York Latin scene with his band Oro Sólido. Others include the hardcore rappers Zona 7, and the New York bands Proyecto Uno and Fulanito, which combined hip-hop with *merengue típico*. Meanwhile, Cuban, Venezuelan, and Puerto Rican musicians were also incorporating *merengue* into their own styles, leading to hybrids such as *merengue-bomba*, espoused by the Puerto Rican Elvis Crespo.

> **Recommended Listening:** "Guallando" by Fulanito, from the CD *El hombre más famoso de la tierra*.

> **Recommended Listening:** "Esta cache" by Oro Sólido, from the CD *Oro sólido: Best of the Best*.

> **Recommended Listening:** "El Tiburón" by Proyecto Uno, from the CD *Proyecto Uno: Todos éxitos*.

> **Recommended Listening:** "Brinca Pa'Rriba" by Zona 7, from the CD *Brinca Pa'Rriba*.

> **Recommended Listening:** "Suavemente" and "Para darte mi vida" by Elvis Crespo and Millie Quezada, from the CD *Elvis Crespo – Greatest Hits*.

BACHATA   The Dominican Republic has an important—though relatively recent—popular song tradition called *bachata*. The term refers to outdoor rural get-togethers that were held in the countryside in the middle of the twentieth century. Like domestic celebrations everywhere, *bachatas* typically started on Saturday afternoons and would often last through the night. They always included food and drink and could become raucous and unruly. The upper classes looked down on these gatherings as occasions for decadent indulgence, lacking the elegance and refinement of their own society balls. *Bachata* also came to refer to the music that was played at these get-togethers, mostly romantic song forms that were popular throughout the Spanish Caribbean: *trovas* and *boleros* played by guitar trios, Puerto Rican *jíbaro* music, and of course *bachata's* Dominican cousin *merengue*. Soon Dominican musicians began composing and performing songs whenever festivities were at hand, often compensated only by a meal and good company. Their songs were at first known as *boleros campesinos* ("country *boleros*") but soon adopted the name *bachata*.

Bachata became the music of the rural working classes, popular throughout the countryside. At first, they consisted of romantic songs of tragic love, cheating, and bitter heartbreak, accompanied by a guitar, *cuatro* or *tiple*, bass or marimba, *maracas, claves*, bongo drums and the obligatory *güira*, and various wind and string instruments. Though *bachata* had long been part of local celebrations, it was not recorded until the 1960s because the dictator Trujillo, strong proponent of *merengue*, controlled the music industry with a tight fist. Upon his assassination in 1961, the industry was suddenly free to expand, and the decades-old *bachata* finally made it into the studio. The first recording artist was José Manuel Calderón, who that year released several *bolero*-influenced songs with guitar accompaniment. Other artists quickly followed including Rafael Encarnación, Fabio Sanabia, and Luis Segura.

> **Recommended Listening:** "Condena" and "Borracho de amor" by José Manuel Calderón, from the CD *14 éxitos*.

> **Recommended Listening:** "No me celes tanto" by Luis Segura, from the CD *La Bachata: Disco de oro*.

Also in the early 1960s, unemployed farm workers migrated to urban areas where they often lived in substandard living conditions. They brought with them the *bachata*, which quickly began to reflect these changing conditions, moving away from the slow romantic country style to a harder edge typical of the urban *barrio*. The romantic view of life depicted in the *boleros* gave way to one of desperation and social isolation. Lyrics reflected the concerns of the working classes: poverty and injustice, as well as more sordid aspects of life such as alcoholism, violence, crime, and prostitution. *Bachata* also reflected growing machismo and misogyny, with songs that celebrated men's sexual prowess and their disrespect for women. Lyrics consisted of coarse street jargon, humorous but vulgar double entendres, and profane insults to cheating lovers or rival singers. Songs were set in working-class bars or seedy houses of prostitution, the same places many of them were now being performed. The refined *bolero* gave way to a coarse, gritty style with simple harmonies, a faster tempo and a discordant vocal technique. Wind and string instruments were discarded, and guitars and percussion came to dominate (though the *bolero*'s elaborate solo guitar passages were retained). Recordings were done poorly and cheaply, with unpolished production values.

As a result, *bachata* continued to be reviled as lowly, unworthy music by mainstream Dominicans and especially by the elite upper classes. As the style rose in Dominican consciousness, so too did its derision and condemnation. *Bachata* became a derogatory term filled with contempt, perhaps akin to the North American word "redneck." *Bachata* recordings, popular among the working classes, would rarely if ever get radio or television airplay, and were ignored by newspaper critics and social commentators. Ensembles could not compete with the *merengue* bands that monopolized the Dominican recording industry and nightclub scene. But *bachata* was also some of the most vibrant music to come out of the Caribbean, without any artifice, pretense, or mannerisms. The style's marginalization provided it with a great degree of freedom of expression. Dominican slang and Spanish vulgarities were the norm, performed by candid musicians who were expressing their identity, accepted by a like-minded audience and uncensored by a musical establishment and recording industry that would have nothing to do with it. Throughout the 1960s and 1970s, many artists wrote and performed lively *bachatas* in this style, including Marino Pérez, Bolivar Peralta, Mélida Rodríguez, and especially Edilio Paredes, one of the most important arrangers and guitar players who shaped the course of *bachata* for more than 30 years.

> **Recommended Listening:** "Ay mami" by Marino Pérez and "Pena por ti" by Luis Segura, from the CD *La bachata: Disco de oro*.

> **Recommended Listening:** "Sufrida" by Mélida Rodríguez from the CD *Mujer bachata*.

By the 1980s, *bachata* began to emerge from its working-class netherworld. Dance rhythms, particularly *merengue*, started to seep in, and it became faster and more danceable. New instruments were added, notably electric guitars, which replaced acoustic ones. The sexual double entendre, which had characterized much *bachata* since its early days, now became an industry in itself, to the point where it received a distinct name: *doble sentido* ("double meaning"). One of the artists responsible for this emergence was Blas Durán, whose hit "Consejo a las mujeres" is widely regarded as the first modern *bachata* song, with a brisk and bouncy feel and a strong *merengue* beat. Recorded with better production values than the average *bachata* song, it was also the first to pierce the artificial ceiling established by the upper classes and the recording industry. Yet in spite—or perhaps because—of this minor success, the style continued to inflame the wrath of the cultural guardians who felt threatened by its advance. Durán, who had had a long career as a *merengue* artist and as a singer of *doble sentido bachata*, was still reviled by the Dominican musical establishment. Other artists who were contributing to the style's evolutions were Ramón Cordero, Eladio Romero Santos, and Julio Ángel.

Recommended Listening: "Consejo a las mujeres" by Blas Durán, from the CD *Blas Durán: 15 éxitos*.

In the 1990s, *bachata*'s success finally exploded, both at home and in the United States. Any lingering resistance faded away and *bachata* at last gained social acceptance, becoming popular with Dominicans of all walks of life. A new generation of musicians emerged who, in contrast to the humble origins of their predecessors, were mostly from the educated middle classes. Their music was not as coarse and ribald, and had a smoother sound that reclaimed some of the elements of the *bolero*. These artists included Luis Dias, Sonia Silvestre, and especially Juan Luis Guerra, whose 1992 album *Bachata rosa* won a Grammy award and was a turning point in the fortunes of the style. Henceforth, *bachata* was mainstream, popular in the New York and Miami dance scenes, as well as in Dominican radio station, television programs, and upscale nightclubs in Santo Domingo.

Recommended Listening: "Como abeja al panal" by Juan Luis Guerra, from the CD *Bachata rosa*.

Inevitably, fusions with other style began appearing. New York *bachateros* adopted *salsa*, commercial pop and techno formulas, relying on synthesizers and drum machines, and in the process turning *bachata* into a dance form, in contrast to its earlier lyrical version. Another hybrid style combined *bachata* with another romantic song form, the Colombian *vallenato*. Meanwhile, a group of *bachateros* arose from the Dominican northwest region of Montecristi, and who followed in the footsteps of the more raunchy *bachatas* of Blas Durán and Eladio Romero Santos, incorporating *merengue* and *doble sentido* into their music. These included Teodoro Reyes, Luis Vargas, Anthony Santos, and Raulín Rodriguez. This style also became increasingly romanticized throughout the 1990s, shedding its rough sound in favor of a smoother ballad sound, and in the process increasing its popularity among upperclass Dominicans. In the new millennium, some of the most important *bachata* artists include the duo Monchy y Alexandra and the R&B influenced group Aventura, who had an international hit with "Obsesión".

Recommended Listening: "Inténtalo tú" by Joe Veras from the CD *Carta de verano*.

Recommended Listening: "Volvió el dolor" by Luis Vargas, from the CD *Luis Vargas: 12 éxitos, Vol. 1*.

Recommended Listening: "Obsesión" by Aventura, from the CD *We Broke the Rules*.

CDI, Track 19: *Bachata*: "Dos locos"

Music and Lyrics: Alejandro Martínez
Instrumentation: electric guitar, bass, keyboards, drum set/drum machine
Notes: *Bachata* stars Monchy (Ramón Rijo) and Alexandra (Alexandra Cabrera de la Cruz) perform this dialogue between two former lovers who still yearn for each other. The twangy guitar figure and the almost hypnotic percussive rhythm underscore the unapologetic romanticism of the lyrics.

El tiempo no ha logrado que te olvide.	*Time has not caused me to forget you.*
No ha borrado las huellas de tu amor.	*It has not erased the traces of your love.*
Todavia siento el sabor de tus besos en mi boca.	*I still feel the taste of your kisses on my lips.*
Todavia siento tus manos acariciandome la piel.	*I still feel your hands caressing my skin.*
Y yo no quiero seguir asi,	*And I don't want to continue like this,*
Estando con ella y pensando en ti.	*Being with her and thinking of you.*
A mi me esta pasando igual:	*The same is happening to me:*
No dejo de pensar en ti.	*I can't stop thinking about you.*
El dia que me levanto contigo en la cabeza,	*When I wake up with you in my mind,*
Lo llamo por tu nombre.	*I call him by your name.*
Y yo no quiero seguir asi,	*And I don't want to continue like this,*
Estando con ella y pensando en ti.	*Being with her and thinking about you.*
Chorus	
Que tontos, que locos somos tu y yo,	*How foolish, how senseless, you and I,*
Estando con otros y amandonos. (x2)	*Being with others and loving each other.*

Many of the styles that emerged in the Spanish-speaking Caribbean were also influential on neighboring English-, French- and Dutch-speaking islands, which also developed important traditions of their own. These traditions are explored in the next chapter.

5

The English-
and French-
Speaking
Caribbean

CHAPTER SUMMARY

The French-Speaking Caribbean

Haiti

- Historical Overview
- Vodou
- *Rará*
- Secular Dances
- *Compas* and *Cadence*

Martinique and Guadeloupe

- Drumming in the French Antilles
- African-Derived Dances
- European-Derived Dances
- Carnival
- *Zouk*
- Contemporary Trends

The Garífuna

- Garífuna Music
- *Punta Rock*

THE ENGLISH-SPEAKING CARIBBEAN

JAMAICA

Musically, the most important and influential English-speaking island in the Caribbean is Jamaica. It is the third largest island in the region, after Cuba (50 miles to the north) and Hispaniola (100 miles to the west). Jamaicans speak both English and a mixture of English, Spanish, French, and African languages called *patois*. The original Arawak inhabitants, now extinct, have left behind some traces of their presence in Jamaican culture, including famous culinary dishes, several words adopted by the English language (e.g., *hammock* and *canoe*) and perhaps most prominently the name of their island *Xaymaca*, which means "land of springs."

A Spanish settlement was established on Jamaica in 1510, and for the next century and a half, the island remained in Spanish hands. Slaves were quickly imported to work the tobacco and sugar plantations, mostly from Fante, Akan, Ashanti, and Yoruba tribes of West Africa. In 1655, the British captured the island, which remained their possession until the twentieth century. The capital was the legendary town of Port Royal, home of pirates and buccaneers, such as the Englishman Henry Morgan. Port Royal inspired the imagination of novelists and filmmakers in the twentieth century, but by most accounts it was not a pleasant place to be, for despite its great economic wealth, it was also a place of cruelty and bloodletting, where drinking, gambling, prostitution, and murder were commonplace. In 1692, the entire "city of sin" was swallowed by the sea as the result of an earthquake or—some say—divine retribution. Thereafter the town of Kingston, across the bay, became the capital. In 1834, slavery was abolished, and to fulfill the demand for labor, Jamaican plantation owners were quick to "hire" indentured servants from Africa, India, China, and, later, the Middle East. One of the last vestiges of the British Empire, Jamaica achieved its independence in 1962. Jamaicans retain a racial, cultural, and musical diversity that reflects their turbulent past. Most of the 2.5 million Jamaicans are Black or Mulatto, with a sizable fraction of Europeans, Chinese, and East Indians. Most subscribe to various Protestant denominations, including prominently the Anglican and Baptist churches. Fewer than 10 percent are Catholic. There are also Jewish, Muslim, and Hindu communities, and of course a sizable portion of the population subscribes to African-derived religions.

Jamaica evolved its music from its rich African and European folk traditions and from its Caribbean neighbors—notably Trinidadian calypso—as well as American soul, jazz, and rock and roll. In turn, the island's music has been very influential on the world scene, particularly in the second half of the twentieth century. Reggae is the style most associated with the island, but Jamaica is also the home of many other popular styles such as *mento*, ska, *dub*, and *ragga*, as well as numerous folk traditions. As everywhere in the African Diaspora, the drum is the predominant instrument, but Jamaica also has the *rumba box*, a lamellophone related to African thumb-pianos such as the *mbira* (Zimbabwe), *kalimba* (Kenya), and *likembe* (Congo). Known on Spanish-speaking islands as the *marimbula*, it consists of a large wooden resonator box with several metal prongs placed over a hole cut into the wood. The player sits on the box, reaches down between his legs and plucks the prongs, which are tuned to specific pitches and have a low, bass sound.

Afro-Jamaican Traditions

The religious syncretism found in Cuban Santería, Brazilian *candomblé*, and Haitian vodou is also present in traditional Jamaican religions such as *obeah*, *kumina*, and *pocomania*, as well as the more recent Rastafarian movement. An important difference, however, is the European side of the syncretic equation, for unlike the Spanish, French, and Portuguese possessions, Jamaica's religious heritage was predominantly Protestant, which greatly affected the religious, cultural, and musical development. In Catholic countries, the veneration of saints lent itself well to the integration of *orishas*, deified ancestral African spirits who provide spiritual help and practical advice. In Protestant countries, by contrast, saints were not a central part of worship, and *orishas* were far less pronounced.

MAROON NATION: *OBEAH* As in other parts of the Caribbean, escaped slaves called Maroons had an important role in Jamaican history. They formed communities in the mountainous interior, where they became farmers and hunters. Their villages served as fighting camps against the government and often staged raids against the White plantations, freeing more slaves in the process. Maroons quickly acquired a reputation for courage, ferocious fighting, and a determined refusal to submit to subjugation, all strongly intertwined with their spirituality and the memory of their African homeland, so that their struggle quickly took on a religious component. They became such a potent force that in 1739 they obtained a peace treaty from the British that granted their freedom, basic human rights, and the land they had traditionally occupied. Since then, their descendants have remained in these more-or-less isolated communities, which continue to be important strongholds for Afro-Jamaican culture, though often under economically depressed conditions. Descendants of Maroons look upon their legendary ancestors with uncommon pride, one of the central aspects of their cultural identity.

Many Maroons speak a dialect called *Kromanti*, derived from the Akan and Ashanti languages. They practice an African-based religion called *obeah*, also known as the "Shango cult" after the Yoruba deity also found in vodou, Santería, and *candomblé*. The spirits and the ancestors are contacted by an "Obeahman," a shaman who serves as intermediary. *Obeah* is often infused with elements of folk medicine to support the struggles of the Maroons and to combat the magical spirits of the White plantation owners and the British government. One of the most famous practitioners of *obeah* was Queen Nanny, a legendary figure in Jamaican history, who is portrayed on today's currency. Queen Nanny, supposedly of African royal blood, was a clever military and spiritual leader who used her faith to strengthen the resistance movement. Her magical powers were such that, according to legend, she taught warriors to stop bullets with their hands.

Obeah (or Maroon Nation) ceremonies include dancing, singing, and complex drumming. They can include light-entertainment styles such as *tambu* ("drum") or *Sa Leone* (after the African country Sierra Leone), or more serious religious styles such as *Kromanti, Ibo*, and *Mandinga*. These ceremonies are traditionally accompanied by two upright drums: a leader ("male") and a follower ("female"). A third drummer plays ostinato patterns on a *kwat*—a bamboo shoot played with two sticks. On the anniversary of the Treaty of 1739, *obeah* ceremonies honor Maroon ancestors (including Queen Nanny herself), who are said to appear to the faithful. *Obeah* is still practiced not only in Jamaica but also in other English-speaking islands such as Barbados, the Bahamas, the Virgin Islands, and Trinidad, where it has come to be associated with Spiritual Baptist rites.

Recommended Listening: "Tambu: Hear When de Dubby Baw" and "Mandinga: Banda Gone a Wood" by Group of Maroons of Moore Town, from the CD *Drums of Defiance: Maroon Music from the Earliest Free Black Communities of Jamaica.*

CDI, Track 20: Afro-Jamaican Ritual: "Anabo Yedeng"

Music and Lyrics: Traditional
Instrumentation: two drums, *kwat* bamboo drum
Notes: This song, performed by members of the Maroon community of Moore Town, is an integral part of Kromanti Play tradition. It tells the story of an escaped slave who invokes the help of his *obeah* spirit to elude his pursuers. The two drummers imitate the speech patterns of the Kromanti language of West Africa, complemented by the ostinato pattern played on the *kwat*.

BONGO NATION: *KUMINA* Another important Afro-Jamaican tradition is *kumina*, developed by the Bongo (or Kongo) Nation. These were Africans who came much later, in the mid-nineteenth century, not as slaves but as indentured servants (though the distinction was in many ways only technical). The Bongo came from the Bantu-speaking people of Central Africa, in modern Angola and Congo. *Kumina* refers both to religious elements and to the music that accompanies them. As in vodou and other African-derived rites, *kumina* ceremonies seek to induce a trance state in the dancers that permits communication with and possession by the spirits. These spirits can be representations of earthly (i.e., secular) ancestors, or they can be specific deities from Central Africa called *Nkisi* (or *Inquices*), equivalent to the West African *orishas*. The supreme deity is called *Nzaambi Mpungu* (King Zaambi), who gives the ancestral spirits their power. The ceremonies often call both good spirits (i.e. *Myal*, the healer) and bad spirits (i.e., *obeah*, the spirit of shadows), for both can provide spiritual guidance and wisdom. Prayers and incantations precede the ceremony, along with rum libations poured for the deities. Male and female dancers perform in a circle accompanied by increasingly intense drumming and call-and-response chanting that summons the ancestral spirits. A pole, similar to vodou's *potomitan*, stands in the center of the circle, connecting the spiritual realm to the earthly one. The enticed spirits descend through the pole into the ground, to the drums and bodies of the dancers. The spirits have arrived when the dancers' movements become more intense and frenzied, occasionally violently so. At this point, the singing and drumming guide the actions of the spirit guests, who will provide messages or warnings to the assembly. *Kumina* incorporates not only African customs and beliefs but Christian ones as well. Like vodou practitioners who recite Catholic prayers before the ritual, *kumina* incorporates Protestant hymns and Bible readings into its music. The belief system became very influential in the development of Rastafarian *nyabinghi* music and of the rhythms of reggae.

Kumina rites can be performed for both religious and entertainment purposes as well as to mark special occasions such as wakes and funerals, weddings, births, national holidays, and other important occasions. The two principal ceremonies are *bailo* and *country*. *Bailo* songs are in Jamaican *patois*, and, like the Maroon *tambu*, reflect a lighter, more informal style, usually for entertainment. *Country* songs, by contrast, are closer to the Congo dialect of the ancestral land, reflecting a more serious, formal, and sacred attitude, and are more apt for possession by the spirits. Goatskin drums are played by two principal drummers who face each other, sitting astride their drums, striking them with bare hands, and altering the pitch with their heels—a technique called *mek bar*. The lower pitched *kbandu* plays a continuous supporting rhythm; the higher pitched *playin kyas* provides complex rhythms and exciting improvisations, guiding the spirits with its tempo and rhythmic patterns. Meanwhile, a third drummer strikes the back of the drum with *katta* sticks, providing an ostinato figure, similar to the *ti-bwa* of the French Caribbean, discussed later in this chapter. *Kumina* music is complemented by makeshift *güiros*, often made from common kitchen graters scraped with a metal comb, as well as shakers made from gourds or metal.

> **Recommended Listening:** "Kumina 'Country' and 'Bailo' Songs" from the CD *Folk Music of Jamaica* (Folkways Records).

REVIVAL ZION AND *POCOMANIA*   Jamaica's Protestant background greatly affected the island's religious evolution, and many Jamaicans could relate to the Biblical Jewish struggle for liberation. Starting in the 1860s, several revivalist groups emerged that fused Old Testament Judeo-Christian beliefs with Black nationalism and even the Hinduism of the East Indian immigrants. Many of these groups are still active, and their services rely heavily on hymn singing, usually accompanied by drums and tambourines. A prominent group is *pocomania*, a Pentecostal movement that also includes possession rituals with frenetic dancing, chanting, and drumming. (*Pocomania* means "little madness," in reference to the dancers' possession by spirits.) Another important ritual is Revival Zion, which leans more towards Judeo-Christian doctrine, for example seeking the guidance of heavenly spirits such as angels rather than earthly ancestral spirits. None of these revival groups has had much impact outside of Jamaica. But in the first half of the twentieth century, another religious movement emerged that would eventually find its way to distant corners of the world, and that would greatly influence the course of Jamaican music: Rastafarianism.

> **Recommended Listening:** "Pukkumina Prayer and Chorus" and "Zion Chorus and 'Groaning'" from the CD *Folk Music of Jamaica* (Folkways Records).

RASTAFARIANISM   Rastafarianism was born in the 1930s as a syncretic mixture of Christianity, African ritual, and Black Messianic Judaism. It had a stronger social consciousness than the nineteenth-century revival religions, as its adherents were intent on achieving social justice, fighting oppression, and developing a Black national identity. Rastafarians look to two key figures in the emergence of their spiritual liberation. The first is the Jamaican political leader Marcus Garvey, who led important Black-power organizations in the United States in the 1920s and who founded the anti-colonial African Orthodox Church. Rastafarians consider Garvey a divine prophet who predicted the second coming of Jesus Christ. The second key figure was the emperor of Ethiopia: born Lij Tafari Makonnen, he claimed to be a direct descendant of King Solomon, and upon his coronation in 1930, Ras Tafari ("Prince Tafari") became emperor Haile Selassie ("Might of the Trinity"). Many Jamaicans saw Selassie as the fulfillment of Garvey's prophecy, the incarnation of God (Jehovah or Jah) on Earth, who would restore an empire where all Blacks could achieve a national identity. Ethiopia came to be seen as the Promised Land, and many Jamaicans sought to emigrate there.

Rastafarianism never coalesced into an organized religion. Rather, it became a collection of spiritual pronouncements and principles. Rastafarians are called *dreads* (because they are "fearful of God"), and their long tresses or dreadlocks reflect a search for purity in a severe and ascetic lifestyle. They draw on *ganja* wisdomweed (marijuana) as a meditative tool in their rituals, though they do not support its recreational use. Rastafarianism remained local and relatively obscure for the first few decades of its existence, but as it emerged into a popular movement in the 1950s, it became the subject of persecution by the British Colonial government. Many Rastafarians emigrated to Britain and the United States, where they were repressed as well, often for their ritual use of *ganja*. The movement finally emerged unto the international consciousness with the popularization of reggae in the late 1960s and has since spread worldwide.

RASTAFARIAN MUSIC   Contrary to popular belief, reggae is not the only—or even the primary—Rastafarian musical style. That privilege belongs to *nyabinghi*, a type of African drumming that emerged in the nineteenth century. According to legend, a Ugandan healing-woman named Muhumusa was possessed by the queen spirit *Nyabinghi* and was inspired to lead an ultimately unsuccessful revolt against the European colonial powers. Thereafter, *Nyabinghi* would always respond when summoned, possessing the faithful (usually women) and inspiring revolts, not only in Africa but in Jamaica as well. Rastafarian ceremonies are called *grounations*, which consist of prayer, dancing, drumming, and a style of chanting that resembles an angry and melancholy wail. *Nyabinghi* drumming draws heavily on *kumina* traditions, with a bass drum, a supporting drum called *funde*, and a principal, improvisatory drum called *akete* that relies on heavy syncopations. As in *kumina*, the divine spirit of Jah is believed to be present in the drums themselves, as well as the dancers.

Nyabinghi provided much of the rhythmic and melodic roots of ska, *rocksteady*, and reggae, discussed later in this chapter. In the late 1960s and 1970s, as reggae dominated Jamaican airwaves and record sales, Oswald "Count Ossie" Williams sought to preserve the original *nyabinghi* drumming and chanting in several early recordings. He and his band The Mystic Revelation of

Rastafari infused *nyabinghi* into their distinctive brand of popular music, with hits such as "Oh Carolina" and "Thirty Pieces of Silver."

> **Recommended Listening:** "Keep Cool Babylon" by Ras Michael and the Sons of Negus, from the CD *Trojan Box Set: Nyahbinghi.*

> **Recommended Listening:** "Rasta Reggae (I'm Going Home)" by Count Ossie, from the CD *Trojan Box Set: Nyahbinghi.*

CDI, Track 21: Nyabinghi: "Got to Move"

Music and Lyrics: Traditional
Instrumentation: *funde* and *akete* drums, rattle
Notes: Unlike many of the African drumming traditions in Latin America, *nyabinghi* is often slow and deliberate to emphasize the suffering conveyed by the wailing singers. In spite of this, the cyclic drumming patterns remain complex. This recording was made in the hills of Trelawney as the U.S. President Ronald Reagan visited Jamaica in 1982. The wailing not only bemoans the spiritual suffering of the Rastafarians but is also a form of political protest, emphasizing social justice and Black solidarity.

JONKONNU   From Jamaican slave culture emerged a colorful masquerade festival called *jonkonnu* (or *junkanoo*). The term may originate from an eighteenth-century African leader named John Canoe or from African religious terms for ancestral spirits. In any event, *jonkonnu* traces its origins to West African harvest and fertility rituals, which it syncretically combined with Christian elements and homegrown folklore. *Jonkonnu* celebrations are held on the days after Christmas, notably on Boxing Day (December 26) and New Years' Day. Revelers parade in the streets wearing elaborate European costumes and gigantic African masks that represent animals, kings and queens, and various historical and mythological figures. The festivities often include makeshift dance, drama, or mime representations, with stock characters like the Devil, Belly-Woman (i.e., pregnant woman), Policeman, Pitchy-Patchy, House-Head, and animals such as Cow-Head and Horse-Head. Revelers and spectators dance to the music provided by fifes, conga drums, and other percussion instruments. Dance moves, including the two-steps-forward-one-step-backwards motion, have been traced to African warrior marches. Similar celebrations can be found in Barbados, Bermuda, Turks and Caicos, Guyana, North Carolina, and among the Garífuna people in Central America. But the most important *jonkonnu* celebrations are now found in The Bahamas, where they are more popular than in Jamaica. Bahamian *jonkonnu* parades are called *"jump up,"* and often include a traditional saw-based style called *ripsaw*. Bahamian exponents of *jonkonnu* include We Funk Junkanoo Group, The Predators, Ronnie Butler, Sweet Emily, and Kirkland Bodie. The international super-hit "Who Let the Dogs Out?" by The Baha Men incorporates a mixture of *jonkonnu* and *mento* rhythms.

> **Recommended Listening:** Jamaica: "Good Mornin, Good Mornin" ("John Canoe" processional) by J. Hamilton Grandison, from the CD *The Long Road to Freedom: An Anthology of Black Music*.

> **Recommended Listening:** Bahamas: "Queen of Junkanoo" from the CD *Queen of Junkanoo*, by Sweet Emily.

For a discussion of other Jamaican folk styles, including *Bruckin's Party* and *Wake Complex*, see www.mymusickit.com.

Jamaican Popular Music

Jamaica's rich folk and Afro-Jamaican music tradition developed over the course of several centuries. But important shifts began to occur in the 1950s as the island became increasingly urbanized. Many Jamaicans migrated to Kingston, Richmond, and other cities where they encountered styles from other Caribbean islands and the United States, particularly rhythm and blues and rock and roll. In the process, they developed an urban sound that was boosted by the emergence of the Jamaican recording industry. A fairly clear evolutionary line can be traced in Jamaican popular music, as the earliest pop songs and Harry Belafonte's calypso were influential on *mento*, which led to ska and continued on through *rocksteady*, reggae, *dub*, and dancehall, ultimately resulting in dozens of stylistic offshoots.

HARRY BELAFONTE By the 1940s, Trinidadian calypso (discussed later in this chapter) had invaded Jamaica, where several artists adopted it as their own. However, the most famous early proponent of Jamaican calypso, and of Jamaican music in general, was not actually born in the Caribbean. Harry Belafonte was born in 1927 in Harlem, New York, to a Jamaican mother and a Martinican father. He returned with his mother to Jamaica for five years in the late 1930s, during which Belafonte picked up a lot of the sounds and rhythms that he would later incorporate into his style. Starting in the 1950s, he had a number of hits that brought this music to the world's attention, with folk-like ballads such as "Jamaica Farewell" and "Island in the Sun," and *mento* and calypso songs such as "Jump in the Line" and the super-hit "Banana Boat Song" (popularly known as "Day-O"), which is based on the Jamaican work-song tradition. Belafonte popularized calypso and Caribbean music in general in both the United States and Britain, but his music was often criticized in Trinidad and Jamaica for its lack of authenticity and its pandering to non-Caribbean audiences, particularly in his use of American English over the more traditional Creole or *patois*. In addition to (and perhaps because of) his musical success, Belafonte became an important actor in American films, one of the first Black actors to break the color barrier in Hollywood, and he was also a prominent civil rights activist.

Recommended Listening: "Banana Boat Song," "Jamaica Farewell," "Island in the Sun," and "Jump in the Line" by Harry Belafonte, from the CD *Harry Belafonte–All Time Greatest Hits, Vol. 1.*

MENTO The early calypso-rooted success of Belafonte inspired other Jamaicans to advance their own homegrown style: *mento*, one of the most influential genres in Jamaica, affecting most of the music that would come later. Early *mento* can be traced as far back as the 1920s, with roots in rural folk traditions such as *quadrills, pocomania,* and *jonkonnu,* as well as Jamaican work songs. *Mento* remained a mostly local phenomenon until the early 1950s, but after the first Jamaican recording studios were established in 1951, it became the first Jamaican style to be extensively recorded. Thereafter it quickly became popular throughout the island, and in the late 1950s it piggybacked onto the calypso craze spurred by Belafonte.

Mento and Trinidadian calypso are closely related (and often confused), because both styles became internationally popular more or less simultaneously and because there was much cross pollination between them. *Mento* songs are often lighthearted and humorous depictions of daily life, animal tales, social issues, and current events. Rarely are they love songs, though they can include humorous bawdy lyrics with not-so-subtle innuendos and double-entendres. Reflecting its rural origins, early *mento* was typically played with acoustic instruments such as guitars and banjos, as well as harmonicas, fiddles, flutes, and whistles and the peculiar sounds of bamboo clarinets and the rumba box. Percussion was usually provided by a single drum, maracas, and shakers. A more cosmopolitan *mento* style also developed in the cities, performed by dance bands in popular nightclubs. Influenced by North American jazz, it relied heavily on clarinets, saxophones, piano, and a full drum set, with the rumba box replaced by a double (or electric) bass.

Like calypso artists, *mento* singers often adopted nobility titles. The first *mento* recordings were made by a veritable musical aristocracy, including Count Lasher, Lord Tanamo, Lord Lebby, Lord Composer, and Count Owen. Other prominent artists included Stanley Motta, Harold Richardson, George Moxey, and Chin's Calypso Sextet. In the 1960s, Lord Flea, Lord Foodos, and The Silver Seas Calypso Band popularized *mento* abroad. By the middle of the decade, as Jamaican music continued to evolve, the popularity of *mento* subsided, and in the 1970s *mento* bands (often deliberately mislabeled calypso bands) were mostly relegated to entertain tourists in Jamaican hotels. In the 1980s and 1990s, however, a resurgence led to various new recordings and concerts, notably those by The Jolly Boys and The Hiltonaires. Today, *mento* is still thriving, although it has not regained the popularity it enjoyed during its "Golden Age" in the 1950s.

Recommended Listening: "Glamour Gal" by Harold Richardson, from the CD *Mento Madness: Motta's Jamaican Mento 1951–1956.*

Recommended Listening: "Matilda" by Lord Foodos, from the CD *Steel Band Calypso Music.*

Recommended Listening: "Slide Mongoose" and "No Money No Music" by Count Lasher's Calypso Quintet, from the CD *Boogu Yagga Gal: Jamaican Mento 1950s*.

SKA Part of the reason for *mento*'s decline was the desire for a more urban, danceable sound. As rhythm and blues and rock and roll became increasingly popular, clever entrepreneurs such as Sir Coxsone Dodd and Duke Reid developed ways to provide these styles to poor Jamaicans who could not afford to buy recordings. Their solution was a series of portable sound systems that were set up in outdoor dancing and party venues and that played the latest North American and Caribbean tunes. This practice became extremely popular throughout the island, and came to be known as *sound system*. It was not long before a new Jamaican urban style—ska—replaced the North-American sounds at these events, the next step in the evolution of Jamaican popular music.

Ska has had several waves of popularity both within and outside of Jamaica. Early iterations can be traced to the late 1950s, influenced by *mento* and calypso. Once these styles began to fade (and just as Jamaica was celebrating its newly acquired independence in 1962), the rock-influenced ska quickly filled the void, particularly in sound system parties in Jamaica's poorer urban areas. Originally, ska was almost entirely instrumental, with a heavy emphasis on woodwinds and brass. It is distinguished from *mento* and calypso by its fast danceable tempo and highly syncopated style, the latter foreshadowing the emergence of reggae. It heavily emphasizes the second and fourth beats—the offbeats—with short but pronounced banjo, guitar, or piano chords, which supposedly gave the style its name: 1–*skak*–3–*skak*–1–*skak*–3–*skak*, a practice known as "skanking." A walking bass further gives ska its bounce.

Some of the early proponents of ska were The Skatalites, who would cover instrumental versions of North-American and British hits. Others included Alton Ellis and the Flames and Prince Buster. Many subsequent reggae artists started their careers with ska, including Jimmy Cliff, Toots and The Maytals, and The Wailers. Ska's popularity outside the Caribbean was assured by the British label Island Records, which promoted Jamaican styles abroad, as well as by the increasing presence of Jamaican immigrants in Britain and the United States. The first ska song that became a hit abroad was Millie Small's "My Boy Lollipop" in 1964. Many others soon followed, including Desmond Dekker's "Israelites." The presence of Dekker and other artists in England in the late 1960s planted the seeds for ska's second wave of popularity. This occurred in the late 1970s with a faster and harder style called *Two-Tone*, named after a record label of the same name, founded by The Specials' keyboard player Jerry Dammers. Dammers sought racial harmony among disenchanted poor British youth, and his ideal is reflected in both the name of the label and in the racial diversity of the artists it produced. For the next few years, the Two-Tone label would sign important artists including Madness, The Specials, The Bodysnatchers, The English Beat, The Selecters, and the Apollinaires. Two-Tone ska was quickly adopted by English Mods, as well as by fringe elements of the punk and skinhead scenes, all of which contributed heavily to the style's resurgence. In the early 1990s, ska became popular yet again, in a version loosely called *third-wave ska*. It now traveled from Britain to the United States, where it combined with elements of punk, rock, and rap, making it even edgier that its Two-Tone iteration but also increasingly obscuring its Jamaican identity. Important proponents of third-wave were The Mighty Mighty Bosstones, The Slackers, Sublime, Pressure Cooker, The Blue Meanies, No Doubt, and Catch-22. It also evolved into hybrid styles such as punk-ska and hip-hop-ska.

> **Recommended Listening:** "Occupation" and "Lucky Seven" by The Skatalites, from the CD *Guns of Navarone: Best of The Skatalites.*

> **Recommended Listening:** "Blessings of Love" by Alton Ellis and The Flames, from the CD *Trojan Ska Box Set.*

> **Recommended Listening:** "Judge Dread" by Prince Buster, from the CD *Prince Buster—Fabulous Greatest Hits.*

> **Recommended Listening:** "A Message to you Rudy" and "Ghost Town" by The Specials, from the CD *The Specials: The Singles Collection.*

ROCKSTEADY   Back in the 1960s, though, ska was still popular in Jamaican urban slums such as Trenchtown and Riverton City, which were increasingly populated by unemployed rebellious youth called "rude boys" and where Rastafarianism was beginning to proliferate. Around 1966, the "rude boys" transformed their music into an important form of cultural identity and social protest against the poor economic conditions that plagued Jamaica after independence, echoing similar youth movements around the world during this period. They kept ska's brass instrumentation but adopted a slower beat and a heavier bass, which emphasized the first and third beat and allowed for Rastafarian chanting. Drums decreased in importance and a new emphasis was put on vocals and harmony, which permitted more direct communication with the audience, sending messages of social protest. Another stepping-stone had been reached: *rocksteady*, a smoother, slower, soul-influenced version of ska. The first prominent *rocksteady* musician was Alton Ellis, who with his band The Flames coined the name of the style and who had a hit with "Girl I've Got a Date." Other important *rocksteady* groups included The Gaylads, The Ethiopians, The Wailers, The Melodians, The Techniques, The Tennors, Jackie Mittoo, The Clarendonians, and Desmond Dekker. One of the most prominent *rocksteady* artists was John Holt, whose song "The Tide is High" became a hit by the British group Blondie. Like ska before it, *rocksteady* also became popular in England in the 1970s.

> **Recommended Listening:** "007 (Shanty Town)" by Desmond Dekker and "Dance Crasher" by Alton Ellis and The Flames, from the CD *Trojan Box Set: Rude Boy.*

> **Recommended Listening:** "The Tide Is High" by John Holt, from the CD *The Tide Is High: Anthology 1962–1979.*

REGGAE The origins of the term *reggae* are unclear, as various sources relate the term to words in English, Spanish, Bantu, and *patois*. Its earliest recorded mention occurred in the 1968 song "Do the Reggay" by Toots and the Maytalls. In any event, several factors coalesced to form the phenomenon that became reggae in the late 1960s. Rastafarianism had made inroads in urban slums for about a decade and now became prevalent everywhere in Jamaica. *Rocksteady* had slowed down and smoothed out the syncopated ska beats, and now more powerful and complex electric bass patterns were added. More instruments enhanced the rhythmic complexities of *nyabinghi*, including drums and other percussion, organ, piano, and especially electric guitars, which became prominent on the syncopated offbeats. Vocal lines adopted *nyabinghi*'s wailing style. Lyrics, which had already become more personal with *rocksteady*, reached a new level, combining overt religious messages with highly political and social causes, often related to Black liberation. The music and the religion became inexorably merged, which only increased the popularity of both: Rastafarian ideals of peace, Black unity, freedom, and liberation appealed to many of the world's subjugated people, particularly in Africa and the Caribbean but also in urban areas of London and New York. Reggae became the most famous style of music associated with Rastafarianism, indeed the most famous of all Jamaican musics, and one of the most popular styles in the entire world. Much of the explosion of both Rastafarianism and reggae can be attributed to the success of one band, and especially of one man: Bob Marley and his group The Wailers.

BOB MARLEY AND THE WAILERS Bob Marley did not invent reggae single-handedly: it was in the air, waiting to coalesce out of *rocksteady* and ska. But it needed a musician and personality of Marley's caliber to give it a final push. Part of Marley's success was due to the fact that, since the advent of the worldwide youth movement in the late 1950s, no music superstar had emerged from an underdeveloped country—what was then called "the Third World." Marley was seen as a hero to millions of the earth's poor, a symbol of pride. More importantly, though, he achieved what he did through raw talent and the force of his personality, combined with an appealing religious message that emphasized peace, love, redemption, liberation, and self-determination. Like just about every musician of his generation, Marley partook of the long succession of Jamaican musical styles, including *mento*, *rocksteady*, and ska. By the time he got to reggae, he was a seasoned musician whose sound had matured over the course of many years.

Marley was born Nesta Robert Marley on February 6, 1945 in the village of Nine Miles, of a White father and Black mother. His first recording came in 1961 at age 16. Two years later, in Kingston, he formed The Wailers (originally called The Wailing Wailers, after the Rastafarian chanting style) and had some early successful recordings, including the song "Simmer Down." Several factors then combined to transform The Wailers from a competent *rocksteady* band into the most important reggae group on the planet. One was the visit of Ethiopian emperor Haile Selassie to Jamaica in 1966, which changed the band's musical and spiritual course. They embraced Rastafarianism, began growing dreadlocks, and incorporated its music traditions into their own. They also shed their purely vocal identity, added several instrumentalists, hired the brilliant local Jamaican producer Lee "Scratch" Perry, and began putting out a new style that was unlike the current *rocksteady* heard at sound system parties. The Wailers' success instantly reached new heights, and firmly established their reputation as the best band in Jamaica. The new style was widely imitated and would soon become a powerful force in the development of international music. Reggae had been born.

In the early 1970s, The Wailers were signed by the British label Island Records, who quickly released two albums: *Catch a Fire* and *Burnin'*. The latter included the hits "Get Up, Stand Up" and "I Shot the Sheriff," which was covered by Eric Clapton in 1974, further propelling The Wailers' reputation in Britain and the United States. Their international success soon matched their popularity in Jamaica. Reggae had become an international phenomenon, and Marley was its principal star. At this point, Peter Tosh and Bunny Livingston left the group to pursue solo careers. Marley carried on, adding more personnel to the band, renaming it "Bob Marley and The Wailers" and releasing the album *Natty Dread*, which became a huge hit in 1975. Other albums followed, including *Rastaman Vibration* (1976), *Exodus* (1977), and *Survival* (1979).

Marley was a consummate performer. His tours took him all over Europe and the United States, as well as to Africa, Japan, Australia, and New Zealand. But in Jamaica, his reputation exceeded that of a music superstar. He was seen as a messianic prophet, venerated by the Rasta community, adored by fans from all walks of life, and respected by politicians. In 1978, he played at a political rally in Jamaica called One Love Peace Concert, which sought to reconcile the bitterly divided parties and for which he received the United Nations Peace Medal. His visit to Ethiopia that same year brought him spiritual renewal. Shortly after the release of *Uprising* (1980), at the beginning of a North American tour, Marley was diagnosed with melanoma. He died eight months later, in May 1981, at the age of 36. He was mourned across Jamaica and the world, honored at his funeral by tens of thousands, and buried in his Native village Nine Miles. A posthumous album called *Confrontation* was released in 1983, which contained the hit single, "Buffalo Soldier," followed in 1984 by the "greatest hits" album *Legend*.

> **Recommended Listening:** Early period: "Simmer Down" by The Wailing Wailers, from the CD *Simmer Down at Studio One, Vol. 1*.

> **Recommended Listening:** Middle period: "Soul Rebel" by The Wailers, from the CD *Soul Rebel*.

> **Recommended Listening:** Late Period: "Wake Up and Live" by Bob Marley and The Wailers, from the CD *Survival*.

The Wailers were not the only reggae band around, only the most prominent. Former Wailers Peter Tosh and Bunny Livingston went on to have very successful careers. Other important reggae artists in the late 1960s and early

1970s included Toots and the Maytals, Jimmy Cliff, Ras Michael, Inner Circle, The Light of Saba, The Abyssinians, Gregory Isaacs, The Congos, and Burning Spear. By the 1980s and 1990s, reggae had evolved into dozens of hybrid styles throughout the world. It was also no longer just a Jamaican phenomenon, as fine musicians and bands emerged worldwide who had never set foot on the Caribbean island and who had no relation to Rastafarianism. European reggae bands included Steel Pulse, Maxi Priest, Los Pericos, and UB40, whose song "Red Red Wine" became an international hit. Many African reggae bands also emerged, including Alpha Blondy, Sonny Okosuns, and Lucky Dube. British and U.S. punk and rock bands were heavily influenced by reggae during this period, notably The Clash, The Police, and Elvis Costello. Reggae festivals began (and continue) to be held regularly throughout the world, featuring European, African, Australian Aboriginal, Latin American, Japanese, and North American bands. Just as Cuban salsa appealed to global audiences with its lively rhythms, reggae's lilting syncopated beat and its powerful message of spiritual love and social justice became equally infectious.

> **Recommended Listening:** "Funky Kingston" by Toots and the Maytals, from the CD *Very Best of Toots and the Maytals*.

> **Recommended Listening:** "Treat the Youths Right" by Jimmy Cliff, from the CD *We All Are One: The Best of Jimmy Cliff*.

> **Recommended Listening:** "Columbus" by Burning Spear, from the CD *Burning Spear Ultimate Collection*.

> **Recommended Listening:** "Babylon Makes the Rules" by Steel Pulse, from the CD *Steel Pulse-Ultimate Collection*.

> **Recommended Listening:** "Some Guys Have All the Luck" by Maxi Priest, from the CD *Maxi Priest-Best of Me*.

DUB MUSIC   The evolution of Jamaican music continued unfettered into the 1970s with the emergence of *dub*, which was the logical extension of the sound system that emerged a decade earlier, now with a pronounced reggae inclination and with increasingly sophisticated state-of-the-art equipment. Of particular importance at these events was the DJ (disc jockey), the singer/speaker who would "toast" the audience, improvising extemporaneously over the recorded rhythms coming out of the sound system. Record producers such as King Tubby and Scratch Perry would often release two versions of ska and reggae hits, the A-side with the full vocal version and the B-side that only had the instrumental tracks—literally a "dub." This version would then be played at sound system parties, allowing the DJ to improvise alliterative rhyming lyrics over the dubs. This system was economically advantageous for the producers, who could reuse recordings they already owned: An A-side that became a commercial hit would become even more lucrative by yielding many more B-side versions. It was not long before instrumental tracks of pre-existing songs were electronically remixed with new vocal and lead instrumental lines, sound effects, and prerecorded sounds. Talented DJs became respected and popular, including Count Matchuki, Sir Coxsone, King Stitch, and Sir Lord Comic. Subsequent proponents of dub were U-Roy, Dreadlocks Fay, and Big Youth, who injected Rastafarian rhythms and chanting into dub. In the late 1970s, a related art form emerged called *dub poetry*, in which stories and poems were spoken over bare reggae rhythms (by now known simply as "dub riddims"). Contrary to dub's dance and party roots, however, dub poetry was a more serious movement, addressing important political and social issues. Notable dub poets included Linton Kwesi Johnson, Queen Majeeda, and Mikey Smith.

It was not long before dub and remixing became popular in Britain and the United States. One of the most significant DJs to come out of the Jamaican ska scene was DJ Kool Herc, later known as the Godfather of Hip-Hop, who began toasting in New York City in 1967. He started a heavy bass style called *break-beat*, during which he would improvise vocally over segments of existing popular songs. Break-beat is universally recognized as one of the sources for break dancing, rap music, and hip-hop. The practice of sampling and setting new vocals and lyrics over a pre-existing song can be traced directly to the Jamaican tradition. (The Jamaican dub DJ is not to be confused with the hip-hop DJ. The former performs vocally, the latter manipulates sound recordings. In hip-hop culture, the vocal performer, or rapper, is known as the MC—Master of Ceremonies.)

> **Recommended Listening:** "Natty Cultural Dread" by Big Youth, from the CD *Ride Like Lightning: Best of 1972–1976*.
>
> **Recommended Listening:** "Inglan Is a Bitch" by Linton Kwesi Johnson, from the CD *Independent Intavenshun: The Island Anthology*.
>
> **Recommended Listening:** The CD *Rough Guide to Dub* contains many remixes by King Tubby, Scratch Perry, and others, though the lack of a DJ's improvised lyrics illustrates dub's quintessential nature as a live performance style.

DANCEHALL AND *RAGGA* By the 1980s, dub became absorbed by the massive proliferation of techno, electronic, dance, and hip-hop music, all of which it had originally influenced. At the same time, Jamaican attitudes towards popular music began changing. The idealism of the 1960s, most evident in reggae's social consciousness, now gave way to a harsher, more conservative and materialistic view of life, one that often espoused a violent reactionary message. From this discontentment emerged dancehall, a reggae/rock style that often included a DJ but replaced recorded tracks with a live band that usually included synthesizers and electric drums. A strong emphasis was put on the percussion and the bass line. Dancehall lyrics rejected the social causes and Rasta-based spiritual messages of 1970s reggae in favor of a cruder, more pop-oriented language and as a result were often denounced by intellectual critics and the Jamaican ruling class. One of the first proponents of this style was Barrington Levy and his band Roots Radic. Others included Wailing Souls, Yellowman, Charlie Chaplin, and General Echo. Similar to dancehall was a more electronic-based style called *ragga*, which used digital computer sequences to produce its melodies and rhythms. It also spawned a youth cultural movement, the *raggamuffins* (*patois* for "villain" or "rogue"), who were akin to the "rude boys" of the 1960s, but now more cynical and hard-edged.

By the 1990s, dancehall, *ragga*, and other reggae-oriented styles had traveled the now-familiar path to Britain and the United States, where they gained a harder edge as they became heavily infused with rap and hip-hop. Variations and hybrids quickly emerged, with such styles as the British Jungle and Butterfly. Recent dancehall artists include Buju Banton, Sean Paul, and Shaggy, whose remake of the *nyabinghi*-influenced "Oh Carolina" was a big hit. Artists such as Bounty Killa and Beenie Man have successfully fused dancehall and gangsta rap. After more than half a century of influence, Jamaican popular music is still at the roots of much of the music of Europe and the United States.

> **Recommended Listening:** Dancehall: "How The West Was Won" by Ranking Toyan, from the CD *The Biggest Dancehall Anthems, 1979–82: The Birth of Dancehall.*

> **Recommended Listening:** *Ragga:* "Under Me Sleng Teng" by Wayne Smith, from the CD *Under Me Sleng Teng.*

> **Recommended Listening:** "Willy (Don't Be Silly)" by Buju Banton, from the CD *The Voice of Jamaica.*

> **Recommended Listening:** "Next Millennium" by Bounty Killa (Bounty Killer), from the CD *Next Millennium.*

> **Recommended Listening:** "Oh Carolina" by Shaggy, from the CD *Mr. Lover Lover: The Best Of Shaggy.*

TRINIDAD

In 1962, Trinidad and the nearby island of Tobago achieved their independence from Britain and joined together, forming a single nation in the southern Caribbean off the coast of Venezuela. In a region of the world that is already diverse, Trinidad stands out for its diversity, reflected in its people, customs, religion, language, and music. Known as "The Land of the Hummingbird," it was occupied variously by the British, Spanish, French, and Dutch. In 1802, it became a possession of Britain, which made efforts to anglicize the island. Two years later, during the Haitian Revolution, many French families and their slaves migrated to Trinidad, infusing the island with pronounced French Creole traditions. East Indians workers were also brought in to work the plantations after slavery was abolished in 1834, followed in the twentieth century by Chinese and Syrian workers. Trinidad has the greatest concentration of East Indians in the hemisphere, greatly affecting the island's culture and music. The continuous colonial merry-go-round brought a strange cultural mix to Trinidad. English is the spoken language, though many people speak French Creole, Spanish, and Hindi. Both Catholic and Protestant traditions are prevalent, as well as important Muslim and Hindu elements. Though in the past the Trinidadian economy was based on agriculture, the most important modern industry in Trinidad is petroleum and its by-products, which in the twentieth century had an important impact on the development of steel pans.

Trinidadian Carnival

The majority of the prominent musical traditions in Trinidad are related to its most important celebration. Trinidadian carnival has become as famous as those in Rio de Janeiro, Venice, and New Orleans. Carnival was brought to Trinidad by the Catholic French and remained popular even after the Protestant British took possession of the islands. After abolition in 1834, increased urbanization caused the elite, fearful of the increased Black presence in the cities, to keep carnival private, upper class, and White. In response, a separate public carnival called *jamette* emerged in the streets, embraced mainly by the migrant former slaves as an important signifier of Black culture and identity, a way of resisting control by the ruling class and the Church. The newly freed Blacks formed music and parade bands, often segregated by language. Nineteenth-century accounts described *jamette* as rowdy and unruly, often turning violent as gangs of French- and English-speaking merrymakers clashed with each other and with authorities, whose attempts to ban it proved fruitless. But by 1900, carnival had become more "respectable," appealing to a cross-section of Trinidadians, and adopting English as the predominant language at the expense of French Creole. It was also around this time that formal music competitions emerged, a feature that would come to define Trinidadian carnival in subsequent years and that in modern times has become a huge commercial enterprise. Throughout the course of the twentieth century, the celebration continued to evolve, though always retaining the popular elements it inherited from its street origins. It would also become infused with three musical styles that have made it one of the most distinctive—and popular—celebrations in the world: calypso, steel pans, and *soca*.

Early Song Forms: *Kalinda* and *Lavway*

Kalinda was a Yoruba oral tradition of song and storytelling from West Africa, usually in call-and-response form. In Trinidad, *kalindas* emerged as slave work songs but also served for entertainment, for example to accompany stick-fighting contests, another African tradition. They were also a secret means of communication among slaves who were unauthorized to speak with each other. The caller of the songs was the *griot*, a traveling musician who often assumed a position of leadership and authority, and who was valued for his singing, storytelling, and instrument-making abilities. *Kalindas* were usually sung without instrumental accompaniment, though rattles, shakers, and even drums would occasionally provide a rhythmic background. After abolition in the 1830s, the *kalinda* tradition continued, and by mid-century, singing competitions had emerged and become popular, particularly during the carnival *jamette*. The *griot* leaders then became known as *chantwells*, and when they started performing in carnival celebrations, their songs became known as *lavways* ("confessions"). *Lavways* were in simple strophic form, providing the *chantwells* the opportunity to show their improvisatory skills during the verses, which the chorus would then try to match during the refrain. Both *kalindas* and *lavways* were enormously influential in the development of calypso, the singing style that would dominate Trinidadian music for much of the twentieth century.

> **Recommended Listening:** "Regimen Mwen De Leon Mama" by Matthew Thomas and Kalenda Band, from the CD *The Caribbean Voyage: Trinidad, The 1962 Field Recordings.*

Calypso

In Greek mythology, Calypso was the sea nymph who rescued the shipwrecked Odysseus and then held him captive for seven years. But there seems to be no connection between the Caribbean musical style and the Greek myth. Rather, the origin of the term *calypso* has been connected to various languages and dialects, notably the French Creole word *carrousseaux* ("carousers" who engage in drunken revelry), the Spanish *caliso*, and the Carib *carieto* (both referring to a type of joyful song), as well as the West African *kaiso* (a cheer of celebration). In any event, *kaiso* has come to be used almost interchangeably with calypso to refer to the musical style.

Calypso is a singing style that combines many aspects of the old *kalindas* and *lavways*, including the improvisatory and call-and-response elements, though the latter is somewhat less pronounced, and more often than not both verse and refrain are sung only by the soloist. Like the *lavways*, some early calypso songs were in French Creole, though English quickly became the language of preference. Songs can be slow or fast and usually have two beats to the measure, with the emphasis on the second beat providing a syncopated feel. Calypso is intricately, though not exclusively, linked with carnival. The style emerged in the second half of the nineteenth century, when it became a potent and popular cultural signifier. Its songs retained the themes of struggle and resistance inherited from the legacy of slavery. They also became important sources of communication, spreading news from town to town and commenting on political and social issues of the day. Today they remain strong expressions of protest and social justice.

Above all, calypso highlighted the oral abilities of its performers, the former *chantwells* who were now called *calypsonians*. Their verbal dexterity determined the success of their songs and stories, which were often peppered with ribald and humorous plays on words, innuendos, and double meanings. Early calypsonians engaged in *picong*, a competition of improvised singing in which singers verbally fought and insulted each other with great skill. The artistry of a calypso song often depended much more on its lyrics than on its rhythms or melodies. Early calypsonians accompanied themselves with a guitar, occasionally backed by a percussionist or two. In the early twentieth century, tents were erected during carnival celebrations where calypsonians would practice their songs. The tradition of the tent became widespread, and soon it became the place where calypso songs were actually performed, along with storytelling, pantomime, skits, and so on. Today, the calypso tent has become one of the two main venues for the style, and the term "tent" now refers to any theater or other large setting where calypso is performed. But calypso was not only intended for a sitting audience: It was also meant to be danced, particularly in the midst of carnival celebrations. Thus, the other venue for calypso performance was the carnival parade itself, in a tradition known as the "road march." Because performers do not remain stationary, the character of the road march calypso is different than that of the tent calypso. Gone are the skits and clever storytelling acts, as the road show relies on the music itself and the antics of the masqueraders. Road march musical accompaniment was originally provided by brass or *tamboo bamboo* bands and later by steel pans (discussed below).

The first calypso recordings occurred in the 1910s, at a time when middle-class carnival celebrations were flourishing, and the music's popularity quickly became widespread. By 1930, the so-called "Golden Age of Calypso," many calypsonians had become stars, often taking fanciful animal names or titles of the nobility such as Lord Executor, Lord Pretender, Lord Invader, Attila the Hun, the Roaring Lion, and The Growling Tiger. Their songs had a decidedly political bent, usually in support of the budding independence movement, and as a result were often repressed by the British authorities. The best performers won awards such as the National Calypso Monarch, Calypso Queen, and Junior Monarch. During this period, the musical accompaniment had now grown to include several guitars, bass, and a larger percussion section. Traditional jazz instrumentation, including brass, woodwinds, and a drum set, now also became popular.

> **Recommended Listening:** "Money Is King" by The Tiger and "Treasury Scandal" by Attila the Hun, from the CD *Calypsos From Trinidad: Politics, Intrigue, and Violence in the 1930s.*

In the 1940s and 1950s, calypso became popular throughout the Caribbean, transported by trading ships and migrant workers and disseminated by the proliferation of radio stations and recordings. Various forms were adopted and adapted by neighboring islands, notably Barbados, Jamaica, Antigua, Grenada, Dominica, and the Virgin Islands, as well as Costa Rica and the Venezuelan mainland. The local folksong traditions of many of these islands were strongly influenced by calypso, which became the quintessential street music of Caribbean carnival. Calypso reached the United States when Lord Invader's song "Rum and Coca-Cola" was covered by the Andrew Sisters during World War II and quickly became a hit. A few years later, it received a huge international boost when the Jamaican-American Harry Belafonte recorded a number of calypso hits.

> **Recommended Listening:** "Rum and Coca Cola" by Lord Invader, from the CD *Calypso Calaloo: Early Carnival Music in Trinidad.*

The post-war period saw great changes in the music of Trinidad, particularly with the increasing popularity of the steel pan. The two greatest calypsonians of the mid-century were Lord Kitchener and Mighty Sparrow, both of whom wrote important songs that would remain influential for decades. Lord Kitchener (Aldwyn Roberts) had his first hit "Green Fig Man" in 1943, which catapulted him to stardom. Kitchener spent much time in Britain, popularizing calypso throughout Europe. With hits such as "Rain-O-Rama" and "Sugar Bum Bum," Kitchener brought a marked vitality to calypso, particularly in his use of the steel pan. The Grenada-born Mighty Sparrow (Slinger Francisco) was recognized as the Calypso King throughout the 1950s and 1960s. Many of his songs, including 1956's "Jean and Dinah," offered strong social and political criticism that influenced the growing independence movement. The first prominent female calypsonian was Calypso Rose, who emerged as a major force in the 1960s and 1970s, and whose success, particularly with the politically charged hit "Fire in Me Wire," led to her being called Trinidad's "Calypso Queen." Though Trinidadian calypso remains a male-dominated world, other female artists have managed to break through and follow in Calypso Rose's footsteps, most prominently Singing Sandra, who was also crowned Calypso Monarch in 1999.

The advent of soca and the worldwide explosion of Jamaican reggae in the 1960s and 1970s somewhat depressed calypso's popularity abroad, though it never went out of style in Trinidad. Modern calypso continues on many of the islands, now performed with modern instruments such as electric guitars, bass, keyboards, and drums. It has also been strongly affected by myriad influences including Indian chutney, reggae, and dancehall, as well as North-American jazz, rock, and hip-hop. These syncretic influences have only served to enrich a style that was syncretic to begin with, in the process perpetuating its vitality and popularity.

Recommended Listening: "Jean and Dinah" by The Mighty Sparrow and "Rain-O-Rama" by Lord Kitchener, from the CD *Mighty Sparrow and Lord Kitchener: 16 Carnival Hits.*

Recommended Listening: "Fire in Me Wire" by Calypso Rose, from the CD *Calypso Rose–Soul on Fire.*

Recommended Listening: "Voices From the Ghetto" by Singing Sandra, from the CD *Rough Guide to Calypso and Soca.*

CDII, Track 1: Calypso: "No Money No Love"

Music and Lyrics: The Mighty Sparrow (Slinger Francisco)
Instrumentation: brass, electric guitar, bass, drum set, tambourine, keyboards
Notes: Mighty Sparrow's calypso is backed by the Jamaican band Bryon Lee and the Dragonaires. The song's humor and lightheartedness ironically colors the serious issues of poverty and domestic abuse that were rampant in Trinidad.

Ivy pack up she clothes to leave because John was down and out.
All alone he was left to grieve, she had a next man in South.
She said openly, she say, I really love you Johnny,
But you ain't have no money, so what will my future be,
Even though you say you love me?

Chorus
We can't love without money.
No we can't make love on hungry belly.
Johnny, you'll be the only one I am dreaming of.
You're my turtledove, but no money, no love.

If you hear how he plead with she to get her to understand.
Listen, mister, she tell Johnny, leggo me blasted hand.
And make up your mind, we got to break up this time.
She said poverty is a crime, you got no money,
Still you tanglin' me all the blinkin' time.

Gentlemen, let me tell you plain, she said, I don't want to make a scene.
But if you only touch me again, police will intervene.
You ain't got a blasted cent, I couldn't even pay me rent.
I had to give up me apartment, you give me nothing to eat.
Now you want me to sleep on the pavement.

Tamboo Bamboo

Back in the nineteenth century, colonial authorities in Trinidad were suspicious of African elements that they saw as a potential threat to the slavery-based plantation system. They attempted to discourage revolt and stamp out African religions by banning drums and controlling celebrations. As a result, a strong drumming tradition is less obvious in Trinidadian culture than in slave cultures of neighboring islands. Instead, Trinidadian music absorbed more of the melodic and harmonic elements of European music, with nonetheless a strong percussive beat. In the nineteenth and early twentieth centuries, Black Trinidadians trying to get around the drum ban were able to improvise, finding instruments and developing techniques wherever they could. One result was an instrument called *tamboo bamboo* ("bamboo drums"), which can also be found in West Africa. Bamboo shoots are either held horizontally in one hand and struck with a stick, or held upright and pounded on the ground, producing a muffled sound. They are several inches in diameter and two to six feet in length, producing a wide variety of pitches. Like the human voice, *tamboo* are divided according to range, with *cutters* (corresponding to the sopranos), *fullers* (altos), *chandlers* (tenors), and *boom* (bass). The various pitches, not organized in any specific tonal system, produce an indeterminate harmonic hum. *Tamboo bamboo* bands became popular during carnival parades around 1900. They consisted of dozens or even hundreds of musicians playing various rhythms and singing in syncopation as they paraded. The lively and exciting orchestra was complemented by *shack-shack* graters, *gwaj* metal shakers, and glass bottles filled with water and struck with metal spoons. *Tamboo bamboo* players became very adept, and in due time their technical skills were transferred over to the steel pan, though some *tamboo bamboo* bands still parade in rural areas of the island.

> **Recommended Listening:** "Congo Bara" by Vasco De Freitas and Tamboo Bamboo Band, from the CD *The Caribbean Voyage: Trinidad, The 1962 Field Recordings*.

Steel Pan

In a culture already infused with quintessentially Caribbean sounds, the instrument that truly places Trinidad at the center of the Caribbean musical culture is the *steel pan*. (The instrument is also known as the *steel drum*, though the correct technical term is *pan*.) The instruments were traditionally made from discarded 55-gallon oil drums, though in modern times most are manufactured specifically as musical instruments. The top of the drum is carefully pounded until it sinks inwards into a concave shape, like the inside of a bowl.

Steel Pan Player from Tobago.

This is the pan, whose surface is then hammered into ovals that produce clean, sharp notes when struck. The size of the ovals determines the pitch: the smaller the oval, the higher the pitch. If the ovals are large, fewer of them will fit on the pan. Some pans will contain only three bass notes, while others can contain more than two-dozen high-pitched notes. As a result, more pans—and thus more players—are required to play the bass notes than the treble notes: Higher-pitched pans will have a single player; in the middle ranges, one player might play two or three pans, whereas a bass player might play 8 or 10 pans. A normal steel band will span about five octaves. There are at least six different types of pan, differing in size, shape, range, and tone. Sometimes, the full body—or skirt—of the drum is preserved to add resonance. Other times, the skirt is cut off halfway or two-thirds of the way to allow the sound to escape more quickly and to make the pan lighter, allowing for greater mobility.

Steel bands can range from just a few instrumentalists to hundreds of players. Some steel bands are stationary; others are itinerant, particularly those in carnival parades, with the pans held by a strap around the players' neck. A rhythm section called the *engine room* usually accompanies steel bands. It usually consists of a drum set, one or two conga drums, timbales, cowbells, *shack-shack* graters, and *gwaj* shakers. The most important element of the engine room and perhaps of the entire steel band is the iron: a brake drum taken from an old car and struck with metal rods. The iron brings much of the energy to the steel band, providing a complex rhythmic background.

The immediate precursors to the steel bands were *tamboo bamboo* ensembles. Legend has it that the steel pan was invented in 1942 by a 12-year-old boy named Winston "Spree" Simon, who had been experimenting with discarded oil drums. More likely, the steel pan was already in the air in the late 1930s, as various bands and musicians, seeking to expand their musical expression, were trying out different percussion instruments made from a variety of materials, including dustbins and biscuit tin cans. They began using oil drums discarded by Trinidad's important oil industry. At first, these drums were unpitched and used only as rhythm instruments. As time passed, however, the pans were tuned to produce a deep booming sound and complex harmonies that supported the melody and eventually became melodic instruments themselves. When the steel pans emerged as viable instruments, Trinidadian musicians took to them as if they had always been a part of the culture. The British authorities, characteristically, looked upon them with suspicion, fearing the debauchery and negative influences that might ensue from these unfamiliar, uninhibited sounds.

Whether or not Spree actually invented the steel pan, he did form important bands in the 1940s that incorporated the new instrument—notably Destination Tokyo, Tropical Harmony, and the Fascinators Band. Within a decade, steel pans were an established tradition, prominent in carnival celebrations, and they began appearing on other Caribbean islands as well. In 1951, The Trinidad All Steel Percussion Orchestra traveled to England and instantly became a hit among the normally conservative British public, which gained the instrument a measure of respect and brought it to the forefront of

Caribbean sounds. A few years later, the U.S. Navy Steel Band was formed, further enhancing the popularity and global recognition of the instrument. By the time Trinidad achieved independence in 1962, steel pan musicians had established numerous competitions, festivals, and touring bands. The following year saw the establishment of the Panorama competition, which would quickly become the most important venue for steel pan performance. Held each year in Port-of-Spain, Panorama lasts over a month during the carnival season, culminating in the crowning of the Panorama Champions on the Saturday before carnival. Today, the steel pan remains one of the most important and popular Caribbean instruments. Ensembles can be found worldwide, and carnivals throughout the Caribbean now typically include many steel pan performances. Its repertoire has incorporated that of other traditions, including classical music, pop, rock, and jazz.

> **Recommended Listening:** "Sixty-Nine" by The Westland Steel Band, from the CD *Trinidad: The Sound of the Sun*.

> **Recommended Listening:** "You Can Call Me Al" by Trinidad Cement Limited Skiffle Band, from the CD *Trinidad Carnival: Steel bands of Trinidad and Tobago*.

CDII, Track 2: Steel Pan: "Pan in A Minor"

Music and Lyrics: Lord Kitchener (Aldwyn Roberts), arranged by Jit Samaroo
Instrumentation: steel band
Notes: This driving steel pan tune was performed at the 1987 Panorama competition. The multi-part theme reappears in numerous variations in the full recording (which is almost 10 minutes long). Notice in particular the thick texture and the virtuosity of the dozens of pan players who stay together throughout the piece. The engine room, consisting of a variety of percussion instruments, drives the rapid, almost dizzying tempo.

0:00	Tempo is set by the cowbell
0:05	Introductory theme(a) over falling bass, in minor key
0:12	Introductory theme(b) over falling bass, in minor key
0:20	Transition, shift to major key, exploration of different keys
0:42	Theme 1(a) in the key of a minor
0:58	Theme 1(b)
1:12	Theme 1(c)
1:28	Theme 1(d)
1:42	Theme 1(c)
1:59	Theme 1(d)

Soca

Supposedly, *soca* melds North-American **so**ul music with **ca**lypso. Its origins, however, are more complex, and go back at least to 1963, when Lord Shorty (Garfield Blackman) added elements of East Indian music to calypso, notably instruments such as the sitar, dholak, and dhantal, and the tabla and tassa drums. Shorty's new style soon became popular, particularly after his hit song "Clock and Dagger." By the 1970s, Trinidadian artists in New York began infusing soca with the soul and funk (and later, disco) music that was emerging in the United States. In the process, the Indian elements were minimized and ultimately abandoned. Electric guitars, bass, and synthesizers became standard, and soca became anchored to a fast and syncopated bass line. Tempos were more upbeat than calypso's, the rhythms faster, steadier, and more intense. Soca also moved away from calypso's vocal and lyrical virtuosity, its slower, more relaxed attitude and its political and social commentary, in favor of a more lighthearted, "party" identity. As a result, it quickly became popular throughout the Caribbean and in the United States, though purists have criticized it as an empty, diluted form of calypso. It achieved worldwide popularity with the 1983 international hit "Hot! Hot! Hot!" by the Montserrat artist Arrow, who often combined calypso and soca with other styles such as *zouk* and even reggae. Another song that helped popularize soca was "Under the Sea," from the 1989 Disney film *The Little Mermaid*. A slew of soca artists became prominent in the 1980s, shedding the nobility titles of their predecessors in favor of one-word names: Shadow, Swallow, Xtatik, Superblue, Square One, and Ajala. Conversely, some of the old-time calypsonians like Lord Kitchener also became important soca musicians. Competitions quickly emerged, where soca artists vied to outperform each other with ornate outfits and dramatic theatricality. It wasn't long before soca, itself a hybrid, began combining with other styles such as gospel, spirituals, and hip-hop to produce even more complex styles. Hyphenated names began emerging such as *chutney-soca* and *ragga-soca*, which infused the style with Jamaican reggae, *ragga*, and dancehall music.

> **Recommended Listening:** "Free Up" by Chris 'Tambu' Herbert, from the CD *Rough Guide to Calypso and Soca*.

> **Recommended Listening:** "Caribbean Party" by David Rudder, from the CD *Rough Guide to Calypso and Soca*.

> **Recommended Listening:** "Bassman" by Shadow, from the CD *Rough Guide to Calypso and Soca*.

> **Recommended Listening:** "Bring the Rhythm Down" by Ajala, from the CD *Rough Guide to Calypso and Soca*.

> **Recommended Listening:** "Outa Space (UFOs)" by Machel Montano and Xtatic from the CD *Any Minute Now*.

> **Recommended Listening:** "Let's Get It On" by Bunji Garlin, from the CD *Revelation*.

CDII, Track 3: Soca: "Get On Bad"

Music and Lyrics: Ozzie Merique and Robin Imamshaw
Instrumentation: electric guitar, bass, synthesizers, brass, drum set, cowbell, timbales
Notes: The fast tempos and unrelenting percussion rhythm underscores the exuberance of this soca tune, performed by Denyse Plummer. The party atmosphere is accentuated by the lyrics, which make specific references to carnival, festivals, and the ancient Roman celebration of Bacchanalia.

Carnival you reign (let me see you).
Bacchanal, bacchanal, bacchanal (it's time to rumble).

The time has come once again, bacchanal, sun or rain.
Festival, we having fun, bare yourself, and tell everyone.

Hottie, hottie, all boys and girls, hottie, hottie, I'm sure you will.
Carnival you reign, carnival you reign.
Bring your bambalam with your flag, no time to be sad.
Get on bad, get on bad, get on bad.

Chorus
Jump, jump, jump up like crazy.
Jump, jump, jump in the party.

When the music play, jump up in a way
Like a hooligan, anyhow you can.

Rapso

Rapso emerged in the urban centers of Trinidad in the 1970s, at a time of political and social turbulence. It combined calypso with Jamaican dub and, later, U.S. hip-hop. (Contrary to popular belief, the term *rapso* is not a combination of **rap** and **so**ca.) Never as popular as soca, it retained the lyrical originality and vocal dexterity at the heart of early calypso. It emphasized serious and socially conscious principles like the Black Power and Pan-Africa movements and was closely linked to the rise of labor unions in Trinidad. Early proponents of the style include Lancelot Layne, with his seminal 1971 hit "Blown Away," and Cheryl Byron, the "Mother of Rapso." In the 1980s, the most important *rapso* artist was Brother Resistance (Roy Lewis) and his Network Riddim Band. It was on his 1980 album *Busting Out* that the term *rapso* first appeared. Brother Resistance's output reflects *rapso*'s socially minded proclivities, and he has infused his music with bold poetry and lyrics. Recent artists such as 3 Canal, Kindred, and Black Lyrics have taken rapso in new directions, adding soul, reggae, and dancehall influences.

Recommended Listening: "Cyar Take Dat" by Brother Resistance and The Network Riddim Band, from the CD *Rough Guide to Calypso and Soca*.

Recommended Listening: "Ring De Bell" by Brother Resistance and The Network Riddim Band, from the CD *D Rapso Nation: Anthology of Best of Rapso*.

Recommended Listening: "Doh Stop" by Kindred, from the CD *D Rapso Nation: Anthology of Best of Rapso*.

Parang

Trinidad's Spanish—and Roman Catholic—heritage is also reflected in its music, particularly with a traditional acoustic folk style called *parang*, derived from the term *parranda*, which refers to an ambulating group of serenading musicians. Akin to the Mexican *posada*, Puerto Rican *aguinaldo*, and Dominican *arguinaldo*, *parang* is performed during the Christmas season by serenaders who play and sing from house to house and neighborhood to neighborhood. The songs are Christmas carols, usually religious in nature, and sung in proper Spanish language. The style was heavily shaped by Spanish colonial music, as well as by the sounds of nearby Venezuela, which also has its own *parranda* tradition. The *parang* season starts before Christmas—sometimes as early as mid-November—and lasts until Three Kings' Day on January 6. As few as four and as many as a dozen *paranderos* sing and play guitars, mandolins, bandolins, violins, and the small high-pitched *quatro* guitar. Occasionally, percussion instruments accompany the *paranderos*, such as *chac-chacs* (gourd maracas), tambourines, clappers, *toc-tocs* (wood block), and *güiros*. Traditional *parang* rhythms are distinct from Trinidadian styles such as calypso and soca, and more akin to Caribbean rhythms in places such as Venezuela, Cuba, Puerto Rico, and the Dominican Republic, which use the Latin *clave* as their basis. *Parangs* start in the evening and can last for several hours. Specific rituals are followed, according to which the hosts welcome the singers, songs are dedicated to various causes or people, and the serenaders are offered food and beverages. Different kinds of songs are used, for example the *aguinaldos* (serenades), which relate to the Nativity, the secular *guarapos*, and the *despedidas*, by which the musicians take leave of their hosts.

As with just about every other Trinidadian style, the continuous popularity of *parang* has led to the establishment of competitions and the naming of *parang* kings and queens. Perhaps the most prominent *parang* artist was Daisy Voisin, dubbed the "Queen of Parang." Others include Henry Perierra, Marcia Miranda, Sharlene Flores, Leon Caldero, The Lara Brothers, and Los Niños del Mundo. Given Trinidadian's propensity to meld musical elements, it was almost inevitable that hybrid styles emerged, for example the English-language *soca-parang*, which often dealt with secular subjects and North American Christmas icons such as Santa Claus. Another hybridization mixed *parang* with East-Indian styles such as chutney. Many purists often lament that these modern styles are over-commercialized and do not reflect the true spirit of the Christmas season. Yet many of the traditional styles and customs are still practiced in Port-of-Spain and other areas of the islands, preserving them for future generations.

Recommended Listening: "Aguinaldo" from the CD *West Indies: An Island Carnival.*

Recommended Listening: "Pasen Pasen" by the Lara Brothers, from the CD *Sweet Parang.*

Recommended Listening: "El Nacimiento" by La Casa de Parranda, from the CD *Christmas Parang.*

Recommended Listening: "Parang Soca Medley" by Crazy, from the CD *Parang Soca Christmas (JW)Volume 1.*

Chutney

After abolition in the 1830s, plantation owners in Trinidad, Jamaica, and Guyana hired thousands of indentured servants from India, China, and the Middle East. Upon regaining their freedom, these workers formed tight-knit communities that remained in relative isolation, retaining many of their original traditions. In Trinidad, descendants of East Indians now comprise over 40 percent of the population (descendants of Africans are another 40 percent, the rest being a mixture of Europeans and other ethnic groups). Their particular style of music has come to hold an important place in Caribbean culture. In 1962, the ethnomusicologist Alan Lomax made field recordings of East Indian music in Jamaica and Trinidad that included a wide assortment of wedding songs, works songs, and funeral songs in a variety of vocal, instrumental and drumming styles, offering important insights into much of East Indian Caribbean culture.

Recommended Listening: Alan Lomax's field recordings on the CD *Caribbean Voyage: East Indian Music In the West Indies.*

Most prominent is chutney, a style that arose in the 1970s, not only in Trinidad but throughout the Indian Diaspora, including notably Guyana. Chutney, which was named after the spicy pickled sauce of Indian cuisine, combined Indian music with calypso. Unlike most of the Caribbean styles, which tend to be male-dominated, chutney was first composed and performed by women, in the privacy of their homes. Originally, the music consisted of religious songs, traditional folk tunes, and wedding songs called *bhajans*. Later, music from Bollywood films was incorporated. Early chutney lyrics were in Hindi but increasingly were written in English or Trinidadian Creole, often combining all three. A distinct singing style was also part of early chutney, with melodies and ornaments characteristic of classical Indian music, though in time it began adopting Western harmonies and melodies, relying more on major and minor scales than Indian *ragas*. In traditional chutney, the melody was played by a hand-pumped organ called a *harmonium*, accompanied by Indian percussion such as the double-headed *dholak* drums, the traditional *tabla* drums, *jhal* cymbals, and the *dhantal*, a metal rod struck with a small U-shaped metal stick.

Particularly prominent during the Muslim Hosay festivals were the conical *tassa* drums, made with goatskin and clay shells, that provide fast and loud rhythms. When chutney started gaining popularity in nightclubs and at public events, many of the acoustic instruments were replaced by electric guitars, bass and synthesizers, which mimicked the booming sounds of the *tassa* drums.

The first important chutney star was Sundar Popo, whose 1970 hit "Nana and Nani" brought the style to the attention of the world. Popo combined Indian instruments with electronic keyboards and electric guitars, melding a predominantly Indian sound with the lyricism of calypso. The style soon became widespread throughout the Indian Diaspora, and Popo was dubbed the "King of Chutney." As calypso evolved into soca in the 1970s, so too did chutney develop into a new fusion called *chutney-soca*, adopting soca's fast tempos and lively rhythms and adding the sounds of the steel pan to the traditional Indian instruments. Chutney now gained traction with Trinidadians who were not of Indian descent, such as Mighty Trini and Mighty Sparrow. One of the most important proponents of chutney-soca was Drupatee Ramgoonai, with hits such as "Pepper Pepper" and "Mr. Bissessar." In the 1990s, chutney and chutney-soca from Trinidad and Guyana made a worldwide splash, becoming popular in London, New York, and even India itself. Successful chutney artists included Sonny Mann, Chris Garcia, and Rikki Jai. The inevitable competitions quickly emerged, including the naming of the annual Chutney Monarch. Today, chutney, like soca and calypso, is heard everywhere in Trinidad, emanating from lively dance clubs, car radios, and popular television shows. As chutney continues to grow in popularity, it is becoming increasingly syncretic, resulting in *chutney-ragga*, *chutney-hip-hop*, and *chut-kai-pang* (chutney, calypso, and *parang*). Some artists have even injected the Punjabi folk dance *bhangra*, resulting in chutney-*bhangra*, soca-*bhangra*, *bhangra*-wine, and *bhangragga*, all energetic dance styles with heavy percussion and lively rhythms.

> **Recommended Listening:** "Tassa" from the CD *West Indies: An Island Carnival*.
>
> **Recommended Listening:** "Nana and Nani" by Sundar Popo, from the CD *The Ultimate Sundar Popo*.
>
> **Recommended Listening:** "Pepper Pepper" and "Mr. Bissessar" by Drupatee Ramgoonai, from the CD *Drupatee Mix*.
>
> **Recommended Listening:** "Lootala" by Sonny Mann, from the CD *Caribbean Carnival: Soca Party, Vol. 4*.
>
> **Recommended Listening:** "Ah Love Meh Nannie" by Sharlene Boodram, from the CD *New Kid In Town*.
>
> **Recommended Listening:** "Chutney Ragga Soca," from the CD *The Rhythms of Trinidad and Tobago*.

For discussion of the music of other English-speaking Caribbean islands, see www.mymusickit.com.

THE FRENCH-SPEAKING CARIBBEAN

HAITI

Haiti is located on the western third of the island of Hispaniola, which it shares with the Dominican Republic. Though it is one of the poorest and most densely populated countries in the world, it has also produced some of the most imaginative and evocative music, art, and literature, and it has traditionally been a major presence in Caribbean culture. An important facet of Haiti is the Creole language, called *Kwéyol*, a mixture of French, Spanish, and African words, originally used by Haitian slaves as a means of communication that the French could not understand. Today, both Creole and French are official languages in Haiti, though most Haitians speak Creole first, and French only as a secondary language. Haitian culture, and particularly its music, have been heavily influenced by its Caribbean neighbors, particularly the Dominican Republic on the Eastern side of the island, as well as Cuba, a mere 50 miles across the sea.

HISTORICAL OVERVIEW   The Spanish conquered Hispaniola early on, lured by its bountiful gold mines, which were worked at first by the aborigines, then by African slaves. In the mid-seventeenth century, French settlers began displacing the Spanish on the western third of the island. In 1697, after several European conflicts between the two powers, the territory was ceded by treaty to France, who promptly renamed it St. Domingue. Under the French, St. Domingue became one of the richest colonies in the world. Over a million slaves were brought in during the eighteenth century. The gold mines long depleted, immense plantations now arose which became extremely wealthy, producing coffee, cotton, and especially sugar. St. Domingue's plantations were also notorious for having some of the most brutal and inhumane living and working conditions in the New World. As a result, many Marrons (escaped slaves) fled into the island's mountainous and heavily forested interior, which provided ideal terrain to hide and form communities, which then became bases for rebellious activity and revolt.

Haiti's was the second successful struggle for independence in the hemisphere (after the U.S. Revolution). It was also the first successful Black freedom movement in the world. Spurred on by the ideals of the French Revolution, a large number of *marrons* and free Mulattos undertook a massive rebellion in 1798 that was spearheaded by the legendary former slave Toussaint L'Ouverture. After much struggle, the country finally declared its independence in 1804, and promptly renamed itself Haiti, a Taíno word that means "High Mountains." During the war and its aftermath, most of Haiti's White inhabitants either were killed or emigrated, so that today most of Haiti's population is Black or Mulatto. Between independence and 1860, the Catholic Church did not have an official presence in Haiti, which enabled African religions to become very prominent for several generations of Haitians. The two centuries since the revolution have been tumultuous, and have included dozens of civilian, military, and dictatorial regimes. The wealth generated by the agricultural system has mostly been squandered by inefficiency, corruption, and the effects of economic embargos. Beginning in 1915, Haiti suffered a twenty-year occupation by the United States, a period which saw the introduction of jazz and swing to Haitian music. Upon the U.S. withdrawal in 1935, a series of short dictatorships followed, culminating in the 1957 power-grab by François "Papa Doc" Duvalier, who ruled Haiti until his death in 1971, after which his son Jean-Claude "Baby Doc" assumed power. The Duvalier dynasty was finally toppled by popular uprising in 1986. Today, Haiti remains the poorest country in the hemisphere, though amid continuing political struggles and the recent devastating earthquake, there remain efforts to stimulate Haitian agriculture, mineral exploitation, and tourism.

Négritude and Haitian Art

In the 1930s and 1940s, important artistic and literary developments emerged in the French-speaking islands of the Caribbean, and quickly spread through much of the African Diaspora. This was *Négritude*, an anti-colonial movement that sought to define and advance Black identity in the colonies, and to re-connect their inhabitants with their African origins. In literature, the most prominent proponents of *Négritude* were Aimé Césaire, the Martinican poet, dramatist and mayor of Fort-de-France, as well as the poet Léopold Sédar Senghor who became president of Senegal. *Négritude* engendered and influenced many other movements around the world, including the Harlem Renaissance in the United States, and the pre-eminence of Haitian art, which in the twentieth century reached an unprecedented level of world-wide acclaim. Haitian art embraced *Indigenisme*, the search for African roots, which was reflected in a style that has variously been labeled "naïve," "primitive," and "intuitive." The style emphasizes bright colors and depicts forest or village scenes of every day life, as well as vodou rituals and the Haitian revolution.

VODOU   Like other countries that were heavily populated by African slaves, Haiti came to develop its own blend of African and European rites and beliefs. Vodou (sometimes spelled *voudou, vaudou, voodoo,* or *vodun*) is a syncretic belief system that emerged in the seventeenth century on sugar plantations and *marron* communities. The religious mix found in Brazil, Cuba, and elsewhere was also present in Haiti, as African and Catholic rites and deities quickly intermingled, hidden from the prying eyes of European clerics. Catholic initiation and funeral rites provided the basic framework for vodou rituals, which were of course repressed by the French, who were concerned both with religious profanity and slave uprisings. Several slave-revolt leaders were themselves vodou priests, for example the Guinean François Mackandal, who led a six-year rebellion that culminated in his execution in 1758, as well as Boukman, who led a similar uprising in 1791. Born in slave plantations, vodou came to symbolize the struggle for independence in the late eighteenth century. It became an important expression of Haitian self-determination that helped propel L'Ouverture's revolutionary movement. After independence and the expulsion of the Catholic Church, many societies emerged in Haiti that openly promoted vodou rituals. Today, most Haitians practice vodou, though many are also Roman Catholic.

The term vodou means "spirit" or "deity" in the Fon language of Benin. The Haitian equivalents of the *orishas* of Cuban Santería and the *orixas* of Brazilian *candomblé* are the *lwa*, ancestral spirits that command their own rituals and music. Thus, *Agwe*, the spirit of ships, seafarers, and the sea, is associated with the Christian St. Ulrich, while the patriarch *Danballah*, the serpent spirit of rain and fertility, is associated with St. Patrick, who is also associated with snakes. *Ogun* is the equivalent of St. Jacques (Santiago), as they both bear a sword and have great courage and ferocity. Over the centuries, plantation owners and Catholic priests often associated vodou with evil and Satanism, though of course Satan is strictly a Judeo-Christian deity, with no connection to the ancient African rites, and much of vodou is concerned with warding off—rather than instigating—evil.

Various vodou rituals exist, such as *manjé lwa* ("spirit eating") and *manjé mò* ("death eating"), which revolve around food offerings, or initiation ceremonies such as *lav tèt* ("head-washing," i.e., baptism) or *maryaj* (a marriage to a specific *lwa*). Ceremonies occur in ritual circles, with concentric levels of spectators, drummers, dancers, and officiants. At the center is the *potomitan*, a wooden pole that connects the earth, water, and sky, and through which the ancestral spirits travel. Rituals often begin with Catholic prayers such as the *cantique* (the Rosary) recited in French, followed by vodou prayers in Creole or African languages. There follows the pouring of libations—alcoholic beverages that are offered to the drums, the *potomitan*, and the *lwas*. The officiants acknowledge and greet the drums, the *potomitan*, the four cardinal directions, and the assembly. The drumming and dancing then begin, with various styles in succession, culminating with the arrival of the *lwas*. Like *candomblé* and Santería, vodou rituals aim for a trance state that opens the doors to the spirits, allowing communication with, and even direct possession by, a specific *lwa*. The purpose is to request assistance of the ancestors, in questions of both the spiritual plane and of everyday life in the corporeal plane. If a vodou rite is done properly, the *lwa* will attend and participate in the ritual, and even request what kind of music is to be played. The initiates (males are called *ougan*, females *manbo*) will dance frenetically to the rhythms of the drums, opening themselves to the *lwa*. Once possession takes place, the initiates reach a state of trance called "mounting the horse," with rapid jerking motions that signify the presence of the *lwa*. Food, drink, candles, and animal sacrifice serve important roles. Ceremonies can last from dusk to dawn, and occasionally even for several days.

Vodou rituals have developed important drumming, dancing, and call-and-response singing traditions to honor and communicate with the *lwa* spirits.

The *tanbou* drums are considered actual deities, respected while in use, put to "sleep" at other times. They are made of hardwood, with heads made from either cowhide attached by wooden pegs or goat-hide attached with rope that produce a louder, brasher sound. Both can be played with sticks, bare hands, bows called *agidas*, or any combination of the three. Vodou drumming typically requires three drummers with added percussion such as *ogans* (bells) and *chachas* (gourd or metal shakers). Several distinct drumming styles are linked to particular areas of the country, with hundreds of local variations. The most predominant are the energetic *petwo*, derived from Central African countries such as Congo, Angola, and Mozambique, and associated with the violent clashes of the war of independence; and the more subdued *rada*, derived from West African countries such as Ghana, Nigeria, Togo, and Benin. *Rada* rhythms use three cow-skin drums called *manman, segon,* and *boula* ("mother," "second," and "small"), which are played with sticks. *Petwo* rhythms are played barehanded on conical goatskin drums called *manman, ralé,* and *kata,* usually smaller than the *rada* drums. Other styles include *bizango, dahomey, mayi, gédé,* and *banda*. Drums enter in a pre-determined order, dialoguing with each other and the dancers. An important element in most vodou drumming is the *kasé*, an improvisatory section played over the main rhythm. The *kasé* displays the drummer's virtuosity and improvising skill, and signals particular structural points in the dance.

In the twentieth century, vodou has gained a greater level of international notoriety than its Cuban, Jamaican, or Brazilian cousins, particularly through Hollywood horror films and tourist attractions, and because it can also be found among the French-speaking Creoles of Louisiana. Popular culture has added a sense of mystery to vodou, interjecting exotic myths involving vodou dolls, zombies who have returned from the dead, and liberal amounts of chicken blood, though much of this is perpetrated by the tourism industry and Hollywood films. (See for example the 1932 film *White Zombie* or 1988's *The Serpent and the Rainbow*.)

Recommended Listening: "Gangan Move Tèt O" by Rasin Mapou de Azor, from the CD *Rhythms of Rapture: Sacred Musics of Haitian Vodou*.

Vodou Ritual: "Gangan Move Tèt O"

Music and Lyrics: Traditional
Instrumentation: three *petwo* drums, *ogan* bell
Notes: In this energetic *petwo* rhythm, the drummers, dancers, and singers attempt to communicate with the *lwa* spirits. Each verse is repeated several times by the leader and chorus. In the second verse, the lead singer Azor refers to himself, while in the third verse the *lwas* themselves are invoked.

0:04	Gangan move tèt O, m'a relé,	*The healer priest is mean, Oh I'm calling,*
	Gangan move tèt O.	*The healer priest is mean.*
	Prete m fizi ou la pou m'ai tire zwazo.	*Lend me your shotgun so I can go shoot a bird.*
	Prete m fizi ou la pou m'ai tire zwazo nan bwa.	*Lend me your shotgun so I can go shoot a bird in the woods.*
	M'a pote ke—a bay yo, gangan move tèt O.	*I'll bring its tail back to them, the healer priest is mean.*
2:04	Lè Azor mouri O, n'ap sonje dantan'l,	*When Azor dies, Oh you'll miss his good times,*
	Lè Azor mouri O, n'ap sonje dantan'l palmanan,	*When Azor dies, Oh you'll miss his good times palmanan,*
	O se pou jou-a.	*Oh, on that day.*
2:59	Se lwa k fè m sa Anye,	*It's the lwas who did this to me Anye,*
	Se lwa k fè m sa Waiy,	*It's the lwas who did this to me Waiy,*
	Se lwa k fè m sa anmwe,	*It's the lwas who did this to me, help me,*
	Se lwa mamman m nan ki fè m mand charité.	*It's my mother's lwa who made me go beg for charity.*

RARÁ Unlike their English, Spanish, and Portuguese neighbors, the French colonies developed the custom of having a second carnival in the middle of lent called *Mi-Carême* (mid-Lent). In Haiti, this gave rise to the *rará* fertility festival, a heavily ritualized event that is closely related to vodou. A rural celebration that has sometimes been called Haiti's "peasant" carnival, *rará* consists of enthusiastic bands that parade in costume on the roads between small towns. They first appear after Ash Wednesday and continue throughout the Lenten season, at first only on weekends, but more frequently as Good Friday approaches. On that day much of the countryside is replete with *rará* bands that parade for several miles, delighting onlookers who throw coins and other small donations to the revelers. Parades reach their climax as they approach the town, and since many bands will have been parading simultaneously, the town center is filled with thousands of revelers and performers, each band trying to outdo the others and curry favor with the crowd.

Though a secular celebration, *rará* is nonetheless infused with Afro-Haitian and Catholic religious symbolism. Some studies claim it is meant to represent the crowds that lined the streets when Jesus rode his donkey into Jerusalem; others claim it symbolizes the Jews who jeered at Christ as he was carrying the cross to the crucifixion. *Rará* bands will often include an entire vodou congregation, displaying their unity and wealth, and praising the strength and protection of their particular *lwa*. Parades often begin with extended ceremonies, prayers, and libations, and the distributions of protective charms. Men, women, and children all participate, ranging in number from a few dozen to several hundred. Participants are dressed in bright costumes with sequins, colorful headgear, and elaborate lacing. Many dress up as the opposite gender. Some juggle sticks, batons, or machetes. Unlike Brazilian samba schools, *rará* bands do not march in an orderly fashion, but rather project an image of uncontrolled chaos that only adds to the excitement. Yet this impression is misleading, as strict rules control the playing, singing, and dancing. The masked leader of the parade holds a whip and a whistle to lightheartedly "whip" the participants into some kind of ordered march, but also to protect the parade from the *lwa* of other *rará* bands they might encounter.

Rará music is played on large horns made from sheet metal and on long bamboo tubes called *vaksins*, because of their similarity to vaccination syringes. *Vaksins* have leather mouthpieces and require a great amount of breath to play, and they sound much like foghorns or muted trombones. Each instrument produces a single low note, and when they are all played in rapid succession, the overall effect is one of a continuously repeating melodic pattern, an interlocking layering technique called *hocketing*. The *vaksins* are complemented by *petwo* drums held by shoulder straps, and bells, rattles, whistles, and metal scrapers. Participants sing and dance, either individually or in groups. Songs often have bawdy and suggestive lyrics. The frantic dancing can lead to a frenzy like that of vodou ceremonies, and it is not uncommon for spirit possessions to occur at *rará* parades. The closing dance is performed by the leader as a salute to the town, to the assembled company, and of course, to the protective spirits. *Rará* traditions have developed throughout Haiti, but certain areas have become important centers, such as Léogane in the south, or the Artibonite valley in the north. Like Brazilian samba schools, some *rará* organizations such as La Sainte Rose and Ti Malice have had a continuous tradition for decades, though they have remained almost unknown outside Haiti. The neighboring Dominican Republic has developed a similar style of celebration called *gagá*.

> **Recommended Listening:** "Rará: Notre Dame de 7 doleurs" from the CD *Caribbean Revels: Rará and Gagá*.

> **Recommended Listening:** "M Pap Mache a Tè Anye" by Rará La Bel Fraicheur De'Langlade, from the CD *Angels in the Mirror:* Vodou *Music of Haiti*.

SECULAR DANCES   The French introduced courtly dances such as gavottes, minuets, and waltzes, which in time were "Africanized"—infused with Afro-Haitian rhythms from vodou and other slave styles such as the *calenda* and the *chica*. A prominent syncretic style is the triple-meter *menwat*, derived from the minuet. Another is the *méringue*, related to the frenetic *merengue* on the other side of the island, though it is slower, softer and smoother than its Dominican cousin. The *méringue* emerged in eighteenth-century formal balls and informal get-togethers, and remained popular for the next two centuries among Haitians of all social, economic, and racial classes. Because they are so widespread, *méringues* can be played with virtually any instrumentation, from piano-and-violin chamber ensembles to rural wind bands, high-society ball orchestras and even vodou drum ensembles. Popular singers in the twentieth century successfully recorded their versions of *méringues*, which became widespread even beyond the island. By the 1940s, however, the *méringue* and other traditional Haitian folk styles had lost some popularity on the island, replaced by Cuban and Dominican sounds and rhythms and by jazz and swing bands that had been introduced during the U.S. occupation. Everywhere in Haiti, one could hear *sones, mambos*, and Dominican merengues. Haitian groups themselves began imitating the sounds and rhythms of their neighbors, including most famously the Orchestre Tropicana d'Haiti and the Orchestre Septentrional.

> **Recommended Listening:** "Menwat Dance" by Gwoup Premye Nimewo, from the CD *Angels in the Mirror:* Vodou *Music of Haiti.*
>
> **Recommended Listening:** "Mizisyen" by Ti Band L'avenir, from the CD *Haiti Cherie: Méringue.*
>
> **Recommended Listening:** "Haiti, Perle des Antilles" by Orchestre Tropicana, from the CD *The Rough Guide to the Music of Haiti.*

COMPAS* AND *CADENCE It was from this heavily Latinized context that there emerged in the 1950s a new Haitian style called *compas direct* ("direct rhythm"), often shortened to just *compas* (or *konpa*). Primarily a dance style, it combined the *méringue* with a profusion of foreign influences, including Dominican merengue, Cuban *son*, Trinidadian *calypso* and *soca*, Jamaican *reggae*, and the Congolese Afro-pop style called *soukous*. Its main proponent was Jean-Baptiste Nemours, whose fresh energetic sound and controversial use of the electric guitar appealed to a younger generation of Haitians. Nemours's style was characterized by a simpler but unrelenting merengue dance beat, which he infused with carnival rhythms. In addition to the electric guitar, *compas* made use of Cuban bongos, conga drums, shakers, bells, and bamboo shoots played with sticks in *ti-bwa* fashion.

Nemours's friend and rival Wébert Sicot developed a similar style named *cadence rampas* (or *kadans*), which also combined some of the musical strains that were floating about, namely the Martinican *mazouk* and *biguine*, and the rhythms of the small Creole-speaking island of Dominica. *Cadence* is a more sophisticated style than *compas*, featuring jazz-derived harmonies played by guitars and brass instruments, with a lyrical singing style supported by a lightly syncopated rhythm. Together, Nemours's and Sicot's bands made *compas* and *cadence* the most popular music of Haitian youth in the 1960s. By the 1970s, the styles were exported to other French-Speaking islands such as Martinique and Guadeloupe, often by Haitians who emigrated for political or economic reasons. Later, various hybrid forms emerged including *cadence-lypso* and *Kadans Dous*. *Compas* was popularized outside the

Caribbean by several bands that traveled internationally, including Tabou Combo, who caused a sensation in Paris in the 1970s and 1980s. A popular *compas* artist was Jean Gesner Henri, nicknamed "Le Roi Coupé Cloué" and "The King of *Konpa*." Coupé's songs were infused with traditional African dance rhythms, and his humorous and satirical lyrics emphasized everyday Creole language, often with sexual double-meanings.

> **Recommended Listening:** "Manman Tyoul La Sou" by Jean-Baptiste Nemours, from the CD *The Rough Guide to the Music of Haiti*.

> **Recommended Listening:** "Gacon Bozo" by Coupé Cloué, from the CD *The Rough Guide to the Music of Haiti*.

> **Recommended Listening:** "Tabou Mania" by Tabou Combo, from the CD *The Best of Tabou Combo: Le son Haiti*.

MARTINIQUE AND GUADELOUPE

The other influential French-speaking islands are Martinique and Guadeloupe (often called the *French Antilles*), small islands with fewer than one million inhabitants between them. The French arrived in 1635 and established important sugar plantations. Between 1794 and 1814, during the Napoleonic wars, Martinique was occupied by the British, and then recaptured by the French. Thereafter, the islands' economic fortunes began to decline, and after slavery was abolished in 1848, former settlers and slaves alike saw much poverty for the next century. In 1946, the islands (along with French Guiana) were incorporated as equal constituents of the French Republic, making their inhabitants French citizens. Starting in the 1960s, the economy increasingly relied on tourism and less on agriculture, though there still remain important banana and sugar crops, most of which are sold in France. Most of the population is Black or Mulatto, with a few pockets of White descendants of the French. In addition to the official French language, the mostly Roman Catholic population speaks a form of Creole that combines French, Spanish, and African languages. While Haiti achieved its independence in 1804, enabling its inhabitants to freely pursue African-based religions, neither Martinique nor Guadeloupe have ever been independent, and the colonial authorities have had a continuous effect on their religious—and thus musical—traditions.

> **Recommended Listening:** Alan Lomax: *Caribbean Voyage: The French Antilles: We Will Play Love Tonight*.

> **Recommended Listening:** Alan Lomax: *Caribbean Voyage: Martinique: Cane Fields and City Streets*.

DRUMMING IN THE FRENCH ANTILLES   The Martinican *bélé* and the Guadeloupan *Gwo ka* are single-headed goatskin drums that lay horizontally on the ground and are often played by two drummers. The master drummer—*tambouyé*—straddles the drum, which he plays with his hands between his legs. He alters the pitch and adds subtle variations in tone by pressing his heels into the

FIG. 5.1: *Ti-bwa* **Rhythm patterns.**

drumhead. Behind him, the second drummer—*bwatè*—plays a steady ostinato rhythm on the body of the drum with a pair of sticks called *ti-bwa* (*petit bois*—"little sticks".) This style of playing—altering the pitch with the heel and having two percussionists on a single drum—is derived from Central African traditions in Congo and Angola and can be found in many cultures derived from these regions, for example the Jamaican *kumina*, the Haitian *djouba*, and in certain coastal styles of Venezuela. The *ti-bwa* marks the main rhythmic patterns, either in duple or triple meter, and is found in virtually every form of Creole music, including Haiti, where it is called *kata* (see Fig. 5.1).

Other common percussion instruments include *chachas* (shakers), triangles, *malakach* (maracas), whistles, and the *sillac*, a *güiro*-like grooved instrument made of bamboo that is scraped with a stick or metal comb.

AFRICAN-DERIVED DANCES

Bamboula   During the early colonial period, slaves and free Blacks would congregate on Saturday evenings and Sundays after Mass. Despite the hardship of the previous week, the weekend was often spent not resting but rather in spontaneous get-togethers called *bamboulas* or *gwo tanbous* ("big drums"). At the center of these get-togethers were circle dances that were social and secular in nature, since African worship was not tolerated by plantation owners (though subtle aspects of African religions inevitably seeped into the

A 19th-Century *bamboula*.

music and rituals). These celebrations were also opportunities to organize re-
bellions, and after several such incidents, *bamboulas* were temporarily banned
in Martinique in 1654. Today, similar sessions occur for entertainment purposes, for social events such as weddings, births, or funeral wakes, political
meetings, and even fundraisers. Whatever the occasion, the rituals remain an
important part of the cultural heritage and identity of the French Antilles.

Kalinda   It was in the *bamboulas* that emerged the traditional Creole drumming, dancing, and singing sessions that are still ongoing on the islands.
Various African-derived secular dances were performed at these events, with
names such as *chica* and *juba*. The most popular was the *kalinda* (or *calenda*), a
courtship dance found throughout the Caribbean, particularly on French-
speaking islands. *Kalinda* is derived from *calends*, the Roman New Year
mid-winter festival, from which we get the word "calendar." It was roughly
equivalent to modern New Year celebrations, but in time, the dances came to
be performed at any time of year. The *kalinda* dance itself is derived from
Guinean dances: a circle is formed by the singers/spectators, with a second
circle of dancers inside, and the drummers at the center. A lead singer—
chanté—improvises a song, and the assembly claps and sings in response.
Dancing couples perform elaborate twirling steps, which involve coming in
close contact, kissing, and touching legs. In 1698, the traveling priest Père
Labat described the *kalinda* as "dishonest, lascivious and indecent," in contrast
to the more wholesome minuets he espoused.

Bélé   The Martinican *bélé* (*bel air*—"good countenance") has its origins in
slave work songs performed in the fields. In time, it became an ensemble production that includes the lead singer (*chanté*), chorus-members (*répondè*),
dancers (*dansè*), as well as the *tanbouyé* drummer straddling his *bélé* drum and
the obligatory *ti-bwa* player (*bwatè*) behind him. *Bélé*'s basic framework is a
call-and-response song, with the *chanté* singing in a nasal voice, answered by
the *répondè* in quick rhythm and with careful coordination. During slavery times,
bélé songs had important communication functions, sung in Creole, which
plantation owners could not understand. Today, they typically speak of love,
death, or other events of everyday life. The dances are carefully choreographed,
with set steps and movements. The entire production revolves around the
drumming, which determines the sequence of steps and the unfolding of the
dance. The *ti-bwa* marks the basic rhythm, which all must follow. Modern *bélé*
organizations and schools perform *swaré bélé* ("*bélé* evenings"), joyful get-togethers that have become very popular in Martinique. They are also sometimes performed for funeral rites. Tourist-oriented, non-participatory *bélé*
presentations can be seen in the luxury hotels of the capital Fort-de-France.

> **Recommended Listening:** "Malavwa" by Florent Baratini, from the CD
> *Caribbean Voyage: The French Antilles: We Will Play Love Tonight.*

Gwo ka   Similar to the Martinican *bélé* is the Guadeloupan *gwo ka* ("large
drum"), a musical style performed by a drum ensemble of the same name. It
features a master drummer called *maké* (*marqueur*—"leader"), who improvises

complex polyrhythms on an upright high-pitched drum. The *maké* is accompanied by one or more supporting drums called *boula*, which are short and stocky, and played in the manner of the *bélé* drum, with the drummer sitting on it and controlling the pitch with his heel, and complemented by the *ti-bwa*. Like the Martinican *swaré bélé*, Guadeloupan musicians gather in communal get-togethers called *swaré léwòz* (*soirées les rose*—"rose evenings"), often in rural settings. These joyful occasions include drumming, dancing, and call-and-response singing, with musicians and spectators forming a circle and solo dancers performing within. *Gwo ka* includes seven traditional rhythms called *léwòz* (incantation rhythms), *graj* (food production), *woulé* (work song), *toumblak* (love and joy), *padjanbèl* (slave work song), *menndé* (carnival song), and *kaladja* (mourning and funeral wakes). All have many local variations. In recent years, a style has emerged that mixes elements of *gwo ka* and *zouk*, called *gwo ka moderne*, with added percussion and electric instruments.

> **Recommended Listening:** "Soulajé Do-A Katalina" recorded by Alan Lomax, from the CD *Caribbean Voyage: The French Antilles: We Will Play Love Tonight*.

Both Martinique and Guadeloupe have martial arts, wrestling, and stick-fighting traditions, not unlike Brazilian *capoeira*. The most prominent are *damié*, *ladija*, *sauvé-vaillant*, *bénadem*, *chatoux*, and *koévalin*. Once violent fighting bouts that took place during weekend celebrations, they have now mostly become stylized dances. The audience forms a circle called *lawonn* (*la ronde*) in which the fighters/dancers meet. Energy and excitement are provided by improvised drumming, which at first mimics and then commands the actions of the fighters, ultimately reaching a frenetic pace.

> **Recommended Listening:** "Robè Machine" by Florent Baratini, from the CD *Caribbean Voyage: The French Antilles: We Will Play Love Tonight*.

EUROPEAN-DERIVED DANCES French plantation owners, nostalgic for the homeland, often imported dances such as the English contra-dance, the Polish mazurka, and the German polka and waltz, which then became popular in their ballrooms and salons. They were typically accompanied by small orchestras made up of slaves or former slaves. After the ball, the musicians would take the music they learned in the White salons and make it their own, performing it at their get-togethers, now infused with their complex rhythms and African instrumentations. French authorities, always suspicious of slave drums and drumming, encouraged these European dances, though they frowned upon their "Africanization." As with the Cuban *danzón*, the Brazilian *chorro*, and others, the dances left the high-society ballrooms behind and became popular dances performed in rural settings, where they would continue to thrive long after the elite had moved on to other styles.

Perhaps the most famous Native of Martinique was Josephine Beauharnais, who in 1796 married Napoleon Bonaparte and became empress of France. As a result of this union, the island in the 1790s and early 1800s reached an unprecedented level of style and sophistication. Martinique became the "in" place to be, and Parisian fashions came to be greatly influenced by the island. One of these fashions dictated that the waist in women's clothing should be worn high, accentuating the bosom. As a result, a type of contra-dance emerged called the **haute-taille** ("high-waist"), which became very popular on the island. Another popular dance was the waltz, which now became the **valse créole**, played with the traditional string and wind orchestra, either in standard triple meter or, more rarely, duple meter. In the 1830s, the mazurka made its way to the French Antilles where it became the **mazouk**, though the intricate steps of the European version were modified considerably. Similarly, the English contra-dance became the **quadrille** (or *kwadril*), a stylized formal dance for four couples similar to the square dance found in the United States. *Quadrilles* are typically in duple meter, and in formal balls usually alternate with triple-meter *valses*. They were originally played with piano and violins, but as they became rural Black dances, other instruments were added, notably the accordion, the *tanbou d'bas* ("bass drum") and *ti tanbou* ("small drum"), as well as various percussion instruments including maracas, *chacha* shaker, and triangles. A prompter called *kommandé* called the dance figures in French or Creole, often improvising moves and interjecting colorful routines. There are traditionally five dance figures, with fanciful names such as *l'entrée* ("entrance"), *le pantalon* ("trousers"), *l'été* ("summertime"), and *la poule* ("hen"). The caller of *quadrilles* and *haute-tailles* eventually fell out of fashion, replaced by standard verse-and-refrain songs that were

A 19th-Century Afro-Caribbean Dance from the Island of Dominica.

humorous and satirical in nature. Today, formal *quadrilles* still take place at events called *balakadri* ("quadrille balls"), while informal ones are called *kout kadri* ("quadrille stroke").

Another important dance which alternated with the staid waltzes and mazurkas at these events was the lively **biguine**, a syncopated dance in duple meter that emerged in Martinique at the end of the eighteenth century. The *biguine* was played informally in White salons by string and piano chamber ensembles and at formal balls by string and wind orchestras, including prominent roles for the clarinet and trombone. It also found its way to the slave quarters, where it was infused with *bélé* rhythms and instruments. By the nineteenth century, it became popular in Saint Pierre, the former capital of Martinique in the northern part of the island, which was destroyed by the eruption of Mount Pelé in 1902. The church authorities took the disaster as a sign from God and were quick to blame the raucous dance, among others. The ban was mostly unsuccessful, and the *biguine*'s popularity continued to grow. In the 1920s, it was infused with the syncopated rhythms and instrumentation of Dixieland jazz: banjos, saxophones, clarinets, pianos, guitars, and drum sets. *Biguines* also began appearing at carnival celebrations.

The most important twentieth-century proponent of French Antillean dance music was the clarinetist Alexandre Stellio, whose orchestra included Ernest Léardée and Archange Saint-Hilaire, and the singer and composer Léona "Strella" Gabriel. In 1931, Stellio's orchestra went to Paris for the Colonial and International Exposition and presented the Caribbean *valses créoles*, *mazouks*, and *biguines*. The latter, in particular, met with instant success and popularity, which soon expanded to the United States and much of the rest of the world. In 1935, the U.S. composer Cole Porter wrote his famous song "Begin the Beguine" for the Broadway show *Jubilee*, though its similarity to the Caribbean dance is tenuous at best. Back on the islands, the *biguine* remained a popular dance for the next few decades, until the 1950s when Haitian *konpa* replaced it in popularity. As with virtually every Caribbean genre, many hybridizations of the *biguine* have appeared, infused with various elements from jazz and Cuban music to reggae and commercial pop. Recently, a more modernized version called *biguine moderne* has emerged, influenced by other styles such as *zouk* and reggae.

Other folk styles include the Martinican **chouval bwa** (*cheval de bois*— "wooden horse"), originally played by small orchestras in the center of hand-pushed merry-go-rounds, usually during feast-day celebrations. Spectators brought their children to ride the wooden horses and hear the hypnotizing music. Traditionally, the orchestra consisted of guitars, saxophones, and accordions. Subsequently, flutes and percussion were added, including triangles and *chacha* shakers. *Chouval Bwa* is often in fast triple meter, imitating the galloping horses of the merry-go-round. The intricate rhythm is played by a barrel-shaped, two-headed drum called *tanbou dé bonda* of likely Yoruba origin and not unlike the Cuban *bata* drums. This drum is played by both a *tambouyé* and a *ti-bwa* player. The style has been very influential and was a major contributor to the development of *zouk*. The most celebrated *Chouval Bwa* artist in recent years has been the Martinique musician André (Dédé) Saint-Prix. *Chanté a véyé* (*chants de veillées*) are funeral wake songs in which singers recite poems and stories in honor of the recently deceased, accompanied by clapping and sometimes drumming. These songs take place either on the evening of the death, or, following Catholic tradition, eleven days later. They can often last all night.

Recommended Listening:

- Valse Créole: "Oh! Douce Martinique" by Alexandre Stellio, from the CD *Intégrale, 1929–1931*.
- Valse Créole: "Valse" (Guadeloupe) and "Fleur des Antilles" (Martinique) recorded by Alan Lomax, from the CD *Caribbean Voyage: The French Antilles: We Will Play Love Tonight*.
- Mazouk: "Yaya Moin Ni L'Agent" by Alexandre Stellio, from the CD *Intégrale, 1929–1931*.
- Quadrille: "Ti-Anne" by Francius Laurence, from the CD *Caribbean Voyage: Martinique: Cane Fields and City Streets*.
- Quadrille: "Quadrille" recorded by Alan Lomax, from the CD *Caribbean Voyage: the French Antilles: We Will Play Love Tonight*.
- Haute-Taille: "Vous me faites plaisir" by Reynoir Casimir, from the CD *Quadrille of Guadeloupe*.
- Biguine: "Serpent maigre" by Alexandre Stellio, from the CD *Intégrale, 1929–1931*.
- Biguine: "Jilo Fout ou Jalou" recorded by Alan Lomax, from the CD *Caribbean Voyage: The French Antilles: We Will Play Love Tonight*.
- Biguine: "Mettez I Déhrô" by Apphonso et Son Orchestre Typique Antillais, from the CD *Au Bal Antillais: Franco Creole Biguinesf From Martinique*.
- Biguine: "Ti Paul" by Loulou Boislaville, from the CD *Caribbean Voyage: Martinique: Cane Fields and City Streets*.
- Biguine Moderne: "Parfum des îles" by Kali, from the CD *Putumayo Presents: French Caribbean*.
- Chouval Bwa: "Balanséy Lala" by Dédé Saint-Prix, from the CD *Chouval bwa sans frontières*.
- Chanté a véyé: "Bo! I Pati" (Guadeloupe) and "Ti Lisyen" (Martinique) recorded by Alan Lomax, from the CD *Caribbean Voyage: The French Antilles: We Will Play Love Tonight*.

CARNIVAL   As in most countries with a strong Catholic heritage, Haiti, Martinique, and Guadeloupe traditionally had a vibrant Mardi Gras season. In recent years, the *karnaval* in Haiti has declined in popularity, supplanted by the *rará* celebrations that begin after Ash Wednesday. It is mostly relegated to Port-au-Prince, where one nonetheless still finds exuberant parades with masked revelers and impressive floats. Conversely, in Martinique and Guadeloupe, Mardi Gras celebrations are more prevalent and energetic. Parade organization and marching ensembles called *Groups a pied* ("walking groups") consist of dozens or even hundreds of percussionists, brass players, and dancers. Like the Brazilian *escolas da samba*, they are social organizations closely associated with specific neighborhoods. Various *vidés* (parades) occur on the islands, including *Gand Vidé* ("large parade") and the colorful *Vidé tout koulè* ("parade of all colors"). They are typically spectacular affairs with lively *biguine*-style music and extravagant costumes. The Guadeloupan tradition *Mas a Saint-Jean* has become very popular, particularly with the rhythms of the group Akiyo. In Martinique, everything revolves around Le Roi Vaval—the King of carnival. On the Saturday before Mardi Gras, the Queen of carnival is elected among representatives from the entire island. On Sunday, King Vaval is introduced as a large wooden effigy. On Monday, the Burlesque Wedding Parade includes a mock wedding between the King and Queen, with men and women dressing in outrageous costumes of the opposite gender. On Mardi Gras proper, the Red Devil Parade takes place, with everyone dressing as a Devil—or at least in red—and engaging in exciting and exotic dancing, jumping, and singing. The culmination of Martinican carnival is not on Mardi Gras but on Ash Wednesday, a custom common throughout the French Caribbean. The dying King Vaval makes his funeral procession, parading through the streets, with costumed revelers following him through the city, dressed in Black and White. Rum flows freely, and the streets are filled with dancers. A funeral pyre is built, and at dusk, Vaval's effigy is set aflame in a huge bonfire, to the joyful cries of "*Vaval mô, vaval mô*" ("Carnival is dead") and "*Vaval pa quitté nou*" ("Carnival, do not leave us"). The revelry continues through the night, finally bringing an end to the carnival season.

Recommended Listening: "Déboul" by Akiyo, from the CD *Mouvman*.

ZOUK Because Haiti and the French Antilles share similar African roots and Creole languages, many of the islands' styles cross-pollinated and influenced each other. Starting in the 1950s, waves of Haitian immigrants brought styles such as *compas* and *kadans* to Martinique and Guadeloupe. These styles quickly came to dominate the islands, and local musicians began to compose and perform their own versions. The eventual result was a style that would put Martinique and Guadeloupe on the musical world map: *zouk*, the French Antilles's answer to Trinidadian soca. Named for an African term for a social gathering, *zouk* has at its roots the African rhythms of *bélé* and *gwo ka*, as well as the European-based dances like the *quadrille, buiguine*, and *mazouk*. It emerged in the early 1980s, most prominently with the group Kassav, with hits such as "Soleil" ("Sun") and "Zouk-La-Se Sel Medikaman Nou Ni" ("Zouk Is the Only Medicine We Know"), and quickly became the most popular style on the islands. Its joyful party atmosphere and hot dance beat are drawn from local Mardi Gras celebrations, but also from the syncopated bass lines of Trinidadian calypso, Jamaican reggae, and *cadence-lypso* from Dominica. Its traditional rhythms also incorporate Dominican merengue, Haitian *konpa*, Cuban salsa, and Congolese *soukous*. Though it is often played with traditional drums, *ti-bwa*, and *chacha* shakers, a great amount of energy is provided by Western instruments such as keyboards, French horns, electric guitars, and bass.

Zouk has become an important style not only in the French Antilles and within the Caribbean itself, but worldwide, including in Europe and the United States. Perhaps more importantly, the African-based music has gone full circle and returned to Africa, where it has been very influential on the popular music. Yet because of its meteoric rise in popularity, many of the traditional Martinican and Guadeloupan styles have been eclipsed, and even the process of music making has been altered. Folksy *quadrille* balls and traditional *swaré bélés* have often been replaced by spectacular flashy performances on par with North American rock concerts, emphasizing lighting, choreography, visuals, and costumes, as well as high-tech commercial studio recordings, often guided by marketing considerations. Kassav remains the premiere *zouk* band, but other important proponents include Les Aiglons, Malavoi, and Kali, as well as Haitian bands such as Zin and Top Vice.

> **Recommended Listening:** "Kaye Mamman" and "Zouk-La-Se Sel Medikaman Nou Ni" by Kassav, from the CD *The Best of Kassav*.

> **Recommended Listening:** "L'Histoire du Zouk" by Kali, from the CD *Putumayo Presents: Caribbean Party*.

Zouk: "Zouk-La-Se Sel Medikaman Nou Ni"

Music and Lyrics: Jacob Desvarieux and Georges Decimus
Instrumentation: electric guitar, keyboards
Notes: This 1985 recording by the group Kassav was one of the first zouk songs to gain worldwide popularity. The lyrics are in French Creole from Martinique and Guadeloupe (different from that of Haiti). Though African drums have been replaced with guitars, synthesizers, and drum machines, elements of Afro-Caribbean music remain: the repeating ostinato patterns, the call-and-response singing, and the infectious dance beat derived from carnival dancing.

Kijan zot fé? M'pa ka konpran'n!	*How do you do it? I don't understand!*
Zot ka viv' kon si pa ni pwoblém.	*You live as if there were no problems.*
Poutan zot sav' lavi la réd.	*And yet you know that life is hard.*
Kijan zot fé pou pé sa kenbé?	*How are you able to stand it?*

Chorus

Zouk la sé sel médikaman nou ni.	*Zouk is the only medicine we need.*
(Sa kon sa.)	*(That's the way it is.)*
M'pa té konnet sécré lasa.	*I don't know your secret.*
Ban mwen plan la p'mwen pé sa konpran'n.	*Tell me the plan so I can understand.*
Ban mwen plan la m'poko sézi'i.	*Tell me the plan, I still don't get it.*
Si janmé on jou mwen tonbé malad . . .	*If ever some day I get sick . . .*
Si sé sa mwen an nou zouké.	*If that's the case, let us go play zouk.*
Mi'i kon sa, Mi'i kon sa,	*That's the way, That's the way,*
An malad.	*I am sick.*

CONTEMPORARY TRENDS Today, the music of Haiti, Martinique, and Guadeloupe continues to explore new territory. Musicians are looking to the islands' rich roots for sources of inspiration, combining folk elements like the *biguine* with a modern popular language and foreign elements such as jazz and Jamaican raggamuffin. In Haiti, vodou and *rará* have inspired jazz and rap styles, including a recent roots music phenomenon called *racine* (or *rasin*). Unlike the carefree party music of *zouk* and *compas*, *racine* often adopts a seriousness of purpose that combines traditional acoustic sound with social and progressive political causes. One of the most prominent *racine* groups is Boukman Eksperyans, which incorporates reggae, jazz, carnival, and vodou rhythms into its particular brand of music. In 1991, their hit "Ke-M Pa Sote" ("I am Not Afraid") played an important part in mobilizing the Haitian population for the first free elections after the fall of the Duvalier dictatorship. Another important proponent of Haitian pop music is Eméline Michel, nicknamed the "Haitian Queen of Creole Song." Her eclectic hits also combine traditional rhythms with *compas* and jazz.

> **Recommended Listening:** "Ke-M Pa Sote" by Boukman Eksperyans, from the CD Vodou *Adjae.*

> **Recommended Listening:** "Baron" by Boukman Eksperyans from the CD *Rough Guide to the Music of Haiti.*

> **Recommended Listening:** "Plezi Mize" by Eméline Michel, from the CD *Eméline Michel: The Very Best.*

As everywhere in the African Diaspora, rap and hip-hop have had an important presence in the French Caribbean, particularly in that there already existed various storytelling traditions that lent themselves well to the style. Prominent among these is the Martinican *kont* (*comte*—"story") whose free-style melodious speech and lyric virtuosity foreshadowed by many decades rap's urban beat. *Kont* includes an impressive vocal percussion effect called *bouladjel* (mouth drumming). Haitian rap has also made important inroads, particularly with its attractive brand that incorporates reggae and *zouk*. The most prominent hip-hop artist to emerge from Haiti is Wyclef Jean, whose band The Fugees play an eclectic style that reflects the multifaceted traditions of his native island. In Martinique and Guadeloupe, rap songs with Creole lyrics are often infused with *bélé* drumming, syncopated reggae beats, and the ever-present *ti-bwa*. As everywhere, Creole rap is concerned with social and political issues, and is an important signifier of Black identity.

> **Recommended Listening:** "Jean Mano di 'Bouwo Dèhyè-Mwen Alé'" by Malcousu Florius, from the CD *Caribbean Voyage: Martinique: Cane Fields and City Streets.*

> **Recommended Listening:** "Ti Chans (Pou Ayiti)" by Masters of Haiti, from the CD *Rough Guide to the Music of Haiti.*

THE GARÍFUNA

One of the Caribbean styles that has achieved great popularity in recent years is not actually found in the Caribbean Sea, but rather on the coast of Central America. The Garífuna are an important ethnic group whose music has been very influential throughout the region. According to popular myth, the Garífuna originated when two slave ships from Nigeria were grounded off the island of St. Vincent in 1635. The survivors swam ashore where they were adopted and protected by the local Carib tribe. The European slave runners, Natives and Africans subsequently intermingled, resulting in a new ethnic group called *Garinagu* or, more commonly, *Garífuna*. (They are also known as the "Black Caribs.") They were joined by escaped slaves from neighboring islands such as St. Lucia and Grenada, and for more than a century and a half formed an independent, self-sufficient mixed community. In the late eighteenth century, Britain, unhappy with the Garífuna's tradition of welcoming escaped slaves, began a campaign to conquer St. Vincent. After years of conflict, the Garífuna were finally defeated and in 1797 were forcibly removed to the Bay Islands off the coast of Honduras. From there, they crossed over to the mainland and populated a large section of the Caribbean coast of Central America.

The Garífuna are one of the few syncretic groups in the Americas that have virtually no European cultural influence, as well as the only Afro-American group whose ancestors were never slaves. They have inherited numerous West African traditions, transmitted uninterrupted to the present day. Key to Garífuna culture is the sense of community that pervades their society. Personal successes, failures, problems, and achievements are shared by the entire community, and often entire villages will come to the aid of an individual. Their language is a mixture of Carib and African dialects, though over the centuries it acquired some French, Spanish, and English. Today, there are an estimated 200,000 Garífuna spread out over the Caribbean coasts of Belize, Guatemala, Honduras, and Nicaragua, as well as the Bay Islands they've occupied since 1797. Though the Garífuna have traditionally been rural dwellers, many have recently sought opportunity in urban areas, and some have also emigrated to the United States, where they maintain an important cultural presence.

Garífuna Music

Garífuna drums, called *garawon* (or *garaju*), are made from hardwoods and deer skin and often have wires stretched over the heads to provide a distorting buzzing effect, much like a snare drum. The traditional ensemble consists of three drummers: the *garawon primera* ("first" or lead drum) plays intricate improvisations over the set patterns played by the *segunda* ("second"), while the *tercera* ("third") provides a continuous bass. Shakers called *sinsiras* accompany the drummers, as do scrapers, *claves*, *weiwintu* (conch shells), and turtle shells, all instruments of Caribbean origin.

The Garífuna religion melds African, Native, and, to a lesser extent, Catholic elements in elaborate rituals that always include drumming and dancing. The festivities revolve around the evocation of spirits and ancestors, whose souls are always present, giving guidance, advice, and protection, and who thus must be cared for and honored with specific rituals. Funeral celebrations called *Beluria* are important events involving the entire community, since mourning is communal, not individual. *Beluria* rituals last nine days during which the still-living soul of the deceased enters the spiritual world even as the lifeless body is prepared for burial. Bereaved women ambulate through the village lamenting the departure of the deceased, accompanied by drummers. The honoring continues indefinitely after the funeral.

Amuyadahani ("bathing of the ancestors") is an ancestral rite during which troubled spirits return to ask for help and are then cleansed by the living. A makeshift grave is dug and a gourd representing the spirit is washed with various natural substances. Another ritual is *chuga*, during which prayer, food, and refreshments are provided for restless souls. The most prominent ancestral ceremony is *aduguruhani* ("the feasting of the ancestors"), often just shortened to *dugu*. It is an elaborate healing ritual designed to cure both physical illnesses that afflict individuals and social problems that plague an entire community. Preparations for *dugu* can last up to a year and involve several families. Shaman healers called *buyae* contact the deceased; food and drink offerings are made; drumming, singing, and dances such as the *hunguhungu* follow and eventually reach a fever pitch. Female dancers achieve a frenzied state and become possessed by the ancestral spirits who then partake of the festivities. After a while—*dugu* ceremonies can last from three days to up to several weeks—the ancestors are satisfied, and the ailments that afflicted the community, whether physical or social, have been alleviated.

As in other parts of the African Diaspora, Garífuna religious music engendered secular styles that eventually surpassed it. The *charikaw* is a secular dance that recreates a hunt in pantomime. In the suggestive *chumba*, women display their most attractive—and erotic—features, to counter the humiliation traditionally inflicted on them by Europeans. The *parranda* is a widespread, boisterous dance in duple meter that combines traditional drumming with Spanish guitars. The *wanaragua* is a Christmas-season dance related to the Jamaican *jonkonnu*, during which large masks are worn and colorful scenes are pantomimed, recreating for example working conditions on plantations or a famous battle during which women disguised as warriors defeated the Spaniards. Work songs are performed in call-and-response form without instrumental accompaniment and have a nasal quality that some have attributed to the Garífuna's Native practices. Usually composed by women, they embrace a female point of view, speaking for example of family issues, gender-based injustice, pointed social commentary, and the unfaithfulness and betrayal of men. Examples include *Eremwu Eu* and *Abaimajani*, sung by women preparing cassava bread, while the men sing *Laremuna Wadauman* when they are engaged in communal tasks.

But the most prominent secular style is *punta*, a suggestive courtship dance based on African fertility rites. The music is in duple or $\frac{6}{8}$ meter, accompanied by the traditional *garawon* drums, *sinsira* shakers, and conch shells. The *primera* drum improvises over the repeating duple-meter patterns of the *segunda*, and there is continuous dialogue between dancers and drummers. *Punta* is a sexually charged re-creation of a cock-and-hen dance, with couples trying to outdance each other. The upper body remains motionless while the lower body exhibits sharp hip movements, pelvic thrusts, and shaking buttocks, an element found in many West African dances.

One of the most important proponents of traditional Garífuna music is Aurelio Martinez, who in 1989 formed the group Lita Ariran. As a child, Martinez learned to drum in Garífuna rituals in a small fishing village in Honduras. Now an international star, he conveys through his music the sacred and secular character of Garifuna culture with virtuosic drumming and a powerfully expressive vocal style. Others proponents include Lugua Ceteño and the band Lanigi Mua, both from Honduras, and the Guatemalan group Baruda.

> **Recommended Listening:** "Naguara" by Andy Palacio, "Lugua Hama Lurudu" by Lugua Ceteño and "Wabouga" by Lincoln Lewis and the Original Turtle Shell Band, from the CD *The Rough Guide to the Music of Central America*.
>
> **Recommended Listening:** "Came Badugey Un" by Baruda and "Madulun" by Lanigi Mua, from the CD *Music from Honduras, Vol. 2*.
>
> **Recommended Listening:** "Bugudura Wuritu" and "Africa" by Lita Ariran, from the CD *Honduras: Songs of the Garífuna*.
>
> **Recommended Listening:** Good compilations of traditional Garífuna styles include:
>
> - *Garífuna Music: Field Recordings from Belize.*
> - *Music from Guatemala, Vol. 2: Garífuna Music*
> - *Paranda: Africa in Central America.*
> - *The Spirit Cries: Music Of the Rain Forests Of South America and the Caribbean.*

CDII, Track 4: *Punta*: "Santo Negro"

Music and Lyrics: Traditional, arranged by Aurelio Martinez and Ivan Duran
Instrumentation: guitar, bass, *garawon* drums, turtle shells, *sinsira* shakers, *güiro*, *clave*
Notes: Aurelio Martinez's "Santo Negro" ("Black saint") is in the Garífuna language and combines traditional singing and drumming with modern pop features. It opens with call-and-response singing accompanied only by a *clave* playing the familiar Caribbean pattern. At 1:19, the other instruments enter, highlighted by complex polyrhythms and the distinctive buzzing sound of the *garawon* drums.

Liru laludun weyo,	*How sadly the sun sets.*
Lubuidun lafuachu hate hae,	*How lovely the moon rises,*
Liru laludun weyo.	*How sadly the sun sets.*
Ñudunugua hamuga, lidon lubengui baba e.	*I wish I could go to my father's fishing spot.*
Gañen nugyamee, aba nisandu wuritu nibugaña,	*I will buy myself a Black statue,*
Roga nuuamee, tuagu nuwarugumania e,	*I will pray for my soul,*
Owa liroulan yadina ubao hae.	*Today, I am the carriage for the people.*

Punta Rock

Punta rock is *punta*'s modern electric equivalent, a style that has placed the Garífuna squarely on the international popular music map. There is some dispute as to the origins of *punta rock*. Some claim it emerged when Garífuna immigrants in New York first heard modern styles such as rock and rhythm and blues, and Caribbean styles such as soca, calypso, and reggae. Others point to the Honduran group Góbana as the creator of the style. Still others claim *punta rock* was developed in Belize in the late 1970s by Pen Cayetano, who sought to create a style that would appeal to Garífuna youth without sacrificing their heritage. Cayetano combined the *punta* folk dance with electric guitars and a more upbeat tempo and developed an innovative percussion section based not only on Garífuna drumming but also on turtle shells of various sizes. In 1979, he formed the first *punta rock* band, the Turtle Shell Band, and began performing at local clubs and community parties called *roadblocks,* then in larger venues across Belize.

Whatever its origins, *punta rock* (often just called *punta*, despite the risk of confusion with its rural folk precursor) has become the most popular Garífuna style, developing into a national phenomenon in Belize and Honduras. Much of its lyrical content, particularly that of Pen Cayetano, addresses the cultural and economic marginalization of the Garífuna, and of Belizeans and Hondurans in general, and the style has helped dissolve Mestizo prejudice. Sung in the Garífuna language, *punta rock* provides a strong sense of pride and identity and seeks to preserve and promote awareness of Garífuna culture, which until recently had been virtually unknown to the rest of the world.

Several *punta rock* musicians have explored the possibilities of the style, adding instruments such as piano, synthesizers, bass guitars, and wind instruments, and providing more harmonic sophistication. Drum sets and drum machines usually complement—and sometimes replace—the *Garawon* drums. Inevitably, *punta rock* has melded with the music of other cultures, becoming infused with elements of jazz, salsa, reggae, soca, and harder-edged rock. It has also developed regional variations, with Belizean style differing significantly from those emerging in Honduras and Guatemala. But one element that has remained constant in *punta rock* is the erotic, sensual dancing that has its origins in Garífuna dances such as *chumba* and *punta*.

Punta rock was first introduced to the outside world when the Turtle Shell Band performed at the New Orleans Jazz and Heritage Festival in 1983. After the compilation album *Punta Rockers* was released in 1987, it was firmly established in Central American and Caribbean consciousness, and became something of an international sensation throughout Latin America and the United States. In Belize, Andy Palacio, Jursino Cayetano, and Peter "Titiman" Flores have become important proponents of the style, along with the Turtle Shell Band. In Honduras, Aurelio Martinez, Banda Blanca, Fuerza Garífuna, and Chico Ramos have been at the forefront of the *punta* and *punta rock* movement. Guatemalan musicians include Sofia Blanco and the groups Suamen and Ugandani. Meanwhile, *punta rock* has become an important style in the United States, with groups such as Garífuna Kids and Garífuna Boyz.

Recommended Listening: "Balandria" by Jursino Cayetano, "Lamiselu" by Andy Palacio, and "Alaporio" by Titiman Flores, from the CD *The Rough Guide to the Music of Central America*.

Recommended Listening: "Milagrosa" and "Luweyuri Waguyo" by Fuerza Garífuna, from the CD *Music from Honduras, Vol. 2*.

6

Brazil

CHAPTER SUMMARY

Introduction
- Historical Overview
- *Saudade*
- Religious Syncretism

The Roots of Brazilian Music
- Brazilian Musical Instruments
- Afro-Brazilian Folk Dances
- *Capoeira*

Carnival
- History of Brazilian Carnival
- *Samba*
- The *Escolas de Samba*
- Carnival Today

The Northeast
- *Baião* and *Fossa*
- *Forro*
- Other Rural Styles

Musica Popular Brasileira
- *Modinha, Lundu,* and *Maxixe*
- *Choro*
- The Golden Age of *Musica Popular Brasileira*
- The *Bossa Nova* Phenomenon
- After the *Bossa Nova*
- *Tropicália*
- The Post-*Tropicália* Explosion

INTRODUCTION

Almost everything about Brazil, and its music in particular, is extremely diverse. It is the largest country in Latin America—the fifth largest in the world—and is home to 170 million people. It borders on every country in South America except Ecuador and Chile and has advantageous natural features such as ports, rivers, and rich natural resources. It remains the largest producer of coffee and sugar, has important cocoa and tobacco crops, and enjoys a robust economy based on industry, agriculture, and tourism. It contains some of the most populated and sophisticated cities in the world as well as Amazonian Native groups who have had little contact with the outside world. Its massive urban centers, such as São Paulo, Santos, Recife, and Rio de Janeiro, contain a diversity of culture, race, social conditions, religion, and music that is unmatched anywhere in Latin America. Because there are hundreds of folk, classical, and popular musical styles in Brazil, this chapter only touches on some of the principal ones, omitting by necessity many worthy musical traditions.

Historical Overview

Unlike the territories of Mexico and Peru, no dominating civilizations emerged in what is now Brazil before the arrival of the Europeans. Instead, the land was populated by millions of semi-nomadic hunter-gatherers, divided into many language groups, including the Gé of the eastern coast and central plateau, the western Pano tribes, and the Caribs of northern Brazil and Arawaks of the Amazon River basin, both related to tribes in the Caribbean and Central America. The period of unprecedented European exploration in the fifteenth century was led by the Portuguese, who had a virtual monopoly on the water routes along the coast of Africa to India and China. After Columbus landed in America, Portugal, determined to protect its interests, demanded its share of the newly discovered lands. In 1494, Spain and Portugal signed the Treaty of Tordesillas, which established an imaginary line running north/south 1,770 kilometers west of the Cape Verde islands. Spain would have possession of unclaimed territory west of the line, while eastern lands would go to Portugal. No one knew, of course, how much land was actually in question. In the end, Spain got the larger portion, though for the next century, the Portuguese continuously attempted to move the Brazilian border farther west into Spanish territory. The first European to actually set foot in Brazil was the Spanish navigator Vicente Yáñez Pinzón, who did so on January 26, 1500. The following April, the Portuguese Pedro Álvares Cabral formally claimed the land for Portugal. A year later, the Italian Amerigo Vespucci explored the coast, naming many of the landmarks he encountered, including the bay he named Rio de Janeiro ("January River"). When he returned to Portugal, Vespucci carried with him samples of the timber resources of the coastal forests, including the valuable brasilwood. As a result, the new land was to be called Brazil. (Brazil is spelled with a "z" in English, with an "s" in Portuguese and Spanish.)

Portuguese colonization quickly followed, with a central government and an extensive administrative bureaucracy. In 1554, São Paulo was founded in the south, and in 1567 the city of Rio de Janeiro was established on the bay of the same name. At first, the Portuguese relied on the Natives to work their mines and plantations, but soon these were almost completely annihilated, mostly by disease. Starting in 1570, and over the course of the next three centuries, more than 3.5 million Africans were brought to Brazil to provide free labor to the plantation owners. As a result, almost half of modern Brazilians are Black or Mulatto. Brazil's colonial economy was based on the production of wood and forest products, sugar, tobacco, cotton, coffee, and, later, rubber, gold, and precious gems. In particular, the region of Minas Gerais yielded many rich mineral deposits, including gold and diamonds. By the 1600s, expansion began towards the south and into the interior, particularly by Jesuit missionaries who began their work in the Amazon River valley. The Jesuits led a mostly successful fight to prevent the enslavement of the Natives who lived in the rainforest, but because of their growing influence and economic power, the Jesuits were expelled from the entire American continent in 1767.

Recommended Viewing: For a vivid depiction of the Jesuit presence in the Amazonian forest, see the 1986 film *The Mission*, which also contains a remarkable music score.

In 1808, after Napoleon Bonaparte had invaded Portugal, the Portuguese king Dom João VI fled to Brazil with his court, and there reestablished the seat of the Portuguese government. In 1815, he declared Brazil a kingdom on equal footing with Portugal. In 1822, Dom João was restored to the Portuguese throne and left Brazil, leaving his son Pedro as regent. Portugal then attempted to return Brazil to its former status as a colony. Emboldened by the independence movement in neighboring Spanish colonies, Dom Pedro proclaimed Brazil's independence, declared its status as an empire and assumed the throne as emperor. His son, Dom Pedro II, reigned effectively for nearly 50 years, during which Brazil became modernized, the economy—which relied mainly on coffee, sugar, and rubber—grew rapidly, and the population expanded. In the second half of the century, parallel abolitionist and republican movements emerged. Brazil abolished the slave trade in 1853 and slavery itself in 1888, the last country in the world to do so. In 1889, Dom Pedro II was deposed, and a federal republic was proclaimed. A series of dictatorial regimes, and various periods of unrest and stability followed. In 1930, Getulio Vargas led a successful military coup against the government and seized absolute power as dictator, which he maintained on and off for the next quarter century. Democratic civilian rule was restored in 1954, only to be thwarted by yet another military coup in 1964. Meanwhile, the capital, seated in Rio de Janeiro since 1808, was moved to Brasilia in the interior, in an effort to decentralize the vast city. A civilian regime was restored again in 1985.

Today, one can find almost every lifestyle imaginable in Brazil, from chic urban neighborhoods of coastal cities to impenetrable rainforests in the interior, from tropical paradise beaches to endless shantytown slums, from harsh desert landscapes to charming historical towns such as Salvador de Bahia. Its most famous city, Rio de Janeiro is punctuated by the fabled natural splendor of its magnificent harbor and by famous landmarks such as Sugar Loaf Mountain, the statue of Christ the Redeemer overlooking the city, and the golden sunshine and sultry beaches of Ipanema and Copacabana. Yet it also has had its share of political and economic problems, having been plagued by hyperinflation, poverty, and a poor civil rights record for much of the twentieth century. Brazil has been on the brink of becoming an economic world power for decades without actually managing to do so. In many ways, Brazil remains a contradiction, a paradox of wealth and poverty: its urban mega-cities are home to some of the wealthiest and some of the poorest people in the hemisphere. The country's mostly White aristocracy inhabits rich, sophisticated neighborhoods while millions of poor Brazilians (Black, White, and Mulatto) eke out a daily living in immense shantytown slums called *favelas*. Brazilian life is also affected by its vast interior: Its territory includes more than half the Amazon rainforest, irrigated by a huge network of rivers and tributaries, at the center of which lies the mighty Amazon river, more than 2,000 miles long. One of the most important problems facing Brazil—and the world—is the deforestation of Amazonia. The ecosystem is home to countless plant and animal species, as well as 200,000 indigenous inhabitants who continue to depend on nature to preserve their traditional culture. The ongoing defoliation of the Brazilian rainforest, along with foreign infectious diseases, constantly threatens them with extinction.

Recommended Viewing: For a glimpse of the bleak life in the *favelas* of Rio de Janeiro, see the 2002 Brazilian film *Cidade de Deus*.

Saudade

Brazilians have a reputation—a stereotype, perhaps—for knowing how to have a good time with a combination of music, dance, sensuality, and soccer. This attitude surfaces particularly during the carnival season, which incorporates the greatest combination of music, revelry, costumes, and dancing in the world. Indeed, much of Brazil's musical life has historically revolved around carnival. An exotic, sensual, and carefree lifestyle, dotted by images of beautiful and scantily clad men and women, are part of the Brazilian myth, perhaps best illustrated by one of the country's most famous song, "Garota de Ipanema" ("Girl from Ipanema").

Conversely, and perhaps paradoxically, Portuguese and Brazilian culture is also colored by the concept of *saudade*, a Portuguese word that is hard to define, and which many claim is untranslatable. *Saudade* is a feeling akin to sorrow, homesickness, melancholy, nostalgia, or regret, and particularly refers to a constant feeling of longing or absence for something, someone, or someplace. It affected much of colonial culture, expressed in the sorrow of the wives and children of discoverers who left them behind, the longing and nostalgia the colonists felt for the home country few would ever see again, and the despair of the Black slaves and Native Brazilians who lamented their fate. Today, *saudade* permeates many Brazilians' worldview; their attitudes, dreams, and aspiration; their ideals about love and beauty; and especially their music. Perhaps it is best compared to "the blues" in the southern United States, though even that does not convey the meaning adequately. Thousands of songs have been written about *saudade*, notably Cesária Évora's "Sodade," which attempts to express the longing she has for her home.

> **Recommended Listening:** "Sodade" by Cesária Évora, from the CD *Sodade, Les plus belles mornas*.

Religious Syncretism

Like much of Latin America, Brazil has a strong Roman Catholic heritage, due mostly to the work of European missionaries, as well as to immigration by Portuguese—and later Italian and German—Catholics. More than 90 percent of Brazilians are Roman Catholic, making it the largest Catholic country in the world. And, once again, religious syncretism was instrumental in the development of Brazilian identity. Over the centuries, Catholicism blended with various African and Native religions to produce a hybrid religion and culture. Though the slave drivers and plantation owners could be as brutal as anywhere else on the continent, the Brazilian ruling class was relatively tolerant of the culture and religion of the subjugated Blacks and Natives. African religions were banned in theory by the Catholic Church, and any hint of slave autonomy was brutally suppressed, but in practice, many Afro-Brazilian rituals, particularly those related to music, were allowed to exist, even thrive.

As in much of the rest of the continent, slaves were brought from both Central Africa—Congo, Angola, and Mozambique—and West Africa—Togo, Benin, Ghana, Ivory Coast, and Nigeria. They came from different ethnic groups including the Bantu, Ewe, Fon, and Yoruba tribes. As a result, their language, culture, religious beliefs, and musical traditions were varied and diverse. Spread throughout Brazil, they eventually organized into brotherhoods based on ethnic origin called *irmandades*, not unlike the Cuban *cabildos*. Though formally Catholic in nature, these organizations provided opportunities for the preservation and development of African culture. Additionally, escaped slaves would take refuge in Native villages called *kilombos* where they would share their African religion with the local *pajés* (shamans) and in turn partake of the rich Native spiritual world, which included an intricate mythology and an advanced homeopathy based on vast knowledge of the forest. Native and African deities were compatible, since both cultures were polytheistic and, more importantly, both sets of spirits were intricately linked with nature. As a result of the officially sanctioned *irmandades* and the underground *kilombos*, Afro-Brazilian religions thrived, combining elements of European, African, and Native beliefs.

Eventually, highly individual cults emerged called *nações* ("nations"), whose ritual practices varied in language, deities, and musical characteristics. These *nações* numbered in the hundreds, with regional and local variations. For example, the *Ketu* nation in the Bahia region follows Yoruba rites, whereas the *Mina Jejé* nation in Maranhão follows Ewe and Fon rituals. These rites are similar to Afro-Caribbean religions such as vodou in Haiti and Santería in Cuba. Though they developed independently, they have a common origin in the ethnic tribes of West and Central Africa. Thus, Santería deities called *orishas*, derived from Yoruba mythology, are also represented in some Brazilian *nações*, now with the name *orixás*. Afro-Brazilian spirits are individually linked to specific elements in nature and have specific personal characteristics and idiosyncrasies. For example, *Yemanja*, the spirit goddess of motherhood and the ocean, is celebrated every New Year's Eve by dipping one's feet into the water. In most cases a supreme deity rules all others, for example the Yoruba *Olorún*. Afro-Brazilian religions also included important elements of Native spirituality such as *pajelança, catimbó*, and *tambor-de-mina*. As occurred in other parts of the continent, African and Native beliefs were hidden under a Christian veneer and thus thrived under the zealous eyes of the religious authorities. Afro-Brazilian spirits became associated with Christian deities, for example the Yoruba water-goddess *Nanan*, identified with the Catholic Saint Anne, while Jesus became identified with *Oxala*, the god of the sky and the universe. The most prominent and widespread Afro-Brazilian religion is *candomblé*, which originated in the state of Bahia, and in the twentieth century expanded to most parts of Brazil, including Rio de Janeiro. *Candomblé* literally refers to a dance in honor of the spirits, and the ritual is centered on a public banquet that takes over a week to prepare. Food is a major part of the ritual, which begins in the evening and often continues until dawn. Animals are sacrificed; priestesses perform divinations with *jogo de búzios* (cowry shells) and invoke the spirits, who then take over the body, placing it into a deep trance.

Many Afro-Brazilian religions were banned in the nineteenth century, and though there was a resurgence in the twentieth century, open worship was not allowed until the 1970s. That resurgence included the development of a new religion called *umbanda*, which melded Afro-Brazilian rituals with European spiritism and philosophy and which was quickly embraced by the society elite in Rio de Janeiro. *Candomblé* and other Afro-Brazilian beliefs are practiced regularly by about two million Brazilians from all social classes, though up to fifty million people of other faiths occasionally participate. *Candomblé* is so widespread that its ceremonies and its music are part of everyday life. Like Cuban Santería and Haitian vodou, the rituals have been co-opted by the tourism industry, and slick, glossy ceremonies are often performed for wide-eyed tourists in search of an exotic thrill. Recent controversies and debates have emerged on whether to "de-syncretize" Afro-Brazilian religions, in essence removing the Christian elements and restoring them to their African purity.

CDII, Track 5: *Candomblé* Ritual: "Aluja de Zangó Aira"

Music and Lyrics: Traditional
Instrumentation: three *atabaque* drums, *agogó* bell
Notes: As in the Santería example (CD 1, Track 11), this *candomblé* ritual consists of complex rhythmic cycles played on drums, intricate dancing, and call-and response singing. Zangó is the Brazilian equivalent of the Yoruba *orisha* of fire, thunder, lightning, war, and masculinity.

THE ROOTS OF BRAZILIAN MUSIC

As in much of Latin America, Brazilian music is a mixture of European, African, and Native elements that percolated for 400 years, ultimately yielding a syncretic mix that incorporates, to various degrees, the elements of all three root traditions. Innumerable styles and genres have emerged, including *choro*, *maxixe*, *lundu*, *forro*, and most famously, *samba* and *bossa nova*. Brazil's musical diversity has surpassed every other country on the continent, with the possible exception of the United States. The two most important musical centers in Brazil are Rio de Janeiro, the giant urban melting pot, home to the biggest carnival celebration in the world, and the northeastern state of Bahia, considered by most the center of northeastern music and indeed of all Brazilian music. A key aspect to the nature of Brazilian music is the Portuguese language itself. Its romantic lilt and distinctive articulation of vowels and consonants, which cannot be found in other Romance languages such as Italian, French, or Spanish, colors the music in a unique way, lending it a laid-back melodiousness seemingly free of time and lagging behind the beat. The same feeling can be found in the doleful *fados* of Portugal—haunting melancholy laments sung in the drinking houses of Lisbon. But it was only when the language began incorporating African and Native words and adopting lively African rhythms that Brazilian music came into its own and became one of the most romantic and sensual musics in the world.

Brazilian Musical Instruments

As in much of the African Diaspora, drums and percussion dominate Brazilian Music. Though many of these instruments are not necessarily Brazilian or African in origin (like the jazz drum kit), others are particular to Brazil, to specific regions, and even to specific towns. Traditionally, Brazilian drumheads were made of goat or cowhides, though in recent decades plastic has come to be the material of choice for both the body and head. *Atabaques* are conical drums of African origin, with calfskin heads, not unlike Cuban conga drums, and come in three different sizes. They are prominent in *capoeira*, *candomblé*, and *umbanda* rituals all over Brazil.

Bombo is a general term for bass drums. Categories of *bombos* include *surdos* ("deaf drums"), often used in *samba baterías* (percussions ensembles). They are cylindrical two-headed drums that produce a deep and low sound akin to a heartbeat. The right hand strikes one head with a padded stick, while the left hand dampens the other head. *Alfaias*, also known as *surdos de cordas* ("rope-drums"), are smaller than *surdos*, and are played with two mallets. The two heads are held tightly by hoops and are tuned with ropes whose tension is increased or decreased. *Alfaias* are originally from the state of Pernambuco, and are prominently used in *mangue* and *maracatú*. *Zabumbas*, traditionally used in northeastern styles like *forro* and *baião*, have a low sound and two heads, used to mark both the downbeat and the backbeat. The right hand plays the accented bass tone with a mallet, while the left hand plays the syncopated higher-pitched unaccented beat with a stick.

Other drums include *repiniques*, high-pitched drums popular in carnival *baterías*, often used as lead instruments and in displays of solo virtuosity. *Repiniques* are played with a stick in the right hand and with the bare left hand, both beating on the same head, often in very rapid syncopation. *Tamborins* are small, handheld drums with a single head, played with a thin stick in the right hand, while the left hand dampens the inside of the head. Their high pitch combines well with the *repiniques*, and the two are often used together in the samba schools. *Pandeiros* are single-headed hand-drums with jingles, similar to tambourines, used in many facets of Brazilian music, including *capoeira* and *samba*.

Several shakers are used to mark the rhythm, including the basket-like *caxixi*, made from straw and filled with seeds or beads that produce a rough sound appropriate for *samba*; the *ganzá*, a metal tube that contains finer beads, producing a smooth sound that is appropriate for *bossa nova*; the *chocalho*, made from either gourds or metal jingles; the *xequebum*, a gourd covered with a web of beading, akin to the Cuban *chekere*; and the *afoxé*, a cylindrical instrument with corrugated grooves, loosely covered with strings of beads that scrape the grooves. The *reco-reco* (or *raspador*), of African origin and similar to the Cuban *güiro*, consists of a hollow bamboo, wood or metal tube with grooves on which a scraper is grated. Cowbells are common in Brazil—as they are throughout the African Diaspora—including the Yoruba *agogó*, a set of double cowbells, and the *gonguê*, a single large cowbell. Brazilian music also makes use of various whistles, most prominently the high-pitched *apito*, which sometimes has one or two finger holes.

A singular instrument is the *berimbau*, a wooden bow with one metal string, originally from Angola. The string is attached to a gourd to increase the resonance. The right hand strikes the string with a bamboo stick and may also hold a *caxixi* shaker. The left hand holds a coin or metal ring that is pressed against the string, altering its pitch and producing an unusual timbre. *Berimbaus* come in different sizes and are used extensively in *candomblé* and *capoeira*. Another unusual instrument is the *cuíca*, a friction drum with a small bamboo stick attached to the inside of the drumhead, named after a small amphibious jungle mouse. Sound is produced by the right hand rubbing the stick

Berimbau.

back and forth with a damp cloth. The pitch is altered by pressing on the drumhead with the left hand. The resulting eerie sonority, which some describe as a "jungle" or "monkey" sound, has become very popular in many Brazilian styles, especially *samba*.

Afro-Brazilian Folk Dances

African rituals and rhythms were ubiquitous in Brazilian slave quarters, and drumming was—and remains—the central facet of Afro-Brazilian music, which also included complex rhythms and syncopations, call-and-response forms, and specific ritual dances. Over the course of four centuries, hundreds of styles emerged, often in conjunction with the Afro-Brazilian religions and social organizations described earlier. After abolition, many of these continued to thrive in the town squares and poor urban neighborhoods, still dedicated to various religious and secular purposes. They include *batuques*, dances accompanied by intense rhythmic drumming and hand clapping, predecessors of the carnival *batucadas*, and influential in the development of *samba*. *Batuque* dancers typically form a circle, clapping hands and playing various percussion instruments. At the center, men and women dance suggestively, pressing their bellies together in a move called the *umbigada* ("navel dance"). The overt sexuality of the *batuques* caused them to be banned numerous times. *Cucumbis* are dramatic representations or pantomimes from Bahia, named after Bantu and Congolese dances that occurred at funerals and male puberty rituals (puberty representing the "death" of the child and the "birth" of the man). They tell stories about mythological and religious characters drawn from both African and Native-Brazilian myths. Music consists of singing and drumming, with dancers that are intricately dressed, decorated with necklaces made from coral or animal teeth, and wielding traditional weapons. They remain popular during Christmas and carnival celebrations.

Maculeles are stick dances that originated in Bahia, based on an ancient Yoruba war legend. Combat is simulated with sticks, and intricate choreography accompanies the dance. It is often associated with *capoeira*, and has some semblance to the *frevo* from Pernambuco.

Bloco afro and *afoxé* refer to social organizations dedicated to Afro-Brazilian culture, among which drumming and dance play a central role. Both *blocos afro* and *afoxés* parade in street festivals, among which carnival is the most popular. These organizations began to appear in Brazilian society in the late nineteenth century to celebrate African culture and religion and were among the first to introduce African rhythmic organization to carnival. Subject to governmental repression since the 1930s, they made a comeback in the 1970s as social movements that aimed to strengthen Afro-Brazilian identity. The term *afoxé* also refers to a dance rhythm called *ijexá* (ee-jay-SHAH), which is closely associated with *candomblé* rituals. (And, as mentioned earlier, *afoxé* is also the name of a gourd-like instrument that is central to the performance of the *afoxé* rhythms.) The most important and long-lived *bloco afro* is *Filhos de Gandhy* ("Sons of Gandhi"), founded in 1949. *Bloco afro* and *afoxé* became familiar to U.S. audiences when Paul Simon included some of their rhythms on his 1990 album *Rhythm of the Saints*. The *bloco afro* revival has also generated new compositions by recent stars such as Virginia Rodrigues, whose entire album *Nós* contains lyrics and rhythms related to *candomblé*.

Maracatus, from the northeast state of Pernambuco, developed from the seventeenth-century *nações* and specifically from the coronation ritual of the leader of the slaves. *Maracatus* can be fast or slow and can sometimes have brass instruments in addition to the percussion. There are literally hundreds of other localized styles of Afro-Brazilian music and dance, such as the *congada*, the *semba*, the *coco*, the *jongo*, and the infamous *lambada*, a bona fide style from the Amazonian town of Belém that was the object of much ridicule when it was co-opted by European entrepreneurs in the late 1980s, who dubbed it "the forbidden dance of love" and artificially transformed it into a rather oily but thankfully short-lived "international sensation."

Recommended Listening: "Ijex" by Filhos de Gandhi, from the CD *Afros e afoxés da Bahia*.

Recommended Listening: "Oludum" by Margareth Menezes, from the CD *Afros e afoxés da Bahia*.

Capoeira

Perhaps the most prominent and famous Afro-Brazilian dance tradition is *capoeira*. It is an ancient martial art, though in modern times it is rarely used in actual conflict or competition and has mostly developed into a stylized dance form. The word *capoeira* is an indigenous name for a small male bird that engages in fierce mating contests with its challengers. Escaped slaves in the interior of Brazil, particularly in the mountain community of Palmares, developed the tradition, and after abolition, *capoeira* left the mountains and jungles and made its way to urban slums, causing unrest and criminal activity. Its practitioners successfully used it to resist authorities, and as a result the government banned *capoeira*. In the twentieth century it metamorphosed into an art form that quickly became popular around the world. Today, it remains an important signifier of Brazilian cultural identity, with a strong international following. *Capoeira* blends elements of dance, music, acrobatics, and martial arts. Music sets the rhythm of the dance, impelling and encouraging the participants. It is played by a percussion ensemble called a *batería*, whose main instruments are three *berimbaus* tuned to different pitches called *gunga*, *mêdio* and *viola*. The *berimbaus* are often complemented by *atabaque* drums, *pandeiro* tambourines, *agogó* bells, triangles, shakers, and *reco-recos*. Part of the challenge of *capoeira* practitioners is following the complex rhythms of the *batería*. They form a circle called a *roda*, in which the fighters/dancers engage in energetic and acrobatic moves. All participants sing and play the instruments of the *batería*. Various types of songs, including *ladainhas*, *chulas*, and *corridos*, some of them improvised, are performed during set portions of the *capoeira* ritual.

Capoeira performance from Bahia, Brazil.

Recommended Listening: "Santa Maria" by Mestre Bimba, from the CD *Batucada and Capoeira*.

Recommended Listening: "Berimbau and Capoeira" by Luciano Perrone, from the CD *Batucada and Capoeira*.

Recommended Viewing: For an intricate—and fascinating—view of *capoeira*, see the 1998 documentary *Pastinha! Uma vida pela capoeira*.

CDII, Track 6: *Capoeira*: **"Paranaê"**

Music and Lyrics: traditional
Instrumentation: three *berimbaus*, *pandeiros*, *atabaque*, *reco-reco*, *agogô*
Notes: Paraná refers to the river between Brazil and Paraguay, and the region is an important center of Afro-Brazilian culture. The slow tempo and hypnotic call-and-response singing of this capoeira song impels the moves of the dancers.

CARNIVAL

In contrast to the economic inequality that historically pervaded Brazilian society, the late nineteenth century saw the poorest and most disenfranchised members of society gain a certain measure of control over much of the cultural and musical establishment. Even before the abolition of slavery in 1888, Black and Mulatto popular culture began to gain ascendancy, exemplified in a hundred different ways, but perhaps most prominently in the two passions that have occupied most Brazilians for the last hundred years: soccer and carnival. The carnival season, which usually begins right after the New Year, paralyzes the country and attracts millions of tourists. The greatest celebration of all occurs in Rio de Janeiro, but most cities and towns have their own version of carnival. Music and dance are important facets of every carnival celebration, and each region has its own type of carnival music: the traditional sambas in Rio de Janeiro, the *frevo*-influenced dances in Recife-Olinda, the *maracatus* from Pernambuco, the reggae-like sambas from Bahia, and so on. In all cases, intense carousing spontaneously erupts in nightclubs and beaches, on city streets and in town squares. Enormous parades with dazzling costumes, splendid floats, and hundreds of frenzied dancers and musicians take over the main thoroughfares of cities large and small. Spectators routinely join in the singing and dancing, using any available object as makeshift percussion. All participants and most spectators dress up as a matter of course. Often the costumes will be dictated by the theme of a specific parade. Some are sophisticated representations of kings and queens, animals and mythological creatures, or traditional old-world commedia dell'arte characters. More modern costumes reflect elements of popular culture. Some—mostly stunningly beautiful

Carnival drummers from Rio de Janeiro.

women—dress up very minimally, or not at all. A hedonistic attitude affects much of the celebration, and the emphasis on pleasure is a theme embodied by all and in evidence in much of the festivities. The celebrations can be overwhelming both to the participants and spectators. But the purpose of carnival is not only one of entertainment. It is an important tradition that anchors Brazilians—and particularly Afro-Brazilians—to their cultural institutions, providing social stability and historical continuity with their music, dance, costumes, and ritual celebrations. It is also a social equalizer and a national unifier: inequalities disappear, as revelers from every socio-economic class and every part of the country are included.

Recommended Viewing: For an impression of the atmosphere of the carnival in Rio de Janeiro, see the 1959 film *Orfeu negro* (*Black Orpheus*).

History of Brazilian Carnival

During the colonial period, the Portuguese brought their unruly pre-Lenten celebration called *entrudo*, which included the curious custom of drenching all participants with water, mud, soot, flour balls, rotten eggs, and other unsavory substances. By the nineteenth century, carnival celebrations had become festive and stylish, with traditional masked balls emerging by mid-century, followed soon thereafter by the first parades which were called *Zé pereiras*, with energetic songs and lively drum accompaniment. On the one hand, the wealthy aristocracy formed groups called *grandes sociedades* ("great societies") that held European-style parades that included luxurious costumes, flowers and masks, and artfully sculpted horse-drawn floats. They also included military band music, marching string and wind orchestras, and male and female choirs. Invariably the *sociedades* festivities culminated in a fancy ball, where the music typically consisted of salon dances or opera themes.

Conversely, Blacks, Mulattos, and poor Whites were routinely excluded from the mostly White *sociedades*, except as street spectators. Barred from their balls and parades, they quickly formed their own associations, called *cordões carnavalescos*, male-dominated carnival circles whose revelry, infused with *candomblé* and *capoeira*, often turned violent. Eventually, gentler, more gender-diverse carnival clubs emerged called *ranchos carnavalescos*. The first *ranchos*, which were not unlike the Cuban *comparsas*, emerged in Rio de Janeiro in 1893. Far removed from the salons of the aristocracy, they emphasized street celebrations and parades organized around specific themes, often telling stories or exploring ancient myths. Revelers would wear costumes and huge papier-mâché puppet masks, dancing to Afro-Brazilian songs and dances such as *cucumbis* and *afoxés*. The *ranchos* competed with the White *sociedades* in popularity, and eventually gained the upper hand when they began holding competitions, which quickly became immensely popular and drew spectators from all social classes. In 1899, a *rancho* called *Rosa de Ouro* commissioned the composer Chiquinha Gonzaga to compose a carnival march. She wrote "Ó abre alas" ("Open Wings"), the first official march of Brazilian carnival. Its catchy rhythm turned it into an instant sensation, and it spawned an entire new carnival tradition. In the following decades, thousands of *marchas* and *marchinhas* were written, usually with strong downbeats and straightforward rhythms, though as time went on, syncopated elements of ragtime and Dixieland jazz began to creep in. But the most important influence was Brazilian in nature, one that would revolutionize carnival and Brazilian music in general for the rest of the century: samba.

Recommended Listening: "Ó abre alas" by Chiquinha Gonzaga, from the CD *Chiquinha Gonzaga: A Maestrina*.

Samba

The dichotomy of *samba* is that it can be simultaneously frenzied and romantic, mischievous and well mannered, elegant and chaotic, savage and civilized. It can express at once the urban angst of the poor *favelas* and the elegant grace of high society; it can simultaneously embody a vehement remonstration against social inequality and a fashionable embrace of authority. The term samba is derived from *semba* and before that *mesemba*, an African *candomblé* dance first recognized in Rio de Janeiro in the first half of the nineteenth century. In subsequent decades, the dance was heavily influenced by other Afro-Brazilian forms such as *maxixe*, *lundu*, and *choro* (discussed below), as well as the carnival *marchas*. The main historical event responsible for the emergence of samba—and for the ensuing immense popularity of carnival—was the abolition of slavery in 1888. As a result of this, tens of thousands of former slaves, primarily from Bahia, made their way to the *favela* slums of Rio de Janeiro, seeking their fortune. These favelas became focal points for Afro-Brazilian religion and culture, where different styles and genres of music percolated. Soon, samba became the most prominent dance of the favelas, and its popularity quickly infected the rest of the city and the country. The first samba recording occurred in 1916, with a song called "Pelo telefone" by Ernesto "Donga" dos Santos, followed by other artists, including José Barbosa da Silva, aka Sinhô, who was known as the "king of the samba." In the 1920s, samba left Brazil for the first time when the *choro* singer Pixinguinha introduced it to ecstatic Parisian audiences. From there, samba's worldwide popularity rocketed. A version of the samba called the *carioca* became immensely popular in the United States, first as a result of the 1933 Fred Astaire and Ginger Rogers film *Flying Down to Rio*, and subsequently due to the many films of Carmen Miranda.

> **Recommended Listening:** "Pelo telefone" by Donga, from the CD *Musica de Donga*.

> **Recommended Listening:** "Bemzinho" by Ary Barroso, sung by Carmen Miranda, from the CD *1930–42: Ary Barroso Compositions*.

Like the Cuban conga, samba gained popularity primarily as a carnival dance, and would even come to define carnival. It is characterized by fast tempos, heavily syncopated rhythms, and is typically in $\frac{2}{4}$ meter with a strong emphasis on the second beat. Several forms of samba exist, including *canção de samba* (a sung samba with elevated, almost poetic lyrics), *samba pagode* (in which competitors rapidly improvise lyrics), and the reggae-like *samba breque*. But the style that characterizes the Rio de Janeiro carnival is the *samba enredo*, performed by the famous *escolas de samba*.

> **Recommended Listening:** "S.P.C." by Zeca Pagodinho, from the CD *Brazil Classics, Vol. 2: O samba*.

Samba: "S.P.C."

Music and Lyrics: Zeca Pagodinho and Arlindo Cruz
Instrumentation: *cavaquinho* ukulele, guitar, *pandeiro*, *surdo*, *cuica*
Notes: This samba by Zeca Pagodinho tells the story of modern economic hardships, as the narrator threatens to denounce his former partner to the S.P.C. (credit protection service), a blacklist of bad debtors. The typical samba shuffle is provided by the energetic *pandeiro* tambourine and the continuous *cavaquinho* in the background. The choir responds to the lead singer in the chorus. The first verse is repeated several times throughout the song.

Precisei de roupa nova, mas sem prova de salario.	*I needed new clothes but had no proof of salary.*
Combinamos, eu pagava, você fez o crediario.	*We agreed, I would pay, you would use your credit.*
Nosso caso foi pra cova e a roupa pro armario. (x2)	*Then our affair would be done, with the clothes in the closet.*
E depois você quis manchar meu nome dentro do meu metiêr.	*And then you tried to tarnish my name among my circle.*
Mexeu com a moral de um homem.	*You messed around with a man's good name.*
Vou me vingar de você.	*I'm going to take revenge on you.*

Chorus

Porque, eu vou sujar seu nome no seu S.P.C.	*Because, I'm going to soil your name in the S.P.C.*
Tu vai ver, eu vou sujar, seu nome no S.P.C.	*You'll see, I'm going to soil your name in the S.P.C.*
Quis me fazer de otario mas o crediario já está pra vencer.	*You tried to make a fool out of me, but your payments are almost due.*
Sei que não sou salafrário mas o numerário você não vai ver.	*Even though I'm not a crook, you won't see any of your cash back*
Com o aumento dos juros, você em apuros pra mim vai correr.	*As the interest rate goes up, you'll be in trouble and come to me.*
Pra me vingar dos teus furos, juro que estou duro não pago carnê.	*To get revenge from your offenses I'll swear I'm broke and won't pay you.*

The *Escolas de Samba*

Descended from the *ranchos carnavalescos, escolas de samba* ("samba schools") are organizations of thousands of singers, dancers, brass and woodwind instrumentalists, drummers and percussionists that prepare year-round for the carnival season. They then perform spectacular events, with songs and parades organized around a specific *enredo* ("theme"), which is often on Brazilian history or popular culture. The *escolas* typically compete for top prizes, which are awarded, after a complex process, for musical performance, harmony, individual singers, conductors and paraders, samba composition, percussion ensembles, visual artistry, costumes, floats, dancing, and thematic originality. *Escolas* include all races and economic classes, and Afro-Brazilians in particular have adopted them as cultural institutions. In modern times they have become important social and political organizations whose influence extends beyond the revelry of the carnival season, particularly in low-income communities, where they perform valuable social service and assistance. *Escolas* empower the members of the organization, providing a feeling of accomplishment, particularly if the *escola* is triumphant in the competition. Many Brazilians passionately identify with a specific *escola*, in the same way that they identify with a specific soccer team.

The first *escola de samba* was *Deixa Falar* ("let us speak") founded in 1928 by Ismael Silva, though it was short-lived. In the next decades, several *escolas* became an integral part of Rio's carnival, including *Estação Primeira de Mangueira, Império Serrano*, and *Portela*, which are still among the most popular. Cities all over Brazil began developing them, and Rio de Janeiro alone had more than 50 officially recognized *escolas* in 1990. Many long-standing rivalries have developed between various *escolas*, and most have developed a rich history and folklore, often with bizarre customs. Some emphasize their musical abilities, others are famous for the ostentatiousness of their costumes and floats; still others pride themselves on subtle differences in their drumming or dancing. The culmination of every *escola* is the carnival parade, a complex enterprise that involves not only the thousands of paraders but also an even greater number of behind-the-scenes administrators, skilled workers and tradesmen. Preparation for the parade usually occurs immediately after the end of the previous year's carnival. Around September and October, appropriate sambas are then composed, selected, rehearsed, and even recorded and prereleased to ensure the audience's enthusiastic participation during the parade. The visual and musical elements must be connected to that year's specific *enredo*. Parades also include the highly ornamented floats called *carros alegóricos*, which are also related to the *enredo* and on which stand exuberantly costumed *destaques*—men and women who are typically in the higher ranks of the *escola* organization.

At the heart of the *escolas* are immense percussion ensembles called *baterías* that perform complex *batucadas*, providing the rhythmic underpinning of the entire parade. A typical *bateria* can consist of up to four hundred drummers and percussionists. The rhythmic complexity of these ensembles is anchored by the deep *surdo* drums, and complemented by *caixa* snare-drums, *pandeiro* tambourines, *cuíca* friction drums, *agogó* cowbells, as well as assorted *repiques*, *reco-recos*, *tamborims*, *pratos*, and *tarols*. Members of the *bateria* are heavily recruited for their talent, are required to pass difficult admission tests, and must undergo intense training before the parade. The principal singer is called the *puxador*, who sings the *escola*'s chosen sambas throughout the parade. The *bateria* is typically in the middle of the parade, and it performs exciting *batucadas* in between the sambas. When the parade reaches the jury box, the *bateria* goes to a designated area, where it plays its most impressive *batucada*, allowing the rest of the *escola* to parade through. This is typically the highlight of the parade, with tremendous displays of energy, excitement and volume. One of the best *baterías* is *Mocidade Independente de Padre Miguel*. Led by Mestre André, it consists of more than three hundred drummers and percussionists and is often recognized as the most rhythmically exciting of the carnival ensembles.

Recommended Listening: "Apresentaçao" by Mocidade Independente de Padre Miguel, from the CD *Batucada and Capoeira*.

Recommended Listening: "Demonstraçao de grupos" by Batería Fantastica da Portela, from the CD *Batucada and Capoeira*.

Carnival Today

Since their emergence in the 1920s, *escolas de samba* have expanded into enormously extravagant affairs, artistically grandiose and technically sophisticated. Daily participation in carnival regularly tops 25,000. Hundreds of thousands of spectators line the streets, and millions more watch on television. In 1984, the immense Sambadrome was constructed in Rio de Janeiro, a half-mile long stadium that seats 90,000 spectators and that has become carnival's official parade ground. The Brazilian national and local economies have become increasingly dependent on the revenues generated during the pre-Lenten season. The advent of television in the 1960s infused carnival with huge sums of money, and since the 1990s, million-dollar broadcast contracts and lucrative recording deals have inevitably transformed the character of the *escolas* and of carnival in general. Many decry its growth and over-commercialization, lamenting that spontaneous traditions have given way to purely commercial considerations. Moreover, large amounts of money often attract unsavory relationships: Allegations of corruption and involvement of mafia and drug cartels have become prevalent in recent years.

Another problem is that the domination of the *escolas da samba* has stifled other traditional, less lucrative aspects of carnival. Thus the old *ranchos*, long ago supplanted by the *escolas*, have continued to decline steadily during the last several decades, to the point where the last *rancho* competition was held in 1990. Yet some of the old standbys remain a part of the celebration. The balls of the *grandes sociedades* still survive in some places. *Marchas* are still performed in many carnival parades, primarily by informal *bandas*, makeshift drum-and-brass ensembles that perform in the neighborhoods without fancy floats or costumes, more interested in providing vibrant and colorful music than in making a fashion statement. Other, non-carnival celebrations are also making inroads, including the folklore festival called *Parintin*, held every June in the Amazon rainforest, as well as traditional celebrations such as Christmas and All-Saints' Day.

THE NORTHEAST

Brazil's northeast—the "hump" that projects into the Atlantic ocean—has proved to be a fertile ground for diverse musical styles and talented musicians. It includes the states of Bahia and Pernambuco, and the cities of Recife, Fortaleza, and Salvador, which is one of the most important centers for African culture on the continent. Salvador was the first capital of Brazil, and for centuries was the center of the slave trade and sugar industry. Beyond the coastal regions lies the *sertão*, the semi-arid backlands that have produced a distinct rural culture.

The influence of the northeast in Brazilian culture can loosely be compared to that of the American south in terms of its predominantly rural heritage, its mixed population, and as the source of both White country music and Black African-derived styles. The analogy can be extended somewhat further, with the state of Bahia and the city of Salvador corresponding to Louisiana and New Orleans. Both places have been cradles of musical and cultural diversity, drawing styles from various sources and transforming them into new influential hybrids. It was in the northeast, and Bahia in particular, that African, Native, and European culture most freely mixed, yielding syncretic styles and traditions that were instrumental in the evolution of the country's music. The Afro-Brazilian rhythms of *candomblé* first originated in Bahia, as did the *maracatu,* *bloco afro*, and *afoxé*, the rural *forro* and *fossa*, and the urban *baião* and *xote*. Emigrants from the northeast first developed the sambas that drove the carnival parades in Rio de Janeiro and developed their own styles of carnival music, such as the *frevo* from Recife. The region was also the cradle of *tropicália*, the movement that propelled Brazilian popular music into the modern era, and many modern styles (such as *axé*) as well as modern artists (including Carlinhos Brown and Margareth Menezes) have their roots in the northeast.

Baião and Fossa

The northeast rural style is easily recognizable: the rhythms are less subtle and the accents more pronounced, giving the music a working-class appeal far removed from the trendy jazz of Brazil's urban nightclubs. The three most important rural styles from the northeast are *fossa, baião,* and *forro. Fossa*, which became prominent in the 1950s and 1960s, is melancholy in nature, with songs of heartbreak, longing, and disillusion, originally performed by a single singer accompanying him- or herself with a guitar, but increasingly with a wind and string orchestra. Important proponents of *fossa* included the despondent Dolores Duran, who had a short and tragic career, the child prodigy Maysa Matarazzo, and the wistful Antônio Maria, whose "Manha de Carnaval" ("Morning of Carnival") was featured in the 1959 film *Black Orpheus*. It later yielded a more sophisticated version called *fossa nova*, paralleling the bossa nova phenomenon.

> **Recommended Listening:** "So por castigo" by Dolores Duran, from the CD *Dolores Duran: Reconstituicao com orquestra e coro em 16 canais*.

> **Recommended Listening:** "Manha de Carnaval" by Antônio Maria, from the sound track of the film *Orfeu negro (Black Orpheus)*.

Baião is a lively dance style based on European ballroom dances, traditionally played by small ensembles at local dances and celebrations. The ensembles usually consist of bamboo flutes called *pífanos*, accompanied by the *sanfona* accordion, the syncopated rhythm of the small *zabumba* bass drum, and other percussion, notably the triangle. The peculiar melodic and harmonic character of the *baião* relies on the musical capabilities of the *pífano* flutes. The brilliant accordionist Luíz Gonzaga developed *Baião* in the 1940s and 1950s. From the state of Pernambuco, Gonzaga was also a composer and is considered the father of both *forro* and *baião*. Other important composers were Jackson do Pandeiro and the *cavaquinho* (ukulele) player Waldir Azevedo, whose "Delicado" became a big hit in Brazil and in Europe.

> **Recommended Listening:** "Baião dos namorados" by Luíz Gonzaga, from the CD *Xodo*.
>
> **Recommended Listening:** "Delicado" by Waldir Azevedo, from the CD *Waldir Azevedo: Serie Warner 25 años*.

Forro

Forro is a dance that originated in the interior but became popular in dancehalls in towns and villages throughout the northeast, and later in the entire country. *Forros* occur almost every weekend in these regions and are especially popular during the June festivals. In contrast to the urbane and sophisticated bossa nova, or the urban samba of the favela slums, *forro* is more of a country-music style, embraced in rural areas, and was traditionally looked down upon by urban sophisticates as earthy, back-country music. As in *baião*, the standard instrument of *forro* is the *sanfona* accordion, complemented by the *zabumba* and triangle and occasionally by a guitar. As in many places on the continent, Europeans immigrants introduced the accordion in the nineteenth century. Indeed, *forro* has often been compared to other styles such as Mexican *norteño*, Colombian *vallenato*, and Louisiana *zydeco*, not only because of the prominence of the accordion but also because of the fast lively rhythms and the rural "country" ethos.

Forro provided a release for field workers and ranch hands who met adversity and tough times with good humor. At its core, it is upbeat, cheerful music for country dancing, though like everything else in Brazil, these dances tend to be suggestive, with couples joined at the hips and moving sensually to the music. The lively dances reach fast and frenzied tempos that leave participants perspiring and exhausted, both from its physical and sensual aspects. The unrelenting accordion drives the Afro-Brazilian syncopated rhythms. Yet *forro* can be both humorous and melancholy: lyrics lament (but also celebrate) the harsh life of the bleak rural northern interior, often with an ironic tone. Heartbreak is a common theme. What provides the irony is the liveliness of the music: sad, dark lyrics are often juxtaposed with happy, even festive music that is almost irresistible.

Forro was present in the northeast at least as earlier as the turn of the twentieth century. But the same demographic trend that brought about the prominence of samba was also responsible for the popularization of *forro* outside its place of origin, namely the migration of poor rural northeasterners to urban centers in search of jobs and a future. The advent of radio and recording technologies in the 1930s further extended the reach and influence of northeastern styles. *Forros* and *baiãos* emerged onto the national consciousness when Luíz Gonzaga started to record and perform them throughout Brazil in the 1940s. He was instantly successful with both genres, but it was particularly his *forros* and their celebration of northeastern rural life that became popular. Another early proponent of *forro* was Jackson do Pandeiro. By the 1940s, *forro* and *baião* had become less rural, more accessible to urban Brazilians, and ultimately more commercialized. But after World War II, Brazilians turned their attention to a succession of foreign-influenced popular styles, culminating in the bossa nova onslaught. *Forro* fell into relative disfavor, or, more accurately, left the spotlight and returned to the rural dancehalls where it had thrived for decades.

But when the *tropicália* movement supplanted bossa nova in the 1960s, artists such as Caetano Veloso, Gilberto Gil, and Gal Costa, all from the northeast, embraced *forro, baião*, and Gonzaga's original style, adopting many of their elements into their music, and even covering many of Gonzaga's classics. Both styles—but especially *forro*—quickly regained popularity, now with a more modern approach. Today, *forro* has once again become popular throughout the country with Brazilians of all races, classes, and walks of life. Radio stations completely devoted to *forro* broadcast the latest hits from their favorite artists. The accordion-based style recently received a huge boost among the urban middle class when a *forro* song was used as the theme song for a popular soap opera. Some of the most popular modern *forro* artists include Elba Ramalho, Falamansa, Chama Chuva, and Colher de Pau. A recent compilation of *forro* titled *Music for Maids and Taxi Drivers* was released internationally and proved to be a big hit around the world, particularly in the United States. Yet in spite of its recent popularity, much of contemporary *forro* has remained true to its roots. Most *forro* artists still hail from the northeast, which lends them authenticity and credentials. They perform in local live bands in dancehalls in Pernambuco or Bahia, where the style remains rough, casual and "authentic," and thus accessible to its core rural audience. In Salvador, *forro* and *baião* emerge from just about every window and night club, infecting passers-by with the sensuality of their rhythms and the excitement of their accordion licks, providing yet another experience of the diversity of Brazilian music.

Recommended Listening: "Morena da Palmeira" by Jose Orlando, from the CD *Brazil forro: Music for Maids and Taxi Drivers*.

CDII, Track 7: *Forro*: "Asa branca"

Music and Lyrics: Luíz Gonzaga and Humberto Teixeira
Instrumentation: *sanfona* accordion, guitar, *zabumba* drum, triangle
Notes: Luíz Gonzaga's "Asa branca" ("White Wing") refers to the picazuro pigeon common in the *sertão* backlands of the Northeast. The narrator speaks of the desolation of the region, and, like the dove, must leave, promising his love he will return. The prominent triangle and bass drum complement the syncopated melody of the accordion.

Quando oiei a terra ardendo,	*When I saw the burning land,*
Qual a fogueira de São João,	*Like the fires of Saint John,*
Eu preguntei a Deus do céu, ai,	*I asked God in heaven,*
Por que tamanha judiação?	*Why such cruel pain?*
Que braseiro, que fornaia!	*What a brazier, what a furnace!*
Nem um pé de prantação.	*Not even a square foot of arable land.*
Por farta d'água perdi meu gado,	*For lack of water I lost my cattle,*
Morreu de sede meu alazão.	*My horse died of thirst.*
Inté mesmo a asa branca	*Even the white-winged dove*
Bateu asas do sertão.	*Flew away from the backlands.*
Entonce eu disse: "adeus Rosinha,	*So I said: "Goodbye, sweet Rosinha,*
Guarda contigo meu coração."	*I leave my heart with you."*
Hoje longe muitas légua,	*Today many leagues away,*
Numa triste solidão,	*In sad solitude,*
Espero a chuva cair de novo	*I wait for the rain to fall again*
Pra mim vortar pro meu sertão.	*So I can return to my backland.*
Quando o verde dos teus óio,	*When the green of your eyes,*
Se espanhar na prantação	*Spreads across this land again,*
Eu te asseguro não chore não, viu	*I assure you, so don't cry,*
Que eu vortarei, viu, Meu coração	*That I will return, my dear.*

Other Rural Styles

The northeastern *forró* and *baião* are not Brazil's only country music. A rural style called *música caipira* could be heard throughout the interior of Central and Southern Brazil for much of the twentieth century. Accompanied by 10-string guitars called *violas*, its sentimental songs spoke of love and the simplicity of rural life. Another, more modern genre evolved from it called *sertanejo* (music from the *sertão*—backlands music), which is not unlike Mexican *norteño* and Tex-Mex music. Whereas *música caipira* is rougher and simpler, *sertaneja* incorporates modern instruments such as electric guitars and synthesizers and makes use of modern recording and performance technology. Like *forró*, it has recently become very popular throughout Brazil. Several duos have become important proponents of *sertanejo*, including Chitãozinho and Xororó, Leonardo and Leandro, and Pena Branca and Xavantinho.

MUSICA POPULAR BRASILEIRA

Brazil has developed a strong tradition of popular music over the last century, with dozens of styles and genres, all known generally as *Musica popular brasileira*—typically referred to simply as MPB. It began taking shape in the nineteenth century with the growth of the major urban centers, particularly Rio de Janeiro, Recife, Salvador, and São Paulo. After abolition, these centers grew tremendously as former slaves emigrated there in search of a better life. They brought their musical traditions to the cities, where they combined with European styles to become the precursors of a popular music tradition that would affect Brazil—and much of the rest of the world—for the next hundred years. Along with soccer and carnival, no element of popular culture has managed to more accurately embody Brazil's passion than MPB.

Modinha, Lundu, and Maxixe

Three forms were particularly popular during the second half of the nineteenth century. The first was the *modinha*, an aria-like art song popular with the White Portuguese elite and derived from the Portuguese *moda*. *Modinhas* had vocal melodies that were lyrical and greatly ornamented, reflecting a sentimental, romantic—and occasionally melancholy—aesthetic that often spoke of courtly love. The second was the *lundu*, originally an Afro-Brazilian courtship dance form that pervaded the slave quarters and low-income section of Brazilian cities. Considered indecent by the church, its rhythms were squarely derived from Afro-Brazilian styles, and its melancholy poetry and lyrics addressed hardship and adversity. Later on, however, in its instrumental form, the *lundu* became popular among the Brazilian elite. The third style was the *maxixe*, a suggestive dance that combined the *lundu* with European dances such as the polka and the Cuban *habanera*. It emerged in Rio de Janeiro in the 1870s and became prominent in the carnival balls of the elite *grandes sociedades*. Named after a kind of cactus, it was one of the early Brazilian dance forms to become popular in the United States and Europe at the beginning of the twentieth century, though in these incarnations it was most often danced like a tango. One of the first proponents of *lundu*, *modinha*, and *maxixe* was the Mulatto Xisto Bahia, who wrote and performed for middle- and upperclass audiences, including at one point the emperor himself, though his fortunes turned with the end of the empire.

> **Recommended Listening:** "A duas flores" by Xisto Bahia and Castro Alves, from the CD *Modinhas brasileiras: Songs from 19th Century Brazil*.

Choro

The *lundu*, *modinha*, and *maxixe* were soon eclipsed by yet another style. By the 1860s and 1870s, wind and string ensembles were all the rage in the dancehalls of Rio de Janeiro and other Brazilian cities. Their principal repertoire included European dances like polkas and waltzes, as well as Argentine tangos, often performed with Afro-Brazilian syncopations. These ensembles slowly began developing their own lively improvisational style, combining the European dance forms with African rhythms and Portuguese *fados*. The result was the *choro*, which literally means "cry" or "weeping." *Choro* has been compared to other styles that blended European song and dance forms with African rhythms, such as the Cuban *danzón* and North American ragtime. It has also been likened to New Orleans Dixieland jazz because of its virtuosity and complexity, its reliance on improvisation, and its marked syncopations. Like Dixieland and ragtime, *choro* is often entirely instrumental, makes use of fast tempos and unconventional melodies and harmonies, and can be prodigiously difficult while simultaneously sounding simple and spontaneous. Unlike Dixieland, however, *choro* typically has only one improvising soloist, usually a flute or clarinet. The first *choro* was "Flor amorosa" ("Amorous Flower"), written in 1868 by Joaquim Antonio da Silva Calado, a virtuoso flute player who led the popular Choro Carioca ensemble. Calado, who was influenced by the New Orleans composer Louis Moreau Gottschalk, placed great emphasis on improvisation, and demanded great virtuosity from his soloists. His singular instrumental combinations produced a unique sound, with the flute providing the solo, the *violão de sete cordas* (seven string guitar) providing the bass, and the *cavaquinho* (small Brazilian ukulele) providing samba-like African-based rhythms. In the twentieth century, a *pandeiro* tambourine and occasionally even a drum set were added to *choro* ensembles.

> **Recommended Listening:** "Flor amorosa" by Joaquim Antonio da Silva Calado and Catulo da Paixão Cearense, from the CD *Chorinhos de ouro, Vol. 6.*

Calado's style was greatly imitated and adapted, so that by the turn of the century *choro* had become the most popular genre in Brazil. Most prominent among the new generation of composers was Chiquinha Gonzaga, who became a mythical figure in the musical and social history of Brazil. Known as "the first lady of *choro*," she was a talented and versatile pianist, guitarist, composer, and conductor. With her ensemble Grupo Chiquinha Gonzaga, she recorded numerous popular songs and often combined European dance styles with Afro-Brazilian popular influences. She also injected Brazilian elements into musical theater, writing over 70 operettas that incorporated *choro* and other Native dance forms, starting with *The Court in the Country* (1885). Of the more than 2000 works she composed, prominent standouts include the first official march of Brazilian carnival, "Ó abre alas" ("Open Wings," 1899), the tango "Corta jaca" ("The Flatterer"), and the *modinha* "Lua branca" ("White Moon"). She was also one of the most interesting and bold characters of her day, an independent spirit who hobnobbed with emperors and street musicians alike, using her fame and influence to promote social causes such as abolition. She thrived on stretching and breaking entrenched gender roles, was fond of creating national scandals, and was prone to popular gossip in the salons of Rio de Janeiro.

> **Recommended Listening:** "Atraente" by Chiquinha Gonzaga, from the CD *Chiquinha Gonzaga: A Maestrina.*

Choro: "Atraente"

Music: Chiquinha Gonzaga (1877)
Instrumentation: piano, guitar, bass, *ganzá* shaker
Notes: In "Atraente" ("attractive" or "captivating"), Chiquinha Gonzaga fused the *choro* with the polka. The piece consists of three themes, each divided in two almost identical parts, remaining unresolved in the first part, then reaching a harmonic resolution. The guitar and shaker lend the *choro* its traditional shuffling motion. Gonzaga herself made this recording a few years before her death in 1935.

0:00	Introduction
0:10	Theme 1a
0:24	Theme 1b
0:38	Theme 1a
0:51	Theme 1b
1:02	Theme 2a
1:14	Theme 2b
1:23	Introduction
1:32	Theme 1a
1:46	Theme 1b
1:57	Theme 3a
2:08	Theme 3b
2:20	Theme 3a
2:30	Theme 3b
2:44	Theme 1a
2:58	Theme 1b

Another important figure during this period was Ernesto Júlio Nazareth, an original composer, fine pianist, and an important pioneer of Brazilian popular music. Like Gonzaga, Nazareth adopted many styles and genres and continuously blurred the border between classical and popular music, though throughout his life he retained an elitist view of art music, denying any popular elements in his style. Though his early studies led him to European-style waltzes and polkas, he quickly became influenced by African rhythms and popular styles such as *maxixe* and *lundu*. In time he became one of the greatest proponents of *choro*. His "Rogue" is widely considered the first Brazilian *tango*, though, like Gonzaga's "Atraente," it too was for the most part a *choro*. He would classify many of his subsequent songs as *tangos*, though they bore only slight resemblance to their Argentine cousin. Among his important contributions to the *choro* repertoire are the classic "Apanhei-te cavaquinho"

("Play That Ukulele") and *Odeón*, written in the parlor of the Odeón movie theater, where famous musicians would come to hear him play.

Recommended Listening: "Odeón" by Ernesto Nazareth, from the CD *Nazareth: Brazilian Ragtime*.

From the 1920s to the 1940s, the most important proponent of *choro* was the flute player Alfredo da Rocha Viana Filho, better known as "Pixinguinha." A child prodigy, he became a renowned flute virtuoso, as well as the most prolific composer of *choro*, with nearly a thousand compositions to his name. His intricate and complex musical forms led subsequent critics to dub him "the Bach of *choro*." As a result of Pixinguinha's contributions, *choro* reached great heights of both complexity and popularity. In 1922, with his group Os Oito Batutas, he traveled to Europe (one of the first Brazilian musicians to do so), where he presented *choro*, samba, and *maxixe* to enthusiastic audiences. It was in Paris that Pixinguinha and his group became familiar with—and readily incorporated into their own music— many of the jazz instruments and arrangements that were then in style. After World War II, with the rise of popular styles such as samba and bossa nova, *choro* fell out of favor with Brazilian audiences, who viewed it as old-fashioned and inaccessible because of its lack of lyrics. In the 1970s, it had a resurgence of sorts, and today, one can once again find modern performers of this important Brazilian style.

Recommended Listening: "Carinhoso" by Pixinguinha, from the CD *Pixinguinha 100*.

The Golden Age of *Musica Popular Brasileira*

The 1930s was the Golden Age of MPB. As elsewhere in the world, this surge was propelled by new recording technology and by the advent of the first radio broadcasts. This was also a period when dozens of talented singers, artists, and composers led carefree bohemian lifestyles, composing fabulous sambas, *choros*, and romantic songs. Their center of operations was the famous Café Nice in Rio de Janeiro. They included singers such as Carmen Miranda, Araci Cortes, and Mário Reis, and composers such as Ataulfo Alves, Dorival Caymmi, and Noel Rosa. One of the greatest composers of the Golden Age was the multitalented Ary Barroso, whose most famous hit "Aquarela do Brasil" (commonly known simply as "Brazil"), went on to become the most famous Brazilian song in the world, with over a thousand recordings. Barroso's fame was partly due to the Portuguese-born Carmen Miranda, who sang many of his songs both in Brazil and in a number of Hollywood films. She was an important contributor to the so-called "Latin Craze" in the United States in the 1940s, and as such was one of the most successful artists on the continent before her premature death at age 46. Always exotically attired and wearing her signature fruit-laden headdresses, Miranda became famous as "The Brazilian Bombshell" and "The Lady in the Tutti-Frutti Hat."

Recommended Listening: "Tico-Tico" by Carmen Miranda, from the CD *Brazilian Bombshell: 25 Hits (1939–1947)*.

Recommended Listening: "Com que roupa?" by Noel Rosa, from the CD *Feitio da vila*.

Recommended Listening: "O mar" by Dorival Caymmi, from the CD *Mar e terra*.

CDII, Track 8: Popular Song: "Aquarela do Brasil"

Music and Lyrics: Ary Barroso (1939)
Instrumentation: wind orchestra, percussion
Notes: Originally written as a carnival samba, "Aquarela do Brasil" became one of the most famous Brazilian songs in the world. Its soaring melody and familiar rising motive (at 0:57) convey its contagious joy and exuberance. The song is ultimately a celebration of the country itself, with subtle references to various aspects of Brazilian culture: the Black Mother is an important Afro-Brazilian religious figure; *congado* is the feast of the Lady of the Rosary; and the Congo King refers to an important carnival figure.

Introduction

Brasil, meu Brasil brasileiro,	*Brazil, my Brazilian Brazil,*
Meu mulato inzoneiro,	*My good-looking Mulatto,*
Vou a cantar-te nos meus versos.	*I'm going to sing you in my verses.*
Ô Brasil, samba que dá	*Oh Brazil, samba that gives*
Bamboleio que faz gingá.	*A swing that makes you sway.*
Ô Brasil do meu amor,	*Oh Brazil that I love,*
Terra do Nosso Senhor,	*Land of Our Lord,*
Brasil, Brasil, prá mim, prá mim!	*Brazil, Brazil, for me, for me!*
Ô abre a cortina do passado.	*Oh, open the curtain of the past.*
Tira a Mãe preta do cerrado.	*Bring the Black Mother down from the mountain.*
Bota o rei congo no congado.	*Return the Congo King to the Congado.*
Brasil, Brasil, prá mim, prá mim!	*Brazil, Brazil, for me, for me!*
Deixa cantar de novo o trovador	*Let the troubadour sing again*
Á merencória luz da lua	*To the melancholy light of the moon*
Toda canção de meu amor.	*Every song of my love.*
Quero ver essa Dona caminhando	*I want to see that lady walking*
Pelos salões arrastrando	*Through the ballrooms, wearing*
O seu vestido rendado.	*Her garments of lace.*
Brasil, Brasil, prá mim, prá mim!	*Brazil, Brazil, for me, for me!*

Many MPB styles extended their popularity into the 1940s, at the same time—not coincidentally—that romantic song traditions like the *trova* and the *bolero* were emerging in other parts of Latin America such as Cuba, Mexico, and Chile. These styles were in turn influencing popular music in Brazil. Additionally, the influence of North American music was being felt more and more in Brazil (as in much of the rest of the world), in the form of jazz, swing, and, later, rock-and-roll. By the 1950s, Brazilian popular music was reverting to an increasingly impersonal—even foreign—style of fluffy and glossy popular song that did little to inflame the passions of Brazilians. Change was clearly needed, and it was only a matter of time before a more modern popular style would make it onto the Brazilian scene. That style was the bossa nova.

The *Bossa Nova* Phenomenon

Bossa nova was just one of the developments that began reshaping Brazilian life in the late 1950s and 1960s. A sense of optimism and modernization pervaded much of the country, and the construction of the new capital Brasilia signaled a new economic boom. Brazil's soccer team engendered immeasurable national pride by winning successive World Cups. New important literary, artistic, and cinematic movements were emerging. The future looked bright, and there was a euphoric feeling that Brazil was entering a new modern age with a head start. It was in this climate that young artists, poets, musicians, and intellectuals began gathering in universities, apartments, and nightclubs, mostly in Rio de Janeiro. Akin to the Beat Generation that was concurrently emerging in the United States, these were usually White, middle-class students who espoused progressive political and social views. And they worshipped American jazz, particularly the sophisticated styles of Stan Getz and Charlie Byrd, which were being publicized by the radio and recording industry. Musicians began adapting these new sounds to their traditional samba rhythms and harmonies, which quickly led to the emergence of the cool urbane *bossa nova* (literally the "new way" or "new trend"), which showed the world that, as in many other aspects, Brazil remained a major musical power.

In contrast to the frenzied and frenetic pace of carnival dances, and to the hundreds or even thousands of musicians that typically make up a *batucada*, bossa nova was a softer, more personal, and decidedly more romantic style, often consisting of only one singer accompanying him- or herself on the guitar. Like the Beat poets and jazz musicians they emulated, bossa nova singers began appearing regularly in Rio nightclubs, dressed in Black and singing their sophisticated and sultry songs to an attentive public. The swinging and syncopated rhythms of the bossa nova combined well with the more personal and intense poetry that was emerging. Though Afro-Brazilian rhythms are unquestionably at the root of bossa nova, it is primarily a style created by and for the White middle class: For the first time since the days of the nineteenth-century empire, a major MPB style was drawn not from the working classes in the shantytown favelas or the street rhythms of carnival,

Antonio Carlos (Tom) Jobim.

but rather from the social and political concerns of Brazilian middle and upper classes. Typical bossa nova lyrics reflect this difference, emphasizing not the gritty hardships of street life but rather the languid lifestyle of love, romance, and the pleasurable good life.

The advent of bossa nova cannot be attributed to one person alone, but three artists are certainly at the center of its creation: the Bahia guitarist João Gilberto, whose difficult, off-center—but slow—rhythms gave the movement its cool feel; Antônio Carlos (Tom) Jobim, whose powerful and sexy melodies and complex harmonies appealed to the jazz generation; and the Rio poet Vinícius de Moraes, who provided lyrics that were perfectly in tune with bossa nova's ethos of pleasure and seduction. Their first collaboration was the 1958 album *Cancão do amor demais* (*The Song of Too Much Love*) with vocals by Elizeth Cardoso. The album contained the song "Chega de saudade," the first bossa nova hit.

North American jazz musicians, already enthralled by Caribbean rhythms, quickly became aware of the mesmerizing new Brazilian style. They soon began making important contributions, for example Charlie Byrd's and Stan Getz's 1962 album *Jazz Samba*. Though many Brazilians welcomed the presence and contributions of the jazz greats, both for artistic reasons and because they lent validation to the fledgling movement, some bossa nova artists, notably Carlos Lyra, opposed them, insisting jazz was co-opting bossa nova and diluting its Brazilian roots.

In 1964, the most famous bossa nova song emerged and instantly became an international sensation. This was "Garota de Ipanema" ("Girl from Ipanema"), another writing collaboration by Jobim and Moraes. With lyrics in both English and Portuguese, "Garota de Ipanema" became an instant phenomenon worldwide and established bossa nova as an international genre, though some condemned it as a vapid and empty exercise in sensuality. Other bossa novas have reached classic status, including "Desafinado" ("Out of Tune") and "One Note Samba," both written by Jobim and Newton Mendonça in response to critics who insisted that bossa nova challenged "correct" definitions of melody and harmony. Bossa nova gave Brazilian popular music an international boost and led to the emergence of the first Brazilian superstars since the days of Carmen Miranda. Gilberto, Jobim, and Moraes, together and individually, would continue to make enormous contributions to Brazilian music for decades. Other important bossa nova artists include Nara Leão, Luíz Bonfa, Carlos Lyra, Sergio Mendez, Oscar Castro-Neves, and Baden Powell. In subsequent years, bossa nova would expand, spawning a number of hyphenated new styles, and would even come to embrace the street sambas it had originally reacted against.

> **Recommended Listening:** "Chega de saudade" by Antônio Carlos Jobim and João Gilberto, from the CD *Antonio Carlos Jobim's Finest Hour*.

> **Recommended Listening:** "A felicidade" by Antônio Carlos Jobim and Vinícius de Moraes, from the soundtrack of the film *Orfeu negro* (*Black Orpheus*).

> **Recommended Listening:** "One Note Samba" and "Desafinado" by Antônio Carlos Jobim, from the CD *Antonio Carlos Jobim's Finest Hour*.

CDII, Track 9: Bossa Nova: "Garota de Ipanema"

Music: Antônio Carlos Jobim
Lyrics: Vinícius de Moraes (Portuguese) and Norman Gimbel (English)
Instrumentation: guitar (João Gilberto), piano (Antônio Carlos Jobim), saxophone (Stan Getz), drum set
Notes: This 1964 recording of "The Girl from Ipanema" is sung in Portuguese by João Gilberto and in English by his wife, Astrud Gilberto. The sparse and subtle orchestration, and particularly Astrud's sultry tone, lends this song a warm sensuality that is evocative of Brazil's beaches and love of life. João Gilberto's guitar provides the shuffling bossa nova rhythms, embellished by Jobim's subtle piano figures and later by Stan Getz's saxophone improvisation.

Verse 1 (Portuguese)

Olha que coisa mais linda,	*Look, such a beautiful thing,*
Mais cheia de graça.	*And so full of grace.*
É ela a menina que vem e que passa,	*And this girl comes and goes*
num doce balanço a caminho do mar.	*walking sweetly towards the sea.*
Moça do corpo dourado do sol de Ipanema,	*The girl with the body golden by*
	the Ipanema sun
O seu balançado é mais que um poema,	*Her walk is more than a poem*
É a coisa mais linda que eu já vi passar.	*It is the most beautiful thing I've*
	ever seen go by.

Chorus

Ah, por que estou tão sozinho?	*Ah, why am I so alone?*
Ah, por que tudo é tão triste?	*Ah, why is everything so sad?*
Ah, a beleza que existe,	*Ah, the beauty that exists,*
A beleza que não é só minha,	*A beauty that is not mine,*
Que também passa sozinha.	*And which also passes by alone.*
Ah, se ela soubesse	*Ah, if she only knew*
Que, quando ela passa,	*That when she passes by,*
O mundo sorrindo se enche de graça	*The smiling world fills up with grace*
E fica mais lindo por causa do amor.	*and remains more beautiful*
	because of love.

Verse 2 (English)
Tall and tan and young and lovely,
The girl from Ipanema goes walking,
And when she passes,
Each one she passes goes "ah."
When she walks, she's like a samba,
That swings so cool and sways so gently,
That when she passes,
Each one she passes goes "ah."

Chorus
Oh, but he watches so sadly,
How can he tell her he loves her?
Yes, he would give his heart gladly.
But instead when she walks to the sea,
She looks straight ahead not at he.
Tall, and tan, and young, and lovely,
The girl from Ipanema goes walking,
And when she passes,
He smiles, but she doesn't see.

After the *Bossa Nova*

After the wave of bossa nova had subsided, several important artists appeared in the 1960s who took MPB in different directions. These artists did not emerge from the streets of carnival, as *samba* had done for generations, nor did they rise out of the rural dancehalls that had spawned *forro* or from the sophisticated nightclub scene as had the bossa nova singers. Rather, they became popular in a new musical venue that was perfectly in tune with youth-oriented culture: the pop music festival. These were (and remain) immensely popular, sleek, televised productions where ambitious singers and songwriters competed for top prizes in the hopes of launching their musical careers. Organized and sponsored by the recording industry, festivals would produce winners who were then offered lucrative recording contracts, though in truth they were not always selected for their musical talent, and many winners, along with their often glossy and empty pop songs, quickly returned to obscurity. Nonetheless, these music festivals often had their finger on—and even propelled—current trends of popular culture. They occasionally became launching pads for important careers, including, early in the 1960s, Edu Lobo, Chico Buarque, Sergio Mendez, and Jorge Ben.

The landmark year of 1967 was particularly fruitful, as music festivals revealed three enormous talents that would dominate much of MPB for the next several decades: Milton Nascimento, Gilberto Gil, and Caetano Veloso. (Significantly, none of them actually won the festivals they competed in.) One of the most popular contemporary Brazilian artists, Nascimento was from the interior province of Minas Gerais, a stronghold of both African and Catholic culture, and his background is often reflected in his powerful poetry. He combined jazz and rock and roll with samba, and continued to expand the Brazilian style and reinvent himself over the years, appearing for example on Paul Simon's 1990 *Rhythm of the Saints*. Chico Buarque was one of the most successful writer of popular songs in the 1960s and 1970s. He also received critical acclaim for the score to the 1976 film *Dona Flor e seus dois maridos* (*Dona Flor and Her Two Husbands*"), which included the popular samba "O que sera" sung as a duet by Buarque and Nascimento. Jorge Ben (aka Benjor) was intent on bringing samba back to popular music, and he did so in 1962 with a series of hits that included "Taj Mahal," "Pais tropical," and his best-known song "Mas que nada" ("What the Heck, Let It Go"). Ben's original nasal delivery and combination of samba, bossa nova, and pop rhythms was a huge success in Brazil. In 1966, "Mas que nada" reached worldwide popularity after it was covered by Sergio Mendes and his group Brasil '66.

Recommended Listening: "A banda" by Chico Buarque, from the CD *Chico Buarque de Hollanda, Vol. 1*.

Recommended Listening: "Travessia" by Milton Nascimento, from the CD *Travessia*.

Recommended Listening: "Ponta de lanca africano (Umbabarauma) by Jorge Ben, from the CD *Brazil Classics 1: Beleza Tropical*.

Recommended Listening: "Mas que nada" by Jorge Ben, from the CD *Samba esquema novo*.

Recommended Listening: "Mas que nada" by Sergio Mendes, from the CD *Sergio Mendes and Brasil 66: Greatest Hits*.

Tropicália

As in virtually every country in Latin America (indeed, in most of the world), Brazilian popular culture in the 1960s could not fend off the onslaught of British and American rock and of youth culture in general. The optimism and stability of the 1950s gave way to the turbulent pessimism of the 1960s, and the generational contrast that emerged in Rio and Bahia could have been lifted straight out of the London or San Francisco scenes. Short-haired, black-clad jazz aficionados with serious demeanors and acoustic guitars gave way to long-haired, psychedelic, unruly rock fans with rebellious attitudes and electric guitars. Like youth movements everywhere, they challenged authority and conformity, melding a political and social consciousness with liberated attitudes towards drugs and sex, all lubricated by a raucous brand of protest music.

Just as North American jazz had earlier shaped the bossa nova phenomenon, the rock-and-roll explosion begat an important cultural movement called *tropicália*. The movement aimed to bring a creative seriousness of purpose that would alter the course of MPB. Like the reemergence of folk music in the United States and of the *nueva trova* throughout Latin America, the first iterations of *tropicália* were introduced by a younger generation of politically and socially conscious singer-songwriters, literate intellectuals who were passionate about philosophy and existential poetry and who aimed to seamlessly marry the text with the music. Reacting to the urbane, middle-class bossa nova, they readily embraced the rebellious sound of North American rock and roll, and melded it with Afro-Brazilian characteristics. In keeping with the long tradition of Brazilian syncretism, they aimed for an inclusive, crossover style that sought to combine diverse elements of art, from Western literature to Afro-Brazilian culture, from traditional samba to the creativity of rock icons such as the Beatles, the Rolling Stones, and Jimi Hendrix. *Tropicália* espoused youth-oriented modernity not only in music but also in every aspect of popular culture including literature, poetry, sculpture, painting, theater, and cinema. The name of the movement was derived from a 1967 modern-art exhibit that aimed to establish an artistic ideal for Brazil. Frankly leftist in ideology, *tropicália* opposed consumer society, social contradictions, and the politics of the military regime then in power. It also sought to expand the image of Brazil beyond Rio de Janeiro, and significantly, many of its adherents were from the northeast, where nonconformity was almost a way of life.

The key figures of *tropicália* were a group of Bahia artists that included singer-songwriters Caetano Veloso and Gilberto Gil, composer Tom Zé and singers Gal Costa, Elis Regina, and Maria Bethania (Veloso's sister). Veloso's melancholy lyrics and soulful renditions have entranced much of Latin America and the world. He was one of the first Brazilians to embrace

the rock-and-roll sound, championing new instrumentations and arrangements. Like Bob Dylan a few years earlier, Veloso embraced the electric guitar which shocked the musical establishment; also like Dylan, Veloso has
been the unofficial poet laureate of his generation. Gilberto Gil, by contrast,
developed a harder sound that emphasized rhythmic diversity, with
pointed emotional protest songs. In October 1967, the third festival of MPB
featured entries by both Veloso and Gil. Veloso's "Alegria, alegria" ("Joy,
Joy") had a rock style and disjointed lyrics that criticized much of Brazilian
establishment. It did not sit well with the audience, who were expecting
more traditional music, and they booed accordingly. Gil's entry, "Domingo
no parque" ("Sunday at the Park"), was equally disjointed, combining a
raunchy electric guitar style with *capoeira* rhythms, and met a similar fate.
But Gil and Veloso had launched a warning shot across the bow of traditional MPB, and the statement had been made that *tropicália* was here to
stay. (Both "Alegria, alegria" and "Domingo no parque" have since become
classics of MPB.) In 1968, Gil, Veloso, and many of their Bahia colleagues
released their landmark concept album *Tropicália ou Panis et circensis*
(*Tropicália, or Bread and Circuses*). The controversial collection came to define
the movement in terms of aesthetic sound and ideology. With songs such as
"Geléia geral" and "Baby," the album quickly became to Brazilians of a
certain age what the Beatles' *Sgt. Pepper's Lonely Hearts Club Band* was to
British and American youth. Veloso and Gil's songs shined a light on the ills
of modern society, confronted authority and conformism, and specifically
attacked the political order of the times with songs such as "Questão de
ordem" ("Question of Order") and "É proibido proibir" ("It Is Forbidden
to Forbid").

Recommended Listening: "Geléia geral" by Gilberto Gil, from the CD
Tropicália ou Panis et Circensis.

Recommended Listening: "Alegria, alegria" by Caetano Veloso, from
the CD *Tropicália Essentials*.

Tropicália: "Alegria, alegria"

Music and Lyrics: Caetano Veloso (1967)
Instrumentation: electric guitar, bass, keyboard, drum set
Notes: Caetano Veloso's psychedelic song is a strong counterculture critique, as the
alienated narrator decides to drop out of a superficial, decadent, and repressive society.
The song is replete with contemporary allusions, for example to starlets Claudia
Cardinale and Brigitte Bardot, as well as to *The Sun*, a famous counterculture publica-
tion. The mention of Coca-Cola is a reference to the insidious pervasiveness of U.S.
corporations.

Caminhando contra o vento,	*Walking against the wind,*
Sem lenço, sem documento,	*Without handkerchief, without documents,*
No sol de quase dezembro, eu vou!	*In the almost December sun, I go!*
O Sol se reparte em crimes,	*The Sun serves up crime*
Espaçonaves, guerrilhas,	*Spaceships, guerillas,*
Em Cardinales bonitas. Eu vou!	*Pretty Claudia Cardinales. I go!*
Em caras de presidentes,	*In the faces of presidents,*
Em grandes beijos de amor,	*In great passionate kisses*
Em dentes, pernas, bandeiras	*In smiles, legs, flags,*
Bomba e Brigite Bardot.	*Bombs and Brigitte Bardot.*
O Sol nas bancas de revista	*The Sun on the newspaper stands*
Me enche de alegria e preguiça.	*Fills me with joy and laziness.*
Quem lê tanta notícia? Eu vou!	*Who reads all that news anyway? I go!*
Por entre fotos e nomes,	*Among photos and names,*
Os olhos cheios de cores,	*My eyes filled with colors,*
O peito cheio de amores vãos.	*My breast filled with empty loves.*
Eu vou! por que não? por que não?	*I go! And why not? Why not?*
Ela pensa em casamento,	*She thinks of marriage,*
E eu nunca mais fui escola.	*I never went back to school.*
Sem lenço, sem documento, eu vou!	*Without handkerchief, without documents, I go!*
Eu tomo uma Coca-Cola,	*I drink a Coca-Cola,*
Ela pensa em casamento.	*She thinks of marriage.*
E uma canção me consola. Eu vou!	*And a song comforts me. I go!*
Por entre fotos e nomes,	*Among photos and names,*
Sem livros e sem fuzil,	*Without books and without rifles,*
Sem fome sem telefone,	*Without hunger, without telephone,*
No coração do Brasil.	*In the heart of Brazil.*
Ela nem sabe até pensei	*She doesn't even know that I thought*
Em cantar na televisão.	*Of singing on television.*
O sol é tão bonito. Eu vou!	*The sun is so beautiful. I go!*
Sem lenço, sem documento,	*Without handkerchief, without documents,*
Nada no bolso ou nas mãos,	*Nothing in my pockets or in my hands,*
Eu quero seguir vivendo, amor.	*I want to go on living, love.*
Eu vou! por que não? por que não?	*I go! And why not? Why not?*

The Post-*Tropicália* Explosion

Not surprisingly, these protest songs ran afoul of the military government that had been established by the coup of 1964. In 1968, a law was passed that severely restricted human rights, aimed at the youth movement in general, and at *tropicália* in particular. Censorship, intimidation, imprisonment, and torture quickly followed. Chico Buarque and Geraldo Vandré fled the country. Caetano Veloso and Gilberto Gil were arrested in 1968 and sent to London in exile, where they remained until 1972. The crackdown spelled the end of *tropicália* as an organized movement, though it was unable to halt its influence. Veloso, Gil, and their supporters had succeeded in bringing about a major shift in the course of popular music, liberating it from the constraint of tradition, and allowing for widespread aesthetic and intellectual experimentation. The movement was a crucial turning point in the evolution of MPB.

Like English and American rock, Brazilian styles quickly diverged in thousands of different directions in the late 1960s and 1970s, with *tropicália* remaining at the root of everything that was being produced. Singer-songwriters soon enough abandoned their reaction against bossa nova and sought out new sources of inspiration. MPB became a mish-mash of styles, drawing from Brazil's rich musical past, with songs that defy categorization, but which always strive for a combination of modernity and Brazilian roots. Gil and Veloso themselves have had very productive careers, never relying on their past glories but continuing to reinvent themselves as versatile and creative artists. Other members of *tropicália* also continued to enjoy popular success, including Maria Bethania and Gal Costa; Costa, more than thirty years later, still remains Brazil's most important female singer. Other women gained prominence during this period, including Fafa de Belem, Simone, Zizi Possi, and Maria Creuza. Perhaps the most celebrated singer of this era was Elis Regina, whose poignant voice and soulful demeanor made her a favorite with Brazilian audiences. In 1979, Regina recorded a collection of duets with Tom Jobim titled simply *Elis and Tom*, which remains one of the most successful Brazilian albums ever released. Tragically, she died of a drug overdose in 1982 at age 37. More recently, important MPB singers have included Margareth Menezes and Virginia Rodrigues, whose sultry voice has taken the style in new directions, including the incorporation of *bloco afro* elements.

> **Recommended Listening:** "O bebabo e a Equilibrista" by Elis Regina, from the CD *Elis, Essa Mulher*.

> **Recommended Listening:** "Noite de temporal" by Virginia Rodrigues from the CD *Sol negro*.

Brazilian rock also became phenomenally successful in the 1970s and 1980s, reaching new heights of record sales. Hundreds of rock artists and thousands of albums took Brazilian music in uncountable directions. One of the most prominent rockers was Raul Seixas who had a number of hit albums, including *Fool's Gold* and *I'm the Fly in Your Soup*. The singer Cazuza also represented the angst of youth. Others bands and artists include Ney Matogrosso, Renato Russo, Barão Vermelho, Blitz, Legião Urbana, the Titãs, and Vimana. Rita Lee, one-time member of the *tropicália* band Os Mutantes has had a successful solo career as a rock singer.

Recommended Listening: "Lança perfume" by Rita Lee, from the CD *Lança perfume e outras manias: The Greatest Hits.*

In the 1980s, the rap and hip-hop movements, spawned by the economic hardships of African-Americans in U.S. inner cities, quickly emerged in Brazil, where a vast underclass lived in the favelas under similar conditions. Brazilian rap makes use of the natural rhythms and inflexions of the Portuguese language, though the subject matter of the songs can be equally coarse. As always, Afro-Brazilian rhythms give Brazilian hip-hop a particular identity.

Recommended Listening: "Minha Mina" by Thaide and DJ Hum, from the CD *Rap from Brazil-Iris Music.*

Another important and extremely popular style emerged in Bahia in the 1990s. This was *axé*, an alternative and continuously evolving style that drew from a mixture of sources including *tropicália*, *choro*, and samba as well as non-Brazilian styles such as jazz, rock, and reggae. *Axé* is a Yoruba word, which means "peace" or "life." It is often heard in trendy bars in Salvador and throughout Bahia. Like so many other styles before it, *axé* has met stiff resistance from entrenched critics who see it as soul-less and empty. Yet if anything, *axé* incorporates every style imaginable, providing—once again—a syncretism of various traditions. Its most prominent practitioner, Carlinhos Brown, proudly refers to *axé* as "Afro-Brazilian popular music without prejudice." Another important *axé* artist is Daniela Mercury, who also continuously redefines the style.

Recommended Listening: "O bode" by Carlinhos Brown, from the CD *Alfagamabetizado.*

The new directions taken by MPB have failed to displace traditional Brazilian music. Rural styles such as *forró, baião,* and *sertanejo* have continued to remain popular nationwide. Bossa nova is still going strong, with a new group of artists that include Rosa Passos. A recent album called *Red Hot + Rio* was a compilation of contemporary American pop stars doing modern renditions of 1960s bossa novas. Traditional samba, exiled from the headlines but still omnipresent in daily life, was revitalized in the late 1960s and 1970s, particularly with the works of Paulinho da Viola and Martinho da Vila, both of whom brought it into the music festival scene, and thus into commercial success. Others samba artists quickly appeared, including Marisa Monte, Clara Nunes, Nelson Cavaquinho, Cartola, Beth Carvalho, Alcione, Jovalina Perola Negra, and the innovative team of Aldir Blanc and João Bosco. Most of the commercial recordings by these artists are *cançãos da samba* (samba songs), not the street dances heard during carnival. They took the *escola* tradition into the studio and turned it into a stylized and polished samba that is slower, more musically diverse, relying on melody, orchestration, and lyrics rather than on the frenzied Afro-rhythms of the carnival dances. In 1988, Vila's *Kizomba, Festa da Raça* won the carnival competition and became a nationwide anthem against racism.

Recommended Listening: "Kizomba, festa da raça" by Martinho da Vila, from the CD *Festa da raça autentico*.

Recommended Listening: The CDs *Brazil Classics 1: Beleza tropical* and *Putumayo: Brazilian Groove* offer a wide variety of MPB styles from the last few decades.

Brazilian music has continued to diversify and cross-pollinate for centuries, and there is no sign that this trend will stop any time soon. This is for the better, for the country's contributions to the music of the world have been among the most important—and the most infectious. Like Brazilians themselves, the music is rarely derived from a single source, but usually is the product of wildly diverse historical, geographic, ethnic, cultural, and religious elements. Perhaps more than anywhere else on the continent, Brazilian music can be likened, not to the proverbial melting pot, where individual ingredients lose their specific characteristics to form a new homogenous whole, but rather to a rich gumbo, where each flavor retains its own identity while simultaneously affecting every other element in the pot.

7

Colombia and Venezuela

INTRODUCTION TO HISPANIC SOUTH AMERICA

Nine countries make up Hispanic South America, all of them sharing cultural elements inherited from their background as Spanish colonies. They can be broadly divided into three areas: the north, which includes Colombia and Venezuela; the Andean region, which encompasses Peru, Bolivia, and Ecuador; and the Southern Cone region, which includes Paraguay, Uruguay, Chile, and Argentina. (The other countries in South America—Brazil and the Guyanas— have a separate, non-Hispanic cultural background and are examined in other chapters.) Yet in spite of their Hispanic background, important differences remain between these countries, beginning with their widely diverse ethnic composition. Broadly speaking, the northern countries have a stronger African presence; in the Andean region, Native influences are more pronounced; while European ancestry often predominates in the south. Beyond these broad gener- alizations, however, each country has a complex panoply of syncretic elements that historically contributed to the emergence of each individual culture. Moreover, even the culture within a given country is not uniform and can often vary drastically between regions, towns, and villages.

The South American continent also has important geographic features that have greatly influenced its history and culture. Most prominent is the *cordillera de los Andes*—the Andes mountain range—which follows the west- ern coast from Colombia to the southern tip of Chile. The western slopes of the Andes fall fairly abruptly into the Pacific Ocean, while the enormous amount of water run off from their eastern slopes irrigates the largest rainfor- est in the world: the Amazon basin, with large and imposing rivers which in- clude the Amazon, the Orinoco, and the Paraná. As one progresses south on the continent, the rainforest gives way to fertile plains called *pampas*, and then to the desolate plains of Patagonia. At the extreme southern tip, dipping to- wards Antarctica, is an archipelago of rugged and barren islands called Tierra del Fuego, first navigated by Magellan in 1520.

During the colonial period, Hispanic South America was divided into three colonial entities: the Viceroyalty of New Granada (encompassing what is today Colombia, Ecuador, Venezuela, and Panama), the Viceroyalty of Peru (Peru and Bolivia), and the Viceroyalty of Rio de La Plata (Argentina, Uruguay, Paraguay, and Chile). The most important military and political fig- ures in South America were the Venezuelan Simón Bolívar and the Argentine José de San Martín, who in the 1820s led revolutionary movements that freed much of South America from the Spanish yoke. San Martín fought for the lib- eration of Argentina, Chile, and parts of Peru. Bolívar, known throughout the continent simply as *El Libertador*, liberated Colombia, Venezuela, Panama, Ecuador, Peru, and Upper Peru, which was renamed Bolivia in his honor. However, Bolívar's dream of a united continent that would mirror— and rival—the United States fizzled soon after independence, disrupted by nationalist attitudes and regional enmities. Instead, the continent quickly be- came a fractured collection of states that more often than not were at war with each other. The post-independence era in every South American country has been marred by political and economic instability, as violent swings occurred between left- and right-wing governments. Democratically elected leaders were regularly overthrown by military regimes led by power-hungry dictators called *caudillos*. Thus, Bolivia famously had 192 governments between 1825 and 1981, each lasting an average of 10 months.

In the twentieth century, this instability often led to guerilla insurgencies from both the right and the left, as well as to the rise of powerful drug-trafficking cartels, particularly in Colombia, Peru, and Bolivia, where they often became a potent cultural and political force. South America today remains a collection of distinct countries, each with its own culture and musical tradition. Yet geographical and political classifications are not always neat and satisfying, since musical elements and styles often overlap multiple areas.

COLOMBIA

A striking example of this multifaceted culture is Colombia (capital: Bogotá). It lies at the crossroads of the American continent, with both a Pacific and a Caribbean coast, and is the gateway to Central America. The upper extremities of the Andes extend into Colombia, and its mountainous interior, dotted with high altitude lakes, has much in common with the Andean traditions to the south. Its southeastern flank reaches into the Amazon Basin, with thick rainforests and extended plains called *llanos*. Its coastal areas share elements of the Afro-Caribbean traditions and are often as pristine as that of the islands. In the south lies the famous Putumayo region, along the river of the same name, which forms the border with neighboring Ecuador and Peru.

Historical Overview

Colombia's original inhabitants included hundreds of Native tribes, most prominently the Chocó, the Kuna, the Quimbaya, and the Chibcha. Many of the original inhabitants were able goldsmiths whose artistry led to the legend of El Dorado, a mythic and much-sought-after kingdom of gold. The Spaniards first landed on the Colombian coast in 1499, and the territory was named after Christopher Columbus, though the explorer never set foot there. Vasco Nuñez de Balboa began surveying the territory in 1508, and five years later he sighted the Pacific Ocean, the first European to do so in the Americas. This opened the gateway for the exploration of the rest of the continent, which, notably, brought the Inca Empire to the attention of the Spaniards. The first Spanish settlement in Colombia was Santa Marta in 1525, soon followed by Cartagena in 1533 and Bogotá a few years after that. In 1717, the Spaniards organized the entire area as the viceroyalty of New Granada. The importation of African slaves began early in the sixteenth century and lasted until abolition in 1851. African populations were concentrated on the tropical lowlands, on both the Atlantic and Pacific coasts.

In 1819, led by Simón Bolívar, New Granada achieved its independence, forming a new country called Gran Colombia. After the death of Bolívar in

1830, Colombia, Venezuela, and Ecuador separated, and New Granada formally became an independent country, ultimately adopting the name Republic of Colombia in 1886. The years since independence have seen dictatorships alternating with democratic periods and a surfeit of civil wars and guerrilla movements, including an especially bloody conflict in the 1940s and 1950s called *La Violencia*, which killed an estimated 300,000 Colombians. The latest conflict began in 1970, with various paramilitary groups from both the left and the right trying to unseat successive unpopular governments, all influenced in one way or another by the lucrative drug trade. Today, Colombia has about 42 million people, about 25 percent of whom are of African or *zambo*—African and Native—ancestry, with 20 percent of European ancestry and 55 percent Mestizo. Native Colombians number about 700,000—slightly over one percent of the population.

Historically, Colombia has been a culturally divided country. Its coastal areas were home to agricultural plantations, cattle ranches, and a large slave population. An important *zambo* presence became prominent after the abolition of slavery in 1851, centered in the cities of Cartagena and Barranquilla, and in the town of San Basilio de Palenque, which was founded by escaped slaves and was thus an important center for the preservation of African culture and music. It is this culture that has been extensively recounted and explored by the Nobel Prize–winning author Gabriel García Márquez, whose novels are infused with the magic realism that pervades the unique coastal way of life. Meanwhile, in the mountainous interior, in the cities of Bogotá, Medellín, and Cali, Hispanic and Mestizo customs and traditions prevailed, dominating the country's cultural life during the colonial period and after independence. In the twentieth century, however, the roles were reversed, and it was the coastal culture, including especially the music, which became more pronounced in the rest of the country, eventually taking over as the leading national influence.

But Colombia also shares much of its musical heritage with neighboring countries. Thus, because the country lies at the northern tip of the Andes, a good deal of its music and culture is similar to that of Peru and Ecuador. On the eastern border, Colombians have also developed their own version of *música llanera*, including the harp-based *joropo*, the quintessential style of neighboring Venezuela. And the Pacific coast has seen the development of a *marimba* tradition that is akin to those in Central America and Southern Mexico.

Music of the Interior

As in much of Hispanic America, colonial Colombia inherited many of its ballads and *romances* from Spain, as well as more cosmopolitan European genres such as opera and salon dances such as the *contradanza*, polka, quadrille, *jota*, and waltz. Eventually, White and Mestizo Colombians developed their own dances, such as the *guabina*, the *torbellino*, and especially the *pasillo*, a type of waltz that became very popular in the nineteenth century throughout the northern part of the continent, including Venezuela and

Ecuador. Music from the Caribbean was also popular, including *boleros*, *habaneras*, and *fandangos*. These styles were at first played with guitars, mandolins, and other string instruments, and in time were played on pianos and string orchestras.

BAMBUCO   The most important style from Colombia's interior was *bambuco*, a rural folk dance that was heavily influenced by European, African, and Andean characteristics. Its exact origins are still debated: The name possibly comes from a Native word for "canoe," suggesting that it was derived from the waterborne cultures of Colombia's interior. Also sometimes known as *música carrilera*, or "railroad music," *bambuco* emerged in the southern regions bordering Peru and Ecuador. Though it later evolved into an urban dance, the rural folkloric version is still preserved in many parts of the country, as well as in neighboring Venezuela. It is a lively courtship couples dance in $\frac{3}{4}$ or $\frac{6}{8}$ meter, which recreates a flirtatious meeting of an amorous couple. The dance has the requisite advances by the man and rejections by the woman, but inevitably ends with the successful union of the two. A red handkerchief is an obligatory prop in the playful movements of the dance. The steps are vigorous and precise and include the flamenco-like *zapateado*. Dancers wear traditional folk costumes, including flower garlands in the woman's hair, while the man wears the typical white sombrero.

In its earliest forms, the country *bambuco* was performed with cane flutes called *chirimías*, accompanied by drums and raspers called *carrascas*. In the nineteenth century, guitars, lute-like *bandolas*, and small *tiple* guitar were added, and the dance was also adopted by the string orchestras of the urban elite, which infused it with the characteristics of elegant salon music, such as prominent flutes and percussion. By the 1920s, it had become popular throughout Colombia and thereafter in other parts of Latin America, including Central America and Mexico, though it never reached the international popularity that coastal styles such as *cumbia* and *vallenato* later achieved. Still later, it became infused with popular styles, both foreign and domestic, including salsa, jazz, and rock. *Bambuco* also became an important element of Colombia's nationalist art music movement, and its presence in Colombian concert halls is still felt to this day. Early popular proponents of *bambuco* included Emilio Sierra, Efraín Orozco, Jorge Añez, Justiniano Rosales, and the duo Calle y Ochoa, who were among the first to record the style. Subsequent performers included Manuel J. Bernal, El Dueto de Antaño, Fulgencio Garcia, Dario Gómez, the trio Pedro Morales Pino, Las Hermanitas Calle, and Jorge Villamil. Despite its overshadowing by *cumbia* and other styles, *bambuco* remains the national dance of Colombia. Important festivals have emerged, notably the Festival Nacional del Bambuco, held every June during the feast of St. John the Baptist.

> **Recommended Listening:** "Coplas del Rajaleña" by Los Tolimenses, from the CD *Música de Colombia*.
>
> **Recommended Listening:** "Soy colombiano (Bambuco)" by Garzón y Collazos, from the CD *Los grandes duetos de Colombia*.

CDII, Track 10: *Bambuco* (*Chirimías*): "Brisas del Pamplonita"

Music and Lyrics: Elías Soto and Roberto Irwin
Instrumentation: *chirimías*, *tambora* drums, *carrasca* raspers
Notes: The Colombian *chirimía* is different than the double-reed oboe-like instrument that was popular during the colonial period. It is a cane flute that emerged in Southwestern Colombia, where it is still popular today. "Brisas del Pamplonita" was composed in 1892, and this 1951 recording is from the town of Popayán, Colombia. The title refers to the curative effects of the breezes on the Pamplonita river. In both this example and the next, the *sesquiáltera* is evident from the very beginning, as the $\frac{6}{8}$ meter (**one**-two-three-**four**-five-six) quickly alternates with $\frac{3}{4}$ meter (**one**-and-**two**-and-**three**-and).

Recommended Listening: "Agáchate el sombrerito (Bambuco)" by Los Tolimenses, from the CD *Las 30 colombianas de la historia*.

Bambuco: "Agáchate el sombrerito"

Music and Lyrics: Jorge Añez
Instrumentation: guitar, *tiple* guitar
Notes: This *bambuco* is both an energetic folk dance and a sweet love song. Each verse is repeated, as the singer narrates the flirting and loving advances that are also reflected in the handkerchief dance.

Agáchate el sombrerito	*Lower your hat,*
Y por debajo mirame,	*And look at me beneath it,*
Y con una miradita	*And with one look*
Dí lo que quieras hablarme.	*Say what you want to tell me.*
Chorus	
Que me voy a morir,	*I am going to perish,*
Que me muero de amor,	*I'm dying of love.*
Que me muero de amor	*I'm dying of love,*
¡Hurria! por las colombianas.	*Hurrah! for Colombian women.*
Tengo que subir, subir,	*I must sail up*
Las aguas del Magdalena,	*The waters of the Magdalena River,*
Pa' llegar a Bogotá	*To get to Bogotá*
Y besar a mi morena.	*And kiss my dárk woman.*
Aún conservo el pañuelito	*I still keep that embroidered*
De cenefa moradita,	*Purple handkerchief,*
Aquel que tanto mordías	*The one you used to bite*
Cuando te ponías bravita.	*When you got mad.*

Aquí tengo el clavelito	*I still have the carnation*
Del jardín de tu casita,	*From the garden of your little house,*
Que al despedirme llorando	*That yours truly kissed*
Lo besó su mercesita.	*As he said goodbye in tears.*

The Caribbean Coast

In contrast to the Hispanic- and Mestizo-influenced interior, several styles have emerged on Colombia's Caribbean coast that are either rooted directly in African traditions or adopted from Caribbean cultures with similar characteristics. African drums and percussion instruments, complex polyrhythms, syncopated dances, and call-and-response songs recreate ancient rituals and practices of African origin. Yet, as in many parts of the African Diaspora, these rituals also have in common the adoption, to various degrees, of European and Native elements, forming a new syncretic style. Throughout the coastal region one can find work songs, initiation ceremonies, courtship and harvest rituals, ancestral communication rites, funeral observances (such as the Bantu mourning ritual *lumbalú* and the lively *buyerengue*), and the *mapalé*, a dance that celebrates the bounty of the sea. Colombia's carnival, which dates back to colonial times, is centered on the city of Barranquilla, at the mouth of the Magdalena River. In the southern town of Pasto, a celebration called the Blacks-and-Whites carnival is held between December 28 and January 6, with the main celebrations occurring on January 5, *Día de los Negros*, commemorating the one day every year in which slaves were free to do as they pleased.

But the most prominent of the Afro-Colombian styles are the *porro*, the *vallenato*, and especially the *cumbia*, which has reached a level of international fame and popularity that rivals that of salsa. All three started as rural, drum-based folk styles. In the 1930s and 1940s, with the advent of the international "Latin Craze," they became representative national symbols, competing on the world market with other styles such as Cuban *son* and rumba, Argentine tango, and Brazilian samba. In order to compete, however, they often had to shed much of their rural, ethnic identities, becoming sophisticated band music led by cosmopolitan, elegantly dressed leaders. African drums, being antithetical to this process, were usually discarded. By the 1960s and 1970s, these styles transformed yet again, becoming pop phenomena influenced by the advent of worldwide youth culture, and adopting the electric bass, guitars, and drum sets of American rock and roll.

CUMBIA   Like so many Latin American styles that have risen to national and international prominence, *cumbia* began as a folk dance among the Black, Native, and mixed populations of the Caribbean coast. Specifically, it was a *zambo* courtship dance that drew from the *cumbe* rituals of Guinea, as well as from coastal indigenous groups such as the Kuna. (Some historians claim that the movements of the dance represent slaves trying to shed their shackles.) Though the term *cumbia* did not appear until the nineteenth century, the dance first emerged during the colonial period in the coastal regions around Santa Marta, Barranquilla, and Cartagena, the port of entry for most slaves, and continued to thrive in post-independence Colombia. In its traditional form, *cumbia* is a heavily syncopated style, usually in duple meter, and purely instrumental, played by *maracas*, *guaches* (seed-filled metal or cane tubes), and three drums of African origin. The *tambora* (or *bombo*), a large two-headed drum played with mallets, provides the bass; the *llamador*, a smaller and higher-pitched drum, provides a continuous repeating pattern. The *mayor* (or *alegre*), held between the legs and played with the hands, provides intricate improvisations above the patterns of the other two. They are carved from wood of the *ceiba* tree, with goatskin heads tied by a henequen fiber rope called *sisal*. *Claves* and *güiros* occasionally join the ensembles.

Like many other courtship and fertility rituals in the Caribbean region, such as the Cuban *rumba*, the Martinican *kalinda*, and the *tambú* from Curaçao, folk *cumbias* are sensual and suggestive, danced by flirtatious couples. Ceremonies called *cumbiambas* begin at twilight and often continue until daybreak, celebrated on warm beaches and for that reason are danced barefoot. Drummers gather around a fire built near the water. The dancing couples form two circles around the musicians, men on the inside, women on the outside. The women, wearing long colorful flowing skirts and flower garlands in their hair, entice the men with their suggestive *zarandeo* movements in which

Man and Woman dancing the *cumbia*.

they twirl their skirts in a fan-like movement. The men wear white shirts—or sometimes dance bare-chested—and rolled-up white trousers, red handkerchiefs around their necks, and straw sombreros, which they repeatedly take off and on to signal their seductive intentions. At a crucial moment in the dance, the men hold white candles high in the air that represent their semen and that they offer to the women as signs of fertility.

A specific type of folk *cumbia* is the *cumbia de gaita* (or *gaitero*), distinguished by the presence of two long indigenous flutes that play alongside the drums and percussion. The term *gaita* (pronounced GA-ee-tah) originally referred to the Gaelic bagpipes found in the Spanish province of Galicia. When the Spaniards arrived in Colombia, the nasal sound of the indigenous flutes reminded them of the Galician *gaitas*, and the term has applied to them ever since. These flutes, made from wood or bamboo cane, are also known by their indigenous name *kuisi*, or more commonly, as *flautas de millo* ("millet-cane flutes"). As in other Latin American traditions, *gaitas* are often identified with genders, with the lead *gaita* called *macho* (male) and the follower *hembra* (female).

CDII, Track 11: *Cumbia de gaita*: "Fuego de cumbia"

Music and Lyrics: Rafael Pérez García
Instrumentation: two *gaitas* (*hembra* and *macho*), three drums (*alegre*, *llamador*, and *tambora*), *guache* shaker
Notes: "Fuego de cumbia" ("cumbia fire") is a traditional *cumbia de gaita* that celebrates the European, African, and Native origins of the style. The two *gaitas* improvise passages between the verses, as the drums dialogue with each other in syncopation and complement the singer.

¡Un fuego de sangre pura que con lamento se canta!	*A fire of pure blood, which is sung with sorrow.*
Se encienden noches oscuras con un jolgorio que encanta.	*The dark nights are set alight with an enchanting celebration.*
Los repiques de tambores, la raza negra levanta.	*The Black race plays the strokes of the drums.*
Y el indio pasivamente con su melódica gaita,	*And the Indian, with his melodious gaita,*
Interrumpe en el silencio cuando una fogata baila.	*Passively interrupts the silence as a fire dances.*
Y yo siento por mis venas un fuego que no se apaga.	*And I feel in my veins a fire that endures.*
Chorus	
Es el fuego de mi cumbia, es el fuego de mi raza.	*It is the fire of my cumbia, it is the fire of my people.*

¡Un fuego de sangre pura que con lamento se canta!	A fire of pure blood, which is sung with sorrow.
¡Un fuego de sangre pura que con lamento se canta!	A fire of pure blood, which is sung with sorrow.
Mi tierra guaca explorada, sin tribus y sin cacique.	My Indian homeland explored, without tribes or ruler.
La raza negra ha quedado que con alegría nos viste.	The Black race has remained, which you witnessed with joy
Porque con fuerza y valor ganaron el paso libre.	For they gained their freedom with strength and courage.
Hay mezclas de su cultura con la del indio aborigen.	They mixed their culture with the aboriginal Indians.
Hacen vibrar el lamento que hoy nuestra tierra vive.	Today our land lives their vibrating lament.
Por aquí hay grandes señales de tiempos precolombinos.	There still remain great signs of pre-Colombian times.
Porque hablar de la gaita es retroceder caminos,	Because to speak of the gaita is to retrace our steps.
Es meterce en el ayer y en la ciencia del indio,	It is to return to yesterday and to the knowledge of the Indian.
Es recordar muchos tiemps que hace siglos se han ido,	It is to remember many eras now gone for centuries,
Pero dejando la mezcla de cultura y de civismo.	But which have left a mixture of culture and civic pride.

Artists began recording the folk *cumbia* in the 1950s, including prominently Antonio Fernández and his group Los Gaiteros de San Jacinto. Though they have been overshadowed by their modern popular versions, folk *cumbias* can still be heard on the coast and in the interior, still danced with traditional costumes, occasionally with just the drum, flute, and percussion accompaniment but also with more modern accompaniment such as the acoustic *orquesta típica*. Though they still retain their ancient courtship elements, they have mostly evolved as vehicles for community celebrations, occasions for the village to celebrate a patron saint, wedding, baptism, or simply a good time on a Saturday night. An important traditional *cumbia* celebration is the feast of San Martín, held every November 11 in and around the city of Barranquilla.

Recommended Listening: "El pescador" and "Dáme la mano Juancho" by Totó la Momposina, from the CD *La candela viva*.

MODERN *CUMBIA* As was often the case with African-derived rituals, the White elite of Bogotá and the interior looked down upon the folk *cumbia* from the coast and considered it crude and lower class. In the first half of the twentieth century, high society White and Mestizo Colombians listened to Cuban *boleros* and *guarachas* and to the jazz and foxtrot rhythms emanating from the

FIG. 7.1 *Cumbia* Pattern:

United States. Yet it was also during this period that many Afro-folk styles—including the Cuban *son*, Trinidadian calypso, and Brazilian samba—were transformed into commercial genres that became popular beyond their country of origin. *Cumbia* soon joined them: its transformation from a rural, African-based courting ritual to a popular dance style was a necessary step for its acceptance by the White and Mestizo middle and upper classes in urban areas of the interior, particularly in Bogotá. Only after shedding its African and Native folk characteristics did it became popular in nightclubs and eventually play on the radio throughout the country. Starting in the 1940s, it began absorbing elements of *son*, mambo, and jazz and incorporating instruments such as guitars, accordions, bass, harps, organs, pianos, and wind instruments such as trumpets, trombones, and saxophones. More percussion was added, including *güiros*, *claves*, and cowbells, and Afro-Colombian drums were abandoned in favor of Cuban instruments such as timbales and conga drums. With the increase in instrumentation, the rhythms paradoxically became simpler and thus more danceable, often shunning their improvised complexity in favor of straightforward—though still highly syncopated—lilting rhythms. The typical *cumbia* rhythm pattern is usually played by a prominent electric bass, which outlines an arpeggiated chord (see Fig. 7.1).

One of the first musicians to popularize *cumbia*—as well as its cousins *porro* and *vallenato*—was Pacho Galán, who had several hits, including "Ay cosita linda," which was later recorded in the United States by Nat King Cole. Lucho Bermúdez, a clarinetist whose musical roots were in early twentieth-century military wind bands, and whose orchestra was widely recognized as the best of its time, spread *cumbia* throughout the country as well as in Chile and Argentina. Another proponent was the short-lived but immensely popular Guillermo Buitrago, who performed not only *cumbia* but *vallenato* as well. By the 1950s *cumbia*, *porro*, and *vallenato* were firmly ensconced in Colombian popular culture. It was also during this time that the styles came to be recorded, notably by the legendary Colombian label Discos Fuentes. Some of the first *cumbias* to be recorded and broadcast on the radio included "El caimán" and "La cumbia cienaguera," which became the style's first international hits, and innumerable cumbia bands have covered both since then.

CDII, Track 12: *Cumbia*: "Cumbia cienaguera"

Music: Andrés Paz Barros
Lyrics: Esteban Montaño
Instrumentation: accordion, guitar, bass, *güiro*, maracas, conga drums, timbales
Notes: "Cumbia cienaguera" (from the coastal town of Ciénaga in Northeast Colombia) is so popular that it is often considered Colombia's unofficial national anthem. This

recording features call-and-response singing derived from African practices, while the drumming patterns are more straightforward, if still highly syncopated. The first verse is addressed to the male chorus, the second to the female chorus, and each responds to the lead singer with slightly different lyrics.

Muchachos bailen la cumbia porque la cumbia emociona.	*Boys, dance the cumbia because the cumbia is exciting.*
Chorus	
La cumbia cienaguera que se baila suavesona.	*The cumbia cienaguera, which is danced smoothly.*
La bailan en Santa Marta y la bailan en toda la zona.	*They dance it in Santa Marta and throughout the countryside.*
Y la bailan en mi tierra porque la cumbia funciona.	*And they dance it in my homeland because the cumbia succeeds.*
Muchachas bailen la cumbia porque la cumbia emociona.	*Girls, dance the cumbia because the cumbia is exciting.*
Chorus	
Vamos a bailar la cumbia, es la cumbia suavesona.	*Let's all dance the cumbia, the cumbia that is smooth.*
Quiero que prendan la vela porque la cumbia emociona.	*I want to light a candle because the cumbia is exciting.*
La bailan en Santa Marta y la bailan en toda la zona.	*They dance it in Santa Marta and throughout the countryside.*

In the 1960s, with the worldwide rise of youth culture and the influence of rock and roll and other Caribbean styles, *cumbia* continued to evolve, abandoning its big band sound in favor of smaller groups that included electric guitars, keyboards, and bass. An important figure was Ernesto "Fruko" Estrada who, with his band Fruko y Sus Tesos, began incorporated elements from the Cuban *son* and continued *cumbia*'s meteoric rise in popularity. The most prominent *cumbia* group to come out of Colombia was La Sonora Dinamita, an ensemble that originated in the 1960s and was subsequently taken over by Estrada. It had a number of important international hits, including "Mi cucú" and "A mover la colita," and was largely responsible for popularizing *cumbia* in other parts of Latin America, notably in Mexico, where it became a phenomenon of its own. In the 1970s, *cumbia* once again was transformed, adopting many of the elements of *salsa*, due in large part to the songs of Joe Arroyo, a protégé of Estrada who succeeded in incorporating the style into his own blend of *música tropical*. In turn, *cumbia* was adopted by salsa bands and rode the coattails of the salsa explosion, achieving immense popularity throughout Latin America and in the United States, to the point where the styles have become virtually interchangeable. Today, in almost every part of the continent, *música tropical* consists of three basic styles: Cuban salsa, Dominican merengue, and Colombian *cumbia*, interspersed with slower romantic ballads.

Other countries have developed their own important *cumbia* traditions, notably neighboring Venezuela and Panama, as well as the Andean region, where it combined with traditional Andean features and led to styles such as *chicha* and *cumbia andina*. In Argentina, a specific style called *cumbia villera* has emerged while in Mexico, *cumbias* have come to rival the Colombian versions in popularity. It is mostly the Mexican version of *cumbia* that is popular today in many parts of the United States (See Chapter 3). Yet, paradoxically, *cumbia* has somewhat fallen from its lofty perch within Colombia itself. The meteoric rise of *vallenato* in the 1980s to some extent eclipsed the style's popularity among Colombians, who in any event still consider *bambuco* the national dance. Though some recent modern *cumbia* artists have emerged, such as Arturo Jaimes, La India Meliyara, and the group Perla Colombiana, no leading figure has emerged to carry the *cumbia* mantle forward into the new millennium. Modern critics have lamented the excess influence of foreign elements into Colombia's most famous style and advocate a return to the folk traditions that are at its roots. Many artists have taken this charge to heart and traditional *cumbias* continue to regain the popularity they once had. Important festivals have also emerged, including the Festival Nacional de la Cumbia, held annually since 1975 in the town of El Banco.

> **Recommended Listening:** "Las mujeres a mí no me quieren" by Guillermo Buitrago, from the CD *Diciembre y Año Nuevo*.
>
> **Recommended Listening:** "Tolú" by Lucho Bermúdez y Su Orquesta, from the CD *El maestro: Los más grandes éxitos del maestro Lucho Bermúdez*.
>
> **Recommended Listening:** "La pollera colorá" and "La cumbia sobre el mar" by Carmen Rivero, from the CD *La época de oro de la cumbia*.
>
> **Recommended Listening:** "Mi cucú" and "El africano" by La Sonora Dinamita, from the CD *Super éxitos, Vol. I*.
>
> **Recommended Listening:** "Cumbia del caribe" by Orquesta de Edmundo Arias and "El ciclón" by La Sonora Dinamita, from the CD *Putumayo Presents: Colombia*.
>
> **Recommended Listening:** "El caimán" by Los Tigrillos, from the CD *Cumbias con garra, Vol. 2*.

CDII, Track 13: *Cumbia*: "A mover la colita"

Music and Lyrics: Wilfrido Vargas
Instrumentation: trumpets, piano, bass, *güiro*, conga drums, drum set
Notes: Performed by La Sonora Dinamita, this *cumbia* became extremely popular in dance clubs and discos in Mexico and the rest of Latin America. Though the lilting bass and Margarita Vargas's vocals identify it as a *cumbia*, it nonetheless borrows salsa's basic format and instrumentation: the *montuno* piano pattern is heard prominently at

the beginning and throughout the song; trumpet flourishes introduce the melody and adorn the phrases of the verses; and the chorus recalls the call-and-response *montuno* of salsa.

(spoken) Y ahora vamos todos a mover la colita!	(spoken) *And now let's all shake our tails!*
Chorus	**Chorus**
A ver, a ver! a mover la colita!	*Come on, come! let's shake our tail!*
si no la mueve se le va a poner malita.	*If you don't shake it, it will begin to ail.*
La mueve el tiburon y la mueve la ballena.	*The shark shakes it, and so does the whale.*
La mueve el cocodrilo y Tarzan all en la selva.	*The alligator shakes it, and so does Tarzan in the jungle.*
Tambien la mueve mi perro, para que le tire un hueso,	*My dog also shakes it so that I throw him a bone,*
Y la mueve el pato Donald cuando se mira al espejo.	*And Donald Duck shakes it when he looks in the mirror.*
Hay que mover la colita al ritmo de esta canción,	*You have to shake your tail to the rhythm of this song,*
Pa'que se vayan las penas y se alegre el corazon.	*So that your sorrows go away and your heart livens up.*
La mueve la sirena y el caballito de mar,	*The mermaid shakes it, and so does the seahorse,*
y la mujer maravilla al bailar con Superman.	*And so does Wonder Woman when she dances with Superman.*
Pa'que se vayan las penas y se alegre el corazon,	*So that your sorrows go away and your heart livens up,*
Vamos todos a moverla al compas de esta canción.	*Let's all shake it to the rhythm of this song.*
¿Y usted que espera para moverla?	*And what are you waiting for to shake it?*
¿No ve que el ritmo es general?	*Do you not see the rhythm is widespread?*
Mover la colita está de moda;	*Shaking your tail is in style;*
Mover la colita es popular.	*Shaking your tail is popular.*
(spoken) Izquierda, derecha, izquierda, derecha, síguele!	(spoken) *Left, right, left, right, keep going!*

PORRO *Porro*'s origins and relationship to *cumbia* are unclear, as some maintain that *porro* is merely a faster version of *cumbia*, while others claim it developed as an independent style. In any event, it was influenced by indigenous *gaita* wind instruments, African rhythms and percussion, and European brass and woodwind instruments. It is both a singing and dancing style, usually in duple time, with a livelier rhythm than *cumbia*. In its traditional form, it is performed by wind-band ensembles whose roots are in the military brass bands and wind orchestras that emerged in the coastal regions of Colombia in the nineteenth century, including prominently in the regions of Sucre and Córdoba. Instrumental improvisation is common, with wind instruments trading off in the manner of a Dixieland jazz band. By the first decades of the twentieth century, the wind bands adopted indigenous flutes and Afro-Colombian *bombo* drums, similar to those used in *cumbia*. With the international popularization of Latin music during the 1940s, *porro* underwent the same transformation as *cumbia*, leaving behind its folk orchestration in favor a more sophisticated, big-band style, which was readily adopted by the urban elite. Within a decade it had become immensely popular in Colombia.

The most important *porro* orchestra was that of the aforementioned Lucho Bermúdez, who composed and performed all styles including *bambucos*, *pasillos*, *cumbias*, and jazz. He was particularly known for his *porro* compositions, arrangements, performances, and recordings, as well as for his virtuosic improvisations on the clarinet. Bermúdez took the sound of the rural folk wind band and polished it into a sophisticated cosmopolitan style that became popular among Colombians of all social classes. Other important *porro* artists during this period included Pacho Galán, Pedro Laza y sus Pelayeros, La Sonora Cordobesa, La Sonora Cienaguera, Banda de 11 Enero, Edmundo Arias, Climaco Sarmiento, Bovea y sus Vallenatos, and Rufo Garrido. Many of these artists also became *cumbia* and *vallenato* artists, performing in popular nightclubs and dancehalls. After the 1960s, *porro* began losing popularity among Colombians, who came to consider it a relic of the past, at the expense of *cumbia* and *vallenato*. Yet some of the old bandleaders continued—and continue—to perform and compose *porros*, mostly on the Caribbean coast. Additionally, various festivals have emerged including the Festival del Porro, held yearly in San Pelayo and dedicated to the traditional style, as well as the Encuentro Nacional de Bandas, held every August in the town of Sincelejo, in the Sucre region.

> **Recommended Listening:** "Carmen de Bolívar" and "Prende la vela" by Lucho Bermúdezy Su Orquesta, from the CD *Los más grandes éxitos del maestro Lucho Bermúdez*.

> **Recommended Listening:** "Fiesta de negritos" by Lucho Bermúdez, from the CD *Putumayo Presents: Colombia*.

VALLENATO   The third important folk style from Colombia's Caribbean coast is the *vallenato*, a song and dance form that emerged in the 1930s and 1940s in the area surrounding the city of Valledupar in northeastern Colombia, a mountainous area on the Venezuelan border. The region's remote rivers and valleys make it ideal for the cultivation and production of drugs, and it has become one of the most notorious centers of Colombia's enormous narcotics industry. The origins of the term *vallenato* are unclear. Literally, it can mean "born in the valley," but also "like a small whale," perhaps in reference to a skin discoloration caused by a mosquito-borne disease that affected inhabitants of the Valledupar region. In any case, *vallenato* was originally a derogatory term for the poor rural residents of Valledupar, akin, perhaps, to the term "redneck" in the United States.

Vallenato is distinguished by its reliance on the diatonic button accordion, an instrument adopted in the nineteenth century by rural farmers on the Caribbean coast. *Vallenato* ensembles are complemented by the *caja* ("box"), a mid-sized drum of African origin similar to the *tambora*; and by the *guacharaca*, an indigenous scraping instrument made from long narrow canes or palm wood, and scraped with a wire fork, intended to imitate the song of a particular bird. *Vallenato*, with its syncretic blend of European, African, and Native instruments, became a national symbol of the multifaceted Colombian population. Often played at town dances, where amorous couples take the floor in romantic embraces, or in storytelling circles called *parrandas*, *vallenato* is hot, lively, and exciting, sustained by driving melodies and rhythms. As in other accordion-based styles, virtuosity on the instrument is a much sought-after and admired trait. The accordion must simultaneously play the melody, provide the harmony and bass line, and even supply a percussive rhythm with the buttons played by the left hand. The best accordionists are revered figures in Colombia, and competitions pit players against each other. Like *cumbia*, *vallenato* is strongly syncopated, reflecting its partial African origins. *Vallenatos* can be divided into four main categories, each with specific rhythmic and narrative characteristics: the stately and melancholy *paseo*, the duple-meter *son*, the triple-meter *merengue* (both unrelated to the eponymous Caribbean dances), and the fast-paced *puya*, much favored by accordion players because of its virtuosic demands.

Vallenatos began as rural ballads and cowboy songs, and most often used the *décima* Spanish classical poetic form. The lyrics, often improvised, reflect the poor rural lifestyle that is at its roots: village scenes, tales of violence and betrayal, and the ubiquitous romantic love serenades. Songs are often celebration of love and of good times, pride for one's region, or humorous local gossip and political commentary. As such they have become important representations of cultural identity, expressing the hopes, fears, joys, and aspirations of, at first, the poor inhabitants of the Valledupar region, and in time of Colombians everywhere. An important element in *vallenato* is its competitive aspect, with singers challenging each other's verbal virtuosity. This is known as *la piquería*, an informal competition in which improvised verses ridicule and mock the opponent. Similar verbal contests can be found in other parts of Latin America, for example the Cuban *controversia*, the Argentine *payada*, or the Trinidadian calypso *picong*. Many of the duels between famous *vallenato* singers have became legendary and many of their improvised songs were subsequently recorded and have become classics, for example "La gota fría," recounting the verbal duel between Lorenzo Morales and Emiliano Zuleta Baquero.

Not surprisingly, many of the early proponents of *vallenato* were also *cumbia* and *porro* artists, and the three style are linked not only in their historical and geographical origin, but also in their evolution from provincial folk traditions to urban popular styles and even into international commercial success. By the 1950s, *vallenato* had expanded from its rural areas into cities such as Valledupar, Santa Marta, and Riohacha, and thereafter slowly made its way to other areas. It was during this period that the writer Gabriel García Márquez began bringing attention to the style in the country's newspapers, greatly contributing to its popularity. Márquez's novels themselves have been linked to the *vallenato* in their depiction of the customs and mores of Colombia's coastal regions. Some of the important early proponents of *vallenato* included Francisco el Hombre, Abel Antonio Villa, Rafael Escalona, and the virtuoso accordionist Alejo Durán. Another was Guillermo Buitrago, Colombia's first pop star, who was also instrumental in developing *cumbia*. His contributions to the country's popular music became mythical after his untimely death in 1949 at age 27. Starting in the 1950s other instruments were gradually added to the accordion-and-percussion ensembles, notably electric bass, guitar, and flute. By the 1970s, new artists continued to update and popularize the style outside the Valledupar region, including Lisandro Meza and Julio Bovea, whose group Bovea y Sus Vallenatos became one of its most important proponents.

Yet *vallenato* continued to be scorned and derided by the middle and upper classes even as *cumbia* gained social acceptance by Colombians of all ages and social status. One important factor that affected the perception of the *vallenato* was its association with the drug cartels in the second half of the twentieth century. Like the *narcocorridos* in the Mexican borderlands, *vallenatos* commented on the opulent but deadly lifestyle of the drug traffickers. Oddly, the historical evolution of the drug trade has matched the country's musical progression, as the older marijuana traffickers of the 1950s and 1960s preferred the more traditional *vallenato*, whereas the cocaine traffickers that supplanted them in the 1970s favored the more popular *cumbia* style. National acceptance of *vallenato* finally occurred during the 1980s and 1990s, when a new generation of Colombian youth adopted it. After almost half a century, *vallenato* had finally conquered Colombia's pop music scene, surpassing even *cumbia* in popularity, with skyrocketing record sales and entire radio stations devoted to it. This new popular form of *vallenato* entails much larger production values than the original three-instrument ensembles. It retains the accordion, but adds heavy electric guitars and bass, a woodwind section, a larger percussion section that included congas and timbales, and electronic keyboards. It also has a more strident singing style. Its most important modern proponent is Carlos Vives, who with his virtuoso accordionist Egidio Cuadrado infused it with rock elements and turned it into an international sensation, particularly after the release of his 1994 album *Clásicos de la provincia*. Other important modern *vallenato* artists include Alfredo Gutierrez, Jorge Celedón, Los Diablitos, and Binomi de Oro, and foreign artists have adopted it as well, notably Rubén Blades and Gloria Estefan.

Yet traditional *vallenato* has also grown in the Colombian public's esteem, and small ensembles can still be heard throughout the country, as well as on radio and television. In contrast to the glossy, commercial *vallenato* heard in Bogotá, New York, and Miami, the more traditional form seeks a return to its earlier roots, themes, and orchestration. Proponents of the traditional style include some of the children of older *vallenato* stars. Important *vallenato* festivals have also emerged and helped to reestablish the traditional style, including the Festival de la Leyenda Vallenata, held in Valledupar since 1968 (when it was won by Alejo Durán) and the Festival Cuna de Acordeones, held in the town of Villanueva.

> **Recommended Viewing:** For a fascinating view of the development of *cumbia* and *vallenato*, see the documentary film *Shotguns and Accordions: Music of the Marijuana Growing Regions of Colombia* (1983).
>
> **Recommended Listening:** "Víspera de Año Nuevo" by Guillermo Buitrago, from the CD *Diciembre y Año Nuevo*.
>
> **Recommended Listening:** "La gota fría" and "Pedazo de acordeón" by Carlos Vives, from the CD *Clásicos de la provincia*.

CDII, Track 14: *Vallenato*: "Altos del Rosario"

Music and Lyrics: Alejandro Durán
Instrumentation: accordion, bass, *caja* drum, *guacharaca* scraper
Notes: This classic *vallenato* was composed and performed by Alejo Durán, one of the best musicians in the genre. The title refers to a town in northern Colombia. The song is self-referential, as Durán places himself at the center of attention, both by name and nickname (he was known as "El Negro Grande"—"the big Black man"). Durán was particularly famous for his virtuosity on the accordion, which is reflected in this song, particularly with some interesting harmonic departures (for example at 0:34). The first half of each phrase is repeated three times.

Lloraban los muchachos, cuando di mi despedida.	*The boys were crying when I said my goodbyes.*
Yo salí del Alto, de la alegre María.	*I left the town of Altos, I left happy María.*
Decía Martín Rodríguez, lo mismo su Papá,	*Martín Rodríguez said, as did his father,*
Que la fiesta sigue, Durán si no se va.	*Let the party continue, for Durán is not leaving.*
Durán si no se va, que la fiesta sigue.	*Durán is not leaving, let the party continue.*
Pobrecito Avendaño, lo mismo Zabaleta,	*Poor Avendaño, the same for Zabaleta,*
Quedaron llorando y se acabó la fiesta.	*They were crying, and the party was over.*

Se acabó la fiesta, quedaron llorando.	*The party was over, and they were crying.*
Lloraban las mujeres, ya se fue el pobre negro.	*The women were crying, the poor Black man has left.*
Dinos cuando vuelves, y nos dará consuelo.	*Tell us when you'll return, that will give us comfort.*
Nos dará consuelo, y dinos cuando vuelves.	*That will give us comfort, tell us when you'll return.*

The Pacific Coast

Colombia's Pacific coast, and in particular the state of Chocó, has had a stronger Black presence than even the Caribbean coast, with close to 90 percent of its inhabitants of African origin. But since most of Colombia's prominent folk and popular music originated from the Caribbean coast and the interior, the music from the Pacific coast has often been overlooked. Because of geographical proximity and historical correlations, the culture of Afro-Colombians on the Pacific coast is similar to that of Black populations in northern Ecuador, in the provinces of Esmeraldas, Carchi, and Imbabura.

CURRULAO The most prominent style from the Pacific coast is *currulao*, a couples' dance that, like some of its Caribbean cousins, is derived from African courtship rituals. It is also a vocal style whose syncopated melodies are sung and accompanied by a *marimba chonta*, named after the palm tree from which the instrument is made. As in Central American marimbas, bamboo tubes are placed under each key, adding a certain resonance to the instrument. It is a diatonic instrument (with only the white keys of the piano) played by two *marimbistas*, one of whom plays a repeating phrase on the lower keys called *bordón*, the other an improvisatory part above called *tiple*. The marimba is accompanied by two *cununos*—upright drums of different sizes with deerskin heads played with one hand and a stick hitting the side of the instrument; and by two *bombos*, large two-headed drums played with mallets. The *cununos* provide the rhythmic framework, typically in $\frac{6}{8}$, while the *bombos* provide the bass. Finally, the ensemble includes numerous shakers called *guasas*: bamboo tubes filled with seeds or pebbles that are not unlike the *guache* used in traditional *cumbia*. Singers are usually female, and include the *cantadora* (soloist) and *respondadoras* (chorus) who play the *guasas* and accompany the soloist in call-and-response form. Songs address issues of local gossip, the praising of a patron saint, and tales of love and marriage, particularly involving the local practice of polygamy.

Currulao is a lively but intense courtship dance, with the obligatory cat-and-mouse game played by the amorous couple who never touch but instead rely on the required handkerchief without which the ritual could not proceed. The dance is tightly choreographed, reflecting African steps and rhythms and European elements such as quadrille-like figures and the ubiquitous *zapateado*. Various versions of *currulao* can be found on the Colombian and Ecuadorian pacific coast, each with specific choreography, tempo, rhythms and melodies: *abosao, bámbara negra, torbellino, andarele, berejú, caderona, caramba, contradanza, jota chocoana, makerule, pango,* and *patacoré,* as well as the ever-present *bambuco,* now infused with African characteristics. *Currulao* underwent a similar process of popularization as its Caribbean counterparts. In the 1960s, it complemented its marimba-based orchestration with a more electric sound and began penetrating the Colombian popular consciousness. One of the first artists to bring it to national attention was the saxophonist Enrique Urbano Tenorio, known as "Peregoyo," who with his ensemble Combo Vacaná became the style's first recording artist. His 1960s recordings with Discos Fuentes quickly gained radio play throughout the country, and *currulao* achieved a respectable level of popularity, though it never reached the heights of *cumbia* or *vallenato*. In 2002, Peregoyo and various octogenarian members of his ensemble returned to the studio and recorded a new album, *Tropicalismo*, which became a hit and introduced *currulao* to a new generation of Colombians. Today, traditional forms of *currulao* are in danger of disappearing, replaced by more glossy productions geared mostly to tourists.

> **Recommended Listening:** "Bambuco" by Tierra Caliente, and "Arrullo" by La Voz de Niño Dios, from the CD *Ecuador and Colombia: Marimba Masters Sacred Songs.*

> **Recommended Listening:** "El botellón" and "Mi gallo corococó," from the CD *Arriba suena marimba: Currulao Marimba Music from Colombia.*

> **Recommended Listening:** "Mi Buenaventura" and "Descarga Vacaná" by Peregoyo y su Combo Vacaná, from the CD *Tropicalisimo.*

Popular Styles

SALSA African rhythms and styles on both the Pacific and Caribbean coasts lent themselves well to similar styles in other parts of the Caribbean, so when the salsa explosion hit in the 1970s and 1980s, Afro-Colombians whose musical identity lay in *cumbia* or *currulao* now quickly embraced the new phenomenon. Not surprisingly, Discos Fuentes was at the heart of the salsa explosion in Colombia, finding new artists and disseminating the style throughout the country. Many of the *salseros* were from the Pacific coast, from the region of Chocó and costal town of Buenaventura. Prominent *currulao* artists such as Peregoyo began infusing the Colombian style into salsa. Others quickly followed, including the Orquesta Guayacán and Grupo Niche. Meanwhile, on the Caribbean coast, artists such as Fruko y Sus Tesos and Joe Arroyo were combining salsa with *cumbia* rhythms. Another band formed by Fruko, The Latin Brothers, became important exponents the style. In time the *salsa* capital of Colombia became the city of Cali.

> **Recommended Listening:** "Delia la cumbiambera" by The Latin Brothers, "Soy como soy" by Fruko y Sus Tesos, and "Yamulemau" by Joe Arroyo, from the CD *Putumayo Presents: Colombia*.

CHAMPETA   Another recent fusion of styles is *champeta*, also known as *terapia criolla* ("creole therapy"), which emerged in the 1980s in the port city of Cartagena and the nearby town of San Basilio de Palenque. In the 1980s, the influx of traders and sailors in Colombia's coastal areas introduced African pop styles such as *juju*, *soukous*, *makossa*, *bikutsi*, and highlife. Live acts from Africa and Haiti began performing at local festivals, and recordings of these musicians began circulating throughout the poor neighborhoods of Cartagena, particularly at outdoor dance gatherings, with loud throbbing music provided by enormous sound systems called *picos* (from the English "pick-up"). Like Jamaican *sound system* and *dub*, these parties were led by flashy record-spinning DJs who remixed the African music with local styles such as *cumbia* and *buyerengue*, and with popular Caribbean styles such as reggae and ragamuffin, Haitian *compas* and Trinidadian *soca*, as well as U.S. rap.

In time, these amalgamations were recorded in makeshift home studios and garages, resulting in *champeta*, a complex, urban, youth-oriented style. *Champeta* features a prominent bass, electric guitar, synthesizers, a drum set, and added percussion. Like their Jamaican *dub* counterparts, *champeta* DJs engage in energetic verbal one-upmanship, often peppered with sexual double-entendres. Though Spanish is the language of choice, African and English words are liberally interjected into the songs. Lyrics address crime, drugs, and violence and are often sexually charged, designed to be both humorous and offensive. *Champeta* is played at parties with hot and lively—and often overtly sexual—dance moves. Because of its origins as a working-class "street" sound, *champeta* was resisted and looked down upon by the middle and upper classes, particularly by the older generation, who considered it obscene, in the same way that *cumbia* and *vallenato* had previously been. In time, *champeta* became a hit on local radio stations and gradually made its way into middle-class nightclubs and discothèques, first in the coastal areas, and then in Bogotá, Medellín, and Cali, and eventually across the country. It has since become embraced by all levels of society, an alternative to the mainstream *cumbia*, *vallenato*, and salsa that still dominate Colombian popular music.

The first artists to put *champeta* on the musical map included Viviano Torres, Justo Valdés, and Hernán Hernández, all from San Basilio, as well as Anne Swing, Son Palenque, and Kusima. Subsequent *champetuos* have included Melchor Pérez, Luis Towers, Francisco "Elio Boom" Corrales, Shaka el Rey Zulu, El Afinaíto, El Sayayín, El Pupy, and El Razta, and groups such as Boogaloo, BIP, and Chawala. The style first came to the attention of the outside world with the 1998 release of the compilation album *Champeta criolla— New African Music from Colombia*, followed a few years later by a second volume. Yet in spite of the success of these two albums, *champeta* has yet to emerge as a prominent international style.

> **Recommended Listening:** "Mini ku soto" by Viviano Torres and Anne Swing, "Unyé Unyé" by Justo Valdez and Son Palenque, and "La cita" by El Afinaíto and Charles King, from the CD *Champeta criolla, Vol. 2*.

Meanwhile, several Colombian pop artists have had international success, notably former *salsero* Charlie Zaa and Juan Esteban Aristizábal, commonly known as Juanes. The most successful Colombia pop artist, however, is Shakira, the multiple-Grammy winning singer who rose to Colombian popularity in the 1990s, then became a star throughout Latin America with the 1998 album *Dónde están los ladrones?* She made her U.S. debut with the well-received 2001 album *Laundry Service*.

> **Recommended Listening:** "Florecita rockera" and "Baracunatana" by Aterciopelados, from the CD *Evolución*.

> **Recommended Listening:** "Estoy aquí" and "Pies descalzos, sueños blancos" by Shakira, from the CD *Pies descalzos*.

VENEZUELA

Venezuela (capital: Caracas) lies east of Colombia, with a Caribbean coastline that is more than 1,700 miles long. Venezuela also contains diverse landscapes, including high plateaus, deserts, mountains, Caribbean islands, and the northern edge of the Andes mountain range. Much of the country is irrigated by the monumental Orinoco River and its many tributaries, one of which contains Angel Falls, the world's highest waterfall. To the south, along the Brazilian border, begins the Amazon rainforest, whose continuing deforestation remains a major environmental problem and a threat to the indigenous populations. Areas that have been influential in the development of Venezuelan culture include the basin around Lake Maracaibo, as well as the *llanos*, fertile plains that lie between the coast and the Orinoco and that occupy a third of Venezuela's territory.

Historical Overview

Columbus landed on the coast in 1498, claiming it for Spain, and, seeing the natural beauty of the land, called it *Tierra de Gracia* ("Land of Grace"). The first colony in Venezuela—and on the South American continent—was established in Cumaná in 1522, and the capital Caracas was founded by Diego de Losada in 1567. The slave trade saw the forcible importation of a significant number of Africans whose descendants by-and-large remained on the fishing villages and cacao plantations along the coast. In 1821, Venezuela became part of Gran Colombia and then achieved its independence in 1830. There followed a series of military dictatorships and democratic governments, notably that of Juan Vincente Gómez, which lasted from 1909 to 1935. It was during this period that Venezuela developed its rich oil fields, which led to a rapid economic expansion and urbanization, particularly after the price of oil rose substantially in the 1970s. Despite the country's oil-derived economic wealth, social inequality has remained at the forefront of Venezuelan politics. It is partly for this reason that in 1998 the presidency was won by the left-leaning Hugo Chávez, who sought to institute a series of social reforms, in the process cooling the country's relationship with the United States. Chávez has been a champion of indigenous people, for example by amending the Venezuelan constitution to guarantee indigenous rights, the first constitution on the American continent to do so, and by replacing the traditional Columbus Day with Indigenous Resistance Day. Chávez's government has been very supportive of musical life in Venezuela, for example with a law that requires radio stations to allocate 50 percent of their airwaves to Venezuelan folk music. The government also sponsors local traditional festivities such as Saints' days celebrations, and has continued to support the wildly successful music education program called "El Sistema," which subsidizes hundreds of schools and youth orchestras throughout Venezuela. Attended by over a quarter-of-a-million children, El Sistema's most famous alumnus is the celebrated conductor Gustavo Dudamel.

Most Venezuelans live in the coastal cities—a third of them in Caracas alone—while the southern areas are sparsely populated. The area south of the Orinoco River constitutes more than half the country's landmass, but contains less than 5 percent of its inhabitants. Sixty percent of Venezuelans are Mestizo, 30 percent of European descent, about 8 percent of African descent, and about 2 percent of Native descent. Prominent Native tribes include the Wayúu, the Warao, and the Guajibo who live in the *llanos*. In the Amazon region live the Piaroa and the famous Yanomamo, who until relatively recently had had no contact with the outside world and who have been the subject of well-known anthropological studies. Venezuelan society is dominated by two major, contrasting cultures. The first is that of Caracas, a modern sprawling city, with all the amenities and drawbacks of modern twenty-first–century society, and where European, Black, Mestizo, and Native elements (as well as those of several other immigrant groups) have melded and evolved for the better part of four centuries. The second dominant culture is that of the *llanos* in the south (as well as in neighboring Colombia) whose inhabitants are affectionately called *guates*. It is in the *llanos* that extensive cattle ranches developed during the colonial period, yielding a distinct cowboy culture not unlike that of the *gauchos* who roam the *pampas* in the southern part of the continent.

Venezuelan Instruments

Several instruments are particular to Venezuelan culture, including the *arpa*, *cuatro*, and *bandola*, though these can often also be found in neighboring Colombia. Brought over from Spain, the *arpa* (harp) was popular throughout Spanish America, and by the nineteenth century at least three different regions in the hemisphere had developed important folk traditions, all of which continue to this day: the *arpa jarocha* from Mexico, the *arpa Paraguaya* from Paraguay, and the *arpa Venezolana* from Venezuela. (There are also scattered harp traditions in the Andean region.) The Venezuelan harp is called generally *arpa criolla*, reflecting its adoption by White descendants of the early Spanish immigrants, perhaps as early as the seventeenth century. During the colonial period, it was used in Catholic worship—particularly in Jesuit missions—and to accompany the songs and dances of the Spanish aristocracy. Though it lost some popularity after Venezuela's independence, it resurged in the middle of the twentieth century. Today, it remains an important element of cultural identity and national pride.

There are many versions of the instrument, each reflecting a specific geographical and historical origin. The most popular and widespread is the *arpa llanera* ("from the llanos"), which typically has 32 strings made of goat- or cow-gut (or, in modern times, nylon) and loudly resonating bass strings. Its triangular wooden frame is made from cedar or pine, and occasionally from mahogany. It is usually accompanied by an ensemble called *conjunto criollo*, which consists of a *cuatro* guitar, maracas, and a singer. Another important harp tradition comes from the Caracas region, known as the *arpa central* (also known as *aragüeña* or *tuyera*). Its resonating chamber is slightly larger than the *llanera* and it has 35 strings, including 12 or 14 steel strings in its upper register, giving it a bright, tinny sound. Because of its greater size and brightness of tone, the *arpa central* does not require the *cuatro*'s harmonic accompaniment, leaving only the singer who usually plays the maracas. Both the *llanera* and the *central* are diatonic harps (playing only the white keys of the piano) and their range is around three octaves. The harp player provides his or her own harmony with a fast syncopated style called *rasgueado*, reminiscent of flamenco guitar strumming. The right hand typically plays the melody in the higher range while the left hand plays both the accompaniment and a second melody that complements the first contrapuntally.

The national instrument of Venezuela is the *cuatro*, a small four-string guitar that is prominent in every aspect of folk music, particularly *música llanera*. It is primarily an accompanying instrument, providing both rhythm and harmony with its fast percussive strumming technique also called *rasgueado*. The *cuatro* can also be found in other cultures in Latin America, notably in Puerto Rico, though that instrument usually has ten strings arranged in five pairs. The *bandola* is a lute-like guitar related to the Spanish *bandurría*, smaller than the *cuatro*, with a distinctive pear shape. Like the *arpa*, it has regional variations (*llanera*, *oriental*, etc.). It typically has either four strings or pairs of strings, though occasionally it can have 12, 14, 16, and even 18 strings,

Traditional *joropo* ensemble: harp, *cuatro*, and maracas.

arranged in pairs. Played with a plectrum, it has a more percussive character than the *cuatro*. Other string instruments include the *requinto* and the *tiple*, guitar-like instruments of various sizes that can have either melodic or harmonic functions. The *bandolín* is even smaller and related to the mandolin, though it has an arched—rather than flat—back.

Música llanera

Much of the country's folklore emerged in the *llanos*, the extensive inland prairies in Venezuela and eastern Colombia. The musical traditions from this rural, cattle-based, agricultural society came to be called *música llanera*, a generic name that encompasses many styles. For much of the last two centuries, *música llanera* became an expression of Venezuela's rural folklore, embracing instruments and dances that reflected traditional customs and songs that focused on rural themes, with a particular Spanish idiom that came to be associated with the *llanos*. The second half of the twentieth century, however, saw the rise of a more urban style of *música llanera*, with more—and more modern—instruments, and whose songs addressed modern cosmopolitan subjects. *Música llanera* is predominantly Mestizo in origin, with a few Black influences nonetheless, most notably a predominance of syncopated rhythms. The typical *llanero* ensemble consists of an *arpa llanera*, a *cuatro*, and maracas, though virtually every ensemble today includes an electric bass. The harp is sometimes substituted with a *bandola*, and a *requinto* often replaces the *cuatro*. The *maracas* player will often double as the singer, and the ensemble accompanies a dance with a lively beat.

JOROPO   The most prominent form of *música llanera* is the *joropo* (ho-RO-po), a style that incorporates poetry, singing, and dancing and that the *llaneros* themselves call *guafa*. It is the national dance of Venezuela and has reached a greater level of international prominence than any other Venezuelan style. The name *joropo* (like the Mexican *jarabe*) is derived from the Arabic word *jarop*, which literally describes a sweet liquid mixture used for medicinal purposes. The key word here is "mixture," and like the *jarabe*, the *joropo* is technically not one single dance but rather a suite of dances that appear in a predetermined succession. In common usage, *joropo* can refer to a single dance, to the entire suite, to the music that accompanies it, or to the event at which it is performed. The terms "*joropo*" and "*música llanera*" have often been used interchangeably, but in fact *joropo* is just the most well-known subcategory of *música llanera*. To confuse matters further, other regional variations of the *joropo* later emerged in other parts of the country, notably the *joropo central* and the *joropo oriental*.

The *joropo* has its roots in the Spanish dances of the colonial period, notably the fandango, and even a casual listener can detect influences from Andalusia and Southern Spain, where the music was in turn heavily influenced by the Moorish occupation. The percussive elements of Andalusian flamenco, along with its fancy *zapateado* footwork, are still in evidence in traditional *joropo*. At the same time, *joropo* is also a quintessentially Venezuelan dance, similar but distinct from colonial dances of other countries, derived from the specific characteristics of Venezuelan culture. By the nineteenth century, it had become engrained in rural folk life, performed during religious feasts or village *fiestas*, at neighborhood parties or family gatherings. In its traditional form, a *joropo* is both sung and danced, accompanied by the standard *arpa, cuatro*, and maracas ensemble. Tempos are usually fast, with *sesquiáltera* rhythms that juxtapose $\frac{3}{4}$ (in the upper register of the harp and *cuatro*) and $\frac{6}{8}$ (in the bass) meters, lending the *joropo* an exciting, almost enthralling rhythmic component. Improvisation is an important aspect of *joropo*, both for the singers who make up lyrics based on established rhyming schemes and for the instrumentalists who engage in intricate melodic and rhythmic exchanges, resulting in a complex aural texture.

Joropo texts often reflect the simple but harsh lifestyle of the *llanos*: the macho attitude of men who succeeded in dominating nature, their heroic tales of war and patriotism, and their love of the land and of the faithful women who stood by their side. They often refer to nature in an allegorical way, speaking obliquely about bittersweet love and despair while reflecting on the beautiful rural landscapes in which they live: rivers, mountains, forests, and the animals that inhabit them. Often, many sets of lyrics, their origins lost in history, exist for a single *joropo*, and new ones are continuously improvised. Other *joropos* are purely instrumental. The rural life of the *llanos* is also reflected in the traditional costumes. Women wear colorful blouses and long flowing skirts embroidered with flowers, their hair weaved with delicate lace. The men wear a traditional costume called *liquiliqui*, consisting of white cotton pants and long-sleeved shirts buttoned to the neck. Footwear consists of canvas *alpargatas*—espadrille-like shoes with soles made from leather or hemp. A distinctive felt sombrero called *pelo-de-guama* complements the ensemble.

The forms of the *joropo* dances were inherited from their colonial ancestors. In a typical *joropo*, various couples—called *joroperos*—dance close together. There are three principal steps: The dance begins with the men, right hand on their partner's waist, leading a waltz-like step called *valseo*; the partners then face each other, holding hands, alternately coming together and separating in sliding motions called *escobillao*; at a certain point, the *arpa* and the *cuatro* will play a rapid percussive passage called *repique*, a signal to the men to begin their intricate forceful *zapateado*, while the women maintain the more graceful *escobillao*. (These steps, or variations thereof, can be found throughout the continent, for example in the Peruvian *zamacueca*, the Argentine *zamba*, the Chilean *cueca*, and the Mexican *jarabe*.) There are many sub-categories of *joropos*, including:

- the fast and lively *golpe*, usually in triple meter. In a *golpe*, a four- or eight-measure ostinato is repeated continuously, over which melodic and rhythmic elements are improvised, providing great flexibility over a rigid structure. Many traditional *golpes* have become part of *llanero* culture, with colorful names such as *el Gavilán, la Periquera, la Jurupera, el Carnaval, el Grillo, el Zumba Que Zumba, la Quirpa, el Gaván, la Montuna Torpe, el San Rafael, el Seis Corrido, la Catira, el Seis por Derecho, el Pajarillo*, and the graceful *Guacharaca*, each with its own rhythmic, melodic, harmonic, and textual characteristics. The *golpe* is also popular in the central region of Venezuela.
- the *pasaje*, also popular in the central region, is more stately and lyrical, typically with a more elevated poem that addresses intimate themes of romantic love or nostalgic yearning; it can also function as a serenade. In a *pasaje*, the harsh percussive passages in the *cuatro* are replaced by softer, more defined melodies in the harp or the *requinto*.
- the *corrido* (or *corrío*) is a narrative song similar to the Mexican genre of the same name. In *corridos*, which are rarely danced, the singer recounts a personal story of bravery or accomplishment, of violence and war, or else stories of unrequited love, all set in the rural backdrop of the *llanos*.
- the *contrapunto* (or *contrapunteo*) is an improvisatory singing contest similar to the Colombian *piquería* that rewards the verbal and musical abilities of the singers. In a *contrapunto*, a specific subject is chosen—typically an aspect of the *llano* lifestyle—and explored in depth. Singers respond back and forth with rapid-fire delivery, expanding on the chosen theme, with made-up verses that are often humorous and ribald, though never obscene. Strict rhyming schemes must be respected, as must be the tempo, rhythm and melody. Singers who fail to do so—or who deviate from the subject matter—are considered to have lost the contest.

Though the *joropo* is quintessentially a style from the *llanos*, regional variations have emerged in other parts of Venezuela. Thus, the *joropo central*, popular in coastal states such as Miranda and Aragua, has been more strongly influenced by African characteristics, with short, improvisatory verses, more intricate melodies, and a brighter tone provided by the metal strings of the harp. It often foregoes the *cuatro* and its percussive effects and instead consists only of the *arpa*, *maracas*, and *buche* (voice). The dances of the *joropo central*, distinct from those of the *llanos*, can be combined into a suite called a *revuelta*, and include a lyrical three-part *pasaje*, an improvisatory *yaguazo*, a *guabina*, a fast-paced instrumental *marisela*, and a short, closing, comical dance called *llamada del mono*. These dances preserve the basic *valseo*, *zapateado*, and *escobillao* steps of the joropo. Meanwhile, in eastern coastal regions, the *joropo oriental* adds guitars and small accordions called *cueretas* to the traditional instrumentation, and features a more graceful dancing style and a more subtle form of *zapateado*. Still other types of *joropo* have emerged on the Guyana border to the east, in the Amazon region and in the Andes, each with their own characteristics, yet each preserving the basic orchestration and dance elements.

As in most folk music, the authorship of many traditional *joropos* is mostly unknown. In the twentieth century, several important composers emerged who penned many of the works that remain at the heart of the repertoire. The most popular *joropo* is "Alma llanera," composed by Pedro Elías Gutiérrez and Rafael Bolívar Coronado as part of a *zarzuela* light opera and first performed in Caracas in 1914. With countless versions and recordings, "Alma llanera," has become a classic, almost the unofficial anthem of Venezuela. Another important composer was Hugo Blanco, who combined many facets of *música llanera* with Cuban music. His most famous song is "Moliendo café," which has achieved immense international popularity. Other notable composers include Ignacio "el Indio" Figueredo, who in the 1940s and 1950s wrote important classics such as "El gabán," "La periquera," "Guayabo Negro," and "Los Caujaritos." In the 1950s, Luis Ariel Rey formed a guitar trio with his brothers called Los Llaneros and was one of the first artists to record the *joropo*, with important hits such as "El jilguero del llano" and "El coplero." In the 1960s, Eneas Perdomo wrote and sang popular *joropos*, notably "Fiesta en Elorza" and "El Verdun." An important composer and zealous guardian of *llanero* culture is the legendary Simón Díaz, who set out to preserve this important folklore tradition. Díaz had a distinguished television, radio, and film career that revolved around *llanero* culture and has come to be known as "Tio Simón" ("Uncle Simón") to generations of Venezuelans. His most famous *joropo* is "Caballo viejo," a heartfelt and lyrical *pasaje*.

The second half of the twentieth century saw the rise of an increasingly urbanized style of *música llanera* due to the continuous migration between Caracas and the *llanos*, the advent of recordings, and the style's appearance on radio and television. Urban versions add instruments such as guitars, pianos, violins, and woodwinds. The style has entered the concert hall in fully orchestrated versions, and versions with electronic instruments are no longer uncommon. At the same time, *joropos* have been infused with various foreign styles, including Cuban salsa and rumba, jazz, rock, and pop. This new generation of Venezuelan and Colombian composers includes Ignacio Rondón, the harpist Juan-Vicente Torrealba, Arnulfo Briceño (who wrote famous *joropos* such as "Ay mi llanura," "Adiós a mi llano," and "Canto llano"), and especially Reynaldo Armas, who has had great international success as a folk artist.

In recent years, promoters have jumped on the *llanero* bandwagon, presenting *joropos* and other styles in flashy, exotic spectacles—men wearing whips and pistols, women wearing skimpy, revealing outfits—that have little in common with the traditional folklore of the *llanos*. As in myriad other stylistic evolutions, tensions have emerged between those who consider traditional *música llanera* the pure "authentic" form and those who espouse a more modern approach. Yet in its various identities, *llanero* culture continues to be preeminent in Venezuela and Colombia. The *llanos* themselves are growing in population. Radio stations throughout Venezuela and Colombia are dedicated exclusively to *música llanera*, which can also be heard in bars, restaurants, and nightclubs in Caracas, Bogotá, and throughout the interior. Important *joropo* festivals and competitions have emerged including the Festival Internacional de Bailadores Reyes del Joropo and the Festival Nacional del Joropo, both held in Venezuela, and the Torneo Internacional del Joropo, held annually in Colombia.

> **Recommended Listening:** "Alma llanera," from the CD *Traditional Songs from Venezuela: De norte a sur*.
>
> **Recommended Listening:** "Moliendo café" by Hugo Blanco from the CD *The Rough Guide to the Music of Venezuela*.
>
> **Recommended Listening:** "Caballo viejo" by Simón Díaz, from the CD *Mis canciones: My Songs*.
>
> **Recommended Listening:** "El gavilán" and "Seis por derecho" by Mandingo y Su Familia, from the CD *Music from South America: Venezuela*.
>
> **Recommended Listening:** "Madrugada llanera" and "Sinfonia del Palmar" by Juan-Vicente Torrealba, from the CD *Concierto en la llanura*.

CDII, Track 15: *Joropo*: "Alma llanera"

Music: Pedro Elías Gutiérrez
Lyrics: Rafael Bolívar Coronado
Instrumentation: *harp, cuatro* guitar, bass, *maracas*

Notes: Venezuela's most famous *joropo* is performed here by the legendary harpist and composer Juan Vicente Torrealba. The song glorifies the landscape and lifestyle of the llanos. Distinctive features are the familiar rising arpeggios in the harp (after the introduction, at 0:12), and the prominent pause immediately before the accented chorus (at 1:11 and 2:04). In this typical *sesquiáltera* rhythm, the bass emphasizes $\frac{6}{8}$ meter (**one**-two-three-**four**-five-six), while the harp and the strumming *cuatro* suggest $\frac{3}{4}$ meter (**one**-two-**three**-four-**five**-six), providing a compelling syncopated feel.

Yo nací en esta rivera	*I was born on this shore*
Del Arauca vibrador.	*Of the vibrant Arauca.*
Soy hermano de la espuma,	*I am brother of the froth,*
De las garzas, de las rosas y del sol.	*Of the herons, the roses, and the sun.*
Me arrulló la vida diana	*I was lulled by life's reveille*
de la brisa en el palmar.	*Of the breeze in the palm trees.*
Y por eso tengo el alma	*And that is why my soul*
Como el alma primorosa del cristal.	*Is like the delicate soul of crystal.*
Chorus	**Chorus**
Amo, lloro, canto, sueño,	*I love, I cry, I sing, I dream,*
Con claveles de pasión.	*With carnations of passion.*
Para ornar las rubias crines	*To embellish the fair mane*
Al potro mas corredor,	*Of my lover's stallion,*
Yo nací en esta rivera	*I was born on this shore*
Del Arauca vibrador.	*Of the vibrant Arauca.*
Soy hermano de la espuma,	*I am brother of the sea froth,*
De las garzas, de las rosas y del sol.	*Of the herons, the roses, and the sun.*

Venezuelan Christmas Music

Venezuela has an important Christmas tradition that is similar to that in other parts of Latin America, characterized by joyful celebrations and a cheerful atmosphere. Throughout the country, in both rural and urban areas, communities come together to celebrate the Christmas season or simply to venerate life, family, and friendship. The festivities often begin in early December and do not end until well into the new year, sometimes even until February. Every day seemingly brings a new reason to celebrate. An important tradition is that of the *pastorellas*, dramatic pastoral plays in which participants dress up as shepherds or other biblical and historical figures, as well as animals and other characters from Venezuelan folklore. Revelers reenact the nativity, accompanied by age-old shepherd dances such as "La Burra," in which a dancer playfully imitates a donkey. Food and drink flow freely, especially the *hallacas*, a seasonal specialty dish consisting of cornmeal wrapped in banana leaves, similar to Mexican *tamales*. The preferred beverages are the *carato de acupe*, made from fermented corn, as well as an eggnog-like drink called *leche de burra*— "donkey milk."

Parranda and Aguinaldo The most important musical Christmas tradition is the *parranda*, a festive event at which Christmas carols called *aguinaldos* are sung. *Parrandas* are related to other similar celebrations found throughout Latin America, such as the Mexican *posada*, the Puerto Rican *aguinaldo*, the Dominican *arguinaldo*, and the *parang* of neighboring Trinidad. *Parranda*, which literally means "revelry," also refers to an informal group of singers that ambulates in the evening throughout a village or neighborhood, serenading passers-by and singing door-to-door in exchange for food and drink. They will stop at Nativity scenes which have been deliberately set up for this purpose and perform specific *aguinaldos*, asking the owners of the house for permission to sing, honoring the infant Jesus, saluting the assembled audience, and finally requesting refreshments. The *parranda* first emerged in the central coastal region, though it can now be found virtually everywhere throughout Venezuela. *Parranda* organizations have distinctive names, identities, and histories, some of which go back half a century or more. Some of the most venerable include *La Flor de Cojedes* (from the state of Cojedes), *la Verde Clarita* (from Carabobo), and *Turpiales de Aragua* (from Aragua). The parading groups dress in their colors, waving their historic banners and wearing large neckerchiefs that represent their identity. One member of the *parranda* always leads the way, carrying a lamp or a star that symbolizes the Star of Bethlehem.

Aguinaldos feature a solo singer alternating with the *parranda* choir. They usually have six verses, but the soloist is often expected to improvise a few more. The improvisations can be melodic, textual, and even extend to the rhythm, which can be free and unmetered. They are accompanied by ensembles that can differ from group to group (often reflecting local custom) but usually include a *cuatro*; a guitar and/or smaller instruments such as a *tiple* or a *requinto*; percussion instruments such as maracas, triangles, tambourines, and *güiro*-like *charrascas*; and drums such as the *tambora* and the *furro*. In some *parrandas*, violins, woodwinds, and accordions—and even keyboards and electric bass—are popular. Though they are integral part of the Christmas season, not all *parrandas* or *aguinaldos* are religious in nature, and they can often be joyful secular celebrations as much as religious observances, exploring popular, social, and political themes, or resolutions for the new year. Some popular artists have recorded *aguinaldos* with great commercial success, performing them well after the Christmas season. The most prominent is the folklore group Un Solo Pueblo, which has had a number of hits since the 1970s, notably "El cocuy del Alumbra."

> **Recommended Listening:** "El cocuy del Alumbra" by Un Solo Pueblo, from the CD *Un solo pueblo: De collección, Vol. 2.*

> **Recommended Listening:** "La burra" by Un Solo Pueblo, from the CD: *La música de un solo pueblo, Vol. 4.*

Recommended Listening: "Parranda" from the CD: *Venezuela: Diablos Songs and Drums*.

Gaita   On the shores of Lake Maracaibo, in the western part of the country near the Colombian border, there emerged another singing style closely associated with Christmas celebrations. This is *gaita*, also known as *gaita de furro* in reference to the particular drum that accompanies it. Though its exact origins remain unclear, it is a syncretic mix of African characteristics—notably in the use of drums and percussion—as well as Spanish song forms and Catholic hymns, particularly Christmas and Easter *villancicos*. Though *gaitas* emerged in western Venezuela, they are now popular throughout the country, and though they are associated with the Christmas season, they can be heard on radio stations beginning as early as October. (The Venezuelan *gaita* Christmas celebration is not to be confused with the *gaita* flute used in some Colombian bambuco traditions, explored earlier in this chapter.)

Gaitas are performed when the local inhabitants of a village or neighborhood congregate by an ornate Christmas altar dedicated to the Nativity or a particular saint. They are traditionally accompanied by four instruments: *cuatro, charrasca, tambora,* and *furro*. The *cuatro* provides the harmony, though sometimes two *cuatros* perform: one to provide intricate melodic passages, the other to provide a percussive strumming called *charrasqueado*. The *tambora* is a large single-headed upright drum made from cowskin, played with sticks that alternately hit the head and the body of the drum. Several *tamboras* can be played in *gaita* ensembles, complementing each other's rhythms as well as that of the *güiro*-like *charrasca*. But the most distinctive instrument used in *gaita* is the *furro* (also known as *furroco*), a large friction drum that provides the bass of the ensemble. The *furro* has a sheep- or goatskin head from which protrudes a meter-long reed cane. It is related to the *zambomba*, an instrument of Congolese origins used in Spain to accompany Christmas *villancicos*, as well as to the Brazilian *cuíca*. With both the Brazilian and the African instruments, however, the cane protrudes inside the drum, and the player must reach into the body of the instrument to produce sound. By contrast, the *furro*'s cane extends outward from the drum head, and the player's hand, covered with wax, rubs it in a vigorous, recurring motion that produces a deep, distinctive sound and that, according to some commentators, reveals important issues of sexual power and identity. Other instruments such as maracas, pitched in pairs, are often added to the ensemble, and modern ensembles typically include percussion such as conga drums, as well as electric bass and keyboards.

A typical *gaita* is in duple meter, either in $\frac{2}{4}$ or $\frac{6}{8}$, with lively tempos. The *gaita* is quintessentially a song and literary form, though some *gaitas*, particularly those with more pronounced African influences, have developed corresponding dances. Like the *aguinaldos*, *gaitas* generally consist of a solo singer improvising octosyllabic verses, alternating with the choir of instrumentalists who sing the refrain that identifies that particular *gaita*. Verbal agility and improvisation is once again an important part of the tradition, and *gaiteros* often compete to determine who is the most talented singer, with occasional disparaging and insulting verses directed at their opponent. The most wide-spread version is the *gaita Zuliana* ("from Zulia") from the northern shores of Lake Maracaibo, but several other stylistic variations have become popular over the decades. Others, in turn, have disappeared completely from Venezuela's cultural consciousness. On the southern shores of the lake, where there is a stronger Black presence, the *gaitas* tend to have more African influences. Thus, the *gaita de tambora* and the *gaita perijanera* consist of a succession of dances and songs in call-and-response form, with a more pronounced drum and percussion accompaniment, and with a wind instrument such as a clarinet replacing the *cuatro*, playing melodic passages between verses.

Though its roots are religious, and it is associated with Christmas season, the *gaita* is actually a secular genre. It has also become a means for the poor underclass to express itself, a vehicle for social protest, and a means for identity. Themes of *gaitas* can address historical events or cultural issues. They can be romantic ballads and serenades, protest songs against the government, or performed merely for celebration. Often *gaitas* are dedicated to specific saints and feast days, such as the *gaita de Santa Lucia* (December 13), the southern *gaita de tambora* dedicated to San Benito (December 29), and the *gaita chiquinquireña*, dedicated to the Virgin of Chiquinquirá, the patron saint of the Zulia region (November 18). Many *gaita* ensembles have succeeded in achieving national exposure, including Maracaibo 15, Estrellas de Zulia, and Gran Coquivacoa. Starting in the 1970s, *gaitas* were adopted by Venezuela's vibrant *música tropical* movement and infused with elements of salsa and *son*. *Gaita* is also popular beyond the western areas (for example the *gaita oriental* from the eastern coastal region), as well as in neighboring Colombia. Several Colombian artists, notably the famous band-leader Lucho Bermúdez, were instrumental in popularizing the genre in that country.

> **Recommended Listening:** "Gaita a Santa Lucia" by Quinto Criollo, from the CD *Musica popular y folklórica de Venezuela*.

> **Recommended Listening:** "Palo palo" by Maracaibo 15, from the CD *The Rough Guide to the Music of Venezuela*.

For a discussion of other Venezuelan styles, including *Tonos de Velorio* and *Cruz de Mayo*, see www.mymusickit.com.

Afro-Venezuelan Music

As in neighboring Colombia, Venezuela's coastal region was greatly influenced by a pronounced African presence scarcely felt in the interior. But, as in Colombia, few generalizations can be made regarding Afro-Venezuelan culture and music, which vary from region to region, sometimes from village to village. A key difference between Black communities in Venezuela and similar ones in Brazil and the Caribbean is that African religions are not as prominent as they are in those areas. Though traces of African deities remain in Catholic worship, there is little evidence of any widespread African-based religious system such as vodou, *candomblé*, or Santería. Most Afro-Venezuelans are

Catholic, and much of the African music is manifested in Catholic rituals such as the *gaita*, with little or no connection to the ancestral African deities.

Besides the Christmas *gaita*, the four most important Afro-Venezuelan celebrations are dedicated to St. John the Baptist, St. Benedict-the-Moor, St. Anthony of Padua, and the feast of Corpus Christi. Each has its own traditions, though all usually involve a Mass and a procession which takes the saint's statue to an elaborately ornamented altar. Singers and dancers precede or follow the saint, accompanied by drums and other percussion. Syncopated African rhythms predominate, as do call-and-response songs. Dances can either be community events—with large numbers of dancers forming circles or lines—or courtship rituals danced by individual couples, who then alternate with other couples in the audience. These celebrations are often performed by *cofradías*—religious and social organizations whose origins typically go back to colonial slavery. But the entire assembly of townspeople and guests normally partake of the celebration, joining in the dancing, music making, singing, and hand and stick clapping, with liberal amounts of food and drink, including rum and a tequila-like beverage called *cocuy*. Afro-Venezuelan traditions have become very popular in recent years with tourists—both domestic and foreign—and have had a sizable presence on the country's television coverage.

San Juan Bautista   The feast of St. John the Baptist is celebrated on June 24 throughout Venezuela, but particularly in the central region. It has traditionally been associated with the summer solstice, which occurs a few days earlier, and often marks the end of the planting season. St. John is particularly important among Black Venezuelans, who consider him a healer and a protector. In colonial times his feast day became a holiday for many coastal slaves, an opportunity for them to perform ancestral rhythms, songs, and dances. At the center of the celebration is the procession, during which the statue of the saint is "stolen" from its original altar, paraded through town, stopping at various places along the way. During these stops, colorful dances are performed, and the statue is sometimes sprinkled with rum, so that by the end of the procession, he is known as *San Juan Borrachero*—"St. John the Drunk."

The rhythms are played on a variety of cylindrical drums, usually made from hollowed-out hardwood trees. Perhaps the most prominent is the *tambor cumaco*, a large drum that lays on the ground horizontally, similar to the Haitian *djouba*, the Martinican *bélé*, and the Jamaican *kumina*. The drummer straddles the instrument, playing the cow or deer drumhead between his legs with his hands. Meanwhile, one or two other drummers using drumsticks stand behind him, playing ostinato rhythms directly onto the body of the drum. This playing technique is derived from the Bantu people of the Congo region of central Africa. Another important set of drums is the *mina y curbata*. The *mina*, often more than six feet in length, rests diagonally on a supporting frame, with the principal player standing in front of it striking the head, while one, two, or even three additional drummers strike the body of the drum. The smaller *curbata* stands vertically, with the player standing or sitting before it. Both drums have deer drumheads and are played with either hard sticks or softer, flexible twigs. These drums originate from West Africa and are related to other regional drum traditions, for example Haitian *rada* and the Dominican *tambora*. Much of the music relies on the dialogue between the two drums, with the *curbata* playing a basic pattern, the *mina* improvising above. (This dual approach to drums and drumming styles—horizontal drums from Central Africa, vertical drums from West Africa—is evidence of the diverse ancestry of Afro-Venezuelans, and can be found throughout the continent.)

In other coastal regions, one finds a set of Central African drums called *tambores cul e' puya* (or *tambores redondos*). This is a set of three smallish, horizontal double-headed drums, straddled by drummers who play them with one bare hand and one stick. The drums have names that reflect their size, pitch and rhythmic function: the smaller and high-pitched *prima* (or *corrío*), which sets the basic rhythm and tempo; the medium-sized *medio* (or *cruzao*), which complements the *prima*; and the larger *grande* (or *pujao*), which improvises over the patterns of the other two. Together, the drums form a complex rhythmic texture. Many other local variations have emerged in the coastal region to celebrate San Juan, such as the slow, *cumbia*-like *sangueo*, the *guaraña*, *canto de sirena*, *llamada*, *lejío*, *jinca*, *lucero*, and many others. Each has its own singing, dancing, and drumming characteristics. Some are solo songs, and others are in call-and-response form. Some are secular, others are religious, and some are both. Some are sung by women while the men play the drums, and others are performed entirely by men.

San Benito el Moro   Because he was Black, the sixteenth-century St. Benedict-the-Moor (also known as San Benito de Palermo) has traditionally been the patron saint of many parts of the African Diaspora, notably in various communities in the western part of Venezuela, in the state of Zulia, and the areas surrounding Lake Maracaibo. The feast of San Benito occurs on December 29, and because of the proximity of the dates, it is associated with Christmas celebrations. As a result, Christmas *gaitas* are often included. In the days and weeks leading up to the feast, one can often find small but beautifully decorated altars with the effigy of San Benito outside many homes on the coast. Various rituals involve specific prayers called *novenas*, which are either recited or sung, followed by extended colorful processions, whose participants often dress completely in black—even painting their faces—complementing their attire with a red cape and colorful hats. During the procession, the statue of San Benito is taken to the altar in the town church, while revelers sing, dance, and light fireworks. In some areas, the procession includes a performance of the *chimbanguele*, a set of dances and songs that are accompanied by drums of the same name, as well as nose-flutes, maracas, and conch shells called *guaruras*. A *chimbanguele* drum set consists of seven conical instruments, four large ones called *mayor*, *respuesta*, *cantante*, and *segundo*, and three smaller, higher-pitched ones called *primera requinta*, *segunda requinta*, and *media requinta*. The drums stand vertically—or sometimes they hang from the shoulder with a strap—with the players standing or sitting in front of them, playing them with one hand and a stick. The drums play set rhythms that result in a complex polyphonic texture, with names such as *agé, chocho, chimbanglero, misericordia*, and *sangorongó*.

Another ritual dedicated to San Benito is the *gaita perijanera*, from the district of Perijá, in the state of Zulia. Once again, prayers and petitions are made to the saint at his altar, followed by a procession that includes a succession of courtship dances, now accompanied by a *cuatro*, maracas and *charrasca*, and the *tambora* and *furro* drums. The dances include props such as sticks and a white handkerchief that is suggestively dropped and picked up at appropriate times. The first dance is the actual *gaita*, where the dancers form a circle, each dancer whirling about. Other dances include the fast, triple-meter *sambe* (danced by couples who do not come in contact with each other), the *guaracha* (a traditional couples dance), and the *chimbanguele* (in which San Benito himself is one of the participants). In some communities, the *gaita perijanera* can comprise up to 10 dances including the *galerón* (a traditional couples dance accompanied by a *cuatro*), the *cumbiamba* (an instrumental couples dance with suggestive steps), the *paloma* (often sad and in a minor key), and the *uruguuto*. The *gaita perijanera* typically ends with another fast *guaracha*, which the assembled multitude sings energetically.

San Antonio de Padua Among the Black communities of the state of Lara, there emerged a celebration in honor of St. Anthony of Padua, whose feast falls on June 13. This is the *tamunangue* (or *son de negros*), a celebration whose centerpiece is a series of eight dances that incorporate singing, complex choreography, prayers, and Catholic and African religious rituals. On the previous night, a vigil is held at church in honor of the saint, which includes prayers and rosaries, and the singing of various *tonos* and *salves*. Prayers of thanksgiving for the rainy season are made, as well as petitions for continued health and wealth and for the recovery of lost objects. Early the following morning, a Mass is held, followed by a procession through town, in which the statue of St. Anthony is accompanied by singers, dancers, and the assembled townspeople who clap their hands or sticks together. Following medieval practice, bread is distributed to the spectators in honor of one of the miracles attributed to St. Anthony. The procession culminates at an altar where the statue of St. Anthony is placed.

The *tamunangue* is a curious mix of secular and religious elements, as well as a syncretic mix of African and European rituals, making it one of the most interesting folkloric dances of Venezuela. It is accompanied by a *cuatro, requinto*, and *tiple* guitar, as well as maracas and *tamunango* drum. Performed by one or two soloists, the songs often follow Spanish poetic forms, but also include call-and response elements, allowing the assembled congregation to participate, using African words to punctuate the refrains. The dances have specific choreographic elements, combining African rhythms with the steps of European salon dances. Most are performed by one couple, each dancer carrying a baton or stick that is part of the choreography. When that couple has finished, the batons are passed to another couple, who then jump into the fray. Women wear white shirts and flowery skirts, while the men wear white shirts and black pants, and the obligatory neckerchiefs and sombreros.

The order of the eight dances that make up the *tamunangue* can change from town to town. *La batalla* is always first, and can occur many times throughout the procession. After an instrumental prelude, two men sing a number of verses in a duet, while two warriors simulate a fierce combat with wooden sticks, symbolically protecting the statue of St. Anthony. *La bella* ("the beautiful woman") occurs after the procession has come to an end, and the effigy of St. Anthony has been placed on the altar. This is a lively dance, with spectators joyfully singing the verses, clapping and yelling "Bella, Bella!" In the center, a couple begins a dance of pursuit, the man continuously—but unsuccessfully—chasing the beautiful woman, until the baton is passed to another couple. *El chichivamos* (or *yiyivamos*) is another lively courtship dance, with the assembled spectators quickly responding to the call of the drum with repeated African phrases. In *La juruminga*, the couple holds the baton and dances around it in a flirtatious manner, to the point where it is unclear if they are flirting or continuing the battle first seen in the opening dance, while the spectators enthusiastically encourage them with various Africanized phrases. In the humorous *El poco a poco*, the man, tired from his relentless pursuit, pretends to suffer a cramp, and must be helped onto a horse by the woman. He then becomes the galloping horse and is mounted by the woman, to the delight of the crowd. *La perrendenga* is a lively dance in which the couple uses the batons to portray the trials and tribulations of their relationship. *El galerón* is an informal competition between various couples. *El seis figuriao* (or *seis por ocho*), the closing dance of the *tamunangue*, is interpreted by six dancers, four of whom surround the central couple in complex 32-step sequences.

Corpus Christi One of the most prominent Afro-Venezuelan celebration is that of *Los diablos danzantes*—the "dancing devils"—which occurs on the feast of Corpus Christi to commemorate the sacrament of the Eucharist. It occurs on the Thursday after the feast of the Holy Trinity, most often in the months of May and June, in proximity to the summer solstice and the feast of San Juan. Perhaps paradoxically, the central figure of this medieval celebration of Christ is the Devil, who, at the end of the day, will submit to the supremacy of the body of Christ. The *diablos danzantes* is a syncretic folklore commemoration that vividly illustrates the opposition between the forces of good and evil. At the center of the celebration are the *diablos*, male revelers of all ages who impersonate the Devil. Unlike the joyful feasts of San Juan or San Benito, *diablos danzantes* is more subdued, for the danger of confronting the Devil is taken very seriously. Magic and the supernatural are prominent. Dancers representing the Devil protect themselves from evil, regularly crossing themselves, carrying protective charms such as crosses and rosaries, and praying continuously throughout the processions. A candlelight *velorio* is held the previous night. The celebrations culminate with a Mass, the ultimate celebration of the Eucharist. The *diablos* dress up in colorful costumes with long red capes, and a bell at the end of their long tail. They don menacing masks with horns (an African custom), typically made of wood or papier-mâché, the number of horns indicative of the dancer's sins. Various jingling bells, rattles, shakers

Diablos danzantes during Corpus Christi celebrations in San Francisco de Yare, Venezuela.

and cowbells hang from a *diablo's* belt, mask or cape. Each *diablo* carries a single maraca in his right hand and a defensive stick in the left hand, which he uses to ward off anyone—or anything—who would interfere with him. Somewhat ironically, the costumes and masks that represent the Devil are also meant to scare him away.

 Diablos danzantes are popular in the central coastal region, with particularly prominent celebrations in San Francisco de Yare (in the state of Miranda), Naiguatá (Vargas), and Chuao (Aragua). They are usually organized and performed by *cofradías* called generally *Sociedades del santísimo*—social and religious organizations whose main goal is to promote a sense of community and identity. Planning for the *diablos* celebration can take several weeks or months. Each *cofradía* has a set number of dancers, a number that is closely monitored during the actual procession, for an extra dancer could indicate that the Devil himself has joined in the celebration, while a missing dancer is deemed to have been (temporarily) abducted. The music is almost exclusively instrumental, and usually performed by a single *cuatro* player (though in San Francisco de Yare and Naiguatá, a snare drum called *caja* or *redoblante* is used), complemented by the various maracas and cowbells played by the dancers themselves. The rhythms are steady, almost monotonous, to highlight the potential danger lurking in the person of the Devil. The colors of the Devil costumes vary from region to region. In San Francisco de Yare, costumes are red and yellow, while in Naiguatá, they are white and painted with protective symbols, with no capes. The *diablos* and *diablas*—for Naiguatá's is one of the few traditions that include women—wear menacing masks that represent monstrous sea creatures. They also carry crucifixes instead of sticks, since they are perhaps more effective defensive weapons. In Chuao, masks can be of any color, decorated with paper garlands and sometimes ornamented with beards. In recent years, the *diablos danzantes* have transcended their local identity and become national celebrations. On the day of Corpus Christi, throughout the central coast, sidewalks are invariably lined with tourists from Caracas or the interior, or even from foreign countries, and the *diablos* regularly make television appearances. A few ensembles have emerged from the coastal areas that have popularized much of the music of Afro-Venezuelan celebrations, though none of them have yet acquired an international following. These include Guaricongo, Huracán De Fuego, Grupo Madera, and Los Vasallos del Sol.

> **Recommended Listening:** "Golpe de cumaco," "Canto de sirena," and "Golpe de hamaca," from the CD: *Venezuela: Diablos Songs and Drums*.

> **Recommended Listening:** "Tonadas de quitiplás" by Jackeline Rago and the Venezuelan Music Project, from the CD *El campanazo*.

> **Recommended Listening:** "Canto de mina," "San Juan," and "Tambores y quitiplás" by Grupo Madera, from the CD *Serie lo máximo: Tambores*.

> **Recommended Listening:** "Tambor de Aragua," "Sirenas" and "Golpe de ajé" by Vasallos del Sol, from the CD *Cantos de sirena*.

> **Recommended Listening:** "Mosaico tradicional" by Tambor Urbano and "Julio Moreno/Linda Mañana" by Vasallos Del Sol, from the CD *The Rough Guide to the Music of Venezuela*.

> **Recommended Listening:** "Tumba la caña bomba que bomba" by Huracán de Fuego, from the CD *Vamos a darle*.

Caribbean Styles

CALIPSO Because of its proximity to Trinidad, Venezuela has developed its own version of the island's most famous style: calypso, which it spells *calipso*. Calypso emerged in Trinidad at the end of the nineteenth century, and was quickly exported by immigrants to Venezuela, where it became popular not, as one might expect, in coastal communities, but rather in the interior, where the discovery of important gold mines led to a gold rush among Trinidadians and other islanders. The epicenter of *calipso* is the district of Bolívar in the southeastern part of the country, and particularly in the town of El Callao, not far from the Guyana border, and is therefore sometimes known as *calipso* *guayanés*. The predominantly Black population of El Callao has developed one of the most important carnival celebrations in Venezuela, one with a markedly Caribbean feel to it, with much revelry and colorful parades that include floats, musicians, and dancers. The obligatory sumptuous costumes are everywhere, with scantily clad women wearing the enormous, feather-laden outfits that have become emblematic of South American carnival. Revelers dress as mythological or historical figures such as *diablos*, kings, and queens, or characters from local folklore or modern popular culture.

Venezuelan *calipso* is usually accompanied by drums, a characteristic not present in Trinidad, where the instrument was banned by colonial authorities. The ensemble consists of two large drums and a smaller one called the *bumbac*, held by the player over the shoulder during carnival parades with its head perpendicular to the ground, and struck by both hands. The large drums play traditional calypso rhythmic patterns, while the higher-pitched *bumbac* plays rapid improvisatory passages above. Additionally, guitars, *cuatros*, cowbells, and whistles accompany the songs, as do percussion instruments made from the iron wheels of a car or bicycle. *Calipso* lyrics are in a mix of English, Spanish, and French *patois*, though as time goes by, there are fewer English-speakers in southeastern Venezuela, and new compositions tend to be exclusively in Spanish. Songs consist of clever verses and a chorus, with a marked rhyme scheme that must be respected. As in Trinidad, *calipso* songs are humorous commentaries on current or national events, a century-old method for spreading news rapidly. Paralleling Trinidad's musical evolution, the area adopted the island's steel pan tradition in the 1950s, as well as the energetic *soca* in the 1970s, which continues to be popular today at carnival in El Callao, but also in various other parts of Venezuela, predominantly in the coastal areas. As in Trinidad, modern instruments such as synthesizers, electric guitars, and bass are common in modern *calipso* and *soca*, as are, increasingly, brass instruments.

> **Recommended Listening:** "Calipso de El Callao" by Alberto Naranjo y Su Trabuco, from the CD *The Rough Guide to the Music of Venezuela*.

> **Recommended Listening:** "Calypsos" by Un Solo Pueblo, from the CD: *La música de Un Solo Pueblo, Vol. 4*.

MÚSICA TROPICAL   Venezuela, like Colombia, has developed its own tradition of *música tropical*, adopting the Cuban *son*, Dominican merengue, and (later) salsa, and infusing them with its own characteristics. During the "Latin Craze" of the 1940s and 1950s, prominent musicians who had migrated from Cuba and the Dominican Republic populated Venezuela—particularly Caracas and other parts of the coast. The popularization of *música tropical* was due principally to the rivalry between two bandleaders: the Dominican Luis María Frómeta—known as "Billo"—and his orchestra Billo's Caracas Boys; and the orchestra of Luis Alfonso Larrain, known as "El Mago de la Música Bailable" ("the Magician of Dance Music"). In the 1940s, these two orchestras achieved a degree of sophistication that increased their popularity not only in

Venezuela but abroad as well. Other groups included Porfi Jiménez y su Orquesta and Los Melódicos, led by Renato Capriles. These big band orchestras, consisting of clarinets, trumpets, saxophones, and trombones, along with guitar or cuatro, bass and a drum set, played *sones*, merengues, rumbas, mambos, and *cumbias*. They also developed their own styles of Latin music (including the Venezuelan *guasa*) and incorporated Afro-Venezuelan (as opposed to Afro-Cuban) drumming.

By the time salsa was emerging from New York in the 1970s, the big-band orchestras were giving way to smaller ensembles such as Sexteto Juventud and especially Dimensión Latina, a group that firmly established Venezuela as an important contributor to the genre. Dimensión Latina was founded in 1972 by José Rodríguez, César Monge, José Antonio Rojas, and bass-player and singer Oscar d'León, who would become Venezuela's greatest *salsero*. Known as "El Sonero del Mundo," d'León would later form another band, Salsa Mayor, with which he would achieve superstardom status, not only in Venezuela but worldwide. Older orchestras such as Billo's Caracas Boys (with new personnel—Billo died in 1988) also continued to play *música tropical*. In the new millennium, salsa, merengue, *cumbia*, and *música tropical* in general continue to have a vibrant presence in Venezuela, popular in nightclubs and discos, and heard 24 hours a day on radio stations throughout the country.

> **Recommended Listening:** "Cómo se baila el merengue" and "Nació un bebé" by Billo's Caracas Boys, from the CD *Billo's Caracas Boys: 1941–44*.
>
> **Recommended Listening:** "La negra Celina" and "El vampiro" by Porfi Jiménez y Su Orquesta, from the CD *Puro Chucu-Chucu*.
>
> **Recommended Listening:** "Los nenes con las nenas" and "Traca que traca" by Los Melódicos, from the CD *Puro Chucu-Chuc*.
>
> **Recommended Listening:** "Lloraras" and "El frutero" by Dimensión Latina, from the CD *Una dimensión de éxitos*.
>
> **Recommended Listening:** "Me voy pa'Cali" and "Mi mujer es una bomba" by Oscar d'León, from the CD *Pura salsa*.
>
> **Recommended Listening:** "Ariel" and "Los Cadetes" by Oscar d'Leon, and "Gavilán" by Dimension Latina, from the CD *The Rough Guide to the Music of Venezuela*.

For a discussion of other Venezuelan popular styles, see www.mymusickit. com.

8

The Andean Region

CHAPTER SUMMARY

Peru
- Historical Introduction
- Afro-Peruvian Music
- *Música Criolla*
  - *Criollo* Songs
  - *Criollo* Dances
  - *Estudiantinas*
- Peruvian Popular Music
  - *Chicha*

INTRODUCTION

The most prominent geographical feature of the western coast of South America is the Andes mountain range, which extends as far north as Colombia and Venezuela and as far south as Chile and Argentina. Particularly prominent is an extended plateau in the central Andes called the *altiplano* (literally the "high plains"), at an average altitude of 11,000 feet, where the Andes are at their widest, and where many of the civilizations in the region lived and continue to live. Yet in spite of the prominence of the mountains, much of the region's population can be found in coastal areas on the western slopes. Meanwhile, on the eastern flank, a series of valleys called Yungas fall dramatically from the highlands into the Amazonian basin, where a host of Native cultures have lived for thousands of years in the midst of the rainforest. The warm, humid, and fertile Yungas have immense cultivated terraced fields that gradually climb up the mountain range, where coffee, sugarcane, bananas, corn, potatoes, rice, and other staples are grown, as well as the controversial coca plant. They are also geologically dramatic, with high cliffs and raging rivers, and contain a great amount of plant and animal biodiversity, making them prime locations for biological preserves and national parks.

The Andean region does not fit neatly into political or cultural boundaries, and every country in South America has been affected to varying degrees by the mountain lifestyle, and particularly by the cultures that predominated there prior to the arrival of the Spaniards. However, the three countries that have developed a particular Andean character are Peru, Ecuador, and Bolivia. Colombia, Venezuela, Chile, and Argentina also have important Andean music traditions, which are discussed here, though the bulk of the music of those countries is explored in their respective chapters.

THE INCAS

As in Mesoamerica, the Andean region had been populated by 3000 BCE by numerous ethnic and linguistic groups, some achieving a great amount of cultural and economic influence. These included the Norte Chico and Chavín civilizations in Peru, who built important structures and artistic legacies, as well as the Valdivia civilization on the coast of Ecuador. Later, the Mochica became prominent on the northern Peruvian coast, while in the south, the Nazca left important archeological remains, including the famous Nazca Lines, a series of enormous etchings in the shape of animals carved into the desert, which can only be appreciated from the air. In the past 20 years, enormous Nazca settlements have been spotted by satellite lying under the sandy landscape, and archeological investigation has thus far revealed important information about musical culture. In Bolivia, the archeological ruins at Tiwanaku remain some of the most splendid on the continent. Around 1500 BCE, the Aymara civilization occupied the shores of Lake Titicaca, which straddles the border between modern Peru and Bolivia. Several other groups attempted to conquer adjoining lands and form extended empires, including the Wari from the central Andes and the Chachapoyas of the Amazon region. Each cultural or military conquest increased the region's accumulated knowledge, which in the end was inherited by—and contributed to the supremacy of—the Incas.

The Inca kingdom first emerged during the twelfth century in the ancient city of Cuzco. By the 1430s, King Pachacuti had conquered most of the mountainous areas in modern Peru and Ecuador and established the Inca Empire he called the *Tahuantinsuyo*, meaning "four regions" in reference to the four sectors that made up the empire and which all met at Cuzco, the capital. Pachacuti's son Túpac and grandson Huayna Cápac continued the expansion, so that by 1500 the Inca dominated virtually the entire Andean region. The empire spanned over 3000 miles along the west coast of South America, from Colombia in the north to central Chile. It encompassed both the Andean highlands and the coastal lowlands, and their influence further reached into many outlying areas. Like the Aztec Empire, the Inca Empire was not monolithic but consisted of various cultures, languages, and political entities, all loosely—but efficiently—held together by the central administration. The official language of the empire was Quechua, but after the Inca conquered the Aymara, their language became an important component of the empire, as did several others. Today, both Quechua and Aymara are still spoken by millions of the descendants of the Incas, and are, along with Spanish, the official languages of Bolivia and Peru.

As in Mesoamerica, the Inca religion centered on the worship of nature. But whereas the rainforest-dwelling Mayas considered rain the most important deity, the Incas, living in the cold, high-altitude world of the Andes, considered the sun the giver of life. The principal Inca deity was the sun god Inti, preeminent over all things, and the emperor was considered his direct descendant, the Son of the Sun. Inti's wife Pachamama was the goddess of the earth, to whom animal sacrifices were made. The principal ceremony of the sun god was called *Intip Raymin*, celebrated during the winter solstice, when it appeared the sun was abandoning the people, which would lead to famine and the disintegration of the empire. After fasting for several days, the people gathered at the temple of the sun in Cuzco called Koricancha, the most spectacular and beautiful monument in the ancient city. They presented gifts and offerings to Inti, imploring him to return and provide a good harvest in the coming season. The ceremony honored not only the god but also his progeny the emperor, who then presented a sumptuous feast to his people, accompanied by song and dance.

The Incas were master architects and engineers, developing a building technique that rarely used mortar, relying instead on large polished stones that interlocked so perfectly that it is famously impossible to stick a knife blade between them. Sacred locations called *huacas* were believed to be permeated with certain spirits and were thus worshiped and revered. Cuzco was—and remains—a beautiful city, as impressive to Spanish eyes as was Tenochtitlán. The most famous Inca archaeological site is Machu Picchu, a city that lies 8,000 feet on a mountaintop about 50 miles from Cuzco and that was forgotten by the outside world until it was "rediscovered" in 1911, when it was dubbed The Lost City of the Incas. Perhaps the most impressive Inca achievement was its vast system of roads, spanning more than 22,000 kilometers from Ecuador in the north to Chile and Argentina in the south, and from the mountains to the sea. It allowed fast communication with a network of runners that quickly relayed information, so that news could reach the other end of the empire in a matter of days. The roads enabled the efficient administration of the empire, the distribution of food on llamas and alpacas (the only draft animals on the continent), and the rapid deployment of the army. Conversely, the road system also led the conquistadors easily and directly to Cuzco, which resulted in the empire's eventual downfall. Many of these trails are still used, and are popular with trekkers and backpackers, particularly the trail to Machu Picchu.

Inca Music

Andean cultures had distinct myths relating to music's relationship with the spiritual world. Even after the advent of the Incas, music, dancing, and costumes were not uniform across the region, just as they are not today. Various groups within the empire continued to rely on their own musical traditions to preserve a sense of identity that deflected the imposed Inca culture, just as their descendants would do in the face of Spanish colonialism and, later, modern globalization. Music was not used exclusively for grand-scale religious purposes as it was in Mesoamerica and could be performed for any occasion, religious, or secular. The agrarian Inca society, like its modern-day descendants, closely followed the yearly agricultural cycle, celebrating the harvest, sowing, the rainy season, and celestial events such as solstices, cycles of the moon and eclipses. Village, neighborhood, and family celebrations invariably included music and dance, not only for special occasions but also in the course of everyday life. Citizens often had their own flutes or small drums they would bring out for any occasion, and local shamans would lead small ceremonies that sometimes involved mind-altering substances.

Celebrations at the Inca court were of course enormous affairs, and they drew much of the focus of colonial writers. Held at the sacred *huaca* sites, they could be huge, elaborate, and bombastic public displays for the benefit of the entire city. Lively celebrations would be staged for the visit of an important dignitary, a birth in the royal family, festivals dedicated to particular deities, rituals of initiation, or offerings of thanksgiving for the harvest or for continuing good health. Particularly exuberant were victory processions, when a triumphant general would return to Cuzco with great fanfare, accompanied by hundreds of flutes, trumpets, drums, conch shells, singers, and dancers. The Incas also had monthly religious festivals, a tradition that continues in many places in the Andes. During feasts and ceremonies, streets and plazas would be intricately adorned with flowers and colorful feathers, and participants would wear their finest clothing. Musical instruments were decorated and painted, usually in vermilion, the royal color of the Inca, because it symbolized blood. A solemn dance called the *guayaya* called for a large drum to be carried by a slave on his back and played by a woman, accompanying a slow procession of hundreds of dancers and singers. One of the most famous and shocking practices of the Incas involved making drums from the cured skin of their defeated enemies. Grizzly colonial accounts tell of captured warriors who were flayed and turned into drums called *runatinyas*. The body, head and arms were stuffed, and the arms were used to beat on the stretched stomach membrane, as a means to showcase a triumph over a conquered enemy and intimidate the survivors.

Numerous singers, dancers and instrumentalists performed at these events with an extended repertoire of songs and dances appropriate for various occasions. Colonial writers describe the emperors and their wives as being very fond of music and dance, often participating in the ceremonies themselves. As in the Aztec Empire, a school for young musicians was maintained at court. The temple of the sun-virgins included six houses, in which privileged maidens from the empire lived and performed various functions. In the fourth house—the *taquiaclla*—girls between the ages of 9 and 15 were trained to sing and play musical instruments and to perform at the emperor's leisure. Also employed at the Inca court were composers called *amauta*, as well as *haravecs*, official poet/storytellers who sang or narrated historical epics to the emperor. From the *haravecs* are descended the mournful Native songs of modern times called *yaravís*, discussed later in this chapter.

THE MODERN ANDEAN REGION

The Inca Empire came to an end at the hands of Francisco Pizarro, who first encountered it in 1526. By the time he returned to the region six years later, the empire was in disarray due to civil war and a smallpox epidemic that had spread quickly along the Inca's efficient road system, ultimately claiming as many as 90 percent of the inhabitants of the empire. As Cortés had done in Mexico, Pizarro quickly found allies in various Native groups that were disenchanted with Inca domination, and with his small expeditionary force proceeded to conquer the empire already weakened by disease and internal dissension. After executing the emperor and much of the nobility, he established the Viceroyalty of Peru and became its first viceroy. Inca resistance continued for several years, but was finally quashed in 1572.

The fall of the Incas forever changed the character of Andean civilizations. The marginalization of Native groups, present everywhere on the continent, was particularly felt in the Andean region during the colonial period and continues to various degrees today. Many areas remained isolated by mountains, deserts, and thick jungles, which often made them inaccessible to Europeans on the coast. Most inhabitants of the highlands still embrace precolonial traditions and speak only Native languages. As in Mexico, the large Native population was sufficient, even after it had been decimated by disease, to work the mines and ranches of the Spanish landowners. African slaves were mostly limited to coastal areas, with a few small pockets in some parts of the highlands, for example around the Potosí area of Bolivia. Though the African influence has been less pronounced than in other parts of the continent, Afro-Andeans—called *morenos* by Native Andeans—have had an important effect on the region's culture and music, an effect that has often been overlooked or altogether denied.

Today, Native inhabitants constitute 25 percent of Ecuador's total population, 45 percent of Peru's, and 55 percent of Bolivia's. The remainder are mostly Mestizos (often called *cholos*), with minorities of European and African descent, and recent immigrants from China and Japan. The two principal Native groups are the Aymara and the Quechua, descendants of populations that constituted the bulk of the Inca Empire. Whereas the Quechua can be found throughout the Andean region, the Aymara are concentrated around Lake Titicaca in southern Peru, Bolivia, and northern Chile. But hundreds of other Native groups can also be found in the region. Moreover, the Aymara and the Quechua, like the Maya in Mesoamerica, are not homogenous, monolithic groups. Most Natives do not consider themselves part of a national or even regional ethnic unit but rather identify with local communities. There are dozens of dialects of both Quechua and Aymara, so distinct that neighboring regions and even adjacent villages often cannot understand each other. By the same token, there is a large variety of musical styles that have evolved independently.

The music of the region can be generally divided into four categories: European-derived music of urban areas, African-based music of coastal areas, Native music of the Amazon, and Native and Mestizo music of the highlands—what is generally referred to as "Andean music." Whereas the first three categories have somewhat specific national characteristics, the fourth transcends the entire region and can be found in the mountainous regions of Peru, Bolivia, Ecuador, Venezuela, Colombia, Argentina, and Chile. Political boundaries are almost irrelevant to a study of the hundreds of Andean styles, many of which cross freely across borders. This chapter will explore this music as a quintessentially Andean phenomenon and then turn to more localized styles on a country-by-country basis.

Andean Music

There are hundreds of Andean musical traditions, with millions of musicians in towns and villages throughout the region. Neighboring villages might have traditions based on completely different instruments, tunings, rhythms, texts, languages, and dances. Much of this music has not been studied or recorded and thus remains unknown to the outside world. There is potential ethnomusicological and anthropological work in the Andes for decades to come. To cover even a small fraction of this diverse musical culture would be beyond the scope of this textbook. Instead, this chapter discusses general characteristics and examines a few localized traditions.

General Characteristics

The following features are commonly, though not universally, found in the region's music:

- Vocal and instrumental music tends to be high pitched. Female singers tend to have a very high vocal range, often singing falsetto, a feature that goes back to Inca times. Men, by contrast, often have a very low vocal range, considered strong and masculine.
- Repetition is an important structural feature. A typical verse might have an ABAB or AABB structure. Short phrases are repeated to form a melody which itself might be repeated dozens of times during a performance, each version subtly different from the preceding one.
- Melodies often reflect the pentatonic scale that is famous to the region, but ancient musical instruments themselves negate the idea that all music was always pentatonic. Another common feature is *bimodality*, the alternation—and occasionally even the juxtaposition—of major and minor keys in a piece.
- Native rhythms and dances tend to emphasize syncopated duple meters, while Mestizo rhythms tend to use the Latin American *sesquiáltera*, juxtaposing duple and triple meters.

A Note on Recommended Listening

Undoubtedly the most comprehensive compilations of traditional Native Andean music are the two sets of recordings released by the Smithsonian Folkways Series titled *Traditional Music of Peru (Vols. 1–8)* and *Mountain Music of Peru (Vols. 1–2)*. Together, these collections contain almost three hundred tracks of field recordings that display the amazing variety of Andean rituals, styles, and instruments. Other good compilations of traditional Andean music include the CDs:

- *Kingdom of the Sun: The Inca Heritage*
- *Festival of the Andes: Paucartambo*
- *Peru and Bolivia: The Sounds of Evolving Traditions*
- *Soul of the Andes: Strings and Flutes from Ecuador*

Andean Instruments

Archaeologists have found musical instruments and other artifacts from pre-Inca civilizations such as the Chavín, Nazca, and Mochica cultures, many of which were later adopted by the Incas and continued to be used after the arrival of the Spaniards. Andean cultures had a greater variety of instruments than Mesoamerican cultures. Particularly important were wind instruments of various shapes and sizes, and evidence suggests that the Incas emphasized melody more than percussion (although the percussive elements of Andean music may have been suppressed by Europeans chroniclers who mostly valued melody). Specific aesthetic ideals were sought by combining instruments to produce a desired timbral effect. Images on pre-Columbian artifacts show musicians playing multiple instruments simultaneously, for example with a panpipe in one hand while beating a drum with the other, or with a panpipe and trumpet in each hand, while their legs and feet play drums and rattles. Some surviving Inca instruments suggest pentatonic melodies, a feature that is still prevalent in much of Andean music today. Yet other instruments hint at more complex harmony, and ethnomusicologists assert that the wide variety of instruments negates the idea that Inca melodies were exclusively pentatonic. In any case, the tuning of the instruments was important, often juxtaposing neighboring tones and relying on microtonal intervals—those that exist, for example, between the keys of a piano. The high pitch and the tuning system, perceived as dissonant, led some Europeans to characterize Inca music, as they had in Mesoamerica, as a "barbarous noise" that was harsh and out of tune.

The two most important instruments among the Native inhabitants of the Andes, both ancient and modern, are the notched flute and the panpipe, which are known by a variety of names in the highlands and in the coastal regions.

NOTCHED FLUTES During Inca times, flutes with a notched blowhole were generically called *pincullu*, which simply means "flute" in both Quechua and Aymara. The earliest Andean *pincullus* go back 2,500 years to the Chavín culture. They came in various shapes and lengths and were made from the bones of pelicans, pumas, llamas, deer, and condors, as well as from cane or wood from the Amazon jungle. The first *pincullus* had four finger holes, but more were gradually added, with varied spacings to produce multiple tunings, thus providing great versatility in terms of expression and melodic content. Depending on their size, number of holes and construction material, they bore different names such as *tarka*, *pipo*, and *quenaquena*. Transverse flutes also existed but were rarer. *Pincullus* were always part of Native festivals, whether sumptuous large-scale ceremonies or intimate family celebrations, and were usually associated with bringing rainfall. *Pincullu* orchestras could number over a hundred players, accompanied by drums, dancers, and singers.

During the colonial period, some *pincullus* adopted features from European recorders, in particular the mouthpiece that directs the player's breath into the pipe. These modern duct-flutes are still called *pincullus*. But it is the notched instrument, in which the player blows directly into an indentation at the top of the pipe, that remains the primary flute of the Andes. It is now called *quena* (sometimes spelled *kena*), derived from the *quenaquena*, which means "hollow" in Quechua. Modern *quenas* are usually made from cane or wood. They come in many sizes, with an obligatory thumbhole in the back, and they can have between four and eight holes in the front. The most common *quena* is a small, high-pitched instrument measuring 10 to 12 inches long, with five finger holes in the front. The intermediate-sized *choquela* measures 18 inches and has six finger holes. The larger, lower-pitched *pusipia* is 21 inches long and has only four holes. The tuning of *quenas*, determined by the size of the instrument and the spacing of the finger holes, differs greatly throughout the region. *Quenas* are often deliberately overblown, generating a brilliant sound with sharp harmonics and loud dynamics that is an octave higher than if it were played in the normal range.

The *quena* is used in both Mestizo and Native traditional folk styles and is widely disseminated in various forms throughout the continent, for example in the Amazon basin and the River Plate area. In ancient Inca tradition, only men played *quenas*, a practice that has prevailed for centuries in traditional Native societies, though women performers sometimes play in the more entertainment-oriented Mestizo forms. As a result of the popularity of Andean music in the last few decades, new forms of the instrument have emerged, along with performance practices that often draw more from contemporary Western art and pop music than from traditional customs.

Zampoña and *quena* players, Peru.

PANPIPES   Perhaps the instrument most associated with Andean cultures, both ancient and modern, is the panpipe, though it also developed independently in many different parts of the world, as far away as Greece, China, and the South Pacific. Yet panpipes were popular among pre-Inca cultures well before the Greeks constructed the cult of Dionysus around a similar instrument they called *syrinx*. The coastal Nazca had a class of artisans whose only job was to construct panpipes, which were impeccably tuned the same. Due to the high altitude and low oxygen of the Andes Mountains, its inhabitants have developed some of the largest lung capacities in the world, providing them with the considerable air volume necessary to play the instrument. A panpipe consists of one or two rows of pipes of increasing length, attached side-by-side, arranged in order of size (and therefore of pitch). The pipes are end-blown, lacking a mouthpiece and finger holes, and their extremities are sealed. The sound is produced by placing the pipe on the lower lip and blowing across the opening. The pipes are made from bamboo or a type of cane called *chuqui*, and occasionally also from feather quills and wing bones of condors and other birds of prey.

The panpipe is prevalent throughout the entire region. It is called ***antara*** in Quechua, ***siku*** (or *sico*) in Aymara, and ***zampoña*** in Spanish. Additionally, there are dozens of local and regional names for the instrument, often indicating size or number of pipes. Thus, a small high-pitched Peruvian panpipe, about six inches in length, is called *ika* or *chulli*; a medium one, measuring about twelve inches, is called *malta*; a two-feet instrument is called *sanka*. The *toyo* is often four or five feet long and is very difficult to play, requiring much more breath to produce each sound. Other names include *orqo, laca, pusa*, and *jilawiri*. The Aymara have a large double-row instrument called *chiriguano*. Meanwhile, Bolivia and Chile have the four-pipe *jula-jula* and the eight-pipe *lakita*, Ecuador has the *rondador*, and Colombia has the *capador*. (For the sake of convenience, the generic Spanish term *zampoña* will be used here.)

Zampoñas come in a variety of sizes, shapes, tunings, and number of pipes. Some in the Peruvian Amazon consist of only three or four pipes a few inches long, while in Ecuador they can have as many as 43 pipes arranged in a single row. Most modern instruments often consist of 10 or 12 pipes. Over time, a second row of pipes was often attached adjacent to the first, a technical advance which gave the player faster access to a given pitch, thus allowing for faster melodies. The second row of pipes is sometimes open-ended, providing a different timbre and greater volume than the melody played on the first row. (An open-ended pipe sounds an octave higher than a closed-ended pipe of the same length.) In some *zampoñas*, the row of pipes is not arranged in a straight line, but rather curves slightly around the player's face, making them easier to play.

Traditionally, panpipes played from three-to seven-tone scales, depending on the number of pipes, and recently they have been constructed to yield a diatonic scale (e.g., the white keys on the piano) or even a full chromatic scale (both the white and black keys). In contrast to the huge *pincullu* orchestras, *zampoña* players during Inca times would often form small ensembles of four instruments, often in the soprano/alto/tenor/bass configuration that was then taking root in Europe around the time of the Conquest, which for that reason surprised some colonial commentators. Modern ensembles often consist of just a pair of instruments, though they sometimes re-form the quartet of Inca times. Melodies are often doubled at the octave, or at the third, fourth, or fifth degree of the scale. In some areas, three *zampoñas* are tuned a third and a fifth apart, thus playing melodies in parallel thirds and fifths. Pipes are usually arranged in strict ascending order of size and pitch, and the instrument assumes a fairly standard triangular shape. An exception is the Ecuadorian *rondador*, in which each pipe is followed by a larger one (tuned a third below) before going up to the next scale degree on a smaller pipe. The lower side of the triangle is thus crenellated with an up-and-down, zigzag pattern. This arrangement of pipes allows a player to play a pitch and its lower third simultaneously, adding to the melody a sense of harmony based on parallel thirds.

During Inca times, Native players reached a high level of virtuosity on the *zampoñas*, a tradition that still continues to this day. Because *zampoñas* require a lot of air, which is scarce in the high altitude of the Andes, it is often difficult to play an entire melody or phrase with a single breath. As a result, a particular technique evolved, mostly in the southern Andes, in which two players play alternate notes in quick succession, producing a smooth, interlocking melody that appears to originate from a single instrument. This interlocking technique (called *hocket*—"hiccup"—in Western art music), is known in the Andes as *trenzado* ("braided"), as the two parts intertwine into a figurative melodic tress. *Trenzado* playing is particularly prominent with the larger panpipes, which require proportionately much more breath. The principal player is called *ira* (Aymara for "leader") while the secondary player is called *arca* ("follower"). In some traditions, the *ira* is identified with the male gender, while the *arca*, in its traditional subordinate role, is associated with the female one.

CDII, Track 16: Panpipes: "Los jilacatas"

Music: Traditional
Instrumentation: panpipes, *bombo* drum
Notes: "Los jilicatas"—"the village leaders"—demonstrates the interlocking *trenzado* technique, as the various panpipes play different parts of the melody in quick succession, accompanied by the drum.

OTHER WIND INSTRUMENTS Modern Andeans have adopted a vertical duct-flute called the **tarka**, with a mouthpiece and six finger holes. *Tarkas* come in several sizes, with the small *ch'ili* measuring less than foot, the medium *mala*

CORE ON · MAJOR · I MENOR
HATVNCHASQVICHVRV
MVLLO · CHAS QVI · CVRACA ~

1609 depiction of an Inca courier announcing his arrival by blowing a conch shell.

about a foot and a half, and the large *licu* over two feet long. Made out of wood from the Amazonian rainforest, they have a square shape and are often intricately and beautifully carved and decorated. Like *quenas*, they are deliberately overblown, producing a high, tinny sound. In some regions, for example in northern Chile and on the Bolivian shores of Lake Titicaca, *tarkas* are traditionally played only during the rainy season to thank the deities for the harvest. In

Mestizo cultures, they can be played on any occasion, but particularly in special competitive dances called *tarkeadas*, often accompanied by *caja* and *bombo* drums. The *tarkas'* slight variations in tuning lend the large *tarka* ensembles a captivating density of sound. The *tunda* ("cane"), also made from cane or wood, is a transverse flute, held horizontally to the side of the player's mouth. *Quepas* were straight or curved trumpets used by the Inca, made from copper, bronze, silver or even clay, with fancifully carved and decorated bodies. The modern *clarín* is similar to a bugle, usually made from brass but sometimes from animal horns, whose brash sound is believed to initiate the frost and hasten the advent of the winter season, and is thus typically heard after the harvest.

An important Inca instrument was the conch shell called *churu* (or *guayllaquepas*). It was used as a ceremonial trumpet, and especially in battle (along with drums) to rally the warriors and intimidate the enemy. Conch shells were rare and thus highly valued. Hunters were sent as far as Central America to find the valuable marine animal. When the hunters returned empty-handed, clay imitations were made, many of which have survived. Because of the instrument's scarcity and important place in Inca ritual, conch players enjoyed a high status among their musician peers. *Pututu* (or *erke*) cow horns are now used throughout the region to signal the beginning of summer and carnival ceremonies, a role once reserved for the *churu*. Another pre-Columbian wind instrument is the *ocarina*. Instead of an elongated pipe, the body of the *ocarina* consists of a rounded clay vessel with as many as eight finger holes plus one or two thumbholes, resulting in a mellow, darker tone. The inherent difficulty in both manufacturing and playing *ocarinas* has caused their popularity to gradually decrease, though they can still be found in various regions of the Andean *Altiplano*, particularly in Bolivia. Various whistles also contributed to Inca music, notably the *chiucas* and *uaucos*, made from the skulls of dogs and other animals.

CHARANGO   The most notable example of musical syncretism in the region is the *charango*, which combines a European instrument with Andean materials and performance ideals. It is a small guitar descended from the Spanish *vihuela* whose resonating chamber is made from the shell of a small armadillo called a *quirquincho* (Quechua for "armadillo"). Since wood was rarer than armadillos in the often treeless *Altiplano*, Natives during the colonial period used whatever materials were at hand. (In recent decades, though, the endangered status of the Andean armadillo has caused *charangos* to be constructed more often from imported wood.) The neck is fretted, and there are usually 10 llama-gut (or—more recently—metal or nylon) strings tuned in pairs, though a *charango* can have as few as 4 and as many as 15 strings. Because it is a relatively small instrument, its strings are short and therefore high-pitched, though the neck, about two feet long, looks disproportionately large. *Charangos* are typically accompanying instruments, strummed vigorously with fast rhythmic patterns that lend a driving percussive rhythm to a piece. In traditional Native societies, the *charango* (like the *quena*) is played exclusively

Charango, front and rear views.

by males, primarily in courting rituals and dances and in harvest fertility rituals. In Mestizo traditions, it is used in conjunction with other instruments as a
form of entertainment, for special occasions such as weddings and parties.
The *charango* is the national instrument of Peru, though it can be found
throughout the region, with various names such as *chillador* (Spanish for
"weeping instrument") and *mulita* ("small mule").

CDII, Track 17: *Charango*: "Love Song of the Animals"

Music: Traditional
Instrumentation: *charango*
Notes: This song, titled "Alpaca" in the Aymara language, is an example of the important traditional link that exists in the Andes between music and nature, and animals in particular. The strumming high-pitched *charango* accompanies the chorus of men who describe and imitate the animals.

DRUMS The general term for drum in the Inca Empire was *huancar*, referring to a wooden instrument made from a hollowed trunk, with a head typically made from llama or alpaca skin. Unlike some of the wind instruments, drums could be played by either men or women, usually with one stick. They were often played in groups of four or eight, numbers that held great spiritual meaning for the Incas. Unlike Mesoamerican drums, Andean drums probably did not have a melodic function but rather served an exclusively rhythmic role in ceremonies to accompany songs and dances and in warfare to encourage warriors and intimidate the enemy. The largest *huancar* was 10 feet in length, played with the hands, and used in triumphant processions and for communication, since they could be heard for long distances across the Andean highlands. Smaller drums were played with sticks, often accompanying flutes to mourn those who perished in battle. A popular drum was the *tinya*, a shallow-frame, double-headed instrument about the size of a tambourine played with a single mallet. The *tinya* remains popular in the Andes, where it is also known as *wankara*, one of the few instruments played by women in traditional Andean societies. Another drum was the *pomatinya*, made from the cured skin of a puma. In modern times, the principal Andean drums are the *bombo* and the *caja*, both found throughout the region. The *bombo*, derived from military marching bands, is a large, circular bass drum made from a hollow tree trunk, with one or two drum heads made of llama, alpaca or cow skin, and which are often intricately decorated with Native ritualistic designs. The *caja* ("box") is a shallow frame drum with two heads, similar to a snare drum, which produces a deep, booming sound. Both the *bombo* and the *caja* are held with the head perpendicular to the ground and struck with a single leather mallet.

PERCUSSION Inca and other Andean ceremonial music was complemented by several percussion instruments not unlike those found in Mesoamerica, and indeed, throughout the American continent. These included arm and leg rattles made from seedpods called *zacapas*, metal jingles, and hand bells called *chanraras*, and rattlesnake tails called *catauri*. Many Inca percussion instruments were reportedly made from gold and inlaid with precious stones, though few of these survive, as they were for the most part looted by the conquistadors. Modern Andean musicians use assorted triangles, bells, and other percussion instruments. Bolivia has a *güiro*-like scraper called ***coancha***, also known as ***reke-reke*** on the Amazonian side, related to the Brazilian *reco-reco*. Cowbells—as well as llama bells—are also widely distributed in the Andean region, on the animals themselves, but also as independent percussion instruments. Rattles called ***chac-chas*** (or *chullus*) are made from animal hooves, while the ***chaucha*** is a seed-filled gourd, shaken like a maraca. The rain stick called ***palo de lluvia*** is made from a dried cactus whose spines have been pushed in, and filled with seeds or pebbles. Not surprisingly, it is used in ceremonies to entice the rain spirits.

OTHER ANDEAN INSTRUMENTS   During the colonial period, Africans introduced drums and marimbas and their song and dance forms, while Spaniards brought wind and string instruments such as harps, violins, lutes, guitars, mandolin, and *vihuelas*. Native populations quickly adopted them and eventually developed their own syncretic, hybridized versions, for example the *charango* discussed above, but also the ***jitara*** and the ***guitarilla***, the ***violín chapaco***, and the mandolin-like ***bandola*** and ***bandolín***. The *bandolín* usually has five sets of two (or sometimes three) strings, while the *bandola* often has four sets of four strings. The manufacture of violins has become an important tradition in the Andean region, particularly in northern Peru, where larger and coarser versions of the instrument can be found, with a heavier sound in the upper register. Though overshadowed in the Andes by the *quena* and *zampoña*, the harp nevertheless has an important presence, for example in the Ecuadorian provinces of Imbabura and Tungurahua where it has been present since at least the 1700s. It can be played as a solo instrument or to accompany song and dance rituals, and it is often paired with a violin. Harps are typically accompanied by a *golpeador*, a second musician who accentuates the rhythms on the harp's sound box with his hands.

Andean Ensembles

Because of the great musical and ritual diversity in the region, there is no such thing as a typical Andean ensemble: any combination of instruments can be found. While Mestizo groups will often blend *zampoñas, quenas,* and *charangos,* Native ensembles performing traditional rituals tend to not mix these instruments. Some combinations are appropriate for specific rituals in specific areas, whereas others can perform year-round for any occasion. In all cases, however, instrumental music tends to have a complex texture, with a lot of features occurring simultaneously.

Native ensembles called *tropas* have traditional performance practices that yield a particular timbral quality. Some *tropas* include 4 to 6 *quenas*, others up to 25, with or without *cajas* and other percussion. *Quenas* are also played as solo instruments, or accompanied by guitars and *charangos*, but always carrying the principal melody. Small, three-hole *quenas* are sometimes played by a single musician who also beats a small *tinya* drum. Occasionally, *quenas* will perform in ensembles with violins, accordions, and harps. Ensembles consisting exclusively of *zampoñas* are common, performing at weddings and feast days, playing in parallel octaves, thirds or fifths, sometimes accompanied by a *caja* or a *bombo*. *Zampoña* players often dance while playing their instruments. In some areas, one or two *tunda* transverse flutes can be accompanied by a single drum, or more than a dozen can play together in octaves or fifths, accompanied by an equal number of *bombos* and *cajas*. *Tarkas* can play in *tropas* of twelve or more instruments of different sizes plus the percussion instruments.

While *tropas* usually perform Native rituals, Mestizo groups called *conjuntos* have recently popularized Andean music in Latin America, Europe, and the United States. *Conjuntos* often incorporate all the Andean instruments, typically consisting of a *quena*, two or three *zampoñas*, a *charango*, a guitar, and a *bombo*. Another popular manifestation of Mestizo music, often heard at community festivals or local feast-day celebrations, is the *orquesta típica*, a string ensemble in which violins carry the melody and a harp provides the bass and rhythmic accompaniment. But the *orquesta típica* is not actually typical at all, and its size and composition often varies from region to region. It can include string instruments such as guitars, mandolins, and *charangos*, wind instruments such as saxophones, clarinets, *quenas*, and accordions, and percussion such as *bombos*, snare drums, and cymbals. Other prominent ensembles are the brass bands derived from nineteenth-century military bands, which can be found in virtually every town square in Peru, Bolivia, and Ecuador. They usually consist of several trumpets, cornets, trombones, and tubas, complemented by drums and cymbals.

Andean Rituals

As in much of Latin America, a syncretic religion emerged during the colonial period which survives to this day and which combines aspects of Christianity with Native beliefs. Catholic celebrations are juxtaposed with Native rituals: the feast of St. John the Baptist (on June 24), for example, is associated with the southern hemisphere's winter solstice. Prayers and supplications reflect both Christian concerns for the afterlife and practical everyday considerations such as tilling, sowing, or harvesting. Native deities, usually related to nature and the earth, are equated with Catholic deities, the most prominent example being the Inca earth goddess Pachamama. Just as Tonatzin, mother of the Aztec gods, became identified with the Mexican Virgen de Guadalupe, so too did Pachamama (literally "earth mother") become identified with the Virgen de la Candelaria and the Virgen del Carmen. Shrines to this Virgin/Mother can be found throughout the Andean region.

The Native worldview revolves around an annual cycle that combines agricultural events with recurring religious festivities. An important dichotomy is the division of the year between the rainy and dry seasons. The rainy season occurs in the summer, which in the southern hemisphere lasts from All Saints' Day (November 1) through carnival in March. Since Inca times, the two seasons have been identified with genders. The rainy season, associated with growth and fertility, is, not surprisingly, the "female" part of the year. Various feasts dedicated to the Virgin occur during this period, including the Immaculate Conception (December 8), the Nativity (December 25), the Purification (February 2), and the Annunciation (March 25). By contrast, the "male" season occurs during the dry winter, and is associated with the celebrations of the (male) sun god, as well as Easter, Corpus Christi, and the feasts of male saints such as St. Peter and St. John the Baptist.

As do most agrarian societies, Native Andeans have a close relationship with nature. Agriculture is at the center of life, and much of the culture—including the music—revolves around the planting season. Specific dances, melodies, songs, and instruments are appropriate for each season and agricultural occasion. Thus, *tarka* duct-flutes, believed to attract rain and fertility, are typically played at the beginning of summer, though later in the season, as harvest approaches, they are used to temporarily halt the rain. Meanwhile, *quenas* and *zampoñas* are associated with the winter season. Rituals are performed for sowing or harvesting, for raising and branding cattle and sheep, for the construction of a town structure, or for specific crops such as corn or potatoes. Fertility rituals occur at the beginning of the rainy season, and affect both personal interrelationships—courtship dances are prominent—and communal concerns such as the size of the harvest or the fertility of animals. As the harvest season wraps up, rites of thanksgiving become common, followed by winter rituals, including the sun-god celebrations.

Catholic rituals became popular within a few decades after the conquest, quickly becoming infused with Native elements. Some saint days, like the feasts of St. James and St. John the Baptist, are widely celebrated throughout the region, but every town and village has its own patron saint, so that on any give day one can find somewhere in the Andes dozens of local festivals. Celebrations usually include elaborate processions and religious plays and dance-dramas, with costumed participants depicting mythical, biblical and historical scenes. Holy Week festivities include dramatic representations of the Crucifixion and Resurrection, with participants playing *quenas* or *zampoñas* and chanting in Spanish, Quechua, and Aymara.

Yet not all Native rituals are religious, and there are also family or community commemorations of life-cycle events: birth, coming-of-age, courtship, marriage and fertility, and death. Many are dedicated to specific professions, such as the *kullawada*, an ancient Bolivian dance that celebrates the textile industry, performed by weavers, knitters, and wool spinners whose costumes are—not surprisingly—beautifully ornamented. Another is the *kallawaya*, a lively and vigorous dance that reflects the physical health and condition of the healers and herbalists who wandered the Inca Empire. Yet another is the *llamerada* (or *karwani*), a ritual dance in honor of llamas and llama herders, offered to ensure the health of the animals, and performed by male and female dancers who mimic the movements of the llamas and their herders. And of course celebrations also occur for social entertainment and community purposes, in neighborhood social gatherings or get-togethers held in private dwellings. In contemporary Native societies, these rituals and celebrations, in addition to their spiritual and practical considerations, often have an added political dimension, as they have come to represent indigenous identity—and at time indigenous resistance—at the local, regional and national level.

As in Inca times, music making in Native societies is generally a public and community-based activity rather than a private individual pursuit. Many festivals and rituals are called *encuentros*—encounters between various members of a Native community or between different communities. In some areas, musicians will simply show up to public celebrations and on the spot agree to begin playing, without prior arrangement or rehearsal. The assembly will be convened by the loud wailing of the *pututu* cow horn (or occasionally the *churu* conch shell), announcing the beginning of the festivities. The first order of business is usually the *challa*, where alcoholic drinks are poured onto the earth, sometimes in the four directions of the compass, as an offering to the ancestors, to Pachamama or to any of the other gods, to thank them for an abundant crop or for the health of family and community. The ceremony then begins, with activities that invariably include music, dance, prayer, and ritual offering to the deities: food and drink are most common, as is incense burning and occasionally animal sacrifice. Dancers often partake of the coca leaf that is prominent in the region, as well as various alcoholic beverages such as *guarapo*, made from sugar cane, and *chicha*, made from fermented corn and popular since Inca times.

Costumes can vary from village to village, ranging from simple white trousers and shirts to extremely ornamented outfits and immense headdresses. Masks and face painting are common, as are bird feathers and animal skins. In the northern Andes, participants often wear the famous multicolored woven ponchos made from llama or alpaca wool. In the south, typical Aymara costumes are more prevalent: women wear white blouses and large, multi-layered, colorfully embroidered skirts called *polleras*, a shawl and the traditional derby hat. Men's attire is simpler, with wool, flannel, or silk shirts, a colorful girdle around the waist, trousers that reach the knee, and alpaca hats called *chullos*, with flaps that cover the ears.

Andean dance is as varied as the music, with innumerable traditions, each with its particular movements, steps, accompaniment, and ritual symbolism. Some are couples' dances, with partners dancing either in close contact or separately; others are circle dances (*ruedas*) in which dancers form a circle, dancing in single file in the direction of the sun, before turning in the other direction. Still others are line dances (*trencitos*—"little trains"), involving rows of dancers in straight lines. Steps often include the vigorous Spanish *zapateado*. Many slower forms end with a fast upbeat section called a *fuga*. Whereas instrumental music is played almost exclusively by men in traditional Native societies, dancing and singing requires participation by both genders, particularly during courting rituals, where gender-based choruses often playfully sing back and forth. While music in Native societies still revolves around specific rituals, Mestizo music is often a function of entertainment. Native musicians might use traditional instruments in a harvest ceremony, while in the next town the same instruments will be used for a Mestizo Saturday night party. Native traditions also tend to be more localized, whereas Mestizo styles tend to be more spread out throughout a region, and even in large cities such as Quito, La Paz, and Lima.

INTI RAIMI   The most important celebration in the Andes is the Festival of the Sun. As discussed above, the principal Inca ceremony was *Intip Raymin*, celebrated on June 24, the winter solstice of the Inca calendar. It marked the beginning of the new year, as the sun, which on that date was thought to be at its furthest from the earth, began its slow return. With the advent of Catholicism, *Intip Raymin* became associated with both Corpus Christi, which often occurs in late June, and the feast of St. John the Baptist, which is always on June 24. Today, it survives under the name *Inti Raimi*, a colorful celebration that lasts a full week. Its principal (and semi-official) manifestation occurs in Cuzco, but similar celebrations can be found throughout the region. During *Inti Raimi*, most of downtown Cuzco—and particularly the main square, called Plaza de Armas—is filled with ambulating strollers, markets, expositions, singing, dancing, parades, and food and drink peddlers. Entire streets are overlaid with intricate flower designs, a tradition derived from European Corpus Christi celebrations. Dozens of Andean groups perform on official stages in the Plaza de Armas, or unofficially on street corners.

The celebration peaks on June 24, and involves elaborate dramatic presentations, with hundreds of actors personifying historical figures, the most important of which are the Sapa Inca (the Sun God/Emperor), and his consort Mama Occla (the Sun Queen). Other actors embody high priests and members of the Inca court, all dressed in lavish costumes. The ritual begins at the Koricancha, the ancient temple of the sun whose remains are still in downtown Cuzco, under and in front of the church of Santo Domingo. After the requisite prayers and invocations, a procession begins in which the Sapa Inca and his consort are carried on a golden throne through the streets to the ancient Inca fortress of Sacsayhuamá, on the hills overlooking the city. Here the emperor and other dignitaries address the assembled crowd in Quechua. This is followed by the "sacrifice" of a llama to implore the sun god to return and to ensure a good harvest. Much dancing and singing follow, and the ceremony concludes with a celebratory bonfire and a return procession to Cuzco.

Some have criticized modern *Inti Raimi* celebrations as being convoluted spectacles of questionable authenticity, performed by mostly Criollo and Mestizo actors mainly for tourists. (The llama, for example, is not actually put to death so as to not offend tourist sensibilities.) While there is undoubtedly some truth to this, it does not detract from the festival's prominence in the region's culture. Moreover, one can find many other such celebrations throughout the Andes that, while they are probably no closer to the practices of the Ancient Inca, provide a more accurate view of contemporary Native identity.

Dancers and musicians celebrate the ancient *Inti Raimi* ritual, Cuzco, Peru.

LA FIESTA DEL APÓSTOL SANTIAGO The feast of St. James the Apostle is the second most important ceremony in the central and southern Andes, particularly in the Mantaro Valley of Peru. The celebration begins on the eve of July 25 and often continues for several weeks. The Catholic celebration is infused with practical agricultural purposes, namely the branding of cattle. It is a fertility ritual to thank St. James, the patron saint of cow herders, for the abundance and health of the cattle, of the crops and of the land in general. It is also a joyful time of celebration and courting, with amorous couples strolling under the moonlight and warming themselves by the bonfires that line the streets. On the actual feast day, altars are erected and intricately decorated with flowers and ribbons, with offerings of food and drink. The names of family or community cows are written on ribbons or coca leaves and presented at the altar, and the saint's protection is invoked. Afterwards the ribbons are affixed to the ears of the animals, while women sing songs of thanks, accompanying themselves with the small *tinya* drum. Other fertility rituals follow, including reenactments of weddings and culminating in the rounding up of the cattle into their corrals. Music is often played by *wakrapukus* ("cow trumpets"), *waka pinkillu* ("cow flutes"), *llungurs* (transverse flutes), and by *orquestas típicas* consisting of saxophones, clarinets, violins, and harps. The festivities end with an extended party, with suggestive—even erotic—dances in which men represent the bulls and women the cows. The work at hand having been accomplished, the revelers partake of much food, including a tripe soup called *mondongo,* as well as alcoholic beverages.

The feast of Santiago is both a symbolic ritual and a practical agricultural event, as it provides an opportunity for a census of the region's cattle. While its origins are squarely derived from Native traditions in rural areas, the celebrations have over time migrated to Mestizo urban settings, no longer concerned with actual cattle, but still maintaining the same symbolisms, particularly those related to fertility and courtship. These celebrations still include some of the traditional music, but as the evening wears on, modern styles such as *chicha, cumbia,* and *salsa* will begin to make their appearance on the host's sound system.

> **Recommended Listening:** "Song to wankar on tinya" and "Vaca y vaca, toro y toro," from the CD *Traditional Music of Peru, Vol. 6: The Ayacucho Region*.

LA FIESTA DEL GRAN PODER   In Bolivia, a prominent ritual is *La Fiesta del Señor Jesús del Gran Poder* ("The Feast of the Almighty Lord Jesus"). Its origins have been dated to 1663 with the arrival of a painting of Christ at a newly founded convent in La Paz. The image showed the three faces of Christ, representing the Trinity, with obvious Native traits, including darker skin. Over the centuries, this Native Christ became venerated as a religious icon that granted protection and well-being. In the 1920s, religious fraternities began organizing processions and other celebrations to honor the image. These organizations consisted of both Andean groups, who worshipped the Almighty with their traditional instruments and dances, and Afro-Bolivian groups, who did so with their intricate drumming and dancing. By the 1970s, the celebration had grown to encompass much of La Paz, and it became a national phenomenon, celebrated by Bolivians all over the country. Today, the feast of the Almighty is a large-scale street celebration that takes place in early June, engulfing much of the city with music, food, and free-flowing alcoholic beverages. It has become a commemoration of diversity, honoring Native, African, and European ethnicities and religions. Dozens of organizations participate in parades and processions, with a vast array of dances and musical forms, and with thousands of musicians, tens of thousands of dancers, and hundreds of thousands of spectators. Particularly impressive are the flamboyant costumes and colorful masks and headdresses, the men wearing glittering robes, the women magnificently embroidered *polleras*. Prayers to the Almighty are appended to rituals dedicated to Pachamama and other Native deities. Though it is predominantly an Aymara celebration, Quechua and Amazonian groups are also represented. Likewise, Afro-Bolivian dances such as *sayas, tundiquis, morenadas,* and *caporales* are an important component of the celebration.

PACHALLAMPE   The Andean region is home to up to 5,000 varieties of potatoes, each with different nutritional values. Historically, one of the most prominent Native celebrations among the Aymara has been the *Pachallampe*, the potato-planting festival, though it is becoming increasingly hard to find in the region. *Pachallampe* ("to loosen the earth") is derived from an ancient pre-Inca agricultural ritual. It takes place in November, at the beginning of the sowing season, just as the summer rains are set to begin. It is a community ritual in which the entire village comes together to plant the season's potato seeds. The opening procession begins at the village church where images of the Virgin or of the local patron saint are carried to the fields. Pack animals carry the potato seeds that will be at the center of the ceremony. The assembly sings fertility songs accompanied by guitars and sometimes violins and accordions. Prayers implore Pachamama to grant abundant rain and a fruitful harvest. The participants and even the animals are intricately ornamented with flower garlands. A ceremonial leader called *mayordomo* is typically dressed in white with an elaborately decorated sombrero, his face painted black. After the procession arrives at the ceremonial field, the seeds are laid out with garlands and other decorations. The *mayordomo* makes offerings of incense, food and drink during an opening ceremony that sanctions the planting. The men plow the earth with a steel shovel called *chonta*, the women—symbols of fertility—following close behind, planting the seeds. Afterward, the assembly gathers to sing and dance the actual *pachallampe*, as well as other couples dances such as *huaynos* and *valses*. Some of the men will dance with images of the Virgin or of various saints. Single men will court young maidens, who signal their interest by gifting them flower garlands. The celebration's fertility character is thus present in both the agricultural and social aspects of the ceremony. Sowing can last all day, and even several days, culminating in one final celebration, as the saints are returned to the church, after which much music and dancing occur, with plenty of food and free-flowing alcohol.

Bolivian dancers and musicians at a traditional wedding.

> **Recommended Listening:** "For Potato Growing: Pascalle" by Leoncio Miranda, from the CD *Traditional Music of Peru, Vol. 2: The Mantaro Valley*.

Andean Song: *Yaraví*

Among the hundreds of song forms that can be found in the region, perhaps the most prominent is the *yaraví* (or *harawí*). In pre-Columbian times, *yaraví* songs were performed by the *haravecs*, professional poet/storytellers at the Inca court. In colonial times, the genre continued to develop a poetic style that reflected the melancholy of Native existence. The *yaraví* was particular to Quechua speakers of the *Altiplano*, since Aymara groups tended to place little importance on vocal music. It gradually incorporated Hispanic elements, and towards the end of the colonial period became increasingly common in the coastal regions, particularly in Arequipa in southern Peru, where it was infused with Afro-Peruvian elements. In the eighteenth century, it was adopted by Peruvian Criollos, who developed their own versions called *canción triste* and *cumanana* (discussed below). In the nineteenth century, various poets, authors, and musicians embraced the *yaraví*, as it conformed nicely to the emotional romantic ideal they espoused. Most prominent among these was the Peruvian poet Mariano Melgar, who is closely associated with the war of independence.

Today *yaravíes* can be found in both Quechua and Spanish, though the latter is become increasingly predominant. Texts are symbolic, imbued with metaphors of nature and the animal world. Pessimism and fatalism are prevalent, as are laments for lost or unrequited love. Death is also an important subject, and some have characterized the *yaraví* as primarily a funeral lament. Yet like the North American blues, the *yaraví* is intended to comfort rather than to sadden, and there is occasionally ironic humor in the genre. Tempos are slow, melodies are usually in the minor key, and sometimes use a pentatonic scale. There are usually only one or two verses that are repeated in turn, though in some cases an upbeat second section is added to diffuse the sad mood. *Yaravíes* can be accompanied by virtually any combination of Andean instruments, and can be performed by both men and women, though the latter are preferred because of their high vocal range.

> **Recommended Listening:** "Saru, Saruy" and "Harawi," from the CD *Traditional Music of Peru, Vol. 6: The Ayacucho Region*.

> **Recommended Listening:** "Llajctaimanta" and "Corazon adolorido" by Tinku, from the CD *Music of the Andes*.

> **Recommended Listening:** "Los ruegos" by Los Morochucos, from the CD *Evocación a la patria vieja*.

> **Recommended Listening:** "Mi madre tierra," "Me consolara la soledad" and "Soy de sangre kolla, quechua y aymara" by Fortaleza, from the CD *Soy de sangre kolla, quechua y aymara*.

> **Recommended Listening:** "Trova de amor" by Alpamayo, from the CD *Magic Flutes and Music from the Andes*.

> **Recommended Listening:** "A vuestros pies madre" by Los Jairas, from the CD *Los Condores and Los Jairas: El condor pasa*.

Yaraví: "A vuestros pies madre"

Music: Traditional
Instrumentation: *quenas, charango*, guitar, *bombo* drum
Notes: This sorrowful *yaraví*, here performed by Los Jairas, is often used in Bolivian religious processions in honor of the Virgin. The *quena* plays the mournful melody in the introduction and between verses, accentuating the singer's implorations. After the second verse, a second *quena* complements the first.

A vuestros pies, Madre, llega un infeliz,	At your feet, dear Mother, an unfortunate arrives,
Cercado de angustias y de penas mil.	Laden with anguish and a thousand sorrows.
Escuchad, benigna dulce Abigail,	Hear me, good and sweet Abigail,
Mis graves delitos, mi pena y sentir.	My grave sins, my sorrow and pains.
¿A quien, dulce madre, podrán acudir	To whom, dear Mother,
Estos tristes hijos, a quien sino a ti?	Can these sad children turn to if not you?

Andean Dances

HUAYNO The *huayno* (often spelled *wayno* or, in Bolivia, *huayño*) is said to derive from pre-Columbian dances. During the colonial period it became widespread among both Natives and Mestizos, engendering dozens of versions throughout the Andes. It has become the most prominent dance form in Peru, particularly in the central part of the country, where it has acquired a more modern popular tinge, as opposed to more traditional styles in the south. It is both a dance and song form, with lyrics that often reflect Andean identity and demonstrate an intense emotion: laments about one's lot in life, unrequited love, or mourning the recently deceased. But it can also be a witty commentary on local political issues or current events. The *huayno* can be danced in religious feasts, both Catholic and non-Catholic, but also at any get-together or celebration, by both Natives and Mestizos. Like *yaravíes, huaynos* can be sung in both Quechua and Spanish, though the former is heard less and less. They have moderately fast tempos and binary meters with frequent momentary borrowing of triplets in the middle of a passage. The form is strophic, with verses set to the same melody, and the lyrics are usually unrhymed. They can be accompanied by *quenas, zampoñas, charangos*, and *guitars*, though violins, trumpets, and harps are also common in some regions, and some *huaynos* are performed by marching brass bands that also feature accordions. Dances are performed by couples, with steps that differ from region to region: sometimes there is a fast *zapateado*, other times the dance is much more graceful. Couples forming a line or a circle hold hands or are united by the handkerchief that is ubiquitous in Latin American dances. Often, *huaynos* are followed by a faster *fuga*, which produces livelier dancing.

Recommended Listening: "Huayno" from the CD *Traditional Music of Peru, Vol. 6: The Ayacucho Region*.

Recommended Listening: "Hirpastay," "Nobleza india" and "Linda compañerita" from the CD *Songs and Dances of Bolivia*.

Recommended Listening: "Chonginada" by Los Románticos de Sicaya and "Quisiera olvidarte" by La Pasoria Huarac, from the CD *Huayno Music of Peru, Vol. 1*.

Recommended Listening: "Huayno de la Roca" by Los Incas, from the CD *Los Incas: Best Selection*.

Recommended Listening: "Patamanta" and "Ukamau" by Ukamau, from the CD *Music of the Indios from the Andes*.

CDII, Track 18: *Huayno: Río de Paria*

Music and Lyrics: Ernesto Sánchez Fajardo
Instrumentation: *quenas*, violins, guitars
Notes: El Jilguero del Huascarán ("the goldfinch of Mount Huascarán") was a folk singer from Ancash Province in northern Peru, along the shores of the Paria River. He wrote and popularized many *huaynos*, including this one, which is accompanied by high female voices, a common feature both in Inca and modern times. This *huayno* also displays the melancholy and resignation typical of songs and dances in the region.

Qué hermoso Río del Paria,	*Beautiful Paria River,*
Cómo llevas tantas piedras,	*As you take so many stones,*
¿Porqué no me llevas a mí,	*Why don't you take me,*
Para quitarme la vida?	*To do away with my life?*
Amores tengo de sobra,	*I have more than enough loves,*
Como las piedras del río.	*Like the stones in the river.*
Lloraré porque te quiero,	*I'll cry because I love you,*
No será porque me falta.	*But not because I lack love.*
Ahora, ahora, ¿qué vas a hacer?	*Now then, what will you do?*
Ya soy cazada, ¿qué vas a hacer?	*I am now married, what will you do?*
Seré tu amigo, sí cómo no.	*I'll be your friend, sure, why not?*
¿Volver contigo? ya no, ya no.	*But to go back to you? no more, no more.*

SANJUÁN The *sanjuán* is the most prominent genre in Ecuador, primarily among the Quechua Natives in the northern province of Imbabura. Some historians claim the dance was already ancient when the Incas invaded the region, whereas others assert it evolved from the *huayno* that was brought by the Incas. In any event, it remained prominent during the colonial period, and has since been adopted by every area of the country as well as parts of northern Peru. The name ("St. John") comes from its association with the *Inti Raimi* celebrations performed on the feast of St. John the Baptist. Today the *sanjuán* is still part of the solstice rituals, but can also be performed at any time of the year, for religious or life-cycle rituals, or purely for entertainment. In some areas, it is linked to a specific event called the "taking of the square" or the "taking of the church," in which Natives from rural areas come to the village or town and reclaim from the Mestizo culture what they consider lawfully theirs. It is a symbolically important ritual, as men—also called *sanjuanes*—compete with vigorous dances in order to claim influence and power for the coming year. More than friendly dance competitions, these dances are important political events, sometimes seen by local authorities as acts of rebellion.

The *sanjuán* is an upbeat dance typically in $\frac{2}{4}$ rhythms, with a strong accent on the first beat marked by a *bombo* drum. It is usually in a minor key, though some include a second section in a major key. The melody is usually played by *quenas* and *zampoñas*, accompanied by guitars, mandolins, harps, and a single drum, though sometimes it is preformed with *tunda* transverse flutes and a drum. *Sanjuánes* are also ballads that recount personal, historical, or current events. Variations include the *sanjuán de blancos*, associated with Mestizo culture, and the *chucchurillu*, which is primarily in a major key. Other cultures, for example the Afro-Ecuadorian of the Chota Valley, as well as the Amazonian tribes in eastern Ecuador, have developed their own version of the *sanjuán*. In the twentieth century, Ecuadorian Mestizos developed the *sanjuanito*, with important differences in form and structure. The *sanjuán* has become popular internationally, and it appears prominently in the repertoire of Andean groups who travel to Europe and the United States.

> **Recommended Listening:** "Sanjuanito de Pujili" by Arturo Aguirre, Ricardo Aguirre, and Jorge Yepez, from the CD *Arte musical del Ecuador*.

> **Recommended Listening:** "Yamor" and "Nuca Llacta" by Viento de los Andes, from the CD *Sanjuanitos*.

> **Recommended Listening:** "San Juanito de medianoche" by Inkuyo, from the CD *Temple of the Sun*.

> **Recommended Listening:** "Lluvia" and "Llamor" by Alpamayo, from the CD *Music from Peru and Ecuador*.

DANZA DE LAS TIJERAS Another prominent dance in the Andean region is the *danza de las tijeras* ("scissors dance") a spectacular and crowd-pleasing demonstration that requires a great amount of physical agility and athleticism. It is performed by the *danzaq*, male dancers who perform complex acrobatic movements that some have compared to hip-hop break dancing and that often include imitation of animals, somersaults, headstands, and spinning the whole body. The dance is further complicated by metal scissors that the *danzaq* must hold in his right hand throughout the performance, adding an element of danger to the acrobatics. The scissors dance is accompanied by a harp and violin that perform seemingly endless formulaic melodies, accompanied by the snapping scissors that keep the beat. Often performed during feast days or carnival celebrations, the *danza de las tijeras* is competitive in nature, with *danzaq* trying to outdo each other. The grueling competition can last several days, and the winner is ultimately determined by the applause of the assembled audience.

Recommended Listening: "Tijeras: Pacha tink" and "Tijeras: Qawachan" from the CD *Traditional Music of Peru, Vol. 6: The Ayacucho Region*.

CARNIVAL DANCES   Various carnival traditions mark the culmination of the harvest season in March, though some communities have a carnival some six months earlier, in November, at the beginning of the summer, thus transforming it from a harvest ritual into a fertility one. The most prominent carnival dance in the southern Andes, popular in Peru, Bolivia, northern Chile, and Argentina, is simply called **carnavalito**, a dance related to the *huayno* whose origins go back to pre-colonial times. Like most carnival dances, it is a joyful and lively communal dance, accompanied by *quenas* and *bombos* with dancers forming *ruedas* (circle figures) as well as *trencitos* (line dances), though occasionally breaking into couples. Andean communities in Chile have specific carnival dances such as the **cachimbo** and **tonos de carnaval**, accompanied by guitars or bandolas, or sometimes by ensembles that include guitars, violins, accordions and *quenas*. The melancholy **cacharpaya** is a farewell Bolivian dance sometimes used to honor a departing member of the community or to close the festivities, but also used as the dance that sends-off the carnival season, sung to the accompaniment of *quenas* and *zampoñas*.

But the most important carnival tradition in Bolivia, centered in the mining city of Oruro, is undoubtedly the colorful **diablada**, which rivals Rio de Janeiro's celebration in terms of pageantry and excitement, if not quite in size. *Diabladas* are performed by dancers called *diablos*—Devils. The representation of the Devil in Christian rituals, particularly around the pre-Lenten season, goes back to medieval traditions, and is thus common to many Latin American traditions, for example the *diablos danzantes* of Venezuela, the *diablitos* dance of Costa Rica and the *red Devil* parades of the French Caribbean. Chile and Peru also have their own versions of the *diablada*. These rituals can take place at night around a campfire, with hypnotic songs and dances that can last until dawn. More often, they consist of large parades with dozens of dance groups, each consisting of several hundred *diablos* who dance and leap energetically to the sound of a wind band or a large *zampoña* ensemble, as spectators heave water bombs on the procession and on each other. The parade also includes dramatic representations of the struggle between good and evil, with actors wearing intricate costumes, masks, and headdresses. Characters include Catholic deities such as the Archangel Michael and the Virgin of Socavón (the patron saint of miners), as well as Native divinities such as the earth-mother Pachamama, and Supay, the Inca demon god of death and the underworld, who during the colonial period became the protector of the miners who spent much of their lives underground. But the struggle also has historical and political implications, as evil characters also include Spanish conquistadors and landowners, and virtuous characters include prominent members of the Inca court, as well as Black slaves and Amazonian Natives. *Diabladas* have thus been seen as important symbols of Native resistance and identity in the face of Spanish and Mestizo culture.

> **Recommended Listening:** "Tarkas de Putina: Carnival Music" from the CD *Mountain Music of Peru, Vol. 2.*

> **Recommended Listening:** "Todos juntos (Carnaval)" by René Villanueva, from the CD *Música de Bolivia.*

> **Recommended Listening:** "Carnavalito quebradeno" by Los Incas, from the CD *Los Incas: Best Selection.*

> **Recommended Listening:** "Tauichi," "Vida ontonal" and "Falsas promesas" by Ukamau, from the CD *Music of the Indios from the Andes.*

> **Recommended Listening:** "Cacharpaya" by René Villanueva, from the CD *Música de Bolivia.*

For a discussion of other Andean dance forms, see www.mymusickit.com.

Andean Music in a Modern Context

For almost half a millennium, Andean music remained mostly relegated to rural settings and provincial towns high in the mountains, relatively isolated and ignored by urban populations in the coastal areas. But in the second half of the twentieth century, many Natives and Mestizos from the highlands, seeking economic opportunity, migrated to Lima, La Paz, Quito, and other cities, which were transformed from Criollo strongholds to primarily Mestizo centers. The new arrivals struggled to maintain a cultural and political identity, so in an effort to combat the process of acculturation, migrants from a particular region often formed organizations dedicated to preserving and promoting the customs, rituals and musical styles of their Native land. As a result, genres that were previously associated with Native or Mestizo traditions of the rural highlands—notably the Peruvian *huayno*, the Bolivian *huayño* and the Ecuadorian *sanjuán*—became urbanized, achieving popularity in poor city neighborhoods, and eventually in the night-clubs of the middle classes. In time, recordings and radio and television broadcasts began disseminating the styles throughout the region.

Often, great efforts were made to preserve the music's original instrumentation and performance practices. Yet increasingly, in an effort to appeal to a wider audience, urban musicians made concessions to modernity, for example by adopting amplification systems in performance, by accepting modifications to traditional instruments, by combining instruments in new ways, or by shedding the original Andean instrumentation altogether, choosing instead *orquestas típicas*, accordions or brass bands to back their songs. New melodies were composed or adopted from foreign styles, including classical music, jazz, and rock, and the Cuban *son* and Colombian *cumbia* also began influencing the music, leading to more popular dance styles, for example the Peruvian *chicha* (discussed below). Most importantly, perhaps, performers often abandoned the ritual and religious context of the music, a process that naturally seems to occur whenever rural folk traditions transform into urban styles, as happened for example with the Brazilian samba and the Cuban rumba. Regional characteristics were also lost, leading to what some commentators have decried as a homogenous "pan-Andean" style.

An important factor in the popularization of Andean music was the emergence of the *peña*, a term that originally referred to a gathering place where village musicians would come together to play. With the urbanization of Andean music, *peñas* became important performance venues—coffeehouses and nightclubs dedicated to folk music, where Andean styles could be heard alongside other Latin America folk genres. *Peñas* deliberately attempted to introduce Andean music to an urban population, as well as to tourists. Key attractions were the extreme virtuosity of the musicians and the music's alleged "authenticity," though as we have seen, its removal from a ritual context, its continuously fluid instrumentation and its commercialization distanced it from traditional highland practices. This deterred neither the performers nor their audiences, particularly middle-class artists and intellectuals who flocked to the *peñas* and readily embraced the music.

By the 1960s, the popularity of Andean music was spreading to other Latin American countries, partly due to its association with other emerging folk styles such as the Chilean *nueva canción* (discussed in Chapter 9), which celebrated Native rights across the continent. Musicians from other countries—notably the Chilean Violeta Parra—became ardent proponents of Andean music and were greatly responsible for its dissemination. Soon, North American and European audiences began embracing Andean music as well. Its international popularity was cemented in the 1970s when one song in particular became a worldwide hit: "El cóndor pasa" ("The Condor Flies By"), the most well-known Andean song, is often mistakenly considered a traditional folk tune. It was actually written in 1913 by Daniel Alomía Robles as part of a *zarzuela* light opera of the same name. In spite of its operatic origins, the song quickly entered the folk repertoire, usually played instrumentally with *quenas* and *zampoñas*, with a tremolo *charango* figure in the background. After hearing it on a London street corner in the 1960s, the North American pop duo Simon and Garfunkel covered the song (with new lyrics) in 1970, propelling it—and Andean music in general—to worldwide recognition. In the 1980s, the popularity of Andean music was further boosted by the emerging New Age movement, which admired it for what it considered its mystical qualities and its association with ancient cultures and natural wonders.

Today, traditional Andean groups can be found throughout the world, but especially in Europe, playing on street corners and subway stations, in concert settings, and in *peñas* and other Latin American nightclubs (L'Escale, in Paris, being one of the most famous). They mostly comprise the basic Andean instrumentation: *quena, zampoña, charango*, guitar, and *bombo*. Ironically, the music's popularity has not been reflected as strongly in its Native countries, which still suffer to various degrees from racial and class prejudice. Unlike other countries, where upper classes have adopted genres that were at one time deemed too ethnic or too working class (for example the Dominican *bachata*, Colombian *vallenato* or Brazilian *forro*), the region's privileged classes have yet to fully embrace Andean music, preferring styles from Mexico, Argentina, the United States, and Europe. Though *quenas, zampoñas,* and *charangos* can be found in *peñas* in Lima, Quito, and La Paz, and while successive governments have declared Andean music a national treasure, it is still too often considered distasteful lower-class "Indian" music by parts of the Criollo urban elite.

Dozens of prominent groups have released their own brands of Andean music in the last several decades, with styles that range from traditional sounds, rhythms and instruments to politically oriented *nueva canción* and to glossy pop sounds aimed at a wider audience. Some of these include Los Jairas, Los Calchakis, Luzmilla Carpio, Grupo Aymara, Grupo Jatari, Savia Andina, Pueblo Nuevo, Los Kjarkas, and the Chilean groups Inti-Illimani and Quilapayún. The group Barroco Andino performed and recorded European classical and Baroque pieces with Andean instruments. A few groups have also emerged which have developed a radically modern style, including the group Arawi, which seeks to combine modern avant-garde techniques with traditional instruments.

> **Recommended Listening:** "El cóndor pasa" by Los Incas, from the CD *Los Incas: Best Selection.*
>
> **Recommended Listening:** "El cóndor pasa" by Los Folkloristas, from the CD *Caminos de los Andes.*
>
> **Recommended Listening:** "El amor y la libertad" and "Llorando se fue" by Los Kjarkas, from the CD *Treinta años solo se vive una vez.*
>
> **Recommended Listening:** "Candombé para José" by Illapu, from the CD *Antología.*
>
> **Recommended Listening:** "La doctrina de los ciclos" by Arawi, from the CD *The Doctrine of Cycles.*

CDII, Track 19: Modern Andean: "Cumbre"

Music and Lyrics: Eddy and Quentin Navia
Instrumentation: guitar, *zampoña* and *toyo* panpipes, *charango, quena, bombo*
Notes: Savia Andina's "Cumbre" ("summit") is a *huayno* that uses some of the largest panpipes in the Andean region: the *toyos*, which can be five feet or longer and have a deep bass sound. Because of the immense quantity of air required to play the *toyos*, the *trenzado* technique is once again used. Listen for each of the *toyos* on the left and right channels of your sound system. The contour of the melody illustrates the title, as the succession of rising themes depicts the ascent (and subsequent descent) of an Andean peak. The "summit" is reached at almost the exact center of the piece (1:52) by the soaring melody of the *quenas.*

0:00	Opening figure in solo guitar.
0:03	Introductory Theme: interlocking toyos doubling guitar figure
0:27	Dramatic pause
0:29	Theme 1 in charango with guitar accompaniment in the background
0:43	Theme 1 played an octave lower
0:55	Introductory Theme: interlocking toyos and guitar
1:18	Transition in guitar
1:24	Theme 2 in quenas and zampoñas, accompanied by guitar, charango, and bombo
1:38	Theme 2 repeated
1:52	Theme 3a, a soaring melody in two quenas in imitation
2:07	Theme 3b, quenas play together, a harmonic third apart
2:30	Theme 3a, charangos playing tremolo
2:48	Theme 3b, guitar
3:09	Introductory Theme, interlocking toyos and guitar, gradually slowing
3:49	End

PERU

Peru stands out not only because of the tremendous diversity of its music, but also because its population has (mostly) embraced it without regard to racial or social origin. While it is true that upper classes have not always been open to certain genres and styles, much of the rest of the country freely absorbs Criollo, Afro-Peruvian, Mestizo, and Native styles, as well as the foreign styles that have made their way to the country, and the hybrids that have inevitably resulted. Peru can be divided into three geographical areas: the Andean mountains that traverse the country from north to south, called generally *la sierra*, the Pacific coast to the west, and the eastern foothills where tropical jungle is the principal feature. Thus, while most people tend to equate Peru with the *altiplano*, the country's diverse landscapes also include vast deserts, thick rainforests, and extensive coastlines with large cities and spectacular beaches.

Historical Introduction

After the fall on the Inca Empire, the Spaniards established the Viceroyalty of Peru in 1542, which became the second-most important Spanish colony, after New Spain (Mexico). It contained virtually the entire west coast of South America, from Chile and Argentina in the south to the Caribbean Sea in the north. Though Cuzco in the mountains had been the Inca capital, the Spaniards founded in 1535 a city on the coast called Ciudad de Los Reyes ("City of Kings"). In time, the Quechua name, *Rimac*, became common and eventually evolved into Lima. It became the capital city and for centuries was the most important Spanish city in South America. Colonial Peru was home to rich gold and silver mines, notably the important mine of Potosí, now in Bolivia. These operations were worked by Native and African slaves who were for the most part brutally exploited. From the Inca Empire the Spaniards retained a system of forced servitude called *mita*, which essentially amounted to slavery. There was also a small but influential Gypsy presence in Peru, which emigrated from the southern Spanish province of Andalusia and which came to influence the country's music.

In the eighteenth century, the unwieldy territory was divided, with the Viceroyalty of New Granada established in Colombia and Venezuela in 1717 and the Viceroyalty of Rio de la Plata in 1776. In 1821, Peru declared its independence, followed by a conflict that culminated in the 1824 battle of Ayacucho, after which Spain was expelled altogether from continental America. Simón Bolívar became president in 1824. For the next century and a half, the country suffered a succession of unstable governments and conflicts, most prominently a war against Spain in the 1860s, as well as the 1879 War of the Pacific, which resulted in Chile's annexation of the Atacama desert. Slavery was abolished in 1854, and in the second half of the nineteenth century, economic development was helped by the construction of an important railroad that connected the coast with the mountainous interior. The twentieth century saw a succession of military coups, though since 1980, Peru has enjoyed free democratic elections. A left-wing guerilla army called *Shining Path* has been active in the Peruvian interior for several decades, and the ensuing clashes with government forces have cause the deaths of over 70,000 Peruvians. Like Colombia, Peru produces a substantial amount of the continent's cocaine, and the drug cartels have had an important influence on both the internal and external affairs of the country. Like its northern neighbor Ecuador, Peru has seen substantial migration from the poorer mountainous interior to the wealthier urban centers on the coast. Native Peruvians constitute 45 percent of the country's population, the largest groups being Quechua and Aymara, but with dozens of others as well. Fifteen percent of Peruvians are White, and 37 percent are Mestizo. There are small but important Black and Asian minorities as well.

Afro-Peruvian Music

Much of the recent musical activity on the part of Afro-Peruvians (as well as Afro-Bolivians and Afro-Ecuadorians) is impelled by an urge to reclaim their Black identity. Their culture has been overshadowed by Andean styles of the *altiplano*, to the point where many outsiders do not realize it even exists. But Black Peruvians have exerted an important and disproportionate influence on the development of the country's musical styles. In turn, the Black population has often adopted elements form European, Mestizo, and Native cultures. Like Native Andeans, they have struggled against marginalization, with the added problem of cultural decline. Colonial authorities repressed the customs, languages, and religions of slave population to such an extent that much of their ancestral cultural heritage was lost, forcing them to adopt

Native customs and language, for example by dressing as their Aymara and Quechua neighbors.

African cultures and religions thus did not evolve in the same way they did in Brazil or the Caribbean. As a result, Afro-Peruvians were mostly Catholic, and their rituals were generally secular and devoid of the religious elements found in vodou, Santería, or *candomblé*. Drums, marimbas, and other traditional African instruments were for the most part banned. Undeterred, the Africans improvised, using household items as percussion instruments, particularly wooden crates that were used to transport goods. In time this led to the development of the *cajón* ("large box"), a wooden box with a sound hole in the back that remains popular not only with Afro-Peruvians but with many other groups as well. The *cajón* player sits on the box and strikes the front of the instrument between his legs with his bare hands. In recent years, the *cajón* has crossed the ocean to Spain, where it can be found in some Flamenco and Jazz ensembles. Another instrument developed by Afro-Peruvians is the *cajita* ("little box"), a small trapezoidal drum made of wood that typically hangs around the player's neck. The *cajita* has a hinged lid that is opened and closed by the left hand while the right hand strikes the instrument with a wooden stick. The *quijada de burro*—the jawbone of a donkey or horse—is used both as a shaker and a scraper and is popular in the Caribbean and other parts of the continent. Other instruments include drums made from gourds called *checos*, as well as assorted rattles and scrapers.

Afro-Peruvian colonial dances, particularly the more sensual and explicit ones, were discouraged and often outright prohibited by religious authorities. Many of them are known only from written accounts, and their choreography and musical features have been lost. However, two prominent dances did survive, undoubtedly influenced by those that came before. The *festejo* ("celebration") is an upbeat, festive dance that traces its origins to the abolition of slavery in 1854, when Blacks celebrated their freedom in exuberant fashion. Part of the *festejo*'s original choreography involved a male martial arts competition, accompanied by lively rhythms played on *cajones*. It then evolved into a competition on the drums themselves, and in time became a frenzied dance, performed by couples who perform suggestive and enticing movements, with pronounced pelvic thrusts, being careful however never to touch each other. The lively rhythms and the physical, almost bawdy nature of the dance is in good humor. The *festejo* retained the *cajón* and *quijada*, and added guitars and singers. The texts of the songs, often in call-and-response form, recall the joyful emancipation of Peruvian slaves, and can be coarse and even vulgar.

The other prominent Afro-Peruvian dance is the *landó*, another fertility dance that probably originates in Angola, and is perhaps related to the Brazilian courtship dance *lundu*. The *landó* is very seductive, mimicking a sexual act and ending with suggestive hip thrusts. It is not as lively as the *festejo*, with slower rhythms that bring a sense of sensuality but also of melancholy. It is often in triple meter, with soft but complex rhythms played on the *cajón*. One of the most famous *landós* is the song "Toro mata," which translates as "the bull kills." Like many traditional folk songs, there are many version of both the tune and the lyrics of "Toro mata," none of which is the "correct" one.

Some accounts claim the song originated in the nineteenth century war between Peru and Chile; others place it in colonial times, with the conflict against the Spanish, the bull in question referring to the dangerous Spanish landowners. The steps of "Toro mata" mimicked and ridiculed European dances such as the waltz and the polka. Always a popular song, it received a boost in 1973 with a hit recording by the percussionist Caitro Soto, a member of the Afro-Peruvian group Perú Negro. It has since achieved national recognition, and it is popular with Peruvians of all ethnicities.

CDII, Track 20: *Landó*: "Zamba malató"

Music and Lyrics: Traditional
Instrumentation: guitars, *cajón, cajita, quijada de burro*
Notes: In the Andes, "zambo" and "zamba" refer to Black men and women. The soft and seductive rhythms of this *landó* by Perú Negro are complemented by the melodic ostinato of the guitar. Though the meter is in $\frac{6}{8}$ (count **one**-two-three-**four**-five-six), the *cajón* and *cajita* drums continuously play against it in syncopation, as do the chorus (indicated in **bold** letters), soloist and dancers in call-and-response form. Most of the lyrics are derived from African dialects, though their meaning has mostly been lost.

(**Zamba malató**)
Ay, Landó (**Zamba malató**)
Landó (**Zamba malató**)
Landó (**Zamba malató**)
Ay, Landó

La negra se pasea por la batea.   *The Black woman strolls along the estuary.*

Landó (**Zamba malató**)
Landó (**Zamba malató**)
Landó (**Zamba malató**)
Ay, Landó

Bailando se menea pa' que la vean.   *She dances and shakes in order to be noticed.*

Landó (**A la mucurú**)
Ay loña loñá (**A la recolé**)
Hoguerequeté (**Babalorishá**)
A la mucurú (**Oyokororó**)
Oyokororó (**A la mucurú**)
Mánde mánde (**A la recolé**)
Ee tirití (**Babalorishá**)
Tan cucurú (**Oyokororó**)
Oyokororó (**A la mucurú**)
Ee Landó

Other Afro-Peruvian traditions popular throughout the nineteenth and early twentieth centuries include the *pregón*, based on a street vendor's cries, and the erotic *alcatraz*, a sensual couple's dance in which the man, carrying a lit candle, attempts to conquer the woman by lighting a piece of cloth that she wears on her backside. Another is the *ingá*, a *festejo*-like dance that simulates a children's ring game, with a dancer holding a doll in the middle of a circle before passing it on. Yet another was the *agua'e nieve* ("melted-snow water"), in which dancers compete with each other with fast and intricate *zapateado*-like steps. Though these dances are now rarely seen in traditional Afro-Peruvian celebrations, modern folk dance troupes have revived them in more formalized performances.

In the second half of the twentieth century, Afro-Peruvian music became more popular throughout the Andean region, with recordings and local radio exposure. Several important groups emerged, including *Cumanana*, a folkloric dance ensemble led by the brother and sister duo Victoria and Nicomedes Santa Cruz. Perú Negro, led by Ronaldo Campos, has recorded both traditional Black rhythms and more modern salsa- and *cumbia*-influenced popular dance music. These groups often combine traditional instruments with modern electric guitars and bass, and add Afro-Cuban percussion such as conga drums and cowbells. The lyrics of their songs typically comment on social issues of contemporary Afro-Peruvians as well as the legacy of colonial slavery. Several Afro-Peruvian female singers have also emerged, including Eva Ayllón, who has been popular in Peru since the 1970s. In recent years, the most prominent Afro-Peruvian singer has been Susana Baca, whose sultry voice and smoky accompaniments have earned her an important international following.

By the turn of the millennium, suggestive Afro-Peruvian dances such as the *festejo* and the *landó* became increasingly popular in nightclubs alongside other Latin American styles such as salsa and Latin rap. First-time listeners of these groups and artists might be surprised by the lack of extensive drumming that is typically found in most traditions of the African Diaspora. Afro-Peruvian music has indeed adopted European instruments—notably the guitar—and occasionally some Andean instruments as well. Other African elements, however, are often present, including call-and-response songs and complex rhythms.

> **Recommended Listening:** "Festejo" from the CD *Pérou: Huayno, valse créole et marinera*.
>
> **Recommended Listening:** "Azucar de caña" by Eva Ayllón and "Enciéndete candela" by Roberto Rivas and Conjunto Gente Morena, from the CD *Afro-Peruvian Classics: The Soul of Black Peru*.
>
> **Recommended Listening:** "Toro mata" by Perú Negro, from the CD *Perú Negro: Zamba malató*.
>
> **Recommended Listening:** "Toro mata" and "A Sacá camote con el pie" by Caitro Soto, from the CD *De cajón*.
>
> **Recommended Listening:** "De los amores" and "Valentín" by Susana Baca, from the CD *Eco de sombras*.

Recommended Listening: "Los tamaleros (pregón)" by Victoria Santa Cruz and "Manonga la tamalera (festejo)" by Gente Morena, from the CD *Gente morena con Victoria Santa Cruz.*

Música Criolla

During the colonial period, those who were born in Peru of Spanish ancestry were known as Criollos to differentiate them from those who had been born in Spain, but also from the Native, Mestizo, and Black populations. Yet, because of the complex syncretic mix found in the coastal regions of Peru, various musical styles—whether their origins are African, European, Native, or Mestizo—have often been lumped together under the generic rubric *música criolla*. In an increasingly globalized world, these categories admittedly come to mean less and less, and in spite of its name, *música criolla* is embraced by Peru's large Mestizo culture, as well as by many Native and Black Peruvians. Nevertheless, if only for historical purposes, it remains important to distinguish the origins of each style.

Criollo culture emerged in coastal areas of northern Peru, in cities like Chiclayo, Lambayeque, Piura, and Trujillo, as well as Lima. Criollos predictably constituted the colonial urban elite, but also included White rural farmers and ranchers, sometimes wealthy, but more often than not scraping a living off small parcels of land. The descendants of the Criollos still continue this urban/rural, wealthy/poor dichotomy, but since the late nineteenth century, much of *música criolla* has been the domain of the working classes.

Música criolla consists of both songs that stand alone, and dances for which songs have been composed. They are derived from European forms and styles, particularly ballroom dances such as the waltz and the polka, Spanish folk dances such as the *jota, fandango,* and *Moros y cristianos*, as well as classical traditions and military band music. Also influential was the music of the Peruvian Gypsies, particularly the guitar, hand-clapping, and flamenco-like *zapateado* dance steps. As virtually everywhere in Spanish America, *zarzuela* light opera was popular in urban centers of nineteenth century Peru. In time, homegrown styles began to emerge, most prominently among them the *tondero*, the *zamacueca*, the *marinera*, the *vals*, and the *polca*, all of which remain at the core of *música criolla*. Though these dances were originally found in the salons of the elite, they came to be seen as plebeian and were thus abandoned, relegated to the poorer neighborhoods, where they were enthusiastically adopted. By the same token, at least as early as the nineteenth century, and probably well before that, *música criolla* began to be influenced by both African and Native characteristics, producing syncretic styles that drew from all three cultures.

Música criolla was—and is—often heard in working-class bars and nightclubs called *fondas* or *chinganas*, as well as in the more folk-oriented *peñas*. An important feature of Criollo culture is the *jarana* (not to be confused with the Mexican guitar of the same name), a prolonged fiesta-like celebration with music, dancing, food, and drink. Usually held in private homes, *jaranas* often become increasingly raucous and uninhibited as the night progresses. The drinks of choice are *pisco* brandy and *chicha* corn beer. It is in these *jaranas* that are displayed the conventional attributes of the Criollo: elegance, ingenuity, and especially *picardía*, a colorful character flaw that implies roguishness, mischief, and craftiness. These traits, which have been so ingrained in the culture that they have almost become a stereotype, are on display in the Criollo's penchant for spectacle, such as cockfighting and bullfighting, and in the songs and dances performed in the uninhibited environment of the *jarana*.

CRIOLLO SONGS   There developed in Peru a singing tradition that is characteristically sad and mournful, and whose origins are not clear. Some historians claim its melancholy nature is the result of the plaintive songs of the Gypsy immigrants, similar to those that still inhabit Andalusia. But these cries are also echoed in the Native *yaraví* songs, discussed earlier in this chapter, which were present in Peru since pre-Columbian days, and which often recall the destruction of the Inca Empire. Still others attribute it to the cries of African slaves who longed for the African continent. This melancholy aesthetic and mournful outlook pervades the song styles of the Andean region, and can be found in colonial church hymns and religious processions, as well as in the *socabón*, the *cumanana*, and the *canción triste* ("sorrowful song"), usually just called simply *triste*. *Tristes* and *cumananas* reflect the harsh existence of poor rural White farmers who sing passionately about a Spanish homeland they have never seen and never will. Their lyrics often reflect wistful scenes of everyday life: loss of love, failed crops, or death of a friend. They can also be political and social complaints, reflecting a working-class point of view. Yet in spite of their melancholy, they are often filled with irony, satire, and humor about their lot in life, much like the blues of the southern United States. There is an important literary component to these songs, whose poetry tends to be more elevated than that of other popular forms. They usually adopt Spanish poetic forms: *tristes* and *cumananas* are typically in *copla* form, while *socabónes* are in *décima* form. Whereas the Native and Mestizo *yaraví* is often in $\frac{6}{8}$ meter and uses the pentatonic scale, the *canción triste* tends to be in $\frac{3}{4}$ and makes full use of the minor scale. The songs are usually accompanied only by guitar, with the occasional *cajón*, though they are sometimes performed without any accompaniment at all. They are often improvisatory, and can involve a competitive aspect, wherein two singers alternately address a specific theme from which they cannot stray, each inventing a four-line *copla* that must preserve the rhyme scheme.

An important singer of *canción criolla* was María de Jesús Vásquez, known as La Reina y Señora de la Canción Criolla ("Queen and First Lady of the Creole Song"). Vásquez was the leader of a generation of singers whose popularity began in the 1940s, which included Alicia Lizárraga, Eloísa Angulo, Delia Vallejos, Esther Granados, and Lucha Reyes. Their success was partly due to the rise of radio—and later television—broadcasts of the genre. Thereafter, Criollo songs could be found throughout the country, particularly in *peña* nightclubs, where both Andean and Criollo music could be heard, as well as other styles such as the Chilean *nueva canción*. In the 1970s, Eva Ayllón and Lucila Campos continued to popularize the style. In recent years, Susana Baca has infused the *canción* with African sensibilities, while Tania Libertad has brought a jazzy torch-song quality to the style. The Peruvian song tradition is still vibrant in the twenty-first century, as evidenced by touring musicians and booming record sales. October 31 is the national Día de la Canción Criolla, a day in which popular festivals and song competitions are held in Lima and other cities.

> **Recommended Listening:** "Cumananas" by Alipio Cruz Ramírez, from the CD *Traditional Music of Peru, Vol. 8: Piura.*

> **Recommended Listening:** "Socavón" by Gente Morena, from the CD *Gente morena con Victoria Santa Cruz.*

> **Recommended Listening:** "La Contamanina" by Tania Libertad, from the CD *Lo mejor de Tania Libertad.*

> **Recommended Listening:** "La herida oscura" and "Cuando llora mi guitarra" by Eva Ayllón, from the CD *Eva! Leyenda Peruana.*

CRIOLLO DANCES   Both African and Native features shaped Criollo dances, as is evident in the use of instruments such as the Afro-Peruvian *cajón* or the wearing of Native-style costumes. Colonial African dances such as the *landó* influenced the nineteenth century *tondero*, the *zamacueca*, and the *marinera*, which are typically accompanied by guitars and *cajones*. They are often courting couples dances, with various degrees of suggestiveness (depending on their origin), which regularly incurred the wrath and censorship of religious and civil authorities. Like some Afro-Peruvian dances, many Criollo dances have disappeared from the culture, including a carnival dance called *son de los diablos*, which portrayed the struggle between good and evil with Devil imagery, but which disappeared in the 1930s. Other dances have survived and continue to be part of the fabric of everyday life—in town feasts, village celebrations, and family get-togethers, particularly in the northern coastal region. But they have also been successfully adopted by professional folk-dance troupes that travel throughout the country and abroad.

Tondero   An important early example of *música criolla* was the *tondero*, which emerged in Peru's northern coast during the colonial period, though some historians claim its origins go back to pre-Columbian days. According to this version, the choreography of the colonial *tondero* was adopted from a now-extinct Native fertility dance called *danza de la pava* ("turkey dance"), which was popular among the Tallan culture along the Peruvian coast. Accompanied by a flute and small percussion instruments, the *danza de la pava* allegedly mimicked the movements of mating turkeys, and later chickens. But another version claims that the *tondero* is derived from the *lundero*, which refers to a *landó* dancer, suggesting the possible influence of the erotic African dance on the Criollo one. Yet another version points to the three-part structure of the *tondero* and claims its origins lie in a similar dance called *canto de Saña* from the colonial city of Saña (or Zaña), which had an important African population.

Whatever its source, there is little doubt that all three cultures were influential in the *tondero*'s development.

Colonial *tonderos* were probably performed by singers accompanied by a lute or harp. In time, the traditional accompaniment of the *tondero* was provided by one or two guitars, a *cajón*, and a chorus, which often accentuated the music with clapping and additional percussion. Some twentieth-century *tonderos* and *marineras* are arranged for and performed by a wind band. *Tonderos* are commonly preceded and followed by *cumanana* songs, which set the melancholy mood of the piece. The dance has three parts: the slow opening *glosa*, the moderately fast *dulce*, and the lively *fuga*. The *glosa* is a lyrical song in a minor key with verses in *copla* form. Its sorrowful nature is related to the melancholy *triste* and *cumanana* song styles. It ends with an accelerated figure in the guitar and percussion called *repique* that transitions to the *dulce*, a song in call-and-response form, in the relative major key. The closing *fuga* is fast and lively, with syncopated rhythms, passionate lyrics, and exciting drumming and instrumental accompaniment, features that supposedly point to a distinct African influence. Yet, *tonderos* differ in lyrics, form, choreography, and accompaniment in many parts of the coastal region. They are still performed at town fiestas held on feast days or at private family gatherings. As in many Latin American courting dances, the handkerchief is an important symbolic prop, swirled by both the man and the woman to signal their intents and desires. The woman flirts but then retreats, the man tries to charm but then assumes a proud macho attitude; the courtship game continues as the dancers imitate the movements of the cock and hen, the former courting the latter until he catches her by the neck. Finally, the woman gives in, the conquest is complete, and the dance is over.

> **Recommended Listening:** "Tondero: Mi burrito" by Leida La Madrid, from the CD *Traditional Music of Peru, Vol. 8: Piura.*
>
> **Recommended Listening:** "San Miguel de Morropón (Tondero)" by Alpamaya, from the CD *Folklore de Perú y Ecuador: America nuestra esperanza.*
>
> **Recommended Listening:** "San Miguel de Piura," "Que viva Chiclayo," and "La perla del Chira" by Banda San Miguel de Piura, from the CD *Marineras and Tonderos.*

Zamacueca and Marinera   Another important example of *música criolla* was the *zamacueca*, a colonial couples dance that was performed in the working class neighborhoods of Lima. The name *zamacueca* supposedly comes from the African words *zamba*, which means "dance," and *clueca* (or perhaps *crueca*), which ostensibly refers to the proud strutting of a chicken. By the end of the colonial period, the *zamacueca* had become popular throughout the coastal region. After independence, its popularity extended to neighboring countries such as Chile, where it became known as the *cueca*, and Bolivia and Argentina, where it is known as the *zamba* (see Chapter 9). Like the *tondero*, the *zamacueca* was influenced by European salon dances such as the *fandango*, as well as the

Afro-Peruvian colonial dances, although the impact of Native features seems to have been limited. It had also originally mimicked a chicken-mating dance, infused with erotic movements. Originally accompanied by a harp or a lute, in time African instruments such as the *cajón* were added, as was the obligatory guitar.

After the 1879 War of the Pacific against Chile, the name of the *zamacueca* was changed to *marinera* in honor of the Peruvian navy that had fought in that war. Yet the differences between the *zamacueca* and the *marinera* extend beyond just the name, and the twentieth-century *marinera* came to have characteristics that distinguish it from its nineteenth century antecedent. The *marinera* soon became a dominant dance of Peruvian folklore, second only to the Mestizo *huayno*. It remains a romantic couples dance, preserving the basic idea of courtship but with a much more elegant sensibility. Couples engage in a stylish ritual, gracefully swirling their handkerchiefs to entice their partner. The courtship begins as the men and women first encounter each other, followed by attempts at seduction, which inevitably lead to a quarrel, and just as inevitably to a reconciliation. A distinctive feature of the *marinera*'s complex choreography is that the woman leads the dance, playing hard to get, while the man pursues her with his forceful *zapateado* until she finally succumbs to his advances, signaled by his wrapping the handkerchief around her.

Women wear shawls, blouses called *anacos* and flowing skirts in the colors of their region, which they twirl in a motion called *zarandeo*. Their hairstyles are indicative of their age and marital status, but usually include flowers or ribbons. In some regions, they also wear distinctive silver earrings called *dormilonas*. Men wear white shirts and black trousers, sometimes covered by the traditional *ponchos*. In some *marinera* traditions, the dancers are barefoot. Like the *tondero*, the *marinera* is in a three-part form, with three verses in *copla* form simply called *primera*, *segunda*, and *tercera*, each part repeated. The choreography shifts at the end of each part. As in most dances, rhythms are usually in $\frac{3}{4}$ or $\frac{6}{8}$ meter, with moderate tempos. The *marinera* retained the guitar-and-*cajón* instrumentation of the *zamacueca*, though in the twentieth century they also began to be performed by brass bands. The assembled audience complements the music with energetic clapping.

Though originally a coastal dance, the *marinera* eventually became popular throughout the country, inevitably leading to local and regional variations. The *marinera limeña* ("from Lima"), also called *canto de jarana*, is slower and more elegant and joyful than some of the other versions, usually in a major key. The *marinera serrana* ("from the sierras"), popular in the mountains and in southern areas, has more Mestizo influences, and its music, costumes, and choreography have been influenced by the *huayno*. Typically in a minor key, it begins slowly and ends with a lively *fuga*, after which the whole dance is repeated. The *marinera norteña* ("from the north") originated in the northern cities of Trujillo and Piura, but has become popular outside of the northern provinces. It is faster and more playful than the one from Lima, with more suggestive moves, and the dancers playing with their hats and handkerchiefs. The sections often alternate between major and minor keys. *Norteñas* sometimes include a trumpet with the traditional instrumentation. Like the *serrana*, the *norteña* is also always repeated.

The first *marinera* was "La concheperla", composed in 1893, with lyrics by Abelardo "El Tunante" Gamarra, the journalist who had first proposed renaming the dance in 1879. An important early composer of *zamacuecas* and *marineras* (as well as *festejos* and *tonderos*) was Rosa Mercedes Ayarza de Morales, who wrote music in both the folk and classical traditions of Peru. Among her notable *marineras* are "Soy peruana" and "San Juan de Amancaes." The *marinera* has continued to grow in popularity throughout the twentieth century and is now considered the country's national dance. Schools of *marinera* are found everywhere across the country. Important *marinera* festivals have emerged, including the Festival Nacional de la Marinera, held every January in the coastal city of Trujillo, and during which the Concurso Nacional de la Marinera competition is held.

> **Recommended Listening:** "La veguera (marinera limeña)" and "La concheperla (marinera norteña)" by Banda San Miguel de Piura, from the CD *Marineras and Tonderos*.

> **Recommended Listening:** "La cholita (brass band)" and "Marinera" from the CD *Pérou: Huayno, valse créole et marinera*.

> **Recommended Listening:** "Son de los diablos" by Juan Criado, "Sueño nomás (resbalosa y fuga)" by Carlos Hayre, and "Jarana para llorar riendo (marinera)" by Alicia Maguiña, from the CD *La Reyna de la jarana: Marineras and festejos*.

> **Recommended Listening:** "Caramba si (marinera limeña)" and "Ven a mi encuentro (zamacueca)" by Victoria Santa Cruz, from the CD *Gente morena con Victoria Santa Cruz*.

Vals Criollo and Polca Criolla   Directly descended from the stately waltzes and lively polkas of the nineteenth century salons of the Peruvian elite are the *vals criollo* and the *polca criolla*, usually just called *vals* and *polca*. The aristocratic dances had been purely instrumental pieces, played by string orchestras or pianos, as they were in Europe. By the turn of the century, they left their elegant surroundings in favor of the streets and bars of poorer neighborhoods in Lima and other cities, where they were adopted by the urban working class. In the process, they were transformed into popular, raucous song forms, with newly composed texts that reflected working class values and experiences: the struggles of everyday life, pessimism for the future, nostalgia for better times, or the anguish of loss, poverty and unrequited love. They were typically sung by one or two singers, accompanied by a guitar or *bandúrria* with intricate virtuosic passages, and, increasingly, by a *cajón*. Like all waltzes, the *vals criollo* is in triple meter, though in the twentieth century, some *valses* have been syncopated (reflecting African influences), or have juxtaposed $\frac{3}{4}$ and $\frac{6}{8}$ meters (reflecting Iberian influences). The *polca* is much faster than the *vals*, and usually in a standard duple meter.

The heyday of the *vals* and *polca* was the early 1900s. Early composers included Rosa Mercedes Ayarza de Morales and José Sabas Libornio. A transitional figure who incorporated modern elements into the dances was Felipe Pinglo Alva, who wrote many of the famous *valses* in the Criollo repertoire, including "El plebeyo" and "Mendicidad." Important *polca* composers included Pedro Espinel, who wrote "La campesina," and Filomeno Ormeño, who is remembered for songs such as "Canción de carnaval" and "Cuando me quieras." In time, the *vals criollo* began to be infused with—and lose popularity to—foreign styles such as U.S. blues and foxtrot, Argentine tango, Mexican *ranchera*, and Cuban *son*. By in the 1950s, it underwent yet another transformation: It ceased to be associated exclusively with the working class and achieved a wider popularity among Peruvians of all classes, who considered it a true representation of Criollo culture, a nostalgic link to a bygone era. This was due in large part to its dissemination on recordings and on radio, performed by a new generation of Criollo singers, the most important of which was undoubtedly Chabuca Granda. With a deep sultry voice and unconventional rhythms, Granda popularized many *valses* that she had written herself, including her most popular hit "La flor de la canela." In the 1960s and 1970s, Granda deliberately infused Afro-Peruvian elements into her compositions. Another famous singer of *valses* and *marineras*—and of *música criolla* in general—was the Afro-Peruvian singer Lucha Reyes (not to be confused with the Mexican *mariachi* singer of the same name). In recent years, singers such as Lucy Avilés and Eva Ayllón have had continued success singing *valses criollos*. The *vals* and the *polca* continue to be popular in Peru, though usually with older generations who still see in them a nostalgic link to the past. To this day, informal get-togethers and family *jaranas* will invariably include *vals* dancing, along with food and drinking. Oddly, many of Peru's soccer teams have adopted *polcas* as their fighting songs.

> **Recommended Listening:** "Estrellita del sud" and "El plebeyo" by Rosamel Araya, from the CD *Perú y sus valses*.

> **Recommended Listening:** "Rosal viviente (vals)" by Banda San Miguel de Piura, from the CD *Marineras and tonderos*.

> **Recommended Listening:** "La flor de la canela" and "Fina estampa" by Chabuca Granda, from the CD *Latinoamericana*.

> **Recommended Listening:** "Ilusiones vanas (vals)" by Victoria Santa Cruz and "Serenata de la guardia vieja" by Gente morena, from the CD *Gente morena con Victoria Santa Cruz*.

ESTUDIANTINAS An important Criollo ensemble is the *estudiantina* (also known as *tuna* or *rondalla*), student organizations associated with various universities in Latin America. The *estudiantina* tradition goes back to the *trovadores*, *goliardos*, and other itinerant musicians of medieval Spain and can be found throughout the continent, including neighboring Ecuador, Bolivia, and Chile but also in Mexico and the Spanish Caribbean. *Estudiantinas* often have the feel of brotherhoods and fraternities, with prankish admission rituals, secrecy oaths, and century-long traditions steeped in mystery. They wear the medieval garb of medieval universities, often with black cloaks, hoods, capes, and three-cornered hats. Though their musical performances are always serious and purposeful, in informal moments there is much irreverent banter and music making that revolves around the consumption of alcohol, and ribald commentaries about the opposite sex. *Estudiantinas* have traditionally been all male, though female *rondallas* are becoming increasingly prominent. They are almost exclusively string ensembles, consisting of guitars, mandolins, and lutes, as well as *charangos, tiples,* and *cuatros*, with the tambourine being the only percussion. Wind instruments such as *quenas* and *zampoñas* occasionally make an appearance. They can sometimes be as small as five or six musicians but usually consist of large bands of several dozen, with a distinctive thick texture of tremolo guitars and mandolins, with unison singing by the entire ensemble. *Estudiantinas* can play slow and romantic serenades, *boleros* and *valses*, lively *pasacalles*, or purely instrumental excerpts from classical music or Spanish *zarzuela* opera. They can also play popular tunes like *huaynos* and string arrangements of Native *quena* and *zampoña* melodies. They perform at university functions, but also in carnival parades and other local celebrations, as well as more formal concert-hall performances. International *estudiantina* competitions occur throughout Spain and Latin America, including one in the Peruvian city of Itaqui, but also in Guanajuato (Mexico), Oporto (Portugal), and Santiago de Compostela (Spain).

> **Recommended Listening:** "Aguila negra" and "Flor de mayo" by Estudiantina Perú, from the CD *Estudiantina Perú (Vol. 1)*.

> **Recommended Listening:** "Carnaval (estudiantina)" by René Villanueva, from the CD *Música de Bolivia*.

> **Recommended Listening:** "Amargo recuerdo" by Estudiantina Quito, from the CD *Música de Ecuador*.

Peruvian Popular Music

Peru has had a number of singers who have successfully drawn from Criollo, Afro-Peruvian, and Native traditions, achieving a degree of commercial success and popularity. Two of the most prominent were Víctor Alberto Gil Mallma, known as *El Picaflor de Los Andes* ("the hummingbird of the Andes"), and Ernesto Sánchez Fajardo, known as *El Jilguero del Huascarán* ("the goldfinch of Mount Huascarán"). Both became popular music icons in the 1950s and 1960s, and even gained important followings among Peru's South American neighbors. But the first Peruvian artist to achieve a worldwide reputation was Yma Sumac. Trained as an opera singer, Sumac had a legendary four-octave vocal range. She had an important career in the 1940s in Argentina, singing Peruvian and other Latin American folk songs. In the 1950s, she went to the United States, where she became part of the "Latin Craze," which had been fueled by an entire generation of Cuban musicians, but also by other artists from South America, notably the Brazilian Carmen

Miranda. Sumac's exotic appearance and stratospheric vocal range made her an instant hit with North American audiences. She recorded many songs with colorful names such as *Virgenes del sol* ("Virgins of the Sun God") whose mysterious exoticism became an important marketing strategy. In truth, much of her North American output was stylized and theatrical and only loosely based on Andean music. She also had a minor career on Broadway and in Hollywood, appearing, for example, in the 1954 epic, *Secrets of the Incas*. For several decades until her death in 2008, she continued to have a cult following, based mostly on the exotic aspects of her career.

> **Recommended Listening:** "Corazón mañoso" by Picaflor de Los Andes, from the CD *Bodas de plata*.

> **Recommended Listening:** "Taita Inty (Virgin of the Sun God)," "Ataypura (High Andes)" and "Xtabay (Lure of the Unknown Love)" by Yma Sumac, from the CD *Voice of the Xtabay*.

CHICHA By the 1960s, the popularity of *cumbia* from neighboring Colombia had spread to most of Latin America. In Peru, it was particularly popular on the eastern foothills of the Andes, where the Amazon basin begins, in cities such as Tarapoto, Moyobamba, Pucallpa, and Iquitos that were rapidly growing because of the emerging oil industry. Soon, Mestizo musicians in these cities began infusing *cumbia* with their own traditional Andean features, including notably elements from the *huayno*. The result was a hybrid style named *chicha*, which derives its name form the fermented corn beer that was popular with the Incas. *Chicha* quickly spread to coastal cities such as Lima, Trujillo, and Arequipa, and thereafter to most of the country, as well as neighboring Ecuador. *Chicha* is Peru's contribution to the continent-wide *música tropical* movement that emerged in the 1960s and 1970s and that includes not only *cumbia* but also Cuban salsa, Puerto-Rican *plena*, and Dominican merengue. It is a youth-oriented style, popular among the teenage children of working-class Native and Mestizo migrants, and consequently addresses themes important to urban youth: songs of love but also of protest, political injustice, and lack of opportunity. *Chicha* preserves some elements of Andean music such as characteristic scales, the juxtaposition of duple and triple meters, and structures of Andean dance forms like the *huayno*. It was originally played with electric guitars, bass and drum set, borrowed from U.S. rock and roll, and complemented by Cuban percussion: conga drums, bongos, timbales, *guïros*, and cowbells. In recent years, synthesizers and electric organs have become the instruments of choice.

Inevitably, various subgenres of *chicha* have emerged. The style that continued to evolve in Amazon cities came to be known as *cumbión* (or *chicha selvática*), and has a much faster tempo than the highlands or coastal styles. It was popularized by groups such as Los Mirlos, Los Demonios de Mantaro, Los Tigres de Tarapoto, and Juaneco y su Combo. Meanwhile, the *chicha limeña* (or *chicha criolla*) from the coastal areas and the *chicha chola* (or *cumbia andina*) from the highlands are strongly influenced by the *huayno* and other elements of Andean music. In Lima, *chicha* was popularized by groups such as Los Shapis, Grupo Alegría, Los Destellos, and Los Hijos del Sol. Perhaps the most prominent *chicha* artist was Lorenzo Palacios Quispe (known as Chacalón, the "pharaoh" of *chicha*), who with his group La Nueva Crema, had several important hits. One subgenre combines elements of salsa and *chicha*, and is thus known as *salchicha*, which translates as "sausage." Another is *tecnocumbia*, which infuses *chicha* with modern techno dance, popularized by groups such as Agua Bella from Peru and Caramelo Caliente from Ecuador, all-female groups that perform songs with a glossy, infectious pop beat. Unlike styles such as the Dominican *bachata* and the Brazilian *forro*, which were originally looked down on by the elite before being enthusiastically adopted throughout their respective countries, *chicha* is often still scorned by the Peruvian upper—and even middle—classes, still considered music for the working classes of Peru's poor urban neighborhoods. One result of this prejudice is that *chicha* has failed to reach the international prominence of other styles such as *cumbia* and *salsa*. Nevertheless, it has managed to cross Peru's borders into neighboring countries, including Bolivia (which has its own version called *saya cumbia*), Ecuador, Argentina, Chile, and, significantly, Colombia, home of the original *cumbia*.

> **Recommended Listening:** "El milagro verde" by Los Mirlos, "Ya se ha muerto mi abuelo" by Juaneco y su Combo, and "Si me quieres" by Los Hijos del Sol, from the CD *Roots of Chicha: Psychedelic Cumbias from Peru*.

> **Recommended Listening:** "Soy provinciano" by Chacalón y la Nueva Crema, from the CD *Lo mejor del faraón de la chicha*.

> **Recommended Listening:** "Cariño loco" and "Lucerito mío" by Agua Bella, from the CD *Cariño loco*.

For a discussion of the musical traditions of Ecuador and Bolivia, see www. mymusickit.com.

9

The Southern Cone Region

INTRODUCTION

Near the southern tip of South America, on the Atlantic coast, two rivers—the Uruguay and the Paraná—come together and form an estuary that is almost 200 miles long and 140 miles at its widest. This estuary is known as *Río de la Plata*, or "river of silver," though in English, it is often called the River Plate. Much of the southern part of the continent is drained by these rivers (as well as by important tributaries such as the Paraguay), reaching as far north as Bolivia and as far east as Brazil. There is so much freshwater flowing into the Atlantic that the estuary has also been called *El Mar Dulce*—"the freshwater sea." In 1536, Pedro de Mendoza founded the city of Santa María de los Buenos Aires on the southern shore of the estuary, which would eventually become the capital of Argentina. Later, Montevideo was founded about 150 miles away on the northern shore, in time becoming the capital of Uruguay. Several hundred miles upriver lies Paraguay, and across the Andes to the west is Chile, encompassing much of the Pacific coast of South America. These four countries in the southern cone of the continent share many historical and cultural characteristics that have come to influence their musical evolution.

As everywhere throughout Spanish America, the importation of Spanish musical culture greatly affected the development of the region's folk music. In colonial Argentina, Uruguay, Paraguay, and Chile, one could find the usual assortment of songs (*romances, guarachas, jácaras, chanzonetas, tonadas, villancicos*, etc.) and dances (*jotas, fandangos, sarabandas, malagueñas*, waltzes, polkas, and mazurkas), as well as literary forms, such as the *copla* and the *décima*. (These are all examined in other chapters.) The guitar was once again the most popular instrument, though the accordion also had an important presence throughout the region. Additionally, all four countries were affected to various degrees by a syncretic mix of European, African, and Native characteristics, though in many parts of the Southern Cone, European influences are more dominant than elsewhere on the continent.

ARGENTINA

Argentina has a geographic and climate diversity that has greatly influenced its cultural and musical development. Within Argentina's borders can be found high Andean landscapes, thick tropical jungles, the Chaco wilderness area, daunting glaciers, and the imposing Iguazú Falls, which form the eastern border with Brazil. In the extreme south are the legendary Patagonia and

Tierra del Fuego, stark and cold landscapes of stunning beauty. An important feature are the famous *pampas*, vast fertile prairies west and south of Buenos Aires that have yielded rich agricultural and cattle industries, and that have been at the center of much Argentine culture.

Historical Overview

Soon after its discovery, the territory surrounding the River Plate became a permanent colony, dependent on the Viceroyalty of Peru. By the eighteenth century, the unwieldy Viceroyalty comprised virtually the entire southern continent except Brazil, so in 1776 it was divided, creating the Viceroyalty of the River Plate that included modern Argentina, Uruguay, Paraguay, and Bolivia. Argentina proclaimed its independence in 1816, led by José de San Martín, revered as the liberator of the area, the southern region's equivalent to Simón Bolívar. There ensued a succession of mostly unstable military and civilian governments. The most significant figures in Argentine politics in the twentieth century were undoubtedly the populist president Juan Perón and his wife Eva Duarte, affectionately known by Argentines as Evita. Perón took charge of the country after a 1943 coup and was elected president in 1946. His nationalist policies were welcomed, particularly as they were championed by his wife, who, though unelected, became the most powerful member of Perón's entourage and the most popular figure in Argentina until her death in 1952. Perón was deposed in 1955, but regained the presidency in 1973, the year before his death. The post-Perón period was one of the unhappiest for Argentina. Starting in 1976, a succession of repressive military dictatorships were marked by the disappearance, torture, and murder of tens of thousands of journalists, writers, and political activists. The ill-conceived and humiliating 1982 war against Great Britain over the *Malvinas*—the Falklands Islands—spelled the end of the military dictatorships, and since then Argentina has enjoyed democratic civilian government, though successive economic crises, with sky-high inflation, have often failed to raise national spirits.

As everywhere on the continent, Argentina's ethnic makeup has been integral to the evolution of its music. Much of the indigenous population was eradicated within a few decades of the arrival of the Spaniards, though some groups continued to offer resistance even after independence. Though there was an important African presence during the colonial period, it was a fraction of that of Brazil to the east. In the nineteenth century, much of the Black population succumbed to yellow fever or to forced conscription into the Argentine army, where they suffered disproportionate casualties in the seemingly endless regional wars. The nineteenth century also saw a large number of immigrants from Europe, principally from Spain and Italy, which affected Argentine customs to a great extent, including the accent: Spanish pronunciation has a very distinctive lilt to it, similar to Italian, so that Argentines can be unmistakably identified throughout the Spanish-speaking world. English, French, German, and Polish immigrants also contributed to the evolving

Argentine identity. Today, Argentines of European descent constitute more than 95 percent of the population, and they have often overshadowed the Black and Native contributions to the culture. Yet it is precisely the Black influences that are at the root of some of the region's more prominent musical styles, including the tango.

There is a clear contrast between urban and rural culture in Argentina. The heart of the country is Buenos Aires, a cosmopolitan city often compared to Paris and Madrid, where tourists mingle with artists, musicians, intellectuals, and businessmen and women. The urban culture that developed in Buenos Aires is called *porteño*, since its port, on the River Plate estuary, is an important economic center, the gateway to much of the region's commerce and industry. But Buenos Aires also has a dark underbelly, with an often-marginalized culture that emerged in working class slums called *arrabales*, such as the famous Boca neighborhood, where poverty and crime are widespread.

Porteños (not unlike New Englanders in the United States) have sometimes suffered from elitism, regarding the rest of the country as backwards, rural, and inferior. Some members of the Argentine elite perceive themselves as avatars of a mostly White Eurocentric culture that must be maintained and protected. Any challenge to this perception is a threat to their status and to what they perceive as a unified society. As a result, Buenos Aires has historically—and sometimes violently—resisted new genres, whether foreign styles like jazz and rock and roll, or folk songs and dances of the interior. Even the tango itself was initially rejected.

Yet Argentina does have an important rural folk tradition, including music that is often referred to as *música del interior*. Much of Argentina's way of life (as in Uruguay, Paraguay, and Brazil) has historically revolved around cattle and horses. The rich and fertile *pampas* are ideal for raising cattle, and Argentina became (and is still) known for the quality of its leather and beef, exemplified by the ubiquitous *churrascos*: enormous steaks grilled on metal skewers. And at the center of this rural culture is the *gaucho*, the mythical cowboy of the pampas.

The *Gaucho*

Though the origin of the term *gaucho* (GA-oo-cho) is in dispute, it seems to have first emerged around the time of Argentina's independence, in the 1810s. The gauchos were at first politically repressed outcasts, sometimes members of traditionally marginalized groups such as immigrants, Natives, Blacks, and Jews, though in time most gauchos were either Mestizos or Criollos. Being outcasts, they naturally gravitated to the solitary rural life of the pampas, which almost inevitably led them to cattle driving. The gaucho heyday was in the mid-nineteenth century, when enormous herds of cattle roamed the pampas that extend throughout western Argentina. Gauchos lived and worked in huge cattle ranches called *estancias*. The cattle industry has declined in recent decades, but the gaucho culture is still very much alive, though it is now often more concerned with artistry and tradition than with actual cowboy work.

The traditional gaucho dress consists of a white shirt, a *corralera* vest, *bombacha* trousers of Turkish origin, and an embroidered loincloth called a *chiripá*. The outfit is held together by a *tirador*—a leather sash studded with gold or silver decorations—and is rounded out with the traditional black hat, neckerchief and *botas de potro* ("colt boots") literally made from horse leather. Whereas U.S. cowboys and Mexican *charros* use the rope as their instrument/weapon of choice, gauchos prefer the *bolas*, three balls or stones tied together with leather strips and used as a sling. They are also skilled with the *rebenque* whip and often carry a small sword called a *facón*. At the center of the gaucho lifestyle is the horse, and the gauchos' legendary riding skills often resulted in their conscription into cavalry units. Very quickly a gaucho folklore emerged that pervaded the culture, music, art, and literature of Argentina.

Gaucho Literature

An important gaucho literary movement emerged in the nineteenth century, encompassing poems, novels, ballads, and plays. The foremost examples are José Hernández's epic poems *El Gaucho Martín Fierro* (1872) and *La vuelta de Martín Fierro* (1879). Others include *Don Segundo Sombra* (1926) by Ricardo Güiraldes and *El inglés de los güesos* (1924) by Benito Lynch, as well as the poetry of Rafael Obligado and Estanislao del Campo. In the twentieth century, the gaucho tradition led to a nationalistic art music movement called *gauchesco*.

These and other works portrayed the gauchos as rugged, freedom-loving, romantic, itinerant, mythical figures who braved loneliness in order to conquer the wilderness. They lived in a violent world where death was common and life was only worth living on one's own terms. Gaucho culture, predominantly male, valued characteristics such a strength and courage, and was imbued with a sense of arrogance and pride. But the gauchos also had a sense of yearning and sorrow, and ultimately of fatalism, cast in a world that they could not control and that would ultimately defeat them. These literary works explored not only the struggle between humanity and the forces of nature but also between the individual and society. The real enemy of the gaucho was not the intractable wilderness but rather a modern urban society that enslaves and corrupts. *Martín Fierro* in particular protested the loss of Argentine traditions to modernization, a theme that is still ongoing, as much of the region still opposes the forces of globalization that assail Latin America. In time, the gaucho became a symbol for Argentine nationalism, even though (or perhaps because) their lifestyle was increasingly at odds with the modern world.

RECOMMENDED VIEWING For a stylized look at the gaucho lifestyle, see the 1968 Argentine film *Martín Fierro*.

PAYADA   The gauchos developed several folk dances, including the lively *gato* courting dance and the *malambo*, a competitive dance for men only, with virtuosic *zapateado* displays. But the primary musical genres of the gauchos were *payadas* and *milongas*. The *payada* was originally a relatively simple ballad, accompanied by guitars, somewhat reminiscent of the cowboy song from the western United States. Like medieval troubadours, *payadores* were often itinerant musicians, traveling the *pampas* from *estancia* to *estancia*, offering their song in exchange for food and shelter, or performing at rural taverns called *pulperías*. Lyrics celebrated the simple, rural lifestyle of the gaucho and the aimless wanderings of the *payadores*. Their dark mood reflected the melancholy solitude of these men who had turned their backs on modern society. But *payadas* could also be protest songs that addressed issues of social injustice and political events. Like the Mexican *corridos*, they were often "traveling newspapers," spreading noteworthy current events or historical tales to a

A nineteenth-century depiction of a *gaucho* playing a guitar.

rural, usually illiterate population. Because they were outdoor songs, they required a loud and raw vocal style, which recalled the melancholy songs of Andalusia.

In addition to the guitar, violins, harps, and smaller tiple guitars can accompany modern *payadas*. As with most songs derived from Spanish traditions, they are usually in *décima* or *copla* form, with octosyllabic lines and strict rhyming schemes. A key element of the *payada* is its improvisatory nature: two *payadores* often engage in a singing duel called *payada de contrapunto*, designed to showcase their verbal and musical virtuosity. It is the vocal counterpart of the competitive *malambo* dance. In gaucho mythology, the greatest *payador* was Santos Vega, a heroic eighteenth-century character whose actual existence is still debated. According to the legend, Vega defeated all comers until the Devil himself, in disguise, finally defeated him and ended his glorious career. Vega has been the subject of many subsequent works, including a 1906 epic gaucho poem by Rafael Obligado, as well as several film productions. The most famous *payador* whose existence can actually be confirmed was the nineteenth-century Afro-Argentine Gabino Ezeiza, nicknamed *el trovador de la pampa* ("the pampa troubadour"), whose fame extended throughout Argentina, neighboring Uruguay, and other parts of the continent. Ezeiza composed more than five hundred *payadas*, and was one of the first Argentine artists to record his music. He also participated in some legendary *payadas de contrapunto*, always emerging victorious. He once defeated another *payador* in a battle that lasted three days. In another contest in Uruguay in 1884, Ezeiza vanquished the famous singer Juan Nava with such skill that the day of the contest, July 23, has since been designated *día del Payador*—National Payador Day—in both Argentina and Uruguay. The song that Ezeiza improvised during that contest, "Heroico Paysandú", has become a staple of the *payada* repertoire.

The twentieth century saw the *payada* singing style eclipsed by the popularity of the *milonga* and especially the tango. Nevertheless, it remains today a living, vibrant tradition, with regular competitions that draw much attention throughout the country. *Payadas* can also be found in neighboring Chile, Uruguay, and Brazil, and similar styles that involve competitive improvised singing can be found throughout the continent, for example in the Cuban *controversia*, the Colombian *vallenato* or the Trinidadian calypso *picong*.

> **Recommended Listening:** "El gatito de Tchaikovsky" (*gato*) and "Malambo santiagueño" (*malambo*) by Hermanos Ábalos, from the CD *Nuestras danzas*.

> **Recommended Listening:** "Mama vieja" and "Mi mala estrella" by El Caballero Gaucho, from the CD *Grandes éxitos del trovador de la pampa*.

> **Recommended Listening:** "Presentación de Eduardo Peralta" and "Contrapunto de los gallos," from the CD *Encuentro internacional de payadores*.

> **Recommended Listening:** "Payada del Martín Fierro y el Moreno" by Héctor Del Valle and Oscar del Cerro, from the CD *Milongas criollas*.

Payada: "Payada del Martín Fierro y el Moreno"

Music: Héctor Del Valle and Oscar del Cerro
Lyrics: José Hernández
Instrumentation: guitars
Notes: This *payada* sets a few verses of José Hernández's 1879 poem *La vuelta de Martín Fierro*, in which the gaucho Fierro has an improvisational duel with a Black payador. Hernández's poetry, with its octosyllabic lines and rhyming schemes, is drawn from the conventions of the *payada* tradition. The lyrics are replete with double entendres and archaic Spanish, as in *mesmo* for *mismo*. In this recording, Héctor Del Valle sings the role of Martín Fierro, while Oscar del Cerro plays the Black payador, each improvising on guitars.

Martín Fierro

Mientras suene el encordado,	*As I find my tuning,*
Mientras encuentre el compás	*As I find my rhythm,*
Yo no he de quedarme atrás	*I shall not fall behind*
Sin defender la parada,	*Without defending the challenge,*
Y he jurado que jamás	*And I have sworn that never*
Me la han de llevar robada.	*Will I yield without resistance.*
A un cantor le llaman bueno,	*A singer is called good,*
Cuando es mejor que los peores	*When he is better than the worst*
Y sin ser de los mejores,	*And without being the best,*
Encontrándose dos juntos	*When two singers meet,*
Es deber de los cantores	*It is their duty*
El cantar de contrapunto.	*To sing a contrapunto (duel).*
Y el cantor que se presiente,	*And the singer who is so inclined*
que tenga ó nó quien lo ampare,	*Whether or not he is protected,*
No espere que yo dispare	*Should not wait for me to draw,*
Aunque su saber sea mucho;	*Though his knowledge may be great;*
Vamos en el mesmo pucho	*We draw on the same cigar,*
A prenderle hasta que aclare.	*We light it until the dawn.*

Black Payador

Yo no soy señores míos	*I am nothing, gentlemen,*
sino un pobre guitarrero.	*But a poor guitar player.*
Pero doy gracias al cielo	*But I give thanks to heaven*
porque puedo en la ocasión	*Because I am able on this occasion*
toparme con un cantor	*To encounter a singer*
que experimente a este negro.	*Who will try out this Black man.*
Mi madre tuvo diez hijos,	*My mother had ten children,*
los nueve muy regulares.	*The first nine of which were normal.*
Tal vez por eso me ampare	*Perhaps that is why I am protected*
la Providencia divina:	*By divine Providence:*
en los güevos de gallina	*Of the eggs laid by a hen,*
el décimo es el más grande.	*The tenth is always biggest.*

Y sé como cualquier otro	*And I know as much as anyone*
el por qué retumba el trueno,	*Why the thunder rumbles,*
por qué son las estaciones	*Why there are seasons*
del verano y del invierno.	*Of summer and winter.*
Sé también de dónde salen	*I also know where the waters come from*
las aguas que caen del Cielo.	*That fall from the sky.*
Yo sé lo que hay en la tierra	*I know what is on earth*
en llegando al mesmo centro,	*Even in its very center,*
en donde se encuentra el oro,	*Where one finds gold,*
en donde se encuentra el fierro,	*Where one finds iron,*
y en donde viven bramando	*And where lie roaring*
los volcanes que echan juego.	*The volcanoes that spew fire.*
Etc . . .	

MILONGA Emerging concurrently with—or, some say, as a direct result of—the *payada* was the *milonga*, a song-and-dance style that is also prominent in neighboring Uruguay. Its origins are still debated, with some historians claiming it is of Afro-Brazilian origin and that the word *milonga* itself means "words" or "verses," in reference to the improvised lyrics of the *payadores*. Others maintain its primary influence lay in Spanish (and specifically Andalusian) dance and song forms, as well as the European polka and the Cuban *habanera* and *danzón*. The term *milonga* has several meanings, often leading to some confusion: it can refer to either the dance or the song, to the venue where these are performed, or to a social event that includes *milonga* dances but also waltzes, *habaneras*, and especially *tangos*. Additionally, there is a difference between the sung *milonga* and the instrumental one, and between the fast, rural *milonga* and the slower form that is related to the tango.

Unlike the soul-bearing *payadas*, *milongas* were social songs and dances, played at community or private gatherings or in *pulperías* and brothels. Singers engaged in melodic and textual improvisation, accompanied by one or two guitars, and occasionally by violins, flutes, and even pianos if they were available. In its traditional, rural form, the *milonga* is a fast and lively dance in duple meter with pronounced syncopated rhythms, unusual accents and asymmetric beats that perhaps reflect African influence. The actual dance is relatively simple and straightforward, with more of a walking feel, lacking the set choreography and intricate turns and figures of the tango. A typical milonga beat can be counted like this: **one**-two-three **four**-five-six **seven**-eight. (See Fig. 9.1).

FIG. 9.1: **Milonga Rhythm Pattern:**

The rural *milonga*, like the *payada*, survived the overwhelming popularity of the tango, and variations of the country dance can still be found in the pampas, as well as in Chile, Brazil, and Uruguay, where it is called *milonga oriental*, marked by heavier rhythms than its Argentine counterpart.

> **Recommended Listening:** "Milonga de ojos dorados" and "Coplas por cifra y milonga" by Alfredo Zitarrosa, from the CD *Milonga de ojos dorados*.

> **Recommended Listening:** "Niño bien" by Tita Merello, from the CD *Tita Merello: Serie de oro*.

Tango

The earliest known reference to the word *tango* occurred in 1616, when the Cathedral diocese in Montevideo prohibited African dances "known by the name of tango, except on feast days, and then only until sundown." Some historians claim the term is of Congolese origin, meaning "place of dance" or "drum," while others maintain the word comes from the Spanish verb *tañer* ("to play an instrument") or from *tangó* (emphasis on the second syllable), a derivation of the Spanish word *tambor* ("drum"). Whatever its origins, the term was widely used to refer to African celebrations, as well as to the drummers, dancers, and dances at these festivities. The River Plate was not the only place where the African tango developed: in Cuba, there was an early reference to a *tango congo*; Brazil had a dance of the same name; Venezuela had a Black carnival tango; and in neighboring Uruguay, Black cultural organizations called *candombés* were also referred to as *tangós*. Many of these dances were probably related to the drum-based, Afro-Argentine dance, which was an integral contributor to the modern urban tango.

ORIGINS   The most important musical process in Argentina was undoubtedly the transformation of the rural *milonga* into an urban genre, for that led directly to the advent of the tango. As in the western United States, Argentina at the end of the nineteenth century saw the vast pampas parceled, privatized, and distributed to recent immigrants, spelling the end of the gaucho lifestyle that had been around for almost a century. Though gaucho mythology would live on, most of the gauchos themselves were forced off the land, eventually settling in poor, working-class *arrabales* in Montevideo and Buenos Aires. The seaport nature of these cities already provided a particularly exotic culture, home to foreign sailors, rootless drifters, gamblers, criminals, and prostitutes, many of whom were often illiterate and sometimes violent. These neighborhoods were also populated by poor working-class White Argentines (many of them recent immigrants), by the few Afro-Argentines that had survived war and disease, and by the disenfranchised and still marginalized gauchos—now called *compadres*, whose only possessions were often their guitar and their *facón* knife. (The next generation of denizens of the arrabales would come to be called *compadritos*.) Particularly popular in the port cities were the taverns, *pulperías*, brothels, and other houses of ill repute that inevitably emerged, precisely the kinds of establishments that traditionally foment the rise of musical genres associated with the marginalized, such as the Cuban *son* and *danzón* and New Orleans jazz. The same process held true in Montevideo and Buenos Aires, which, with their constant flux of cultures and their working class underbelly, were perfect settings for the emergence of the genre that would come to represent the marginalized in the southern part of the continent.

It is in this setting that the rural *milonga* became urbanized, turning into a slow, stately dance. The single guitarist now gave way to an ensemble accompaniment, usually consisting of violins, wind instruments, pianos, and eventually the *bandoneón* (discussed below). More importantly, the *milonga* also encountered Afro-Argentine traditions. Throughout the nineteenth century, Argentine authorities had repressed most African music and dance, and the centuries-old drumming tradition in the River Plate was rapidly fading away. Afro-Argentine dances traditionally were either community or individual activities, whereas those of the White working class were usually couples' dances, with men and women holding each other closely. According to the most popular theory, the tango developed when the White *compadres*, dancing their *milongas*, began mocking—and then mimicking—the dramatic Afro-Argentine dances. Their movements were incorporated into the couple's choreography, and the music altered to accentuate their dramatic nature. The tango thus emerged in the 1870s from this syncretic melding of Afro-Argentine rhythms and gaucho culture. The mournful *payada* and the syncopated *milonga* fit right in with the dance's dramatic and exotic feel, though the previously fast-paced gaucho dance was slowed down considerably to accentuate the drama. But the tango was also heavily influenced by European social dances, by the mournful Flamenco singing from Andalusia, and by the slow, lilting rhythms of the Cuban *habanera*, which most likely entered Argentina via light *zarzuela* productions from Cuba.

Early tangos spoke of the dark underbelly of life in the port cities. They reflected the hardships of immigrants who left their home for opportunity and who sought comfort in a foreign land. Tangos were imbued with the gaucho sense of honor and pride, of nostalgia and yearning for bygone days of glory on the pampas, tempered by a sense of melancholy, fatalism, and resignation. Like the North American blues, tangos emoted anguish, desperation, and hopelessness and explored social ills such as poverty, misery, exploitation, alcoholism, and prostitution. Tales of jealousy, possession, betrayal, vengeance, and murder were common, often charged with a violent sexual energy.

Tango lyrics were permeated by a working-class slang called *lunfardo*, a mixture of rural dialects and foreign languages such as Italian, French, Portuguese, and Quechua brought by sailors and immigrants. Spanish words spelled backwards were common. Some words were substituted with others that had only a distant or subtle association. (A corresponding example in English might be the slang use of the word "axe" to refer to a guitar.) Often, words had suggestive or obscene double meanings. Like most slang, *lunfardo* emerged spontaneously and became a code among the marginalized classes, used to conceal true meaning from outsiders.

The earliest tangos were often played by a single singer accompanying himself on the guitar, in the tradition of the *payada*. In time, flutes, violins, accordions and/or mandolins complemented the guitar. By the turn of the century, the guitar was replaced by the piano, and the flute was replaced by the instrument that came to be emblematic of the tango: the *bandoneón*, an accordion-like instrument with buttons on either side instead of the black and white keys of the piano. The *bandoneón* produces different notes when it is pushed in and pulled out, and each note is doubled an octave above. Together, the two hands have 71 buttons at their disposal, producing a total of 142 pitches.

The *bandoneón* first appeared in Germany around 1850, named after—and perhaps invented by—Heinrich Band, a German dealer who in any case was responsible for popularizing the instrument. It was brought to Argentina by German immigrants towards the end of the century. Soon thereafter, the tango accompaniment became standardized, embodied in a small ensemble called *orquesta típica criolla*, which consisted of *bandoneón*, violin, piano and guitar. Later, this ensemble evolved into the *sexteto*, with two *bandoneónes*, two violins, piano and double bass, a configuration still favored by many proponents of the tango. Still later, the string section was greatly expanded, with several violins and cellos adding a thicker texture to the music.

The tango retained the syncopated duple meters and straightforward harmony of the *milonga*. Most early tangos were in $\frac{2}{4}$ meter, with a basic—now almost stereotypical—rhythmic pattern, shown in Fig. 9.2. In time, more complex rhythmic patterns emerged, particularly with the advent of the *nuevo tango* in the 1950s. Most tangos are also in two parts, with the second half providing rhythmic and harmonic contrasts.

The steps of the tango are slow and dramatic. Born in houses of prostitution, the dance is an erotic representation of the sexual act—not filled with the love and joyful expectations that often accompany courtship dances but rather suggestive of the hard and illicit relationships between prostitutes, patrons, and pimps. The man abruptly pulls the woman to himself, and the two unsmiling dancers embrace almost violently. Their upper bodies are rigid, yet their steps are smooth and elegant, particularly those of the woman, who wraps her legs around her male counterpart in suggestive ways. Implied violence is inherent to the dance, which some commentators have compared to a knife fight, and whose culmination is indeed suggestive of both death and sexual climax. Gender issues are of course paramount to the relationship between the dancers, perhaps more so than in any other dance on the continent, with a pronounced machismo that demands male domination of the

FIG. 9.2: Tango Rhythm Pattern: $\frac{2}{4}$

woman. Though male pride and female surrender are necessary to the unfolding of the drama, the woman nevertheless retains a measure of control, and
for all the male posturing, it is she who will ultimately determine the course of
the relationship. These stylized versions can be very dramatic, but the tango is
also a social couples' dance, often devoid of the theatrical gestures popularized in films. At its core it remains an intimate, sensual dance, with the couples holding each other closely, upper bodies in continuous contact, women
resting their heads on the man's shoulders, the men whispering *mots d'amour*
in their partner's ear.

Though the tango is almost universally associated with Argentina, much
of its development occurred simultaneously across the estuary in
Montevideo, where the African-based *candombé* drumming tradition became
an important influence. The history of the tango is usually divided into three
periods. The *guardia vieja* ("old guard") refers to the time between its origins
and around 1920. The period between 1920 and 1955, dominated by Carlos
Gardel, is known as the *guardia nueva*. The period after 1955, dominated by
Ástor Piazzolla, is known as the *nuevo tango*.

> **Recommended Listening:** Two important compilations that document
> the evolution of the tango during its first half-century are *Argentine vals,
> tango et milonga 1907–1950*, and *Antología noble del tango: Sus grandes
> intérpretes y compositores*.

GUARDIA VIEJA   The first tangos began appearing sporadically around
1870, and within a decade, the dance had more or less achieved a set form.
Most were anonymous and usually preserved the improvisatory character
inherited from the *payada* and *milonga*. Having partially engendered the
tango, the urban *milonga* was quickly absorbed and overshadowed by it, to
the point where it is often hard to distinguish between the urban *milongas*
and the early tangos. Because of their unsavory origins, early tangos were
shunned by Argentine middle- and upper classes. It would have been un-
seemly for upper-class women in particular to be associated with the dance
of pimps and prostitutes. Yet within a generation, the tango began to slowly
edge into middle-class consciousness. This process of gradual acceptance
has been repeated countless times on the American continent, as styles associated with the working class, racial minorities or otherwise marginalized
groups—notably Cuban *danzón*, Dominican *bachata*, Brazilian *forró*, and
North American jazz—steadily gained recognition by the dominant culture.
In this case, the Argentine middle class became enamored with the exotic
and "dangerous" elements of the tango. The dance soon became popular in
middle-class theaters and nightclubs known as *cabarets*. In the process, it
became more refined, polished, and cosmopolitan. To the dismay of some
purists, it had become respectable.

Yet the tango was still unable to break the ranks of the Argentine
upper-class elite. Ultimate acceptance by Argentine society was achieved in
a roundabout way. Around 1900, Argentine musicians took a sanitized version

to Europe, with some of the harsher elements softened to make it more alluring. The dance was enthusiastically embraced in the salons of Paris, Madrid, and London, as well as in ballroom dances and vaudeville theatrical productions. It became closely identified with *belle époque* society, which prized all things exotic and sensual. Only then did the tango come full circle, returning to its native land where it was finally embraced by Argentine high society. Many important artists were responsible for its popularity during this period, both at home and abroad. One of the most prominent was Vicente Greco, one of the pioneers of the *orquesta típica criolla*, and whose important contributions included the tangos "Don Juan," "Don Pedrito," and "Rosendo." Another was the pianist Enrique Saborido, whose 1905 "La morocha" became a hit both in Argentina and in Europe. Some early prominent tangos include "El choclo" and "El porteñito," both written in 1903 by Ángel Villoldo. Another important figure was Roberto Firpo, who set the syncopated rhythms in the piano and assigned the melodies to the violin and *bandoneón*, an arrangement that would become the standard for decades to come.

> **Recommended Listening:** "Don Pedrito" and "El garrotazo" by Vicente Greco, from the CD *Homenaje a la guardia vieja del tango: Vicente Greco 1911–1914*.

> **Recommended Listening:** "La morocha," "El porteñito," and "El choclo" by Juan D'Arienzo, from the CD *Serie de oro: Juan D'Arienzo*.

> **Recommended Listening:** "La cumparsita" and "Desde el alma" by Roberto Firpo, from the CD *De la guardia vieja*.

> **Recommended Listening:** "La cumparsita" by Juan D'Arienzo y Su Orquesta, from the CD *Antología noble del tango: Sus grandes intérpretes y compositores*.

CDII, Track 21: Tango (*guardia vieja*): "El choclo"

Music: Ángel Villoldo (1898)
Lyrics: Enrique Santos Discépolo (1947)
Instrumentation: piano, bandoeón, bass, violins, celesta
Notes: Sung here by Alberto Arenas, "El choclo" is one of the oldest tangos and is typical of the *guardia vieja*. In 1947, new lyrics were added, with various words in *lunfardo* slang of the *compadritos*, such as *bacan* (pimp), *pebeta* (young girl), and *cana* (policeman). The title—Quechua for "corn"—here refers to the singer, who associates the development of the tango with the emergence of life in the *arrabales*. An unusual feature of this recording is the celesta solo (at 1:41), though it is characteristic of Francisco Canaro's orchestra, which often developed interesting arrangements and orchestrations.

Con este tango que es burlón y compadrito,	*With this mocking tango of the compadritos,*
Bateó sus alas la ambicion de mi suburbio;	*The ambition of my home flapped its wings;*
Con este tango nacio el tango y como un grito,	*With this tango the tango was born and like a shout,*
Salio del sordido barrial buscando el cielo.	*It left the sordid mire looking for heaven.*
Conjuro extraño de un amor hecho cadencia,	*Strange spell of a love turned into music,*
Que abrio caminos sin más luz que la esperanza.	*That opened paths with no more light than hope.*
Mezcla de rabia de dolor, de fe, de ausencia,	*A mixture of rage, pain, faith, absence,*
Llorando en la inocencia de tu ritmo juguetón.	*Weeping in the innocence of your playful rhythm.*
Por tu milagro de notas agoreras,	*From the miracle of your divining notes,*
Nacieron sin pensarlo, las paicas y las grelas.	*Were born without a thought, women and young girls.*
Luna en los charcos, canyengue en las caderas,	*Moon on the puddles, canyenque dance on the hips,*
Y una ansia fiera en la manera de querer.	*And a fiery desire in the ways to love.*
Al evocarte, tango querido,	*Evoking you, beloved tango,*
Siento que tiemblan las baldosas de un bailongo,	*I feel the shaking of the tiles of a dancehall,*
Y oigo el rezongo de mi pasado.	*And I hear the grumbling of my past.*
Hoy que no tengo más a mi madre,	*Now that I no longer have my mother,*
Siento que llega en punta pie para besarme	*I feel her coming on tiptoes to kiss me,*
Cuando tu canto nace al son de un bandoneón.	*When your song is born to the sound of a bandoneón.*
Carancanfunfa se hizo al mar con tu bandera	*The early tango took to the sea with your [Argentinean] flag*
Y en un pernó mezclo a Paris con Puente Alsina.	*And in a pernod mixed Paris and Puente Alsina.*
Fuiste compadre del gavión y de la mina	*You were protector of seducers and the seduced*
Y hasta comadre del bacán y la pebeta.	*And even of pimps and young girls.*
Por vos shusheta, cana, reo y mishiadura	*Because of you, dandies, cops, bums, and the poor*
Se hicieron voces al nacer con tu destino.	*Were given voice as they were born with your destiny.*
Misa de faldas, querosen, tajo y cuchillo,	*Mass of skirts, kerosene, slash, and knife,*
Que ardió en los conventillos y ardió en mi corazón.	*That burned in the tenements and burned in my heart.*

GUARDIA NUEVA Around 1920, the tango underwent a transformation that would establish it as the premiere Argentine musical style. It was during this period that a populist and nationalist movement enveloped Argentina and led, for example, to universal suffrage and to the embracing of Argentine folklore.

This movement recognized the tango as the quintessential Argentine art form. With a serious approach that exuded *porteño* qualities, the tango became an important signifier of Argentine cultural identity beyond the *porteño* neighborhoods, one with which Argentines of all ages, social classes, and regional origins could proudly identify. Poets, composers, and performers infused it with a deep emotional content that resonated with Argentine society. In the process, it became more refined and cosmopolitan, shedding many of its coarser elements, but prompting some critics to complain that it was losing much of its authenticity, becoming too closely associated with elevated poetic forms. The crude language and erotic themes became much more subtle and wistful. *Lunfardo* was still maintained, but only as an affectation, since most of its proponents were now middle-class intellectual poets and musicians rather than illiterate denizens of the *arrabal* underclass. Whereas *guardia vieja* tangos had retained the duple meter of the *milonga*, a greater harmonic and rhythmic complexity now enveloped the genre. Lyrics were often sentimental, though they maintained the inherent pessimism and fatalism that pervaded the genre. Unrequited love and betrayal were still common themes, as were melancholy glimpses of life, family and friendship, and social problems and political commentary derived from poverty and social injustice. In time, important poets and writers were influential on tango lyrics, including the Spaniard Federico García Lorca, the Chilean Pablo Neruda, and the Argentine Jorge Luis Borges. The tango also became prominent in political circles, as politicians would wrap themselves in it to demonstrate their patriotism. It had transcended its origins as an amusing exotic dance and become a mainstay of popular consciousness.

This period also saw the rise of professional composers and performers—intensely passionate singer/songwriters who not only became respectable but were also revered throughout the country. Having passed from the bars and brothels of the *arrabal* to the *cabarets* and theaters of the middle class, the tango began to emerge in recordings and particularly in film, which contributed to the dance's popularity. The tango also now became known in the United States, where the free-wheeling "roaring '20s" welcomed the dance's overt erotic nature, particularly after it was danced suggestively by Rudolph Valentino in the 1921 film *The Four Horsemen of the Apocalypse*. The tango—and Argentine culture in general—was a key contributor to the "Latin Craze" that would envelope the United States for the next several decades.

Prominent tango artists that emerged in the 1920s included the Orquesta Típica Select and the Orquesta Típica Victor, as well as the *bandoneón* players Oswaldo Fresedo and Ciriaco Ortíz, frontman of the group Los Provincianos. Important composers of the period included Juan-Carlos Cobián, Enrique Delfino, and Pascual Contursi. Violinist Julio de Caro wrote many of the important tangos of the period, including "Boedo", as did his brother, the pianist Francisco de Caro, whose "Flores negras" became an important *tango-romanza*. Alfredo Gobbi wrote numerous classic tangos, many of them sung by his wife Flora Rodríguez de Gobbi. But it was one singer in particular, Carlos Gardel, who did the most to solidify and perpetuate the tango's reputation throughout Argentine society, and to a new generation of Europeans in the 1920s and 1930s.

Recommended Listening: "Mala sangre" and "Milonguita" by Orquesta Típica Select, from the CD *Orquesta Típica Select . . . 1920: Argentine Tango*.

Recommended Listening: "Mocosita" and "Adiós Argentina" by Orquesta Típica Victor, from the CD *Orquesta Típica Victor: 1926–1931*.

Recommended Listening: "Boedo" and "Flores negras" by Julio de Caro, from the CD *Tangos de rompe y raja*.

Recommended Listening: "Mi noche triste" by Roberto Rufino and "A Orlando Goñi" by Alfredo Gobbi, from the CD *Antología noble del tango: Sus grandes intérpretes y compositores*.

Carlos Gardel   There is some debate as to Gardel's birthplace and date: some claim he was born in France in 1887, others in Uruguay in 1890. In any case, he moved to Buenos Aires as a young child and quickly became immersed in the culture of the *arrabales*. He began his career in the 1910s in the city's *cabarets*, where he acquired a reputation as a dramatic, heartfelt singer. His recording debut occurred in 1917 with Pascual Contursi's song "Mi noche triste," which became an instant hit, selling over 100,000 copies. Thereafter, his career took off meteorically, and he soon became an idol across the continent. Nicknamed *El Zorzal Criollo* ("the creole songbird") and *El Rey del Tango* ("the king of tango"), Gardel became an icon for the working class because of his success in transcending his roots in the misery of the *arrabal*. His good looks and charisma were instrumental in his popularity, and his deep baritone voice, infused with a male sensuality, had a particularly dramatic phrasing that was widely imitated, ultimately becoming the standard for decades thereafter. He toured extensively throughout Latin America, Europe, and the United States and also had an important film career, appearing in over a dozen pictures that helped popularize the tango across the world. Like Rudolph Valentino before him, Gardel became the archetype of the Latin lover, and by the mid-1930s, had become the most famous actor in Spanish language film. He recorded over 500 tangos in his career, many of which he composed himself and became staples of the repertoire, including "Mi Buenos Aires querido," "El día que me quieras," "Volver," "Silencio," and "Cuesta abajo." Gardel transformed the tango from a popular dance into an important song style, embraced by all Argentine society. His career was at the height of its popularity when he died in an airplane accident in 1935 in Medellín, Colombia. He was mourned by millions, and, like other popular figures whose careers were cut short prematurely, his death firmly ensconced him in myth, turning him into a legendary larger-than-life figure. He remains, with Ástor Piazzolla, the preeminent figure in the history of the tango.

Recommended Viewing: Arguably Gardel's best film is *El día que me quieras* (1935), a musical whose title song became one of Gardel's most famous hits. Amazingly, the film also features 14-year-old *bandoneón* player Ástor Piazzolla.

Recommended Listening: "Mi noche triste," "Mi Buenos Aires querido," "Volver," and "El día que me quieras" by Carlos Gardel, from the CD *Carlos Gardel: Sus 40 tangos más famosos*.

Couple dancing the tango in Buenos Aires, Argentina. The billboard depicts Carlos Gardel.

CDII, Track 22: *Tango (guardia nueva)*: "La cumparsita"

Music: Gerardo Mata Rodriguez (1917)
Lyrics: Enrique Maroni and Pascual Contursi (1924)
Instrumentation: guitar
Notes: "La cumparsita" is far and away the most famous of all tangos. First performed as a carnival march in Montevideo, it was subsequently infused with tango rhythms by Roberto Firpo and thereafter became a worldwide hit. Like many tangos, its original bawdy lyrics were changed once it gained popularity. Its title—"the little carnival parade"—suggests a masked procession of endless miseries that afflict the lonesome narrator who has been abandoned by his prostitute lover. Carlos Gardel recorded several versions of the song, some with full tango instrumentation, others, such as this one, with a simple guitar accompaniment. Gardel's plaintive vocals and the sparse chords of the guitar accentuate the song's loneliness and despair.

Si supieras que aún dentro de mi alma,	*If you only knew that deep within my soul*
Conservo aquel cariño que tuve para ti.	*I preserve that affection that I had for you.*
Quien sabe si supieras que nunca te he olvidado,	*Who knows, if you only knew that I never forgot you,*
Volviendo a tu pasado te acordaras de mi.	*Reliving your past, you would remember me.*
Los amigos ya no vienen, ni siquiera a visitarme.	*My friends no longer come, not even just to visit.*
Nadie viene a consolarme en mi aflicción.	*No one comes to comfort me in my affliction.*
Desde el día que te fuiste, siento angustias en mi pecho.	*Since the day that you left, I feel anguish in my chest.*
Deci, percanta, que has hecho de mi pobre corazon?	*Tell me, woman, what have you done to my poor heart?*
Al cotorro abandonado ya ni el sol de la mañana	*Into the abandoned pad not even the morning sun*
Asoma por la ventana como cuando estabas vos.	*Peeks through the window, as when you were here.*
Y aquel perrito compañero que por tu ausencia no comía,	*And that friendly puppy who in your absence would not eat,*
Al verme solo, el otro día tambien me dejo.	*When it saw me all alone, the other day it also left me.*

After Gardel   In spite of —or perhaps because of—Gardel's untimely death in 1935, the tango's popularity continued to rise throughout the 1940s, through radio and recordings, as well as in the film industry that Gardel had helped launch. Not coincidentally, this period also saw the political rise of the populist president Juan Perón, who championed the tango as a true nationalistic genre. The 1930s and 1940s were dominated by artists such as Juan de Arienzo, Alberto Gómez, Oscar Larroca, Hugo del Carril, Juan Carlos Miranda, and Alberto Echague. Agustín Magaldi leaned towards the rural antecedents of the gaucho *payadas*. Enrique Santos Discépolo composed songs such as "Cambalache," "Confesión," and "Yira, yira." Important innovators included the pianist Osvaldo Pugliese, who recorded "La Yumba" and "Recuerdo," and Aníbal Troilo, one of the best *bandoneón* players prior to the emergence of Piazzolla. The 1930s also saw the rise of important female singers of the tango, including Rosita Quiroga, Ada Falcón, Azucena Maizani, Mercedes Simone, and especially Libertad Lamarque, known as "The Queen of Tango." Lamarque also had an important film career, appearing in Argentina's first sound film called *Tango!* (1933). She became popular throughout the continent and in the 1940s continued her career in Mexico, where she made important films and later, several popular soap operas.

Recommended Listening: "Quejas de bandoneón" by Aníbal Troilo, "Nieve" by Agustín Magaldi, "La yumba" by Osvalvo Pugliese y Su Orquesta, "Yira, yira" by Alberto Gómez, and "Malena" by Juan Carlos

Miranda, from the CD *Antología noble del tango: Sus grandes intérpretes y compositores.*

Recommended Listening: "Julián" by Rosita Quiroga, "La última copa" by Ada Falcón, "Estampilla" by Azucena Maizani, and "Volver" by Libertad Lamarque, from the CD *Antología noble del tango: Sus grandes intérpretes y compositores.*

NUEVO TANGO   By the 1950s, the tango was losing popularity. After more than half a century of tradition, it had engendered fairly strict expectations from both its performers and its audiences. Innovations were slow to come by, and a certain amount of stagnation permeated the style. There was widespread recognition that it had abandoned its gritty roots on the street, settling instead for upper-class salons and concert halls. Argentine youth in particular, like their counterparts all over the world, yearned for music that was more relevant to them. After the 1952 death of Evita Perón—a big supporter of the tango—and the country's gradual move towards dictatorship, there was an emerging dissatisfaction with the cultural status quo. This phenomenon was not limited to Argentina, and Latin styles were in decline throughout the continent. The U.S. "Latin Craze" was ending, and traditional Cuban, Brazilian, and Argentine styles, seen as antiquated artifacts of an older generation, were giving way to youth-oriented styles. The immense popularity of Elvis Presley and the Beatles was just around the corner, and Argentina, like every country on the continent, was affected by the gradual importation of foreign styles, notably jazz and rock and roll. Additionally, other styles from Argentina's interior, notably the *zamba* (discussed below) were gaining popularity. The time was ripe for a major revitalization of the genre, and, as if by design, a new style of tango emerged called, somewhat predictably, *nuevo tango*. This change was not as abrupt as some have maintained: older tango artists like Aníbal Troilo and Osvaldo Pugliese and newer groups like Sexteto Tango and Sexteto Mayor had already begun innovations in the late 1940s and early 1950s. Nevertheless, the revitalization is usually attributed to one man, Ástor Piazzolla, who took the tango in bold new directions, and who as a result is considered, after Gardel, its most important proponent.

Ástor Piazzolla   Piazzolla was born in Argentina in 1921 to a family of Italian immigrants. When he was three, his family moved to New York City, where he absorbed much of culture and music, including jazz, Broadway, and Tin Pan Alley songs. His father made sure that he was also educated in the tango and bought him a *bandoneón* when he was nine. Piazzolla quickly became a virtuoso on the instrument, to the point where a few years later, Carlos Gardel, then on tour, heard the 13-year-old play and asked him to join his band. Piazzolla's father refused the invitation, which proved a fateful decision when a year later Gardel and his band were killed in an airplane crash. In 1937, the family returned to Argentina, where Piazzolla joined the orchestra of Aníbal Troilo, then considered the greatest *bandoneón* player.

Yet despite his love for the tango, the young Piazzolla, like many of his contemporaries, did not consider it serious music, and from an early age, he had been intent on becoming a classical composer. Throughout the 1940s, he continued playing in the evenings in *cabarets* while at the same time pursuing his classical studies during the day, notably with the Argentine composer Alberto Ginastera. In 1953, Piazzolla went to Paris to study with the famous composition teacher Nadia Boulanger, which proved to be a turning point in his career. Boulanger encouraged Piazzolla to draw from the melodies and rhythms of his native land, and the young composer, seeing the wisdom of her advice, wholeheartedly embraced the tango he had until then considered no more than a meal ticket. He began infusing it with his other two musical loves—jazz and classical music—creating a style that was wholly original. The *nuevo tango* was born. Until his death in Buenos Aires in 1992, Piazzolla remained an important composer, arranger, and star *bandoneón* player, composing original pieces that continuously stretched the definition of the style.

Piazzolla famously once said: "For me, the tango was always for the ear rather than the feet." His music, complex, and far-reaching, cannot be easily categorized. He consciously developed a style that was mostly instrumental, devoid of singing and dancing, and that became an intellectual aural exercise for the educated listener. His music was not always—and was not meant to be—accessible to the working class denizens of the *arrabal*. Yet, he also rejected the stuffy concert hall atmosphere that the tango had adopted, and preferred an edgier, "street" sound (though eventually, his compositions found their way to the concert hall, where theywere very successful).

Nuevo tango is heavily infused with harmonic, melodic, rhythmic, and instrumental elements drawn from jazz and classical music, particularly those of the 1950s and 1960s avant-garde. Dissonance and even atonality are common. Melodies can be at once harsh and lyrical, and textures often contrast greatly, echoing the dramatic shifts of the earlier tango choreography. Traditional classical techniques such as baroque forms and contrapuntal fugues are also used, far removed from the simple two-part form of the *milongas* of the late nineteenth century. As in jazz, instrumentalists often improvise over set harmonic progressions. Piazzolla's tangos often have a greater rhythmic complexity, playing on the dance's natural dramatic syncopations. He also explored the possibilities of timbre, with unorthodox combinations of instruments and playing techniques. He transcended the standard instrumentation of the *orquesta típica* and began writing works for classical ensembles, though usually preserving the *bandoneón*, which he recognized as integral to the style. Throughout his career, he led various ensembles with an ever-changing number of players. Thus, in 1955, he formed the Buenos Aires Octet (with electric guitar), followed in the 1960s by his famous Tango Nuevo Quintet (piano, violin, double bass, electric guitar, and *bandoneón*), the Nonet in the 1970s, and the Sextet in the 1980s. Recordings of some of these ensembles have become legendary. He also re-introduced Afro-Uruguayan *candombé* drums: the tango, long denied its African percussion, now came full circle.

Piazzolla wrote more than a thousand compositions, and he famously collaborated with prominent artists such as the Kronos Quartet and jazz saxophonist Gerry Mulligan. He wrote several tangos for symphony orchestra, concertos for *bandoneón* and orchestra, as well as a tango oratorio, a tango opera, and important film and theater scores. The classical and jazz avant-garde scenes in Europe and the United States quickly embraced his radical style. In Argentina, by contrast, the reaction was almost universally negative, and at times violently so. The tango had come to represent the cultural identity of several generations of poor immigrants and of Argentine society in general. Altering it was perceived as an attack on the very definition of what it meant to be Argentinean. Piazzolla was seen in some circles not only as an artistic defector, but also as a political traitor whose music verged on the unpatriotic. A powerful anti-Piazzolla movement quickly arose that occasionally resorted to threats on the composer's life. He was despised by purists and traditionalists and ignored by the Argentine government, despite his great international success.

Yet his new edgy sound appealed to a younger generation tired of the traditions of their forefathers. Not coincidentally, *nuevo tango* became associated with a new liberal political outlook, whereas the old tango had been associated with repressive dictatorships. In retrospect, rather than destroying the tango, Piazzolla was rescuing a stagnant style and giving it a boost that made it far more powerful that it would have been otherwise. And despite the fact that he opened the floodgates to innovation and experimentation, Piazzolla managed to preserve what many consider the essence of tango: its profound lyricism and melancholy, its seriousness of purpose, and the sensuality and raw sexual violence it drew from its origins in the harsh life of the *arrabal*. In the end, *nuevo tango* did for the tango what *salsa* did for the Cuban *son*: it infused it with a surge of popularity, though it never regained the glories of its heyday in the 1920s and 1930s. Like the first tangos a half century earlier, the *nuevo tango* had to be accepted first by European and North American audiences before coming full circle and gaining acceptance in its native land. Though Piazzolla's music still meets some resistance in Argentina, he is now generally recognized as one of the greatest exponents of the genre.

Recommended Listening: "Libertango" and "Buenos Aires hora cero" by Ástor Piazzolla, from the CD *The Essential Tangos of Ástor Piazzolla*.

Recommended Listening: "Adiós, Nonino" by Ástor Piazzolla, from the CD *Ástor Piazzolla–Grandes del tango Vol. 1*.

Nuevo tango: "Adiós, Nonino"

Music: Ástor Piazzolla (1959)
Instrumentation: bandoneón, piano, strings, bass
Notes: Piazzolla wrote this piece, which translates as "Goodbye, Grandpa," a few days after the death of his father in 1959. Piazzolla recorded it more than 20 times with different arrangements, and many other artists have covered it as well. In this recording, the *bandoneón* is the star, though the strings and piano take turns carrying portions of the melody. The main theme, an emotional lament, is hinted at early in the recording and is played in full by the bandoneón at 0:59.

Piazzolla was not the only proponent of *nuevo tango*, just its most visible. Other important artists included Roberto Goyeneche, Julio Sosa, and Amelita Baltar. The 1980s and 1990s saw another relative decline in the popularity of the tango, though important artists—including some of Piazzolla's pupils and collaborators—continued to innovate the genre, with artistic and even commercial success. Some of the most prominent are Pablo Ziegler, long-time pianist in Piazzolla's bands, the *bandoneón* players Marcelo Nisinman and Rodolfo Mederos, and the singers Susana Rinaldi and Maria Graña. Meanwhile, traditional tango has not gone by the wayside, and in myriad establishments in Buenos Aires or Montevideo one can still find a traditional *sexteto*, performing mournful songs that accompany sensual dancing. Various academic institutions have emerged dedicated to its preservation, including the Academia Nacional del Tango (founded in 1990), the Academia Porteña del Lunfardo, dedicated to the linguistic study of Argentine slang, and the Universidad del Tango, which has been offering a bachelor's degree in tango studies since 1992. Though the dance might no longer be at the forefront of popular culture, Argentines of all ages still take their tango seriously. More than a century after its inception, it remains a thriving tradition, still the most important expression of Argentine national identity.

> **Recommended Listening:** "Balada para mi muerte" and "Los paraguas de Buenos Aires" by Amelita Baltar, from the CD *Piazzolla y Amelita Baltar*.
>
> **Recommended Listening:** "La rayuela" and "Bajo cero" by Pablo Ziegler, from the CD *Bajo cero*.

Other Folk Dances and Songs

Though the *tango* is easily the most famous Argentine style, it is by no means the only one. In rural areas, Argentine folk songs, ballads, and dances—called generally *música del interior*—reflect traditional Native, Black, and Criollo customs. Folk dances are often in two-part form, and tend to be in the Latin American *sesquiáltera* that combines $\frac{6}{8}$ and $\frac{3}{4}$ meter. Folk costumes, similar to the gaucho attire, reflect the rural nature of the dances: men wear loose ruffled shirts and tight vests and the *bombacha* trousers, all held together by a sash. Hat, riding boots, and a neckerchief round out the costume. Women wear colorful flowing skirts called *polleras* and embroidered blouses and vests. Their hair is often worn in tresses or in a tight bun.

With the urban migration in the first half of the twentieth century, a few rural styles managed to eke out some popularity in urban centers, competing with the enormous popularity of the tango, and after the latter's decline in the 1950s, some of them managed to gain national prominence. Thus, from the southern part of the country came the energetic *loncomeo*, influenced by indigenous Mapuche features. The *pericón*, from the central *pampas*, is a stylized contradance for four couples, with a prompter calling the figures. The *cielito*, also found in neighboring Chile and Uruguay, has its roots in the wars of independence. The *remedio* is a handkerchief dance found in the northern and central areas. But the most prominent Argentine folk dances are the *zamba*, the *chacarera*, and the *chamamé*. Argentine folk music is showcased in important festivals, the most prominent of which is undoubtedly the Festival de Folklore de Cosquín, a nine-day event held every January since 1961 in the central province of Córdoba.

ZAMBA   The Argentine *zamba* is not to be confused with the Brazilian *samba*, though the two words are pronounced the same way. The term refers to the African-derived dance of the *zambos*—those of mixed Native and Black ancestry. The dance is related to the Chilean *cueca*, and both dances are descended from the Peruvian *zamacueca*, which became popular in the first half of the nineteenth century (see Chapter 8). The first *zambas* emerged in the northern and western regions of Argentina, particularly in the provinces of Santiago del Estero and Mendoza. By the twentieth century, the dance had become popular throughout the country. Today, one can find *zambas* virtually everywhere, ranging from glossy, tourist-oriented productions in the hotels of Buenos Aires to the traditional country-dances still performed on a Saturday night in the villages of the interior. It is so widespread that April 7 has been declared national *zamba* day.

Like many folk dances in the region, the *zamba* is a courtship dance that uses the handkerchief as an obligatory prop to express the intentions and desires of the amorous couple. The tempo is stately, the steps graceful, accentuating the *sesquiáltera* rhythms. The choreography reflects a traditional encounter between the partners: the man makes the advances, which are resisted by the woman; the man perseveres, the woman holds out to the very end. The dancers do not hold each other, but are connected by their handkerchiefs. When it is clear the man's advances have been successful, he "possesses" the women by wrapping his handkerchief around her. *Zambas* are also song forms: an introduction typically precedes three verses, often interrupted by an instrumental bridge. Lyrics can have wide-ranging themes, including love songs and commentary on political and cultural events. Several artists have had great success recording the dance, including Argentino Luna, Los Hermanos Ábalos, and especially the legendary folk musician Atahualpa Yupanqui, an important singer and poet who was a great proponent of Argentina's folk music. Yupanqui's lyrics recalled life on the pampas and the romanticism of the gaucho, but he also brought attention to the social conditions of Argentina's marginalized Native people. As a champion of social justice, he was a key player in the emergence of the *nueva canción* in the 1960s. By the same token, many *nueva canción* artists like Mercedes Sosa have embraced Argentine folk dances with great success.

Recommended Listening: "La añera," "La pobrecita," and "Piedra y camino" by Atahualpa Yupanqui, from the CD *Solo lo mejor de Atahualpa Yupanqui*.

Recommended Listening: "Agitando pañuelos" and "La zamba alegre" by Hermanos Ábalos, from the CD *Nuestras danzas*.

Recommended Listening: "Zamba para no morir" and "Luna Tucumana" by Los cantores de Quilla Huasi, from the CD *Sus mejores temas*.

Recommended Listening: "Zamba de la distancia" and "Zamba del riego" by Mercedes Sosa, from the CD *Canciones con fundamento*.

CHACARERA The music of Argentina's northwest has much in common with that of the Andean region, and particularly of its neighbors Chile and Bolivia. Yet one folk dance has transcended its regional origin and become popular throughout the country. This is the *chacarera*, a dance that emerged in the nineteenth century on the *chacras*—farms and rural estates in the northwest. It is a line dance with moderately fast tempos and strongly accented syncopations in $\frac{6}{8}$ or *sesquiáltera* rhythms. Verses alternate with instrumental passages, during which the dancers perform set movements. Couples face each other, advancing and receding, hands held high with palms forward at all times, and only occasionally coming together. One partner performs a turn while the other looks on, keeping the beat with handclaps. Men flaunt their syncopated *zapateado* steps, while the women display the *zarandeo*, twirling their flowing skirts with their hands in a fanning gesture. Despite its festive nature, the music that accompanies the *chacarera* is often wistful and melancholy, reflecting its Andean origins. In the mountains, *chacareras* are often sung in the Quechua language and played with *quena* flutes. But the song and dance form that most Argentines are familiar with is usually sung in Spanish and accompanied by guitars, pianos, violins, and/or accordions, and with the obligatory Andean *bombo* drum. In the beginning of the twentieth century, the *chacarera* could be increasingly found in urban centers, with early composers such as Andrés Chazarreta and Manuel Gómez Carrillo. By the 1950s, it had become a permanent part of Argentine consciousness, with important proponents such as Los Chachaleros, the duo Pepe and Gerardo Nuñez from the province of Tucumán, and especially the Carabajal family, led by the patriarch Carlos, and who have been a major presence in Argentine *chacarera* for over half a century.

Recommended Listening: "Chacarera del rancho" by Hermanos Ábalos, from the CD *Nuestras danzas*.

Recommended Listening: "Nadita" by Atahualpa Yupanqui, from the CD *Solo lo mejor de Atahualpa Yupanqui*.

Recommended Listening: "Chacarera del Pockoy Pacha" and "Santiago del estero" by Los Carabajal, from the CD *Serie histórica*.

Recommended Listening: "Chacarera del 55" by Mercedes Sosa, from the CD *Canciones con fundamento*.

Recommended Listening: "Chacarera del patio" by Cuti y Roberto Carabajal, from the CD *A bailar chacareras*.

Chacarera: "Chacarera del patio"

Music: Carlos Carabajal
Lyrics: P. R. Trullenque
Instrumentation: guitars, violins, *bombo* drum
Notes: This *chacarera* features Cuti and Roberto Carabajal. The *sesquiáltera* rhythm is steadily strummed by the guitar and *bombo*. As you count **one**-two-**three**-four-**five**-six, notice how the seemingly straightforward meter becomes ambiguous as the violins and voices enter off the beat. The nostalgic lyrics allude to the simple but wholesome life in rural patios, with references to some of Argentina's most prominent folkloric groups, including Los Tucu-Tucus ("the gophers") and Los Cuyoyos ("the fireflies").

Pintao de sol y luna, techaditos de estrellas	*Painted with sun and moon, with starlit ceilings,*
Lindos son en mi pago esos patios de tierra.	*These earthen patios where I come from are lovely.*
Patio cara de viejo donde tendía mi mama	*Old-face patio where my mother*
El pan que en la batea lavando lo ganaba.	*Hung her washing to earn her bread.*
Y pa' los carnavales con cuete y chacareras	*And during carnivals, with fireworks and chacareras,*
Embarrando chinitas armabamos trincheras.	*Armed behind fences we threw mud at the girls.*
Chacarera de tierra, luna color de chango	*Chacarera of the land, red-colored moon,*
Sol lleno de coyuyos, son patios de Santiago.	*Coyuyo-filled sunlight, these are the patios of Santiago.*
Siestas chamuscadoras de hombres bichos y plantas	*Burning siestas of men, insects, and plants*
En patios arbolados se hacen agua y tinajas.	*In tree-lined patios alongside water and earthen jars.*
Si habré bebido estrellas que a mi vaso bajaban	*I have drunk the starlight that descends into my glass*
En las noches de amigos, patio, copla y guitarra.	*In the night with friends, patio, song, and guitar.*
Tucu-tucus alumbran las noches de concierto	*The Tucu-Tucus light up the nights in concert*
De grillos trovadores en los patios desiertos.	*Like grasshopper troubadours in deserted patios.*
Chacarera de tierra, luna color de chango	*Chacarera of the land, red-colored moon,*
Sol lleno de coyuyos, son patios de Santiago.	*Coyuyo-filled sunlight, these are the patios of Santiago.*

CHAMAMÉ Meanwhile, a completely different kind of music was emerging in the northeast, a region heavily settled by German and Polish immigrants who brought with them their accordions and dances such as the polka and the mazurka. The region is also populated by Guaraní Natives, the predominant ethnic group in neighboring Paraguay. In the nineteenth century, these influences combined to produce a dance called the *polca correntina* ("polka from the province of Corrientes"). By the twentieth century, it had evolved into the *chamamé*, a term derived from a Guaraní phrase that means "song and dance." *Chamamé* songs are often in the Guaraní language. The dances can be either slow or fast, but the steps are always graceful, and, unlike both the *zamba* and *chacarera*, the couples embrace closely, though at times the man will perform intricate *zapateado* steps while his partner looks on. The most prevalent instrument is the accordion, often complemented by a *bandoneón*, violin, guitars, and double bass. *Chamamé* accordionists traditionally have attained a high level of virtuosity. In the 1940s, the popularity of the *chamamé* began expanding throughout the northeast, and, later, into urban areas. By the 1970s it had become prevalent throughout the country, as well as in Chile, Paraguay, and southern Brazil. As with other genres across the continent, *chamamé* has both a traditional style and a more contemporary pop-oriented version. Perhaps the most renowned *chamamé* artist was Tránsito Cocomarola, who dominated the genre starting in the 1930s until his death in 1974. Other important *chamamé* artists from the early part of the twentieth century included Isaco Abitbol, Ernesto Montiel, the guitarist Antonio Niz, and the singing duo Verón-Palacios. In recent years, the genre has been represented by artists such as Chango Spasiuk, Alejandro Brittes, and Raúl Barbosa, who has been called the greatest accordion player in Argentina. Important *chamamé* festivals have emerged, notably the Baradero Festival, held yearly in Buenos Aires, the Festival Ramallo Pora festival in the town of Ramallo, and the National Chamamé Festival in Corrientes.

> **Recommended Listening:** "Pampa del indio" and "Kilómetro 11" by Trio Cocomarola, from the CD *Colección aniversario*.

> **Recommended Listening:** "Polca rural" and "El casamiento ucraniano testimonio 2" by Chango Spasiuk, from the CD *Polcas de mi tierra*.

Música tropical

Despite its reputation for having slow, dramatic, heart-wrenching music—best exemplified by the tango—Argentina also has its versions of hot and fast *música tropical*, whose origins lie in the Caribbean and other parts of the continent.

CUARTETO In the 1930s and 1940s, Argentine popular music consisted mainly of tangos and milongas (still played by *orquestas típicas*), as well as waltzes, polkas, and other dances performed on Saturday nights by touring ensembles called *orquestas características*. In the city and province of Córdoba, in central Argentina, a musical style emerged that would offer a popular alternative to the predominance of the music from Buenos Aires. This was *cuarteto*, famously born on June 4, 1943, when the group Cuarteto Leo performed on a Córdoba radio station, and subsequently in local dancehalls. Cuarteto Leo was formed by Augusto Marzano, whose daughter Leonor (after whom the group was named) developed the piano pattern called *tunga-tunga* that would become typical of the style. *Cuarteto* was so-called because it consisted of four instrumentalists—piano, accordion, violin, and double bass—plus a vocalist. Its smaller personnel allowed for easier performance and touring than did the cumbersome *orquestas*. The accordion, borrowed from the then-emerging *chamamé*, lent *cuarteto* a distinctive sound that appealed to the rural population of Córdoba. Though it originally drew from rural folk dances, *cuarteto* became a lively urban genre specifically for dancing, with upbeat rhythms that borrowed heavily from the Cuban *son* and the Dominican merengue. *Cuarteto* music is typically in duple meter, with high-speed tempos. The characteristic *tunga-tunga* pattern resembles the *oom-pah oom-pah* of the polka, though it is played very fast, with a continuous, almost hypnotic beat. The *cuarteto* repertoire, then and now, consists mainly of love songs and humorous scenes from everyday life, with melodies usually in the minor mode.

After their 1943 radio premiere, *Cuarteto Leo* became extremely popular in Córdoba and spawned many imitators, particularly after it began recording in 1953. It remained the most important band in the region until the 1980s. In the last half century, *cuarteto* styles and instrumentations have expanded, with various subgenres influenced by jazz and rock, Dominican merengue, and Cuban salsa. By the 1970s, *cuarteto* ensembles had grown to 12 or 15 musicians and included drum sets and Latin percussion, while synthesizers, electric guitars, and electric bass often replaced the violin and bass. The accordion continued to be popular, though in some ensembles it was supplanted by brass instruments borrowed from salsa, such as trumpets, trombones, and saxophones.

Not surprisingly, the Buenos Aires elite, who considered the music common and low class, rejected *cuarteto*. As a result, the style failed to make inroads into *porteño* culture. During the military dictatorships of the 1970s, *cuarteto* was repressed politically and was even banned during the 1978 Soccer World Cup. Yet *cuarteto* remained for the most part apolitical, without the element of social protest that characterized, for example, *nueva canción*. By the mid-1980s, with the end of the dictatorships, and because of popular television broadcasts and recordings, *cuarteto* was finally embraced in Buenos Aires and the rest of country, and even into neighboring countries. Today, Córdoba remains the capital of *cuarteto*, where it is still wildly popular, with dancehalls, radio stations, and record sales specifically dedicated to the genre. Popular *cuarteto* concerts have become almost ritual in nature, with huge fan followings. Perhaps the most important *cuarteto* artist in modern times is the colorful Carlos "La Mona" Jiménez, whose idiosyncratic gestures and singing style became a signature characteristic of his music. Jiménez, an important political figure who opposed the military dictatorships of the 1970s and 1980s, has become a symbol for Argentine youth. Other important *cuarteto* artists include Negro Videla and Rodrigo Bueno, who is usually known by his first name, as well as the *cuartetos* Tru-la-lá, Cachumba, and Banda Express.

Recommended Listening: "Se quema el rancho" and "Del brazo con la suerte" by Cuarteto Leo, from the CD *Cuarteto Leo: 20 grandes éxitos*.

Recommended Listening: "Beso a beso," "Bum bum" and "La novia blanca" by Carlos "La Mona" Jiménez, from the CD *El original Bum bum*.

Recommended Listening: "La Mano de Dios" by Rodrigo Bueno, from the CD *La mano de Dios*.

BAILANTA With the gradual rise of *cuarteto* in the 1970s, dancehalls called *bailantas* emerged in Buenos Aires, where an upscale offshoot of *cuarteto* became popular, also called *bailanta*. The style was influenced by Colombian *cumbia* and Dominican merengue, as well as Cuban salsa, which was in the process of conquering the entire continent. The accordion remained a prominent instrument, accompanied by electric guitars, bass, synthesizers, and the usual Latin percussion. Yet, unlike *cuarteto*, whose roots are squarely in Argentina's rural folk dances, *bailanta* quickly became a pop-oriented urban sound and has been criticized for being superficial, glossy, and excessively commercial. *Bailanta* was politically acceptable to the government and was seen as a Buenos Airean alternative to the Cordoban style. By the late 1980s, it had become a sales phenomenon, rivaling the success of *cuarteto*. Many homegrown *bailanta* bands emerged, including prominently Ykarus and Los Sultanes, though these bands for the most part broke little stylistic new ground. Today, *bailantas* remain fancy Latin discos with multi-colored starlights, showcasing fabulous dancers, where Buenos Airean youth flock to hear the latest imported or homegrown Latin band.

CUMBIA VILLERA But *música tropical* was also popular in the extended slums and shantytowns of Buenos Aires. These were the infamous *villas miserias*—"misery cities"—in reference to the extreme economic conditions that predominated there, exacerbated by Argentina's late twentieth-century economic crises that disproportionately affected the working class. One of the most popular styles in these *villas miserias* was the Colombian *cumbia*. In the mid-1990s, some of the *villas* residents, including notably the *cumbiero* Pablo Lescano, decided to incorporate their own themes, ideas, and experiences into the Colombian genre. The result was the *cumbia villera*, a vibrant, hard-edged style that reflects the misery and harsh living of the shantytowns. Lescano formed several groups including Flor de Piedra and Damas Gratis, which quickly popularized *cumbia villera*, first within the *villas* themselves and then throughout the city. Other groups quickly followed, including Los Pibes Chorros, Bukaneros, Metaguacha, Jalá-Jal, Sacude, La Chala, Dama Negra, and Yerba Brava.

Cumbia villera takes the typical arpeggiated bass-line of the *cumbia* and adds back-rhythms taken from reggae and ska, as well as a harsh vocal style and body language borrowed from hard rock and North American hip-hop. Cuban percussion is complemented by synthesizers and other electronic instruments, as well as by the sampling and "scratching" sounds of rap music.

Like myriad other popular styles born in Latin American slums and shanty-towns, *cumbia villera* addresses the poverty, discrimination, and harsh living conditions of urban existence. Yet an important difference is that there is no marked racial component: the inhabitants of the *villas miserias*—and thus the proponents of *cumbia villera*—are overwhelmingly White. In spite of this, some commentators have characterized the genre as Argentina's "Black music," and some of the artists themselves have deliberately taken on characteristics—even stereotypes—of artists in other Black-oriented styles, typically North American rap and hip-hop. As in those styles, issues of crime and violence, resistance to political and police authority, gang membership and street credibility are paramount to artists of *cumbia villera*. Youth-oriented lyrics reflect their marginalization from society, the raw living of the *villas miserias*, and the problems of the modern underclass. Songs speak of brushes with the law, of incarceration, of treacherous women (for it is a male-dominated genre), of alcoholism and drug addiction, and the glorification of crime. As in the tango, there is a sense of fatalism, of being unable to alter the direction of one's life. Yet while tango songs reflected sorrow and regret, these are songs of desperation.

Unlike the often glossy and superficial *bailanta*, the heartfelt nature of *cumbia villera* made it an important form of social identity for poor Argentines, much as the tango had done a century earlier. Predictably, *cumbia villera* was once again disdained, rejected and condemned by the upper classes, though by the turn of the millennium, it had transcended the *villas* themselves and was embraced by the working classes of Buenos Aires, Montevideo, and neighboring countries, and as far away as New York and Miami. An important step in its evolution was its association with many of the country's soccer teams and individual stars, some of whom emerged from the very slums that gave birth to the style. Since 2005, it has been shaped by Puerto Rican *reggaetón*, thus producing a new subgenre, *cumbiatón*.

> **Recommended Listening:** "Sos un botón" and "La cumbia de los vagos" by Flor de Piedra, from the CD *La vanda mas loca*.

> **Recommended Listening:** "Andrea," "El tano pastita" and "Sentimiento villero" by Los Pibes Chorros, from the CD *Discografía completa*.

CHILE

Chile is hard to classify because of its distinctive geographical features that place it in several cultural spheres. The country has an unusual shape, a thin strip of land 110 miles at its widest yet over 2,600 miles long. Its southernmost tip nears the Antarctic, while its northernmost area reaches north of the Tropic of Capricorn, at the borders with Peru and Bolivia. With the Andes to the east and the Pacific Ocean to the west, most of the territory consists of high mountains that gradually—but sometimes abruptly—fall into the ocean. In between lie fertile plateaus, home to most of the population and the country's economic activity, and rivers that have carved out impressive valleys.

The Inca Empire influenced Chile's northern areas in pre-colonial times. Native groups such as the Atacamas and the Mapuches, whose descendants continued to resist the European presence well into the nineteenth century, populated other parts. First sighted by Ferdinand Magellan in 1520, the Chilean coast was explored by Pedro de Valdivia, who founded the city of Santiago in 1541 and became the territory's first governor. Part of the Viceroyalty of Peru, it was mostly neglected by Spain during the colonial period. Chile's independence movement, led by Bernardo O'Higgins, began in 1810—before any of its South American neighbors—and was ultimately successful in 1818. Since then, Chile has had its share of wars, political instability, and military dictatorships. The country gained much of its northern territory in the 1880s after the successful War of the Pacific against Peru and Bolivia. One of the more notorious chapters in Chilean history occurred in 1973, when socialist president Salvador Allende, who had instituted important land reforms, was overthrown and killed in a military coup widely believed to be orchestrated by the U.S. Central Intelligence Agency (CIA). Allende was replaced by the right-wing military strongman Augusto Pinochet, whose dictatorship lasted until 1990 and was marked by repression, censorship, violence, and economic hardships. In recent years, Chile has achieved a semblance of democratic and economic stability. Today 30 percent of Chileans are of European descent, with 65 percent Mestizo, about 1 percent of African descent, and the remainder mostly Native Chileans.

Chile is usually divided into the northern, central, and southern regions. The fertile central valley is home to Chile's famous vineyards. Almost 90 percent of Chileans live here, one-third of them in the capital Santiago. Other important cities include the seaport Valparaíso and the famous resort Viña del Mar. The rest of the country is sparsely populated: The northern region encompasses the arid Atacama desert, considered the driest area in the world, while the mountainous southern region is characterized by spectacular glaciers, lakes, and fjords, as well as hundreds of islands and rocky outcrops. The music of the northern region is closely related to Andean cultures, and is discussed in Chapter 8. The southern region, despite the paucity of its population, is disproportionately rich in terms of its music and folklore, particularly in the island of Chiloé, which has produced various styles that have become influential in the rest of the country. The central region is musically more similar to the River Plate, though separated from it by the Andean range. It is here that can be found the country's most representative folk culture, that of the *huaso*.

The *Huaso*

Chile has an important cowboy culture, equivalent to—and not unlike—the gauchos of neighboring Argentina. These are the *huasos*, ranchers, and cattle drivers who traditionally lived in rural areas of the central region. *Huasos* are able horsemen, and their skills are displayed at popular rodeos and patriotic parades and holidays. The *huaso*'s female counterpart is the *china*, the young virtuous maiden to whom the *huaso* dedicates his valor and his artistry. (The term "*china*" is unrelated to the Asian country, but rather is derived from the Quechua word for "maiden.") The *huaso*'s costume is characterized by a ubiquitous sash worn around the waist, riding boots with spurs, and a multi-colored poncho. Much of Chilean rural culture and folklore revolves around the *huasos*.

Chilean Folk Songs

As in Argentina and other parts of Spanish America, much of Chile's folk music was derived from colonial Spanish songs like the *villancico* and narrative ballads like the *romance*, as well as the *copla* and *décima* poetic forms. By the twentieth century, they had evolved into forms such as the *corrido*, *verso*, and *tonada*, discussed below. As in Argentina, Chilean folk songs are often sung by two singers in parallel thirds, similar to the doubling of panpipes in the Andean region, though they are usually upbeat and in major keys and do not display the melancholy so often found in Andean and Argentine folklore. Songs tend to be strophic, use *sesquiáltera* rhythms and are often sung in a high-pitched nasal style.

The instrument of choice is once again the guitar, but also the *guitarrón*, a smallish guitar not to be confused with the huge Mexican bass instrument of the same name and used in *mariachi* ensembles. The Chilean *guitarrón*, related to the colonial *vihuela*, is a high-pitched instrument with a wide neck and 25 strings, arranged in five courses of two, three, and four strings each, as well as independent strings called *diablitos*. It is found exclusively in Chile, where it accompanies songs and poetic forms in rural areas, as well as *velorios* (wakes) and other religious genres. Other instruments important to Chilean folklore are the lute-like *bandola*, the harp, and the *rabel*, a bowed instrument with three strings that is related to early violins of the same name. Accordions, either with keys or buttons, are popular mostly in the southern region.

POETAS POPULARES An important factor in the development of Chilean song was the emergence in the second half of the nineteenth century of singer/songwriters called generally *poetas populares* (sometimes referred to as *payadores*, like their gaucho counterparts). These ambulating musicians traveled the countryside and performed in villages, towns, and rural areas, much like the medieval troubadours from whom they are indirectly descended. By the end of the century, many of their poetic songs were printed in sheet music called *lira popular* ("popular lyrics"). *Poetas* accompany themselves with a guitar or *guitarrón* and usually sing with a very loud and emotional vocal style. Their preferred form is the *verso*, an improvisatory poetic form that is moderately slow, in a major key, and typically consists of five verses with an introduction and a concluding section. Their repertoire can be divided between *canto a lo humano* ("songs about humans" or secular songs) and *canto a lo divino* ("songs about the divine" or sacred songs). *Canto a lo humano*, performed at private parties or town celebrations, addresses issues of love, history, or literature but can also be a pointed critique of social ills, local or national politics, or philosophical contemplations of contemporary life. *Canto a lo divino* occurs primarily during children's wakes, but also at religious events such as Cruz de Mayo celebrations held on May 3. A circle of eight to ten *poetas* perform religious-oriented songs that comment on Biblical stories and characters, bidding farewell to the *angelito*, the angelic child who has passed away. The *canto* can sometimes last all night, and in the morning, the *poetas* will switch to the secular *canto a lo humano*.

As in the Argentine *payada*, two *poetas* occasionally square off in a lively contest called *contrapunto*, each performing a verse to which the other must respond, preserving the melody, rhythm, and rhyme scheme of the verse. Several legendary *poetas* have become part of Chilean mythology, most prominently Liborio Salgado, who in the nineteenth century allegedly competed in a *contrapunto* with the Devil himself. Salgado's grandson Lázaro also became an important *poeta*, as did the famous *guitarrón* player Isaías Angulo. In modern times, notable *poetas* include Manuel Sánchez, Francisco Astorga, and Juan Carlos Bustamante. Various festivals dedicated to the genre have emerged, and *poeta cantos* have been published, recorded and studied, forming an important literary genre that has been embraced not only by academics but by Chileans in general as an expression of Chile's rural culture.

> **Recommended Listening:** "Décimas por el nacimiento" by Conjunto Cuncumén, from the CD *Antología de la música folklórica de Chile*.

TONADA Another important folk song is the *tonada* ("tune"), descended from the secular *romances* and semi-religious *villancicos* of the colonial period, and traditionally performed in local village celebrations or feasts of patron saints. *Tonadas* are typically slow and lyrical, though sometimes fast passages alternate with slow ones. They can be sung by one singer or as duets in parallel thirds, accompanied by one or several guitars, but sometimes also by a piano or a harp. *Tonadas* typically consist of several verses and chorus and are in major keys and in *sesquiáltera* meter. They can be sentimental love songs, social commentaries, or work songs related to rural tasks. Like most ballad forms, *tonadas* are not danced. The *tonada* was directly influential on the development of the *nueva canción*, and though the latter has somewhat overshadowed the former in recent decades, the *tonada* continues to remain popular in both rural and urban settings. *Tonadas* are also found in neighboring Argentina, as well as Venezuela, Mexico, and the Spanish Caribbean.

> **Recommended Listening:** "Río, río" by Los Huasos Quincheros and "El rodeo" by Raul Gardy, from the CD *Chile típico, Vol. 4*.

> **Recommended Listening:** "El delantal de la china" by Gladys Briones, from the CD *Chile típico, Vol. 5*.

> **Recommended Listening:** "Mi banderita chilena" by Silvia Infantas and "Tonadas de Manuel Rodriguez " by Coro Chile Canta, from the CD *Antología de la música folklórica de Chile*.

Folk Dances: *Cueca*

The most prominent folk dance in Chile is the *cueca*, a *criollo* dance related to the Argentine *zamba* discussed earlier. Both dances are descended from the Peruvian *zamacueca*, which began infiltrating the southern part of the continent in the 1820s and soon thereafter became popular throughout Chile, Argentina, and Bolivia. The term *cueca* is derived from the African word *clueca*, supposedly a reference to the proud attitude of mating chickens or turkeys, and the dance ostensibly parodies their movements. Yet unlike the *zamacueca*, which tends to reflect the sad melancholy typical of the Andean region, the Chilean *cueca* is upbeat, joyful, lively, and usually in a major key. It is performed in taverns, private parties, town festivities, and during patriotic holidays and other national celebrations. In rural settings, it is prominent at *fiestas* connected with the yearly agricultural cycle or with patron-saint feasts.

The *cueca* is a couples' dance in which the partners only come in contact by means of the ubiquitous handkerchief, held in the right hand. The basic steps resemble those of other dances on the continent, including the Venezuelan *joropo* and the Mexican *jarabe*. Dancers alternate between the waltz-like *valseado*, the graceful *escobillado* ("like a brush"), where the partners come together and separate in a sliding motion, and the percussive *zapateado*, by which the *huaso* attempts to impress—and seduce—his partner. The *cueca* begins with the *huaso* calling out the object of his affections, after which the couple promenades in a circle. As the verses begin, they perform various circular figures, full- or half-turns, and small jumps. As in the chicken mating ritual that originated the dance, the *huaso* circles the *china*, who can signal her interest by coquettishly swirling her skirt with her hands. The *huaso*'s advances are initially rebuffed, but in the end, of course, the couple will ultimately reconcile and the seduction will be successful. As in the Argentinean *zamba*, the dance ends when the *huaso*, on his knees, finally "captures" the *china* by wrapping his handkerchief around her.

The lyrics of *cueca* songs, as befits its nature as a courtship dance, typically speak of love, either fulfilled or unrequited, but can also speak of family and community affairs, historical events, or reminiscences of old times. Urban *cuecas* can address social or political issues such as poverty or injustice. Typical *cuecas* have three parts, each consisting of verses that alternate with the chorus and a concluding section called *remate*. Like the Argentine *zamba* and *chacarera*, rhythms are once again in *sesquiáltera*, and are traditionally accompanied by a guitar and a harp, with another musician doing the *tamborileo*—rhythmic patterns drummed with the hands on the body of the guitar or the harp. They are complemented by the *pandero* tambourine, the *cacharaina* (a donkey jawbone scraped like a *güiro*), and the Andean *bombo* bass drum. The assembled audience is a big part of the festivities, and it is expected to join in with clapping, singing, and yelling.

Though the *cueca* was most famously adopted by *huaso* culture, it also became popular in all regions of the country, in both urban and rural settings, with variations in style and choreography. Thus, the *cueca nortina*, from the northern area, is influenced by some of the Aymara and Quechua dances of the Andean region and accompanied by Andean *zampoña* pan-pipes, *quena* flutes, and *charango* guitars or sometimes a brass orchestra. They are usually faster than the central and southern *cuecas*, but do not emphasize the *zapateado* as much, preferring instead the more graceful *valseado*. The *cueca chilota* ("from Chiloé") in the southern region is a loud and energetic dance with more prominent jumping and *zapateado* steps. It is often accompanied by accordions that complement the guitar and percussion and is sometimes characterized by a reversal in gender roles, as the woman pursues the man, who feigns lack of interest.

The central region, being the most populous, has many variations, including the *cueca campesina*, a slow style found in rural areas, usually sung by women; the *cueca brava*, found in urban working-class neighborhoods; the *cueca porteña* ("from the port," that is, from Valparaíso), whose songs speak of seafarers and the underbelly of port life; the *cueca criolla*, a more urban style which has achieved commercial success; the *cueca chilenera*, another urban style that can be accompanied by guitars, accordions, pianos, and various percussion instruments; the *cueca valseada* ("waltz-like"); and the humorous *cueca cómica*. The *cueca* was declared the country's national dance in 1979, and today remains the most popular dance in Chile.

> **Recommended Listening:** "Huillincana [cueca chilota]" by Conjunto Millaray, from the CD *Chile típico, Vol. 1.*

> **Recommended Listening:** "La Rosa y el clavel" and "Barquilla de amor" by Silvia Infantas y los Baqueanos, from the CD *Heroes y tradiciones.*

> **Recommended Listening:** "Cueca a Balmaceda" by Gabriela Pizarro, from the CD *Canto campesino.*

> **Recommended Listening:** "La cueca del bautizo" and "El huaso enamorado" by Hermanos Campos, from the CD *50 cuecas.*

CDII, Track 23: *Cueca:* "Adiós Santiago querido"

Music and Lyrics: Segundo Zamora
Instrumentation: guitar, accordion, *pandero* tambourine, *cacharaina* scraper, *bombo* drum
Notes: The friendly banter between musicians at the beginning is typical of the informality of *cueca* folk dances. The song makes references to familiar landmarks and sites in Santiago, the capital of Chile, but also to the *huasos*, and it is presumed the narrator is leaving the city for the rural homeland. Though this is a song of longing, it remains upbeat and joyful. As in many such dances, the *sesquiáltera* rhythms combine $\frac{3}{4}$ and $\frac{6}{8}$ meters, with ambiguous syncopations clouding the beat. Try clapping **one**-two-three-**four**-five-six, then **one**-two-**three**-four-**five**-six and notice how in both cases the singing and instruments often play against the meter.

Adiós, Santiago querido,	*Goodbye beloved Santiago,*
Adiós, Parque Forestal, si, ay ay ay.	*Goodbye, Forestal Park, yes, ay ay ay.*
Cerro de Santa Lucía,	*Santa Lucía Hill,*
Tambien la Quinta Normal, si, ay ay ay.	*And Quinta Normal Park, yes, ay ay ay.*
Adiós, Santiago querido, si, ay ay ay.	*Goodbye beloved Santiago, yes, ay ay ay.*
Adiós, calle San Pablo, con Matucana,	*Goodbye, San Pablo street, and Matucana,*
Donde toman los guapos	*Where the good-looking ones go drinking*
En Damajuana, si, ay ay ay.	*In Damajuana, yes, ay ay ay.*
Adiós, calle San Pablo, con Matucana,	*Goodbye, San Pablo Street, and Matucana,*
Si, ay ay ay.	*Yes, ay ay ay.*
En Damajuana, sí, Parque Cousiño,	*In Damajuana, yes, at Cousiño Park,*
Donde toman los huasos, también los niños.	*where the huasos drink and the children too*
Si, ay ay ay.	*Yes, ay ay ay.*
En la calle Bandera, alguien me espera.	*On Bandera street, someone waits for me.*

The Popularization of Chilean Folk Music

As virtually everywhere on the continent, rural folk styles like the *tonada* and the *cueca* were brought by migrants to the cities in the first half of the twentieth century, where they were influenced by urban features, often shedding their connection with the ranchers of the central region. In the 1920s and 1930s, various groups began disseminating and popularizing this music, singing about the romantic *huaso* life in urban bars, restaurants, and nightclubs that catered to the working classes. After they began to be recorded and broadcast on radio, the styles quickly transcended their origins and become popular—even commercially successful—throughout the country, in both rural and urban settings.

Some of the most notable proponents of *huaso* music include Los Cuatro Huasos, Los Huasos Qincheros, Los Hermanos Silva, and Los Provincianos (not to be confused with the Argentine tango group of the same name). Not surprisingly, the music of the *huaso*—even the urbanized version—reflects rural themes, values, and characteristics that have become emblematic of the country itself, even among Chileans who have never lived in rural areas or ridden a horse. Chile's folk music, like that of numerous other countries, has become a symbol of national identity, infused with a variety of emotional meanings such as romance, nostalgia and patriotism.

Recommended Listening: "El tortillero" by Los Cuatro Huasos, from the CD *Lo mejor del folklor chileno*.

An important factor in the popularization of Chilean folk music (as well as *nueva canción* and Andean and Argentine folk music) was the emergence of performance venues called *peñas*. The term *peña* originally referred to a village gathering place where Andean musicians would practice informally. By the

1950s, as folk music became increasingly urbanized, *peñas* had developed into intimate nightclubs and coffee houses in Andean towns and cities, as well as in Chile and the River Plate. Today, *peñas* are popular all over the Americas as well as in Europe. They are specifically dedicated to folk music, whether traditional Chilean or Argentine styles, Andean music, or *nueva canción*. The music is almost invariably acoustic, often consisting of a singer-songwriter with only his or her guitar as accompaniment. The *peña* remains an informal venue for bohemian gatherings where serious conversation or philosophical contemplation are common, a community meeting place for grass-roots left-wing political activists, a place where poetry readings and folk music bring like-minded people together.

It was also in the 1950s that several Chilean folk musicians became popular and commercially successful. These included Margot Loyola, Silvia Infantas, and the husband and wife team of Héctor Pavez and Gabriela Pizarro, who formed the group Millaray. But the leading folk artist was Violeta Parra, who would become an important figure in the emergence of *nueva canción*. In the 1950s, Parra made several recordings that paid tribute to traditional Chilean folk music. One of her songs, "Gracias a la vida," became popular in the United States when it was covered by the folk singer Joan Baez. The daughter of a music professor and classically trained herself, Parra became a world famous singer who continued to record much of Chilean folklore until her death in 1967.

Parra and other folk artists, like their Argentine counterpart Atahualpa Yupanqui, also did important ethnomusicological research, collecting folk songs and dances throughout the region, and publishing important studies. They were driven by a love for their country's music and by a need to instill in their countrymen a similar nationalistic attitude, in order to counteract the enormous influence of foreign—and especially U.S.—culture that pervaded Chile and the rest of Latin America. They are credited with preserving much of Chile's musical patrimony. Prominent folk festivals have showcased Chilean folk music for decades, including the Festival Nacional de Cueca y Tonada Inédita, the Festival del Huaso, and the Festival Folklórico de la Patagonia, held in Punta Arenas, near the southern tip of the continent.

> **Recommended Listening:** Important compilations of traditional Chilean folk music include the two-CD set *Antología de la música folklórica de Chile*, and the five-volume collection *Chile típico*, as well as Violeta Parra's albums *La tonada presentada por Violeta Parra* and *La cueca presentada por Violeta Parra*.

Nueva canción

Had Chile's musical output been limited to its *cuecas*, *tonadas*, and other songs and dances, it would still be considered a major contributor to the world's folk music. But in the 1960s, Chile was only just beginning, and it would soon develop what would become the most important song style in Latin America and one of the most important worldwide. This was *nueva canción* (sometimes called *nueva canción chilena*)—a "new song," so-called to differentiate it from traditional Chilean folklore.

ORIGINS   The rise of *nueva canción* was due to the confluence of three important factors, all of which began to percolate in the late 1950s and 1960s: the work of dedicated folklorists such as Violeta Parra, the Argentine Atahualpa Yupanqui and the Cuban Carlos Puebla, who studied, recorded, and popularized their country's folk music; the growing preeminence of Andean music across the continent; and the hemispheric emergence of a new left-leaning political and social consciousness. Yet it is hard to pinpoint exactly when the new style emerged, for many of its elements surfaced simultaneously across the continent. In Chile, it drew from the country's rich folk music tradition, and not surprisingly some of the prominent folklorists such as Parra and Margot Loyola were involved in the process. One of their most important contributions was their adoption and promotion of Andean music. Parra, especially, had researched many of the styles of Peru, Bolivia, Ecuador, and northern Chile, and began performing them in Santiago. In the process, she became aware of the injustice and oppression of indigenous cultures. Even before *nueva canción*, she was already singing protest songs about these injustices, infusing them with the musical characteristics of the very people she was singing about.

Nueva canción developed primarily in *peñas*, where traditional folk music was already popular. One of the most important was La Peña de los Parra, operated in Santiago by Parra's children Ángel and Isabel. It opened in 1965 and quickly became the epicenter of the movement, where important artists such as Rolando Alarcón, Patricio Manns, and Víctor Jara performed regularly. It established a venue not only for artists to have their music heard, but also for audiences hungry for the new style. *Peñas* quickly multiplied and spread to other countries, as far away as Europe. The musicians themselves began touring and recording, leading inevitably to much stylistic cross-pollination between folk artists from different countries. One famous example occurred in Paris, where Violeta Parra met Gilbert Favre, a French musician who researched and performed Andean music. On Parra's advice, Favre went to Bolivia and founded Los Jairas, one of the most influential groups in both the Andean and *nueva canción* traditions.

As noted earlier, much of traditional Chilean folk music is lively, joyful, and upbeat. *Nueva canción*, by contrast, now adopted the dark melancholy and minor keys borrowed from the *huaynos* and *yaravís* of the Andean region. *Nueva canción* was also infused with a particular poetic sensibility inherited from the *poetas populares*, who used elevated poetry in their *versos* and *décimas*. Some of Chile's most important literary figures, including notably Nicanor Parra (brother of Violeta) and Pablo Neruda, were important influences on the style.

The accompaniment for *nueva canción* is most often a single guitar played by the singer, the medium preferred in the intimate setting of the *peñas*.

In larger venues, and for recording purposes, the guitar is usually comple-mented by traditional instruments such as the Chilean *guitarrón*, the *cuatro* guitar, and the *bombo* drum, but sometimes also by non-traditional instru-ments such as electric guitar and bass. Groups like Inti-Illimani have adopted a more Andean sound, playing traditional instruments such as *zampoñas* (pan-pipes), *quenas* (flutes), and *charangos* (armadillo guitars). Performers often wear regular street clothes but sometimes adopt the traditional Andean dress, marked by multi-colored ponchos and *chullos*—alpaca hats with flaps that cover the ears.

NUEVA CANCIÓN'S POLITICAL OUTLOOK   *Nueva canción* was a youth-oriented style that was solidly grounded in left-wing politics. Not by coincidence, it emerged at a time when political and ideological struggles were occurring simultaneously across the continent. From Canada to Tierra del Fuego, left-of-center principles began to challenge national attitudes, which inevitably affected art and music. Many *nueva canción* artists were political activists, and much of the music consisted of socially committed, politically charged protest songs that were often aimed at Latin American military dictatorships and right-wing governments. Predictably, the music was often repressed by the governments they criticized, who considered it evidence of an insidious and dangerous counterculture.

Lyrics typically displayed concern for peace and social justice and soli-darity with protest movements in other countries, pointing to *nueva canción*'s identity as a hemispheric rather than a national style. Songs were often about revolutionary martyrs (most prominently Che Guevara), fallen comrades such as the singer Víctor Jara, and historical events that highlighted the injustice and violence perpetrated against the working class and indigenous cultures. A common theme was *el imperialismo Yanqui*—"Yankee imperialism"—and many songs attacked the U.S. support of right-wing dictators, the pernicious influence of U.S. corporations, and the Vietnam War. An important rallying cry was: "El pueblo, unido, jamás será vencido!" ("The people, united, will never be defeated!"), from the title of a song written by Sergio Ortega.

> **Recommended Listening:** "El pueblo unido jamás será vencido" by Inti-Illimani, from the CD *Antología, Vol. 1: 1973–1978*.

Nueva canción: "El pueblo unido jamás será vencido"

Music and Lyrics: Sergio Ortega (1970)
Instrumentation: guitar, charango
Notes: This song was first recorded by Quilapayún and used as a song for solidarity dur-ing Salvador Allende's *Unidad Popular* campaign in 1970. After the 1973 coup, this recording by Inti-Illamini turned it into the unofficial anthem of the entire protest move-ment across the continent.

El pueblo unido jamás será vencido . . .	*The people united will never be defeated . . .*
De pie, cantar, que vamos a triunfar.	*Arise, and sing, for we will succeed.*
Avanzan ya banderas de unidad.	*Flags of unity are now making way.*
Y tú vendrás marchando junto a mí,	*And you will march alongside with me,*
Y así verás tu canto y tu bandera florecer.	*And so you'll see your song and flag blossom.*
La luz de un rojo amanecer	*The red light of the dawn*
Anuncia ya la vida que vendrá.	*Already foretells the life that is to come.*
De pie, marchar, el pueblo va a triunfar.	*Arise, advance, the people will succeed.*
Será mejor la vida que vendrá.	*The life to come will be so improved.*
A conquistar nuestra felicidad,	*To realize our joy and happiness,*
Y en un clamor mil voces de combate	*And a clamor of a thousand fighting voices*
Se alzarán, dirán canción de libertad.	*Will rise, will tell a song of freedom.*
Con decisión la patria vencerá.	*With strength of mind the fatherland will win.*
Y ahora el pueblo que se alza en la lucha	*And now the people, arising in the struggle*
Con voz de gigante gritando: ¡adelante!	*With the voice of a giant crying out: Forward!*
El pueblo unido jamás será vencido . . .	*The people united will never be defeated . . .*
La patria está forjando la unidad.	*The fatherland is forging unity,*
De norte a sur se movilizará.	*From north to south, they will rally forth.*
Desde el salar ardiente y mineral	*From the blazing mineral salt mines*
Al bosque austral, unidos en la lucha	*To the southern forests, united in struggle*
Y el trabajo irán, la patria cubrirán.	*And labor they will envelop the fatherland.*
Su paso ya anuncia el porvenir.	*Their steps foretell things that are to come.*
De pie, cantar el pueblo va a triunfar.	*Arise, advance, the people will succeed.*
Millones ya, imponen la verdad.	*Millions now are imposing the truth.*
De acero son ardiente batallón	*Battalions of fire are constructed out of steel,*
Sus manos van llevando la justicia y la razón.	*Taking in their hands justice and reason.*
Mujer con fuego y con valor,	*Woman, with fire and courage,*
ya estás aquí junto al trabajador.	*You are already alongside the worker.*
Y ahora el pueblo que se alza en la lucha	*And now the people, arising in the struggle*
Con voz de gigante gritando: ¡adelante!	*With the voice of a giant crying out: Forward!*
El pueblo unido jamás será vencido . . .	*The people united will never be defeated . . .*

Nueva canción artists sought to create a just, egalitarian society that respected and even celebrated peasants and the working class. A particular concern was the historical struggle of Native cultures against their European oppressors, going back to the days of the Conquest. Víctor Jara, Violeta Parra, and groups such as Inti-Illimani brought attention to the exploitation of the still marginalized and disenfranchised Natives in Chile (though few *nueva canción* artists were themselves of indigenous ancestry). This concern became international, and artists in other countries began doing the same, most prominently Los Jaibas, who infused Native Bolivian styles with a new social consciousness, something that had not been a part of traditional Andean music.

But *nueva canción* also celebrated its folk-music roots as the true music of the people, often exploring traditional themes of *cuecas* and *tonadas*: the natural wonders of the countryside and the yearning for simpler—and more just—times, all imbued with the melancholy that permeated Andean music. At the same time, they were taking a stand against the catchy but vacuous, consumer-oriented rock-and-roll and pop styles that were becoming increasingly popular, particularly those in the English language, and sought to return Latin American music to the folk traditions that engendered it and with which common people could relate.

THE PEAK OF *NUEVA CANCIÓN* By the mid-1960s, *nueva canción* had become a recognizable stylistic movement, with many artists who began their careers under the tutelage of traditional folk musicians such as Violeta Parra and Margot Loyola. They included Héctor Pavez, Gabriela Pizarro, Rolando Alarcón, and the novelist Patricio Manns, as well as Payo Grondona and Osvaldo Gitano Rodríguez from the port of Valparaíso. Another was Luis Advis, who constructed large-scale protest compositions with elements from classical music. But the most prominent exponent was undoubtedly Víctor Jara. Born in 1932, he became a prominent theater director at the forefront of Chile's theatrical scene. In the late 1950s, he joined the group Cuncumén as a singer, and thereafter performed regularly at La Peña de los Parra. He had important collaborations with the groups Quilapayún and Inti-Illimani. After winning the competition at the first Festival de la Nueva Canción Chilena in 1969, he became the most visible symbol of the new generation of folk singers. Jara's songs envision a world without violence and display a deep respect and appreciation for traditional Chilean and Andean folklore and a concern for the welfare of the working class and Native cultures.

Nueva canción being primarily a youth-oriented movement, several universities were closely connected to its development. The group Cuncumén (from a Mapuche word meaning "whispering water") began in 1955 as a traditional folk ensemble at the University of Chile under the guidance of Margot Loyola. It included Rolando Alarcón, who would remain musical director for a decade, as well as Víctor Jara. Quilapayún (Mapuche for "three bearded men") debuted in 1965 at the Catholic University in Valparaíso under Jara's direction. It soon became extremely popular, with uncompromising albums such as *Basta!* ("Enough!) and *X Vietnam*, a denunciation of the Vietnam war. Inti Illimani (Aymara for "sun of Illimani Mountain") was formed in 1967 by students at the Universidad Técnica del Estado. It quickly became one of the most popular *nueva canción* groups, with songs that showed deep respect for Chilean and Andean folk traditions and solidarity with revolutionary

Nueva canción singer Víctor Jara.

movements. Another group that continued the legacy of *nueva canción* was Illapu, formed in 1971.

The year 1965 saw *nueva canción*'s first commercial hit, Patricio Manns's "Arriba en la Cordillera". Songs by Víctor Jara and Rolando Alarcón soon followed. Yet despite these successes, many artists were unable to break through into commercial recordings, due mostly to their left-leaning views, which repelled many media corporations. As a result, a new company called Discoteca del Cantar Popular was founded in 1968 to record and publish the songs of otherwise marginalized musicians. *Nueva canción* soon transcended the *peña* and became popular in larger concert settings, festivals, and political demonstrations. The first festival dedicated to the new style was the Encuentro de la canción protesta in 1967 in Havana, Cuba, which brought together dozens of *nueva canción* and *nueva trova* artists from 18 countries across the hemisphere. Two years later, the Primer Festival de la Nueva Canción Chilena occurred in Santiago and paid homage to Chile's traditional folk roots with the participation of older groups such as Los Huasos Quincheros. The festival's competition was won by Víctor Jara's song "Plegaria de un labrador" ("the worker's prayer"). But the key event that gave the movement national recognition was the 1970 election of Salvador Allende and his Popular Unity Party. The socialist Allende was in tune with the political outlook of the *nueva canción* movement, which as a result flourished under his rule. *Peñas* and festivals continued to grow in numbers and popularity. Chilean musicians were supported at the expense of foreign ones, and some of the most memorable music was composed during this period.

Nueva canción was only the most prominent of a number of folk-song styles that emerged simultaneously across the hemisphere and that all had in common a love for their country's folk roots, a predilection for acoustic instruments, and a deliberate leftist worldview. The second-most major contributor to the movement was Cuba, whose revolutionary songs were known generally as *nueva trova*, composed and performed by artists such as Carlos Puebla, Silvio Rodríguez, Noel Nicola, Vicente Feliú, Pablo Milanés, and Sara González. In Argentina, led by the example of Atahualpa Yupanqui, folk musicians such as Mercedes Sosa, Los Chalchaleros, and Los Fronterizos quickly embraced *nueva canción*, later followed by León Gieco and Víctor Heredia. In Uruguay, Daniel Viglietti and Alfredo Zitarrosa became major figures, as did the group Los Olimareños. Mexico also had important *nueva trova* artists, including notably Amparo Ochoa, Gabino Palomares, and Oscar Chávez. Andean countries, which had contributed to the emergence of the style, were also well represented, notably with the Bolivian group Los Jairas, as well as singers Emma Junaro and Matilde Casazola. In Nicaragua, the Mejía Godoy brothers, Carlos and Luis Enrique, wrote songs that were associated with the anti-Somoza revolution. Other significant artists included Venezuela's Grupo Madera and Ali Primera, El Salvador's Yolo-Camba-I-Ta, and Brazil's Chico Buarque, Milton Nascimento, and Caetano Veloso, whose contributions to that country's MPB popular music were infused with elements from *nueva canción*. One also needs to include in this list U.S. folk artists such as Pete Seeger, Phil Ochs, Bob Dylan, and Joan Baez, who, though they sang in English, nonetheless shared both the musical aesthetics and the political outlook of the Latin American movement.

> **Recommended Listening:** "Gracias a la vida" by Violeta Parra, from the CD *Violeta Parra: Antología*.
>
> **Recommended Listening:** "Si somos americanos" and "Yo defiendo a ai tierra" by Rolando Alarcón, from the CD *Rolando Alarcón y sus canciones*.
>
> **Recommended Listening:** "Arriba en la cordillera," "El cautivo de Til Til," and "Palimpsesto" by Patricio Manns, from the CD *En Chile*.
>
> **Recommended Listening:** "Cantata popular Santa María de Iquique" by Luis Avis, from the CD *Santa Maria de Iquique*.
>
> **Recommended Listening:** "Premonición a la muerte de Joaquín Murieta" by Quilapayún, from the CD *Antología 1968–1992*.
>
> **Recommended Listening:** "Exilada del Sur" and "La denuncia" by Inti Illimani, from the CD *Antología, Vol. 1: 1973–1978*.
>
> **Recommended Listening:** "Preguntas por Puerto Montt," "Te recuerdo Amanda" and "Plegaria a un labrador" by Víctor Jara, from the CD *Víctor Jara: Antología musical*.

Nueva canción: "Plegaria a un labrador"

Music and Lyrics: Víctor Jara (1969)
Instrumentation: guitar
Notes: Víctor Jara's *Plegaria a un labrador* ("The Worker's Prayer") illustrates his commitment to social justice and workers' rights. Using familiar formulas from Judeo-Christian prayers, he provides an imagery that promotes both solidarity and spirituality. Jara initially sings alone, but is quickly joined by other voices, suggesting that strength and justice can be achieved by joining together.

Levantate y mira la montaña	*Stand up, look at the mountains*
De donde viene el viento el sol y el agua.	*Source of the wind, the sun, the water.*
Tú que manejas el curso de los rios,	*You, who change the course of rivers,*
Tú que sembraste el vuelo de tu alma.	*Who sowed the flight of your soul.*
Levantate y mírate las manos,	*Stand up, look at your hands,*
Para crecer estrechala a tu hermano.	*Offer them to your brother so you can grow.*
Juntos iremos unidos en la sangre.	*We'll go together, united by blood,*
Hoy es el tiempo que puede ser mañana.	*Today is the day we can make our future.*
Líbranos de aquel que nos domina en la miseria.	*Deliver us from those who keep us in misery.*
Tráenos tu reino de justicia e igualdad.	*Thy kingdom of justice and equality come.*
Sopla como el viento la flor de la quebrada.	*Blow like the wild flowers of the mountains.*
Limpia como el fuego el cañón de mi fusil.	*Like fire, clean the barrel of my gun.*
Hágase por fin tu voluntad aquí en la tierra.	*Thy will at last be done on earth.*
Danos tu fuerza y tu valor al combatir.	*Give us your strength and courage to struggle.*
Sopla como el viento la flor de la quebrada.	*Blow like the wild flowers of the mountains*
Limpia como el fuego el cañón de mi fusil.	*Like fire, clean the barrel of my gun.*
Levantate y mírate las manos.	*Stand up, look at your hands,*
Para crecer estréchala a tu hermano.	*Give them to your brother so you can grow.*
Juntos iremos unidos en la sangre,	*We'll go together, united by blood,*
Ahora y en la hora de nuestra muerte.	*Now and at the hour of our death. Amen.*
Amén.	

THE 1973 COUP D'ÉTAT An important date in the evolution of *nueva canción* was September 11, 1973, the day Salvador Allende was overthrown by the right-wing dictator Augusto Pinochet, who considered *nueva canción* a pernicious movement and quickly moved to suppress it. *Peñas* were closed, performance and radio play were censored and banned, and artists and intellectuals were arrested and imprisoned. Pinochet even outlawed the playing of *quenas* and *charangos* during his dictatorship, since they were associated with the oppression and marginalization of Native groups. During the dictatorship, the entire movement went either underground or into exile, including both Inti-Illimani and Quilapayún, who were on tour in Europe at the time of the coup and who remained in exile until the 1990s. Isabel and Ángel Parra similarly left for Europe, as did Héctor Pavez, who died in France a few years later. But the biggest blow to the movement occurred a few days after the coup, when Víctor Jara, *nueva canción*'s most famous and important representative, was arrested, tortured, and summarily murdered at a local stadium by a Pinochet death squad.

The repression was so brutal and pervasive that some claim that *nueva canción* essentially ended in 1973, annihilating, if not the artists themselves, certainly the sense of optimism that had pervaded the style. Yet the silver lining was that many of the musicians who left the country—most prominently Inti-Illimani—continued to popularize *nueva canción* in the Andes, Argentina, Mexico, and Europe, turning it into a worldwide phenomenon. Jara's death elevated him and his music to legendary status. *Nueva canción* subsequently became tremendously popular across the world and festivals continued to be held for decades throughout the continent, including some specifically dedicated to Jara himself. His death also advanced the cause of human rights across the world and brought international condemnation on the Pinochet régime, which would nonetheless last for almost two decades.

CANTO NUEVO Meanwhile, in Chile itself, the first years of the dictatorship continued with massive repression of anything resembling protest songs. One way to get around the censorship, espoused for example by the group Barroco Andino, was by performing European classical music with Andean instruments. (The government's prohibition of *quenas* and *charangos* was quickly ignored and never enforced.) Also allowed to re-emerge was traditional—that is, non-political—Andean music, which as a result flourished in Chile, as it did throughout the world during this period. In time, non-political *peñas* gradually re-appeared, and after several years of repression, the censorship began to loosen somewhat. It was in this atmosphere that, in the late 1970s, a new subgenre of *nueva canción* emerged called *canto nuevo* (which also means "new song"). It was generated by the few *nueva canción* musicians who had remained in Chile, as well as by a younger generation of singer/songwriters whose personal memory of Parra, Jara, and others, if it existed at all, was quickly fading. They included Osvaldo Torres, Isabel Aldunate, Eduardo Peralta, Nano Acevedo, and Cristina González, as well as the groups Ortiga, Sol y Lluvia, Aquelarre, Grupo Abril, Santiago del Nuevo Extremo, and the duo Shwenke y Nilo. These musicians learned to navigate the repression of the Pinochet regime and managed to mostly avoid political entanglements.

Whereas *nueva canción* had openly embraced hope and optimism, *canto nuevo* addressed the reality of living under an oppressive regime. Not as overtly political, it nevertheless continued to push the envelope under the suspicious eyes of the military dictatorship, attempting to reassert a nationalistic style. Its political rhetoric was carefully couched in ambiguous symbolism and imagery, which allowed it to exist (if not exactly thrive), for it remained intermittently repressed and tightly controlled. *Canto nuevo* artists were also not as utterly devoted to the purity of folk music as had been the previous generation, and influences of the Chilean and Argentine *rock nacional* scene began to permeate it, as well as jazz and *música tropical*. Slowly, *canto nuevo* began to creep into public consciousness. By 1977, some radio stations and *peñas* were openly showcasing the style. A new record label was founded called Alerce, which released an important album in 1978 called simply *Canto nuevo*. The style also began to appear at music festivals, notably at the Viña del Mar festival, long considered an elite resort city, which dispelled any potential suspicion. *Canto nuevo* never reached the level of exposure and popularity that its predecessor had, but nor did it succumb to government pressure and disappear. It continuously held a middle ground throughout the 1980s, fluctuating back and forth between periods of government permissiveness and repression, until the fall of the dictatorship in 1990.

> **Recommended Listening:** "Yo te nombro" by Libertad Isabel Aldunate, "Canción para el otro exilio" by Sol y Lluvia, "Cuando llega el invierno" by Isabel Aldunate, "Hay que hacerse de nuevo cada día" by Schwenke y Nilo and "Canción de la esperanza" by Ortiga, from the CD *Antología del canto nuevo*.

THE 1990s Democracy was restored in Chile in 1990, which by then had seen many of the right-wing dictators on the continent fall from power, including Nicaragua's Anastasio Somoza regime and the military juntas in Argentina. Exiled artists began to return, often hailed as heroes who had continued the good fight abroad. A new generation of *nueva canción* artists emerged, including the offspring of some of the former folklorists, notably Héctor Pavez Pizarro, son of Héctor Pavez and Gabriela Pizarro. They still sang about social justice, now tinged with a melancholy that reflected the long process of national healing. (The stadium where Víctor Jara was executed was renamed in his honor in 2003.) But by and large the *nueva canción/canto nuevo* movement was over, as it struggled to find its moral and political imperative. Chilean youth, as youth are wont to do, went in new directions, embracing either *música tropical* or the *rock nacional* movement that was overtaking the southern part of the continent.

Nueva canción's effects are still debated. Its message spread across the continent, providing a sense of social and national identity to millions of Latin Americans at a time when the entire region was undergoing enormous social, economic and political changes. Certainly in Cuba, the pro-revolutionary *nueva trova* served to uphold and cement the ideals of the Cuban revolution. In the United States, the corresponding folk style—perhaps best exemplified by Bob Dylan's "The Times They Are A-Changing"—had an enormous influence on the social and political upheavals in the 1960s. In other countries, however, the result was mixed. One could argue that the country that had created the *nueva canción* tradition—Chile—is also the one where the protests were least successful, for its heartfelt sentiment and social optimism were crushed by almost two decades of brutal dictatorship. Yet the message of social justice ultimately did return home and brought belated change to Chile in the 1990s. Perhaps more importantly, by focusing on Chilean folklore, *nueva canción* attempted—and to a great extent succeeded—to connect the present with the past, and to establish a sense of national identity. It also brought a deliberate sense of purpose to music in the face of a tidal wave of foreign and commercial styles. In the end, *nueva canción* transcended its musical features and shaped Latin American and Caribbean societies like no other style on the continent.

For other prominent Argentinean and Chilean styles, and for the music of Uruguay and Paraguay, see www.mymusickit.com.

INDEX